D1518765

GRAPHIS ANNUAL REPORTS 2

GRAPHIS ANNUAL REPORTS 2

THE INTERNATIONAL YEARBOOK OF ANNUAL REPORTS

DAS INTERNATIONALE JAHRBUCH ÜBER JAHRESBERICHTE

LE RÉPERTOIRE INTERNATIONAL DES RAPPORTS ANNUELS

EDITED BY/HERAUSGEGEBEN VON/RÉALISÉ PAR

B. MARTIN PEDERSEN

WRITTEN BY/GESCHRIEBEN VON / ÉCRIT PAR

MARGARET RICHARDSON

PUBLISHER AND CREATIVE DIRECTOR: B. MARTIN PEDERSEN

EDITOR: MARISA BULZONE

ASSOCIATE EDITOR: HEINKE JENSSEN

ASSOCIATE ART DIRECTOR / DESIGNER: RANDELL PEARSON

PHOTOGRAPHER: WALTER ZUBER

"G" FROM THE ALUMINUM ALPHABET DESIGNED BY TAKENOBU IGARASHI

GRAPHIS PRESS CORP., ZÜRICH (SWITZERLAND)

GRAPHIS PUBLICATIONS

GRAPHIS, The international bi-monthly journal of visual communication
GRAPHIS DESIGN, The international annual of design and illustration
GRAPHIS PHOTO, The international annual of photography
GRAPHIS POSTER, The international annual of poster art
GRAPHIS PACKAGING, An international survey of packaging design
GRAPHIS DIAGRAM, The graphic visualization of abstract, technical and statistical facts and functions
GRAPHIS COVERS, An anthology of all GRAPHIS covers from 1944-86 with artists' short biographies and indexes of all GRAPHIS issues
GRAPHIS ANNUAL REPORTS, An international compilation of the best designed annual reports
GRAPHIS CORPORATE IDENTITY, An international compilation of the best in Corporate Identity design
POSTERS MADE POSSIBLE BY A GRANT FROM MOBIL, A collection of 250 international posters commissioned by Mobil and selected by the Poster Society

GRAPHIS-PUBLIKATIONEN

GRAPHIS, Die internationale Zweimonatszeitschrift der visuellen Kommunikation
GRAPHIS DESIGN, Das internationale Jahrbuch über Design und Illustration
GRAPHIS PHOTO, Das internationale Jahrbuch der Photographie
GRAPHIS POSTER, Das internationale Jahrbuch der Plakatkunst
GRAPHIS PACKUNGEN, Ein internationaler Überblick über die Packungsgestaltung
GRAPHIS DIAGRAM, Die graphische Darstellung abstrakter, technischer und statistischer Daten und Fakten
GRAPHIS COVERS, Eine Sammlung aller GRAPHIS-Umschläge von 1944-86 mit Informationen über die Künstler und Inhaltsübersichten aller Ausgaben der Zeitschrift GRAPHIS
GRAPHIS ANNUAL REPORTS, Ein internationaler Überblick über die Gestaltung von Jahresberichten
GRAPHIS CORPORATE IDENTITY, Eine internationale Auswahl des besten Corporate Identity Design
POSTERS MADE POSSIBLE BY A GRANT FROM MOBIL, Eine Sammlung von 250 internationalen Plakaten, von Mobil in Auftrag gegeben und von der Poster Society ausgewählt

PUBLICATIONS GRAPHIS

GRAPHIS, La revue bimestrielle internationale de la communication visuelle
GRAPHIS DESIGN, Le répertoire international de la communication visuelle
GRAPHIS PHOTO, Le répertoire international de la photographie
GRAPHIS POSTER, Le répertoire international de l'art de l'affiche
GRAPHIS EMBALLAGES, Le répertoire international des formes de l'emballage
GRAPHIS DIAGRAM, La représentation graphique de faits et données abstraits, techniques et statistiques
GRAPHIS COVERS, Recueil de toutes les couvertures de GRAPHIS de 1944-86 avec des notices biographiques des artistes et le sommaire de tous les numéros du magazine GRAPHIS
GRAPHIS ANNUAL REPORTS, Panorama international du design de rapports annuels d'entreprises
GRAPHIS CORPORATE IDENTITY, Panorama international du meilleur design de l'identité corporate
POSTERS MADE POSSIBLE BY A GRANT FROM MOBIL, Une collection de 250 affiches internationales commandées par Mobil et choisies par la Poster Society

PUBLICATION No. 198 (ISBN 3-85709-428-1)

Color originated in the United Kingdom by Wace Litho, Birmingham, and in the United States of America by Collins, Miller & Hutchings, Chicago, Illinois.
Printed in the United Kingdom by Brandprint, London, and in the United States of America by The Etheridge Company, Grand Rapids, Michigan, subsidiary companies of the Wace Group PLC, London, England.
Color originated using Dupont film and Crosfield scanning equipment and Howson Algraphy litho plates.
Printed on ikonorex. 135 g/m² by ZANDERS Feinpapier AG
Typeset using Quark XPress® on a Macintosh® computer
Linotron output by Graphic Technology, New York, New York
Set in Bodoni, ITC Garamond and Futura Extra Bold

CONTENTS

INHALT

SOMMAIRE

REMARKS

Our sincere thanks are extended to all contributors throughout the world who have made it possible for us to publish an international spectrum of outstanding work.

Entry instructions may be requested from: Graphis Press Corp., Dufourstrasse 107, 8008 Zürich, Switzerland

ANMERKUNGEN

Unser herzlicher Dank gilt Einsendern aus aller Welt, die es uns möglich gemacht haben, ein breites, internationales Spektrum der besten Arbeiten zu veröffentlichen.

Teilnahmebedingungen: Graphis Verlag AG, Dufourstrasse 107, 8008 Zürich, Schweiz

AVERTISSEMENT

Nos sincères remerciements vont à tous les collaborateurs du monde entier, qui nous ont permis de publier un vaste panorama international des meilleurs travaux.

Demande de participation: Editions Graphis SA, Dufourstrasse 107, 8008 Zürich, Suisse

GRAPHIS ANNUAL REPORTS 2
AND THE GRAPHIS ANNUAL REPORTS AWARDS PROGRAM AND EXHIBITIONS
HAVE BEEN MADE POSSIBLE BY THE GENEROUS SUPPORT AND SPONSORSHIP OF
THE WACE GROUP PLC LONDON

THE WACE GROUP PLC, HEADQUARTERED IN LONDON, IS THE WORLD'S LARGEST PRE-PRESS CORPORATION, WHICH ALSO CONTROLS PRINTING INTERESTS IN EUROPE AND THE UNITED STATES. □ OUR INDUSTRY IS ONE OF ACCELERATING TECHNICAL INNOVATION WHERE CREATIVITY ABOUNDS. SUCCESS IN SUCH AN INDUSTRY CAN BE ACHIEVED ONLY BY COMMITMENT TO CUSTOMERS' CHANGING NEEDS, EXCELLENT QUALITY AND RELIABLE AND PROMPT SERVICE. ALL WACE GROUP COMPANIES ARE ACKNOWLEDGED AS BEING TECHNICAL AND MARKET LEADERS WITHIN THEIR SPECIALIST FIELDS. WACE IS A CUSTOMER-DRIVEN AND INNOVATIVE GROUP, CONTINUOUSLY INVESTING IN THE LATEST TECHNOLOGY TO MAINTAIN AND EXTEND ITS POSITION AS THE WORLD'S LEADING PRE-PRESS GROUP. □ "WE ARE DELIGHTED TO HAVE THE OPPORTUNITY OF BEING PARTNERS WITH THE GRAPHIS PRESS CORP. IN THIS PRESTIGIOUS INTERNATIONAL PROJECT," SAYS THE WACE GROUP MANAGING DIRECTOR, JOHN CLEGG. ■

ZANDERS / WELTWEIT DER NAME FÜR FEINPAPIER / FOR PAPER OF PERFECTION / SYMBOLE DE QUALITÉ DANS LE MONDE ENTIER ■

THIS BOOK HAS BEEN PRINTED ON IKONOREX. 135 G/M² GENEROUSLY PROVIDED BY ZANDERS FEINPAPIERE AG

INTRODUCTION

VORWORT

PRÉFACE

A LETTER TO OUR SHAREHOLDERS

BY RAY DEVOE

Imagine that the "Truth in Packaging Law" has been further extended to apply to annual reports and other corporate communications. Just think what the consequences might be. Take, for example, the fairly typical "President's Report to the Shareholders" that follows. Although this annual report message was drafted by the financial public relations operation ("Hired flacks"), imagine that they are required to include a parenthesis after many items, in this case as they would be interpreted by an anonymous cynical security analyst approved by the Financial Analysts Federation. □ Dear Fellow Shareholders: All in all it was an interesting year. ("An old Chinese curse goes, 'May you live in interesting times.' ") A year full of challenge ("Competition") and stimulating opportunity. ("Except, they missed the boat.") □ We are proud of our policy of promotion within the ranks in virtually all managerial positions. ("Like a septic tank, in this company the really big chunks tend to rise to the top.") As is normal within any organization, various management changes have been affected in the interests of promoting efficiency and harmony. ("The scenery only changes for the lead dog in a dogsled team.") □ Regarding the resignation of my predecessor during the audit, management has endorsed all his actions, and enthusiastically asked him to further serve the company in an advisory capacity. ("If they dumped him, he might squeal to the SEC.") While management believes in qualified promotions from within the organization, during the year certain steps were taken to ensure the long term viability of current management's business philosophy. ("Last year the Chairman of the Board–and largest stockholder–became a grandfather.") □ I might digress from the broad overview to give you an idea of some of the exciting products the company has under development. ("How much is this going to cost?") Malnutrition, overpopulation and dieting are three major world problems, the latter particularly in this country. ("Although obviously it never crossed the minds of those fat cats on the Board.") For the first two, the twin problems of malnutrition and overpopulation, your company is developing an 1800-calorie birth control pill. This should make up for the disappointing sales in the less-developed countries of our recently introduced line of designer condoms–marketed under the name "Sergio Preventé." □ Another new product we hope to be offering soon ("If they can con the FDA") addresses the dieting craze in America. We have developed a unique appetite suppressant. It is a garlic-flavored pill that bloats your stomach and gives you heartburn and indigestion. The sensation is exactly the same as if you had just left the table after a large Italian meal. □ I know you are all interested in hearing about our earnings prospects. ("The moment of truth for the bull has arrived.") I would be less than totally honest if I said I was completely satisfied with our recent earnings results. ("Dishonesty is the second best policy, but they couldn't hide this disaster.") But let's put everything in perspective. Earnings of 25 cents per share for the quarter, while significantly below the $1.47 per share earned in the corresponding quarter last year were, considering your company's long historical record, more reasonable. ("That's what they earned in 1950.") Now I'm aware that many of you were disappointed by these results ("The stock dropped 50 percent in the next week"), particularly since they were well below the estimates projected by management during the quarter. ("They lied.") However, in a business such as this there are a great deal of exogenous variables that can unexpectedly impact our operations. ("They didn't have the foggiest idea what was going on during the quarter.") I would like to emphatically state that your management will never be satisfied with results that are merely "satisfactory." ("At least they didn't go bankrupt–that's reserved for 'unsatisfactory' earnings.") □ As to the future, it has been said that one should not prognosticate, especially about the future. ("They're not even sure what happened in the *last* quarter.") While many in our industry are cautiously optimistic, your management feels that the more prudent course would be to remain optimistic, but proceed with caution. ("They still don't have the foggiest notion of what's going on. Maybe when they get a better idea of the last quarter?") □ In conclusion, your forward-looking management eagerly anticipates your company's confrontation with the future and the challenges that lie ahead. ("New rotten ideas sometimes make people forget the old rotten ones.") □ Very respectfully submitted, Robin N. Cheaton, President. ■ *Raymond F. DeVoe, Jr. is a market strategist with the investment firm of Legg Mason Wood Walker Inc. in New York City. He is also the author of* The DeVoe Report, *a weekly investment service newsletter on any subject affecting securities prices.*

PHOTO BY GARTH VAUGHAN / ARTS COUNSEL

EIN BRIEF AN UNSERE AKTIONÄRE

von Ray DeVoe

Man stelle sich vor, dass Mogelpackungen auch bei Jahresberichter und anderen Firmenkommunikationen verboten wären. Was käme wohl dabei heraus? Nehmen wir einmal den folgenden, recht typischen «Brief des Geschäftsführers an die Aktionäre». Obgleich diese Botschaft von der Finanzabteilung formuliert wurde, stelle man sich vor, dass ein zynischer Finanzanalytiker hinter vielen Angaben etwas in Klammern hinzufügen würde. □ Liebe Mitaktionäre! Alles in allem war es ein interessantes Jahr. («Um es mit den Chinesen zu sagen: «Mögest Du in interessanten Zeiten leben.») Ein Jahr grosser Herausforderungen («Konkurrenz») und grosser Gelegenheiten («leider hat man sie verpasst»). □ Wir sind stolz darauf, dass wir in quasi sämtlichen Management-Positionen Beförderungen vornehmen konnten. («Die Szene ändert sich nur für den Leithund der Schlitten-hunde.») □ Was das Ausscheiden meines Vorgängers während der Berichtsperiode betrifft, so hat das Management alle seine Aktionen gebilligt und ihn gebeten, der Firma weiterhin in beratender Funktion zu dienen. («Falls sie ihn abgeschoben haben, könnte er bei der SEC (Securities and Exchange Commission) singen».) □ Ich möchte kurz abschweifen, um Ihnen eine Vorstellung von einigen der hervorragenden Produkte zu geben, die unsere Firma entwickeln will. («Wieviel wird das kosten?») Unterernährung, Überbevölkerung und Übergewicht sind heute weltweit wichtige Probleme, das letztere vor allem in unserem Land. («Die Fettklösse im Vorstand scheinen sich offenbar nicht angesprochen zu fühlen.») Was die ersten beiden miteinander verbundenen Probleme angeht, so hat unsere Firma eine Anti-Baby-Pille mit 1800 Kalorien entwickelt. Das sollte auch den enttäuschenden Verkäufen unserer kürzlich entwickelten Linie von Designer-Kondomen unter dem Namen «Sergio Preventé» in unterentwickelten Ländern zugute kommen. □ Ein weiteres neues Produkt, das wir bald auf den Markt bringen möchten, («wenn es ihnen gelingt, die Federal Drug Administration hinters Licht zu führen») bezieht sich auf den Schlankheitswahn in den USA. Wir haben einen einzigartigen Appetithemmer entwickelt. Es ist ein Pille mit Knoblauchgeschmack, die Blähungen, Sodbrennen und Verdauungsschwierigkeiten verursacht. Man fühlt sich wie nach einem ausgiebigen italienischen Essen. □ Ich weiss, dass Sie alle erfahren möchten, wie unsere Ertragsaussichten stehen. («Der Augenblick der Wahrheit ist gekommen.») Ich wäre nicht ganz ehrlich, wenn ich behaupten würde, ich sei mit dem kürzlich erzielten Ertrag vollkommen zufrieden. («Unehrlichkeit wäre die zweitbeste Politik, aber sie können dieses Disaster nicht verbergen.») Aber sehen wir alles aus der richtigen Perspektive. Gewinne von 25 Cent pro Aktie in diesem Quartal schienen im Verhältnis zu den vergangenen Jahren angemessener zu sein, wenn sie auch bedeutend unter den $ 1.47 pro Aktie im Vergleichsquartal des Vorjahres liegen. («Das entspricht den Gewinnen von 1950.») Ich bin mir bewusst, dass viele von Ihnen über diese Ergebnisse enttäuscht waren («die Aktienkurse fielen daraufhin um 50%»), besonders weil sie unter den Prognosen der Geschäftsführung während des Quartals lagen. («Sie haben gelogen.») Bei einem Unternehmen wie dem unseren gibt es viele Unbekannte, die uner-wartet einen Einfluss auf den Geschäftsgang haben können. («Sie hatten keinen blassen Schimmer, was in dem Quartal passierte.») Ich möchte ganz besonders betonen, dass sich die Geschäftsleitung nicht mit Ergebnissen zufrieden geben wird, die nur «befriedigend» sind. («Zumindest machten sie nicht Konkurs, das hiesse unbefriedigende Ergebnisse.») Wie man allgemein sagt, sollte man keine Vorhersagen machen, ganz besonders nicht für die Zukunft. («Sie wissen nicht mal, was im vergangenen Quartal passierte.») Während in unserer Industrie ein vorsichtiger Optimismus herrscht, ist unsere Geschäftsleitung der Meinung, dass man bei allem Optimismus vorsichtig sein sollte. («Sie wissen nicht mal, was im vergangenen Quartal passierte.») Während in unserer Industrie ein vorsichtiger Optimismus herrscht, ist unsere Geschäftsleitung der Meinung, dass man bei allem Optimismus vorsichtig sein sollte. («Sie haben immer noch keinen blassen Schimmer, was passiert. Vielleicht bekommen sie eine Vorstellung, wenn sie begreifen, was passiert ist?») □ Der Blick der Geschäftsleitung ist in die Zukunft gerichtet, und wir freuen uns auf die Herausforderungen, die vor uns liegen. («Neue verrückte Ideen lassen die Leute manchmal die alten verrückten Ideen vergessen.») □ Ihr sehr ergebener, Robin N. Cheaton, Präsident. □ *Raymond F. DeVoe Jr. is Marktstratege bei der Investment-Firma Legg Mason Wood Walker Inc. Er ist Autor des DeVoe Report.* ■

PAR RAY DEVOE

Imaginez un peu que la «Loi de l'emballage-vérité» aurait vu son champ d'action accru jusqu'à englober les rapports annuels et autres communictions d'entreprise et essayez de vous représenter les conséquences. Prenez par exemple le «Rapport du Président aux actionnaires», texte typique que vous trouverez plus loin. Bien que le message de ce rapport annuel ait été rédigé par le départment des relations publiques financières, imaginez que leur texte soit assorti, en parenthèses, par le point de vue d'un analyste financier cynique. □ Chers co-actionnaires, cet exercice a été au fond tout à fait intéressant. («Une vieille malédiction chinoise dit: «Je vous souhaite de vivre à une époque intéressante.») Une année pleine de défis («compétition») et d'opportunités stimulantes. («sauf qu'ils ont raté le bateau.») □ En ce qui concerne la démission de mon prédécesseur durant la révision des comptes, la direction a pris toutes ses décisions à son compte avec enthousiasme et l'a invité à continuer de servir notre société en qualité de conseiller. («S'ils l'avaient laissé tomber, il aurait pu aller rapporter à la COB.») □ Je m'écarterai de cet aperçu d'ensemble pour vous donner une idée de certains produits sensationnels qui sont en cours de développement dans notre maison. («Et ça va coûter combien?») La sous-alimentation, la surpopulation et les régimes diététiques constituent trois problèmes majeurs à l'échelle du globe, le dernier en particulier dans notre pays. («Bien qu'évidemment ça n'est jamais venu à l'idée des gros chats repus au Conseil d'administration.») Pour les deux premiers, les problèmes associés de la sous-alimentation et de la sur-population, notre société est en train de mettre au point une pilule de régulation des naissances de 1800 calories. C'est ce qui devrait compenser largement les ventes peu satisfaisantes, dans les pays peu développés, dans notre gamme préservatif design lancé récemment et commercialisé sous la marque «Sergio Preventé». □ Un autre produit nouveau que nous espérons être à même de mettre sur le marché rapidement («S'ils peuvent circonvenir l'Office fédéral de contrôle de médicaments») répond à la vogue extraordinaire des produits diététiques en Amérique. Il s'agit d'une pilule à l'ail qui fait gonfler votre estomac et vous donne des brûlures d'estomac et des indigestions. La sensation est exactement la même que lorsque vous vous lever de table après un copieux repas italien. □ Je sais que vous êtes tous intéressés à connaître les perspectives de nos profits. («Le moment de la vérité est arrivé pour le taureau.») □ Je manquerais à la règle d'honnêteté si je vous disais que j'ai été complètement satisfait de notre dernier chiffre d'affaires. («Ils n'ont pas pu cacher ce désastre.») Pourtant restituons le tout dans la perspective qui convient. Les profits de 25 cents par action et trimestre que nous avons enregistrés sont évidemment bien en dessous du dollar 1,47 par action, pour la période correspondante de l'année passée. Toutefois ces 25 cents paraissent plus raisonnables au vu de la longue histoire des résultats financiers de notre société. («C'est ce qu'ils ont gagné en 1950») Je suis parfaitement conscient que vous êtes nombreux à avoir été déçus par ces résultats («la valeur de l'action va chuter de 50% la semaine prochaine»), surtout puisqu'ils sont nettement inférieurs au projections de la direction au cours du dernier trimestre. («Ils ont menti.») Toutefois, dans une affaire telle que la nôtre, il existe nombre de variables exogènes qui peuvent influencer nos opérations de manière inattendue. («Ils n'avaient pas la moindre idée de ce qui se passait au cours du trimestre.») J'aimerais affirmer ici solennellement que votre direction ne se satisfera jamais de résultats qui ne sont que «satisfaisants». («Au moins ils n'ont pas fait faillite - ce qui est réservé aux résultats «non satisfaisants» ».) □ Pour ce qui est des prévisions d'avenir, l'opinion veut que l'on évite de faire des pronostics surtout en ce qui concerne le futur. («Ils ne savent même pas ce qui est arrivé au juste au trimestre passé.») Alors que nombre de nos concurrents sont prudemment optimistes, notre direction pense que l'attitude la plus prudente consisterait à rester optimiste tout en avançant à pas comptés. («Ils n'ont toujours pas la moindre idée de ce qui se passe. Peut-être pourraient-ils s'informer un peu mieux du trimestre passé?») □ En conclusion, votre direction anticipant l'avenir se réjouit d'ores et déjà de la confrontation avec cet avenir et les défis qu'il nous réserve. («Les idées neuves pourries font parfois oublier au gens les vieilles idées pourries.») Avec l'assurance de mes sentiments distingués. □ Robin N. Cheaton, Président T. ■ *Raymond F. DeVoe, Jr. s'occupe de stratégie de marché au sein de la société d'investissement Legg Mason Wood Walker Inc. à New York. Il est aussi l'auteur du The DeVoe Report, un bulletin d'investissement hebdomadaire sur tout ce qui touche aux valeurs cotées en bourse.*

INTERNATIONAL ANNUAL REPORTS

BY MICHAEL WATRAS

What role does the annual report really play in today's business environment? Is it a financial document? Does it serve a marketing purpose? Should it be the company image piece? And should it have an international perspective? The answer to all of the above is "Yes," and a whole lot more. □ As the world gets smaller and companies compete for businesses on a global level, it becomes quite clear that the role of the annual report must change to meet that need. □ Indeed, more and more companies now produce foreign language annual reports. Several of our own clients, Bell Atlantic, Scott Paper, Guinness and H.J. Heinz, to name a few, produce their reports in a number of languages. □ In a world of instant communication, the annual report must serve many audiences in many tongues. Companies in countries such as Great Britain, France and Spain are racing to produce annual reports that now compete with those produced not only in the United States, but around the world. □ CGI's London office recently celebrated its first anniversary to great success in producing over 15 annual reports for some of that country's largest companies. Our commitment to Great Britain, shown by the opening of this office, was based on extensive research that proved to us that the annual report is a very international document and that Britain was a market in which we could succeed. □ As the selection on these pages clearly show, the annual report, which used to be a purely commercial phenomenon, is now international, serving many audiences. ■

THE BIG BUSINESS OF DESIGN

BY BENNETT ROBINSON

In the past couple of years, something unusual happened in our profession. Big British advertising conglomerates began buying American design offices. Saatchi & Saatchi grabbed Segal & Gale and then Jim Cross, Addison picked up Corporate Annual Reports, and WCRS bought us. American designers were becoming internationalized. □ This movement is related to what's happening with our annual report clients as well. Their marketing is becoming increasingly international in scope. There are business deals out there to be made and, with 1992 fast approaching, it's good sense to think in more worldly terms. □ Now that our arena is widening, the management of a design firm takes on new dimensions. Where once we could walk from drawing board to drawing board, we now monitor the output of our London and Los Angeles offices by fax when we can't do so in person. Daily design conferences by telephone are commonplace. Where once we struggled for a consistency of fresh and original solutions from our home office, we now have three offices to oversee, with more on the way. □ The management of our talent base has become more challenging. And, at this point, we could do a lot worse than to look to our clients and the world of business for new and effective management techniques. ■ *Corporate Graphics Inc. specializes in the design and production of corporate literature, and has offices in New York City, Los Angeles and London. Bennett Robinson and Michael Watras co-founded CGI thirteen years ago, and are still the best of friends.*

INTERNATIONALE JAHRESBERICHTE

VON MICHAEL WATRAS

Welche Rolle spielt der Jahresbericht tatsächlich in der heutigen Geschäftswelt? Sollte er das Firmen-Image stützen? Und sollte er eine internationale Perspektive haben? Ja zu dem oben Gesagten und noch zu viel mehr. □ Während die Welt immer näher zusammenrückt und die Firmen auf einem internationalen Markt konkurrieren, wird es ziemlich klar, dass der Jahresbericht eine Rolle übernehmen muss, die den neuen Bedürfnissen angepasst ist. □ Tatsächlich stellen jetzt immer mehr Firmen Jahresberichte in fremden Sprachen her. Viele der Kunden von Corporate Graphics wie Bell Atlantic, Scott Paper, Guinness und H J Heinz haben mehrsprachige Berichte. □ In einer Welt unmittelbarer Kommunikation muss der Jahresbericht einem grossen Publikum verschiedener Muttersprachen zugänglich sein. In Ländern wie Grossbritannien, Frankreich und Spanien reisst man sich jetzt darum, Jahresberichte für den Weltmarkt herzustellen. □ Corporate Graphics' Londoner Büro feierte kürzlich sein erstes erfolgreiches Jahr, in dem es über 15 Jahresberichte für die grössten britischen Firmen produziert hatte. Unser Erfolg in Grossbritannien ist darauf zurückzuführen, dass wir auf Grund von Studien beweisen konnten, dass ein Jahresbericht ein sehr internationales Dokument ist. □ Ich glaube, es ist eindeutig, dass der Jahresbericht, der einst ein reines geschäftliches Phänomen war, zu einem internationalen Dokument für ein grosses Publikum geworden ist. ■

DESIGN, DAS GROSSE GESCHÄFT

VON BENNETT ROBINSON

In den vergangenen paar Jahren hat sich in unserer Branche etwas Ungewöhnliches getan. Grosse britische Werbeagenturen haben begonnen, amerikanische Design-Studios aufzukaufen. Saatchi & Saatchi schluckte Segal & Gale und dann Jim Cross, Addison übernahm Corporate Annual Reports und WCRS hat uns gekauft. Amerikanische Designer sind international geworden. □ Dieser Trend entspricht der Entwicklung bei unseren Jahresbericht-Kunden. Ihr Marketing richtet sich mehr und mehr an ein internationales Publikum. Angesichts des Jahres 1992 tut man gut daran, in globalen Begriffen zu denken. □ Mit der Ausdehnung unseres Wirkungskreises haben wir im Design-Management mit neuen Dimensionen zu tun. Während wir einst von Zeichentisch zu Zeichentisch gehen konnten, sehen wir die Arbeit unserer Büros in London und Los Angeles heute via Fax, wenn wir nicht persönlich da sein können. Tägliche Design-Besprechungen per Telephon sind an der Tagesordnung. □ Die Führung unserer kreativen Mitarbeiter wird zu einer immer grösseren Herausforderung. Was effektives Management angeht, können wir von unseren Kunden lernen. Design ist jetzt ein Riesengeschäft, und es gewinnen jene, die effizient qualitativ hochstehende Arbeit bieten. ■ *Bennett Robinson und Michael Watras gründeten Corporate Graphics Inc. vor 13 Jahren. Sie sind Spezialisten für Firmenliteratur und haben Büros in New York, London und Los Angeles.*

L'INTERNATIONALISATION DU RAPPORT ANNUEL

PAR MICHAEL WATRAS

Quel rôle le rapport annuel joue-t-il effectivement dans le monde des affaires aujourd'hui? S'agit-il d'un document financier? Se met-il au service du marketing? Est-il destiné à projeter l'image de l'entreprise? Et doit-il s'inspirer d'une perspective internationale? La réponse est oui à toutes ces questions, ainsi qu'à bien d'autres encore. □ Au fur et à mesure que le monde se rétrécit et que les entreprises intensifient leur concurrence à l'échelle de la planète, il est évident que le rôle du rapport annuel doit changer de manière à satisfaire à ces besoins nouveaux. □ Le fait est qu'un nombre croissant d'entreprises publient désormais des rapports annuels en langues étrangères. Plusieurs clients de CGI, Bell Atlantic, Scott Paper, Guinness, H J Heinz, sont sur les rangs avec leurs rapports multilingues. □ Dans un monde où la communication est instantanée, le rapport annuel doit être à la disposition de nombreux publics dans de nombreuses langues. Des pays tels que la Grande-Bretagne, la France et l'Espagne sont très actifs dans la production de rapports annuels qui portent la concurrence sur le plan planétaire. □ Le bureau de Londres de CGI a récemment fêté son premier anniversaire en publiant avec un succès mérité une quinzaine de rapports annuels pour les grandes entreprises britanniques. Notre engagement en Grande-Bretagne est dû à des recherches exhaustives qui ont démontré que le rapport annuel s'est assuré une place de choix comme document hautement international. □ Je pense qu'il est clair dorénavant que ce qui ne constituait à l'origine qu'un phénomène commercial s'est transformé en un document international au service de publics multiples. ■

LE DESIGN REJOINT LE BIG BUSINESS

PAR BENNETT ROBINSON

Ces dernières années, notre profession a été affectée par un phénomène inhabituel. D'importants conglomérats britanniques spécialisés dans le domaine de la publicité se sont mis à racheter des bureaux de design américains. C'est ainsi que Saatchi & Saatchi s'est emparé de Segal & Gale, puis Jim Cross, Addison de Corporate Annual Reports, tandis que WCRS se portait acquéreur de notre groupe. Les designers américains s'internationalisent. □ Cette évolution est en rapport avec ce qui arrive à ceux de nos clients qui nous commandent des rapports annuels. Leur marketing vise de plus en plus la scène internationale. Il y a des affaires à réaliser à cet égard, et la date fatidique de 1992 approchant à grands pas, il est indiqué de se mettre à penser en termes planétaires. □ Maintenant que le champ de nos activités s'élargit, la gestion du design voit s'agrandir ses dimensions. Alors que naguère il suffisait de passer d'une planche à dessin à l'autre, nous surveillons par fax la production de nos bureaux de Londres et de Los Angeles lorsque nous ne pouvons le faire en personne. □ La gestion des talents à notre disposition s'est faite plus ardue, au point que nous pourrions faire bien pire que de rechercher auprès de nos clients les techniques de gestion efficace. Après tout, le design rejoint désormais le big business, et les gagnants de demain seront ceux qui sauront conjuguer une gestion efficace et une production de très grande qualité. ■ *Bennett Robinson et Michael Watras ont fondé Corporate Graphics Inc. il y a 13 ans. Ces spécialistes de la littérature d'entreprise entretiennent des bureaux à New York, Londres et Los Angeles.*

IMPROVING THE MESSAGE

BY DR. PETER WEIBEL

Good design attracts and holds the attention of the reader. It helps to emphasize important messages and it conveys an impression of the attitude and style of management. □ Design should be an aid to the communication of messages contained in the report–so all concerned with the preparation of an annual report must have regard to the content. There are many rules and guidelines relating to the content of annual reports and they vary from country to country. In a short contribution I can merely comment very briefly on two topical issues–making annual reports more forward looking and the problems of reporting to an international audience. □ When shareholders receive the annual report they are interested in forming a view as to how their shares are doing. Reduced to basics they have to decide whether to hold on to their shares or sell them. This decision should be based on a view of what will happen in the future–are dividends and the share price likely to increase faster than those of alternative investments? A good annual report should help the shareholder to take this decision. □ An annual report is mainly concerned with setting out financial and other information about what happened during the year covered by the report. Some reports may contain information about future plans and expectations but this is an area where practices vary and there are few established guidelines. □ In the European Community, the Fourth Directive on Company Law requires annual reports to give "an indication of likely future developments in the business of the company and of its subsidiaries," but this is so general that it has had little effect on published information. □ In the United States, the Securities and Exchange Commission (SEC) made a significant move in 1980 when it strengthened its requirements for "Management's Discussion and Analysis of Financial Condition and Results of Operations" (MDA). An important objective of the revised MDA was to focus on events and uncertainties known to management which would cause reported financial information not to be indicative of future operating results. The MDA is not required to be indicative of future operating results. This is potentially extremely valuable information but a review by the SEC carried out in 1980 revealed a very poor level of compliance. Out of 190 reports review, only 12 were judged to be completely satisfactory. This reluctance on the part of management to reveal information that impacts on the outsider's view of where the company is going is perhaps understandable, if it leads to a less optimistic view being taken. But if the annual report is to be worth all the time and money spent in its preparation, it must provide useful information and this includes bad news as well as good. □ In most cases, words can be translated into other languages and the message remains the same. Unfortunately, the language of accounting is an exception to this general rule. Profit in one country may not mean the same thing in another. The rules of accounting vary from one country to another and, to add to the confusion, some countries require more information to be disclosed in annual financial statements than others. □ The result of this variety of rules is that international companies have to go to the expense of preparing different statements for filing with regulatory authorities in different countries and investors who want to compare the performance of companies operating in different countries have to make their own adjustments to achieve comparability. □ The answer to this problem might seem obvious–get everyone to agree to a common set of accounting rules so that all financial statements are prepared in a common accounting language. □ But it isn't as simple as this. Economics in different parts of the world vary greatly. Obviously rates of inflation differ, but other, less obvious things may affect the interpretation of financial statements as well, such as the size of individual markets and their rates of growth, taxation systems and import controls. A profit, however the accountants calculate it, is not the same thing in a stable, large economy as it is in a small, inflationary one. □ The efforts of international bodies to narrow differences in accounting are worthwhile, but we need not be unduly concerned if they proceed slowly. It is more important that all concerned with setting the standards for annual reports should strive for better quality information in the commentary as well as the figures that it is to develop uniform rules to be applied to a changing world. ■ *Dr. Peter Weibel is Managing Director and Chief Executive Officer of Revisuisse Swiss Auditing Company. In 1989, he also became Partner in Charge of Switzerland of the combined operation of Revisuisse and Price Waterhouse in Switzerland. In the latter capacity, he is a Member of the Price Waterhouse European Policy and Management Board.*

PHOTO BY STEPHAN HANSLIN

GESCHÄFTSBERICHTE - WIE KANN DIE AUSSAGEKRAFT VERBESSERT WERDE?

VON DR. PETER WEIBEL

Attraktiv gestaltete und gut strukturierte Geschäftsberichte ziehen die Aufmerksamkeit des Lesers auf sich. Sie helfen mit, wichtige Botschaften zu vermitteln und widerspiegeln Haltung und Stil des Management. □ Weil Erscheinungsbild und Gestaltung des Geschäftsberichts wichtige Voraussetzungen für eine wirksame Kommunikation sind, müssen alle an der Entstehung Beteiligten eng zusammenarbeiten. Es gibt heute unzählige Regeln und Richtlinien über Inhalt, Aufbau und Gliederung von Geschäftsberichten. Diese weichen jedoch von Land zu Land voneinander ab. In der Folge soll lediglich auf zwei aktuelle Themen eingegangen werden: □ - Wie kann der Blick in die Zukunft geschärft werden? □ - Wie soll eine internationale Leserschaft angesprochen werden? □ Wenn Aktionäre den Geschäftsbericht erhalten, möchten sie sich eine Meinung über die Entwicklung ihrer Aktien bilden können. Im Kern geht es um den Entscheid, ob sie ihre Aktien behalten oder verkaufen sollen. Dies hängt davon ab, wie sich die Aktie entwickeln werden. Ein guter Geschäftsbericht soll dem Aktionär diese Entscheidung erleichtern. □ Ein Geschäftsbericht enthält im wesentlichen finanzielle und andere Informationen über das abgelaufene Geschäftsjahr. Er stellt somit eine historische Aufzeichnung dar. Daher muss ein Aktionär in die Lage versetzt werden, sich aufgrund von Vergangenheitsinformationen ein Bild über die zukünftige Entwicklung machen zu können. Einige Geschäftsberichte mögen bereits Hinweise über zukünftige Pläne und Erwartungen beinhalten, doch bewegen wir uns hier in einem Gebiet, in dem die Gepflogenheiten sehr verschieden sind und in dem es kaum allgemein anerkannte Richtlinien gibt. □ In den Vereinigten Staaten hat die «Securities and Exchange Commission» (SEC) im Jahre 1980 einen bedeutenden Schritt getan, als sie die Vorschriften über die «Management's Discussion and Analysis of Financial Condition and Results of Operations» (MDA) verschärfte. Ein wichtiges Ziel der revidierten MDA war, die Geschäftsleitung zu zwingen, auf Ereignisse und Ungewissheiten hinzuweisen, die der Geschäftsleitung bereits bekannt sind und welche die im Jahresabschluss enthaltenen finanziellen Resultate in Zukunft beeinflussen können. Die MDA verlangt keine Vorhersagen, der Geschäftsbericht soll jedoch Kommentare enthalten, welche dem Leser die eigene Zukunftseinschätzung erleichtern. □ Üblicherweise können Worte in andere Sprachen übersetzt werden, ohne dass deren Bedeutung verändert wird. Leider stellt die Sprache des Rechnungswesens die Ausnahme von der Regel dar. Reingewinn in einem Land darf nicht gleich gesetzt werden mit Reingewinn in einem anderen Land. Die Grundsätze des Rechnungswesens sind verschieden von Land zu Land, und um die Verwirrung noch grösser zu machen, sei darauf hingewiesen, dass einige Länder mehr Informationen in den Geschäftsberichten verlangen als andere. □ Eine Konsequenz dieser Vielfalt von Regeln ist, dass international tätige Firmen verschiedenes Jahresabschlüsse für die Behörden verschiedener Länder erstellen müssen. Eine weitere Konsequenz besteht darin, dass Investoren, welche die Resultate von Firmen verschiedener Länder miteinander vergleichen wollen, eigene Korrekturen vornehmen müssen, um einen solchen Vergleich überhaupt zu ermöglichen. □ Das Problem wäre dann gelöst, wenn jedermann gemeinsamen Standards im Rechnungswesen zustimmen würde, damit in allen Jahresabschlüssen die gleiches Sprache gesprochen wird. □ Aber dies ist nicht so einfach. Auch weniger offensichtliche Faktoren als unterschiedliche Inflationsraten sind bei der Interpretation von Jahresabschlüssen zu berücksichtigen, wie z.B. die Grösse der einzelnen Märkte und deren Wachstumsraten, die verschiedenen Steuersysteme sowie Einfuhrkontrollen. Der gleiche Reingewinn, wie immer er von den Buchhaltern berechnet wird, ist unterschiedlich zu beurteilen, je nachdem, ob er in einer grossen stabilen Volkswirtschaft oder in einer kleinen inflationären Wirtschaft erzielt wird. □ Die Anstrengungen internationaler Institutionen, Unterschiede im Rechnungswesen abzubauen, sind begrüssenswert, doch ist es nicht erstaunlich, wenn sie nur langsam vorankommen. Viel wichtiger als die Erzwingung international uniformer Vorschriften erscheint mir die erklärte Absicht aller Beteiligten, die Aussagekraft der Zahlen und insbesondere der Kommentare verbessern zu wollen.

■ *Dr. Peter Weibel ist Delegierter des Verwaltungsrates und Vorsitzender der Geschäftsleitung der Revisuisse, Schweizerische Revisionsgesellschaft. Ist er auch Partner in Charge of Switzerland von Revisuisse und Price Waterhouse.* ■

RAPPORTER LA GESTION EN AMÉLIORANT LE MESSAGE

PAR DR PETER WEIBEL

Le design de qualité attire et retient l'attention du lecteur. Il contribue à mettre en vedette les messages importants et donne une idée de l'attitude et du style de la direction. □ Le design devrait faciliter la communication des messages contenus dans le rapport. Il faut donc que toutes les personnes participant à son élaboration prennent le contenu en considération. Il existe de nombreuses règles et directives concernant le contenu d'un rapport annuel, et ces règles et directives varient de pays en pays. Dans ces quelques lignes, je ne peux qu'effleurer deux problèmes d'actualité - la manière de renforcer l'élément prospectif des rapports annuels et les problèmes que pose la présentation des rapports de gestion à un public international. □ Lorsque les actionnaires d'une entreprise reçoivent le rapport annuel, il cherchent à se faire une idée de la tenue de leurs actions. En simplifiant à l'extrême, on peut dire qu'ils ont à décider s'ils désirent garder ou revendre leurs actions. Cette décision devrait se fonder sur une vue perspective de l'avenir - les dividendes et le prix des actions ont-ils une chance de croître plus rapidement que ceux d'investissements différents? Un bon rapport annuel devrait pouvoir aider l'actionnaire à prendre cette décision. □ Un rapport annuel tend essentiellement à présenter les informations financières et autres relatives à l'exercice écoulé - sous forme d'un rapport historique sur une année de devenir de l'entreprise. L'actionnaire désireux de connaître le cap que va prendre sa société est obligé de s'inspirer de ces informations historiques pour anticiper sur l'avenir. Certains rapports sont susceptibles de contenir des renseignements et projections au sujet d'opérations futures; pourtant c'est là un domaine où les pratiques diffèrent grandement et où il n'existe qu'un nombre réduit de directives. □ Aux Etats-Unis, la Securities and Exchange Commission SEC a fait un pas important en la matière en renforçant dès 1980 les exigences posées à la «discussion et analyse, par la direction, de la situation financière et des résultats des opérations» (document abrégé en MDA). Un objectif essentiel de la révision du MDA était de mettre à jour les événements et incertitudes connus de la direction et qui, faute d'être rendus publics, affecteraient les projections à partir des résultats financiers publiés. On n'attend pas du MDA qu'il ait un caractère prévisionnel, mais qu'il incorpore des commentaires susceptibles de guider le lecteur dans son interprétation des renseignements sur le passé immédiat de l'entreprise en vue d'en tirer des leçons pour l'avenir. □ Dans la plupart des cas, les mots d'une langue donnée sont traduisibles dans d'autres langues, et le message reste inchangé. Malheureusement le langage de la gestion comptable constitue une exception notable à la règle. Ce que l'on entend par profit dans tel pays risque d'être compris différemment dans tel autre. Les règles de la comptabilité varient d'un pays à l'autre; pour corser la confusion qui en résulte, certains pays exigent la publication d'un volume plus important d'informations que d'autres lorsqu'il s'agit de compiler les résultats financiers annuels. □ La conséquence de cette diversité de règles est que les sociétés œuvrant au plan international doivent assumer les frais de la préparation de messages différents selon l'autorité de tutelle nationale prescrivant les règles de présentation des rapports annuels. Les investisseurs souhaitant comparer les performances d'entreprises opérant dans différents pays sont obligés de réajuster les chiffres pour qu'ils soient comparables. □ La solution semble évidente: amener tous les intéressés à souscrire à un ensemble de règles comptables communes permettant d'établir les rapports de gestion dans un langage comptable commun. □ Ce n'est pourtant pas aussi simple qu'il n'y paraît. Une foule de points moins évidents que les taux d'inflation différentiels risquent d'affecter l'interprétation des résultats financiers, ainsi les dimensions des marchés individuels et leur taux de croissance, les systèmes d'imposition et le contrôle des importations. Un profit donné n'a pas la même signification dans une économie stable de grandes dimensions que dans une économie de dimensions réduites de type inflationniste. □ Les efforts entrepris par les organismes internationaux pour réduire les écarts comptables sont dignes d'intérêt, mais nous n'avons pas à nous soucier des lenteurs du progrès en la matière. Il est plus important que tous ceux qui définissent les normes pour l'élaboration des rapports tendent à valoriser l'information de meilleure qualité, aussi bien le commentaire que dans la partie chiffrée. C'est un impératif qui l'emporte sur le souci de l'uniformisation des règles comptables. ■ *Le Dr Peter Weibel est P.-D.G. de la Société Suisse de Revision Revisuisse. Il est en outre associé, chargé des affaires suisses de l'opération conjointe de Revisuisse et de Price Waterhouse en Suisse.* ■

JURY COMMENTS

KOMMENTARE DER JURY

COMMENTAIRES DU JURY

The annual reports that appear on these pages were selected from over 1,000 entries received by Graphis Press Corp. Judging took place at the School of Visual Arts in New York City during the summer of 1989. In addition to choosing 25 reports from each year, the jury selected one report from each group to receive the Graphis "Best of Show" award.

MICHAEL BIERUT
Vice President, Graphic Design
Vignelli Associates
New York, New York

Michael Bierut was born in Cleveland, Ohio, and graduated from the University of Cincinnati's College of Design, Architecture, Art and Planning. He joined Vignelli Associates in 1980, was appointed Vice President, Graphic Design in 1984, and was made a partner of the firm in 1989. Mr. Bierut's work, which has been widely published, has won awards from the AIGA and the Art Directors Club, and is represented in the permanent collection of New York's Museum of Modern Art. He currently serves as a Director of the Society of Typographic Arts, and as President of the New York Chapter of the AIGA.

JAMES SEBASTIAN
President, Creative Director
Designframe, Inc.
New York, New York

James Sebastian holds a BFA in design from the Rhode Island School of Design as well as a BS in marketing. In 1976, he founded Designframe, Inc., an internationally recognized, multi-discipline marketing and communications consulting firm. Mr. Sebastian's work is included in the Museum of Modern Art Design Collection and the Library of Congress. Among the many awards won by the firm is the IDEA award from the Industrial Design Society of America.

MICHAEL WEYMOUTH
Principal
Weymouth Design
Boston, Massachusetts

Michael Weymouth was born in Maine and studied at The New England School of Art in Boston , Massachusetts. He worked for 10 years in the Boston design community prior to starting Weymouth Design in 1973. The firm presently designs 20-25 annual reports each year as well as other corporate materials, such as capabilities brochures and corporate identity programs for its clients. Mr. Weymouth is well-known for shooting much of his own photography and, indeed both he and his firm have won numerous awards in both photography and design competitions.

Jim Berté
Principal, Design Director
Robert Miles Runyan & Associates
The Nichols Institute Annual Report 1987

A graduate of the Rhode Island School of Design, Jim Berté headed the James Valkus Design office in Montreal for eight years. He then moved to St. Louis, where he worked as an independent design consultant. In 1977, Jim migrated to California, where he joined the Playa del Rey-based firm of Robert Miles Runyan & Associates. As a Principal and Design Director at RMR&A, Berté has been recognized nationally and internationally as one of the foremost designers in the United States.

KIT HINRICHS
Principal
Pentagram Design
(San Francisco)
Immunex Corporation
Annual Report 1988

Kit Hinrichs was born and raised in Los Angeles and studied at the Art Center College of Design. After graduating in 1963, he worked as a designer in several New York design offices before forming the design partnership of Russell & Hinrichs. In 1972, he joined with his wife, Linda, to form Hinrichs Design Associates. In 1976, they joined with B. Martin Pedersen, Vance Jonson and Neil Shakery to form Jonson, Pedersen, Hinrichs & Shakery. He remained a principal of JPH&S until he, Linda and Neil merged with Pentagram Design in 1986. Mr. Hinrichs has received several gold and silver awards from the New York Art Directors Club and the Los Angeles Art Directors Club, in addition to honors from many other organization and associatons. Mr. Hinrichs was recently inducted as a member of AGI (*Alliance Graphique Internationale*).

ANNUAL REPORT DESIGN

GESTALTUNG VON JAHRESBERICHTEN

DESIGN DES RAPPORTS ANNUELS

87

NICHOLS INSTITUTE

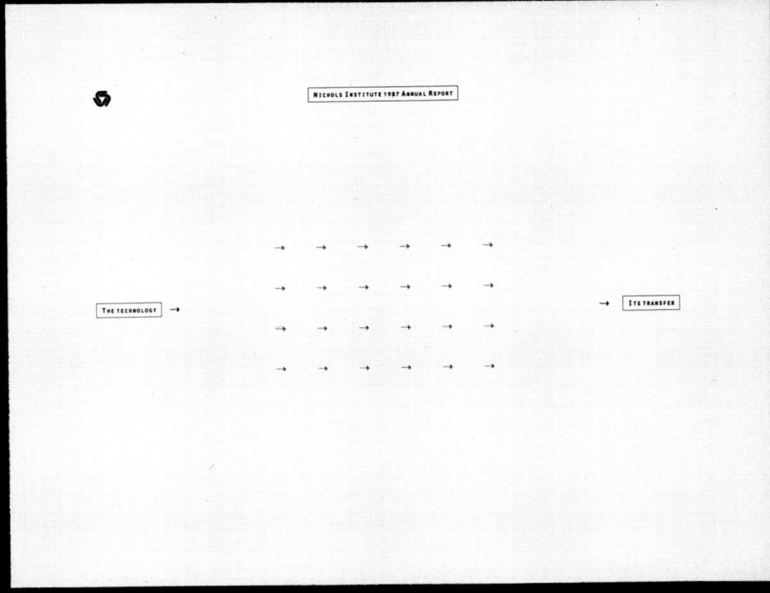

Corporate Profile

Nichols Institute is a for-profit corporation committed to transferring medical technology and information from the research bench to the patient's bedside while maintaining the quality and integrity of the academic research that created it. Nichols Institute provides comprehensive specialized testing services for diagnostic, prognostic, and therapeutic use by physicians and hospitals.

Nichols Institute is comprised of four subsidiaries. Nichols Institute Reference Laboratories works with leading academic researchers and provides specialized diagnostic tests that expedite the transfer of research findings and achieve the highest quality commercial applications. Nichols Institute Network, Inc. brings Nichols Institute's diagnostic capabilities to selected regions of the United States where market conditions demand local presence for satisfactory service. Nichols Institute Diagnostics continues this commitment to quality by creating simplified test kits that may be used by hospitals and laboratories in their own facilities. Finally, Nichols Institute International distributes test kits to international markets.

All four areas are dedicated to the same mission, to transfer and utilize new medical technology with the utmost attention to quality, respect, innovation, service, and efficiency.

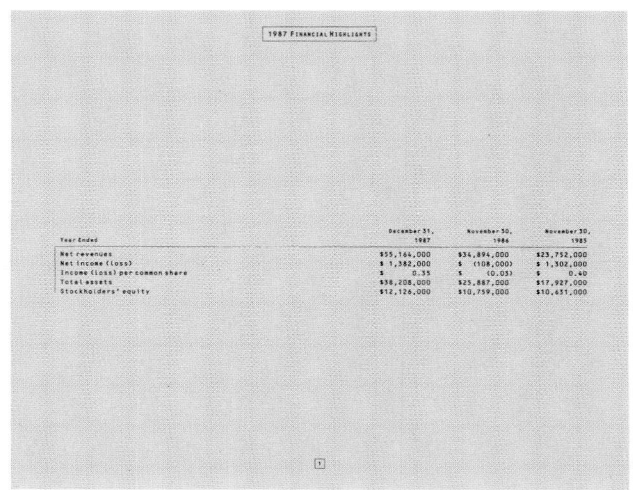

1987 Financial Highlights

Year Ended	December 31, 1987	November 30, 1986	November 30, 1985
Net revenues	$55,164,000	$34,894,000	$23,752,000
Net income (loss)	$ 1,382,000	$ (108,000)	$ 1,302,000
Income (loss) per common share	$ 0.35	$ (0.03)	$ 0.40
Total assets	$38,208,000	$25,887,000	$17,927,000
Stockholders' equity	$12,126,000	$10,759,000	$10,631,000

Message to Shareholders

Medical knowledge is increasing exponentially. Discoveries, new protocols, and valuable information emanate from research institutions across the country and around the world. All possess the same goal – to solve the puzzles of biotechnology that can improve the quality of life.

In the past it has taken as many as 10 years for the average patient to benefit from such work. The effort to harness this technology and make it available quickly to the broadest range of patients forms the ultimate mission of Nichols Institute. Over the past 17 years, Nichols Institute has developed an orchestrated approach to managing this process. Nichols Institute Reference Laboratories, Nichols Institute Network, Inc., Nichols Institute Diagnostics, and Nichols Institute International have sought to serve the medical community in the full breadth of its testing needs.

In 1986, Nichols Institute made a substantial commitment to its future through unprecedented investment that resulted in new labs, equipment, facilities, and computer systems in the fields of microbiology, toxicology, and genetics; existing labs in endocrinology, oncology, and immunology were also augmented. The Nichols Institute approach demands astute management of all resources – people, capital, revenues – to handle the explosive growth and change that has marked the delivery of health care in recent years.

In 1987, this management plan proved particularly successful as Nichols Institute reached a profitable culmination of long-term strategies and goals, with a substantial increase in net revenues over fiscal year 1986. This substantial revenue increase is one result of ongoing efforts to build and maintain the necessary framework that allows the increasing tide of discovery and technology to reach those who need it most with superior quality, accuracy, and efficiency.

At the core of Nichols Institute's mission lies the goal to approach medical issues with proactive management and initiative. At the moment, the medical community struggles with

managing AIDS and AIDS-related complex, with substance abuse, with cancer, and birth defects. Nichols Institute seeks to address these needs, to help physicians care for patients through diagnostic testing procedures and products that provide critical information on which to base medical decisions.

The business of managing science and medicine seems at times to defy the rules of business administration. Strategic planning proves at best frustrating within the health care industry. But Nichols Institute recognizes that such volatility can introduce enormous opportunities and possibilities. Ultimately the timely, appropriate response to recent developments can reap substantial benefits.

The past year reflects Nichols Institute's continuing focus on building a management and technical team that manages change – and volatility – effectively. Several executives have joined the staff, reinforcing the dynamic capabilities of the existing management team.

The ability of Nichols Institute to serve the medical community and its patients relies upon an outstanding team of researchers, directors, managers, technicians, client services representatives, local representatives, and couriers who, at all levels, work to transfer research findings and provide superior services that fundamentally address the needs of the medical community. The focus of this annual report is to illustrate the rich and varied achievements of the people who have enabled Nichols Institute to reach its goals.

Albert L. Nichols MD

Albert L. Nichols, MD
Chairman, Board of Directors
Chief Executive Officer

Williams Jones, MD

Professor of Medicine and Pediatrics
Director, Division of Medical Genetics
University of California, San Diego
Department of Medicine.

The technology

Genetic amniocentesis allows physicians to detect certain chromosomal abnormalities before the birth of a child. Such abnormalities can result in birth defects, such as Down's Syndrome. Before the development of this technology in the early 1970s, there were no means for gaining such information prior to delivery. Making such information available to assist in the care of patients is the goal of diagnostic research. In most amniocentesis cases, women enjoy the reassurance that no chromosomal abnormality exists during pregnancy. Although it cannot rule out all potential birth defects, genetic amniocentesis goes a long way toward managing those abnormalities which have a significant relationship to maternal age.

Its transfer

Developing and building a department of skilled technologists to handle the intricacies of technology such as genetic amniocentesis forms the core of my work. As a Scientific Director, I seek out individuals whose experience and sensitivity make them adept at the very close, labor-intensive detection process that can find chromosomal abnormalities in human genes. It is painstaking and delicate work.

Dr. Jones maintains an intimate link with our day-to-day work. He reviews every patient case, and when urgency dictates, he calls to discuss results with the client. Fully one third of our caseload reflect genetic abnormalities which must be addressed with sensitivity. Quality control is the most critical component of this process to ensure the accuracy of our findings. When dealing with the quality of human life, nothing less would be acceptable.

Marilyn Owens, PhD

Scientific Director
Nichols Institute Reference Laboratories
Genetics, Microbiology, Cellular Immunology, and Flow Cytometry

determine more cost-effective means for clinical testing. The position of Nichols Institute as a comprehensive reference laboratory is opportune since hospitals must turn to such sources in achieving cost containment. Hospitals and health care providers can no longer perform many tests efficiently, particularly costly specialized tests.

Nichols Institute's position as a technology leader and its relationship with major research institutions permit the first commercial application of new technology under the direction of Nichols Institute management. With a national service and sales presence, Nichols Institute maintains a strong vantage point for serving the specialized testing needs of physicians and their patients.

The international market for medical products is growing dramatically. The development of kits by Nichols Institute Diagnostics allows many of the same technologies developed by Nichols Institute's Academic Associates to reach people around the world. Presence in other parts of the world also allows Nichols Institute to be close to emerging sources of new technology outside the United States.

With previous investment in place and working, Nichols Institute has become a truly comprehensive resource for specialized testing, a resource upon which clients and their patients may fully depend.

Profit Strategies

The 1986 investment included computer systems and automation which allowed sample volume increase without concomitant labor increases in 1987. Through these volume increases Nichols Institute managed to achieve improved economies of scale.

By offering comprehensive specialized services, Nichols Institute provides greater value and convenience to the client. The superiority of Nichols Institute's products is widely recognized in the market; clients now value the ease of having one resource for all specialized needs. By continuing to strengthen its comprehensive status, Nichols Institute helps guarantee its position in the marketplace.

Luis de la Maza, MD, PhD

Professor of Pathology
University of California, Irvine
Medical Center

The technology

In microbiology we are trying to gain a better understanding of how sexually transmitted organisms produce infection. We want to improve the methods for detecting these organisms through techniques that are more rapid and sensitive than those currently available.

For example, the number of cases diagnosed with human immunodeficiency virus (HIV) infection or AIDS continuously increases, and methods for making more accurate diagnosis of an HIV infection are under development. Other sexually transmitted infections such as herpes and *Chlamydia trachomatis* have spread quickly throughout the population. The fact that we do have effective therapies for these two infections means rapid, sensitive diagnostic methods can help us curtail their impact.

Its transfer

The stimulating interaction among researchers and professionals at Nichols Institute creates a unique environment for the germination and exchange of ideas. These ideas readily translate into action, into tests and procedures that help patients on a daily basis. There is a freedom here that allows me to manage my area in ways which allow me to make the most of individual talent, to allow each technologist to apply his or her expertise. In doing so, we can help manage the revolutionary changes that are taking place in microbiology, changes that will profoundly affect the diagnosis and management of infectious diseases in years to come.

Sydney Harvey, PhD

Scientific Director
Nichols Institute Reference Laboratories
Microbiology

As a vital resource for product development and enhancement, the Nichols Institute Academic Associate Program consists of 24 distinguished academic researchers who continue to expand and strengthen the commercial application process of new technology for clinical use. In 1987, Nichols Institute Reference Laboratories extended its commitment to the fields of genetics, toxicology, and microbiology – fields which remain at the forefront of medical and public health issues, such as birth defects, substance abuse, and immune deficiency disorders.

To make such expansion possible, new researchers joined the program:

Thomas Casky, MD, FACP, heads the Institute of Molecular Genetics at Baylor College of Medicine; he manages the utilization of DNA probes for studies in genetic disease, such as cystic fibrosis;

William Nyhan, MD, PhD, professor of Pediatrics at the University of California, San Diego School of Medicine manages studies of inborn errors of metabolism;

Sydney Harvey, PhD, also joins the management team; she is Scientific Director in the area of microbiology.

Constant exploration, development, and implementation of new technology place Nichols Institute in a unique, progressive position to serve the medical community. As the economics of health care demand full-fledged dedication to cost effective measures, Nichols Institute benefits from having always approached its work from the vantage point of superior quality.

In 1987, the Voluntary Hospitals of America signed a two-year agreement which allowed Nichols Institute to offer testing services to approximately 750 member hospitals across the country, a meaningful indication of Nichols Institute's position as a recognized provider of quality, well-managed services.

As Nichols Institute Reference Laboratories continues its momentum into 1988, service holds top priority as the means to most effectively satisfy its markets.

The client benefits from three tiers of Reference Laboratory expertise and service. The continuing involvement of the Academic Associates, doctoral-level laboratory

Jerald Nelson, MD

Professor of Medicine

Associate Professor of Pathology, Loma Linda School of Medicine

Medical Director, Nichols Institute Reference Laboratories

Endocrinology

The technology

Accurate diagnosis and effective therapy are the most crucial aspects of health care.

In the past, thyroid problems were often misdiagnosed and mistreated, resulting in worse health–not better. More accurate and sensitive testing procedures can pinpoint disorders and determine the adequacy and effectiveness of particular therapy. Although thyroid disorders are rarely life threatening, they can adversely affect a patient's sense of well-being and function. Our goals now focus on testing information that allows us to treat the individual's unique needs with carefully measured and monitored therapies. As Medical Director for the Nichols Institute Endocrinology Reference Laboratory, I am available to clients and physicians on a daily basis who are faced with complex, confusing cases that need assistance in addressing the needs of patients.

Its transfer

Nichols Institute Diagnostics translates research findings of the Reference Laboratories into simplified, high quality testing kits for diagnosis and therapy. Diagnostic testing technology involves continual modification to achieve new levels of sensitivity. Academic Associates like Dr. Nelson remain highly involved in constantly assessing and modifying the technology that forms the basis for the kits and products we produce. As new information and understanding becomes available, it is integrated into our products. The result–we remain on the leading edge of our field.

12

Richard Zahradnik

Director of Research and Development

Nichols Institute Diagnostics

13

management, and highly trained local representatives, is responsible for maintaining the highest standards of response and reliability.

In addition, these same people work extensively in an educative mode to help physicians understand the procedures so that patients receive optimal diagnostic and therapeutic benefits. In 1987, approximately 1,000 calls from customers were handled each day. Client Services staffing and computer software were substantially enhanced to speed results to the client and to manage increased volume more efficiently.

In 1988, Nichols Institute Reference Laboratories expects to maintain its upward momentum, driving toward new technology and new applications supported by superior expertise and service. With the 1986 expansion in place, Nichols Institute Reference Laboratories is positioned to achieve continued growth in the coming years. The goal, as always, will remain the astute clinical application of biomedical discovery and information.

NICHOLS INSTITUTE NETWORK, INC.

Two objectives remain constant for health care providers in the late 1980s: a continued need to increase cost efficiency while maintaining clinical quality, and a growing preference for the efficiency and convenience of one resource for all testing needs. To help satisfy these objectives, Nichols Institute Network is comprised of selected laboratories through which regional areas of the United States are provided with new technology as it becomes available.

Nichols Institute Network offers hospitals and physicians convenient access to specialized, esoteric tests developed and performed by Nichols Institute Reference Laboratories as well as routine tests of superior quality and clinical correlation of results. Many of these routine medical tests require immediate turnaround. Local presence through Nichols Institute Network meets this need while strengthening awareness of Nichols Institute Reference Laboratories' capabilities.

Part of the philosophy behind this initiative reflects an integrated management approach. Nichols Institute Network laboratories exhibit responsible, effective

CONSOLIDATED BALANCE SHEETS

Nichols Institute and Subsidiaries

	December 31, 1987	November 30, 1986
Assets		
Current assets:		
Cash	$ 1,215,000	$ 196,000
Receivables–trade (net of allowance for doubtful accounts and contractual allowances of $918,000 in 1987 and $608,000 in 1986) (Notes 1 and 4)	10,482,000	7,535,000
Inventories (Notes 1 and 4)	1,953,000	1,564,000
Prepaid expenses	491,000	320,000
Income taxes receivable (Note 9)		515,000
Total current assets	14,141,000	10,130,000
Property (Notes 1, 2, 4, and 5):		
Land	1,417,000	1,154,000
Buildings	2,513,000	1,516,000
Equipment	13,757,000	10,163,000
Leasehold improvements	1,109,000	1,015,000
Total property	18,796,000	13,848,000
Less accumulated depreciation and amortization	(8,263,000)	(5,966,000)
Net property	10,533,000	7,882,000
Other assets:		
Facility development costs (Notes 1 and 2)	3,555,000	2,544,000
Investment in partnerships (Note 3)	69,000	134,000
Goodwill (net of accumulated amortization of $255,000 in 1987 and $86,000 in 1986) (Notes 1 and 12)	4,959,000	3,258,000
Covenants not to compete (net of accumulated amortization of $517,000 in 1987 and $241,000 in 1986) (Notes 1 and 12)	928,000	1,082,000
Customer lists (net of accumulated amortization of $393,000) (Notes 1 and 12)	1,888,000	
Other	2,135,000	857,000
Total other assets	13,534,000	7,875,000
Total assets	$38,208,000	$25,887,000

24

	December 31, 1987	November 30, 1986
Liabilities and Stockholders' Equity		
Current liabilities:		
Current portion of long-term debt (including subordinated debt of $1,860,000 in 1987 and $814,000 in 1986) (Note 4)	$ 3,084,000	$ 1,457,000
Accounts payable	3,227,000	2,596,000
Deferred contract revenues (Notes 1 and 10)		516,000
Accrued compensation and employee benefits	1,459,000	682,000
Accrued interest	445,000	184,000
Other accrued liabilities	794,000	493,000
Income taxes payable (Note 9)	273,000	
Deferred income taxes (Notes 1 and 9)	196,000	175,000
Total current liabilities	9,478,000	6,103,000
Long-term debt (including subordinated debt of $3,640,000 in 1987 and $1,133,000 in 1986) (Note 4)	15,739,000	8,487,000
Deferred income taxes (Notes 1 and 9)	865,000	538,000
Commitments and contingencies (Notes 2, 5, and 11)		
Stockholders' equity (Notes 4, 6 and 7):		
Preferred Stock–$.10 par value:		
Shares authorized, 500,000; Shares issued and outstanding, none		
Common Stock–$.10 par value:		
Shares authorized, 6,000,000		
Shares issued and outstanding, 2,122,803 in 1987 and 2,049,901 in 1986	212,000	205,000
Class B Common Stock–$.10 par value (convertible into common stock):		
Shares authorized, 4,000,000		
Shares issued and outstanding, 1,761,984 in 1987 and 1,824,262 in 1986	176,000	182,000
Additional paid-in capital	7,333,000	7,242,000
Retained earnings	4,484,000	3,222,000
Total	12,205,000	10,851,000
Less notes receivable from issuance of Class B Common Stock	(79,000)	(92,000)
Total stockholders' equity	12,126,000	10,759,000
Total liabilities and stockholders' equity	$38,208,000	$25,887,000

See accompanying notes to consolidated financial statements.

25

NOTES TO CONSOLIDATED FINANCIAL STATEMENTS

Nichols Institute and Subsidiaries

NOTE 1 SUMMARY OF SIGNIFICANT ACCOUNTING POLICIES

GENERAL:
The Institute operates clinical laboratories and specializes in providing ''esoteric'' testing services, manufactures certain diagnostic kits and performs related research and development. The services and kits are sold primarily to domestic customers including hospitals, medical centers, clinics, physicians, and other clinical laboratories.

PRINCIPLES OF CONSOLIDATION:
The accompanying consolidated financial statements include the accounts of Nichols Institute and its wholly and majority owned subsidiaries. All intercompany accounts and transactions have been eliminated.

INVENTORIES:
Inventories which consist principally of diagnostic kits, antisera, laboratory supplies, and packaging materials are stated at the lower of cost (first-in, first-out) or market.

PROPERTY:
Property is stated at cost and is depreciated using the straight-line method over the estimated useful lives of the related assets which range from two to twenty-five years. Leasehold improvements are amortized using the straight-line method over the shorter of the estimated useful lives of the assets or the remaining term of the related lease.

CONTRACTUAL ALLOWANCES:
The Institute provides services to certain patients covered by various third party payor programs including the Federal Medicare and state MediCal/Medicaid programs. Billings for services under these third party payor programs are included in revenues net of allowances for differences between normal billing rates and estimated program rates. Adjustments to the estimated rates based on final settlement with the programs are recorded upon settlement.

RESEARCH AND DEVELOPMENT CONTRACTS:
The Institute recognizes revenue on research and development contracts on the percentage-of-completion method, measured by costs incurred in completing the research to date relative to the total estimated costs of the contract (cost-to-cost method). Changes in estimates may result in revisions to costs and income and are recognized in the period in which the revisions are determined. Contract fees, which are generally funded in negotiated increments, received in excess of revenue recognized are recorded as deferred contract revenue.

INCOME TAXES:
The provision (credit) for income taxes is recorded based upon the reported pre-tax income (loss). Deferred income taxes are provided with respect to transactions that are reported in different periods for book and tax purposes. Investment and other tax credits are recorded on the flow-through method.

INCOME (LOSS) PER COMMON SHARE:
Income (loss) per common share is based upon the weighted average number of shares of Common Stock and Class B Common Stock (collectively ''common shares'') and common equivalent shares (if applicable) outstanding during the period. The weighted average number of common equivalent shares includes shares issuable upon the exercise of stock options and warrants less the number of shares assumed purchased with the proceeds available from such exercise.

INTEREST:
Interest costs of $368,000, $17,000, $243,000 and $93,000 were capitalized during the year ended December 31, 1987, the month ended December 31, 1986, and the years ended November 30, 1986 and 1985 respectively in connection with the Institute's facility development (Note 2).

GOODWILL:
Goodwill represents the excess cost of a purchased business over the fair value of its net assets. Goodwill is amortized using the straight-line method, generally over 25 and 40 years.

30

COVENANTS NOT TO COMPETE:
The cost of covenants not to compete is amortized using the straight-line method over the terms of the agreements (generally five years).

CUSTOMER LISTS:
The cost of customer lists is amortized using the straight-line method over the estimated period of benefit, generally five to seven years.

RECLASSIFICATIONS:
Certain amounts as previously reported have been reclassified to conform to the current period presentation.

CHANGE IN YEAR END:
During 1987, the Institute changed its fiscal year end from November 30 to December 31 to more closely align financial reporting periods to its operating cycle. The accompanying statements of consolidated operations reflect the operating results of December 1986 separately from the year ended December 31, 1987.

NOTE 2 FACILITY DEVELOPMENT COSTS

On January 30, 1986, the Institute exercised a lease option on undeveloped real property intended for a proposed new facility. During December 1986, the Institute consummated the purchase of this land for $1,000,000 in cash.

Costs related to the proposed facility development (primarily master planning, feasibility studies, water facilities, interest, option payments, and architectural and engineering fees) have been deferred until construction of the facility is completed, at which time they will be amortized over the related life of the facility and/or capitalized as part of the land costs.

On January 15, 1987, a petition was filed in the Orange County Superior Court against the County of Orange and the Board of Supervisors of Orange County claiming that the defendants' certification of the environmental impact report and approval of the use permit relating to this project violated the provisions of the California Environmental Quality Act.

A subsidiary of the Company, Nichols Institute Reference Laboratories, is named as a real party in interest in this action. The petition requested, among other things, injunctions restraining all named parties from undertaking any construction or development on the property. On June 2, 1987, the Superior Court denied all reliefs being sought by the plaintiffs. On July 3, 1987, a notice of appeal was filed with the Superior Court by the plaintiffs. The Institute believes that the claims asserted in this action are unfounded, intends to defend this matter vigorously, and expects that the injunctions being sought will be denied.

NOTE 3 INVESTMENT IN PARTNERSHIPS

The Institute and certain of its stockholders are general partners in two limited partnerships that were formed to acquire certain buildings presently leased and occupied by the Institute. The lease agreements have initial terms through 1988, with separate exercisable options to extend the terms for two and five additional years respectively. The Institute has an option to purchase the properties at fair market value, subject to certain adjustments.

The Institute sold the majority of its interest in one of these partnerships during 1985 and 1984. The gain on the sale of the partnership interests of $199,000 in 1985 has been included in other (income) expense–net in the accompanying statements of consolidated operations.

Rental payments made to the partnerships, including payments on capitalized lease obligations, amounted to approximately $600,000 during each of the years 1985 through 1987.

During 1985, the Institute acquired a 19% interest in a limited partnership for $110,000. The Institute is under contract with this partnership to develop and market diagnostic kits (see Note 10). This investment has been accounted for using the equity method of accounting.

31

NOTE 13 SELECTED QUARTERLY FINANCIAL DATA (UNAUDITED)

The following table sets forth selected financial data for the quarters indicated (based on a fiscal year ended November 30 for 1986 and a calendar year ended December 31 for 1987):

	First	Second	Third	Fourth
Revenues:				
1987	$12,652,000	$13,782,000	$14,445,000	$14,285,000
1986	7,625,000	8,827,000	8,923,000	9,519,000
Gross profit:				
1987	5,309,000	5,700,000	5,922,000	5,797,000
1986	3,179,000	3,767,000	3,684,000	4,155,000
Net income (loss)				
1987	238,000	333,000	348,000	463,000
1986	32,000	(60,000)	(181,000)	101,000
Net income (loss) per share:				
1987	$0.06	$ 0.08	$ 0.09	$0.12
1986	0.01	(0.02)	(0.05)	0.03
Weighted average number of shares outstanding:				
1987	3,884,000	3,901,000	3,941,000	3,922,000
1986	3,855,000	3,827,000	3,836,000	3,882,000

Gross profit represents revenues less cost of sales.

Reported results for the fourth quarter of 1987 include a decrease in the effective tax rate from 48% used in previous quarters to 46% as computed for the entire year. This decrease arose largely from tax benefits realized from the disposition of BioDiagnostics Laboratories.

38

SELECTED FINANCIAL DATA

Year Ended	December 31, 1987	November 30 1986	1985	1984	1983
Consolidated summary of operations:					
Total revenues	$55,164,000	$34,894,000	$23,752,000	$19,662,000	$16,735,000
Income (loss) before income taxes	2,542,000	(213,000)	1,801,000	1,190,000	992,000
Provision (credit) for income taxes	1,160,000	(105,000)	499,000	362,000	400,000
Extraordinary credit					69,000
Net income (loss)	1,382,000	(108,000)	1,302,000	828,000	661,000
Net income (loss) per common share	$0.35	$(0.03)	$0.40	$0.30	$0.25
Consolidated balance sheet data:					
Net working capital	$ 4,663,000	$ 4,027,000	$ 5,986,000	$ 1,816,000	$ 1,661,000
Total assets	38,208,000	25,887,000	17,927,000	10,841,000	9,089,000
Long-term debt	15,739,000	8,487,000	3,363,000	3,523,000	3,571,000
Stockholders' equity	12,126,000	10,759,000	10,631,000	3,622,000	2,894,000
Equity per share	$3.12	$2.78	$2.79	$1.36	$1.08

Nichols Institute has never paid any dividends.

See Note 12 in the accompanying consolidated financial statements for a discussion of the impacts of business acquisitions on operating results and Management's Discussion and Analysis of Financial Condition and Results of Operations for a discussion of the anticipated future impacts of the reduction of the maximum Federal corporate tax rate to 34 percent.

MARKET FOR REGISTRANT'S COMMON EQUITY AND RELATED STOCKHOLDER MATTERS

The Institute's Common Stock is listed on the American Stock Exchange and is reported under the symbol ''Lab.'' There is no established public trading market for the Institute's Class B Common Stock. The following table sets forth the reported high and low sales prices for the Common Stock of the Institute for the quarters indicated (based on a fiscal year ending November 30 for 1986, after which the information is based on the calendar ending December 31, to coincide with the change in the Institute's year end) as reported by the Wall Street Journal:

	1987 High	1987 Low	1986 High	1986 Low
First quarter	7 1/2	4 1/2	9 3/4	7 1/2
Second quarter	8 3/8	6	12	8 1/4
Third quarter	10 1/8	7 3/4	11 3/8	7 3/4
Fourth quarter	9 3/8	4 1/8	8 1/4	6 1/8

As of January 31, 1988 there were approximately 390 holders of record of the Institute's outstanding Common Stock, but the Institute believes that the number of beneficial owners greatly exceeds that amount. The approximate number of holders of record of the Institute's outstanding Class B Common Stock at that date was 107.

The Institute has not paid cash dividends on shares of its Common Stock or Class B Common Stock to date and presently intends to retain all earnings to fund its operations. The Institute's current bank agreement prohibits the payment of cash dividends (see Note 4 in the accompanying consolidated financial statements).

39

CLIENT:
NICHOLS INSTITUTE

DESIGN FIRM:
ROBERT MILES RUNYAN & ASSOCIATES

ART DIRECTOR:
JIM BERTÉ

DESIGNER:
JIM BERTÉ

PHOTOGRAPHER:
SCOTT MORGAN

WRITER:
JULIE SUHR

TYPOGRAPHER:
COMPOSITION TYPE

PAPER SELECTION:
REFLECTIONS, CARNIVAL KRAFT, CORONADO SST

PAPER MANUFACTURER:
CONSOLIDATED, CHAMPION, SIMPSON

PRINTER:
RALPH'S PRINTING

NUMBER OF PAGES:
40 PLUS COVER

SIZE:
11" X 8 1/2"

TYPE SELECTION:
OPTICAL CHARACTER RECOGNITION B

ADELE SIMON, MARKETING COMMUNICATIONS MANAGER, NICHOLS INSTITUTE, SAN JUAN CAPISTRANO, CALIFORNIA

Nichols Institute is a corporation which takes academic research and transfers these findings from the academic to the commercial. In other words, from the research laboratory to the bedside.The 1987 annual report presented the idea of this change from the first concept to the finished product. We needed to show our academic associates and their methods in-house, through clinical testing. This was a very good piece, this annual report. It was innovative, not run-of-the-mill. It got a great response in the design community. The firm was going through some corporate changes at this time, and the transition was a little difficult. We had an earlier, more beautiful version planned for this annual report, but the circumstances just were not favorable for it.

ADELE SIMON, MARKETING COMMUNICATIONS MANAGER, NICHOLS INSTITUTE, SAN JUAN CAPISTRANO, KALIFORNIEN

Nichols Institute befasst sich mit akademischen Forschungsergebnissen und deren praktischer Anwendung - mit anderen Worten, vom Labor bis zum Patienten. Im Jahresbericht 1987 geht es um den Weg vom ersten Konzept bis zum fertigen Produkt. Wir wollten unsere akademischen Kollegen zeigen, ihre Laborarbeit bis hin zum klinischen Test. Dieser Jahresbericht ist wirklich gelungen. Er war innovativ, kein Massenprodukt. Von Design-Fachleuten kamen zahlreiche positive Kommentare. In der Firmenstruktur wurden zu jener Zeit gerade einige Änderungen vorgenommen, und die Übergangsphase war ein bisschen schwierig. Wir hatten zuerst eine aufwendigere Version geplant, aber unter den gegebenen Umständen war das nicht angebracht.

ADELE SIMON, MARKETING COMMUNICATIONS MANAGER, NICHOLS INSTITUTE, SAN JUAN CAPISTRANO, CALIFORNIE

Le Nichols Institute est une société qui transpose au plan commercial les résultats de recherches universitaires. En d'autres mots, du labo à la table de chevet. Le rapport annuel pour 1987 incarne l'idée de cette transposition de la conception première au produit fini. Il nous fallait présenter nos associés universitaires et les méthodes qu'ils appliquent à l'expérimentation clinique. Ce rapport annuel est très bien tourné novateur. La communauté de design s'est montrée très favorable à son égard. La société connaissait à l'époque quelques changements au niveau de la direction, et la transition a été quelque peu difficile. Nous avions préparé une première version plus belle, mais les circonstances n'ont pas été favorables à sa publication.

JIM BERTÉ, ROBERT MILES RUNYAN & ASSOCIATES, PLAYA DEL REY, CALIFORNIA

Nichols Institute is a small company primarily involved in transferring information from the research bench to the medical community. For the annual report, we tried to focus on the experts in the company. The Chairman was involved in fine art and influenced our initial direction. The photo collages we originally created were 16 x 10 inches. We felt the bigger pictures better conveyed the seriousness of the medical research. But the Chairman had second thoughts about the images, so we eliminated the collages altogether and in their place used blown-up versions of portraits. We also had to fit in a lot of existing copy when the size of the book was changed at the last minute. We decided to use a computer-printed looking typeface. On the cover, we used the idea of transference of information to product, and we picked up the look of computer-printed type. Ultimately, the report was well-received, both by the client and the communities for which it was intended.

JIM BERTÉ, ROBERT MILES RUNYAN & ASSOCIATES, PLAYA DEL REY, KALIFORNIEN

Nichols ist eine kleine Firma, die sich vor allem mit Forschungsergebnissen medizinischer Experten und deren Vermarktung befasst. Wir versuchten, Fachleute dieser Firma zu zeigen, die für jemanden ein Produkt oder eine Dienstleistung von der Forschung bis hin zur Vermarktung betreut. Wir hatten Porträts in einer Grösse von l6"x10" gemacht. Aber wir mussten sie klein zeigen. Die grösseren Bilder entsprachen zwar der Vorstellung von Medizin und Forschung besser, aber der Geschäftsführer hatte seine Meinung geändert. Der Text musste auch der neuen Grössensituation angepasst werden. Wir erfassten alle Daten auf dem Computer und druckten sie aus. Für den Umschlag benutzten wir die Idee der Übertragung von Informationen auf ein Produkt, und wir übernahmen die typische Computerschrift. Wir haben festgestellt, dass wir die Leute ängstigen, wenn wir etwas Neues machen; es ist schwer, vom Üblichen wegzukommen.

JIM BERTÉ, ROBERT MILES RUNYAN & ASSOCIATES, PLAYA DEL REY, CALIFORNIE

Nichols est une petite société essentiellement active dans les applications pratiques de la recherche médicale. Nous avons voulu dresser le portrait des spécialistes qui y travaillent pour faciliter la recherche en vue de la fabrication d'un produit ou service commercialisable. Les portraits réalisés tout d'abord mesuraient 16" sur 10" mais nous devions les tirer au petit format bien que le grand format aurait mieux décrivé la profession médicale et la recherche. Mais le P.-D.G. a repensé la question des formats. Il a fallu adapter conséquemment les textes déjà rédigés, ce qui nous a amenés à transférer toutes ces données sur ordinateur et à en faire des print-outs. La couverture reprend l'idée du transfert de l'information au produit, avec en gaufrage des caractères d'imprimante. Nous avons découvert que lorsque nous nous hasardons sur des chemins nouveaux, cela commence par faire peur aux gens trop habitués aux présentations standards.

ARTS
COUNCIL
43rd annual
report
and accounts
87
88

The Arts Council of Great Britain was formed in August 1946 to continue in peacetime the work begun with Government support by the Council for the Encouragement of Music and the Arts. The Arts Council operates under a revised Royal Charter granted in 1967 in which its objects are stated as:

(a) to develop and improve the knowledge, understanding and practice of the arts;
(b) to increase the accessibility of the arts to the public throughout Great Britain;
(c) to advise and co-operate with departments of government, local authorities and other bodies.

The Arts Council, as a publicly accountable body, publishes an annual report and accounts to provide Parliament and the general public with an overview of the year's work.

contents

CHAIRMAN'S introduction

Lord Rees-Mogg

David Banks

"Those responsible for the distribution of public monies to the arts must never lose sight of the goal of excellence."

This is my last report as Chairman of the Arts Council, so it may be appropriate if my mind, in valedictory mood, surveys not only the last 12 months, but all my seven years in office. When I arrived, I brought with me to the Council a worthy guide, Samuel Johnson; if there is one achievement of which I have the fondest memory, it is the exhibition in 1984 held at our headquarters in Piccadilly, at my suggestion, to mark the bicentenary of his death.

The Arts Council is in the business of patronage — a subject about which the Doctor had something to say — and I hope that in my time it has learnt to avoid the arrogance of one kind of patron (the aristocrat whose functions the Arts Council has now in large part assumed) and to court the favours of quite another kind, the citizen. We are coming to value the consumer's judgement as highly as that of the official or the expert. So if the institution which I will leave next March on the expiry of my term is in need of a motto, it could do worse than to adopt the lines Johnson wrote for Garrick:

The drama's laws, the drama's patrons give,
For we that live to please must please to live.

The Arts Council is proud of its traditional commitment to judgement by peers. Our panels, boards and committees are well stocked with distinguished representatives from the arts professions. But their advice, although essential, is not sufficient. The voice of the public must also be given due weight. This is the fundamental reason why I support the Council's objective to reduce the arts world's reliance on state subsidy and to lower the proportion (but not of course the absolute amount) of grant to the overall turnover of arts organisations; for the way in which the public discriminates is through its willingness to pay for its pleasures.

An early milestone of my chairmanship was the publication of the Arts Council's strategy document, *The Glory of the Garden*, also in 1984. This represented the first major effort since we closed our regional offices in 1956 to decentralise decision-making — devolving important responsibilities to the 12 English Regional Arts Associations and working even more closely than before with local government. So far we have not shifted as many resources from London to the regions as we would have liked, but in other respects Glory has succeeded in re-drawing the English arts map.

With hardly a pause the Arts Council went on to address the challenge which the abolition of the Greater London Council and the metropolitan county councils presented. Co-operating with the Regional Arts Associations and the successor councils and aided by a generous subvention from government, we were able to ensure that the arts took no harm.

We inherited the South Bank Centre, already a success story under the Greater London Council, we turned it into a triumph. The Arts Council was responsible for the Centre's management for two years, and then, last April, was able to give it independence. It flourishes like the bay tree.

The Arts Council as a bureaucracy is now in good shape to face the challenge of the times. Although there is some streamlining still to do, the reform of our organisational arrangements — and in particular the formation of three new departments for Marketing, for Film, Video and Broadcasting and for Planning — has significantly increased our effectiveness.

The outcome has been a great release of energy. We are moving forward on many fronts; a selection of recent initiatives include a radical reform of the system of client evaluation; help for ethnic minority arts; a code of practice on the arts and disability; the development of incentive funding; the formation of an independent drama production company, Upstart; the opening of our doors to the arts of other nations.

What the future will bring I do not seek to predict with any degree of certainty. But I believe that the imminent reform of broadcasting and the impact of technical advances on the mass media will bring important opportunities for the arts which the Arts Council is now well-placed to seize, and must not shirk.

Finally, those responsible for the distribution of public monies to the arts must never lose sight of the goal of excellence. The word fell into desuetude as the Arts Council, in collaboration with the Regional Arts Associations, developed policies which had the central aim of increasing the accessibility of the arts to all sorts and conditions of men and women. The Council was right to adopt this course, but must always take care not to be seen to abandon those on whose daring and skill — the painters, sculptors, actors, composers, film-makers, writers, musicians, dancers — the whole great enterprise of culture depends.

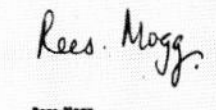

Rees-Mogg

DEPARTMENTAL reports

COMBINED ARTS

Graham Marchant, Director: Arts Co-ordination

Notting Hill Carnival

This was a year of considerable change as the implications of the organisational review became apparent. Now that arts centres and community arts are properly the responsibility of Regional Arts Associations, it has become less necessary for the Council itself to maintain separate resources. Accordingly, arrangements were made for both South Hill Park Arts Centre and Riverside Studios to be funded in future solely by their respective Regional Arts Association, reduced funds for the National Association of Arts Centres are being devolved, and responsibility for Free Form is being transferred to the Visual Arts department. This will leave only two clients: the Notting Hill Carnival and the ICA. From 1988/89 the affairs of these clients will be reported directly to Council and dealt with by the Director: Arts Co-ordination himself. Accordingly the Combined Arts unit has ceased to exist. Responsibility for performance art henceforth reverts to the Visual Arts department, which used to deal with it in the 1970s.

Commissioning funds for new live work were held by Projects UK, Chisenhale Dance Space and a consortium in the North West of England called No Quarter. Performances for railway stations in Manchester, Halifax and Liverpool, and a Halloween project conceived by Mary Prestidge, Fran Cottell and Jan Howarth for a site on a canal in the East End of London, all demonstrated how large-scale live events can successfully operate in outdoor spaces, giving a higher public profile to an area of work which had often been considered inaccessible.

The first performance art summer school was organised by No Quarter, with additional subsidy from the Training section. One of the tutors on the course, Stephen Taylor Woodrow, probably best known for his *Living Paintings*, started his community placement at South Hill Park Arts Centre. He will be based at the centre for two years on a part-time basis with a brief to involve the local community in the practice of live art.

A pilot project with the Education unit established short-term placements for live artists in the fine art departments of three art schools. Much energetic work developed out of these placements, which it is hoped will eventually contribute to strengthening live work within fine art courses and to increasing skills amongst younger artists. Many such artists will be hoping to showcase their work in events such as the National Review of Live Art. The festival this year was hosted by the Riverside Studios and welcomed the largest audience in its history.

An overview of current practice and a brief history of performance is offered by the publication of *Live Art Now*. Copies of this book are available for sale from bookshops in selected galleries and art centres. In addition, the Visual Arts department will continue to update its information on artists and venues interested in live art.

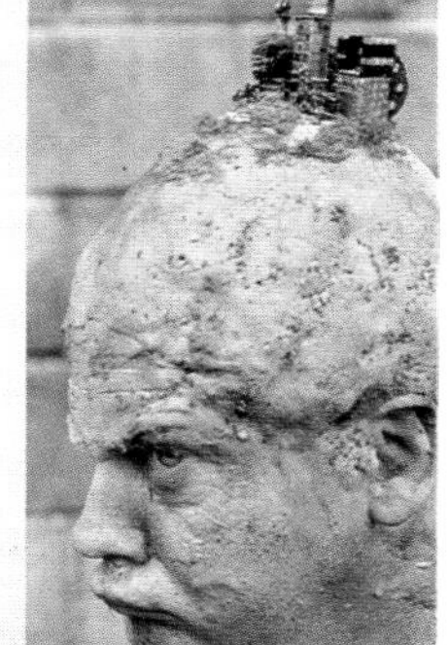

Hypochondria by Forkbeard Fantasy, ICA

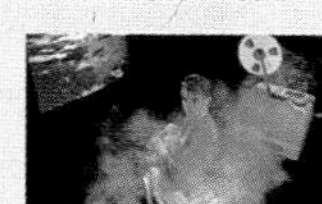

Graeme Miller in Desert in The Garden

INCOME PROFILE OF REVENUE CLIENTS

8

9

DEPARTMENTAL

reports

LITERATURE

Fleur Adcock

Alastair Niven, Director of Literature

In the past year the Council has continued its reappraisal of the role of the Literature department and its confirmation of the value of literature as a major British art form which deserves public subsidy. New attitudes have led to the generation of new life. There are two reasons for this.

First, the new literature policy statements were warmly welcomed by the Council and the literary community, outlining as they did strategies for enhancing access to reading, support for writers and an internationalist view of writing. Secondly, by appointing a new full-time Literature Director, Dr Alastair Niven, after an interim period when the post was under discussion, the Council underlined its commitment to the equality of literature as an artform within its remit. The Council has looked very searchingly at the role of literature within the arts and now takes a positive and optimistic view of it, aware of its particular value to the Council's educational and multi-cultural policies. Underlying this is a recognition that literature, past and contemporary, is one of the glories of the nation.

Certainly there are heightened expectations of us among the public and press, though not all of these can be realised within the modest budget available. Money for literature has, however, risen by 35% for the 1988/89 financial year as a result of seeds sown in the year under review.

One of the year's major themes was internationalism. Plans were laid to establish a multi-cultural policy of support for literary activities, including a fund to assist published translations, backing for projects to extend reading opportunities for children, and a co-ordinating facility for writers' tours.

A report on black and multi-cultural publishing was commissioned and steps were taken to introduce a positive policy of support for literature in education. It is proposed, for example, to bring teachers together to discuss some of the problems they may face when talking about contemporary poetry or black writing in the classroom.

We participated for the first time in Council of Europe discussions to promote poetry and a new policy was introduced of encouraging knowledge of overseas literatures, especially those originating in the English language. Dr Niven also attended the triennial European Conference on Commonwealth Literature.

Much of the year was spent in re-establishing strong links with the Regional Arts Associations. The Director visited many areas of the country to see the range of literary activities – small press publishing, writers' groups, festivals, exhibitions, adult education classes, prison and community attachments, library schemes, etc – which take place in most parts of Britain.

This year we must say goodbye and thank you to Robert Woof, Chairman of the Literature Advisory Panel. He is succeeded by the novelist P D James. We also congratulate the Writers' Awards winners – Fleur Adcock, Ken Smith and Carole Satyamurti – all poets.

It has been a year of new policies within the department, new attitudes towards literature, new overtures abroad – a time of prospects and goodwill. But there is still much ground to be regained before literature at the Arts Council is back at the financial strength it once had. In its defence of literary interests, however, and in its view of literature as integral to the artistic health of Britain, the Council is now more vigorous than it has been for many years.

INCOME PROFILE OF REVENUE CLIENTS

Box Office & Other Earned Income 71%

LA & Other Public Subsidy 1%

ACGB Subsidy 28%

Schools workshop at the Arvon Foundation

16

17

Summary for PARTIALLY SIGHTED people

Government funding of the Council was announced on a three year basis, allowing us to plan further ahead and use resources far more effectively.

An incentive funding scheme was developed out of a special government fund, aiming to improve arts organisations' financial stability by encouraging better management and increased private sector income. An international initiatives fund was created to develop our role in international cultural affairs.

Upstart, an independent touring theatre company, was set up with Arts Council capital-isation to produce plays and musicals on tour.

London's South Bank became independent after two years as part of the Council.

A tape version of this report is available on request. The Arts Council operates an equal opportunities policy.

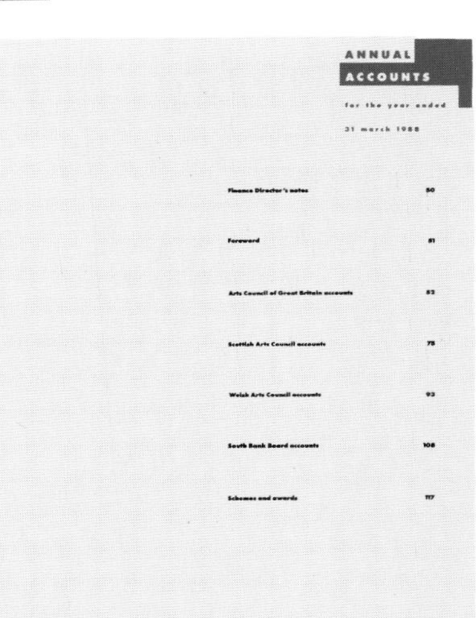

ANNUAL ACCOUNTS

for the year ended 31 march 1988

49

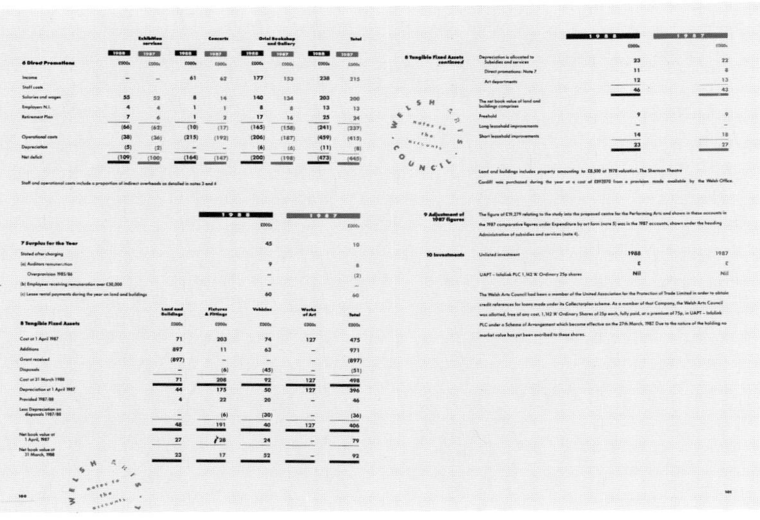

6 Direct Promotions	Exhibition services 1988 £000s	Exhibition services 1987 £000s	Concerts 1988 £000s	Concerts 1987 £000s	Oriel Bookshop and Gallery 1988 £000s	Oriel Bookshop and Gallery 1987 £000s	Total 1988 £000s	Total 1987 £000s
Income	–	–	61	62	177	153	238	215
Staff costs								
Salaries and wages	55	52	8	14	140	134	203	200
Employers N.I.	4	4	1	1	8	8	13	13
Retirement Plan	7	6	1	2	17	16	25	24
	(66)	(62)	(10)	(17)	(165)	(158)	(241)	(237)
Operational costs	(38)	(36)	(215)	(192)	(206)	(187)	(459)	(415)
Depreciation	(5)	(2)	–	–	(6)	(6)	(11)	(8)
Net deficit	(109)	(100)	(164)	(147)	(200)	(198)	(473)	(445)

Staff and operational costs include a proportion of indirect overheads as detailed in notes 3 and 4

	1988 £000s	1987 £000s
7 Surplus for the Year	45	10
Stated after charging		
(a) Auditors remuneration	9	8
Overprovision 1985/86	–	(2)
(b) Employees receiving remuneration over £30,000	–	–
(c) Lease rental payments during the year on land and buildings	60	60

8 Tangible Fixed Assets	Land and Buildings £000s	Fixtures & Fittings £000s	Vehicles £000s	Works of Art £000s	Total £000s
Cost at 1 April 1987	71	203	74	127	475
Additions	897	11	63	–	971
Grant received	(897)	–	–	–	(897)
Disposals	–	(6)	(45)	–	(51)
Cost at 31 March 1988	71	208	92	127	498
Depreciation at 1 April 1987	44	175	50	127	396
Provided 1987/88	4	22	20	–	46
Less Depreciation on disposals 1987/88	–	(6)	(30)	–	(36)
	48	191	40	127	406
Net book value at 1 April, 1987	27	28	24	–	79
Net book value at 31 March, 1988	23	17	52	–	92

100

8 Tangible Fixed Assets continued	1988 £000s	1987 £000s
Depreciation is allocated to Subsidies and services	23	22
Direct promotions: Note 7	11	8
Art departments	12	13
	46	43
The net book value of land and buildings comprises		
Freehold	9	9
Long leasehold improvements	–	–
Short leasehold improvements	14	18
	23	27

Land and buildings includes property amounting to £8,500 at 1978 valuation. The Sherman Theatre Cardiff was purchased during the year at a cost of £897070 from a provision made available by the Welsh Office.

9 Adjustment of 1987 figures The figure of £19,279 relating to the study into the proposed centre for the Performing Arts and shown in these accounts in the 1987 comparative figures under Expenditure by art form (note 5) was in the 1987 accounts, shown under the heading Administration of subsidies and services (note 4).

10 Investments	1988 £	1987 £
Unlisted investment		
UAPT – Infolink PLC 1,142 'A' Ordinary 25p shares	Nil	Nil

The Welsh Arts Council had been a member of the United Association for the Protection of Trade Limited in order to obtain credit references for loans made under its Collectorplan scheme. As a member of that Company, the Welsh Arts Council was allotted, free of any cost, 1,142 'A' Ordinary Shares of 25p each, fully paid, at a premium of 75p, in UAPT – Infolink PLC under a Scheme of Arrangement which became effective on the 27th March, 1987. Due to the nature of the holding no market value has yet been ascribed to these shares.

101

CLIENT:
THE ARTS COUNCIL OF GREAT BRITAIN

DESIGN FIRM:
GIANT

ART DIRECTORS:
NEIL SMITH, MARTYN HEY, ALAN HERRON, MARK ROLLINSON

DESIGNER:
NEIL SMITH

PHOTOGRAPHERS:
GLYN WILLIAMS, CLINT ELEY, DAVID BANKS

ILLUSTRATORS:
NEIL SMITH, MARTYN HEY

WRITERS:
VARIOUS

PRODUCTION MANAGER:
NEIL SMITH

TYPOGRAPHER:
NEIL SMITH

PAPER SELECTION:
HIGH SPEED TINTED PEACH, CONSORT ROYAL MATT

PAPER MANUFACTURER:
WIGGINS TEAPE, THE DONSIDE PAPER CO.

PRINTER:
LINO-TECH, LONDON

NUMBER OF PAGES:
120 PLUS 4-PAGE COVER

TYPE SELECTION:
FUTURA DEMIBOLD, FUTURA EXTRA BOLD

NIGEL SHERVEY, COMMUNICATIONS MANAGER, THE ARTS COUNCIL OF GREAT BRITAIN, LONDON, ENGLAND

In our 1987-88 annual report, we were addressing different audiences. We have an arts audience, and we have a specific message for them–that we are a planning and an enterprising body. We need to project our efficiency and the concomitant artistic quality we provide. We also direct this report to our government here, since the arts need more government money. We give information and we created in this annual report a reflection of the arts in the U.K. We had changed the format of our annual report. It had been dull and dreary, with no color. Then we decided that our annual report could be an effective means of communication, and that it would be more likely to be noticed if it looked attractive. We received favorable responses from a number of politicians.

NEIL SMITH, GIANT, LONDON, ENGLAND

Although the Arts Council is a government organization, we were told that the annual report should also apppeal to businesses for sponsorship. We had to produce quite a hefty document. The specific photographs for each of the sections were provided to us, so we arranged to have the cover photograph and the background photographs taken. We provided unity through color and a continuous backgound running throughout. Although in many ways this was difficult to do from a design point of view, everybody liked it when it was finished.

NIGEL SHERVEY, COMMUNICATIONS MANAGER, THE ARTS COUNCIL OF GREAT BRITAIN, LONDON, ENGLAND

Mit unserem Bericht für 1987-88 wenden wir uns an ein unterschiedliches Publikum. Da ist einmal das kunstorientierte Publikum, dem wir mitteilen wollen, dass wir viel planen und unternehmen. Ausserdem richtet sich der Bericht auch an die hiesige Regierung, weil für die Kunst mehr öffentliche Mittel benötigt werden. Wir informieren und bieten in diesem Jahresbericht einen Überblick über das Kunstschaffen im U.K. Wir hatten den Stil unseres Jahresberichtes geändert. Vorher waren die Berichte langweilig und eintönig. Dann stellten wir fest, dass unser Jahresbericht auch ein effektives Kommunikationsmittel werden könnte und dass er mehr Chancen hätte, beachtet zu werden, wenn er attraktiver aussehen würde. Eine Reihe von Politikern reagierte positiv.

NEIL SMITH, GIANT, LONDON, ENGLAND

Obgleich der Arts Council eine staatliche Organisation ist, sollte der Bericht vor allem Sponsoren aus der Wirtschaft ansprechen Wir mussten ein umfangreiches Dokument zusammenstellen. Die Aufnahmen für die einzelnen Sektoren wurden uns geliefert, während wir für die Umschlagaufnahme und Hintergrundphotos sorgten. Durch den Einsatz von Farbe und den Hintergrund erreichten wir ein einheitliches Bild. Obgleich dies in vieler Hinsicht keine leichte gestalterische Aufgabe war, waren alle mit dem fertigen Produkt zufrieden.

NIGEL SHERVEY, COMMUNICATIONS MANAGER, THE ARTS COUNCIL OF GREAT BRITAIN, LONDRES, GRANDE-BRETAGNE

Dans notre rapport pour 1987-88, nous nous adressons à différentes catégories de lecteurs. D'une part, nous avons un public artistique auquel nous aimerions expliquer que nous sommes une organisation entreprenante. A cet effet, il faut pouvoir démontrer notre efficacité. Ce rapport s'adresse aussi au gouvernement, puisque l'Etat est censé subventionner tout ce qui touche à l'art. L'information que nous accumulons dans ce rapport couvre l'entier des activités culturelles du Royaume-Uni. Nous avions déjà changé le format de nos rapports, qui paraissaient quelque peu ternes. Pour faire de ce document un moyen de communication actif, nous avons cherché à lui donner un caractère plus attrayante. Beaucoup d'hommes politiques nous avons témoigné leur satisfaction avec ce rapport.

NEIL SMITH, GIANT, LONDRES, G.-B.

Bien que l'Arts Council soit une organisation gouvernementale, nous avons été priés de tenir compte également des sponsors potentiels à recruter dans les milieux d'affaires. Il en est résulté un gros document. Pour chaque chapitre, nous avons reçu les photos correspondantes; nous nous sommes occupés de la photo de couverture et des photos d'ambiance, donnant une unité à l'ouvrage par le biais de la couleur et d'une thématique photo continue. La tâche n'a pas été facile du point de vue de la stylique, et pourtant tout le monde a exprimé son approbation.

B E I   E L E C T R O N I C S ,   I N C .

Selected Financial Data

Business Statement

BEI Electronics, Inc. (BEI) is a diversified technology company which designs, manufactures and markets high technology systems and products principally under two subsidiaries: BEI Defense Systems Company and BEI Motion Systems Company. BEI has seven manufacturing facilities located in Arkansas, Texas and California and employs nearly six hundred nationwide.

BEI Defense Systems Company supplies rocket systems, combat and training warheads, electronic fire control systems, field support services and special ordnance components to the U.S. Department of Defense and U.S. allies throughout the free world.

BEI Motion Systems Company supplies precision electronic, optical, magnetic and electromechanical motion control systems and components for a wide range of industrial, commercial and military applications including computer controlled machines, aerospace, and factory automation.

(Dollars in thousands except per share data)

Year Ended 30 September	1987	1986	1985	1984	1983
Net Sales	$47,346	$40,210	$40,507	$36,537	$30,263
Net Income	$ 3,186	$ 1,934	$ 1,909	$ 2,587	$ 1,624
Net Income per Share	$ 2.50	$ 1.49	$ 1.36	$ 1.86	$ 1.15
Working Capital	$ 8,695	$ 5,942	$ 5,526	$ 4,369	$ 3,481
Total Assets	$28,374	$22,659	$22,489	$16,851	$15,795
Long Term Debt	$ 3,160	$ 3,947	$ 3,755	$ 3,047	$ 3,343
Shareholders' Equity	$13,756	$10,562	$10,427	$ 8,669	$ 6,201
Firm Backlog at Sept. 30	$60,661	$57,769	$50,442	$40,611	$51,347

2 3

To Our Shareholders

The Company is pleased to report that Fiscal Year 1987 was a very successful year for BEI Electronics, Inc. Consolidated sales of $47.3 million were approximately 18 percent above Fiscal Year 1986, and net income of $3.2 million was up 65 percent from the prior year. During fiscal 1987 BEI also received $51.8 million in new orders, a 25 percent increase over fiscal 1986. At September 30, 1987, the Company's backlog of unfilled orders was over $60 million. All of these results were new Company records. Continued growth in sales and earnings is projected for the coming year. ◖Significant progress was made during the fiscal year toward consolidating BEI's position as a full systems supplier to its major markets. The Defense Systems subsidiary expanded its role as the lead contractor in the Hydra-70 program. The Hydra-70 is the most advanced free-flight aerial rocket system in the inventory of the United States military forces. It embodies state-of-the art technology in propulsion, warheads, electronic fuzing and rocket fire control systems. New tactical applications were developed and fire control capabilities were extended to encompass integrated management of other armament systems. Extensive bookings were received for new rocket motors and warheads and there has been a growing interest in the system capabilities among other free world forces already generating significant orders. The Motion Systems subsidiary continued to improve and broaden its product lines, extending its ability to respond to customer requirements over a wider range of technical problems. During the year it won prototype orders for new strategic defense, space, and industrial applications; was awarded an important contract in the superconducting super collider project; and developed new systems applications combining BEI technical excellence in optical encoders, brushless motors, actuators and magnetics. ◖The Company is excited about the future growth potential of its products and technology. To prepare for this anticipated future growth, the Company strengthened its organization structure during fiscal 1987 by adding seasoned professionals in critical management skill positions, including a new Corporate Chief Financial Officer, a Corporate Treasurer, a new President for Defense Systems Company, and key marketing and technical personnel at each subsidiary. Production capacity was increased at Defense Systems Company and additional capital was invested in expanding and upgrading engineering, computing and program management capabilities. The Company significantly increased its underlying financial strength through completion of a new banking arrangement effectively doubling its available credit line. During the year the Company began to relocate its corporate office from Little Rock, Arkansas, to obtain the advantages of proximity to major financial services and technological resources available in the San Francisco Bay Area. ◖The Company's long term growth strategy is to reinvest its earnings to increase its available market by extending its role as a systems supplier, improving and expanding on current product offerings, introducing or purchasing complementary new technology, and developing international business. BEI has had consistent success at designing, developing and extending its technology to provide added value to its customers. As you will discover in these pages, the Company possesses strong and diversified technologies and competes at the high-end of its marketplace. The people of BEI Electronics, Inc. are proven in their response to challenge and the Company approaches the future with confidence.

Sincerely,

Charles C. Crocker
Chairman

George S. Brown
President and CEO

(dollars in thousands) *Net Sales* *Net Income* *Shareholders' Equity* *Firm Backlog at Sept. 30*

6 7

Hydra-70 Versatile and Powerful

During 1987, BEI Defense Systems Company enhanced its capabilities as a total systems aerospace contractor. Despite increased competitiveness and reduced budgets BEI has developed the Hydra-70 rocket weapons system into a versatile, low cost force multiplier. The Hydra-70 employs relatively inexpensive rockets with remote settable fuzes and powerful warheads adaptable to many existing launch platforms and combat scenarios. BEI fire control systems allow the Hydra-70 to integrate with other weapons systems. The concepts developed for air-to-ground deployment are now being used for air-to-air, ground-to-ground, and ground-to-air operations to provide a high growth market for free-flight rocket systems. Substantial progress was made this year in extending Hydra-70 capabilities, especially in development of new warheads and fire-control systems. ◖BEI design efforts produced a training warhead with a smoke puff charge for day or night use, which reduces damage to instrumented test ranges from explosive warheads. It is anticipated that sizeable quantities of this training round will be required for many years to train and maintain the proficiency of military pilots and gunners. ◖In addition, BEI was awarded contracts to develop a red phosphorous smoke warhead to provide a highly versatile obscuration capability to US forces; and a special air-to-air warhead to combat the growth of helicopter gunships among unfriendly forces. These will be added to the Hydra-70 arsenal along with the high explosive and multi-purpose submunition warheads currently in production. ◖Another major accomplishment was the development of the Armament Management System for integrated fire control of rockets, guns and other ordnance aboard high performance and rotary-wing aircraft. A number of these systems have been sold to approved foreign forces for use on helicopter fleets.

The HYDRA-70 equipped Cobra attack helicopter provides effective fire power against ground-base targets, and combats the increased threat from unfriendly helicopters.

The Hydra-70 offers a dependable cost effective weapons system that is launched from a wide variety of combat platforms.

To increase the Hydra-70's versatility, BEI offers a broad range of additional warhead/fuze combinations — for providing smoke screens, for illuminating a target with 1 million candle power, or like the chaff warhead shown here, to broadcast radar jamming material.

Gateways to Tomorrow in Motion Control

For fiscal 1988 BEI Motion Systems has three major objectives. First, to participate in the anticipated renaissance of space programs; second, to exploit the innovations flowing from the company's research and development activities and, third, to continue building the industry's strongest team of sales and application engineers. ◖Space applications have been a traditional BEI market and significant business is expected from resumed shuttle flights and foreign space programs with payloads calling for BEI motor-encoder and servo drives. ◖Among the new products are a family of more accurate, smaller and lightweight encoders approved for advanced missile guidance systems and laser defense and communications systems. These are markets not previously addressed where BEI cost-effectiveness and technical excellence are gaining favorable recognition. BEI's strong industrial position is enhanced by new encoders and brushless motors for process control, factory and office automation and medical products. ◖Additional growth will result from work on fiber-optics remotable motion and proximity transducers and on special purpose magnetic devices. Applications include "fly-by-light" controls for advanced aircraft; industrial controls for severe environments; and magnetic levitation, vibration control, and bearing systems for industry, space and defense. ◖BEI's focus on application engineering will result in increasing combinations of BEI motion products and know how, such as new infra-red imaging scanners for missile guidance and driver/pilot vision; computer aided test systems for pointing and tracking components; and electronic drives for a myriad of computer controlled industrial and scientific products.

BEI supplies its new line of mil-spec ruggedized encoders, motors and drive electronics to support infra-red scanning systems employed in missile guidance and navigation systems and airborne or ground based night vision systems.

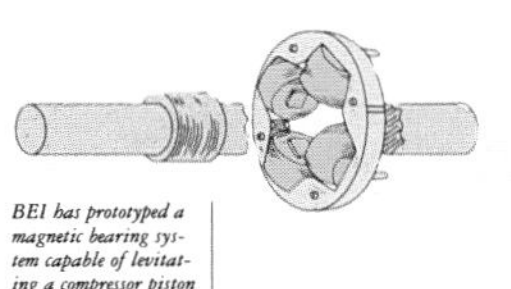

BEI has prototyped a magnetic bearing system capable of levitating a compressor piston for zero-friction applications in space.

BEI encoders using fiber optics provide protection from electronic interference and high temperatures in advanced aircraft.

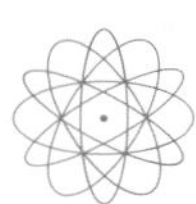

BEI's systems expertise lends a hand to the Superconducting Supercollider project. For Brookhaven National Laboratory, the firm is designing a device capable of checking tiny errors in the bore alignment along the planned collider's 52-mile circumference.

16

17 Management's Discussion and Analysis of Financial Condition and Results of Operations

Results of Operations Fiscal 1987 vs Fiscal 1986

In 1987 the Company earned a profit of $3.2 million, an increase of $1.3 million or 65 percent higher than in 1986.

Revenues increased by 18 percent in 1987 to $47.3 million from $40.2 million in 1986. The increase in revenue was primarily attributable to increased shipments of rockets and rocket motors to the U.S. military. Sales of industrial encoders also increased during the year.

Cost of sales as a percentage of revenue declined to 58.4 percent for fiscal 1987 compared to 60.0 percent in fiscal 1986. This reduction was primarily due to aggressive control of overhead costs as volume increased and through product cost reduction.

Operating expenses in fiscal 1987 of $13.8 million were $1.4 million or 11 percent higher than in fiscal 1986 but declined as a percentage of revenue from 30.9 percent to 29.2 percent. Company sponsored research and development increased to $2.0 million, up 11 percent. Selling expense increased by 8 percent primarily due to the upgrading of BEI Motion Systems sales and marketing organization. General and Administrative expense increased by 15 percent largely due to non-recurring costs associated with relocation of the Corporate office, increased corporate development and related expenses. Interest expenses declined on reduced borrowings resulting from an improved cash flow.

Inflation at current rates does not have a material effect on the Company's operation.

Financial Position

During fiscal 1987, BEI net worth increased to $13.8 million. Cash generated from operations during fiscal 1987 was $4.8 million; of this amount $2.8 million was used to fund growth in working capital due to increased business volume. Capital expenditures for new production equipment used $1.1 million and $0.9 million was used to pay down long term debt.

At September 30, borrowing on the Bank Line of Credit was $2.6 million of which $1.1 million was used to buy certificates of deposit to collateralize outstanding Letters of Credit. Cash was at $1.2 million with $1.1 million invested in the certificates of deposit.

Subsequent to September 30, an agreement was reached with Wells Fargo Bank and Algemene Bank Nederland NV (ABN), to provide an increase in the line of credit to $10 million from $8 million, to include a $5.0 million facility to fund letters of credit in support of BEI marketing programs.

The Company had no material commitments for capital expenditures at the end of fiscal 1987. Based on the financial condition of the Company at September 30, 1987 the internal cash flow will be sufficient to provide the capital resources necessary to fund anticipated growth and if additional funding should be required it could be generated through bank borrowings.

Consolidated Statements of Income 20

(dollars in thousands except per share amounts) Year Ended September 30	1987	1986	1985
Net sales—Note B	$ 47,346	$ 40,210	$ 40,507
Cost of sales	$ 27,660	$ 24,119	$ 24,912
	$ 19,686	$ 16,091	$ 15,595
Selling, general and administrative expenses	$ 11,193	$ 9,886	$ 9,353
Research, development and related expenses	$ 1,982	$ 1,778	$ 1,434
Interest expense	$ 659	$ 772	$ 673
	$ 13,834	$ 12,436	$ 11,460
	$ 5,852	$ 3,655	$ 4,135
Other income	$ 159	$ 90	$ 220
Income from Continuing Operations Before Income Taxes	$ 6,011	$ 3,745	$ 4,355
Federal and state income taxes (credit)—Note G			
Current	$ 3,292	$ 1,583	$ 2,078
Deferred	$ (467)	$ 228	$ (133)
	$ 2,825	$ 1,811	$ 1,945
Income from Continuing Operations	$ 3,186	$ 1,934	$ 2,410
Discontinued operations—Note B			
Loss from operations of discontinued division (less applicable income tax benefit of $287)	—	—	$ (365)
Loss on disposal of discontinued division $(150) and provision $(114) for operating losses during phase-out period (less applicable income tax benefit of $128)	—	—	$ (136)
	—	—	$ (501)
Net Income	$ 3,186	$ 1,934	$ 1,909
Earnings Per Common Share—Note H			
Income from continuing operations	$ 2.50	$ 1.49	$ 1.73
Discontinued operations	—	—	$ (.37)
Net income	$ 2.50	$ 1.49	$ 1.36
Average shares outstanding	1,271,866	1,295,335	1,398,787

See notes to consolidated financial statements.

21 Consolidated Statements of Changes in Financial Position

	(dollars in thousands) Year Ended September 30	1987	1986	1985
Source of Funds	Net income	$ 3,186	$ 1,934	$ 1,909
	Charges to income not requiring current working capital:			
	Depreciation and amortization of property, plant and equipment	$ 1,133	$ 1,126	$ 1,128
	Other amortization	$ 156	$ 158	$ 134
	Deferred income taxes—noncurrent	$ 80	$ 228	$ 57
	Total from Operations	$ 4,555	$ 3,446	$ 3,228
	Long-term debt borrowings	$ 143	$ 916	$ 1,464
	Stock options and warrants exercised	$ 8	$ 28	$ 279
	Net book value of property disposals	$ 42	—	$ 154
	Other	$ 260	—	—
		$ 5,008	$ 4,390	$ 5,125
Application of Funds	Purchase of assets of Kimco, Inc., less net working capital of $219—Note C			
	Property, plant and equipment	—	—	$ 244
	Designs, drawings and related assets	—	—	$ 875
	Acquisition of property, plant and equipment	$ 1,140	$ 985	$ 1,261
	Purchase of Treasury Stock	—	$ 1,827	$ 430
	Reduction of long-term debt	$ 930	$ 725	$ 755
	Increase in notes receivable from officers and other related parties (net)	$ 185	$ 287	$ 164
	Other	—	$ 151	$ 238
		$ 2,255	$ 3,975	$ 3,967
	Increase in Working Capital	$ 2,753	$ 415	$ 1,158
Changes in Components of Working Capital	Increase (decrease) in current assets:			
	Cash and short-term investments	$ 819	$ 170	$ 17
	Accounts receivable	$ 3,600	$ (941)	$ 2,826
	Inventories	$ 972	$ 833	$ 1,381
	Prepaid expenses and other	$ 43	$ (30)	$ 48
	Deferred income taxes	$ 547	—	—
		$ 5,981	$ 32	$ 4,272
	Increase (decrease) in current liabilities:			
	Note payable to a bank	$ (43)	$ (200)	$ 2,250
	Trade accounts payable	$ 1,641	$ (315)	$ 462
	Accrued expenses and other liabilities	$ 1,302	$ (540)	$ 186
	Federal and state income taxes	$ 347	$ 662	$ 10
	Deferred income taxes	—	—	$ (190)
	Current portion of long-term debt	$ (19)	$ 10	$ 396
		$ 3,228	$ (383)	$ 3,114
	Increase in Working Capital	$ 2,753	$ 415	$ 1,158

See notes to consolidated financial statements.

CLIENT:
BEI ELECTRONICS

DESIGN FIRM:
TOLLESON DESIGN

ART DIRECTOR:
STEVEN TOLLESON

DESIGNERS:
STEVEN TOLLESON, NANCY PAYNTER

PHOTOGRAPHER:
STEVEN UNZE

WRITER:
LINDSAY BEAMAR

TYPOGRAPHER:
SPARTAN TYPOGRAPHERS

PAPER SELECTION:
QUINTESSENCE, LINEN, CURTIS FLANNEL

PAPER MANUFACTURER:
SIMPSON, LINWEAVE, JAMES RIVER

PRINTER:
GRAPHIC ARTS CENTER

NUMBER OF PAGES:
28 PLUS COVER

SIZE:
8" X 11 3/4"

TYPE SELECTION:
GARAMOND, HELVETICA BOLD CONDENSED

LAWRENCE W. PARRISH, VICE PRESIDENT AND CHIEF FINANCIAL OFFICER, BEI ELECTRONICS, INC., SAN FRANCISCO, CALIFORNIA

BEI Electronics, Inc had a very successful year in a very sensitive business. The annual report had to capture the seriousness of company's stance, and to inform the BEI audience of our consistent success at designing, developing and extending its technology.

STEVEN TOLLESON, TOLLESON DESIGN, SAN FRANCISCO, CALIFORNIA

BEI Electronics is basically two industries dealing with technology and the government. We needed to appeal to the shareholders, and we tried to keep the book friendly, although, since some of the work is defense-related, we were dealing with a serious subject. Our primary role was to make the annual report accessible to the shareholders, make it understandable, and inviting. We combined some photography with technical drawings and presented a strong type treatment which had a "presence," but did not compete with the other elements on the page.

LAWRENCE W. PARRISH, VICE PRESIDENT UND CHIEF FINANCIAL OFFICER, BEI ELECTRONICS, INC., SAN FRANCISCO, KALIFORNIEN

BEI Electronics hatten ein erfolgreiches Jahr in einem sehr heiklen Geschäft. Der Jahresbericht sollte der Bedeutung der Firma entsprechen und der Leserschaft vor Augen führen, dass die Firma den technologischen Bereich erfolgreich entwickelt und ausbaut.

STEVEN TOLLESON, TOLLESON DESIGN, SAN FRANCISCO, KALIFORNIEN

BEI Electronics, ein technologisches Unternehmen, erfüllt u.a. Aufträge der Regierung. Wir mussten die Aktionäre mit einem freundlich wirkenden Bericht ansprechen, obgleich wir ein ernstes Thema zu behandeln hatten, da ein Teil der Produktion für die Landesverteidigung bestimmt ist. Unser Hauptauftrag lautete, den Bericht für die Aktionäre zugänglich, verständlich und einladend zu gestalten. Wir verbanden Photographie mit technischen Zeichnungen und wählten eine starke Typographie, die eine «Präsenz» hatte, aber die anderen Elemente nicht erschlug.

LAWRENCE W. PARRISH, VICE PRESIDENT ET CHIEF FINANCIAL OFFICER, BEI ELECTRONICS, INC., SAN FRANCISCO, CALIFORNIA

BEI Electronics a connu une année très prospère dans un domaine d'activité sensible. Le rapport annuel se devait de souligner le sérieux de l'entreprise et informer le public des succès continus dans le design, le developpement et l'extension de sa production technologique.

STEVEN TOLLESON, TOLLESON DESIGN, SAN FRANCISCO, CALIFORNIE

BEI Electronics travaille dans deux branches industrielles qui intéressent la technologie moderne et le gouvernement. Il nous fallait séduire les actionnaires tout en préservant l'impression de sérieux qui convient aux militaires, auxquels une partie de la production est destinée. La tâche principale était de nous placer au niveau de compréhension des actionnaires en leur relatant les faits de manière simple et attrayante. Nous avons alterné photos et dessins techniques et opté pour une typographie de poids sans toutefois lui faire concurrencer les autres éléments.

BRITISH

COLUMBIA

1987

FOREST

PRODUCTS

LIMITED

ANNUAL

REPORT

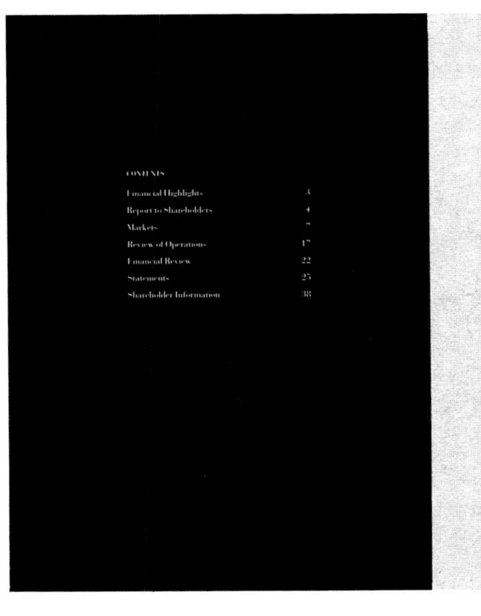

TO OUR SHAREHOLDERS AND EMPLOYEES:

Strong market demand, higher prices and favorable currency relationships helped the Company establish a new milestone in 1987 with four consecutive quarters of record sales and earnings. ■ Consolidated net earnings for the year were $140.2 million, or $2.47 per common share, compared with earnings of $40.2 million or $.79 per common share in 1986. Sales rose 27 per cent to $1.4 billion compared with the sales of $1.1 billion reported for the previous year. Earnings and sales in 1986 were affected negatively by weaker product markets and a lengthy woodworkers' strike. ■ Increased cash flow generated by improved profits and an infusion of capital from the Company's major shareholder, Fletcher Challenge Limited, led to a reduction in long-term debt of $144.3 million. Shareholders' equity grew from $475.8 million to $698.1 million. Consequently, the ratio of long term debt to equity declined to .5:1 from a 1:1 ratio in 1986. The higher income levels achieved in 1987 improved return on shareholders' equity to 22.1 per cent from 8.7 per cent in the previous year. ■ The Company was able to return to regular common share cash dividends in 1987 totalling $28.5 million after several years of inadequate returns. ■ The underlying reason for the excellent results in 1987 was the strong recovery of world economies leading to increased demand for pulp, newsprint and wood products in export markets. The weaker American dollar in relation to some foreign currencies enhanced the competitive position of export sales, the majority of which are conducted in U.S. funds. In North America, forest product sales were generally good but lumber shipments to the United States were subject to a 15 per cent export tax for most of the year which resulted in lower margins. Coated paper demand improved substantially in response to excellent growth in the U.S. commercial printing industry; however prices were depressed for the first half of the year due to several new plants being commissioned. ■ Most of the Company's operations ran at full capacity during the year in response to strong market demand. Increased productivity and efficiency were achieved through the outstanding effort of employees and by the completion of several capital projects aimed at improving our competitive position. Full details of these achievements and other progress are included in the Review of Operations section of this report. ■ Significantly, it was a year of relative labour peace with the exception of a one day general strike in June when union employees throughout B.C. took illegal action to protest the provincial government's new industrial relations legislation. ■ During 1987 the Company and its affiliates embarked upon the most ambitious expansion and modernization program in its history with the start of capital projects totalling more than $700 million. The principal projects are a US$350 million expansion and modernization of Blandin Paper Company; a $212 million newsprint mill and sawmill modernization at Finlay Forest Industries Ltd. (50 per cent owned by BCFP); and, a $32 million thermomechanical pulp mill expansion at Crofton. When all of these projects are completed in 1989, the Company will have improved not only its cost-effectiveness but also its ability to claim a far greater market share in growth businesses such as newsprint and coated paper. ■ BCFP's new major shareholder, Fletcher Challenge Limited, of New Zealand, has brought new stability to the Company with access to greater capital resources. Fletcher Challenge has acquired a 69

Ian Donald, *Chief Executive Officer*

Kenneth P. Benson, *Chairman*

The recession taught us some new lessons about marketing forest products. Fundamentally, it is the same business with the same products and many of the same international markets. Strategically, it's a whole new ball game. Today, our products must match the needs of the customer because it is the buyer, not the producer, who rules the marketplace. BCFP's manufacturing plants are responding to the challenge, meeting more exacting specifications and setting new standards for quality and consistency. We are extracting more value from our timber resources and in the process creating earnings and security for our shareholders and employees. Behind this market-driven strategy, is the placement of more than $700 million in announced capital spending to achieve the economies of scale and efficiency that will help us compete in Beijing or Baton Rouge. As you will see on the next few pages, new market opportunities are coming into focus as a result of these changes.

MARKETS

REVIEW OF OPERATIONS

FORESTRY AND WOOD SUPPLY

As part of the Company's long-term commitment

1987

other forest product companies on the B.C. coastline

WOOD PRODUCTS

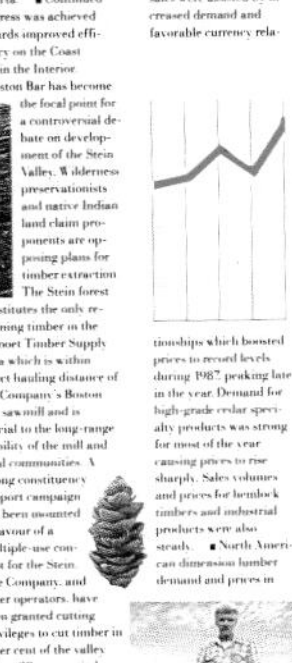

CONSOLIDATED BALANCE SHEET

as at December 31, 1987 (in thousands of dollars)

	1987	1986
ASSETS		
CURRENT ASSETS		
Cash and short term investments	$ 15,498	$ 5,091
Accounts receivable	141,065	109,683
Inventories (Note 2)	183,016	170,757
Prepaid expense	6,169	8,598
	345,748	294,129
LONG TERM INVESTMENTS AND ADVANCES		
Investment in associate companies (Note 3)	76,204	52,013
Other investments and advances (Note 4)	42,227	37,423
Project funds invested (Note 5)	77,988	—
	196,419	89,436
FIXED ASSETS (Note 6)		
Property, plant and equipment	602,838	591,639
Timberlands and logging roads	159,919	164,271
	762,757	755,910
DEFERRED CHARGES (Note 7)	19,903	28,209
	$1,324,827	$1,167,684

Approved by the Directors:

Director

Director

CONSOLIDATED BALANCE SHEET

BRITISH COLUMBIA FOREST PRODUCTS LIMITED

as at December 31, 1987 (in thousands of dollars)

	1987	1986
LIABILITIES		
CURRENT LIABILITIES		
Bank loans (Note 8)	$ 21,577	$ 61,117
Accounts payable and accrued liabilities	126,053	95,691
Dividends payable	8,708	6,164
Income taxes payable	7,332	7,661
Current portion of long term debt	4,397	9,835
	168,067	180,468
LONG TERM DEBT (Note 8)	324,555	470,884
DEFERRED INCOME TAXES	118,619	40,564
PREFERRED SHARES ISSUED BY SUBSIDIARIES (Note 9)	15,498	—
SHAREHOLDERS' EQUITY		
Share capital (Note 10)		
6% cumulative preferred shares of $50 par value redeemable at $53		
Authorized — 240,000 shares		
Outstanding — 77,300 shares (1986 — 84,500 shares)	3,865	4,225
Common shares without par value		
Authorized — 60,000,000 shares		
Outstanding — 57,661,515 shares (1986 — 50,836,417 shares)	299,523	174,717
	303,388	178,942
Earnings reinvested in the business	371,660	262,749
Foreign currency adjustment	23,040	34,077
	698,088	475,768
	$1,324,827	$1,167,684

Commitments and Contingencies (Notes 10 and 13)

CLIENT:
BRITISH COLUMBIA FOREST PRODUCTS

DESIGNER:
JOHN VAN DYKE

PHOTOGRAPHER:
TERRY HEFFERNAN

WRITER:
STU CLUGSTON

STU CLUGSTON, DIRECTOR OF COMMUNICATIONS, FLETCHER CHALLENGE, VANCOUVER, BRITISH COLUMBIA, CANADA

The 1987 annual report for British Columbia Forest Products Limited was the last for this company prior to its becoming part of Fletcher Challenge, and the overiding theme was this was a company in transition to serve a bigger, global market. We have very high regard for John Van Dyke, and he managed to create an annual report which distinguished itself from other annual reports. It also allayed the anxiety accompanying the proposed change of ownership. The feedback I had from the audience, especially the shareholders, was that this annual report made them feel good about the company.

JOHN VAN DYKE, VAN DYKE COMPANY, SEATTLE, WASHINGTON

What British Columbia Forest Products wanted to show in their 1987 annual report was the company's positioning in the the world market, and the firm's product application. So we showed these themes through photography. The photographer was Terry Heffernan, with whom I often work. So, for example, we showed newsprint using Chinese newspapers; for pulp, we used writing paper from Germany. We portrayed light-weight paper through an American magazine. Each paper product had its own spread, and we introduced a graph with each one. The company had just been purchased by a firm in New Zealand, so we wanted to emphasize the year of this annual report, because it was a milestone. So we did a die cut of the year on the cover, and we had a globe of the world showing through the die cut, which emphasized the global theme. We heard the response to this was favorable. The client knew exactly what it wanted in this annual report and that helped to make it a success.

STU CLUGSTON, DIRECTOR OF COMMUNICATIONS, FLETCHER CHALLENGE, VANCOUVER, BRITISH COLUMBIA, KANADA

Der Jahresbericht 1987 für British Columbia Forest Products Limited war der letzte für die Firma in ihrer damaligen Form (jetzt gehört sie zu Fletcher Challenge), und das zentrale Thema war deshalb die Übergangsphase, die einem grösseren, globalen Markt gerecht werden will. Wir halten sehr viel von John Van Dyke, und es gelang ihm, einen Jahresbericht zu produzieren, der sich deutlich von anderen unterscheidet. Zudem wurden damit die mit der Änderung der Besitzverhältnisse verbundenen Befürchtungen abgebaut. Die Empfänger äusserten sich positiv über diesen Bericht.

JOHN VAN DYKE, VAN DYKE COMPANY, SEATTLE, WASHINGTON

British Columbia Forest Products wollten in ihrem Jahresbericht für 1987 ihre Stellung auf dem Weltmarkt und die Anwendung ihrer Erzeugnisse zeigen. Wir benutzten Photos, um diese Themen zu verbildlichen. Ich arbeitete, wie so oft, mit Terry Heffernan. Beim Thema Zeitungsdruck verwendeten wir eine chinesische Zeitung, als Beispiel für Papierbrei zeigten wir Briefpapier aus Deutschland, als Beispiel für leichtes Papier ein amerikanisches Magazin. Jeder Papierqualität wurde eine Doppelseite mit einem Diagramm gewidmet. Die Firma war gerade von einem neuseeländischen Unternehmen gekauft worden. Darum wollten wir deutlich machen, dass dieses Jahr ein Meilenstein in der Geschichte der Firma ist. Die Jahreszahl wurde durch eine Ausstanzung auf dem Umschlag betont, durch die man eine Weltkugel erkennt, die wiederum das globale Thema unterstreicht. Wir erfuhren, dass das Echo positiv wâr. Der Kunde wusste genau, was er mit diesem Bericht wollte.

STU CLUGSTON, DIRECTOR OF COMMUNICATIONS, FLETCHER CHALLENGE, VANCOUVER, COLOMBIE BRITANNIQUE, CANADA

Le rapport annuel 1987 pour British Columbia Forest Products Limited a été le dernier à être publié avant son rachat par Fletcher Challenge. Le thème principal en était l'étape de transition qui allait faire de l'entreprise un fournisseur encore plus apprécié sur les marchés mondiaux. John Van Dyke a réussi à réaliser un rapport annuel sortant de l'ordinaire, qui a contribué à apaiser les craintes que le public pouvait avoir face au changement de propriétaire. La réaction du public, et notamment des actionnaires, m'a montré que ce rapport annuel leur a inspiré confiance au sujet de notre société.

JOHN VAN DYKE, VAN DYKE COMPANY, SEATTLE, WASHINGTON

Ce que British Columbia Forest Products entendait démontrer par le biais du rapport annuel pour 1987, c'était la place de l'entreprise sur les marchés mondiaux, ainsi que la gamme d'applications de ses produits. Nous avons donc illustré ces thèmes en photos. A cet effet, je me suis assuré l'aide de Terry Heffernan. Nous avons entre autres montré du papier journal en utilisant des journaux chinois; pour la pâte à papier, nous avons utilisé du papier à lettres venue d'Allemagne, pour le papier mince, un magazine américain. Chaque qualité de papier a eu droit à une double page entière illustrée d'un graphique. L'entreprise venait d'être rachetée par une société néo-zélandaise; il nous fallait donc présenter l'exercice passé en revue comme un jalon essentiel. On a découpé le millésime sur la couverture, avec la mappemonde visible par derrière pour souligner l'aspect global de l'opération. Nous avons appris que les réactions à cette publication ont été favorables.

EQUITY & LAW

Equity & Law

JAARVERSLAG 1987

I N H O U D

I N L E I D I N G

Ons bedrijf is in 1987 opnieuw sterk gegroeid. Het premie-inkomen steeg in vergelijking met 1986 met 24% tot *f* 318,8 miljoen. De premiereserve van onze portefeuille nam met 18% toe tot *f* 1.342 miljoen en de omzet met 21% tot *f* 416,1 miljoen. Wij beschouwen deze vooruitgang in het licht van de groei van de levensverzekeringsmarkt in Nederland met circa 10% en de matige groei van de nationale economie als zeer bevredigend. Het aandeel van *Equity & Law* in de levensverzekeringsmarkt is daardoor opnieuw gestegen.

Deze groei is, naar onze mening, de resultante van een consequent bedrijfsbeleid, van een blijvend grote belangstelling van verzekeringnemers voor onze Verzekerd Groei-fondsen (VGF) en van ons streven naar een optimale dienstverlening aan onze cliënten. Het aantal Verzekerd Groei-fondsen werd in 1987 uitgebreid van acht tot elf. Hierdoor kunnen wij nog beter aan de preferenties van onze verzekeringnemers tegemoet komen.

Het fraaie resultaat over het afgelopen jaar is mede te danken aan de enthousiaste inzet van de met ons samenwerkende verzekeringsadviseurs en van al onze medewerkers. Wij zijn hen zeer erkentelijk voor hun toewijding.

O N D E R N E M I N G S F I L O S O F I E

- Specialist zijn op het terrein van levensverzekeringen in Nederland.
- Produkten aanbieden met 'value for money', die 'helder als glas' zijn.
- De distributie van die produkten laten verlopen via de professionele verzekeringsadviseur.
- Functioneren als innovatieve en flexibele organisatie, snel reagerend op veranderingen en op behoeften in de markt.
- De kwaliteit van de dienstverlening en een mentaliteit van klantgericht denken en handelen combineren met een hoge mate van effectiviteit en efficiency.
- Medewerkers door gelijke kansen en een stimulerend bedrijfsklimaat optimaal mogelijkheden tot ontplooiing bieden.
- Streven naar een groei die hoger ligt dan de groei van de markt.
- Streven naar het hoogste premie-inkomen per medewerker in de levensverzekeringsbranche.
- Optimaliseren van winstgevendheid op lange termijn.

M A R K T O N T W I K K E L I N G E N

De markt voor levensverzekeringen werd in het jaar 1987 in hoge mate gedomineerd door het wetsvoorstel 'Brede Herwaardering'. Op 10 juli 1987 vond de publikatie plaats van het voorontwerp van dit wetsvoorstel voor onderhoudsvoorzieningen en spaarvormen. Dit bracht de gehele (levens)verzekeringsbranche in rep en roer, gezien het ingrijpende karakter van de voorgestelde maatregelen. Hierover is de laatste maanden zoveel gepubliceerd, dat wij in herhaling zouden vervallen door het hier nog eens uitgebreid te behandelen. Duidelijk is, dat waneer de voorstellen ongewijzigd zouden worden overgenomen, onze bedrijfstak, en dus ook ons bedrijf, in het hart zou worden getroffen. De consument heeft de weg naar onze bedrijfstak gevonden, waar het gaat om het veilig stellen van zijn/haar belangen ten aanzien van de oudedag. Onderzoeken bevestigen dat het hier nagenoeg altijd gaat om belangen op lange termijn en dat daar ook het verschil zit met het zogenaamde banksparen. Meer en meer worden er vraagtekens gezet – als gevolg van de toenemende vergrijzing – achter de haalbaarheid in de toekomst van de huidige hoogte van de AOW-uitkeringen. Bovendien neemt de belangstelling voor een flexibele pensioneringsleeftijd hand over hand toe. Daarom bevreemdt het des te meer, dat de overheid hier een halt aan zou willen toeroepen.

Alle bij de herwaardering betrokken partijen hebben, vaak goed onderbouwd, heftig geprotesteerd tegen de plannen van de bewindslieden van financiën. Het voorontwerp dat als een discussiestuk wordt aangemerkt kan, als tenminste recht wordt gedaan aan de bezwaren vanuit alle lagen van de bevolking, niet in zijn huidige vorm worden ingevoerd. Ook leden van de vaste kamercommissie voor financiën hebben laten blijken geen voorstander van deze voor alle partijen ingrijpende beleidswijziging te zijn. Inmiddels heeft het departement laten weten, dat het indienen van het wetsvoorstel is uitgesteld tot het tweede kwartaal van 1988, teneinde recht te doen aan de vele en indringende reacties die zijn ontvangen naar aanleiding van het voorontwerp.

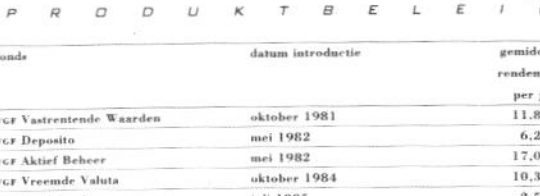

P R O D U K T B E L E I D

fonds	datum introductie	gemiddeld rendement per jaar
VGF Vastrentende Waarden	oktober 1981	11,87%
VGF Deposito	mei 1982	6,20%
VGF Aktief Beheer	mei 1982	17,09%
VGF Vreemde Valuta	oktober 1984	10,38%
VGF Aandelen I	juli 1985	-2,54%
VGF Obligatie	juli 1985	7,62%
VGF Kombinatie	oktober 1985	6,98%
VGF Vastgoed	juni 1986	3,78%
VGF Aandelen II	oktober 1987	
VGF Uiterboei	oktober 1987	
VGF Algemeen Fondsenbezit	oktober 1987	

In de pensioensfeer zorgde de wetgever voor extra druk op de bedrijfstak door het aanbrengen van wijzigingen in de Pensioen- en Spaarfondsenwet. Die hebben vooral tot gevolg, dat ontslag voor de ex-werkgever het betalen van een forse premie of koopsom kan betekenen, om te kunnen voldoen aan de eis van het meegeven van een tijdsevenredig pensioen. Wellicht zal dit in de toekomst leiden tot minder pensioenovereenkomsten, die zijn gebaseerd op een combinatie van salaris en diensttijd, maar zal worden overgestapt naar een beschikbaar premiesysteem. De concurrentie op de pensioenmarkt is groot, doch de combinatie van maatwerk en grote deskundigheid bij onze medewerkers op de pensioenafdeling heeft gezorgd voor een grote toename van het aantal contracten. Verdere automatisering en constante aandacht voor de kwaliteit van de dienstverlening doen ons 1988 met vertrouwen tegemoet zien, te meer omdat nu de basis is gelegd voor een verdere flexibilisering van ons aanbod, overeenkomstig de wensen van onze cliënten en de met ons samenwerkende verzekeringsadviseurs.

Het Verzekerd Keyman-projekt, een verzekering die door een onderneming wordt gesloten voor opvang van de financiële gevolgen van overlijden of algehele blijvende arbeidsongeschiktheid van een sleutelfiguur, is verder aangepast aan wensen uit de markt, zoals die kenbaar werden gemaakt. Er is tegemoet gekomen aan de wens de mogelijkheid te openen gedurende meerdere jaren een uitkering te kunnen ontvangen bij het onverhoopt wegvallen van de keyman. Naast een eenmalige uitkering kan thans worden gekozen voor een uitkering

18

'T BETERE LEVEN V

ONTWIKKELING RESULTATEN

Het saldo vóór toewijzing van winst en overrentedeling aan polishouders nam in 1987 ten opzichte van 1986 met ruim ƒ 2,9 miljoen af tot ƒ 33,5 miljoen. Deze daling is veroorzaakt door de grote instroom aan nieuwe produktie, die een negatief effect op het resultaat heeft als gevolg van de door ons bedrijf gehanteerde netto-reserveringsmethode. Deze methode houdt in dat in het jaar van afsluiten alle kosten worden genomen, waardoor de baten pas in de toekomst zichtbaar worden. Een tweede factor die een negatief effect op de winst heeft gehad, is het resultaat op herverzekeringen. Tot slot dient te worden vermeld dat de post 'Overige baten en lasten' ruim ƒ 2 miljoen lager is uitgevallen dan in 1986.

Van het resterende saldo ad ƒ 33,5 miljoen wordt ƒ 30,8 miljoen aangewend ter verhoging van de rechten van polishouders, terwijl het restant als versterking van het eigen vermogen aan het vermogensoverschot wordt toegevoegd.

24

PREMIE-INKOMEN EN BELEGGINGSOPBRENGSTEN

Premie-inkomen en beleggingsopbrengsten zijn in 1987 gestegen van ƒ 345 naar ƒ 416 miljoen. Deze stijging kan als volgt worden weergegeven (in miljoenen guldens):

	1987	1986	%
Premies en koopsommen:			
Verzekeringen in beleggingseenheden	157,6	122,1	+29,1
Overige levensverzekeringen	161,2	134,7	+19,7
	318,8	256,8	+24,1
Beleggingsopbrengsten, exclusief waardestijgingen:			
Verzekeringen in beleggingseenheden	29,4	22,6	+30,1
Overige levensverzekeringen	67,9	65,7	+ 3,4
	97,3	88,3	+10,3
	416,1	345,1	+20,6

Uit dit overzicht blijkt dat zowel verzekeringen in beleggingseenheden als overige levensverzekeringen op zeer bevredigende wijze zijn gegroeid. Ook de beleggingsopbrengsten toe te rekenen aan verzekeringen in beleggingseenheden ontwikkelden zich voorspoedig; bij de overige beleggingsopbrengsten werden de gevolgen van de dalende kapitaalmarktrente steeds duidelijker. Dit effect werd nog versterkt door het vrij hoge aantal hoogrentende leningen dat vervroegd is afgelost.

25

T O E L I C H T I N G J A A R R E K E N I N G

3 **Bedrijfsmiddelen**

	Computer en -systemen	Auto's	Kantoormachines, inventaris	Verbouwingen	Totaal
Aanschafwaarde 01-01-1987	9.841	270	2.834	6.249	19.194
Investeringen 1987	3.295	203	855	2.564	6.917
	13.136	473	3.689	8.813	26.111
Desinvesteringen 1987	565	–	614	–	1.179
Aanschafwaarde 31-12-1987	12.571	473	3.075	8.813	24.932
Cumulatieve afschrijvingen per 01-01-1987	2.809	33	1.210	343	4.395
Afschrijvingen 1987	2.788	83	391	629	3.891
	5.597	116	1.601	972	8.286
Desinvesteringen 1987	175	–	614	–	789
Cumulatieve afschrijvingen per 31-12-1987	5.422	116	987	972	7.497
Boekwaarde 31-12-1987	7.149	357	2.088	7.841	17.435
Boekwaarde 31-12-1986	7.032	237	1.624	5.906	14.799

De afschrijvingen worden bepaald als een percentage van de aanschafwaarde zonder rekening te houden met een restwaarde. De volgende afschrijvingspercentages worden gehanteerd:

- Computers, computersystemen en auto's: 20% van de aanschafwaarde per jaar.
- Kantoorinventaris en verbouwingen: 10% van de aanschafwaarde per jaar.
- Kantoormachines: 25% van de aanschafwaarde per jaar.

Over aanschaffingen die gedurende het boekjaar plaatsvinden is naar tijdsgelang afgeschreven. De tot en met 1986 gevolgde methode om ook zelfgebouwde software te activeren is in 1987 verlaten. In plaats daarvan wordt alleen de gekochte systeemsoftware geactiveerd en over een gelijke periode als de bijbehorende apparatuur afgeschreven. Deze wijziging resulteert in een extra afschrijving van ruim ƒ 700, waarvan ƒ 399 aan voorgaande jaren kan worden toegerekend en dientengevolge onder 'Overige baten en lasten' is verantwoord.

4 **Deelnemingen**

Dit betreft een aantal belangen in andere maatschappijen, alsmede een aan één van deze verstrekte lening, die zijn gewaardeerd tegen de verkrijgingsprijs c.q. lagere intrinsieke waarde.

32

5 **Beleggingen**

	1987	1986
5.1 Onroerend goed		
Deze post is als volgt samengesteld:		
Kantoorgebouwen	8.400	7.935
Winkelpanden	16.230	15.937
Woonhuizen	780	780
	25.410	24.652
5.2 Leningen op schuldbekentenis		
Deze portefeuille is als volgt samengesteld:		
Overheid en door overheid gegarandeerd	336.466	310.750
Hypotheekbanken	36.951	37.660
Banken	28.409	28.253
Industrie	291	390
Overige	6.000	5.820
	408.117	382.873
5.3 Obligaties		
De post obligaties is als volgt samengesteld:		
Overheid en door overheid gegarandeerd	84.399	79.910
Hypotheekbanken	3.725	1.513
Banken	87.870	85.459
Industrie	2.638	3.558
Gezondheidszorg	290	317
Converteerbare obligaties	1.107	1.401
Internationale instellingen	29.581	35.895
Aangehouden in de vorm van participaties in beleggingsfondsen	374.037	302.777
Verzekerd Groei-fonds portefeuille	94.594	70.205
	678.241	581.035
5.4 Aandelen		
Deze portefeuille is als volgt opgebouwd:		
Internationals	19.273	21.759
Banken en verzekeringsmaatschappijen	18.599	25.380
Overige genoteerde fondsen	15.685	20.666
Niet genoteerde fondsen	7.569	2.725
Aangehouden in de vorm van participaties in beleggingsfondsen	9.098	3.509
Verzekerd Groei-fonds portefeuille	67.260	60.521
	137.484	134.560
Opties	242	260
	137.726	134.820

33

CLIENT:
EQUITY & LAW

DESIGN FIRM:
HENRIK BARENDS

DESIGNER:
HENRIK BARENDS

PHOTOGRAPHER:
PAUL DE NOOIJER

TYPOGRAPHER:
HENRIK BARENDS

PRINTER:
EQUIPAGE

A.H.LIEUWMA, MARKETING AND SALES MANAGER, EQUITY & LAW, THE HAGUE, THE NETHERLANDS

Our main theme for the Equity & Law 1987 annual report was "a better way of life." We wanted to convey the fact that we believe insurance is the financial guarantee to a better way of life after retirement. In order to portray this, we chose to photograph a young, enthusiastic man reacting to his dreams of the future in a contemporary way. Our company has a clear and well-defined philosphy, and we believe that insurance is more than just insurance. We were very positive about how these ideas were presented in the annual report, and our audience was very enthusiastic about the modern look of this report.

A.H. LIEUWMA, MARKETING AND SALES MANAGER, EQUITY AND LAW, DEN HAAG, NIEDERLANDE

Unser Hauptthema für den Jahresbericht 1987 war «ein besserer Lebensstandard». Wir wollten sagen, dass unserer Meinung nach eine Versicherung die finanzielle Garantie für einen besseren Lebensstandard nach der Pensionierung ist. Um dies darzustellen, beschlossen wir, einen jungen, lebensfrohen Mann zu zeigen. Unsere Gesellschaft hat eine klare, genau umrissene Politik, und wir glauben, dass Versicherung mehr als nur Versicherung ist. Wir waren von der Art, wie die Ideen im Jahresbericht umgesetzt wurden, sehr angetan, und unser Publikum war vor allem von dem modernen Stil des Berichtes begeistert.

A.H. LIEUWMA, MARKETING AND SALES MANAGER, EQUITY & LAW, LA HAYE, LES PAYS-BAS

Le thème principal choisi pour notre rapport annuel 1987 était «une vie plus agréable.» Nous avons voulu faire partager notre conviction que les assurances garantissent une vie plus agréable aux retraités. Pour mettre ce concept en image, nous avons opté pour la photo d'un jeune homme enthousiaste et réaliste. Notre société s'inspire d'idées claires et bien définies, et nous sommes persuadés que l'assurance, c'est bien plus qu'une simple assurance. Nous avons été très heureux de voir comment ces idées ont été présentées dans le rapport annuel. Notre public a réagi avec enthousiasme à l'aspect moderne de ce document.

HENRIK BARENDS, AMSTERDAM, NETHERLANDS

What we were to emphasize in the 1987 annual report for Equity & Law was the "better way of life" theme. In taking the photographs, the photographer, Paul de Nooijer, used themes which had been used for an Equity & Law publicity campaign as a starting point, and he created an interesting contrast of the publicity photography within his own. The design was contemporary, with each photograph getting its own page. The type was leaded, and we used a lot of white space. We tried to harmonize the photography and the typography as closely as possible.

HENRIK BARENDS, AMSTERDAM, NIEDERLANDE

Thema dieses Jahresberichtes war ein «besserer Lebensstandard». Bei seinen Aufnahmen ging der Photograph Paul de Nooijer von den Themen aus, die Equity & Law für eine Werbekampagne verwendet hatte. Es entstand ein interessanter Kontrast mit der Werbephotographie. Die Gestaltung war zeitgemäss, wobei jeder Aufnahme eine Seite gewidmet wurde; bei der Schrift verwendeten wir einen grossen Durchschuss, und auf den Seiten liessen wir viel Leerraum. Photographie und Typographie wurden so gut wie möglich aufeinander abgestimmt.

HENRIK BARENDS, AMSTERDAM, PAYS-BAS

Ce qu'il nous fallait mettre en relief, c'était la thématique d'«une vie plus agréable.» Pour ses prises de vues, le photographe Paul de Nooijer s'est inspiré des thèmes utilisés pour une campagne de publicité en faveur d'Equity & Law en créant un contraste suggestif entre la photo publicitaire du départ et sa propre réalisation. Le design est résolument contemporain avec une photo par page, un interlignage pour la composition et une abondance de blancs. Nous avons cherché à harmoniser dans la mesure du possible l'élément photo et l'élément typo.

GOUCHER COLLEGE

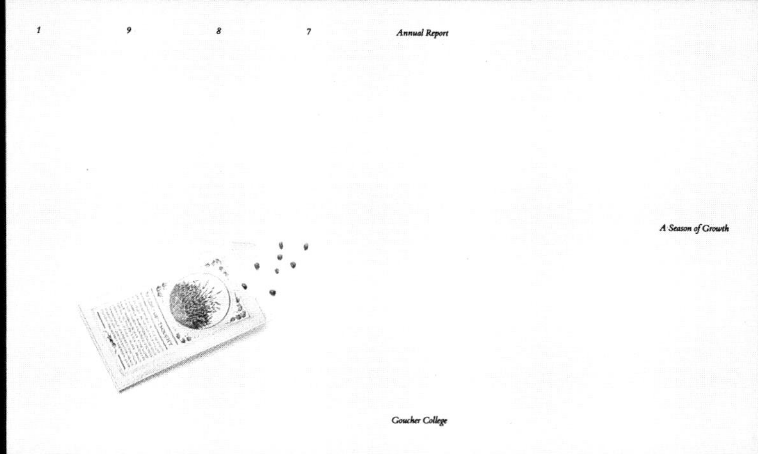

The Goucher Quarterly
Fall 1987
Volume LXVI/Number 1

The Goucher Quarterly (USPS 233-920) is published quarterly by Goucher College, Towson, Baltimore, Maryland 21204. Subscriptions $3.00. Second class postage paid at Baltimore.

A SEASON OF GROWTH

For thousands of years flowers and plants have served as tokens of affection, cures for injuries and diseases, and as purely decorative objects. They have so enchanted us that we have assigned specific meanings to many species of plants. In this annual report, plants symbolize a successful season of growth at Goucher College and the promise of many fruitful seasons to come.

Peppermint — wisdom, virtue

PRESIDENT'S LETTER

"There is a springtime feeling in the air, a joyous sense of awakening, a free creativeness, an unconscious pride . . ."
Van Wyck Brooks

The words, penned by early twentieth century literary critic Van Wyck Brooks, describe the cultural "flowering of New England" in the nineteenth century. But they also seem remarkably applicable to Goucher at the start of its second century. Indeed, it strikes me that in the past year we at Goucher have been witness to our own flowering. We have seen many programs, ideas, and even physical facilities that were long in the planning come to fruition, and we have seen tremendous growth in many other areas. ◆§ On the surface, it would seem that there have been many new additions to Goucher during the past year — the Decker Center for Information Technology, the Hughes Field Politics Center, the Todd Dance Studio, the Presidential Leadership Seminars, among others. Yet, a closer inspection reveals that each of these new features of the Goucher campus has its roots deep in the college's past. The Decker Center, for example, with its ventures into such exotic areas as artificial intelligence, computer music, and satellite technology, is simply the logical extension of an almost 30-year-long commitment to integrating computer science and technology with the liberal arts. The Field Politics Center at Goucher was established in the 1940s. A bequest from Sarah Tilghman Hughes '17 and the dedicated efforts of the political science faculty and an alumni advisory board have given the center new life and purpose along with a new name. Similarly, the sparkling new Todd Dance Studio is merely the physical evidence of the great strides Goucher's dance program has made since the first dance studio was built in 1967. ◆§ The Alumni Admissions Recruiting Program enjoyed its most successful year to date, as alumni recruiters saw years of high school counselor and college fair visits rewarded with an unprecedented surge in attention, applications, and enrollment. The newly inaugurated planned giving program, under the able chairmanship of Dorothy Lamberton Clapp '39, is the fruit of fund-raising labors that have carried the college in recent years through record-breaking capital and annual giving campaigns. ◆§ During 1986-87 there were some new roots established at Goucher as well — the roots of a truly coeducational, coequal academic and social environment. These roots have been planted with the same care that has characterized Goucher programs in the far and recent past, and they will be nurtured with equal attention. The research efforts of Psychology Department members Richard Pringle and Katherine Canada, described in this report, indicate Goucher's commitment to encouraging this flowering of spirit and energy for many seasons to come. ◆§ The springtime feeling lingers in the air on the Goucher campus. We embark on a new beginning, but our roots are strong and deep and will provide the source of a long and fruitful growing season.

Rhoda M. Dorsey
Rhoda M. Dorsey
President, Goucher College

FINANCIAL REVIEW

The foresight and generosity of Goucher's alumni and friends have contributed tremendously to the successful growth of the college.

"Not a having and a resting, but a growing and a becoming, is the character of perfection as culture conceives it."
Matthew Arnold, Sweetness and Light

Strawberry — foresight, good works

◆§ *Nancy-Bets Rowe Hay '63 has been an active volunteer in the Alumni Admissions Recruitment Program since its inception in 1974.*
§◆ *Psychology professors Richard Pringle and Katherine Canada are conducting research they hope will make Goucher "the best possible coeducational environment."*

Chrystelle Bond, Dance Department chair, calls the new Todd Dance Studio "a physical manifestation" of the vibrant dance program.
Anna Marie Christello '89 is a centennial scholarship winner, political science major, and student leader.

Financial Review

Giving Results
The singular success of annual giving for 1986-87 speaks to our alumni's continuing commitment to Goucher and provides the most traditional kind of support for the college. Alumni annual giving for 1986-87 increased by nine percent over 1985-86. In a time of transition and change, such support is vital to the financial health of the college. In the previous year, Goucher received two extraordinary bequests totaling more than $1,000,000. As a result, comparison of this year's figures for Restricted Funds, Endowment and Plant show a decline when compared to 1985-86; however, when compared to the 1984-85 year, funds allocated to those accounts increased by a healthy $180,126. The Women of Promise Campaign, reflecting the increased number of outstanding pledges on which donors have completed their payments, has come to a close.

Operating Results
For the sixth year in a row the college achieved an operating budget surplus. This success was particularly noteworthy as the surplus was realized in a year of low student enrollment and some extra expenditures as the college began the transition to coeducation.

An excellent year in annual giving and strong endowment performances, combined with good budget control and low inflation, resulted in a financially successful year. The college also was able to augment compensation increases, provide needed computer and scientific equipment, and maintain overall standards of excellence in facilities and programs.

Perhaps most importantly in a time of increasing concern with the costs of attending college, the percentage of tuition and fee increases announced for 1987-88 were the lowest since 1972, and well below national averages. These increases represented the fourth year in a row of decreasing percentage increases in tuition and fees.

Endowment Results
Goucher's endowment value moved to $54.1 million, a 7.7 percent increase over the endowment value at the end of the prior year. This increase represented a small slowdown in the recent growth trend of the endowment, as the investment objectives for the year centered more on yield than growth. The income generated from the endowment did contribute 17 percent of the total revenues for the year, which is a strong fiscal indicator by national standards. Indeed, on the ratio measure of endowment value to number of students, the college continues to rank among the top 50 colleges in the country.

Endowment and Similar Funds Market Value

Year	Market Value
1983	$33,124,146
1984	$33,472,464
1985	$40,892,650
1986	$50,244,394
1987	$54,109,945

Summary of Voluntary Support

	1982-83	1983-84	1984-85	1985-86	1986-87
Capital Campaigns	$3,085,890	$1,160,982	$ 972,757	$ 304,521	$ 43,961
Restricted Funds, Endowment and Plant	1,238,280	1,265,007	1,526,043	2,155,840	1,706,169
Annual Giving Operating Funds	732,932	783,003	1,395,391	987,107	1,031,816
Total	$5,057,102	$3,208,992	$3,894,191	$3,447,468	$2,781,946

The Financial Report 1986-87

Statement of Current Revenues and Expenditures Years Ended June 30, 1986 and 1987

Revenues	1987	1986
Student Tuition & Fees	$ 6,609,142	$ 6,803,563
Government Grants	1,041,265	992,208
Endowment Income	2,747,732	2,751,784
Gifts	2,006,410	1,371,567
Other Sources	595,663	732,009
Auxiliary Enterprises	3,159,926	3,204,886
Total Revenues	$16,160,138	$15,856,017

Expenditures and Mandatory Transfers	1987	1986
Instruction and Research	$ 4,784,183	$ 4,572,698
General Administration	762,820	726,118
General Institutional	2,399,462	2,219,039
Student Services	1,466,761	1,064,221
Student Aid	1,682,169	1,772,456
Library	457,221	457,677
Physical Plant	1,439,200	1,602,223
Auxiliary Enterprises	2,308,520	2,405,031
Mandatory Transfers	198,624	210,102
Total Expenditures and Mandatory Transfers	$15,498,960	$15,029,565
Excess of Revenues over Expenditures Prior to Non-Mandatory Transfers	$ 661,178	$ 826,452
Non-Mandatory Transfers (to)/from Other Funds	(637,074)	(751,270)
Net Surplus (Deficit)	24,104	75,182

Goucher College Board of Trustees

Goucher College Board of Trustees

Officers
CHAIR
Patricia A. Goldman '64
Vice Chair
National Transportation Safety Board

VICE CHAIR
Douglas W. Dodge
President
Mercantile-Safe Deposit & Trust Company

SECRETARY
Mary Katherine Scarborough Scheeler '49
Attorney

TREASURER
George E. Thomsen
Partner
McKenney, Thomsen and Burke

Trustees Emeriti
Donald L. DeVries
Charlotte Bush Failing '27
Janet Jeffery Harris '30
Frank A. Kaufman
John A. Luetkemeyer
Emma Robertson Richardson '34
Ruth Blaustein Rosenberg '21
Thomas R. Rudel
Walter Sondheim, Jr.
Claire von Marees Stieff '21
Roszel C. Thomsen
Elizabeth Conolly Todd '21

Members
Bruce D. Alexander
Senior Vice President
The Rouse Company

Susan Smith Baldwin '61
Proprietor
SHE

Ethel Weber Berney '46
Berney Travel Service

J. Henry Butta
Vice President
C&P Telephone Company

Dorothy Lamberton Clapp '39

Andre Davis
Associate Judge
First District Court of Maryland

Leslie B. Disharoon
Chairman of the Board and President
Monumental Corporation

Rhoda M. Dorsey
President
Goucher College

Joseph C. Eanes, Jr.
President and Chief Executive Officer
Fidelity and Deposit Co. of Maryland

Martha Howell Eck '60

James A. Flick, Jr.
Managing Partner
Ernst and Whinney, Baltimore

Hilda E. Ford
Secretary of Personnel
State of Maryland

Judith Nogi Goldstein '49
President
Goucher Alumni Association

Virginia Dondy Green '65
Partner
Reed Smith Shaw & McClay

Alice Falvey Greif '51

Ann Burgunder Greif '39

Edmund F. Haile
Partner
Daft, McCune, Walker, Inc.

Nancy-Bets Rowe Hay '63
Director of Admissions
Garrison Forest School

Donald B. Hebb, Jr.
General Partner
Alex Brown and Sons

Fern Karesh Hurst '68

Mary Bloom Hyman '71
Director of Education
Maryland Science Center

Kenneth N. Kermes

Ann Galperin Leibowitz '60
Senior Corporate Attorney
Polaroid Corporation

Jack Moseley
Chairman of the Board
U.S.F.&G. Company

William C. Mules
Headmaster
McDonogh School

Ann Baer Pearlstone

Lawrence R. Rachuba
General Partner
DeChiaro Limited Partnership

Anica B. Donnan Rawnsley '51

Barbara Bagden Roberts '69
President
Roberts & Co.

Russell R. Reno, Jr.
Partner
Venable, Baetjer and Howard

Henry A. Rosenberg, Jr.
Chairman of the Board and Chief Executive Officer
Crown Central Petroleum Corporation

Moira Rynn '85

Sheila Kleinman Sachs '61
Attorney
Gordon, Feinblatt, Rothman, Hoffberger and Hollander

Marinella D. Sarmiento '86
Research Assistant
George Washington University

Elizabeth Sarvello '87
Graduate Student
University of Virginia

Marcia K. Sharp
Chairman
Hager, Sharp & Abramson, Inc.

Jean Flah Silber '54

J. Richard Thomas
Thomas Associates

Robert E. Vogel
Vice President
Rexnord Automation, Inc.

Semmes G. Walsh
Executive Vice President
Monumental Corporation

Mary Southard Warshawsky '68
Owner
Coveralls

Murray Weingarten
Vice President & Group Executive
Aerospace Sector
Bendix Field Engineering Corp.

College Officers
Rhoda M. Dorsey
President

Gerald Duff
Dean and Vice President

Julie Collier-Adams
Dean of Students and Vice President

Barbara Fritze
Dean of Admissions and Financial Aid

David G. Healy
Vice President for Finance and Planning

Judith T. Phair
Vice President for Public Relations

Wesley H. Poling
Vice President for Development and Alumni Relations

twenty-five

CLIENT:
GOUCHER COLLEGE

DESIGN FIRM:
RUTKA WEADOCK DESIGN

ART DIRECTORS:
KATE BERGQUIST, ANTHONY RUTKA

DESIGNER:
KATE BERGQUIST

PHOTOGRAPHER:
BILL DENISON

ILLUSTRATOR:
KATE BERGQUIST

WRITERS:
JUDITH TURNER PHAIR, ANN LANO

JUDITH T. PHAIR, VICE-PRESIDENT FOR PUBLIC RELATIONS, GOUCHER COLLEGE, BALTIMORE, MARYLAND

There were many things the college was hoping to convey with our 1987 annual report. Of course, this is a financial report, but it has additional uses like for the alumnae, for the development office, the parents. So we needed to communicate to many audiences. We try a fresh approach every year, and for this year our "growth" into a co-ed institution from a women's college was a crucial part of our overall communication project. We needed to give both an assessment of that transition and show the stability after that transition. We needed words and images which symbolized our growth financially, academically and physically.The choice of seeds, flowers–the creative graphics–were Rutka Weadock Design's inspiration. The photographs of the staff members and students got a great reception. We got an excellent response from our various audiences.

ANTHONY RUTKA, RUTKA WEADOCK DESIGN, BALTIMORE, MARYLAND

Since Goucher College had gone co-ed, we took the idea of growth as the theme for the college and started doing the research by looking up various quotes on growth, and we thought of treating this theme literally with the planting of seeds. The idea of plants came first, then seeds for growth, then we started researching the meaning of various plants, for example, peppermint stands for wisdom and virtue. Of course, there was almost no money at all, so we did the illustrations in-house, and we put a lot of energy into the production of the piece. It isn't perfect bound, and we had to work the photos into a center spread. Photography was done on the campus and we propped everything. We made the stilts, the swing, got in a trampoline, the ladders. We photographed for two days. The subjects were very involved. They had a good time, and the whole report turned out to be a lot of fun.

JUDITH T. PHAIR, VICE-PRESIDENT FOR PUBLIC RELATIONS, GOUCHER COLLEGE, BALTIMORE, MARYLAND

Es gab sehr viele Dinge, die das College im Jahresbericht 1987 auszudrücken hoffte. Natürlich ist dies ein Finanzbericht, aber er sollte auch die Absolventen des College, die Verwaltung und die Eltern ansprechen. Jedes Jahr bemühen wir uns um eine unverbrauchte Lösung. Dieses Jahr war die Umwandlung von einer reinen Mädchenschule in eine gemischte Schule eines der wichtigsten Themen. Wir mussten unsere Einschätzung der Übergangsphase darlegen und die darauf folgende Stabilität glaubhaft machen. Wir brauchten Worte und Bilder, die den Ausbau im Hinblick auf Finanzen, Ausbildung und physische Grösse darstellen. Die Idee der Samen, der Blumen - des ganzen Designs - stammt von Rutka Weadock Design. Die Aufnahmen der Angestellten und der Schüler kamen ausgezeichnet an. Die Reaktionen waren äusserst erfreulich.

ANTHONY RUTKA, RUTKA WEADOCK DESIGN, BALTIMORE, MARYLAND

Da das College in eine gemischte Schule umgewandelt worden war, machten wir Wachstum zum zentralen Thema. Wir sahen uns zuerst verschiedene Zitate zu diesem Begriff an und überlegten, ob wir das Thema im wahrsten Sinne des Wortes durch das Säen von Samen umsetzen sollten. Die Idee von Pflanzen entstand zuerst, dann dachten wir an die Samen, und schliesslich befassten wir uns mit der Bedeutung verschiedener Pflanzen. Es standen kaum finanzielle Mittel zur Verfügung, deshalb machten wir die Illustrationen selbst und befassten uns intensiv mit der Herstellung des Berichtes. Er ist nicht perfekt gebunden, und wir mussten die Photos im Mittelbund unterbringen. Die Aufnahmen wurden auf dem Schulareal gemacht. Zwei Tage lang photographierten wir. Alle Beteiligten machten mit, und sie hatten Spass daran - der ganze Bericht wurde schliesslich ein Vergnügen.

JUDITH T. PHAIR, VICE-PRESIDENT FOR PUBLIC RELATIONS, GOUCHER COLLEGE, BALTIMORE, MARYLAND

Le College entendait utiliser son rapport annuel 1987 pour faire passer toute une série de messages. Il s'agit bien entendu d'un rapport financier, mais qui répond aussi aux besoins des étudiants, du bureau de développement et des parents. Cette année, c'est notre transformation de collège féminin en collège mixte qui a eu la place vedette dans notre projet de communication global. Il nous fallait évaluer l'impact de cette transformation et faire état des résultats obtenues après sa stabilisation. Nous avions besoin de mots et d'images symbolisant notre croissance au plan financier, universitaire et physique. Le choix des semences et des fleurs - l'aspect graphique créatif - est dû à l'inspiration de Rutka Weadock Design. Les photos des enseignants et des étudiants ont été accueillies avec enthousiasme, et nos divers publics ont très bien réagi à cette publication.

ANTHONY RUTKA, RUTKA WEADOCK DESIGN, BALTIMORE, MARYLAND

Du fait de l'accession de Goucher College au statut d'une institution mixte, nous avons opté pour le thème central de la croissance et avons entrepris des recherches sur les différents lexèmes associés à la croissance, pour fixer notre choix sur l'aspect végétal. L'idée des plantes a surgi d'abord, puis celle des semences, puis nous avons déterminé les significations symboliques des différentes plantes. Comme il n'y avait presque pas de budget à disposition, nous avons réalisé les illustrations nous-mêmes et investi pas mal d'énergie dans la production du rapport. La reliure est cousue, et les photos sont regroupées sur une double page au centre. Les prises de vues se sont faites sur le campus même, et nous avons fourni tous les accessoires. Les prises de vues ont duré deux jours. Les modèles se sont bien amusés, et la fabrication du rapport a finalement été une source de plaisir pour tous les participants.

H.J. HEINZ COMPANY

H.J. Heinz Company 1987 Annual Report.

Field Reports:

Heinz U.S.A. Accelerates in an Era of Radical Change.

The Surprising Assets of Weight Watchers.

Barrier Breaking Makes Star-Kist a Fast Running Leader.

Venezuela: A Study in Small Bigness.

Foresight + Flexibility = The Big Payoff in Britain.

Ore-Ida's Method is to Sell by the Billion.

Plada's Productivity Engine Slips into High Gear.

From Eden to Dandenong, Australia is Another World.

Chilled Food is Red Hot in Central Europe.

The Goods Pour Out in Heinz's Canada.

Henry J. Heinz II: A Eulogy for an Uncommon Man.

Chairman Henry J. Heinz II was in the 56th year of service to what he liked to refer to as "the old firm," when he died on February 23, 1987 at the age of 78. Characteristically, he attended both the January board and executive committee meetings, although he was in rapidly deteriorating health, such was his dedication to duty.

Mr. Heinz served as president and chief executive officer from the death of his father, Howard C. Heinz, in 1941, until he became chairman in 1965. Thereafter, while actively playing a management role, his main energies were directed toward philanthropy. He presided over the distribution of more than $300 million to educational, cultural, health, wildlife preservation, urban renewal and nutritional programs that enriched the lives of millions in his native Pittsburgh and elsewhere. His eulogizers could, therefore, quite honestly point to his as a life of continuing generosity to good causes.

To three generations of Heinz men and women, "the Chairman" was a connecting link with the company's beginnings. His presence served as a reminder that traditional company values—*quality products, fair business practice, brand reputation*—are sacred and inviolable. The preservation of these values in his name appeals to his colleagues as the most fitting of all memorials.

Highlights.

H. J. Heinz Company and Consolidated Subsidiaries

(dollars in thousands except per share data)	*1987*	*1986*	*1985*
Sales	$4,639,486	$4,366,177	$4,047,945
Operating income	592,985	532,583	474,598
Net income	338,506	301,734	265,978
Per common share amounts:			
Net income	$ 2.47	$ 2.20	$ 1.93
Dividends	1.00½	.87½	.77½
Book value	10.81	10.17	8.98
Capital expenditures	$ 184,730	$ 206,331	$ 158,830
Depreciation expense	99,218	85,524	78,833
Net property	1,036,760	923,520	759,708
Cash and short-term investments	$ 564,676	$ 405,255	$ 346,485
Working capital	822,059	704,479	686,955
Total debt	876,620	540,588	463,413
Shareholders' equity	1,392,949	1,360,007	1,230,454
Average number of common shares outstanding	131,665,217	134,125,804	136,102,374
Current ratio	1.79	1.77	1.91
Debt/invested capital	38.6%	28.4%	27.4%
Pretax return on average invested capital	29.5%	31.0%	30.5%
Return on average shareholders' equity	24.6%	23.3%	22.6%

Return on Average Shareholders' Equity
(in percent)

Dividends and Earnings per Common Share
(in dollars)
■ Dividends   Earnings per share
Five-year compound growth: Dividends 16.5%, Earnings per share 12.5%

To Our Shareholders.

Dr. Anthony J. F. O'Reilly – Chairman, President and Chief Executive Officer

Our 23rd consecutive year of new financial records is confirmed by the highlights digest on the preceding page. Somewhat obscured, but reflected also, are the results of dramatic changes during the year, many of which flowed from your company's quest of low cost operator status in each of its operating subsidiaries. This effort, now entering its third year, added a total of $109 million to our consolidated operating income, much of which was reinvested in marketing support for our products and services in a fiercely competitive world marketplace.

It is proper, and overdue, that Heinz shareholders be introduced to our excellent field managers in this year's annual report. Each of the subsidiary company presidents and managing directors, whose photographs highlight the report, speaks to the present and to the future of his company, setting forth the challenges in his particular market.

When, more than two years ago, I summoned our field managers to the first low cost operator conference, I pointed out that changing competitive and economic conditions called for an examination of every last existing practice with an eye to improvement. They were told that even the most time-sanctified practices were to be scrutinized and, if new, more economical, methods and procedures were available, were subject to total elimination. I bade them to be irreverent of established practice and adventuresome about the future.

As is true of any sweeping mandate, the low cost operator program required time for absorption into the management mentality. Immediate savings were generated in what many at first regarded as an accelerated profit improvement program. When fully understood, however, changes of a more fundamental nature began to occur. Inefficient production facilities and low-margin products were closed out. Marketing strategies were revamped with the objective of achieving more clout for every dollar spent. New product introductions and line extensions of existing products were accelerated. Capital expenditures were more accurately directed to technologies susceptible of higher productivity and less labor intensity. Company managers everywhere squared off against competitive challenge from whatever quarter, marshaling all of their respective resources against such problems as declining rates of inflation, trade concentration, changing consumer demographics and direct competitive challenge. What was initially regarded, then, as stepped-up profit improvement evolved into the creation of a new entrepreneurial spirit within the universe that is Heinz. Viewed from another vantage point, what is happening within the company can be seen as the most vigorous kind of preparation for company growth initiatives in the final decade of the 20th Century and beyond.

This year the low cost operator effort saw creation of intra-company task forces, each presided over by a senior corporate officer and peopled with experts drawn from each of our companies. These task forces are foraging for basic change in crucial operational areas—general and administrative expense, manufacturing, sales-marketing and procurement—that are common to all Heinz subsidiaries. In a company that prides itself on granting complete autonomy to its operating subsidiaries, this horizontal integration is itself reflective of a profound corporate culture change, a test of our cherished notions of collegiality. I am happy to say that the program was embraced by an enthusiastic field management.

This concerted effort by Heinz management to reinvent the corporation is being carried out against a backdrop of continuing financial success. During the past decade, our gross profits almost tripled, while our gross prcfit margin in relation to net sales rose from 33% to 40%.

Our market capitalization expanded more than eightfold, from $680 million to $5.4 billion. An investment in Heinz shares, if dividends were reinvested, increased more than 11 times. At fiscal year end, our balance sheet was stronger than at any time in our 118-year history.

We continue to pursue vigorously an acquisition search for middle-sized companies that fit comfortably into niches within our present structure and that are attuned to ever changing consumer needs. At the same time, we remain adamant in our determination not to dilute the financial interest of present shareholders. The past year saw the purchase for cash of a number of companies at home and abroad that fitted well into strategic planning. Company resources, as reflected in our robust balance sheet, ensure our ability to take advantage of new acquisition opportunities. Acquisition of such companies during the last 10 years cost us $416 million. These properties, at current multiples, are worth $1.3 billion in today's marketplace. Put another way, we bought $3.20 in value for every dollar spent.

Details of marketing developments during the year are set forth in the section that follows. Worthy of comment, however, is the general observation that all Heinz major product lines ended the year at or near historic highs, a result that is reassuring, given the intensified competitive climate that prevailed in the world marketplace. Once again, Heinz increased its outlay for marketing support of its existing and new products to $380 million, as compared with $348 million in fiscal 1986 and $123 million a decade ago. New products and innovative line extensions were introduced, many in the fastest-growing segments of the industry.

We have gone through a period that saw sustained growth in all of the measurements that serve as indicators of management effectiveness. Net sales, net income, earnings per share, return on average invested capital, return on average shareholders' equity, gross profit and total return to shareholders – all of these gauges of management achievement have yielded results that place Heinz on a comparative basis in the top rank of its industry. Wall Street has recognized this performance, according a high price-earnings ratio to our shares.

As for the future – always the concern of an alert management – I believe company shareholders have every right to be optimistic. Our core business is strong and growing, while new products and line extensions multiply in response to consumer needs. We back all of our brands with ever-larger marketing expenditures. We pursue our policy of niche acquisitions with diligence. We are planting the Heinz flag in countries such as The People's Republic of China, the Republic of Korea, and, most recently, in Thailand. And, most importantly, we are using our low cost operator initiatives to prepare our company everywhere for the future. Small wonder, then, that company management attitudes are animated by confidence and a pervasive sense of great expectations.

The continuing support of company shareholders is counted a major resource that is never taken for granted. Management understands that its first loyalty runs to those who have invested funds in our shares, including thousands of Heinz employees at all levels. Our activities to achieve a new era of growth for the company are calculated to nurture this vital management-shareholder partnership.

Foresight + Flexibility = The Big Payoff in Britain.

John F. Hinch – H.J.Heinz Company Ltd.

The most important change in the markets, the popular press tells Britain, is the return of the "good old competitive buyers' market." Well, the good old competitive spirit has returned, but in food it is anything except "the good old market."

To come at once to the most arresting point about Heinz-U.K: in productivity, performance and competitiveness the company is unique in the food industry. Indeed, it has few, if any, counterparts anywhere in British business. Without much fanfare at all, we have transformed the oldest overseas unit of Heinz into an advanced organization, where every employee is a highly capitalized, highly productive, highly motivated team member with the outlook of an aggressive entrepreneur.

Three years ago, it was clear that Heinz-U.K. was running full speed into the most challenging era of its existence. Discounting by six national retail chains and cooperatives, each possessing its own generic or private labels, had become a permanent condition. For Heinz this meant not only a loss of bargaining power with its biggest customers, but a threat to the clear-cut character, prestige and reputation of its brands. The company was in danger of dropping into a position of secondary importance.

The difference in strategy between Heinz and the food retailers could not be sharper. We have to be preoccupied with profit margins rather than volume. We have to meet the orgies of price cutting. We have to survive in a world where the buyer is a discriminating consumer, not a mere bargain hunter.

By contrast, Britain's food retailers act and think in terms of units. A chain's management judges its performance and charts its future in terms of units and constantly aims for higher unit sales. So powerful is the assault from retailers that the private label knocked out some food processors unable to break with the past.

In 1985, the largest single capital appropriation in company history was necessary to finance the transformation of every Heinz-U.K. function. Large and small structural alterations in manufacturing, distribution and marketing were put into place. Every system and process was reshaped. To integrate the whole business into a finely tuned system, we make heavy use of computers and automation.

In the short run, we needed enormous improvements in productivity to meet the assault of private labels. In the long run, we needed to protect the competitive strength of our major brands – beans, soup, ketchup, pasta, baby foods and salad dressings. Some facts and figures show that the £100 million solution is working in revolutionary fashion.

Productivity, measured in tons per employee, is up almost 70% over the past five years. Investment in technology has enabled us to reduce the number of employees from 5,000 in 1983 to 2,500. At the same time, we have increased or stabilized the market share of our volume lines, while aiming to increase the company's overall gross margin.

The sum total of progress in Britain in just three years is that we have an existing springboard into any facet of a "lowest cost imaginable" program. The people who are transforming Heinz tend to be young, unabashedly brainy, ambitious and aggressive. Nothing hems them in – neither a rigid organization structure nor time-honored operating practices. They are building our future.

A Londoner who spent some years in Pittsburgh as vice president and controller of Heinz U.S.A., John F. Hinch is now managing director of Heinz-U.K.

21

Financial Charts.

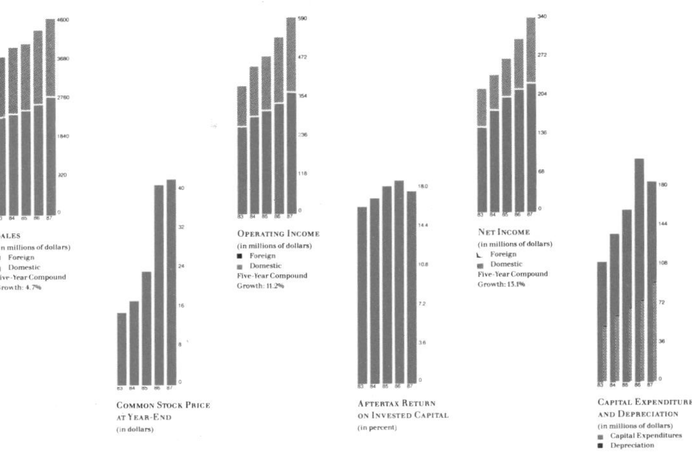

56

Financial Review.

H.J. Heinz Company and Consolidated Subsidiaries

Operating Results

Net sales rose 6.3%, or $273.3 million, in 1987. The weaker U.S. dollar used in the translation of foreign currencies contributed approximately two-thirds of the sales increase. Unit volume growth and acquisitions accounted for the remaining one-third. Price increases in some foreign markets were offset by lower prevailing prices in the U.S. The acquired companies included Near East Food Products, Inc. (a producer of flavored rice mixes and other specialty food products), The Pro-Mark Companies, Inc. (a distributor of Weight Watchers-brand dairy products) and Scaramellini S.p.A. (an Italian confectioner).

Foreign volume growth, particularly in the United Kingdom, Canada, Venezuela and Japan, provided over 60% of the consolidated volume gains. Domestic volume gains came primarily from Weight Watchers meeting and food operations, tuna products and Amoré gourmet canned cat food.

In 1986, volume gains provided 75% of the sales growth, with foreign increases contributing approximately one-half of the total volume growth. These gains were complemented by the effect of a weaker U.S. dollar versus certain major foreign currencies.

The gross profit margin continues to improve, reaching 40.1% in 1987 from 39.5% in 1986 and 38.4% in 1985. Lower commodity costs and volume growth in certain higher profit margin products and services contributed to margin expansion.

Marketing expenditures grew 9.1% to $379.8 million in 1987, from $348.0 million in 1986 and from $303.0 million in 1985. In addition to a continuing commitment to its established brands, the company spent heavily on growth opportunities in new product areas, such as Candle Lite dinners and microwavable potatoes. Other operating expenses increased 5.0% in 1987, compared with increases of 8.6% in 1986 and 2.4% in 1985. These expenses reflect the effect of the company's efforts to reduce costs.

Operating income increased 11.3% in 1987, with the operating margin improving to 12.8% in 1987 from 12.2% last year and 11.7% in 1985. This improvement was achieved despite restructuring charges of $27.4 million in 1987, $18.5 million in 1986 and $16.9 million in 1985. The restructuring charges included in prior periods have been reclassified to operations from other expense, in accordance with the provisions of the SEC Staff Accounting Bulletin No. 67, Income Statement Presentation of Restructuring Charges. The current year's restructuring charges primarily result from redundancy-related costs at Heinz-U.K., costs associated with the closure of Ore-Ida's Greenville, Michigan facility and further consolidation of Star-Kist production facilities at Terminal Island, California. Operating income in 1987 benefited from sales volume growth in the company's higher profit margin products and services, from the effect of the company's cost reduction efforts and from a weaker U.S. dollar.

The foreign companies contributed approximately 37% of total operating income in 1987. Heinz-Italy's double-digit local currency operating income growth was supplemented by a nearly 30% increase in the average lira exchange rate. Heinz-U.K.'s local currency operating income growth was achieved despite higher redundancy-related costs in 1987, as it benefited from its emphasis on reducing factory costs. This local currency growth was complemented by a stronger sterling exchange rate. Significant operating income growth, in local currency and U.S. dollars, also was achieved at Heinz companies in Portugal, Central Europe, Japan, Venezuela and Zimbabwe.

57

Eleven-Year Summary of Operations and Related Data.

H. J. Heinz Company and Consolidated Subsidiaries

(dollars in thousands except per share data)	*Fiscal Year*	*1987*	*1986*	*1985*
Summary of Operations:	Sales	$ 4,639,486	$ 4,366,177	$ 4,047,945
	Cost of products sold	2,779,781	2,640,777	2,492,384
	Interest expense	50,978	57,956	52,821
	Provision for income taxes	226,070	197,594	179,325
	Net income	338,506	301,734	265,978
	Net income per common share	2.47	2.20	1.93
Other Data:	Dividends paid:			
	Common	132,278	117,351	105,489
	per share	1.00⅔	.87⅓	.77⅓
	Preferred	177	227	291
	Average number of common shares outstanding	131,665,217	134,125,804	136,102,374
	Capital expenditures	184,750	206,331	158,830
	Depreciation	99,218	85,524	78,633
	Total assets	3,364,197	2,837,364	2,473,774
	Total debt	876,620	540,588	463,413
	Shareholders' equity	1,392,949	1,360,007	1,230,454
	Pretax return on average invested capital (%)	29.5	31.0	30.5
	Return on average shareholders' equity (%)	24.6	23.3	22.6
	Book value per common share	10.81	10.17	8.98
	Price range of common stock:			
	High	50½	44	24½
	Low	38¾	22⅝	16¼

50

1984	*1983*	*1982*	*1981*	*1980*	*1979*	*1978*	*1977*
$ 3,953,761	$ 3,738,445	$ 3,688,500	$ 3,568,889	$ 2,924,774	$ 2,470,883	$ 2,159,436	$ 1,877,300
2,456,159	2,368,302	2,397,546	2,359,760	1,917,677	1,640,128	1,453,025	1,268,297
46,417	50,354	58,851	59,585	40,010	29,471	18,859	16,332
164,725	136,122	108,145	126,879	59,583	72,164	69,554	72,967
237,530	214,250	192,802	160,827	131,497	108,404	95,277	96,598
1.70	1.51	1.37	1.16	.96	.79	.68	.69
94,210	78,352	65,755	54,841	48,131	41,309	32,143	24,260
.67½	.55⅔	.47	.40	.36	.31	.23⅔	.17¾
387	805	1,220	2,198	3,075	3,138	3,147	3,166
139,662,554	142,050,768	140,322,840	136,755,120	134,329,482	133,979,586	133,657,678	136,459,398
136,971	111,385	140,451	128,604	98,061	111,623	85,441	50,679
70,245	64,196	59,232	56,362	49,259	38,371	30,755	27,743
2,342,970	2,178,693	2,129,570	2,059,578	1,956,736	1,607,181	1,322,406	1,256,052
448,676	384,049	455,672	432,451	502,465	342,918	228,002	220,779
1,120,659	1,139,610	1,029,830	944,668	843,839	755,599	678,877	630,218
29.0	26.8	25.0	25.5	19.6	20.9	20.9	22.6
21.0	19.8	19.5	18.0	16.4	15.1	14.6	16.1
8.19	7.90	7.16	6.58	5.87	5.21	4.65	4.20
19¾	15⅛	11⅛	9¼	7⅜	7⅜	6¾	5¾
13⅞	9¾	8⅝	6⅜	5¾	5⅞	4⅞	4⅞

51

CLIENT:
H.J. HEINZ COMPANY

DESIGN FIRM:
CORPORATE GRAPHICS

ART DIRECTOR:
BENNETT ROBINSON

DESIGNERS:
BENNETT ROBINSON, ERIKA SIEGEL

PHOTOGRAPHER:
RODNEY SMITH

ILLUSTRATOR:
ROSEMARY WEBBER

PRODUCTION MANAGER:
NAYDA JIMENEZ

TYPOGRAPHER:
TYPOGRAM

PAPER MANUFACTURER:
THREE CROWNS AB TUMBA BRUK

PRINTER:
ANDERSON LITHOGRAPH

NUMBER OF PAGES:
56 PLUS COVER

DEBBIE FOSTER, GENERAL MANAGER, CORPORATE COMMUNICATIONS, H.J. HEINZ COMPANY, PITTSBURGH, PENNSYLVANIA

In our 1987 annual report, we wanted to introduce the heads of our affiliates, our field managers. We wanted to show our leadership on a personal basis, unit by unit. We had interviews done with each of the affiliates and in these conversations, each looked to the future as he saw it. We found a photographer whose work appeared in fine art galleries. This was his first commercial job. We felt the design by Corporate Graphics gave the report an elegant look. We had an excellent response to the report.

BENNETT ROBINSON, CORPORATE GRAPHICS, NEW YORK, NEW YORK

For H.J. Heinz's annual report we wanted to show the essence of what that company was doing and we focused on the management as the theme. We wanted to make this look individual and fresh. We pictured the field managers, not at the corporate headquarters, but scattered around the world. We found a photographer, Rodney Smith, who was a successful gallery and art book photographer. He was not commercial, but he related well in portrait work, and we thought he could handle corporate executives. So we had these wonderful black-and-white portraits centered on black pages opposite the interviews. This was our thirteenth annual report for H.J. Heinz, and we try to make it different each year in an interesting way.

DEBBIE FOSTER, GENERAL MANAGER, CORPORATE COMMUNICATIONS, H.J. HEINZ COMPANY, PITTSBURG, PENNSYLVANIA

In unserem Jahresbericht für 1987 wollten wir die Leiter unserer Filialen vorstellen. Unsere Kaderleute sollten auf ganz persönliche Weise präsentiert werden. In jeder Filiale wurden Interviews durchgeführt, und dabei sprach jeder einzelne über seine Sicht der Zukunft. Wir fanden einen Photographen, dessen Arbeit in Galerien gezeigt wird. Dieses war sein erster kommerzieller Auftrag. Dank der Gestaltung durch Corporate Graphics erhielten wir einen stilvollen Jahresbericht, und wir hatten ein ausgezeichnetes Echo.

BENNETT ROBINSON, CORPORATE GRAPHICS, NEW YORK, NEW YORK

Beim Jahresbericht für H.J. Heinz wollten wir deutlich machen, womit die Firma sich hauptsächlich befasst, wobei wir die Geschäftsführung zum Thema machten. Wir wollten eine persönliche, frische Darstellung. Also liessen wir die Filialleiter in aller Welt photographieren. Wir engagierten den Photographen Rodney Smith, der nicht an kommerzielle Aufgaben gewöhnt war, wohl aber an Porträtaufnahmen, und wir glaubten deshalb, dass er für die Aufnahmen der Kaderleute geeignet sei. Das Ergebnis waren wunderbare Schwarzweissaufnahmen, die wir auf schwarzen Seiten gegenüber den Interviews plazierten. Dies war unser dreizehnter Jahresbericht, und wir lassen uns jedes Jahr eine interessante, neue Lösung einfallen.

DEBBIE FOSTER, GENERAL MANAGER, CORPORATE COMMUNICATIONS, H.J. HEINZ COMPANY, PITTSBURGH, PENNSYLVANIE

Dans notre rapport annuel pour 1987, nous avons désiré dresser le portrait de nos directeurs régionaux sur un plan personnel. Chacun a fait l'objet d'une interview où il a pu s'exprimer sur sa vision de l'avenir. Nous nous sommes assuré l'aide d'un photographe dont les œuvres sont introduites dans le circuit des galeries d'art, et dont ça a été la première réalisation commerciale. Le design conçu par Corporate Graphics confère à ce rapport une élégance certaine. Nous avons enregistré des réactions très favorables à sa publication.

BENNETT ROBINSON, CORPORATE GRAPHICS, NEW YORK, NEW YORK

Pour le rapport annuel de H.J. Heinz, nous avons voulu représenter la quintessence de cette entreprise et nous sommes tournés vers ses dirigeants choisis comme thème représentatif. Il nous en fallait une présentation individuelle pleine de fraîcheur. C'est ainsi que nous avons dressé le portrait des directeurs régionaux dans leur zone d'action aux quatre coins du monde. Nous avons trouvé un photographe, Rodney Smith, qui n'est pas un commercial, mais excellait au portrait, et nous étions convaincus qu'il saurait faire le point sur des dirigeants d'entreprise. C'est ainsi que sont nés ces admirables portraits noir et blanc centrés sur des pages noires en regard des interviews. C'est le 13e rapport annuel que nous avons eu à réaliser.

IMMUNEX

1987 ANNUAL REPORT

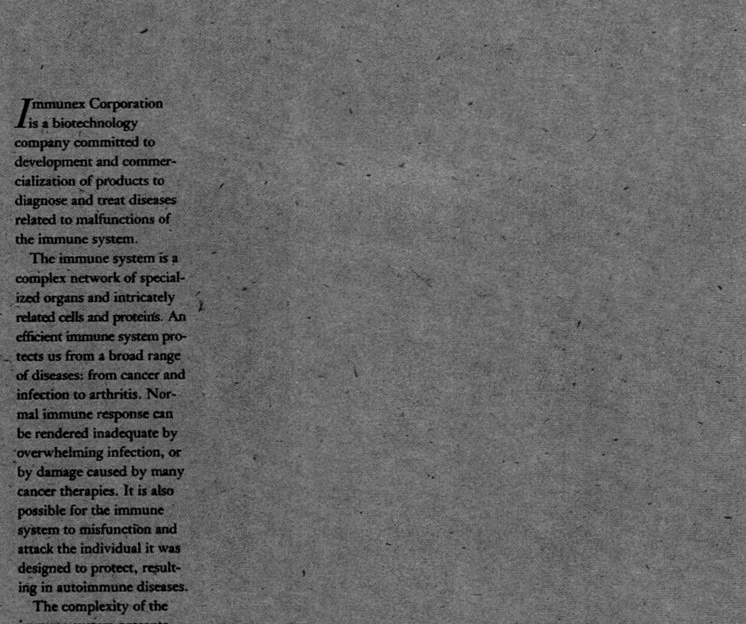

*I*mmunex Corporation is a biotechnology company committed to development and commercialization of products to diagnose and treat diseases related to malfunctions of the immune system.

The immune system is a complex network of specialized organs and intricately related cells and proteins. An efficient immune system protects us from a broad range of diseases: from cancer and infection to arthritis. Normal immune response can be rendered inadequate by overwhelming infection, or by damage caused by many cancer therapies. It is also possible for the immune system to misfunction and attack the individual it was designed to protect, resulting in autoimmune diseases.

The complexity of the immune system presents great challenges matched by great opportunities. Immunex's leadership in immunology, coupled with a capable and experienced management team, has positioned the company to capitalize upon the opportunities provided by an increasing understanding of the immune system.

FINANCIAL HIGHLIGHTS

Immunex Corporation

Selected Financial Data

	1987	*1986*	*1985*	*1984*	*1983*
Revenues	$15,703,964	$ 9,481,872	$ 3,226,830	$ 3,471,159	$ 1,712,927
Net loss	(175,488)	(1,415,268)	(4,441,768)	(2,464,497)	(1,856,989)
Net loss per common share	(.02)	(.20)	(.75)	(.42)	(.48)
Total assets	73,641,296	72,661,582	12,707,934	17,293,048	18,660,119
Long-term debt, including current portion	42,595,581	42,185,907	1,416,396	1,765,550	583,861
Shareholders' equity	28,265,290	28,259,268	10,879,173	15,145,148	17,599,699

Research Revenues ($ millions)

1987	11.3
1986	6.6
1985	2.4
1984	2.2
1983	.8

Research Expenses ($ millions)

1987	10.1
1986	7.9
1985	6.5
1984	4.8
1983	2.6

Shareholders' Equity ($ millions)

1987	28.3
1986	28.3
1985	10.9
1984	15.1
1983	17.6

Working Capital ($ millions)

1987	57.4
1986	60.9
1985	7.3
1984	11.2
1983	15.8

Our manufacturing capabilities will become reality with the spring 1988 completion of a pilot-scale fermentation plant, a major asset of Immunology Ventures, our successful 50/50 joint venture with Eastman Kodak Company. Immunology Ventures was formed in 1986 to develop and manufacture certain lymphokine therapeutic products. The pilot plant, located at Immunex's headquarters in downtown Seattle, is designed to meet Good Manufacturing Practices requirements as established by the FDA and has the capacity to manufacture products for both clinical trials and commercial sale.

STEPHEN A. DUZAN
President and CEO

*D*uring the last year, while work in the production plant has been left primarily to workers with hardhats and drills, our manufacturing needs have been met by extraordinary efforts of the scientific staff. Using equipment intended for production of experimental amounts of our products, the staff produced sufficient quantities of GM-CSF, G-CSF, IL-3, IL-1, and IL-4 for clinical testing.

This production work, which often required extended periods of 'round-the-clock attention, was accomplished in addition to Immunex's continuing and substantial scientific progress.

In 1987, Immunex researchers were the first to clone genes encoding human Interleukin-7 and the Interleukin-1 receptor. Patent applications have been filed to protect these discoveries, and scientific papers have been submitted for publication. We are excited about these developments, but have withheld detailed public disclosure to permit peer review and publication prior to public discussion of these achievements. Additional information concerning these proteins and their potential therapeutic applications will be included in upcoming quarterly reports to our shareholders.

Our screening lab, which uses proprietary techniques to screen Eastman Kodak's library of organic compounds, has also met with success. Our efforts to identify organic molecules that mimic or block immune system activities have produced two "hits." We have identified classes of compounds which help predict the structure of second and third generation products, including potential therapeutics in the area of allergies. These organic compounds could have even greater market potential than recombinant protein products because it might be possible to give them orally rather than via injection.

Details of these and other significant accomplishments are included in the Operations Review, which begins on page six of this report. In connection with this review, we've invited several investment analysts to ask questions which they would like us to address. These questions, and our answers, appear within the same pages.

STEVEN GILLIS, CHRISTOPHER S. HENNEY
Executive Vice Presidents

*P*lanning for our future, we have continued to invest in research in new technologies. In addition to screening organic compounds, we are following promising avenues in the areas of transgenics, oncogenes, and protease inhibitors, and we maintain an active interest in developing the possibilities of rational drug design.

The composition of Immunex's Board of Directors changed over the year with the retirement of one of our board members and the addition of a new director. We extend our thanks and appreciation for the guidance given to us by Martin S. Gerstel, president of Alza Corporation, who stepped down from the Board in May. And we welcome Kirby L. Cramer, Ph.D., chairman of Hazleton Laboratories and Kirschner Medical Corporation.

1987 was an exciting year for Immunex. Our expectations for the year ahead are equally high. We will have more products in clinical trials than ever before and will be playing a greater role in managing the trial process. At the same time, we are continuing to develop new research opportunities for future product development.

During this period of growth, we share stockholder concerns that current stock prices don't reflect an appropriate value for the company and we are mindful of the scarcity of additional new capital for emerging firms. Our plans are based on the assumption that the market will not recover soon, and our objectives are balanced with the need to carefully marshal our financial resources.

A final challenge to be met in the coming year is a challenge to our management of Immunex's internal culture. As we add new functions and make the transition to a larger, more versatile company, we must continue to nurture the energy and enthusiasm of the scientists who take the lead with cutting edge research. It is upon their discoveries that Immunex will build its future as an independent pharmaceutical company.

Stephen A. Duzan
President

ERATIONS REVIEW

A key component of the Immunex story for 1987 is the progress made in moving our recombinant products from the laboratory into the man clinical testing process.

Three products developed at Immunex were tested in man patients in 1987. Six new products were readied begin clinical trials, the process by which approval btained to market a pharmaceutical.

Our collaborative partner for Interleukin-2 (IL-2), ffmann-La Roche, is documenting the potential of this lymphokine as a cancer therapeutic. IL-2 causes proliferation of T-cells, a type of white blood cell that is capable of destroying malignant tissue. IL-2 clinical trials have moved into advanced stages, measuring the effectiveness of the protein administered alone, in combination with activated immune cells (LAK therapy) and with other agents.

Clinical testing is also progressing on Immunex's monoclonal antibody against the IL-2 receptor, under the direction of Becton Dickinson. The antibody may serve to prevent graft-versus-host disease, an often fatal result of a bone marrow transplant.

GM-CSF, developed in collaboration with Behringwerke A.G., a subsidiary of the West German pharmaceutical leader Hoechst A.G., entered clinical trials in 1987. Our agreement with Behringwerke covers the family of colony stimulating factors (CSFs) developed by Immunex. Clinical testing of GM-CSF, (granulocyte-macrophage colony stimulating factor) began early in 1987 and has now entered an advanced phase, with studies carefully designed to generate data required for regulatory approval.

GM-CSF stimulates the bone marrow to produce two types of white blood cells, granulocytes and macrophages. These cells, which play a crucial role in combatting infection, are depleted by chemotherapy and certain disease conditions. The first phase of clinical testing has investigated the usefulness of GM-CSF in treating a variety of naturally-occurring and cancer therapy-induced white blood cell deficiencies. These

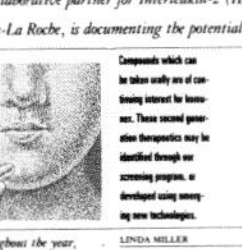

Compounds which can be taken orally are of continuing interest for Immunex. These second generation therapeutics may be identified through our screening program, or developed using emerging new technologies.

IL-3, an early colony stimulating factor, is vialed and ready for clinical trials. Testing will begin in 1988 to evaluate the protein's effectiveness in restoring levels of infection fighting white blood cells.

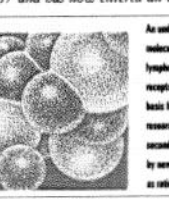

An understanding of the molecular structure of lymphokines and their receptors will provide the basis for Immunex researchers to develop second generation drugs by new techniques, such as rational drug design.

For preclinical tests in burn and wound healing settings, an Interleukin-1 gel was formulated under sterile conditions. This product will be the first Immunex proprietary product to begin testing in human clinical trials.

Throughout the year, meetings take place between Immunex senior management and members of the financial community. This section of our report was prepared with the assistance of four investment analysts.

These questions were contributed by: Linda Miller, Vice President, PaineWebber; Michael Sorell, Equity Research, Morgan Stanley & Co.; Eugene Rothman, Vice President, Alex. Brown & Sons; and Stu Weisbrod, Biotechnology Analyst, Prudential-Bache Securities, Inc.

LINDA MILLER

Q How quickly must Immunex develop production and marketing capabilities? How great an investment will be made in these areas?

A The timing and cost of developing these capabilities will depend on the timing of regulatory approval and the nature of the products first approved. We are gearing up to ensure that our capabilities in both production and marketing keep pace with our growing needs.

While our laboratory scale fermenters have met needs for clinical trial quantities of products, construction is nearing completion on our pilot-scale manufacturing plant. This facility is a major asset of Immunology Ventures, and the cost of its construction is shared with Eastman Kodak. Future plans for Immunology Ventures include construction of a larger manufacturing plant. Once that plant is complete, the pilot-scale facility will be used primarily for process development and scale-up.

Successful marketing of a new product begins well before the actual approval of the new drug. With that in mind, we added product managers and a planning coordinator to our staff in 1987. These individuals are involved in the management of the products, including marketing research and analysis of the competitive situation.

MICHAEL SORELL

Q Will you be able to develop and market new products of your own?

A Certainly. We have been engaged in proprietary product development since our inception. One-third of our 1988 research and development budget is targeted for continued work on projects that we own and will develop without collaborative agreements. [illegible] of the ten products scheduled for clinical or field trials in 1988 belong totally to Immunex. Additionally, the target markets for our first proprietary products do not require an extensive sales force. For example, Interleukin-1 as a topical healing agent for burns could be distributed nationwide through a concentrated number of burn centers. IL-1 as a vaccine adjuvant will initially be sold directly to vaccine manufacturers.

EUGENE ROTHMAN

Q Elaborate on Immunex's proprietary new product candidates, for example, the rhinovirus program.

A The rhinovirus project is an example of one of our first forays outside the field of pure immunology research. We have isolated and characterized a rhinovirus protease. We are investigating ways to neutralize the virus by halting its replication. It is a challenging project, and the resulting product may be a treatment for the common cold.

The two applications of IL-1 for which Immunex has retained full rights are closer to the clinical testing process. Immunex is now conducting advanced preclinical studies of IL-1 as a wound healing agent and vaccine adjuvant.

STU WEISBROD

Q How does the current drug screening program with Kodak fit into your strategy? Why not rational drug design instead?

A We view the screening program as an important component of our strategy for the future, and a critical component of a rational drug design program. The screening program is designed to identify immunologically active molecules in Kodak's library of organic compounds using Immunex bioassays. Immunex continues to screen 1,000 compounds a week, and has screened a total of 50,000 compounds to date. In 1987 the screening program was expanded and we increased both lab space and personnel committed to this project.

The information obtained from screening, coupled with our growing molecular understanding of both lymphokines and their receptors will illuminate our search for second generation drugs by rational drug design.

universal expression and purification system, developed by Immunex scientists, will be sold as a kit, and is now being test marketed to researchers.

The Immunology Ventures production plant is located in Immunex's Seattle facility. The 10,000 square foot plant will manufacture joint venture, proprietary and collaborative products needed for clinical trials. Although its capacity will initially meet our needs for commercial production, our longer-term strategy will be to use this facility for limited production needs and process scale-up.

10 *While our manufacturing plant was under construction, Immunex's scientific staff met production needs. Quantities of recombinant GM-CSF, G-CSF, IL-3, IL-4 and IL-1 needed for clinical trials were fermented and purified to FDA clinical trial standards.*

Two high points of the scientific year were the first successful cloning of genes encoding two proteins: the IL-1 receptor, which has possible therapeutic value in auto-immune diseases and arthritis, and IL-7 which may prove useful in treating cancer or B-cell deficiencies. These endeavors required advanced techniques and relied on expertise from throughout the company.

Under an agreement separate from the joint venture, Immunex has been using proprietary assays to screen Eastman Kodak's library of organic compounds. To date, 50,000 compounds have been screened, and two interesting families of compounds have been identified. In 1987, the screening agreement was expanded to include additional screening for small molecules which may mimic or block lymphokine function.

Projects in earlier development stages include new applications for our established technologies and new directions for pharmaceutical research. We are exploring appropriate possibilities in transgenics, rational drug design, development of protease inhibitors and anti-microbial peptides. These activities will assure that Immunex remains at the forefront of immunology research and product development.

Our management structure has been enhanced to support the increasing complexity of our operations.

Carol L. Epstein, M.D., joined Immunex as Director of Clinical Affairs, to direct the increased number of products in human testing.

In the area of marketing and communications, H. Stewart Parker was elected to Vice President. Katie Weiss was hired to fill the new position of Director of Communications.

James Johnson joined the company as Director of Finance, to focus on budgeting and financial planning.

Jan Gombotz was promoted to Director of Information Systems, responsible for the expansion and operations of our computer system. Carl March, Ph.D., a five-year employee, became Head of the Protein Chemistry Department. Tom Hopp, Ph.D., Vice President and former head of that department, has been named head of the newly established Transgenics Department.

From the laboratory bench to medical practice, new pharmaceuticals face a complex journey.

At Immunex, our primary goal is to successfully guide our products along the entire distance.

BALANCE SHEETS

Immunex Corporation

December 31,	*1987*	*1986*
20 *Assets*		
Current assets:		
Cash and cash equivalents	$ 4,337,735	$ 2,762,510
Marketable securities (Note 2)	54,863,057	60,099,326
Accounts receivable	1,157,387	470,983
Other current assets	480,685	221,175
Total current assets	60,838,864	63,553,994
Property, plant and equipment, net (Note 4)	8,526,841	6,944,466
Other assets, at cost:		
Debt issuance costs, net of amortization	1,357,464	1,405,822
Patent costs, net of amortization	768,869	491,395
Investment in joint venture (Note 3)	2,149,258	265,905
	$73,641,296	$72,661,582
Liabilities and Shareholders' Equity		
Current liabilities:		
Accounts payable	$ 506,615	$ 234,826
Accrued liabilities	587,787	374,831
Deferred revenue	436,023	356,750
Debenture interest payable (Note 5)	1,250,000	1,250,000
Current portion of long-term debt (Note 5)	614,578	454,641
Total current liabilities	3,395,003	2,671,048
Long-term debt (Note 5)	41,981,003	41,731,266
Commitments (Note 9)		
Shareholders' equity:		
Preferred stock, 1,800,000 shares authorized, none issued	–	–
Common stock, $.01 par value, 20,000,000 shares authorized, 7,684,423 and 7,628,389 outstanding at December 31, 1987 and 1986, respectively (Note 6)	76,844	76,284
Capital in excess of par value	39,488,833	39,307,883
Accumulated deficit	(11,300,387)	(11,124,899)
Total shareholders' equity	28,265,290	28,259,268
	$73,641,296	$72,661,582

See accompanying notes.

STATEMENTS OF OPERATIONS

Immunex Corporation

Year Ended December 31,	*1987*	*1986*	*1985*
Revenues:			21
Revenue under collaborative agreements (Note 7)	$11,315,678	$ 6,602,973	$ 2,365,796
Interest	4,388,286	2,878,899	861,034
	15,703,964	9,481,872	3,226,830
Costs and expenses:			
Research and development (Note 7)	12,091,192	7,873,949	6,486,224
General and administrative	2,110,854	1,600,640	1,036,968
Interest	1,280,759	1,413,456	145,406
Loss from joint venture (Note 3)	396,647	9,095	–
	15,879,452	10,897,140	7,668,598
Net loss	$ (175,488)	$(1,415,268)	$(4,441,768)
Net loss per common share	$ (.02)	$ (.20)	$ (.75)
Average number of common shares outstanding	7,659,695	7,222,013	5,942,384

See accompanying notes.

NOTES TO FINANCIAL STATEMENTS

Immunex Corporation

under certain conditions. The Company may redeem the debentures at agreed upon prices at any time, except that no redemption may be made prior to August 15, 1988 unless the closing price of the common stock for a specified period is at least 150% of the conversion price then in effect. Mandatory sinking fund payments sufficient to retire 5% of the principal are required annually commencing August 1, 1996.

Equipment on the accompanying balance sheets, principally laboratory equipment, includes $3,566,847 and $2,712,474 at December 31, 1987 and 1986, respectively, under capitalized leasing arrangements. Accu-
26 mulated amortization was $1,081,903 and $625,526 at December 31, 1987 and 1986, respectively.

Note 6.
Stock Options

The Company has an option plan providing for issuance of incentive and nonqualified stock options to employees, directors and outside consultants. There were 1,300,000 shares of common stock reserved for the plan. Options are granted by a committee of the Board of Directors at the fair market value of the Company's stock at the date of grant. Each outstanding option has a term of ten years from the date of grant and becomes exercisable at a rate of 20% per year beginning one year from the date of the grant.

During 1987, the committee approved an exchange program, under which employees may exchange options granted after 1985 for options granted on December 7, 1987, having an exercise price of $10.00 per share. There are options to purchase 346,180 shares at an average exercise price of $18.02 per share eligible, none of which were exchanged as of December 31, 1987.

Information with respect to options outstanding at December 31, 1987 is as follows:

Year Granted	*Shares Subject to Option*	*Price per Share*	*Total Exercise Price*
1982	38,669	$ .22–$ .57	$ 10,001
1983	61,631	$ .57–$12.75	216,645
1984	164,033	$ 4.25–$ 7.75	955,151
1985	93,240	$ 4.88–$14.63	660,016
1986	129,600	$11.38–$19.63	1,934,386
1987	453,846	$10.00–$23.88	7,068,902
	941,019		$10,845,101

Of the outstanding options at December 31, 1987, 165,125 were exercisable. In addition, at December 31, 1987, 134,552 shares were available for future grants.

Note 7.
Research and Development

The Company's research and development revenues are recorded pursuant to collaborative agreements under which the Company receives varying levels of reimbursement based on costs incurred for the related projects. Once a product is developed and marketed, the Company will receive royalties on sales of the product. Revenues received from Immunology Ventures are included as revenue under collaborative agreements.

The Company's research and development expenses include costs incurred on projects covered by collaborative agreements and on projects for which the Company is funding its own research. Research and development expense in excess of the amounts received under collaborative agreements, if any, on an individual project basis totalled $2,964,307, $3,104,860, and $4,385,500 for the years ended December 31, 1987, 1986 and 1985.

The following table shows the percentage of the Company's total research and development revenue in each of the last three years contributed by each of the Company's partners in collaborative research agreements which contributed 10% or more of such revenue:

Collaborative Partner	*1987*	*1986*	*1985*
A	20%	24%	49%
B	4	6	25
C	30	17	—
Immunology Ventures (Note 3)	43	50	—

Note 8.
Income Taxes

At December 31, 1987, the Company had a net operating tax loss carryforward of $16,300,000 and a carryforward of $1,060,000 for research and experimental credits. The carryforwards expire from 1996 through 2002. For financial reporting purposes, the net operating loss carryforward at December 31, 1987 approximates $10,700,000. The difference between the net operating loss carryforward for income tax purposes and financial reporting purposes is primarily attributable to differences in depreciation rates, the treatment of equipment leases, and methods of recording losses from Immunology Ventures.

Note 9.
Commitments

Minimum rental commitments under noncancellable operating and capital leases at December 31, 1987 are as follows:

Year Ended December 31,	*Operating*	*Capital*
1988	$1,094,805	$ 770,425
1989	1,094,805	732,476
1990	1,094,805	704,455
1991	1,200,754	524,333
1992	1,200,754	233,783
Thereafter	3,378,591	—
Total minimum lease payments	$9,064,514	2,965,472
Less amount representing interest		369,891
Present value of minimum capital lease payments		$2,595,581

Minimum payments under operating leases have not been reduced by minimum sublease rentals aggregating $1,519,790, receivable from Immunology Ventures under noncancellable subleases.

Rental expenses on operating leases for the years ended December 31, 1987, 1986 and 1985 were as follows:

	1987	*1986*	*1985*
Minimum rental expense	$1,044,615	$685,524	$598,033
Sublease rental income	(416,555)	—	—
	$ 628,060	$685,524	$598,033

As of December 31, 1987, the Company has guaranteed $1,448,000 of equipment lease financing for Immunology Ventures.

Report of Certified Public Accountants

The Board of Directors and Shareholders
Immunex Corporation

We have examined the accompanying balance sheets of Immunex Corporation at December 31, 1987 and 1986, and the related statements of operations, shareholders' equity and cash flows for each of the three years in the period ended December 31, 1987. Our examinations were made in accordance with generally accepted auditing standards and, accordingly, included such tests of the accounting records and such other auditing procedures as we considered necessary in the circumstances.

In our opinion, the statements mentioned above present fairly the financial position of Immunex Corporation at December 31, 1987 and 1986, and the results of its
operations and its cash flows for each of the three years in 27
the period ended December 31, 1987, in conformity with generally accepted accounting principles applied on a consistent basis during the period.

Arthur Young & Company

Seattle, Washington
February 5, 1988

Price Range of Common Stock

	1987 High	*1987 Low*	*1986 High*	*1986 Low*
4th Quarter	23⅝	9⅜	14	11⅛
3rd Quarter	24⅝	20¼	19⅝	11
2nd Quarter	25⅝	16⅝	19⅝	12⅞
1st Quarter	20⅝	11½	16½	12⅝

The common stock of the Company is traded on the National Market System under the NASDAQ symbol IMNX. No dividends have been paid on the common stock.

CLIENT:
IMMUNEX CORPORATION

DESIGN FIRM:
PENTAGRAM DESIGN

ART DIRECTOR:
KIT HINRICHS

DESIGNERS:
BELLE HOW,
KIT HINRICHS

PHOTOGRAPHER:
STEVE FIREBAUGH

ILLUSTRATOR:
ED LINDLOF

WRITER:
KATIE WEISS

VALOREE DOWELL, DIRECTOR OF COMMUNICATIONS, IMMUNEX CORPORATION, SEATTLE, WASHINGTON

The Immunex Corporation is a biotechnology company committed to the development and commercialization of pharmaceutical products. The main objective of the 1987 annual report was to provide an in-depth description of the process involved in getting Federal Drug Administration approval for a new product. This was especially necessary since the approval process for therapeutic drugs takes so long, and we needed to remind the investors of the procedure and the time involved. We knew that photography would not adequately convey this, so Pentagram used illustration in a time line centerfold. This was effective and informative and it captured the image of quality we wanted to convey, especially since the centerfold also featured photogaphs of our staff, and somehow the total centerfold captured the artistry in the work done by the Immunex scientists.

VALOREE DOWELL, DIRECTOR OF COMMUNICATIONS, IMMUNEX CORPORATION, SEATTLE, WASHINGTON

Die Immunex Corporation ist ein biotechnisches Unternehmen, das sich mit der Entwicklung und Vermarktung von pharmazeutischen Produkten befasst. Das Hauptziel des Berichtes für 1987 war eine ausführliche Darstellung des Arbeitsprozesses, der mit der Einholung der Zulassungsgenehmigung eines neuen Produktes bei der Federal Drug Administration verbunden ist. Der Bewilligungsprozess für therapeutische Produkte ist so langwierig, dass wir die Investoren an die Prozedur erinnern mussten. Pentagram verwendete deshalb im Mittelbund Illustrationen mit einer Zeitübersicht. Das war eindrucksvoll und informativ und gab den gewünschten Eindruck von Qualität, besonders weil im Mittelbund auch Aufnahmen unserer Angestellten gezeigt wurden. Hier kommt die anspruchsvolle Arbeit der wissenschaftlichen Mitarbeiter zum Ausdruck.

VALOREE DOWELL, DIRECTOR OF COMMUNICATIONS, IMMUNEX CORPORATION, SEATTLE, WASHINGTON

L'Immunex Corporation est une société de biotechnique qui se voue à la mise au point et à la commercialisation de produits pharmaceutiques. L'objectif principal de notre rapport annuel pour 1987, c'était de fournir une description détaillée de la procédure qui mène à l'homologation d'un nouveau médicament par la Federal Drug Administration. Il paraissait utile d'informer les investisseurs de la complexité et de la durée du processus administratif. Nous savions que la photo ne se prêterait pas vraiment à la visualisation, d'où l'organigramme dépliant conçu par Pentagram au centre de l'ouvrage, procédé efficace et riche d'enseignements qui a permis de restituer l'idée de qualité. Toute cette section centrale donne bien l'impression de l'art consommé avec lequel les recherches scientifiques sont poursuivies dans les laboratoires d'Immunex.

KIT HINRICHS, PENTAGRAM DESIGN, SAN FRANCISCO, CALIFORNIA

Immunex is a relatively young biotechnology firm with great expertise, but no products yet. This would be true of any new drug company getting established. For the firm's 1987 annual report, there was the need to explain to the casual investor how long it takes for a pharmaceutical product to be approved (the span is about seven to ten years). In this annual report, we provided an overview of the industry, and we demonstrated that Immunex knew exactly where it was going. We stressed the importance of the young, vital staff but also gave the report a classical feeling for the financials. The contemporary and classical design are combined into one continuous whole. We show the company as on-the-edge, but with traditional financial reporting.

KIT HINRICHS, PENTAGRAM DESIGN, SAN FRANCISCO, KALIFORNIEN

Immunex ist eine relativ junge biotechnische Firma mit einer ausgezeichneten Expertise, aber bisher ohne Produkte. Im Jahresbericht 1987 musste dem weniger informierten Investor erklärt werden, wie lange ein pharmazeutisches Unternehmen braucht, um die Bewilligung für ein neues Produkt zu bekommen (zwischen 7 und 10 Jahren). Wir lieferten einen Überblick über die Industrie und zeigten, dass Immunex genau weiss, was sie will. Wir stellten die Bedeutung der jungen, vitalen Belegschaft heraus, wählten aber für den Finanzteil eine klassische Präsentation. Das moderne und das klassische Design bilden eine schöne Einheit. Wir stellten die Firma als ein ganz modernes Unternehmen dar, das aber im Finanzbereich auf Tradition setzt.

KIT HINRICHS, PENTAGRAM DESIGN, SAN FRANCISCO, CALIFORNIE

Immunex est une société de biotechnique de création relativement récente, qui dispose de spécialistes de tout premier plan sans avoir encore mis de produits sur le marché. Pour le rapport annuel 1987, il s'agissait d'expliquer à l'investisseur le temps qu'il faut compter jusqu'à l'homologation d'un produit pharmaceutique (7 à 10 ans). Nous avons donné un aperçu de la branche et souligné l'importance d'un personnel jeune tout en ne négligeant pas l'aspect classique du respect des impératifs financiers. Le design a un volet contemporain et un volet classique qui s'intègrent en un tout homogène. La société cultive une technologie de pointe, mais fait confiance aux méthodes éprouvées de la gestion financière et de la présentation des résultats.

INDEPENDENCE BANCORP

Independence Bancorp
One Hillendale Road
Perkasie, Pennsylvania 18944
215 257 2402

Buck County Bank & Trust Company
One Hillendale Road
Perkasie, Pennsylvania 18944
215 453 3000

Cheltenham Bank
50 Huntingdon Pike
Rockledge, Pennsylvania 19111
215 379 1800

Freedom Valley Bank
1522 McDaniel Drive
West Chester, Pennsylvania 19382
215 431 3160

Lehigh Valley Bank
65 East Elizabeth Avenue
Bethlehem, Pennsylvania 18018
215 821 5000

Third National Bank & Trust Company
130 Wyoming Avenue
Scranton, Pennsylvania 18504
717 348 8230

Independence Bancorp, Inc. and Subsidiaries
Financial Highlights

(In thousands, except per share data)

December 31,	1987	1986	Percentage Increase	5 Year Growth Rate
Income and Dividends				
Net income	$ 26,767	$ 24,824	7.8%	14.1%
Net interest income (tax-equivalent)	105,608	94,124	12.2	14.9
Cash dividends paid	10,637	8,558	24.3	13.8
Per Share:				
Primary earnings	2.79	2.66	4.9	10.0
Fully diluted earnings	2.63	2.56	2.7	8.7
Cash dividends paid	1.14	1.04	9.6	9.8
Book value	19.15	17.19	11.4	11.4
Financial Condition				
Total assets	$2,902,739	$2,454,215	18.3%	19.6%
Loans	1,362,415	1,103,368	23.5	19.9
Investment securities	1,304,492	1,104,917	18.1	30.7
Deposits	2,101,178	1,761,326	19.3	16.1
Shareholders' equity	187,145	162,066	15.5	16.0
Selected Ratios				
Return on average assets	0.98%	1.14%		
Return on average shareholders' equity	15.27	16.61		
Net interest margin	4.15	4.64		
Average shareholders' equity to average total assets	6.45	6.89		
Primary capital to total assets	7.03	7.10		

market prices. Independence intends to pursue any civil remedies it may have against this broker. We have also advised federal and state authorities of these matters and we intend to cooperate fully in any investigations.

In September of 1987, Independence placed $22.1 million of 10⅜ percent asset-backed bonds held in our investment portfolio on non-accrual status and reclassified them to other assets. This action was taken in response to reports and projections of delinquencies and foreclosures of the underlying collateral and in response to communications from the bond trustee concerning positions being taken by the private credit insurer underwriting the collateral. Future payments will be applied to reduce the outstanding principal amount of the bonds and interest income will not be recorded. In December, Independence commenced legal action against the broker of these investments.

These developments will not significantly affect the stability or long-term outlook of Independence Bancorp.

We are thankful for the five years of direction provided by J. Franklin Hartzel, who left the Independence Board of Directors upon reaching retirement age. With deep regret, we note the death of Leonard L. Genghini—a retired Board member who served Independence since 1983 and was a member of the Board of Directors at Cheltenham Bank since 1968.

As we near the end of the 1980's, Independence Bancorp is positioned for strong growth and development into the next decade. We are strengthened by our clear focus on community banking in dynamic markets, a solid and diversified loan portfolio, and the dedication of our 1,500 employees.

I invite you to review a discussion of our growing markets, clear business direction and elements of our profitability explained in the next several pages.

Sincerely,

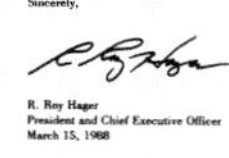

R. Roy Hager
President and Chief Executive Officer
March 15, 1988

page 6

page 7

page 8

Brenda Lucom **Bucks County Bank**

Bucks County Bank, with $1.2 billion in assets, operates 17 offices in a prosperous marketplace in Bucks and Montgomery counties that has convenient access to New York and Philadelphia. It is preparing to open two additional offices this year along with a specialized commercial banking facility. A product of community banking since the beginning of this century, it has been recognized numerous times for its commitment, financial and personal, to Bucks County communities. In the words of one charitable organization's tribute: Bucks County Bank is a "Big Brother and Big Sister to all of us."

"When we were looking for financing to start our health club we inquired at other banks but found the people at Bucks County Bank younger and more aggressive. They had more faith in us than anyone else."

Brenda Lucom, 29, had worked as a travel agent and a legal secretary. At the end of each day at the office, however, she impatiently waited to run to a gym to begin her daily fitness workouts. In 1985 she turned her hobby into a business when she and her partner, also a weightlifter, opened Club Genesis in Souderton, Pennsylvania. Backed by financing from Bucks County Bank, their venture is healthy and strong. The former "Miss East Coast of 1984," has a busy schedule but she does set aside time for other activities—on her days off she lifts weights.

page 9

Independence Bancorp Inc. and Subsidiaries
Distribution of Assets, Liabilities and Shareholders' Equity;
Interest Rates and Interest Differential

(Dollars in thousands)

Year ended December 31,	1987 Average Balance	1987 Annual Rate	1987 Interest Inc./Exp.	1986 Average Balance	1986 Annual Rate	1986 Interest Inc./Exp.
Assets						
Interest-bearing deposits with banks	$ 5,225	9.84%	$ 514	$ 25,098	10.82%	$ 2,716
Federal funds sold and securities purchased under agreements to resell	3,634	6.58	239	11,524	6.55	755
Trading account securities	7,272	8.55	622	4,098	7.25	297
Securities						
U.S. Treasury	147,746	8.11	11,979	122,262	9.26	11,324
U.S. Government agencies and corporations	431,083	8.02	34,578	455,900	8.80	40,132
State and municipal	155,751	12.55	19,554	172,432	13.73	23,667
Other securities and equity securities	535,631	9.28	49,701	254,220	9.31	23,658
Total securities	1,270,211	9.12	115,812	1,004,814	9.83	98,781
Loans						
Commercial and financial	471,219	10.13	47,726	409,691	10.44	42,765
Real estate—construction and mortgage	350,490	10.83	37,955	262,861	11.46	30,122
Installment loans to individuals	398,242	10.28	40,946	293,845	11.61	34,118
Lease financing	40,863	11.40	4,659	16,937	11.80	1,999
Total loans	1,260,814	10.41	131,286	983,334	11.09	109,004
Total earning assets	2,547,156	9.75	248,473	2,028,868	10.43	211,553
Non-interest earning assets	171,194	—	—	142,241	—	—
Total Assets	$2,718,350	9.14%	$248,473	$2,171,109	9.74%	$211,553
Liabilities and Shareholders' Equity						
Interest-Bearing Deposits						
Demand—interest-bearing	$ 138,356	5.25%	$ 7,265	$ 96,469	5.44%	$ 5,250
Savings	622,621	5.36	33,401	528,407	5.70	30,095
Time	426,117	6.96	29,650	420,177	7.92	33,262
Time over $100,000	389,694	6.97	27,174	269,805	6.99	18,858
Total interest-bearing deposits	1,576,788	6.18	97,490	1,314,858	6.65	87,465
Short-term borrowings	584,730	7.02	41,068	398,606	6.92	27,595
Long-term borrowings	61,051	7.05	4,307	33,976	6.97	2,369
Total interest-bearing liabilities	2,222,569	6.43	142,865	1,747,440	6.72	117,429
Demand—non-interest bearing	281,812	—	—	243,185	—	—
Other liabilities	38,665	—	—	31,003	—	—
Total liabilities	2,543,046	5.62	142,865	2,021,628	5.81	117,429
Shareholders' equity	175,304	—	—	149,481	—	—
Total Liabilities and Shareholders' Equity	$2,718,350	5.26%	$142,865	$2,171,109	5.41%	$117,429
Interest income/earning assets		9.75%	$248,473		10.43%	$211,553
Interest expense/earning assets		5.60	142,865		5.79	117,429
Net interest margin		4.15%	$105,608		4.64%	$ 94,124
Selected Ratios:						
Return on average assets		0.98%			1.14%	
Return on average equity		15.27			16.61	
Dividend payout ratio		40.86			39.10	
Average equity to average assets		6.45			6.89	

Year ended December 31,	1985 Average Balance	1985 Annual Rate	1985 Interest Inc./Exp.	1984 Average Balance	1984 Annual Rate	1984 Interest Inc./Exp.	1983 Average Balance	1983 Annual Rate	1983 Interest Inc./Exp.
Assets									
Interest-bearing deposits with banks	$ 43,862	10.61%	$ 4,655	$ 24,801	10.58%	$ 2,623	$ 102,494	10.20%	$ 10,451
Federal funds sold and securities purchased under agreements to resell	18,455	8.10	1,494	17,440	8.65	1,508	46,061	9.09	4,188
Trading account securities	3,239	9.54	309	6,186	14.58	902	15,896	10.27	1,633
Securities									
U.S. Treasury	127,986	10.16	12,998	98,870	10.41	10,293	99,291	10.11	10,038
U.S. Government agencies and corporations	308,489	9.80	30,224	239,214	10.87	26,001	159,375	10.41	16,586
State and municipal	103,980	13.94	14,494	134,897	12.63	17,043	115,149	12.80	14,739
Other securities and equity securities	134,787	10.34	13,938	130,093	11.90	15,483	96,437	11.24	10,839
Total securities	675,242	10.61	71,654	603,074	11.41	68,820	470,252	11.10	52,202
Loans									
Commercial and financial	339,063	12.07	40,932	269,220	13.71	36,918	194,441	12.82	24,924
Real estate—construction and mortgage	214,966	12.02	25,835	200,716	12.18	24,455	208,168	11.35	23,630
Installment loans to individuals	235,078	12.78	30,037	175,977	13.53	23,803	144,587	14.12	20,413
Lease financing	7,086	11.57	820	1,457	9.27	135	765	4.18	32
Total loans	796,193	12.26	97,624	647,370	13.18	85,311	547,961	12.59	68,999
Total earning assets	1,536,991	11.43	175,736	1,298,871	12.25	159,164	1,182,664	11.62	137,473
Non-interest earning assets	116,611	—	—	97,279	—	—	85,772	—	—
Total Assets	$1,653,602	10.63%	$175,736	$1,396,150	11.40%	$159,164	$1,268,436	10.84%	$137,473
Liabilities and Shareholders' Equity									
Interest-Bearing Deposits									
Demand—interest-bearing	$ 78,432	5.92%	$ 4,646	$ 56,279	5.60%	$ 3,154	$ 51,930	5.57%	$ 2,894
Savings	438,421	6.37	27,917	376,896	6.86	25,857	352,560	6.25	22,019
Time	419,809	9.21	38,652	418,754	10.32	43,221	404,431	10.24	41,409
Time over $100,000	171,333	8.62	14,776	113,923	10.55	12,017	75,938	10.53	7,997
Total interest-bearing deposits	1,107,995	7.76	85,991	965,852	8.72	84,249	884,859	8.40	74,319
Short-term borrowings	181,991	8.14	14,819	108,196	10.41	11,259	86,584	9.48	8,209
Long-term borrowings	6,723	7.29	490	9,403	8.97	843	10,919	8.52	930
Total interest-bearing liabilities	1,296,709	7.81	101,300	1,083,451	8.89	96,351	982,362	8.50	83,458
Demand—non-interest bearing	213,593	—	—	196,311	—	—	176,082	—	—
Other liabilities	21,893	—	—	16,589	—	—	18,441	—	—
Total liabilities	1,532,195	6.61	101,300	1,296,351	7.43	96,351	1,176,885	7.09	83,458
Shareholders' equity	121,407	—	—	99,799	—	—	91,551	—	—
Total Liabilities and Shareholders' Equity	$1,653,602	6.13%	$101,300	$1,396,150	6.90%	$ 96,351	$1,268,436	6.58%	$ 83,458
Interest income/earning assets		11.43%	$175,736		12.25%	$159,164		11.62%	$137,473
Interest expense/earning assets		6.59	101,300		7.42	96,351		7.05	83,458
Net interest margin		4.84%	$ 74,436		4.83%	$ 62,813		4.57%	$ 54,015
Selected Ratios:									
Return on average assets		1.20%			1.13%			1.09%	
Return on average equity		16.33			15.75			15.05	
Dividend payout ratio		42.76			46.92			44.22	
Average equity to average assets		7.34			7.15			7.22	

Non-accrual loans are included in the average balances. Loan fees included in interest income for 1987, 1986 and 1985 were $4,694,000, $5,407,000 and $2,886,000, respectively. The indicated income and annual rate are presented on a taxable equivalent basis using the federal marginal rate of 40% for 1987 and 46% for 1986, 1985, 1984 and 1983.

CLIENT:
INDEPENDENCE BANCORP

DESIGN FIRM:
MICHAEL GUNSELMAN, INC.

ART DIRECTOR:
MICHAEL GUNSELMAN

DESIGNER:
MICHAEL GUNSELMAN

PHOTOGRAPHER:
ED ECKSTEIN

WRITER:
JEFFREY C. RICHARDSON

PRODUCTION MANAGER:
MICHAEL GUNSELMAN

TYPOGRAPHER:
COMPOSING ROOM

PAPER SELECTION:
VARIOUS

PRINTER:
LEBANON VALLEY OFFSET

NUMBER OF PAGES:
62 PLUS COVER

SIZE:
8 1/2" X 11"

JEFFREY C. RICHARDSON, VICE-PRESIDENT OF CORPORATE COMMUNICATIONS, INDEPENDENCE BANCORP, PERKASIE, PENNSYLVANIA

Independence Bancorp is a holding company of five community banks with 50 offices throughout Eastern Pennsylvania. In the 1987 annual report, we wanted to stress the concept of community banking, to emphasize our closeness to the customer. Our tellers live in the same communities as the customers. They know the clients by name. This, we feel, is our competitive edge against the bigger, more impersonal banks. To capture this sense of personal service, we showed our chairman without a jacket, and we actually took customers out of lines at the various branches and put them into the photographs. We feel the annual report captured the essence of the company.

JEFFREY C. RICHARDSON, VICE-PRESIDENT OF CORPORATE COMMUNICATIONS, INDEPENDENCE BANCORP, PERKASIE, PENNSYLVANIA

Independence Bancorp ist eine Holding-Gesellschaft von fünf Regionalbanken mit 50 Filialen überall im Osten von Pennsylvania. Im Jahresbericht für 1987 wollten wir den kommunalen Charakter der Banken unterstreichen und unsere Nähe zum Kunden herausstellen. Unsere Schalterangestellten leben in den gleichen Orten wie die Kunden. Sie kennen jeden beim Namen. Das ist unser Vorteil gegenüber den grösseren, unpersönlicheren Banken. Um dies zu verbildlichen, zeigten wir unseren Vorsitzenden in Hemdsärmeln und photographierten verschiedene Kunden. Wir finden, dass die wesentliche Aussage ausgezeichnet zum Ausdruck gekommen ist.

JEFFREY C. RICHARDSON, VICE-PRESIDENT OF CORPORATE COMMUNICATIONS, INDEPENDENCE BANCORP, PERKASIE, PENNSYLAVANIE

Independence Bancorp est une holding qui regroupe cinq banques locales disposant de 50 succursales dans l'Est de la Pennsylvanie. Dans notre rapport annuel pour 1987, nous avons voulu souligner le concept de la banque locale en insistant sur le contact étroit que nous entretenons avec la clientèle. Nos caissiers habitent les mêmes circonscriptions administratives que nos clients, qu'ils connaissent par leur nom. C'est là que réside notre force par rapport aux grandes banques. Ce sentiment d'un service personnalisé, nous l'avons traduit en image en montrant notre président en bras de chemise, ainsi que divers clients pris au hasard dans les files d'attentes de nos guichets.

MICHAEL GUNSELMAN, MICHAEL GUNSELMAN, INC., WILMINGTON, DELAWARE.

We decided that because the banks of Independence Bancorp cater to the small customer, that we would show customers. We emphasized that these were real people in a non-environmental setting, but we did want to have a consistent feeling and texture. The photographer, Ed Eckstein, used 8 x 10-inch film with tight cropping and left the film edge showing. The boy on the cover is a paperboy with an actual account. We talked to him, and found out that he plays the sax. He looks like a real kid. He looks like the future.

MICHAEL GUNSELMAN, MICHAEL GUNSELMAN, INC., WILMINGTON, DELAWARE

Da diese Banken auf den kleinen Kunden ausgerichtet sind, beschlossen wir, die Kunden zu zeigen. Wir wollten hervorheben, dass es sich um ganz normale Leute handelt. Sie wurden konsequent ohne Hintergrund aufgenommen. Ed Eckstein verwendete einen 8 x10"-Film und nutzte die Bildfläche völlig aus, wobei er auch den Filmrand mit einbezog. Der Junge auf dem Umschlag ist ein Zeitungsausträger, der ein Konto bei einer der Filialen hat. Er verkörpert den Jugendlichen von heute. Er ist unsere Zukunft.

MICHAEL GUNSELMAN, MICHAEL GUNSELMAN, INC., WILMINGTON, DELAWARE

Comme ces banques ont une clientèle locale de petites gens, nous avons décidé de mettre ceux-ci en scène. Nous avons souligné le fait qu'il s'agit de clients réels dans un décor non environnemental en maintenant une unité de feeling et de contexte. Le photographe, Ed Eckstein, a utilisé un film de 8"x10" avec une découpe serrée et le cadre du film visible. Le garçon de la couverture est un porteur de journaux qui a un compte bancaire. Il a l'air d'un gars bien intégré dans le réel et qui regarde vers l'avenir.

LEAF, INC. ANNUAL REPORT 1987
Peanut Butter
WE MAKE GOOD FRIENDS

FINANCIAL HIGHLIGHTS

(in thousands)	1984(a)	1985	1986	1987
Financial Results:				
Net Sales	$314,795	$308,562	$317,369	$375,430
Operating Income	$ 13,553	$ 19,319	$ 22,982	$ 24,076
Income Before Tax	$ 1,244	$ 5,031	$ 11,781	$ 15,561
Net Income	$ 495	$ 2,888	$ 5,772	$ 7,244
Financial Position:				
Working Capital	$ 50,748	$ 57,221	$ 52,189	$ 41,910
Property, Plant and Equipment, Net	$ 79,535	$ 77,984	$ 81,672	$ 88,852
Total Assets	$200,544	$211,010	$234,202	$247,790
Long-term Debt	$ 92,137	$ 92,289	$ 81,187	$ 68,862
Stockholder's Equity	$ 75,648	$ 78,708	$ 84,991	$ 94,667
Other Financial Data:				
Capital Additions	$ 10,357	$ 10,713	$ 18,646	$ 19,267
Depreciation and Amortization	$ 14,157	$ 12,040	$ 12,055	$ 13,531
Dividends	$ –	$ 1,000	$ 1,443	$ 1,811
Return on Sales(b)	0.2%	0.9%	1.8%	1.9%
Return on Assets(b)	0.3%	1.4%	2.6%	3.0%
Return on Equity(b)	0.7%	3.7%	6.8%	7.7%
Current Ratio	2.7:1	2.6:1	1.9:1	1.6:1
Debt to Equity Ratio	1.7:1	1.7:1	1.8:1	1.6:1

(a) The financial statements for the period ended December 31, 1984, cover a thirteen month period.
(b) Return computations use net income divided by net sales, average total assets, ending equity.

NET SALES

(in thousands)	
87	$375,430
86	$317,369
85	$308,562
84	$314,795

OPERATING INCOME

(in thousands)	
87	$ 24,076
86	$ 22,982
85	$ 19,319
84	$ 13,553

NET INCOME

(in thousands)	
87	$ 7,244
86	$ 5,772
85	$ 2,888
84	$ 495

LEAF, INC.

Leaf, Inc.'s business is a good one.

That's not just because sales rose more than 18 percent and because profits increased more than 25 percent.

Nor is it just because we added to our already varied lines, improved the quality of our existing products and developed the industry's most sophisticated and effective marketing programs.

Our business is a good one because Leaf makes products that make good friends.

Candy and gum are what we give children to teach them the meaning of the word "share." Sweets are what we bring to a host's home to say "thanks for inviting us." We give candy to friends on Halloween to make them smile. And we give candy to very special people to help say "I love you."

Most of us, regardless of our ages, our incomes or our nationalities, use candy to make friends. And, we always will.

In 1987, Leaf, Inc. improved its relationship with its old friends and made many new ones. This Annual Report describes how.

CONTENTS

LEAF, INC.

In 1983, when Leaf, Inc. was formed by the acquisition of three existing candy and gum companies, we acquired some major opportunities and some major problems.

Included among our opportunities were several well-known and well-established brand names in the United States, Canada, and Europe, and many talented people with significant candy-industry experience.

Listed among our problems were an unmanageable network of more than 300 brokers, an inefficient and expensive distribution system, virtually no customer service organization, literally thousands of product items in our line and several products whose quality and marketing support had been allowed to deteriorate.

We spent the first three years of the company's life solving the problems we inherited. Our broker network is now one-tenth its former size. It includes 30 of the most effective brokers in the United States, all of whom work with Leaf more as a part of the company than as outside agents. Our distribution system has been streamlined, and now our customers may request immediate delivery of all of Leaf's products in a single shipment.

We have continued to cut the number of items in our line, allowing us to concentrate on our 15 leading brands and their most popular sizes and varieties. We have improved the quality of many of our brands, and have continued to increase our advertising and promotional expenditures significantly.

The year 1987, however, was the year to move ahead with building our brands—and we did so aggressively.

In 1987, combined sales of Leaf, Inc., Leaf Sweden and Leaf Finland reached $449 million. Of that, the operations of Leaf, Inc., not including Leaf Sweden and Leaf Finland, were $375 million, an increase of 18.3 percent over 1986. Net income for Leaf, Inc. was $7.2 million, up 25.5 percent over fiscal 1986.

In mid-November 1987, we acquired the trademarks of the former Chuckles Company, including Chuckles® jellied candies and Pine Bros® cough drops, two major brands in the northeastern United States. We are confident that the Chuckles and Pine Bros. brands have great potential for growth nationally.

In early January 1988, we acquired 49 percent of the outstanding shares in L. S. Heath & Sons, Inc., makers of the Heath English Toffee Bar and Heath ice cream product ingredients.

In 1987, Leaf assumed operational responsibility for the candy division of our parent company, Huhtamaki Oy, of Finland. The division, locally known as Hellas, is called Leaf Finland in the international marketplace. In addition, Leaf, Inc. assumed management of Kanolds, a Swedish candy manufacturer in which Huhtamaki, in 1987, acquired the 50 percent of the shares it did not own previously. Kanolds is now known as Leaf Sweden.

Net Sales

(in thousands)	
87	$449,100
86	$317,369
85	$308,562
84	$314,795

Operating Income

(in thousands)	
87	$ 37,900
86	$ 22,982
85	$ 19,319
84	$ 13,553

Leaf, Inc. ■ Leaf Sweden and Leaf Finland

Erkki Railo, President and Chief Executive Officer, Leaf, Inc.

In 1987, two-thirds of the consolidated sales of Leaf, Inc., Leaf Sweden and Leaf Finland came from U.S. operations, while the remaining one-third resulted from operations overseas.

In 1988, Leaf, Inc. will pursue its long-term growth objectives by continuing to improve its products and plants, strengthen its marketing and promotional capabilities, and enhance its already excellent customer service system. We will continue to acquire compatible products with high-growth potential, and increase market share of our leading brands through broader geographic distribution.

Alicia Woo, 7, made friends of everyone who saw her first dance recital at New York's Dance Theatre of Harlem in 1987. And, Leaf, Inc., with its Jolly Rancher hard candies and other childrens-oriented products, made millions of kids happy.

LEAF SPECIAL BRANDS

Leaf, Inc.'s second U.S. domestic marketing group, Leaf Special Brands, markets all Leaf candy and gum products targeted at children. These include Jolly Rancher® hard candies and candy canes, Now & Later® taffy and several major brands of bubble gum, including Rain-Blo® and Super Bubble®

Leaf Special Brands, which formerly was known as the Leaf Jolly Rancher group, was renamed in late 1987 to reflect the addition of several existing Leaf products into its line. With Leaf General Brands now handling products for the teen to adult market, Leaf Special Brands focuses more intently on products targeted to a younger audience.

Jolly Rancher, one of the top-selling branded hard candies in the United States, continued its longtime use of sports marketing to gain exposure and sales. Consistent with this image, Jolly Rancher is a featured brand in Leaf's Major League Baseball sponsorship.

To promote the sponsorship and other brand promotions, Leaf is more than doubling its advertising budget in 1988. Specific plans for Jolly Rancher candy include advertising on television game shows and in children's publications.

Rain-Blo was particularly active in 1987. To stimulate sales and interest from the trade, the brand received new packaging, new sizes and a cherry cola flavor. To reach its target market directly, Rain-Blo bubble gum samples were packed into 200 million cereal boxes.

Super Bubble bubble gum also introduced a cherry cola flavor and, in 1988, will unveil the Super Bubble cartoon character in all packaging and advertising.

Building representation in predominant candy price points plays an integral part in Leaf Special Brand's marketing strategy. Leaf can therefore gain wider distribution, particularly in supermarket outlets, and compete aggressively with similarly-priced items.

During the year, Leaf introduced 40-cent size Now & Later and Jolly Rancher bars, as well as a 35-cent Super Bubble pack. Leaf led the industry by testing Now & Later bars and Jolly Rancher stix at 25 cents. Both are emerging as popular in convenience stores as consumers trade up from the 10-cent level.

Leaf, the largest gum ball manufacturer in the United States, increased capacity at its Memphis plant.

Other brands marketed by Special Brands are Slo Poke® and Black Cow® caramel suckers, Sixlets® candy-coated chocolatey pieces, and Hot Dog® and Bub's Daddy® bubble gums.

It takes a special person to maintain a sense of humor while driving a taxi through the streets of London. But, Tom Smith smiles a lot, especially when he's in his role as a leader of the London Taxi Drivers Fund for Underprivileged Children. He knows how to make friends with a smile. And with sweets, like Mr. Freeze freezer snack.

LEAF INTERNATIONAL

Leaf, Inc., through its Leaf International division, is a major force worldwide in the manufacture and marketing of confectionery products. Leaf International has operations in Canada, Ireland, The United Kingdom, The Netherlands and The Federal Republic of Germany, and manages two operations in Finland and Sweden.

Leaf Canada manufactures and markets Whoppers candy, Mr. Freeze freezer snack and Rain-Blo bubble gum products in that country. Sales in 1987 increased nearly 15 percent to $24 million. A major effort was made during the year to build an internal sales organization in Ontario to supplement the activities of outside distributors serving the Eastern and Western portions of Canada.

Leaf Canada's plant, in Scarborough, Ontario, also produces gum and freezer snacks for Leaf's U.S. operation. The plant's increased capacity and a favorable exchange rate in 1987 made it possible for Leaf, Inc. to import about one-third of Leaf Canada's products to the United States.

Leaf's European operations had aggregate 1987 sales of $135 million, including $77 million from Leaf Finland and Leaf Sweden, affiliates owned by Leaf, Inc.'s parent, Huhtamäki Oy, but managed by Leaf, Inc. personnel.

Leaf Ireland is the company's overseas operation with the greatest expertise in novelty gum production. Among its new products slated for distribution in Europe in 1988 are Bubble King™ bar bubble gum, Jawberries™ candy-coated gum and Bugs Bunny carrot-shaped gum. Mr. Freeze continued to dominate the country's freezer snack category, while entry into supermarkets and strong promotional support helped Leaf Ireland products perform particularly well in France and Belgium.

In the United Kingdom, a country with high per capita candy consumption, Leaf sells gum, Mr. Freeze freezer snack and Hellas™ filled chocolate bars. Sales and marketing, once handled by both Leaf and Chiltern Confections, formerly part of Leaf's parent company, were consolidated under Leaf U.K. at the beginning of the year for greater efficiency.

Maple Leaf, headquartered in Amsterdam, became the leading producer and marketer of gum in Holland ▶

Consolidated Statements of Income

Leaf, Inc. and Subsidiaries

For the years ended December 31, (in thousands)	1987	1986	1985
Net sales	$375,430	$317,369	$308,562
Cost of sales	241,403	206,141	204,027
Gross margin	134,027	111,228	104,535
Selling, general and administrative expenses	109,951	88,246	85,216
Operating income	24,076	22,982	19,319
Other expenses, net	8,515	11,201	14,288
Income before income taxes and extraordinary item	15,561	11,781	5,031
Provision for income taxes	8,317	6,009	3,133
Income before extraordinary item	7,244	5,772	1,898
Extraordinary item			990
Net income	$ 7,244	$ 5,772	$ 2,888

The accompanying notes are an integral part of the consolidated financial statements.

Consolidated Balance Sheets

Leaf, Inc. and Subsidiaries

December 31, (in thousands)		1987	1986
Assets:	Current assets:		
	Cash and short-term investments	$ 3,535	$ 25,732
	Accounts receivable – net of allowances	38,461	32,830
	Notes receivable	1,728	2,078
	Inventories	64,509	48,364
	Prepaid expenses	2,180	2,262
	Other assets	3,625	2,344
		114,038	113,610
	Property, plant and equipment, less accumulated depreciation and amortization	88,852	81,672
	Goodwill, net of accumulated amortization	42,538	36,855
	Other assets	2,362	2,065
		$247,790	$234,202
Liabilities:	Current liabilities:		
	Notes payable	$ 13,133	$ 3,895
	Current portion of long-term debt	11,793	11,804
	Accounts payable	22,255	23,176
	Accrued liabilities	24,947	22,546
		72,128	61,421
	Long-term debt	68,862	81,187
	Capital lease obligations	1,446	1,562
	Deferred income taxes	9,519	3,748
	Other long-term liabilities	1,168	1,293
		$153,123	$149,211
Stockholder's Equity:	Common stock, no par value, authorized 10,000,000 shares, issued and outstanding 9,500,000 shares in 1987; $1 par value, authorized 1,000 shares, issued and outstanding 100 shares in 1986	95	
	Additional paid-in capital	76,550	76,550
	Retained earnings	12,050	6,712
	Currency translation adjustments	5,972	1,729
		94,667	84,991
		$247,790	$234,202

The accompanying notes are an integral part of the consolidated financial statements.

Leaf, Inc. Officers

Erkki Railo
President and
Chief Executive Officer

Finance and Administration
Mark A. Larson
Senior Vice President, Chief Financial and Administrative Officer

Paul R. Naslund
Vice President, Management Information Systems

James P. O'Connor
Vice President, Distribution

Craig M. Smith
Vice President, General Counsel

J. Elliott Wells
Vice President, Purchasing

Leaf General Brands Group, U.S.A.
Paul H. Mullan
Senior Vice President

Michael W. Gretz
Vice President, New Products

Donald R. Hartman
Vice President, Sales

George H. Stege
Vice President, Ford Gum

Edward A. Tortoreo
Vice President, Planning

Douglas V. Wheeler
Vice President, Marketing

International Projects
Martin S. Leaf
Senior Vice President

Leaf Special Brands Group, U.S.A.
Robert W. Anderson
Senior Vice President

George E. Martinelli
Vice President, Sales

Research and Development
Sheldon Siegel
Senior Vice President

Benjamin E. Houston
Vice President, R&D and Quality Assurance

Operations
James S. Grubiak
Senior Vice President

H. Pete Russell
Vice President

Leaf International
Keijo Suila, President

Leaf Canada
Allister Scorgie,
President

Leaf Ireland
Fred Galvin
Managing Director

Leaf U.K.
Charles S. Sproat
Managing Director

Maple Leaf B.V.
Frits van Manen
Managing Director

Leaf Sweden
Christer Stevinger
Managing Director

Leaf Finland
Jyrki Laine
Managing Director

Board of Directors

Chairman
Asko Tarkka
Chairman and Chief Executive Officer, Huhtamäki Oy

Vice Chairman
Erkki Railo
President and Chief Executive Officer, Leaf, Inc.

Eero Aho
Vice President, Administration and Finance, Huhtamäki Oy

James A. Hanlon
Retired President and Chief Executive Officer, Peter Paul Cadbury USA

Philip B. Joyce
Retired Vice President, Sales, M&M/Mars Division, Mars, Inc.

Jarmo Nuotio
Retired Vice President, Confectionery and Beverage Division, Huhtamäki Oy

Leslie Shankman
Retired President, Leaf Confectionery, Inc.

CLIENT:
NW AYER INC.

DESIGN FIRM:
SAMATA ASSOCIATES

ART DIRECTORS:
PAT AND GREG SAMATA

DESIGNERS:
PAT AND GREG SAMATA

PHOTOGRAPHERS:
MARK JOSEPH,
TERRY HEFFERNAN

WRITER:
JOEL FELDSTEIN

ERKKI RAILO, PRESIDENT AND CHIEF EXECUTIVE OFFICER, LEAF, INC., BANNOCKBURN, ILLINOIS

Our message in the 1987 annual report was to tie in with the customer, to connect with the consumer with the theme of "we make good friends." The layout of this annual report was exceptional. Greg and Pat Samata used black-and-white photographs effectively contrasted with color in a way that has been seen since, but then was really the start of a new trend. We intended to build connections in this annual report to our various constituencies as a public relations-type exercise. The response was very favorable to this report.

ERKKI RAILO, PRESIDENT AND CHIEF EXECUTIVE OFFICER, LEAF, INC., BANNOCKBURN, ILLINOIS

Die Botschaft unseres Jahresberichtes für 1987 heisst, dass wir für unsere Kunden da sind, dass wir helfen, «Freundschaften zu schliessen». Das Layout war aussergewöhnlich. Greg und Pat Samata verwendeten Schwarzweissphotos, auf denen einzelne Teile sehr effektvoll koloriert wurden. Wir wollten mit diesem Bericht im Stil von einer Public-Relations-Kampagne mit unseren verschiedenen Kunden und Lieferanten einen guten Kontakt herstellen. Das Echo auf diesen Bericht war sehr positiv.

ERKKI RAILO, PRESIDENT AND CHIEF EXECUTIVE OFFICER, LEAF, INC., BANNOCKBURN, ILLINOIS

Le message de notre rapport annuel pour 1987 a consisté à jeter un pont vers notre clientèle, à établir la communication sur le thème de «nous nous faisons de bons amis». Nous avons bénéficié d'une présentation hors pair. Greg et Pat Samata ont utilisé des photos noir et blanc efficacement contrastées avec la couleur. Nous avons voulu établir des liens avec diverses catégories de clients et donc effectuer un travail de relations publiques. Nous avons enregistré des réactions très favorables à ce rapport.

PAT AND GREG SAMATA, SAMATA ASSOCIATES, DUNDEE, ILLINOIS

This was the second annual report we had done for Leaf, and we developed the theme with the company. Once we decided on "we make good friends," then we highlighted people in their areas of expertise and just had fun with the product. We had each individual photographed and then we hand-tinted the particular candy or brand we wanted to feature with that person. We wanted to show an intimate photograph indicating a close relationship between the person and the product–the photographs made this relationship look like a kind of friendship.

PAT UND GREG SAMATA, SAMATA ASSOCIATES, DUNDEE, ILLINOIS

Dieses war der zweite Jahresbericht für Leaf, und wir erarbeiteten das Grundthema zusammen mit der Firma. Nachdem wir uns auf «Freundschaften schliessen» geeinigt hatten, stellten wir die Leute in ihren Arbeitsbereichen vor. Erst photographierten wir verschiedene Personen, und dann wurde das Konfekt oder die Marke handkoloriert. Wir wollten persönlich wirkende Aufnahmen zeigen, in denen die enge Verbindung zwischen der Person und dem Produkt zum Ausdruck kommt - das Thema der Freundschaft wird damit nochmal angesprochen.

PAT ET GREG SAMATA, SAMATA ASSOCIATES, DUNDEE, ILLINOIS

C'est le deuxième rapport annuel que nous ayons eu à préparer pour Leaf. Nous en avons élaboré le sujet d'entente avec la société. Une fois le thème choisi - «nous nous faisons de bons amis» -, nous avons monté en épingle les différents intéressés. Chaque personnalité présentée a eu droit à sa photo agrémentée de la marque spécifique (coloriée main) qui lui est associée. Nous entendions ainsi faire comprendre le lien essentiel qui relie la personne et le produit, les photos s'employant à faire comprendre la nature amicale de ce lien.

MACEUTICAL AND CHEMICAL WORKS

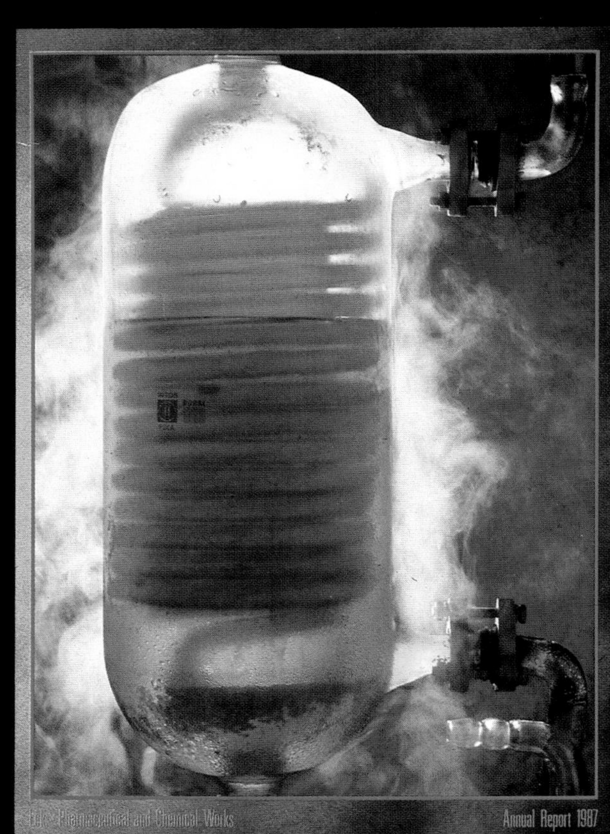

The year 1987 was characterized by an unstable economic situation in Yugoslavia, resulting mainly in high inflation which reached 178% according to the price growth index of industrial products; devaluation of the domestic currency was even higher (the US dollar rose by 172% and the German mark by 232% over the same period).
All this has to be taken into consideration when judging the results of our business operations. One of the characteristics of the domestic market is that the government regulates prices for drugs, the production of which is LEK's main field of operation. Total sales in the domestic market grew by 137%, out of which 18% represents production growth; the rest is due to the effect of price growth. In the domestic market LEK still ranks third in the production of medicaments and is also outstanding for its veterinary, dental, phytotherapeutic and cosmetic products. Due to restrictive price policy the only alternative for LEK was to increase sales in the domestic market and thus neutralize bad profitability.
We succeeded in increasing our exports by 3%; thus the total sales to foreign markets amounted to 84.8 million US dollars. Exports represent 44.3% of total sales and 49.8% of external revenue. It is very important that our position strengthened in some of the most developed countries although we were subject to negative effects resulting from changed relations among the world's most important currencies.
The government adapted the whole budgetary system to inflationary economic conditions. Nevertheless, we cannot ignore the fact that in spite of increased production we could not neutralize the pressure of inflation upon our profitability. Income growth (in dinars) lags behind the growth of total revenue, whereas accumulation (in dinars) is kept at the level achieved in 1986. These results become even more clear if expressed in US dollars, where a drastic fall of our accumulation can be observed. Nevertheless, we consider the increase in depreciation a very positive one since it represents a source of new investment. One of the most important achievements of 1987 is the successful management of operating assets; in spite of increased production, inventories remained at the level of the beginning of 1987.
Expenses for research and development amounted to 2.7% of sales. This is not much compared to other pharmaceutical producers abroad and has demanded a very careful allocation of resources. However, this did not prevent us from launching several new products both in the domestic and foreign markets, the main results of which are expected only in 1988 and in the years to follow. LEK founded two new agencies abroad: one in Warsaw and the other in Singapore, as well as a joint company in Switzerland. This should contribute to improving the presence of LEK in some territories, as well as its confirmation as an international pharmaceutical company.

Metod Dragonja
General Manager

Lek is a company where the amount of physical work is becoming smaller and intellectual work is gaining in importance as the essential driving force behind development and production.

KNOW-HOW

the most vital driving force behind Lek

After 42 years, Lek Pharmaceutical and Chemical Company has 2780 employees working at six different sites in Slovenia: Ljubljana, Mengeš, Prevalje, Lendava, Lipovci and Kranjska gora.
Lek's activity is most sensitive regarding its nature and most difficult regarding its requirements, complexity, market demands and dynamics. It has to integrate knowledge into its work and final products. Thus all progress is possible only by development and exploitation of innovation potential. For Lek this conception is not a novelty since the conditions for innovations are well developed. Lek's business policy is directed towards an organized, innovating mass activity which becomes more and more involved in the income acquiring process.
The company encompasses three production organizations: Pharmacy, Chemistry and Cosmetics; five joint organizations: Research and Development, Maintenance, Quality Control, Hotel and Engineering; and an Administration Division: Personnel and Legal Department, Finance Department, Economics Department, Common Affairs Department and Foreign Trade Department.
In recent years great technological and social changes occurred all over the world, which Lek has to adapt to. Egineering technology has greatly developed, no less in the field of information science and organization, and most of all in the coordination of all three. This is best reflected in management of the production process. New technology has affected Lek primarily in the field of biotechnology and chemical synthesis. In 1982 Lek initiated the fermentation production of ergot alkaloids; this represents a great part of the production programme, as well as of sales. New developments enabled Lek to start the fermentation production of antibiotic gentamycin towards the end of 1985. Among the important products manufactured by means of chemical synthesis is cimetidine, the production process of which has been patented by Lek abroad.

RAW-MATERIALS

The three main technologies in our production are fermentation, chemical synthesis and extraction of medicinal herbs.

Lek's orientation to producing its own pharmaceutical raw materials has proved correct. The ongoing development in the fields of biotechnology, production of new materials, chemical synthesis and extraction of natural active substances will continue to be Lek's priority in the future. The development strategy is based on active participation in the third technological revolution which is taking place in information science, cybernetics and robotics.

RAW-MATERIALS

MEDICINE

Lek produces 122 medicaments in 170 forms treating practically all forms of types of ailments.

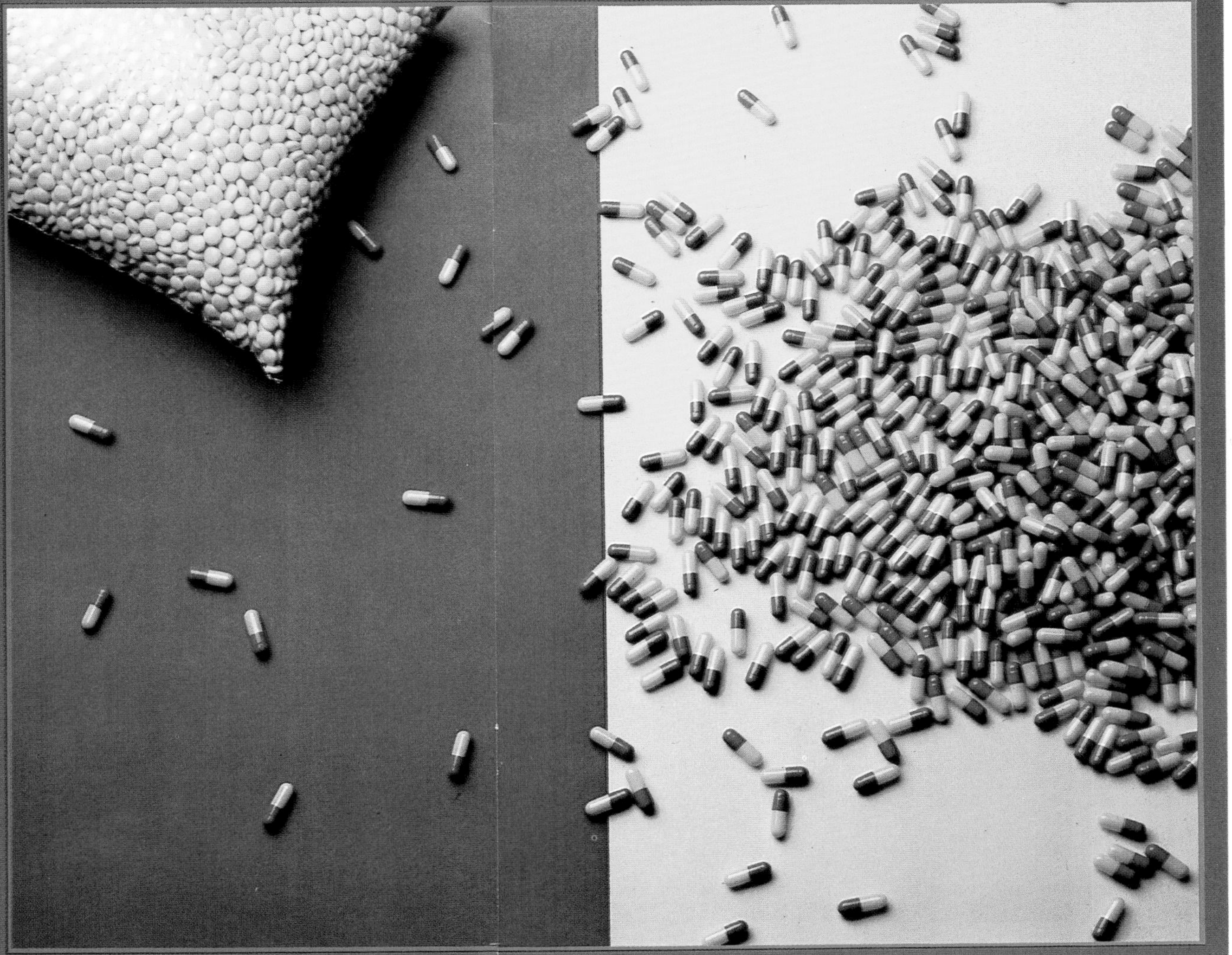

Every individual working in the production process is responsible for product quality; 5% of all employees work in the Quality Control Division

QUALITY

Quality - a duty all workers must attain

Other very important Lek production programmes are chemical products, raw materials and active substances for production of drugs, in which the three main technologies are fermentation, chemical synthesis and extraction of medicinal herbs.
As to varied production of active substances Lek can be placed at the very top of Yugoslav producers. Pharmaceutical raw materials manufactured by Lek include narcotic agents, glucoheptonates, stearates, and cimetidine, as well as other substances for organic synthesis and herbal extracts. The majority of our chemical products are used as an active substance for the production of medicaments. However, some of them are finished products. Chemical production extends to 22 products in 40 forms and represents 14.6% of total production.
Lek is one of the largest manufecturers of dental products in Yugoslavia. We also produce veterinary products. The mineral and vitamin mixtures plant manufectures food additives: premixes containing minerals, vitamins and microminerals, supermixes consisting of minerals, vitamins, microminerals and additives which are given with food. A total of 29 veterinary preparations are available in the form of powders, solutions, tablets, boluses, granulates and sprays, as well as 5 sorts of mixtures based on minerals and vitamins, 21 premixes and 18 supermixes.

Lek's activity also covers the sphere of cosmetics and hygiene products. In recent years more than 150 types of cosmetics have been developed and one quarter of them are exported. Among the Yugoslav producers of cosmetics Lek is in fourth place. The collection comprises 150 sorts of products intended for body care, colour cosmetics, cleansing products and detergents representing 10.9% of Lek's production.

QUALITY CONTROL

All medicaments are produced and controlled in accordance with the FDA, WHO and GMP health standards.

All medicaments are produced and controlled in accordance with the FDA, WHO and GMP health standards. The Quality Centre, Department of Internal Control is a special service created within the established quality assurance system which continuously performs quality control. The Information Department, which exists within the Quality Centre, reports on the quality changes in the production process. Any deviations from set standards, as well as new methods for improving quality are discussed by teams of scientists.

VETERINARY PRODUCTS

In recent years Lek has developed into an international company with exports amounting to ca. 50% of its output and the average annual production growth has exceeded 17%.

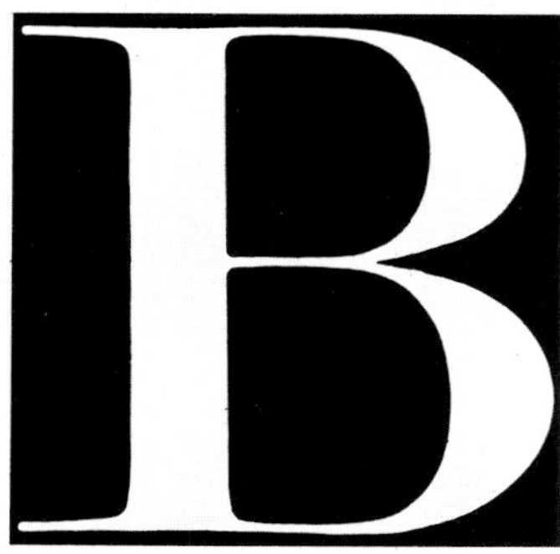

BALANCE

Consolidated Balance Sheet

		(Dollars in Thousands)			(Dinars in Thousands)		
		Dec. 31, 1986	Dec. 31, 1987	%	Dec. 31, 1986	Dec. 31, 1987	%
I.	ASSETS						
1.	Operating Assets	125,085	163,363	31	47,512,250	121,777,155	156
	Cash	7,474	14,914	100	2,838,924	11,117,323	292
	Accounts Receivables	31,629	46,242	46	12,013,967	34,470,373	187
	Inventories	32,893	32,775	(0)	12,494,231	24,432,100	96
	Other Assets	876	6,101	596	332,827	4,547,870	1,266
	Long-Term Investments	8,111	11,525	42	3,080,977	8,591,269	179
	Fixed Assets	41,007	48,830	19	15,575,939	36,399,893	134
2.	Reserves	3,094	2,976	(4)	1,175,385	2,218,327	89
3.	Non-Operating Assets	6,724	5,594	(17)	2,554,020	4,170,319	63
	Total Assets	131,809	168,957	28	50,066,270	125,947,474	152
II.	LIABILITIES						
1.	Operating Resources	125,085	163,363	31	47,512,250	121,777,155	156
	Supplies	9,648	16,431	70	3,664,668	12,248,087	234
	Short-Term Loans	19,023	26,658	40	7,225,642	19,872,000	175
	Other Current Resources	17,209	22,025	28	6,536,520	16,418,301	151
	Business Funds	67,459	84,017	25	25,623,636	62,629,376,	144
	Long-Term Loans	8,525	11,208	31	3,238,141	8,355,183	158
	Other Long-Term Liabilities	127	48	(62)	48,258	35,881	(26)
2.	Reserve Resources	3,094	2,976	(4)	1,175,385	2,218,327	89
3.	Non-Operating Resources	6,724	5,594	(17)	2,554,020	4,170,319	63
	Total Liabilites	131,809	168,957	28	50,066,270	125,947,474	152

Consolidated Income Statement

	(Dollars in Thousands)			(Dinars in Thousands)		
	Dec. 31, 1986	Dec. 31, 1987	%	Dec. 31, 1986	Dec. 31, 1987	%
External Total Revenue	134,015	161,298	20	50,904,213	120,238,075	136
Costs and Expenses	95,152	116,539	22	36,142,468	86,873,170	140
Depreciation	5,021	8,371	67	1,907,092	6,240,114	227
Salaries	16,317	19,642	20	6,197,932	14,641,791	136
Income Before Taxes	17,525	16,746	(4)	6,656,721	12,483,000	88
Taxes and Contributions	9,505	11,909	25	3,610,523	8,877,411	146
Net Income	8,020	4,837	(40)	3,046,198	3,605,589	18
Reserve Funds	1,370	1,419	4	520,514	1,057,491	103
Common Consumption Funds	1,552	957	(38)	589,649	713,147	21
Business Funds	5,097	2,462	(52)	1,936,035	1,834,951	(5)

1 US \$ = 379,84 din in 1986
1 US \$ = 745,44 din in 1987

CLIENT:
LEK LJUBLJANA

ART DIRECTOR:
STUDIO KROG

DESIGNER:
EDI BERK

PHOTOGRAPHER:
DRAGAN ARRIGLER

WRITER:
VESNA ARRIGLER

PRINTER:
UCNE DELAVNICE

NUMBER OF PAGES:
24

MAJDA KUSAR, DIRECTOR OF FOREIGN TRADE DIVISION, LEK, LJUBLJANA, YUGOSLAVIA

Lek's intention for the 1987 annual report was to introduce our readers to Lek's orientation to research and development since we are a pharmaceutical and chemical company. We also featured our export results. The design was very different from the classical type of annual report, which is what we expected from Studio Krog, which acts as our company's house art department. The response of our audience to the annual report was good, but with no special reference to the design.

MAJDA KUSAR, DIRECTOR OF FOREIGN TRADE DIVISION, LEK, LJUBLJANA, JUGOSLAWIEN

Lek wollte das Publikum vor allem auf das Engagement in den Bereichen von Forschung und Entwicklung hinweisen, da wir ein Unternehmen der pharmazeutischen und chemischen Industrie sind. Daneben zeigten wir auch unsere Exportergebnisse. Die Gestaltung unterschied sich wesentlich vom herkömmlichen klassischen Stil, den wir vom Studio Krog erwartet hatten. Wir erhielten ein positives Echo auf den Jahresbericht, wenn auch die Gestaltung nicht speziell erwähnt wurde.

MAJDA KUSAR, DIRECTOR OF FOREIGN TRADE DIVISION, LEK, LJUBLJANA, YOUGOSLAVIE

Dans son rapport annuel pour 1987, Lek entendait présenter au lecteur les efforts de recherche et de développement entrepris par ce groupe chimique et pharmaceutique, tout en n'oubliant pas les succès enregistrés à l'exportation. Le design a été très différent de celui adopté communément pour un rapport annuel, comme on pouvait s'y attendre de la part du Studio Krog. Les réactions favorables enregistrées de la part des lecteurs n'ont pas mentionné particulièrement l'aspect design.

EDI BERK, STUDIO KROG, LJUBLJANA, YUGOSLAVIA

Lek had wanted a conventional annual report that presented them as a high technology company, but we suggested that the emphasis should be that although Lek has a long tradition, the company is young when it comes to ideas. We featured the five main areas of the business, indicating the company's interest in research, and Lek's achievements. We used color and black and white to separate the information from the financials.

EDI BERK, STUDIO KROG, LJUBLJANA, JUGOSLAWIEN

Lek hatte an einen konventionellen Jahresbericht gedacht, der den hohen technologischen Standard zum Ausdruck bringen sollte. Wir schlugen dagegen vor, im Bericht zu betonen, dass Lek trotz der langen Tradition im Hinblick auf Ideenreichtum ein junges Unternehmen ist. Wir stellten die fünf wichtigsten Betriebsbereiche dar und verwendeten Farbe und Schwarzweiss-Darstellungen, um die Informationen vom Finanzteil abzusetzen.

EDI BERK, STUDIO KROG, LJUBLJANA, YOUGOSLAVIE

Lek avait en vue un rapport annuel conventionnel pour se positionner comme groupe high-tech, mais nous avons suggéré une autre approche en montrant que la longue tradition chez Lek n'exclut pas une profusion d'idées neuves dignes d'une société de création récente. Le rapport est centré sur cinq domaines d'activité. La couleur et le noir et blanc identifient séparément l'information générale et les résultats financiers.

L&N Housing Corp.

Annual Report

1987

CONTENTS

SELECTED FINANCIAL DATA

	Year Ended December 31				
	1987	1986	1985	1984	1983
Income	$ 6,031,000	$ 6,667,000	$ 7,915,000	$ 7,507,000	$ 6,912,000
Expenses	1,668,000	1,752,000	1,282,000	1,252,000	1,197,000
Net income	$ 4,363,000	$ 4,915,000	$ 6,633,000	$ 6,255,000	$ 5,715,000
Net income per share	$1.98	$2.23	$3.02	$2.84	$2.60
Average number of shares outstanding	2,200,000	2,200,000	2,200,000	2,200,000	2,200,000
Cash dividends per share	$2.40	$2.46	$2.94	$2.84	$2.59
Total assets	$71,887,000	$52,512,000	$53,032,000	$53,109,000	$53,321,000

FOURTH QUARTER FINANCIAL HIGHLIGHTS

	Quarter Ended December 31	
	1987	1986
Income	$2,388,000	$2,013,000
Expenses	759,000	774,000
Net income	$1,629,000	$1,239,000
Net income per share	$.74	$.56
Average number of shares outstanding	2,200,000	2,200,000

MARKET AND DIVIDEND INFORMATION

The New York Stock Exchange trading symbol for the Company's common stock is LHC. At December 31, 1987 there were approximately 1,400 holders of record of the Company's common stock. During the years ended December 31, 1987 and 1986, the high and low stock sales prices and dividends declared on common stock have been:

	Year Ended December 31, 1987			Year Ended December 31, 1986		
	Stock Prices		Dividends Declared	Stock Prices		Dividends Declared
	High	Low		High	Low	
First quarter	$28¼	$22½	$.41	$34⅜	$31	$.59
Second quarter	24⅝	17⅞	.30	34¼	28¼	.59
Third quarter	19⅛	16¾	.50	30½	17	.49
Fourth quarter	20¾	16⅝	.69	27¼	22¾	.50

1

$56,165,000, six have been sold or refinanced, returning $31,850,000 of its original capital and aggregate gain on sales of $3,409,000.

As the markets for multi-family rentals began to decline in 1985, the Company shifted its investment target to commercial projects such as shopping centers, suburban office buildings, warehouse/distribution centers and high-technology or research and development facilities. Furthermore, in 1987 the Company began to invest temporary excess cash in participations in short-term mortgage loans held by Lomas & Nettleton Financial Corporation ("LNFC") in order to achieve higher yields than those available on other short-term investments. In late 1987 it increased its investments in such participations by utilizing borrowed funds available through lines of credit. It is anticipated that the practice of using borrowed funds to enhance the Company's net income will be continued throughout this year.

In late 1987 the Company also made investments in marketable securities through the purchase of shares of two real estate investment trusts managed by LNFC. The shares of both entities — Lomas & Nettleton Mortgage Investors ("LNMI") and Lomas Mortgage Corporation ("LMC") — are listed on the New York Stock Exchange and dividends received by the Company are qualified income to maintain its status for taxation as a real estate investment trust. The Company purchased an aggregate of 300,000 shares of LNMI at an average cost of $20.54 per share with a current dividend

4

yield of 12.5 percent per annum. The Company purchased an aggregate of 10,000 shares of LMC at an average cost of $21.10 per share with a current dividend yield of 12 percent. The decision to make such investments was made because of the attractive yields relative to other investments available to the Company, the liquidity of such securities and the tax status of the income received thereon.

Investment Portfolio

Today the Company's investment portfolio can be divided into four categories. It currently includes one permanent investment in a commercial project of the type that constitutes the Company's current primary investment objective; permanent investments in four multi-family rental projects of the type that initially were the Company's primary investment objective; investments in participations in short-term mortgage loans held by LNFC and other mortgage-related assets; and investments in marketable securities. At December 31, 1987 the Company's investments were as set forth in the following table:

Category	Amount
Permanent multi-family investments	$18,067,000
Permanent commercial investments*	4,747,000
Other mortgage-related investments	2,518,000
Participations in short-term mortgage loans with LNFC	37,481,000
Marketable securities	5,809,000
Cash and cash equivalents	3,057,000
	$71,679,000

*The Company has $453,000 remaining to be funded on this project. Additionally, the Company has commitments outstanding totaling $12,987,500 to fund two additional commercial projects. One previously funded commercial project has been sold and retired, and two previously issued commitments on commercial projects were not funded because of sale or failure to meet leasing requirements.

5

The Coming Year

In 1988 the Company will concentrate its efforts in three areas. First, it will seek to originate and fund an additional $14,500,000 of quality permanent investments in order to invest fully its permanent capital. Second, the Company will closely monitor its investments in multi-family rental projects that are producing less than satisfactory yields with a view to enhancing those yields or retiring the related investments. Finally, it will seek to enhance its net income through profitable sales of its investments and the utilization of leverage to purchase participations in short-term mortgage loans at favorable spreads.

In the current environment it is extremely difficult to project the Company's net income. Without the utilization of borrowed funds to purchase participations in mortgage loans and without any sales of projects, the Company's current portfolio will produce net income of approximately $1.60 per share in 1988. Our plan is to utilize leverage and possibly the purchase of additional marketable securities if attractive yields are available to augment income and produce net income of $1.90 to $2.00 per share for 1988.

Jess Hay
Chairman and Chief Executive Officer

Ted Enloe
President

March 17, 1988

8

REPORT OF ERNST & WHINNEY
INDEPENDENT ACCOUNTANTS

Stockholders and Board of Directors
L&N Housing Corp.
Dallas, Texas

We have examined the balance sheet of L&N Housing Corp. as of December 31, 1987 and 1986, and the related statements of income, stockholders' equity and cash flows for each of the three years in the period ended December 31, 1987. Our examinations were made in accordance with generally accepted auditing standards and, accordingly, included such tests of the accounting records and such other auditing procedures as we considered necessary in the circumstances.

In our opinion, the financial statements referred to above present fairly the financial position of L&N Housing Corp. at December 31, 1987 and 1986, and the results of its operations and its cash flows for each of the three years in the period ended December 31, 1987, in conformity with generally accepted accounting principles applied on a consistent basis.

Ernst & Whinney

Dallas, Texas
January 22, 1988

9

STATEMENT OF INCOME — L&N HOUSING CORP.

	Year Ended December 31		
	1987	1986	1985
Income			
Interest:			
Mortgage loans	$2,309,000	$4,273,000	$4,742,000
Other mortgage-related investments	1,548,000	892,000	1,117,000
Cash equivalents	656,000	135,000	54,000
Land leases	209,000	635,000	797,000
Financing fees	342,000	233,000	305,000
Dividends	198,000	—	—
Rent from foreclosed real estate	273,000	—	—
Gain on sales of land	496,000	499,000	900,000
	6,031,000	6,667,000	7,915,000
Expenses			
Management fees	527,000	625,000	686,000
Stockholder relations	153,000	205,000	164,000
Directors' fees	56,000	58,000	51,000
Legal, audit and other	43,000	42,000	84,000
Franchise tax	181,000	169,000	159,000
Provision for possible losses	179,000	653,000	138,000
Interest	433,000	—	—
Operating expenses on foreclosed real estate	96,000	—	—
	1,668,000	1,752,000	1,282,000
Net income	$4,363,000	$4,915,000	$6,633,000
Net income per share	$1.98	$2.23	$3.02
Average number of shares outstanding	2,200,000	2,200,000	2,200,000

See notes to financial statements.

10

BALANCE SHEET — L&N HOUSING CORP.

	December 31	
	1987	1986
Assets		
Mortgage loans	$12,278,000	$19,729,000
Land	1,220,000	3,136,000
Substandard investments	9,316,000	9,450,000
	22,814,000	32,315,000
Less allowance for possible losses	(766,000)	(1,197,000)
	22,048,000	31,118,000
Other mortgage-related investments	39,999,000	7,481,000
Marketable equity securities	5,809,000	—
Cash and cash equivalents	3,057,000	13,454,000
Accrued interest receivable and other assets	974,000	459,000
	$71,887,000	$52,512,000
Liabilities		
Notes payable to banks	$21,000,000	$ —
Accounts payable and accrued expenses	252,000	243,000
Deferred financing fees	122,000	231,000
Commitment fee deposits	188,000	233,000
	21,562,000	707,000
Stockholders' Equity		
Common stock ($.50 par value, 15,000,000 shares authorized, 2,200,000 shares issued and outstanding)	1,100,000	1,100,000
Paid-in capital	49,457,000	49,457,000
Undistributed income	331,000	1,248,000
Unrealized loss on marketable equity securities	(563,000)	—
	50,325,000	51,805,000
	$71,887,000	$52,512,000

See notes to financial statements.

11

NOTES TO FINANCIAL STATEMENTS — L&N HOUSING CORP.
December 31, 1987

BUSINESS

The Company is engaged in the business of investing in multi-family housing and commercial rental projects. These investments consist of a first mortgage loan which may be accompanied by a purchase and leaseback of the underlying land. In addition, the Company invests in participations in short-term mortgage loans and marketable securities of real estate investment trusts.

ACCOUNTING POLICIES

Income Taxes
The Company believes it has qualified as a real estate investment trust and intends to continue to do so. Accordingly, no provision has been made for federal income taxes.

Recognition of Income
Interest and income from land leases are taken into income when earned. The Company discontinues the accrual of income when circumstances exist which cause the collection of such income to be doubtful. Determination to discontinue accruing income is made after review by the Company's management of all relevant facts including delinquency of principal and/or interest or land rents, credit of the borrower and value of the collateral. Investments classified as substandard are refinanced mortgage loans and related land with interest rates significantly below market.

Deferred interest is taken into income when realized.

Interest on Collateralized Mortgage Obligation ("CMO") residuals is taken into income using the effective yield method.

Loan financing fees are recognized as income by the interest method over the terms of the related loans.

Allowance for Possible Losses
The Company provides for possible losses on its investments in amounts which it believes adequate relative to the risks inherent in such investments. Consideration is given to the net realizable value of the collateral underlying the loan or of the properties owned, which is defined as the estimated selling price a property will bring if exposed for sale in the open market less direct selling expenses.

Marketable Equity Securities
Marketable equity securities are carried at the lower of cost or market computed on an aggregate basis.

14

Cash and Cash Equivalents
Cash and cash equivalents include cash on hand and highly liquid investments with maturities of three months or less.

INVESTMENTS

At December 31, 1987 the Company had investments in six real estate projects. Two of these investments are classified as substandard and one is classified as a note receivable. Of the three remaining investments, one matures in 1989, one in 1994 and one in 1997. The average yield on these three investments at December 31, 1987 was approximately 8.58%.

During 1987 three of the Company's mortgage loans were paid off resulting in recognition of $472,000 of income from deferred interest and financing fees. The underlying land associated with these loans was sold, resulting in a gain of $496,000. The Company financed one of these land sales by retaining a second mortgage on the property. This mortgage is classified as a note receivable and income is being recognized on a cash basis. Additionally, two more of the Company's investments were restructured, whereby the Company financed the sale of the underlying land to the borrower. One other of the Company's investments was similarly restructured as of December 31, 1986. These three investments, having a basis of $14,431,000, produced net income of $1,188,000 and $1,418,000 for 1987 and 1986, respectively, and would have produced net income of $1,796,000 each year had they been current in accordance with their original terms.

Another investment in the amount of $4,500,000 was foreclosed in April 1987. At the date of foreclosure, $300,000 was charged to the allowance for possible losses, reducing the value of the investment to $4,200,000. In November 1987 the property was sold resulting in an additional loss of $310,000. The Company received cash of $254,000 and a mortgage investment recorded at $3,636,000. The yield on this investment at December 31, 1987 was approximately 9%.

Other mortgage-related investments consisted of the following:

	December 31	
	1987	1986
Mortgage loan participations	$37,481,000	$7,481,000
CMO residual	2,018,000	—
Note receivable	500,000	—
	$39,999,000	$7,481,000

The mortgage loan participations were with Lomas & Nettleton Financial Corporation ("LNFC"). These participations are short-term real estate loans with a weighted average rate of 9.35%.

At December 31, 1987 the Company had unfunded mortgage loan commitments of $13,441,000.

15

CLIENT:
L&N HOUSING CORP.

DESIGN FIRM:
RICHARDS, BROCK, MILLER, MITCHELL & ASSOC.

ART DIRECTOR:
CHRIS ROVILLO

DESIGNER:
CHRIS ROVILLO

WRITER:
L&N HOUSING CORP.

TYPOGRAPHER:
SOUTHWESTERN TYPOGRAPHICS

PAPER SELECTION:
ENHANCE

PAPER MANUFACTURER:
BECKETT ENHANCE

PRINTER:
BRODNAX PRINTING

NUMBER OF PAGES:
20 PLUS COVER

SIZE:
8 1/2" X 11"

TYPE SELECTION:
PALATINO

JESS HAY, CHAIRMAN AND CHIEF EXECUTIVE OFFICER, L&N HOUSING CORPORATION, DALLAS, TEXAS

For our 1987 annual report, we had no specific thematic objectives. We just wanted our numbers presented in a pleasant and attractive way. What the designer did with the formatting was attractive, and we were pleased with this design. The response we had to this annual report was favorable.

CHRIS ROVILLO, RICHARDS BROCK MILLER MITCHELL & ASSOCIATES/THE RICHARDS GROUP, DALLAS, TEXAS

The direction for the 1987 annual report from the CEO at L&N was to use all type, and no artwork. This limits what can be done quite a bit. This company trusts us, and we know this company well. So I started playing around with type, and I eventually came up with the idea to vary the paper. I started by making a tiny dummy with interesting textures of paper, and the design evolved from there. There is a three-color configuration whenever you turn a page. We had more complicated trims originally, but it became mathematically impossible to do what was originally plannned. The report has top trims only. Everything else in the report is simple and restrained. Palatino type is always used for this company's annual report, and we placed the text into rectangles. The trims then don't confuse anyone. We used the inside colors for the title on the cover.

JESS HAY, CHAIRMAN AND CHIEF EXECUTIVE OFFICE, L&N HOUSING CORPORATION, DALLAS, TEXAS

Für unseren Jahresbericht 1987 hatten wir kein bestimmtes Thema. Wir wollten einfach, dass unsere Zahlen auf eine ansprechende Art präsentiert werden. Die Art, wie der Designer mit dem Format umging, war attraktiv, uns gefiel die Gestaltung. Das Echo auf diesen Jahresbericht war positiv.

CHRIS ROVILLO, RICHARDS BROCK MILLER MITCHELL & ASSOCIATES/THE RICHARDS GROUP, DALLAS, TEXAS

Die Direktive für den Jahresbericht 1987 war, Typographie statt Illustrationen für die Gestaltung einzusetzen. Das beschränkte die Möglichkeiten erheblich. Also begann ich, mit Typographie herumzuspielen, und dabei kam ich auf die Idee, verschiedene Papiersorten einzusetzen. Beim Umschlagen jeder Seite ergibt sich ein Zusammenspiel von drei Farben. Ursprünglich dachten wir an raffiniertere Formatwechsel, aber das war mathematisch nicht durchführbar. Deshalb sind die Seiten nur oben beschnitten. Alles andere in diesem Bericht ist einfach und zurückhaltend. Wie immer bei den Jahresberichten der Firma wurde Palatino als Schrift verwendet, den Text plazierten wir in Rechtecke. Dadurch irritieren die Beschneidungen der Seiten nicht. Wir verwendeten die Farben aus dem Inhalt auch für den Umschlag. Der Kunde war begeistert.

JESS HAY, CHAIRMAN AND CHIEF EXECUTIVE OFFICER, L&N HOUSING CORPORATION, DALLAS, TEXAS

Pour notre rapport annuel 1987, nous n'avions pas d'objectifs thématiques spécifiques à formuler, nous contenant de souhaiter que les résultats financiers soient présentés de manière agréable, attrayante. Ce que le designer a fait de l'ouvrage est plaisant, et nous avons été très satisfaits du design.

CHRIS ROVILLO, RICHARDS BROCK MILLER MITCHELL & ASSOCIATES/THE RICHARDS GROUP, DALLAS, TEXAS

Les instructions reçues pour le rapport annuel 1987 spécifiaient l'usage de la typo sans aucune illustration, ce qui limite quelque peu les possibilités d'action du designer. Je me suis donc mis à manipuler la typo et suis arrivé à l'idée de varier la qualité du papier. C'est à partir d'une maquette de papiers de différentes textures que la stylique de l'ensemble a été élaborée. Chaque fois qu'on tourne une page, on découvre une configuration tricolore. On avait prévu des rognages plus complexes, mais il s'est avéré mathématiquement impossible de les traduire dans les faits. Le rognage n'intervient que dans le haut des pages. La typo utilise d'un bout à l'autre des caractères Palatino, et le texte est inséré dans des rectangles, ce qui fait que le rognage ne prête nulle part à la confusion. Les couleurs des pages intérieures ont été reprises sur la couverture.

MASSACHUSETTS INDUSTRIAL FINANCE AGENCY

Since 1978, the Massachusetts Industrial Finance Agency has been a driving force in the revitalization of the Massachusetts economy. As an independent public agency, MIFA has issued over $4 billion in Industrial Development Bonds – equivalent to $1.7 million invested every business day.

More than 2,100 industrial expansion and commercial development projects have benefited directly. MIFA financing has spearheaded creation of an estimated 76,000 jobs – one every 15 minutes of the workday.

In the past 18 months, MIFA has dramatically transformed and expanded its role, reflecting the changing nature of the economic development challenge and the impact of federal tax reform.

PAGE 1

A New Era in Public Finance

MIFA links Main Street businesses to Wall Street capital through the design of innovative financing programs and the Agency's reputation in the public credit markets.

In 1986, the Congressional process of federal tax reform threatened traditional tax-exempt funding with extinction and placed the role of public finance agencies in jeopardy.

For MIFA and its small business constituency, accustomed to a straightforward process of tax-exempt funding below the prime rate, massive cutback or outright elimination of tax-exempt Industrial Development Bonds posed a clear danger.

MIFA attacked the challenge, turning it into new opportunity. The Agency sought and found new sources of funds and created innovative financing mechanisms. In fact, the silver lining in tax reform's reduction of tax-exempt IDB financing has been the accelerated development of these new programs.

MIFA is now able to offer access to far broader capital markets with a greater variety of financing possibilities. Dealing in these new arenas necessitates a clear understanding of the dynamics within the public bond markets and heightened sensitivity to market volatility.

One devastating effect of the 1986 tax bill was the removal of incentives for commercial banks to purchase IDBs, which forced them out of the marketplace. Historically, commercial banks had bought over 85% of MIFA's tax-exempt bonds. As a result of tax reform, a primary focus of MIFA's activities has been to identify new buyers for our bond issues.

MIFA turned to the public credit market, where institutions such as pension funds, mutual funds and insurance companies, as well as individual investors, form a very broad and deep pool of capital. It is to these sources on Wall Street that the nation's largest and most credit worthy corporations turn for debt financing, selling corporate bonds to finance capital expansions.

To most individuals and smaller businesses, the public credit market is a great unknown. There is no Dow Jones Average and no "broad tape" listing of trades as in the stock market. Yet the public bond markets are far larger. Public markets also allow far greater flexibility in managing the terms and maturities of financings.

A year ago, the public credit market was uncharted territory for public finance agencies that serve small business borrowers. The prime barriers to entry are size, credit history and recognition – each of which is being overcome by MIFA.

Size of financings in the public credit market is generally many millions of dollars and occasionally billions. MIFA financings have historically

PAGE 8

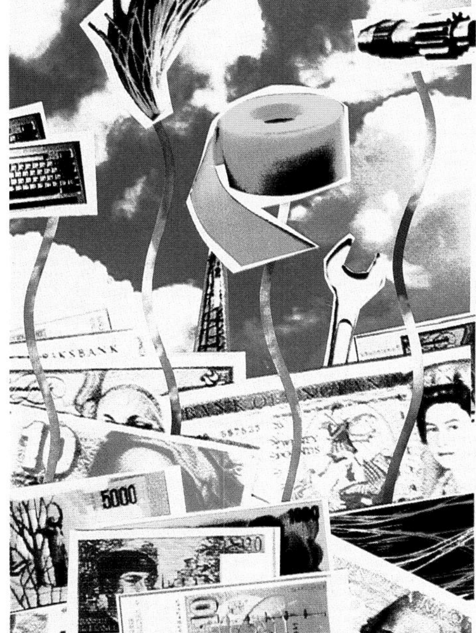

Access to the Eurobond market and credit enhancement from highly-rated banks have provided a new growth medium for Massachusetts businesses.

averaged about one and one-half million dollars – a large sum for a growing business but tiny in the public markets. MIFA has worked to overcome that barrier through pooling.

Pooling is a financial concept common to other financial instruments, such as mutual funds and mortgage-backed securities. Pooling smaller items – stocks or mortgages – together creates size and spreads the risk for investors.

The pooling of smaller bonds into one larger offering is an important new structural financing method for MIFA. The Agency issued more IDB pools in the past year than in the previous eight years.

The recent pools are, moreover, structured as repeatable programs, which will help streamline the bond issuance process and allow MIFA to accommodate increased volume.

Larger sized financings attract more competition for the bonds, which means a lower interest rate for the borrowers. The issuance costs and fees associated with selling bonds in the public market are shared by all participants, lowering the cost for each.

Under the July 1987 legislation, MIFA now has the ability to pool public and private issues in a single financing, which will allow larger bond issues and further ease access to sources such as the Eurobond market, where $100 million is considered the threshold for entry.

Credit history is a second barrier to the public markets for smaller businesses.

The companies MIFA has financed have proved to be strong growth performers and job creators, although they tend to be relatively small and unknown – particularly outside Massachusetts. When bonds are sold publicly on Wall Street or other global financial centers, the strength of a company's credit history or rating directly affects the interest rate the company pays on the capital it borrows.

A critical new component of MIFA's financings is credit enhancement, which uses the guarantee of a strong financial institution to support a bond issue. MIFA has formed relationships with Massachusetts-based, national and international financial institutions that have the high rating and stature needed for credit enhancement.

The initial results of MIFA's efforts have been extremely encouraging. In just six months, three major European banks – each among the top-rated financial institutions in the world – have entered into agreements with MIFA to issue letters of credit (L/C) to back bonds for growing businesses in Massachusetts.

PAGE 11

MIFA's $50 million L/C agreement with AAA-rated Rabobank Nederland marked the first time an international bank supported a public program that exclusively serves smaller companies. AA minus-rated Algemene Bank Nederland N.V. and Aaa-rated Barclays Bank PLC have also committed backing for MIFA bond issues. These agreements have dramatically lowered costs of borrowing and provided prototypes for future offerings.

In addition, Massachusetts banks have also been active in supporting MIFA bond issues, providing credit enhancement and, in some instances, standby letter of credit services for the international agreements.

Recognition in the marketplace is also a vital factor in gaining investor interest and confidence. Fortune 500 companies are well known in the public market. Smaller companies, such as those which MIFA has traditionally assisted, are unknown entities whose bonds are extremely difficult to place in the public market. MIFA's name is known; our $4 billion track record assures recognition in the U.S. for the Agency's bond issues.

Broader recognition has also been created through MIFA initiatives to meet with leading European and Japanese financial institutions. The expanded powers offered by the July 1987 legislation, combined with this improved international visibility, will lead to great opportunities for financing in global capital markets.

MIFA's thrust in the public credit market has been augmented by efforts to distribute bond issues as "private placements" – bonds purchased by a single investing institution. For example, the Massachusetts Pension Reserves Investment Management (PRIM) fund has agreed to purchase bonds directly from MIFA. In this way, PRIM will be investing directly in projects of public purpose through MIFA issues – Massachusetts investing in Massachusetts.

Many commercial banks – no longer bond purchasers – have expressed interest in placing MIFA issues privately, a means of distribution that will become increasingly important in the future.

Expertise is vital to operating in these arenas of public finance. Sensitivity to the marketplace, timing of bond sales and structure of bond issues have a dramatic impact on our borrowers' interest rates. This, in turn, affects their ability to fulfill their expansion plans and create job opportunities.

MIFA now has the organization and the capability to serve in its new role as the public sector investment bank for Massachusetts business and to help sustain the momentum of economic growth.

TAXABLE BONDS

In February 1987, MIFA took a small but critical step by issuing a $7.8 million pool of taxable IDBs on behalf of three North Shore companies. A taxable IDB pool had never before been sold. Even MIFA's underwriters were unsure that the market would accept this new instrument.

On the morning of the sale, doubts remained. Then the issue was announced and sold out in two hours. A critical test had been passed with flying colors. This small bond issue became big news:

- It proved MIFA could interest large investors – who normally buy only the issues of larger companies – in small business credits.
- It demonstrated MIFA could successfully structure an issue with innovative advantages to the borrowers. The bonds, with credit enhancement from Essexbank, were issued with a floating interest rate. The borrowers, however, retained an option to convert to a fixed rate.
- It showed MIFA could obtain advantageous interest rates, with total cost to borrowers near the prime rate.

Tremendous media coverage and national interest followed this sale, and with good reason, for taxable IDBs offer many advantages:

- Exemption from state taxes holds down interest rates and allows MIFA to target potential purchasers who can use that benefit.
- Taxable IDBs can be used for commercial real estate, refinancing and warehouse and distribution projects now excluded from tax-exempt funding – in addition to a wide variety of industrial uses.
- Interest rates are somewhat higher than for tax-exempts but still significantly lower than conventional financing sources.
- Because IRS regulations are not a focal point, issuance costs are lower and the documentation process is faster.

Perhaps the major benefit of taxable IDBs is that no limit on size exists. MIFA can continue to serve the small business borrower who has traditionally turned to the Agency. In addition, MIFA is able to work with enterprises whose size or financing needs have been too great to meet tax-exempt funding rules. MIFA can now aid companies of any size in public purpose, job creating expansions.

A second taxable IDB issue provided $17.2 million for Boston Scientific Corporation, with backing from Aaa-rated Barclays Bank PLC. Boston Scientific, a leader in least invasive surgical instrumentation and medical technology, used bond proceeds to acquire and improve real estate for

BOSTON SCIENTIFIC CORPORATION, WATERTOWN

CENTRAL MASS. JOB TRAINING, WORCESTER

INDUSTRIAL DEVELOPMENT BOND PROJECT LISTING

Company	Location	Board Approval	Bond Amount	Taxable or Tax-exempt	Jobs
Jiffy Packaging Corp.	Beverly IDFA	1/86	$ 1,750,000	T-E	50
Schlott Company, Inc.	Lawrence IDFA	1/86	600,000	T-E	*
The Standish Corporation	Taunton IDFA	1/86	639,800	T-E	50
Technical Plastics Corp.	N. Attleboro	1/86	3,000,000	T-E	16
Volterra, Goldberg & Manzetti	Attleboro	1/86	450,000	T-E	*
Zymark Corporation	Hopkinton IDFA	1/86	1,800,000	T-E	100
Cambridgeport Air Systems, Inc.	Salisbury	2/86	896,000	T-E	22
Clopax Corporation	Easton IDFA	2/86	550,000	T-E	5
Fall River Management	Fall River IDFA	2/86	400,000	T-E	*
Fall River Management	Fall River IDFA	2/86	1,450,000	T-E	*
Graphic Innovations, Inc.	Pittsfield IDFA	2/86	490,000	T-E	4
Iron Mountain Boston, Inc.	Boston IDFA	2/86	4,102,700	T-E	31
ASE Services, Inc.	Holliston	3/86	1,000,000	T-E	15
Atlantic Coast Paperboard Corp.	Lawrence IDFA	3/86	6,150,000	T-E	**
D.J. Fabricators, Inc.	Ipswich IDFA	3/86	1,200,000	T-E	13
LaVigne Press, Inc.	Worcester IDFA	3/86	750,000	T-E	11
Lehi Sheet Metal Corp.	Westborough IDFA	3/86	520,000	T-E	13
Mercantile Printing Co.	Worcester IDFA	3/86	540,000	T-E	7
San Lau Realty Trust	Andover IDFA	3/86	1,400,000	T-E	*
Orbit Plastics Corporation	Salisbury	3/86	600,000	T-E	6
Randolf and Baldwin, Inc.	Ayer	3/86	773,850	T-E	8
Screenprint, Inc.	Wilmington	3/86	1,650,000	T-E	50
Tog Mold Tool & Die Co.	Pittsfield IDFA	3/86	475,000	T-E	7
West Lynn Creamery, Inc.	Lynn IDFA	3/86	5,000,000	T-E	225
Gloucester Landing Associates	Gloucester	4/86	7,800,000	T-E	*
Combined Properties, Inc.	Chelsea	4/86	8,000,000	T-E	200
Cambridge Plating Company, Inc.	Belmont	7/86	1,800,000	T-E	4
Liberty Place Realty Trust	Newburyport	7/86	790,000	T-E	*
Jones Machine Co., Inc.	Danvers	7/86	500,000	T-E	15
Massachusetts AFL-CIO	Boston IDFA	7/86	962,000	T-E	*
Omnirel Corporation	Leominster	7/86	2,910,000	T-E	91
Southeastern Regional NMR Center	Brockton IDFA	7/86	2,300,000	T-E	8
312 Main Street Partnership	Great Barrington	8/86	350,000	T-E	*
Roman Marble, Inc.	Stoughton IDFA	8/86	995,000	T-E	20
M&M Realty Trust	Hudson	9/86	500,000	T-E	*
Massasoit Associates Limited Partnership	Springfield IDFA	9/86	2,500,000	T-E	*

Company	Location	Board Approval	Bond Amount	Taxable or Tax-exempt	Jobs
Richard L. Kinchla	Falmouth	9/86	$ 550,000	T-E	*
Douglas A. King Builders, Inc.	North Easton	11/86	2,250,000	T-E	*
Interpretive Data Systems	Brookline	11/86	4,500,000	T-E	*
Danvers Atrium Trust	Danvers	11/86	800,000	T-E	*
Lynn Fryer Manufacturing	Ipswich IDFA	11/86	1,035,000	T-E	10
Stetson Place Development Trust	Weymouth	11/86	600,000	T-E	*
Union Chemical Co.	Newburyport	11/86	858,000	T-E	4
Tech-Pak, Inc.	Peabody	11/86	4,275,000	T-E	25
Union Machine Co. of Lynn, Inc.	Peabody	11/86	2,100,000	T-E	25
Worcester Manufacturing Co., Inc.	Worcester IDFA	11/86	1,550,000	T-E	45
PAL Realty Trust	Lynn	12/86	4,000,000	T	25
Boston Scientific Corporation	Watertown	12/86	17,200,000	T	193
Hansen Engineering & Machinery Co., Inc.	Danvers	12/86	2,100,000	T	35
M.O.M., Inc.	North Reading	12/86	1,700,000	T	3
Milliken Associates Ltd. Partnership	Fall River IDFA	12/86	4,250,000	T-E	*
Ogden Haverhill Associates	Haverhill	12/86	31,265,000	T	60
Ogden Haverhill Associates	Haverhill	12/86	66,000,000	T-E	-
Ogden Haverhill Associates	Haverhill	12/86	87,535,000	T	-
Astrofoam, Inc.	Holden	12/86	3,510,000	T-E	60
Gilliam Associates	New Bedford IDFA	12/86	6,000,000	T-E	*
Brady Enterprises, Inc.	East Weymouth	12/86	2,080,000	T-E	10
Capri Custom Cabinetry Inc.	Plymouth	12/86	1,150,000	T-E	21
Eastern Container Corporation	Springfield	12/86	1,325,000	T-E	15
G.F. Sprague & Company, Inc.	Holbrook	12/86	680,000	T-E	10
Hero Coatings, Inc.	Newburyport	12/86	760,000	T-E	4
Cambridge Aero Instruments Inc.	Shirley	12/86	545,000	T-E	10
Quality Printing Co., Inc.	Pittsfield	12/86	550,000	T-E	17
Mar-Ell Distributors, Inc.	Walpole	12/86	1,755,000	T-E	25
Mentor O & O, Inc.	Norwell	12/86	2,500,000	T-E	47
Morse Manufacturing Co., Inc.	Sterling	12/86	980,000	T-E	50
Rand McNally & Company	Taunton IDFA	12/86	3,000,000	T-E	62
Richard A. Klein, Inc.	Wrentham	12/86	3,400,000	T-E	22
South Hadley House Care Associates	South Hadley IDFA	12/86	4,800,000	T-E	135
Stonehedge Convalescent	Boston IDFA	12/86	2,000,000	T-E	**
W.C. Bonner Company, Inc.	Hudson	12/86	2,900,000	T-E	25
Wilmington Fabricators, Inc.	Wilmington	12/86	5,165,000	T-E	30

HANSEN ENGINEERING, DANVERS

MARINER PUBLICATIONS, MARSHFIELD

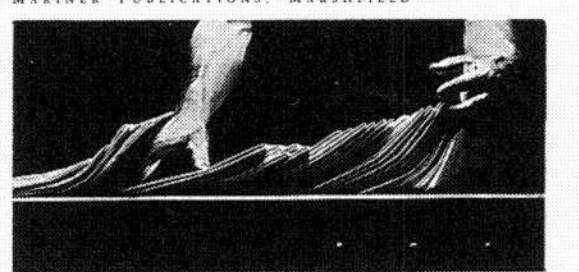

INDUSTRIAL DEVELOPMENT BOND REFUNDINGS

Company	Location	Refunded Amount
Agway Inc.	Bernardston	$ 1,800,000
Aid-Pak, Inc.	Gloucester	1,123,700
Citizens Utility Company	Agawam	31,000,000
Hamilton House Nursing Home	Needham	2,700,000
Lafayette Place Parking Associates	Boston	18,700,000
Museum of Fine Arts	Boston	17,140,000
New England Tape Company	Hudson	920,000
Ogden Haverhill Associates	Haverhill	38,475,000
Polycon Inc.	Woburn	650,000
Polyvinyl Films Inc.	Sutton	550,000
Technical Aid Corporation	Newton	1,745,000
Total: 11 Projects		$114,803,700

BOARD OF DIRECTORS

Chairman
Robert L. Beal
Executive Vice President
The Beal Companies, Inc.

Vice-Chairman
David F. Squire
Trustee and Former Vice President
Brandeis University

Treasurer
Ronald A. Homer
President and Chief Executive Officer
Boston Bank of Commerce

Edward P. McCann
Former Area Director
Communications Workers of America

Janet M. Pavliska
President and Chief Executive Officer
Bank Five for Savings

Joseph D. LoBello
Executive Vice President
Bank of New England - West

Frank T. Keefe
Secretary
Executive Office of Administration and Finance

Joseph D. Alviani
Secretary
Executive Office of Economic Affairs

Paul Tortolani
Commissioner
Department of Commerce & Development

EXECUTIVE DIRECTOR
Brian T. Carty

CLIENT:
MASSACHUSETTS INDUSTRIAL FINANCE AGENCY

DESIGN FIRM:
WEYMOUTH DESIGN

ART DIRECTOR:
MICHAEL WEYMOUTH

DESIGNER:
MARA KALNINS

PHOTOGRAPHER:
GEORGE SIMIAN

ILLUSTRATOR:
MARA KALNINS

WRITER:
DAVID BICKFORD

JUDITH GLASSER, DIRECTOR OF MARKETING, MASSACHUSETTS INDUSTRIAL FINANCE AGENCY, BOSTON, MASSACHUSETTS

In 1986 through 1987, the very nature of the Massachusetts Industrial Finance Agency operations had to change dramatically, due to radical changes in the tax laws and the economy. This annual report, then, had to reflect the changing areas of business. We needed to show this wide array of business and capital markets and what we do: linking, connecting, and providing access for businesses as a state agency. For these various roles, we discussed collage illustrations, because these could link very different concepts together. In this report, it was not enough for us to show products we had provided funding for or our successes in sponsoring businesses as we had before; we needed to show new programs in a new way. This annual report was considered interesting, and it was well-received, especially since the illustrations at the front of the book were followed by photographs in the second half, all of which feature people's hand in the process of working. It showed the businesses, the products, and the jobs at the end. We were very happy with this report.

JUDITH GLASSER, DIRECTOR OF MARKETING, MASSACHUSETTS INDUSTRIAL FINANCE AGENCY, BOSTON, MASSACHUSETTS

In den Jahren 1986 und 1987 musste die Geschäftspolitik der Massachusetts Industrial Finance Agency angesichts einschneidender Änderungen der Steuergesetze und der wirtschaftlichen Entwicklung drastisch geändert werden. Der Jahresbericht musste diesen Veränderungen in den verschiedenen Bereichen Rechnung tragen. Wir mussten den immensen Bereich der Geschäftstätigkeit und der Kapitalmärkte zeigen und was wir tun, um den Unternehmen Verbindungen und Aufbaumöglichkeiten zu verschaffen. Um die vielseitigen Aufgaben darzustellen, dachten wir an Collagen, weil diese verschiedene Konzepte miteinander verbinden würden. Es hätte nicht genügt, Produkte oder Erfolge darzustellen, wir mussten neue Programme auf eine neue Art zeigen. Wir mussten MIFAs neue Finanzmechanismen deutlich machen. Dieser Jahresbericht stiess auf grosses Interesse und wurde gelobt, besonders weil die Illustrationen im zweiten Teil von Aufnahmen abgelöst werden, die Hände von Leuten bei der Arbeit zeigen.

JUDITH GLASSER, DIRECTOR OF MARKETING, MASSACHUSETTS INDUSTRIAL FINANCE AGENCY, BOSTON, MASSACHUSETTS

De 1986 jusque fort avant en 1987, la nature même des opérations de la Massachusetts Industrial Finance Agency a subi des transformations radicales dues à des changements radicaux intervenus dans la législation fiscale et la vie économique. Ce rapport annuel devait impérativement en tenir compte. Il nous fallait montrer l'ampleur des affaires mises en cause, la grande diversité des marchés de capitaux et ce que nous entreprenons en tant qu'agence de l'Etat pour faire le trait d'union, établir des connexions et y introduire les entreprises. Des collages semblaient le moyen graphique le plus adéquat d'assembler en une seule composition des concepts fort différents. Il ne suffisait pas de montrer des produits ou de faire état de nos succès; il nous fallait montrer des nouveaux programmes mis en œuvre de maniere neuve et décrire les nouveaux mécanismes de financement de la MIFA. Notre rapport annuel a suscité l'intérêt et a été bien accueilli, surtout du fait que les illustrations étaient suivies de photos dans la seconde partie.

MICHAEL WEYMOUTH, WEYMOUTH DESIGN INC., BOSTON, MASSACHUSETTS

The Massachusetts Industrial Finance Agency is a state agency that arranges for financing for small businesses in Massachussets, and it has been successful. It was part of what was referred to as the "Massachusetts Miracle" and it was consistent with the growth of the state. The people who head this agency think of themselves as creative and innovative in what they do, and this has to be reflected in the reports. They had been able to create an incentive to invest, but with the new tax laws, there was no incentive. So MIFA had to become more inventive to show that this organization was a big friend to small businesses. In the annual report MIFA expects innovation, expects that cutting edge, expects the annual report to raise eyebrows. I worked closely with Mara Kalnins, the designer, and we came up with thumbnails of the concepts of the business processes. We took the various elements suggested by the client and played with them on a computer, and Mara did the illustrations.

MICHAEL WEYMOUTH, WEYMOUTH DESIGN INC., BOSTON, MASSACHUSETTS

Die MIFA ist eine staatliche Behörde, welche sich mit der Finanzierung kleiner Unternehmen in Massachusetts befasst. Sie ist Teil von dem, was man das Massachusetts-Wunder nennt, und sie wurde dem aufstrebenden Staat Massachusetts gerecht. Die Leute an der Spitze betrachten ihre Arbeit als kreativ und innovativ, und dies sollte in den Geschäftsberichten zum Ausdruck kommen. Es war ihnen gelungen, Investoren anzuziehen, aber die neuen Steuergesetze boten keinen Anreiz mehr. MIFA musste sich deshalb etwas einfallen lassen und zeigen, dass diese Organisation der grosse Freund kleiner Unternehmen ist. Ich arbeitete eng mit Mara Kalnins, der Designerin, zusammen, und wir entschieden uns für eine Darstellung der Hauptmerkmale der Geschäftsvorgänge. Wir nahmen die verschiedenen Elemente, die der Kunde vorgeschlagen hatte, spielten damit auf dem Computer, und dann machte Mara die Illustrationen. MIFA war mit dem Jahresbericht sehr zufrieden.

MICHAEL WEYMOUTH, WEYMOUTH DESIGN INC., BOSTON, MASSACHUSETTS

La MIFA est une institution de l'Etat qui assure le financement des P.M.E. dans le Massachusetts. Elle a été partie prenante de ce qu'on a appelé le miracle économique de Massachusetts et a participé au développement de l'Etat. Les dirigeants considèrent leurs interventions comme dictées par la créativité et l'innovation, qualités qui devaient se refléter dans le rapport. Ils avaient réussi à activer la volonté d'investir, et voici que la nouvelle législation fiscale donnait un coup d'arrêt brutal à cette disponibilité des investisseurs. C'est ce qui a amené la MIFA à se faire plus inventive encore afin de prouver aux P.M.E. qu'elles trouveraient toujours en elle une amie fidèle. J'ai travaillé avec Mara Kalnins pour mettre au point des descriptions concises des concepts inhérents à la vie des affaires. Nous avons pris les divers éléments suggérés par le client et les avons associés sur ordinateur, puis Mara a créé les illustrations. La MIFA s'est déclarée enchantée de ce rapport annuel.

ORTHORP CORPORATION

Northrop Corporation

1987

Annual Report

Prototypes are only now being built, but teams of up to nine pilots have already flown ten thousand sorties in Northrop's U.S. Air Force YF-23A Advanced Tactical Fighter and in other future aircraft—"theirs" and "ours." To refine the ultimate design solution, fighter qualities are varied each time, surviv-ability technologies modified, hostile radars and air-to-air and surface-to-air missiles multiplied and changed. All in our Integrated Simulation Systems Laboratory. All proving the future through advanced technology resources.

12

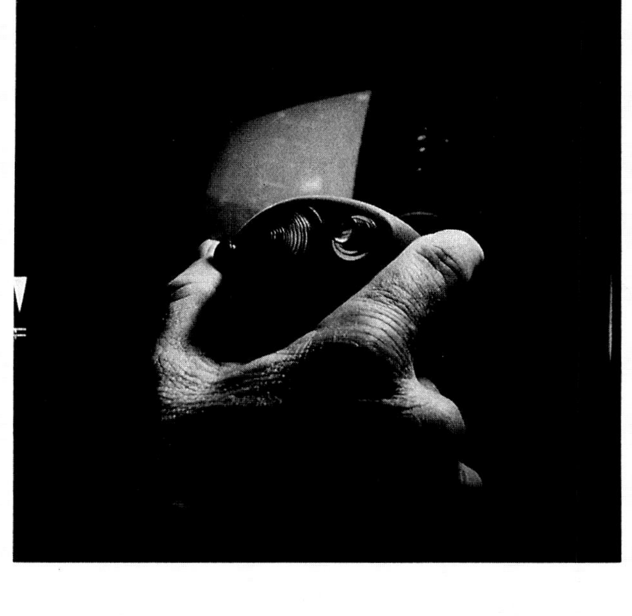

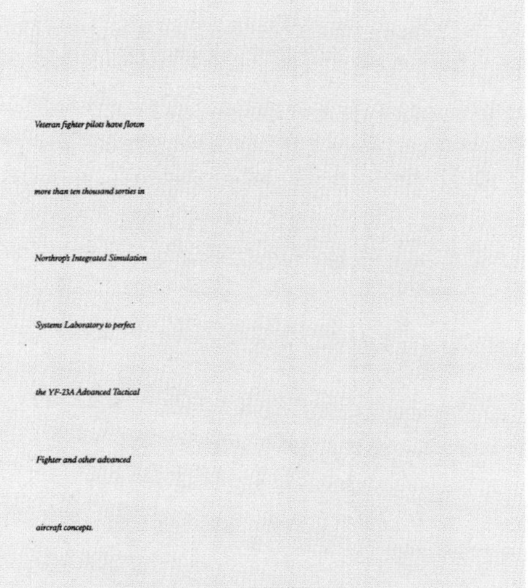

Veteran fighter pilots have flown more than ten thousand sorties in Northrop's Integrated Simulation Systems Laboratory to perfect the YF-23A Advanced Tactical Fighter and other advanced aircraft concepts.

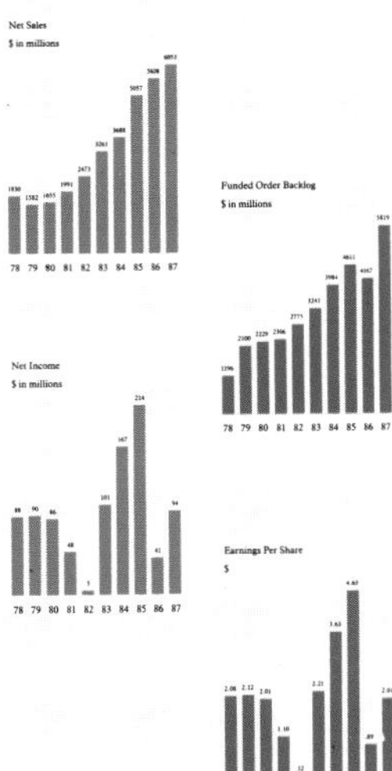

Funded Order Backlog
$ in millions

78 79 80 81 82 83 84 85 86 87

Earnings Per Share
$

78 79 80 81 82 83 84 85 86 87

1

measurement units. Subsequently, the system being built for the MX Peacekeeper was selected for use on the proposed Small ICBM, sometimes known as Midgetman.

We have reported to you on other actions we have taken where we have found violations of practices and procedures. We dismissed the manager and a number of employees at a small plant producing aircraft and missile subsystems after they admitted irregularities in the way they performed tests. We closed that operation in Pomona, California, and moved the work to the Precision Products Division headquarters in Norwood, Massachusetts, for better operational and management control.

We have gained valuable experience from these events and have taken management actions to try to assure they will not recur. We have strengthened senior management responsibilities on a corporate level and reorganized certain functions to provide greater corporate management oversight and direction of the practices, procedures, and program performance in all our operating centers. We have added management experience in key areas of our operating units. If additional changes are needed, they will be made. We recognize that human errors cannot be totally eliminated; but we are improving the management systems that will help to eliminate the effect of those errors.

Many issues remain under investigation. As we have said, we consider every allegation as if it might be true, every suggestion as if it might be valid. Less than 24 hours after allegations were recently raised concerning the Advanced Technology Bomber program, we had assigned a senior corporate management team to examine them. In addition to providing direct oversight, the assignment of a special corporate team assures that the people working on programs are diverted as little as possible from their principal responsibilities. This process will help us determine promptly and completely if there is any substance to claims made about the company or its operating units and what action, if any, is required.

On behalf of all the men and women of Northrop, we are determined that these issues not distract us from the job at hand, namely continuing to meet our commitments to our customers who depend upon us. We recognize that with our increased involvement in large, high-priority programs, the company will undergo a higher degree of scrutiny, a more detailed assessment of performance, and a more demanding level of expectations on the part of our Government, our shareholders, and the American people. We intend to assure that our own rigorous business, procedural, and ethical standards, as well as those of our customers and

6

Frank W. Lynch *Kent Kresa* *Thomas V. Jones*

our Government, are met by every employee in every part of the company.

We have demonstrated the technical skill to win the business responsibilities we have today. We believe that Northrop has the resources, the equipment and, above all, the dedicated, experienced people to carry out those responsibilities successfully, for our customers and thus for our shareholders. That has been Northrop's history, and that, we are convinced, is Northrop's future.

Thomas V. Jones	Frank W. Lynch	Kent Kresa
Chairman of the Board and Chief Executive Officer	Vice Chairman of the Board	President and Chief Operating Officer

March 9, 1988

7

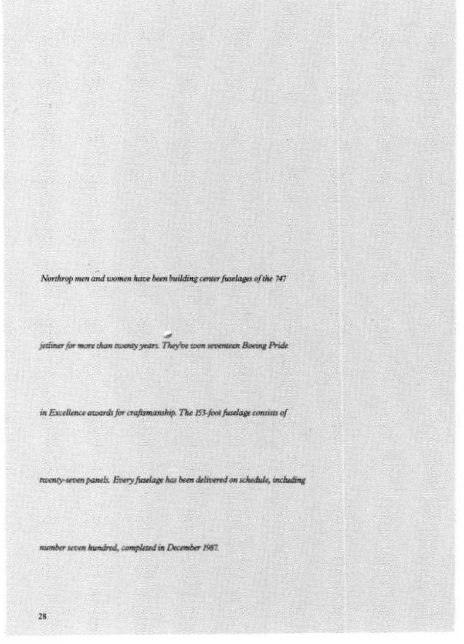

Northrop men and women have been building center fuselages of the 747 jetliner for more than twenty years. They've won seventeen Boeing Pride in Excellence awards for craftsmanship. The 153-foot fuselage consists of twenty-seven panels. Every fuselage has been delivered on schedule, including number seven hundred, completed in December 1987.

28

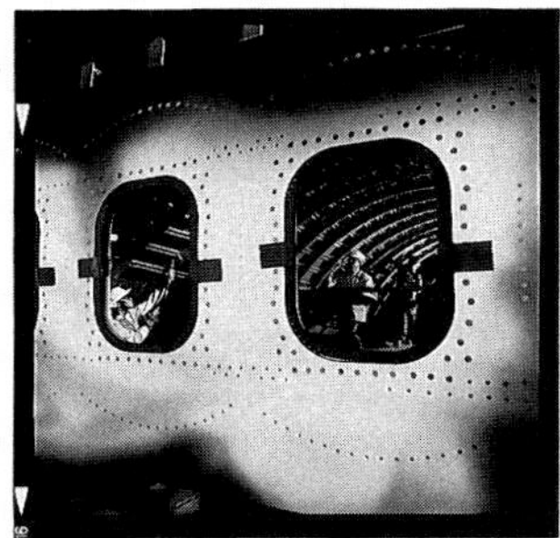

respectively. Overseas customers and the U.S. Government acting on behalf of foreign governments accounted for 9 percent of the backlog at the end of 1987, compared with 16 percent in 1986, 22 percent in 1985, 24 percent in 1984 and 32 percent in 1983. The remaining percentage at each year-end consisted of direct foreign and commercial business.

Funded Order Backlog

	1987	1986	1985	1984	$ in millions 1983
F/A-18	$ 935	$1,154	$1,805	$1,138	$1,475
ECM	631	638	608	456	243
MX Peacekeeper	491	543	508	491	147
747	41	160	133	174	134
ATF		46			
F-5E/F-5F/RF-5E	69	66	141	356	271
Peace Hawk/ATTS			29	73	261
All other	3,652	1,560	1,387	1,296	710
	$5,819	$4,167	$4,611	$3,984	$3,241

Measures of Performance

The primary cause of the higher operating profit in the aircraft segment in 1987 was the absence of F-20 company-sponsored research and development expenditures. Operating profit in the aircraft segment has been reduced in recent years as a result of significant expenditures for several company-sponsored research and development projects, primarily the F-20 Tigershark. As reported in 1986, following the decision by the U.S. Air Force to upgrade existing aircraft rather than buy new F-20s, the company discontinued investing in the F-20. The reduction in operating profit sustained in 1986 due to the F-20 included provision for supplier termination and other estimated close-out costs. The amount of expenditures made in 1985 of $189.1 million was offset by $46.5 million in proceeds from the insured loss of two Tigersharks. The company's total outlay for F-20 research and development, other pre-contract, and close-out costs was $1.15 billion through December 31, 1986—$236 million in 1986, $142.6 million in 1985, $148.5 million in 1984, and $168.1 million in 1983. The costs to develop the F-20 Tigershark—as well as other company-sponsored research and development projects—are charged against income as incurred.

In 1987 the company lowered the amount of operating margin ultimately expected to be earned through completion of a research and development contract. Under the company's accounting policy, it recognizes in the current period the cumulative effects on current and prior periods of changes in both estimated final costs and fees. Based on the latest estimate of the contract's higher final cost and lower margin,

36

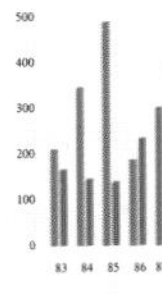

the rate of margin was lowered in 1987 from that used prior to 1987. This resulted in this year's operating margin on the contract being $60 million lower than that recorded in 1986. The effect of a similar adjustment made in 1986 was to reduce that year's operating margin $127 million from that of 1985.

Somewhat higher margin rates achieved on the F/A-18, 747 and F-5 programs were not sufficient to offset the effect of lower sales volume on the 747 and F-5 programs during 1987. Improved performance on F/A-18 contracts during 1986, combined with increased deliveries and performance improvements on 747 work, about offset the effect of lower F-5E and F-5F deliveries in 1986. The higher margin earned on the increased deliveries of F-5E and F-5F aircraft in 1985 versus 1984 was nearly offset by the write-down of inventory resulting from the planned shut-down of this program.

The largest factor in the higher operating profit of the aircraft segment in 1985 came as a result of the settlement of F/A-18 aircraft claims and contractual disputes with the McDonnell Douglas Corporation. In addition to the receipt of $50 million for the settlement, the favorable resolution of other contractual issues regarding, among other things, foreign F/A-18 fighter sales enabled the company to recognize operating margin earned on past and current sales.

Operating units of the aircraft segment invested approximately $66 million in new advanced technology projects, including the ATF, during 1987, compared with $32 million in 1986, and $41 million in 1985. Many of these projects are classified. The company in 1988 intends to make expenditures of approximately $90 million, mainly in the pursuit of winning the next phase of the ATF program. While contractual requirements of the ATF could conceivably be met within the $691 million contract value, the company does intend to make expenditures beyond this amount over the 50 month period of prototype building and testing, which began in late 1986. The company continues to follow its policy of recording all known losses when determined in the performance of its contracts with customers. However, this practice is not appropriate for the ATF program. The amount and timing of ATF expenditure commitments are at the sole discretion of the company. The company takes into consideration the evolution of the design, management authorized enhancements, and its assessment of its competitive posture as the program matures over the next 3 years.

Electronic countermeasures systems contribute most of the operating profit in the electronics segment. Operating profits in the segment as a whole declined in 1987 as a result of a number of problems at the Electronics Division, where IMUs for the MX Peacekeeper missile are produced. Deliveries of IMUs were behind contract schedule and sales were lower than the year before. Consequently, costs rose as a percent of

37

Consolidated Statements of Financial Position

Northrop Corporation and Subsidiaries

December 31	1987	1986	1985	1984	$ in millions 1983
Assets					
Current assets:					
Cash	$ 5.0	$ 4.8	$ 7.1	$ 3.7	$ 60.2
Accounts receivable	905.2	620.3	492.8	306.7	205.4
Inventoried costs	623.6	505.9	405.9	418.0	301.0
Prepaid expenses	32.9	29.5	24.9	15.0	10.7
Total current assets	1,566.7	1,160.5	930.7	743.4	577.3
Property, plant and equipment at cost:					
Land and land improvements	116.4	114.4	111.2	105.6	78.6
Buildings	716.4	666.1	615.9	575.5	479.8
Machinery and other equipment	1,715.2	1,561.7	1,282.1	981.5	777.9
Leasehold improvements	54.5	45.9	36.5	19.3	16.6
	2,602.5	2,388.1	2,045.7	1,681.9	1,352.9
Accumulated depreciation and amortization	(1,105.2)	(901.0)	(694.4)	(510.9)	(379.5)
	1,497.3	1,487.1	1,351.3	1,171.0	973.4
Other assets	59.6	51.2	50.7	42.1	45.3
	$ 3,123.6	$ 2,698.8	$ 2,332.7	$ 1,956.5	$ 1,596.0
Liabilities and Shareholders' Equity					
Current liabilities:					
Notes payable to banks	$ 888.6	$ 499.9	$ 164.0	$ 43.4	$
Trade accounts payable	365.4	341.5	310.9	233.7	214.1
Accrued employees' compensation	153.8	142.6	165.6	149.7	132.9
Advances on contracts	38.2	20.0	44.1	187.0	192.7
Income taxes payable	26.0	34.4	46.0	25.3	26.7
Deferred income taxes	449.3	431.9	449.5	331.5	255.1
Other current liabilities	132.1	223.5	151.3	164.4	104.4
Total current liabilities	2,053.4	1,693.8	1,331.4	1,135.0	925.9
Long-term obligations	31.4	47.8	51.0	50.3	44.0
Deferred income taxes	91.3	58.5	51.3	46.4	49.2
Shareholders' equity:					
Paid-in capital					
Preferred stock, 10,000,000 shares authorized and none issued					
Common stock, 200,000,000 shares authorized, issued and outstanding: 1987 — 46,843,207; 1986 — 46,578,034; 1985 — 46,298,621; 1984 — 46,100,787; 1983 — 15,213,277	190.8	176.8	161.6	150.7	133.3
Retained earnings	777.8	740.9	755.5	596.7	471.1
Unvested employee restricted award shares	(21.1)	(19.0)	(18.1)	(22.6)	(27.5)
	947.5	898.7	899.0	724.8	576.9
	$ 3,123.6	$ 2,698.8	$ 2,332.7	$ 1,956.5	$ 1,596.0

The accompanying notes are an integral part of these financial statements.

44

Consolidated Statements of Income

Northrop Corporation and Subsidiaries

Year ended December 31	1987	1986	1985	1984	In millions, except per share 1983
Net sales	$6,052.5	$5,608.4	$5,056.6	$3,687.8	$3,260.6
Cost of sales:					
Operating costs	5,357.7	4,985.9	4,205.4	3,005.5	2,725.0
Administrative and general expenses	527.6	551.7	543.4	438.9	395.1
Operating margin	167.2	70.8	307.8	243.4	140.5
Other income (deductions):					
Claim settlement			50.0		
Interest income	2.0	2.2	2.2	7.6	6.9
Other, net	18.7	5.4	5.5	(1.5)	19.6
Interest expense	(50.5)	(28.9)	(17.4)	(7.5)	(14.3)
Income before income taxes	137.4	49.5	348.1	242.0	152.7
Federal and foreign income taxes	43.2	8.3	133.7	75.1	52.0
Net income	$ 94.2	$ 41.2	$ 214.4	$ 166.9	$ 100.7
Weighted average common shares outstanding	46.8	46.5	46.3	45.9	45.6
Earnings per share	$ 2.01	$ .89	$ 4.63	$ 3.63	$ 2.21

Consolidated Statements of Changes in Shareholders' Equity

Year ended December 31	1987	1986	1985	1984	$ in millions, except per share 1983
Paid-in capital					
At beginning of year	$ 176.8	$ 161.6	$ 150.7	$ 133.3	$ 128.0
Employee stock awards and options exercised, net of forfeitures	14.0	15.2	10.9	17.4	5.3
At end of year	190.8	176.8	161.6	150.7	133.3
Retained earnings					
At beginning of year	740.9	755.5	596.7	471.1	397.9
Net income	94.2	41.2	214.4	166.9	100.7
Purchase of 40,000 shares	(1.1)				
Cash dividends	(56.2)	(55.8)	(55.6)	(41.3)	(27.5)
At end of year	777.8	740.9	755.5	596.7	471.1
Unvested employee restricted award shares					
At beginning of year	(19.0)	(18.1)	(22.6)	(27.5)	(32.0)
Grants, net of forfeitures	(6.2)	(4.9)	(.3)	(8.8)	(1.9)
Amortization	4.1	4.0	4.8	13.7	6.4
At end of year	(21.1)	(19.0)	(18.1)	(22.6)	(27.5)
Total shareholders' equity	$ 947.5	$ 898.7	$ 899.0	$ 724.8	$ 576.9
Book value per share	$ 20.23	$ 19.29	$ 19.42	$ 15.72	$ 12.64
Cash dividends per share	1.20	1.20	1.20	.90	.60

The accompanying notes are an integral part of these financial statements.

45

CLIENT:
NORTHROP CORPORATION

DESIGN FIRM:
WEYMOUTH DESIGN

ART DIRECTOR:
MICHAEL WEYMOUTH

DESIGNERS:
TOM LAIDLAW,
CORY FANELLI

PHOTOGRAPHERS:
CHARLES HARBUTT,
BURK UZZLE,
JEFF CORWIN

WRITER:
ALLAN A. MYER

ALLAN A. MYER, DIRECTOR OF SPECIAL COMMUNICATIONS, NORTHROP CORPORATION, LOS ANGELES, CALIFORNIA

The Northrop Corporation annual report for 1987 is fundamentally a statement of effort over the course of that year. Northrop does very serious work using the taxpayers' money; we have to portray this hard work. The design by Weymouth Design is interesting because, like an airplane design, there is not an extra ounce of anything it doesn't need. Every design element works with every other design element. Even the photography has no cropping, indicating an honesty and an integrity. The annual report is successful because it is a clear statement about the company and close to the quality of the company's products.

ALLAN A. MYER, DIRECTOR OF SPECIAL COMMUNICATIONS, NORTHROP CORPORATION, LOS ANGELES, KALIFORNIEN

Der Geschäftsbericht der Northrop Corporation für das Jahr 1987 ist eine Darstellung der Anstrengungen, die in jenem Jahr unternommen wurden. Northrop hat eine sehr ernsthafte Aufgabe zu erfüllen, da Steuergelder eingesetzt werden, und wir mussten die harte Arbeit, die dahinter steckt, aufzeigen. Die Gestaltung von Weymouth Design erinnert an die Konstruktion von Flugzeugen, nirgends ist ein überflüssiges Teilchen zu finden. Jedes Design-Element funktioniert in Verbindung mit einem anderen Design-Element. Sogar die Photos wurden unbeschnitten verwendet, als Indiz für Aufrichtigkeit und Integrität.

ALLAN A. MYER, DIRECTOR OF SPECIAL COMMUNICATIONS, NORTHROP CORPORATION, LOS ANGELES, CALIFORNIE

Le rapport annuel de la Northrop Corporation pour 1987 est fondamentalement un message relatant les efforts entrepris au cours de l'année. Northrop fait du travail sérieux avec l'aide de l'argent des contribuables, et nous entendions dresser le tableau des tâches accomplies. Le design réalisé par Weymouth Design est intéressant en ce qu'il ne comporte - pas plus qu'un design d'avion - pas une once de superflu. Chaque élément de l'ensemble est en interaction avec chaque autre élément. Même les photos sont utilisées telles quelles, faisant montre d'honnêteté et d'intégrité. Ce rapport annuel est réussi parce qu'il comporte un message clair.

MICHAEL WEYMOUTH, WEYMOUTH DESIGN, BOSTON, MASSACHUSETTS

Designing for Northrop requires that designer and client be in total sync. They are heavily involved with defense work, and as a result do not lavish a great deal of money on the annual. What really makes it work, however, is Northrop's commitment to excellent photography, printing and paper. If there is one overriding aspect to working with Northrop it is that of chemistry–of working together. The people running the project at Northrop are extremely capable and are intent, within a tight budget, on producing an annual report that they expect to be as precise as the products they build.

MICHAEL WEYMOUTH, WEYMOUTH DESIGN, BOSTON, MASSACHUSETTS

Bei Northrop Corporation handelt es sich um ein Unternehmen der Verteidigungsindustrie. Wir präsentierten eine graphische Lösung in Schwarzweiss, von der wir glaubten, dass sie das Wesen von Northrop reflektiert. Wir benutzten gute Aufnahmen, eine ausgezeichnete Schwarzweiss-Druckerei und hervorragendes Papier. Wir verwendeten die vollständigen Aufnahmen, wobei gegenüber von jedem Bild eine Seite mit klarer, ruhiger Typographie eingesetzt wurde. Dieser Text war wichtig. Wir glauben, dass wir Northrops Bedürfnisse verstanden haben und ihnen gerecht wurden.

MICHAEL WEYMOUTH, WEYMOUTH DESIGN, BOSTON, MASSACHUSETTS

Le Design pour Northrop est un exemple d'osmose réussi. Nos rapports avec cette entreprise ont évolué avec les années. Il s'agissait de réaliser un rapport annuel pour l'industrie de la défense, avec un budget réduit à l'essentiel. Nous avons élaboré un document viable en noir et blanc en utilisant de bonnes photos, les services d'une imprimerie spécialiste du noir et blanc et un papier extraordinaire. Pour le design, nous avons eu recours aux photos complètes en les contrastant avec des pages typo sereines et reposantes. C'est un document important qui en est résulté.

POTLATCH CORPORATION

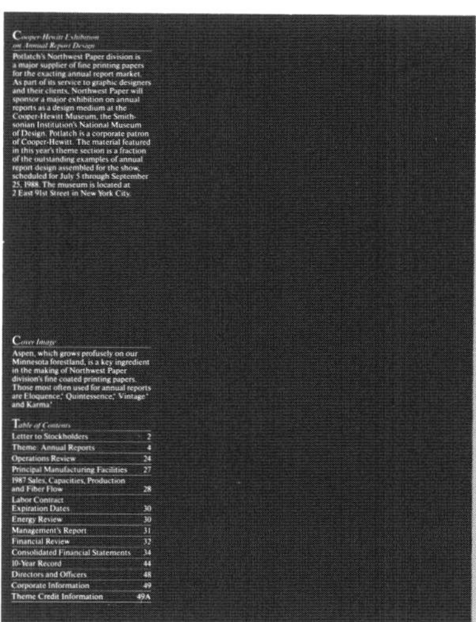

Cooper-Hewitt Exhibition on Annual Report Design

Potlatch's Northwest Paper division is a major supplier of fine printing papers for the exacting annual report market. As part of its service to graphic designers and their clients, Northwest Paper will sponsor a major exhibition on annual reports as a design medium at the Cooper-Hewitt Museum, the Smithsonian Institution's National Museum of Design. Potlatch is a corporate patron of Cooper-Hewitt. The material featured in this year's theme section is a fraction of the outstanding examples of annual report design assembled for the show, scheduled for July 5 through September 25, 1988. The museum is located at 2 East 91st Street in New York City.

Cover Image

Aspen, which grows profusely on our Minnesota forestland, is a key ingredient in the making of Northwest Paper division's fine coated printing papers. Those most often used for annual reports are Eloquence,® Quintessence,® Vintage® and Karma®

Table of Contents

FINANCIAL HIGHLIGHTS

(Dollars in thousands—except per-share amounts)	1987	1986	1985
Net sales	$992,077	$976,373	$950,323
Net earnings	87,623	69,943	37,669
Per common share:(1)			
Net earnings			
Without dilution	$ 3.13	$ 2.49	$ 1.10
Fully diluted	2.98	2.45	1.10
Cash dividends paid	.86	.795	.78
Common stockholders' equity	21.90	19.64	18.13
Working capital	$146,170	$126,426	$ 73,020
Depreciation, amortization and cost of fee timber harvested	65,061	64,391	61,225
Capital expenditures	155,213	95,615	63,089
Long-term debt (noncurrent portion)	364,792	344,312	337,668
Stockholders' equity	638,034	574,566	473,220

(1) Restated to reflect the two-for-one stock split in 1987

Potlatch Corp., founded in 1903 in Potlatch, Idaho, is a diversified forest products company with 1.4 million acres of timberland in Arkansas, Idaho and Minnesota. Our manufacturing facilities convert wood fiber into two main product lines: wood products (lumber, plywood, oriented strand board, particleboard and wood specialties) and bleached fiber products (bleached kraft pulp, paperboard and packaging, printing papers and consumer tissue).

Potlatch's business philosophy is to earn a growing profit and reasonable rate of return, given the normal cycles of our business. This will be achieved by talented, well-trained and highly motivated people who are properly supported by a sound financial structure and a keen sense of social responsibility to all of the publics with whom the company has contact.

Potlatch Corporation and Consolidated Subsidiaries

ANNUAL REPORTS

Over the last half century, the annual report to shareholders has evolved into a design category all its own. A hybrid of many disciplines, annual report design is part industrial art, part photo-reportage, part mixed media, part fine art—and yet unique in its form and purpose.

Before the Securities and Exchange Act of 1934 mandated that all publicly traded companies provide yearly financial reports to investors, few corporations published more than basic financial statements. In complying with the new federal law, companies recognized an opportunity to "piggyback" a marketing message onto this legal document. Several annual reports in the late '30s and early '40s proudly featured photographs of the corporate headquarters building, maps pinpointing regional offices, and bar charts showing sales and earnings growth. In 1940, Sears, Roebuck and Co. produced what may be the first editorial theme section when it published "The Story of Sears." Many companies followed suit with "anniversary" issue reports.

It was not until the late 1950s, however, that most corporations began to realize that graphic design could be a powerful means of establishing a distinct corporate identity, as well as an orderly way to present information.

A handful of designers forged a new perception of annual reports through highly innovative visual elements. Departing from the standard documentation photography of products and manufacturing plants, they began to use art to portray a company's character. Graphic designer Paul Rand expressed IBM's polished and progressive image through the choice of typeface, the use of coated paper stock, the framing of visual elements with white space, and presentation of dramatic pictures by famous photographers. Robert Miles Runyan introduced a montage of ideas through still-life photos in the 1959 Litton report. Erik Nitsche applied contemporary art techniques to the 1959 General Dynamics annual.

These trendsetting reports, according to designers, demonstrated the exciting range of possibilities in annual reports. Quality design proved to be an effective tool for defining corporate style and professionalism. At the same time, compelling images could pull readers into the text, interpret intangible ideas and engage the reader's attention on both an intellectual and emotional level. By the late '60s, annual reports emerged as a most important corporate marketing tool—a visual statement of management goals and philosophy and often a personal expression of the CEO himself.

During this period, dramatic technological improvements helped shape the direction of annual reports and gave designers a sophisticated array of tools with which to ply their craft. Letterpress gave way to lithography. Flexible phototypography replaced hot metal type. Advances in paper manufacturing produced a broad choice of fine coated sheets polished to a glossy sheen. At each step of the production process, technology created new capabilities. Computerization is making changes occur even more rapidly.

The vast amount of original art contracted by corporations today has made them the 20th century patrons of the arts, fulfilling the role once held by the nobility and the church. Contemporary artists are rarely commissioned to paint the grand duchess or ceilings of chapels in Rome. Many great names, however, have at some point produced work that has appeared in corporate annual reports.

But like the Renaissance artist who was given a theme and point of view for the mural commissioned by the church, today's graphic artists have a specific assignment—to tell the company story clearly and memorably. It is in the telling of the story that the designer's creativity shines through. The visual impact of annual reports ranges from elegantly dignified, avant garde or scholarly to emotionally compelling. The interpretations are as unique as the companies themselves.

While graphic designers play a central role in the visual development of an annual report, they by no means can take full credit for the quality of its outcome. Annual report design demands cooperative creativity and skill. The process involves the corporation, designers, writers, photographers, illustrators, typographers and printers, among others. Each is entrusted with preserving the integrity of the corporate message and enhancing the overall design. And each can affect the visual power of the annual report for better or worse.

Over the past quarter century, corporations have discovered it is not just what they say but how they present it that leaves a lasting impression. Each element of design—the feel of the paper, the brilliance or subtlety of color, the choice of typestyle, the mood of the imagery—elicits its own subliminal response from the reader. As a result of this growing awareness, design is no longer viewed as mere window dressing for the financial review. It has become an art form in itself.

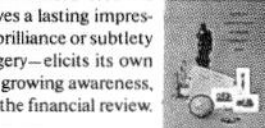

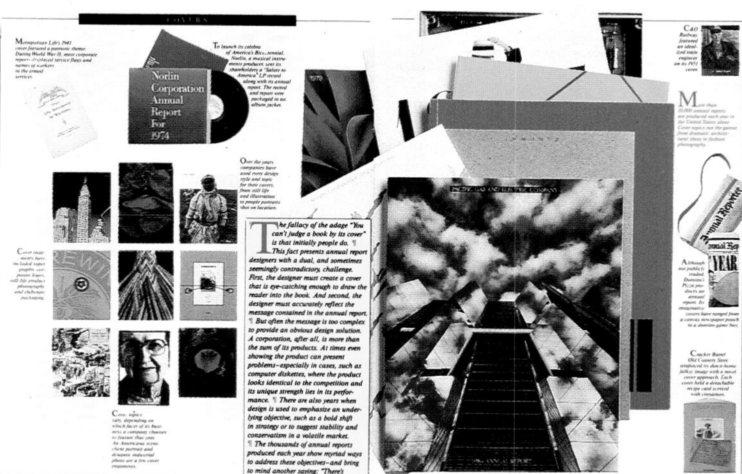

Boy Scouts of America created a very graphic posterized image from a familiar boy scout pose.

This simple silhouette effectively expresses the essence of the mother-child health care services provided by Pennsylvania Hospital.

Metropolitan Life conveyed its support of the arts in a feature about the restoration of paintings by N.C. Wyeth, commissioned in 1940.

Lomas & Nettleton Mortgage Investors invited children to write about ways to improve the future and illustrated their comments with fanciful images.

20

Back to basics" was the title for this illustration in MICOM Systems' 1986 report. Illustrator Guy Billout is noted for his thought-provoking and humorous treatment of subjects.

THEME ILLUSTRATION

GUY BILLOUT

When Multibank Financial highlighted the communities it serves, it combined small black-and-white images with captions relating fascinating historical trivia.

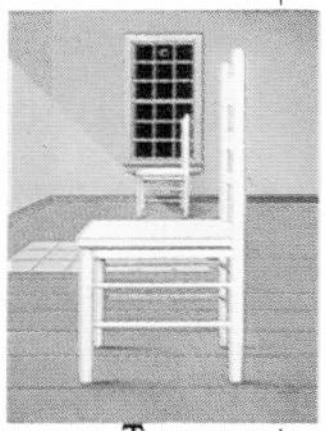

The 1982 Heinz report recognized the off-the-job talents and interests of workers by featuring poems written by employees. Heinz then commissioned well-known artists to illustrate these poems.

Annual report illustrators work in every medium, including oil, watercolor, pen-and-ink, air brush, collage and woodcut. Illustrators are selected as much for their ability to interpret a subject as for their artistic style.

This illustration revealed Activision's participation in the international home computer software market and its products' graphics capabilities.

Sometimes the sensitive nature of a subject is better depicted symbolically. Syntex used this image to illustrate its research into cardiovascular diseases.

For its 1986 annual report, Hewlett-Packard Limited used stylized illustrations with photographic insets to highlight each of its operating units.

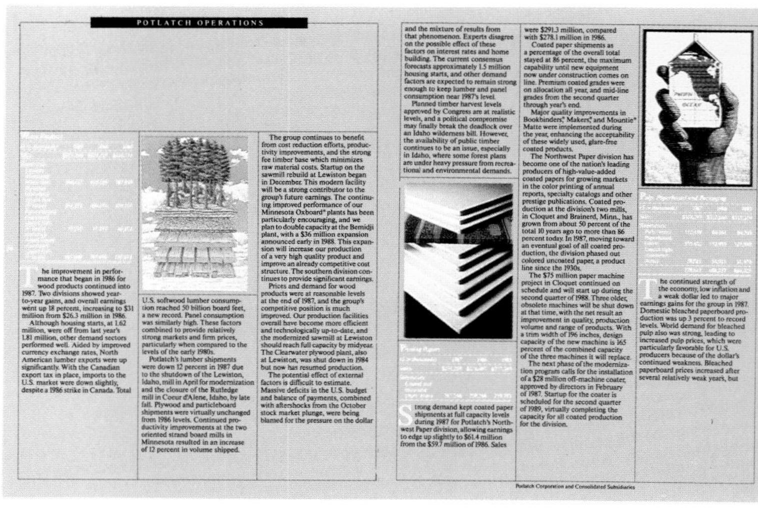

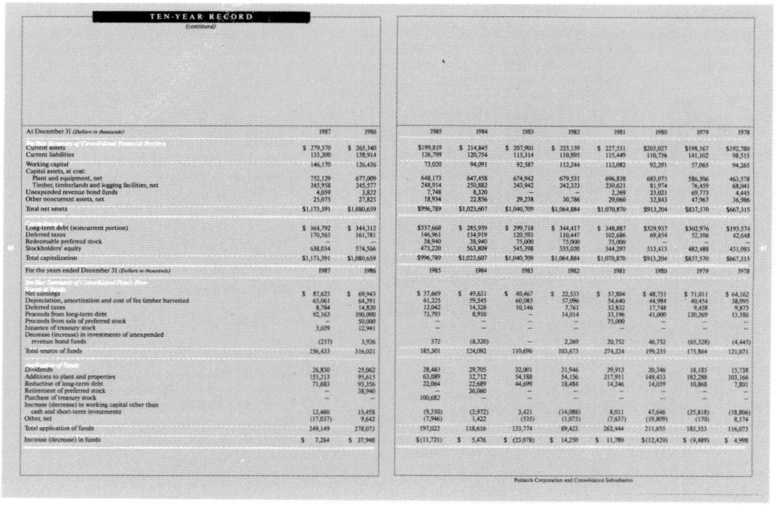

POTLATCH OPERATIONS

The improvement in performance that began in 1986 for wood products continued into 1987. Two divisions showed year-to-year gains, and overall earnings went up 18 percent, increasing to $31 million from $26.3 million in 1986.

Although housing starts, at 1.62 million, were off from last year's 1.81 million, other demand sectors performed well. Aided by improved currency exchange rates, North American lumber exports were up significantly. With the Canadian export tax in place, imports to the U.S. market were down slightly, despite a 1986 strike in Canada. Total U.S. softwood lumber consumption reached 50 billion board feet, a new record. Panel consumption was similarly high. These factors combined to provide relatively strong markets and firm prices, particularly when compared to the levels of the early 1980s.

Potlatch's lumber shipments were down 12 percent in 1987 due to the shutdown of the Lewiston, Idaho, mill in April for modernization and the closure of the Rutledge mill in Coeur d'Alene, Idaho, by late fall. Plywood and particleboard shipments were virtually unchanged from 1986 levels. Continued productivity improvements at the two oriented strand board mills in Minnesota resulted in an increase of 12 percent in volume shipped.

The group continues to benefit from cost reduction efforts, productivity improvements, and the strong fee timber base which minimizes raw material costs. Startup on the sawmill rebuild at Lewiston began in December. This modern facility will be a strong contributor to the group's future earnings. The continuing improved performance of our Minnesota Oxboard* plants has been particularly encouraging, and we plan to double capacity at the Bemidji plant, with a $36 million expansion announced early in 1988. This expansion will increase our production of a very high quality product and improve an already competitive cost structure. The southern division continues to provide significant earnings.

Prices and demand for wood products were at reasonable levels at the end of 1987, and the group's competitive position is much improved. Our production facilities overall have become more efficient and technologically up-to-date, and the modernized sawmill at Lewiston should reach full capacity by midyear. The Clearwater plywood plant, also at Lewiston, was shut down in 1984 but now has resumed production.

The potential effect of external factors is difficult to estimate. Massive deficits in the U.S. budget and balance of payments, combined with aftershocks from the October stock market plunge, were being blamed for the pressure on the dollar and the mixture of results from that phenomenon. Experts disagree on the possible effect of these factors on interest rates and home building. The current consensus forecasts approximately 1.5 million housing starts, and other demand factors are expected to remain strong enough to keep lumber and panel consumption near 1987's level.

Planned timber harvest levels approved by Congress are at realistic levels, and a political compromise may finally break the deadlock over an Idaho wilderness bill. However, the availability of public timber continues to be an issue, especially in Idaho, where some forest plans are under heavy pressure from recreational and environmental demands.

Strong demand kept coated paper shipments at full capacity levels during 1987 for Potlatch's Northwest Paper division, allowing earnings to edge up slightly to $61.4 million from the $59.7 million of 1986. Sales were $291.3 million, compared with $278.1 million in 1986.

Coated paper shipments as a percentage of the overall total stayed at 86 percent, the maximum capability until new equipment now under construction comes on line. Premium coated grades were on allocation all year, and mid-line grades from the second quarter through year's end.

Major quality improvements in Bookbinders,* Makers,* and Mountie* Matte were implemented during the year, enhancing the acceptability of these widely used, glare-free coated products.

The Northwest Paper division has become one of the nation's leading producers of high-value-added coated papers for growing markets in the color printing of annual reports, specialty catalogs and other prestige publications. Coated production at the division's two mills, in Cloquet and Brainerd, Minn., has grown from about 50 percent of the total 10 years ago to more than 86 percent today. In 1987, moving toward an eventual goal of all coated production, the division phased out colored uncoated paper, a product line since the 1930s.

The $75 million paper machine project in Cloquet continued on schedule and will start up during the second quarter of 1988. Three older, obsolete machines will be shut down at that time, with the net result an improvement in quality, production volume and range of products. With a trim width of 196 inches, design capacity of the new machine is 165 percent of the combined capacity of the three machines it will replace.

The next phase of the modernization program calls for the installation of a $28 million off-machine coater, approved by directors in February of 1987. Startup for the coater is scheduled for the second quarter of 1989, virtually completing the capacity for all coated production for the division.

The continued strength of the economy, low inflation and a weak dollar led to major earnings gains for the group in 1987. Domestic bleached paperboard production was up 3 percent to record levels. World demand for bleached pulp also was strong, leading to increased pulp prices, which were particularly favorable for U.S. producers because of the dollar's continued weakness. Bleached paperboard prices increased after several relatively weak years, but

Potlatch Corporation and Consolidated Subsidiaries

TEN-YEAR RECORD
(continued)

At December 31 *(Dollars in thousands)*	1987	1986	1985	1984	1983	1982	1981	1980	1979	1978
Current assets	$ 279,370	$ 265,340	$199,819	$ 214,845	$ 207,901	$ 223,139	$ 227,531	$203,027	$198,167	$192,780
Current liabilities	133,200	138,914	126,799	120,754	115,314	110,895	115,449	110,736	141,102	98,515
Working capital	146,170	126,426	73,020	94,091	92,587	112,244	112,082	92,291	57,065	94,265
Capital assets, at cost:										
Plant and equipment, net	752,129	677,009	648,173	647,458	674,942	679,531	696,838	683,075	586,306	463,578
Timber, timberlands and logging facilities, net	245,958	245,577	248,914	250,882	243,942	242,323	230,621	81,974	76,459	68,041
Unexpended revenue bond funds	4,059	3,822	7,748	8,320	–	–	2,269	23,021	69,773	4,445
Other noncurrent assets, net	25,075	27,825	18,934	22,856	29,238	30,786	29,060	32,843	47,967	36,986
Total net assets	$1,173,391	$1,080,659	$996,789	$1,023,607	$1,040,709	$1,064,884	$1,070,870	$913,204	$837,570	$667,315
Long-term debt (noncurrent portion)	$ 364,792	$ 344,312	$337,668	$ 285,939	$ 299,718	$ 344,417	$ 348,887	$329,937	$302,976	$193,574
Deferred taxes	170,565	161,781	146,961	134,919	120,593	110,447	102,686	69,854	52,106	42,648
Redeemable preferred stock	–	–	38,940	38,940	75,000	75,000	75,000	–	–	–
Stockholders' equity	638,034	574,566	473,220	563,809	545,398	535,020	544,297	513,413	482,488	431,093
Total capitalization	$1,173,391	$1,080,659	$996,789	$1,023,607	$1,040,709	$1,064,884	$1,070,870	$913,204	$837,570	$667,315

For the years ended December 31 *(Dollars in thousands)*	1987	1986	1985	1984	1983	1982	1981	1980	1979	1978
Net earnings	$ 87,623	$ 69,943	$ 37,669	$ 49,631	$ 40,467	$ 22,533	$ 57,804	$ 48,751	$ 71,011	$ 64,162
Depreciation, amortization and cost of fee timber harvested	65,061	64,391	61,225	59,545	60,083	57,096	54,640	44,984	40,454	38,095
Deferred taxes	8,784	14,820	12,042	14,326	10,146	7,761	32,832	17,748	9,458	9,873
Proceeds from long-term debt	92,163	100,000	73,793	8,910	–	14,014	33,196	41,000	120,269	13,386
Proceeds from sale of preferred stock	–	50,000	–	–	–	–	75,000	–	–	–
Issuance of treasury stock	3,039	12,941	–	–	–	–	–	–	–	–
Decrease (increase) in investments of unexpended revenue bond funds	(237)	3,926	572	(8,320)	–	2,269	20,752	46,752	(65,328)	(4,445)
Total source of funds	256,433	316,021	185,301	124,092	110,696	103,673	274,224	199,235	175,864	121,071
Dividends	26,830	25,062	28,483	29,705	32,001	31,946	29,913	20,346	18,185	15,738
Additions to plant and properties	155,213	95,615	63,089	32,712	54,188	54,156	217,911	149,433	182,288	103,166
Reduction of long-term debt	71,683	93,356	22,064	22,689	44,699	18,484	14,246	14,039	10,868	7,801
Retirement of preferred stock	–	38,940	–	36,060	–	–	–	–	–	–
Purchase of treasury stock	–	–	100,682	–	–	–	–	–	–	–
Increase (decrease) in working capital other than cash and short-term investments	12,460	15,458	(9,350)	(3,972)	3,421	(14,088)	8,011	47,646	(25,818)	(18,806)
Other, net	(17,037)	9,642	(7,946)	1,422	(535)	(1,075)	(7,637)	(19,809)	(170)	8,174
Total application of funds	249,149	278,073	197,022	118,616	133,774	89,423	262,444	211,655	185,353	116,073
Increase (decrease) in funds	$ 7,284	$ 37,948	$(11,721)	$ 5,476	$ (23,078)	$ 14,250	$ 11,780	$(12,420)	$ (9,489)	$ 4,998

Potlatch Corporation and Consolidated Subsidiaries

CLIENT:
POTLATCH CORPORATION

DESIGN FIRM:
PENTAGRAM DESIGN

ART DIRECTOR:
KIT HINRICHS

DESIGNERS:
KIT HINRICHS,
LENORE BARTZ

PHOTOGRAPHERS:
TOM TRACY,
BARRY ROBINSON,
TERRY HEFFERNAN

ILLUSTRATORS:
DOUG SMITH,
MARK SUMMERS,
MAX SEABAUGH,
DAVE STEVENSON

WRITER:
DELPHINE HIRASUNA

TYPOGRAPHER:
REARDON & KREBS

PAPER SELECTION:
QUINTESSENCE, ELOQUENCE

PAPER MANUFACTURER:
POTLATCH CORPORATION

PRINTER:
ANDERSON LITHOGRAPH

NUMBER OF PAGES:
48

SIZE:
8 1/2" x 11"

TYPE SELECTION:
TIMES ROMAN

DELPHINE HIRASUNA, PROJECT MANAGER, POTLATCH CORPORATION, SAN FRANCISCO, CALIFORNIA

Potlatch Corporation's Northwest Paper Division sponsored an exhibition on annual reports at the Cooper-Hewitt Museum in New York, so for the company's 1987 annual report we featured annual reports themselves as a theme. We do produce annual report printing paper, and we presented the historical development of annual reports. The cover featured trees, but not any old trees. These are Minnesota Aspen, which are annual report quality trees. The way we approached this theme was by recognizing the annual report as an artistic form in its own right, and we did a lot of research at the Harvard Business School in developing the text.

KIT HINRICHS, PENTAGRAM DESIGN, SAN FRANCISCO, CALIFORNIA

The 1987 Potlatch annual report was a culmination of previous annual reports. Once we heard that Potlatch was doing the exhibition at the Cooper-Hewitt on annual reports, we wanted to make the company's annual report part of that exhibition and a celebration of that display. We did a catalog for the show on the same subject, so we were already culling material on annual reports. We could pick and choose what we liked. It was a ready-made idea, and it had very positive results.

DELPHINE HIRASUNA, PROJECT MANAGER, POTLATCH CORPORATION, SAN FRANCISCO, KALIFORNIEN

Die Northwest Paper Division von Potlatch sponsorte eine Ausstellung von Jahresberichten im New Yorker Cooper-Hewitt-Museum. Wir machten deshalb Jahresberichte zum Thema unseres eigenen Geschäftsberichtes. Wir stellen Papier für Jahresberichte her, und die Darstellung der geschichtlichen Entwicklung schien uns besonders geeignet. Auf dem Umschlag zeigten wir Bäume, und zwar Minnesota-Espen, die sich gut für Jahresbericht-Papierqualitäten eignen. Wir machten deutlich, dass für uns Jahresberichte eine Kunst für sich sind. Der Text ist das Ergebnis von Recherchen an der Harvard Business School.

KIT HINRICHS, PENTAGRAM, SAN FRANCISCO, KALIFORNIEN

Der Geschäftsbericht 1987 für Potlatch übertraf alle bisherigen Berichte. Als wir hörten, dass Potlatch die Ausstellung von Jahresberichten im Cooper-Hewitt-Museum macht, wollten wir gemeinsam den Jahresbericht zu einem Teil der Ausstellung werden lassen. Wir machten einen Katalog über das gleiche Thema und hatten deshalb reichlich Material. Wir konnten aussuchen und nehmen, was uns gefiel. Es war eine schnell getroffene Entscheidung. Wir hatten ein positives Echo.

DELPHINE HIRASUNA, PROJECT MANAGER, POTLATCH CORPORATION, SAN FRANCISCO, CALIFORNIE

La Northwest Paper Division de la Potlatch Corporation ayant organisé une exposition de rapports annuels au Musée Cooper-Hewitt de New York, nous avons choisi ce thème pour le rapport annuel 1987 du groupe. Nous produisons du papier destiné à l'impression de rapports annuels et avions l'intention de montrer le développement historique. On trouve des arbres sur la couverture, plus précisement des trembles du Minnesota, la qualité rêvée pour les rapports annuels. Notre approche a consisté à reconnaître au rapport annuel une forme artistique per se. Le texte est le résultat de recherches à la Havard Business School.

KIT HINRICHS, PENTAGRAM, SAN FRANCISCO, CALIFORNIE

Le rapport annuel de Potlatch pour 1987 est le couronnement des rapports précédents. Dès que nous avons appris que Potlatch organisait l'exposition de Cooper-Hewitt consacrée aux rapports annuels, nous avons voulu intégrer le rapport commandé dans cette exposition et en faire un document à la gloire de l'exposition. Comme nous avions fait un catalogue sur le sujet, il a suffi d'élaguer les matériaux qui y figuraient, choissant et utilsant ce qui nous convenait. Les résultats étaient très prositifs.

Annual Report 1987

The Progressive Corporation

The Progressive Corporation and Subsidiaries 2

Financial Highlights

For The Year (millions — except per share amounts)	1987	1986	Change	Compounded Annual Increase 1983-1987
Direct premiums written	$1,178.2	$830.1	42%	37%
Net premiums written	1,116.5	780.9	43	35
Net premiums earned	994.4	677.2	47	33
Total revenues	999.9	683.3	46	32
Income before security sales	91.3	55.3	65	50
Per share	3.16	1.98	60	46
Total return income	75.4	68.3	10	15
Per share	2.61	2.44	7	12
GAAP underwriting profit margin	5.6%	4.3%		
At Year-end (millions — except per share amounts)				
Consolidated shareholders' equity				
GAAP	$ 395.0	$311.4	27%	40%
Current value	397.4	322.7	23	42
Common shares outstanding	28.7	28.0	3	3
Book value per share				
GAAP	$ 13.75	$11.13	24	36
Current value	13.83	11.53	20	38
Return on average shareholders' equity				
GAAP	24.3%	23.0%		
Current value	18.7	27.4		

Current value/total return accounting is discussed on pages 40 and 41.

3

About Progressive

The Progressive insurance organization began business in 1937. Progressive Casualty Insurance Company was founded in 1956. The Progressive Corporation, an insurance holding company formed in 1965, owns thirty-five operating subsidiaries and has two mutual insurance company affiliates. The companies serve insurance agents, brokers and their customers in the United States and Canada by being a financially strong, stable, service oriented provider of nonstandard automobile and other specialty property-casualty and credit related insurance and services.

Of the approximately 1,000 property-casualty insurance company groups, Progressive ranks thirty-ninth in size. The 1987 industry premiums written were $192 billion. Progressive's share was six-tenths of one percent.

We believe that a superior return on equity and a positive environment are essential to attract quality people and achieve ambitious growth plans. By building a dynamic organization of talented people, governed by core values and guided by clarity about our mutual objectives, we compete successfully. We outperformed the industry again in 1987.

We enter 1988 in strong financial condition with capital adequate to support our premium growth plans. Progressive's financial strength is recognized by an A+ rating from A. M. Best Company and a claims-paying rating of AAA, the highest awarded by Standard & Poor's. Our long-term debt is rated at the second highest level.

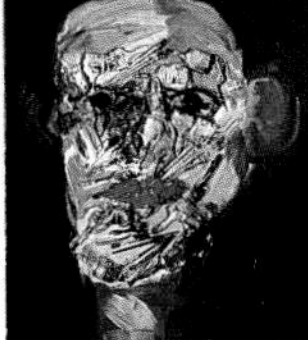

Rainer Fetting
Brush Head
Oil and paint brushes
on canvas
1984

6

of all our people was 30 (compared to 29 at 12/31/86). Their average time with us was 36 months (compared to 29 months at 12/31/86). The low average tenure is a function of the numbers of people hired from 1984 through 1987, not high turnover.

Our strategy is not without risk. We expect industry underwriting standards and pricing to soften and industry combined operating ratio improvement to end in 1988. We are confident enough about the five-year prospects for our strategies that we may experience a higher expense ratio short-term to maintain, even build, service capabilities, and insure fewer risks if we can't sell the value added at our price.

Our investment approach supports our vision of Progressive's long-term prospects. It stresses capital preservation, simplicity and individual responsibility. We will invest in high quality, short-term securities or in stock of companies we know and understand well. This strategy is consistent with our increasing emphasis on partnership.

This report communicates our beliefs to shareholders, customers, our people whose high quality execution is so essential to our success, and many others interested in Progressive. It describes our business strategy emphasizing its new aspects. It is our charter for the future. We update the annual report every year. This report describes more important changes than most. We introduce the important themes of change, service as important as risk transfer, partnership and leadership.

My role now is to articulate Progressive's values and mission, inspire our people to be creative, be a strong leader and to develop strong leaders. Other senior managers increasingly establish and document policy, make decisions and represent Progressive where I was formerly

7

required. Total management participation in the strategy development process builds a consensus which is essential to the strategies' successful execution. In 1987, we took a small step toward dealing with the large issue of building a management succession process when the Board and senior managers reached agreement for the first time on a temporary management plan should I be unable to perform.

Our accomplishments and opportunities are exciting. Our challenges and problems are demanding. We will improve and stay flexible. Much more will be required to accomplish our vision. We start 1988 as we started all other years — excited, respectful of the challenge implicit in our objectives and confident that our excellent people working hard will achieve superior results.

At Progressive, it always seems we are just starting and the future is brighter than ever before. We deeply appreciate the customers we are privileged to serve. Thank you for your business. To Progressive's 5,879 people, thank you for your invaluable contribution to the 198[illegible] results. This is my 23rd letter to shareholders whom we thank for support. For some time I have signed personal and many business lette[illegible] as I do here for the first time. It feels good to wish you

Joy, Love and Peace,

Peter B. Lewis,
Chairman, President, and
Chief Executive Officer

Barbara Kasten
Loyola Law School
Site #8, #9
Cibachrome prints
1986

8

Core Values, Mission and Objectives

Communicating a clear picture of who we are (Core Values), what's important (Mission), what we try to do (Objectives) and how we will do it (Strategies) permits all people associated with Progressive to understand us.

9

Core Values

Progressive is its values. We want them to be understood and embraced by all Progressive people. They dictate our decisions and actions. They cause us to be different and to succeed.

Integrity
We revere truth and practice open disclosure. We adhere to high ethical standards, report completely, encourage disclosing bad news and welcome disagreement.

Golden Rule
We respect all people. We deal with people as we would like them to deal with us. Shareholders, employees, customers, companies in which we invest and suppliers are partners.

Objectives
We carefully document, continually review and clearly communicate Progressive's values, mission, objectives and strategies. Individual objectives are negotiated, documented and are the basis for performance evaluation.

The artist's vision often inspires me to consider crazy alternatives — one of which may be our next marketing innovation.

Deborah Kass
Untitled
Oil on canvas
1986

Transportation Business

1987 net premiums written for the group were $165 million, 65% more than 1986. 1987 underwriting results (12% loss) were worse than 1986 (8% loss) in part because we wrote off the costs of ending several unsuccessful experiments. We are optimistic about the prospects for our continuing businesses. We ended 1987 with 974 people.

Stephen J. Leaman
Group President

The mission of the Transportation Group is to become the leading provider of insurance and related services to motor carriers. We organized by customer for more than twelve different carrier types such as truckload, less-than-truckload, tankers, charter buses and limousines. We serve all fleet sizes. The Transportation Group operates under the trade name of NCI Transportation Services.

In 1987, we more than doubled our staff to 540 people. Many who joined us in 1987 are experienced senior managers in the areas of safety, actuarial, underwriting, sales and claims. Their experience and expertise enhances our ability to respond to customer needs and to manage our growing business. The staff now includes 44 safety services people who have more than 500 years of combined experience in transportation safety, 175 people in transportation claims who work with Progressive's 150 field claims offices to handle each transportation claim in the best way and 50 direct sales representatives. We ended 1987 with more than 300 large fleet and 4,000 small fleet customers, with a total of over 50,000 power units. This staff can effectively manage a nationwide transportation insurance and service business. Growth in staff will moderate in 1988.

Market price declines in 1987 are expected to continue in 1988. We use our loss experience and outside sources to estimate the real cost of exposures. We will not sell insurance or service below our cost estimates.

Results of our comprehensive program to reduce the total cost of accidents for our customers are encouraging. This program includes reducing the frequency of accidents through effective safety programs, reducing claim payments by having specialized claims adjusters handle claims on a timely basis and greater customer risk retention. We will emphasize the benefits of this approach during 1988.

1987 net premiums written for the Transportation Group were $151 million, compared to $66 million in 1986. The GAAP combined operating ratio was 105, compared to 123 in 1986. These results met our expectations.

Bruce W. Marlow
Chief Operating Officer

Sometimes unpredictable and controversial.

Andy Warhol
Truck
Silkscreen
1986

Investment Strategies

What we invest in and how we manage investing is driven by the fact that insurance is our primary business, requiring current value capital always to be adequate to support planned insurance premium volume. For this reason, and because investment assets should be marked to market, we concentrate on high quality liquid assets which could produce lower earnings than would a more volatile portfolio. Because our insurance underwriting is generally profitable, investment income may be subject to maximum taxes, requiring us to consider the tax impact of each investment.

In 1971, when invested assets were $38 million, we retained and relied on Stein Roe & Farnham to suggest and execute investment strategy. Invested assets grew to $98 million in 1977, $357 million in 1983 and $1,354 million in 1987. As invested assets grew, Progressive people became more involved.

By 1984, our people had assumed responsibility for strategy. We increased our common stock holdings. More recently, we began to direct security selection and trading and to use new

investment vehicles. We had success with hedged equity strategies such as forward conversions. We traded baskets of stocks hedged against futures and used portfolio insurance. Our investment manager was primarily responsible for the strategy and results from 1984 through 1987. His recommendations were discussed with and approved by the Chairman and Finance and Investment Committee of the Board.

In investments, like insurance, Progressive searches continuously for better ways to achieve its objectives. Passing $1 billion of invested assets made investment a much higher priority for most senior management. Our new strategy is shaped by debate involving advisors and senior managers. The current strategy, in which partnership is central, is more risk averse and less difficult to account for and understand than our strategy has been in the past. Common

Many of our artists are young and emerging, just like many of us.

Larry Brown
Niagara II
Oil on wood
1987

Ten Year Summary — Consolidated Operating Results

(Not covered by report of independent auditors)

(millions — except per share amounts)	1987	1986	1985	1984	1983	1982	1981	1980	1979	1978
Direct premiums written:										
Personal lines	$ 690.2	$526.2	$3[illegible]6.4	$264.1	$216.3	$221.6	$189.1	$136.2	$121.2	$ 95.0
Commercial lines	488.0	303.9	145.0	47.1	28.4	25.6	22.3	21.1	18.2	17.0
Total direct premiums written	1,178.2	830.1	541.4	311.2	244.7	247.2	211.4	157.3	139.4	112.0
Net reinsurance ceded	61.7	49.2	18.5	2.7	2.3	.3	1.7	1.5	1.3	1.4
Net premiums written	1,116.5	780.9	522.9	308.5	242.4	246.9	209.7	155.8	138.1	110.6
Change in unearned premiums reserve	122.1	103.7	78.1	35.0	(.6)	7.1	22.1	15.7	6.3	17.6
Premiums earned	994.4	677.2	444.8	273.5	243.0	239.8	187.6	140.1	131.8	93.0
Losses and loss adjustment expenses	571.9	406.6	288.4	176.2	147.8	165.9	115.9	72.9	80.7	55.4
Policy acquisition costs	292.6	190.2	130.1	82.5	81.3	77.6	58.7	43.4	42.7	30.5
Other underwriting expenses	74.4	51.8	26.4	21.4	11.3	8.9	6.5	4.1	4.3	2.4
Total operating expenses	938.9	648.6	444.9	280.1	240.4	252.4	181.1	120.4	127.7	88.3
GAAP underwriting profit (loss) before taxes	55.5	28.6	(.1)	(6.6)	2.6	(12.6)	6.5	19.7	4.1	4.7
Provision (benefit) for Federal income taxes	12.2	13.1	(.7)	(3.8)	1.0	(6.1)	2.5	9.0	1.2	2.1
GAAP underwriting profit (loss) after taxes	43.3	15.5	.6	(2.8)	1.6	(6.5)	4.0	10.7	2.9	2.6
Other operations after taxes	.8	—	(.6)	1.9	1.6	2.2	2.1	1.2	.9	.5
Operating income (loss) after taxes	44.1	15.5	—	(.9)	3.2	(4.3)	6.1	11.9	3.8	3.1
Investment income net of expenses	60.7	48.6	34.3	25.5	24.3	25.0	17.6	11.9	10.1	7.2
Provision for Federal income taxes	7.0	5.5	4.1	3.2	3.4	4.1	2.2	1.0	1.1	1.0
Investment income after taxes	53.7	43.1	30.2	22.3	20.9	20.9	15.4	10.9	9.0	6.2
Interest expense after taxes	6.5	3.3	4.8	3.3	3.5	4.7	2.4	1.3	1.4	.8
Net investment income after taxes	47.2	39.8	25.4	19.0	17.4	16.2	13.0	9.6	7.6	5.4
Income before security sales	91.3	55.3	25.4	18.1	20.6	11.9	19.1	21.5	11.4	8.5
Net realized gain (loss) on security sales	(1.5)	9.4	10.0	(4.2)	2.0	(13.0)	(5.3)	1.1	(.8)	(.5)
Extraordinary credit	—	—	.2	—	3.7	—	—	—	—	—
Cumulative effect of accounting change	3.7	—	—	—	—	—	—	—	—	—
Net income (loss)	93.5	64.7	35.6	13.9	26.3	(1.1)	13.8	22.6	10.6	8.0
Net unrealized gain (loss)	(18.1)	3.6	13.0	(.9)	3.3	38.2	(8.9)	(15.0)	(4.8)	(3.8)
Extraordinary credit	—	—	(.2)	—	(3.7)	—	—	—	—	—
Total return income	$ 75.4	$ 68.3	$ 48.4	$ 13.0	$ 25.9	$ 37.1	$ 4.9	$ 7.6	$ 5.8	$ 4.2
Per share:										
Income before security sales	$ 3.16	$ 1.98	$ 1.13	$ .84	$ .83	$ .48	$ .73	$ .79	$ .40	$ .29
Net income (loss)	3.23	2.31	1.57	.64	1.06	(.04)	.52	.83	.38	.28
Total return income	2.61	2.44	2.11	.60	1.05	1.50	.19	.28	.20	.15
Dividends	.230	.058	.051	.047	.045	.040	.038	.036	.027	.021
Average equivalent shares	28.9	28.5	23.5	21.7	24.7	24.8	26.2	27.2	28.1	29.6

All share and per share amounts were adjusted for stock split-ups.

CLIENT:
THE PROGRESSIVE CORPORATION

DESIGN FIRM:
NESNADNY & SCHWARTZ

ART DIRECTOR:
JOYCE NESNADNY

DESIGNER:
JOYCE NESNADNY

PHOTOGRAPHERS:
NESNADNY & SCHWARTZ

ILLUSTRATOR:
VARIOUS

WRITER:
THE PROGRESSIVE CORPORATION

PRODUCTION MANAGER:
MARK SCHWARTZ

TYPOGRAPHER:
TYPESETTING SERVICES INC.

PAPER SELECTION:
CAMEO DULL 100/100

PAPER MANUFACTURER:
SD WARREN

PRINTER:
FORTRAN PRINTING

NUMBER OF PAGES:
62 PLUS COVER

SIZE:
8 1/2" X 11"

TYPE SELECTION:
BODONI

TOBY LEWIS, CURATOR OF THE ART COLLECTION OF CORPORATE ART, THE PROGRESSIVE CORPORATION, MAYFIELD HEIGHTS, OHIO

At the Progressive Corporation, we have wonderful art in our collection. We needed a link of having the art work tie in with Progressive's annual report. We did some brainstorming and we decided to bring the people of the company in by asking what they thought of the art in their offices. The pieces of art we collected over the last few years have added to the Progressive Corporation. In this annual report, we show the art beginning on the front page (with the first part of a Barbara Kruger work) and we continue to feature art pieces throughout the book. In general, the annual report was well-received. The most frequent negative comment was that the annual report was so white that it picked up dirt.

MARK SCHWARTZ AND JOYCE NESNADNY, NESNADNY & SCHWARTZ, CLEVELAND, OHIO

The Progressive Corporation has used art in its annual report for years. What we needed to do in this annual report was to make some sense of the corporate culture and corporate ideals in relation to the art. What we decided on with the firm was to use feedback from the Progressive employees, and this would provide a dialogue about the art within the context of their company, their working lives. The art was a "wish list" of contemporary works, outstanding pieces by exciting artists. With the art featured, we had the quotes from the Progressive staff. We had originally wanted to tie the annual report to key words from management, but the tie-in was more effective as quotes on the art.

TOBY LEWIS, CURATOR OF THE ART COLLECTION OF CORPORATE ART, THE PROGRESSIVE CORPORATION, MAYFIELD HEIGHTS, OHIO

Die Progressive Corporation besitzt eine beachtliche Kunstsammlung . Wir brauchten eine Verbindung zwischen den Kunstwerken und dem Jahresbericht. Wir beschlossen, die Mitarbeiter der Firma miteinzubeziehen und sie zu fragen, was sie von den Kunstwerken in ihren Büros halten. Die Kunstwerke, die wir im Laufe der letzten Jahre gesammelt haben, sind ein Gewinn für die Progressive Corporation. In diesem Jahresbericht zeigen wir von der ersten bis zur letzten Seite Kunst (wir beginnen mit dem ersten Teil einer Arbeit von Barbara Kruger). Der Bericht wurde allgemein sehr gut aufgenommen. Die am häufigsten geäusserte Kritik bezog sich auf die Schmutzempfindlichkeit des Berichts.

MARK SCHWARTZ UND JOYCE NESNADNY, NESNADNY & SCHWARTZ, CLEVELAND, OHIO

Die Progressive Corporation hat seit Jahren in ihren Geschäftsberichten Kunst gezeigt. In diesem Jahresbericht wollten wir die Firmenkultur und Firmenphilosophie in Verbindung mit der Kunstsammlung darstellen. Wir beschlossen, Kommentare der Angestellten einzusetzen, so dass ein Dialog über Kunst im Zusammenhang mit ihrer Arbeit entstehen würde. Wir zeigten zeitgenössische Kunst, besondere Stücke ausgezeichneter Künstler. Daneben erschienen die Kommentare der Angestellten. Ursprünglich hatten wir geplant, den Jahresbericht auf die Hauptaussagen des Managements auszurichten, aber die Zitate zum Thema Kunst eigneten sich besser.

TOBY LEWIS, CURATOR OF THE ART COLLECTION OF CORPORATE ART, THE PROGRESSIVE CORPORATION, MAYFIELD HEIGHTS, OHIO

La collection d'art de la Progressive Corporation contient des œuvres d'une très grande beauté. Nous voulions associer la qualité de cet art au rapport annuel de Progressive. Nous avons décidé de faire participer le personnel en sollicitant son opinion sur les tableaux accrochés dans les bureaux. Les œuvres d'art réunies ces dernières années pour le compte de la Progressive Corporation ont enrichi son partrimoine. Dans ce rapport annuel, nous démarrons dès la première page avec une partie d'une œuvre de Barbara Kruger et alignons des œuvres tout au long de l'ouvrage. Ce rapport a été bien accueilli. La plupart des critiques ont porté sur la blancheur du papier, qui signale cruellement les empreintes.

MARK SCHWARTZ ET JOYCE NESNADNY, NESNADNY & SCHWARTZ, CLEVELAND, OHIO

Depuis des années, la Progressive Corporation illustre ses rapports annuels d'œuvres d'art. Ce qu'il nous fallait dans ce nouveau rapport annuel, c'était de mettre en perspective l'effort culturel de cette société et l'idéal qu'elle poursuit dans ce domaine. Nous avons donc décidé d'utiliser les commentaires du personnel, de manière à obtenir un dialogue sur la place de l'art dans leur vie active. Les œuvres d'art représentées sont des œuvres contemporaines de tout premier plan réalisées par des artistes inspirés. Finalement la mise en parallèle des œuvres et des citations les concernant s'est avérée plus efficace qu'une série d'exposés sans relation directe avec l'illustration.

THE L.J. SKAGGS AND MARY C. SKAGGS FOUNDATION

PRESIDENT'S LETTER

1987 was a very active year for our Foundation in a number of respects. First, we distributed 309 grants, totalling $2,798,192. Second, we moved our offices for the first time since the organization of the Foundation in 1967. Third, the effects of October's activities on Wall Street, which reduced our equity portfolio by almost 30 percent in value, have a great impact upon our grant-making capability. The Directors, from the first days of the Foundation, have used the total return concept for its investment portfolio which meant that most funds for grants came from capital gains on the transfer of securities. In years of a rising market this has been most beneficial, but as you will see from the financial statements in this report, in 1987 there was a decline in our fund balance of over $2,000,000.

The Directors, at their November 1987 meeting, determined to award the grants recommended by the staff of the Foundation for 1988 funding even though there would be a further reduction in our fund balance. However, the Directors also determined that for the next five years the amount of grants awarded would be cut back from the level of the past several years by approximately 20 percent. The Directors recognize that further invasion of principal might occur during this period but, upon advice of our investment counselors, it is believed that at the end of five years our grants can again be funded completely from the total return on the investment portfolio. The staff has been directed to work with our grantees to implement this decision with as little negative impact as possible. I am confident that with creative grantmaking our

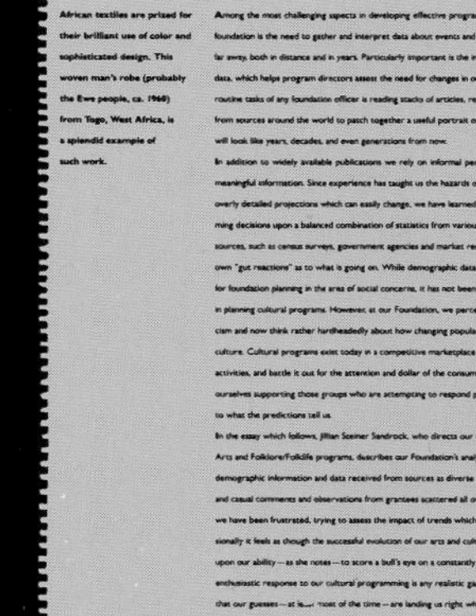

African textiles are prized for their brilliant use of color and sophisticated design. This woven man's robe (probably the Ewe people, ca. 1960) from Togo, West Africa, is a splendid example of such work.

BULL'S EYE ON A MOVING TARGET:
ART FOR A SOCIETY IN TRANSITION

Since the inception of the Foundation's Folklore/Folklife Program eight years ago, we have made new friends all across the nation as we expand and initiate programs. The quotation at right is excerpted from a longer letter from Professor Daniel Patterson, Chairman of the Curriculum in Folklore at the University of North Carolina at Chapel Hill, a longtime colleague and grantee of the Foundation, one of many individuals who have periodically provided us with valuable information on changing times in their regions. Professor Patterson's remarks echo similar observations we are receiving from all around the country—grantees and applicants reporting on the much-publicized changes in our country's demographic makeup.

For decades, researchers and demographers have pronounced that by the year 2000, the United States will have a very different look and feel, as large numbers of immigrants continue to pour in from Asia and Latin America. Many have also predicted the decline of the middle class as we know it, and the emergence of a two-tier society, consisting mainly of well-to-do Baby Boomers, who are beginning their families later and rely on a working woman to help meet the costs associated with a more comfortable lifestyle, and a vast "underclass", many of whom will be the new immigrants and other minorities.

The rise to prominence of the "Baby Boom" generation—those born between 1946 and 1964—has profound implications for our society in general, and—along with social service providers—arts funders have much to gain from studying this population group and their needs and interests. A few facts: there are 80 million of them—and as they reach their peak earning power, they will pump billions of dollars into the American marketplace. The majority are two-income couples; in fact, 69 percent of them need two incomes to make their mortgage payments. Estimates are that over the next few decades more than 75 percent of American women will be in the workforce—and many of them will postpone beginning their families until quite late in life.

This group will be financially cautious and conservative, (80 percent profess having "traditional values" and want their children to attend college) hoping to achieve the very best for the children they have waited so long to have, and many will also—after a long day at work—be willing

Images of death and spirits figure prominently in much of the world's folk art, and many beautiful objects are produced for use in funerary or mourning rites. This 1986 painting by Haitian artist Alberto Bazile has an exuberant and joyful quality, despite the somber topic.

to spend significant sums of money on time-saving devices which will assist in making their time at home more efficient and productive. Not surprisingly, market research projects a huge demand for home computers (15 million are already in use worldwide), telephone answering machines, catalog sales with personalized shopping services attached to "800" toll-free numbers, home entertainment equipment, and other goods and services designed to make domestic life convenient and enjoyable. With growing traffic congestion and longer commute distances, these individuals may be less willing to venture back downtown for evening arts events, particularly when children are young. Sports and weekend "family recreation" activities will compete ever more fiercely with the arts for the consumer's leisure time and dollars as their families grow. Large markets are already developing for quality children's products to satisfy the demand from older parents who want to be assured that their children have "the best".

Together with the influx of a huge number of immigrants who also will develop into a powerful market force, what implications can all this have for a foundation's cultural grant planning? We believe that there will be multiple changes and influences which will be felt by the arts groups we support, but one key factor is that the arts market may well become more conservative as the baby boomers age, less prepared to spend money on the experimental and avant-garde, but with greater interest in theatre, opera, symphony and the larger dance companies. But we expect that there will simultaneously be an increasing interest in the aesthetics of other cultures as Americans see more evidence of international influences all around them in their daily lives. (For example, several California school districts already report as many as thirty languages spoken by students in urban schools—creating both fascinating new opportunities as well as tremendous difficulties for arts educators).

In the coming multi-cultural community, many arts consumers may respond most positively to groups which offer an educational—rather than experimental—experience for them and their children. We also anticipate that the arts and culture of other countries—and our own American folk art—will emerge as strong influences on the cultural life of the next several decades because much of it is immediately comprehensible and accessible to a broad audience, affirms community, family and traditional values and folk morals, and can easily accommodate children's educational activities.

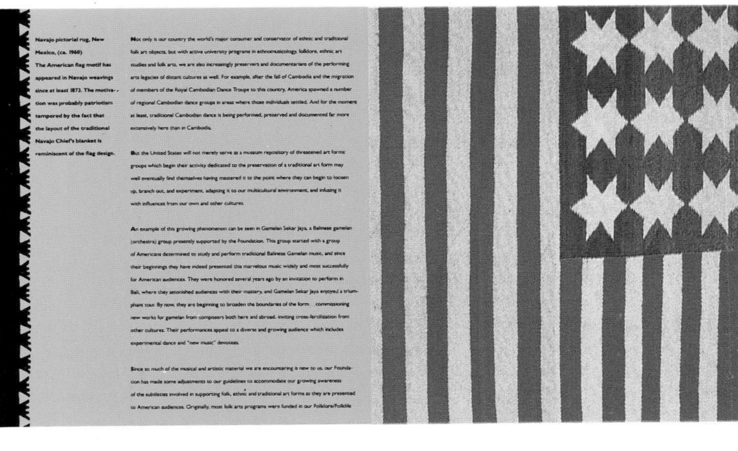

30

Navajo pictorial rug, New Mexico, (ca. 1960)
The American flag motif has appeared in Navajo weavings since at least 1873. The motivation was probably patriotism tempered by the fact that the layout of the traditional Navajo Chief's blanket is reminiscent of the flag design.

Not only is our country the world's major consumer and conservator of ethnic and traditional folk art objects, but with active university programs in ethnomusicology, folklore, ethnic art studies and folk arts, we are also increasingly preservers and documentarians of the performing arts legacies of distant cultures as well. For example, after the fall of Cambodia and the migration of members of the Royal Cambodian Dance Troupe to this country, America spawned a number of regional Cambodian dance groups in areas where those individuals settled. And for the moment at least, traditional Cambodian dance is being performed, preserved and documented far more extensively here than in Cambodia.

But the United States will not merely serve as a museum repository of threatened art forms: groups which begin their activity dedicated to the preservation of a traditional art form may well eventually find themselves having mastered it to the point where they can begin to loosen up, branch out, and experiment, adapting it to our multicultural environment, and infusing it with influences from our own and other cultures.

An example of this growing phenomenon can be seen in Gamelan Sekar Jaya, a Balinese gamelan (orchestra) group presently supported by the Foundation. This group started with a group of Americans determined to study and perform traditional Balinese Gamelan music, and since their beginnings they have indeed presented this marvelous music widely and most successfully for American audiences. They were honored several years ago by an invitation to perform in Bali, where they astonished audiences with their mastery, and Gamelan Sekar Jaya enjoyed a triumphant tour. By now, they are beginning to broaden the boundaries of the form... commissioning new works for gamelan from composers both here and abroad, inviting cross-fertilization from other cultures. Their performances appeal to a diverse and growing audience which includes experimental dance and "new music" devotees.

Since so much of the musical and artistic material we are encountering is new to us, our Foundation has made some adjustments to our guidelines to accommodate our growing awareness of the subtleties involved in supporting folk, ethnic and traditional art forms as they are presented to American audiences. Originally, most folk arts programs were funded in our Folklore/Folklife

24

Signs appearing in village streets throughout the world have provided opportunities for anonymous artists and artisans to express their creativity. Very often signs convey subtle—and not so subtle—clues about the business within—as with this Haitian bar sign (ca. 1960).

category, but we now try generally to keep "authenticity" an important element of eligibility for consideration in that program, so that art forms freely adapting from other aesthetics or borrowing sophisticated lighting or staging techniques from the Western theatrical arts are no longer considered to be appropriate for consideration under that category. Since many of these programs are excellent ones, we have just created a new "World Performance" program within our Performing Arts category to enable us to include groups whose work derives from ethnic and folk traditions—but who present their work in a standard proscenium format "adapted" to the needs of conventional staged presentation.

Within our Visual Arts category we will now also fund programs in folk art as well as receive applications in our ongoing Crafts/Architecture/Design program. This will permit us to fund selected visual arts programs where work is based upon folk or ethnic material but also is not necessarily "traditional" enough to be appropriate for funding within our Folklore/Folklife grant category.

We are certain that the next few years will see exciting and stimulating developments in the arts world and we hope to position ourselves so that we can respond swiftly to the demographic shifts we will be experiencing all around us. Just as Dr. Patterson has reported to us of profound changes occurring in the South, even a simple walk around the area surrounding our offices in Oakland also confirms that our ability to select and support the best offerings of the cultural life of the future will depend upon our ability to absorb new information and respond readily to it. We must be prepared to come to new art forms with open eyes and hearts, and be willing to spend time and energy to learn about other cultures and values as they materialize on our street corners, in schools, homes, concert halls and galleries. Creative arts funding may indeed feel like trying to hit a skittish and ever-changing target, but even with the hopefully rare, but inevitable mistakes we will make, we are still thankful for the opportunity to learn of new customs, values and expressions from artists who have valuable, beautiful and brilliantly colored new threads to weave into the fabric of American society.

Jillian Steiner Sandrock

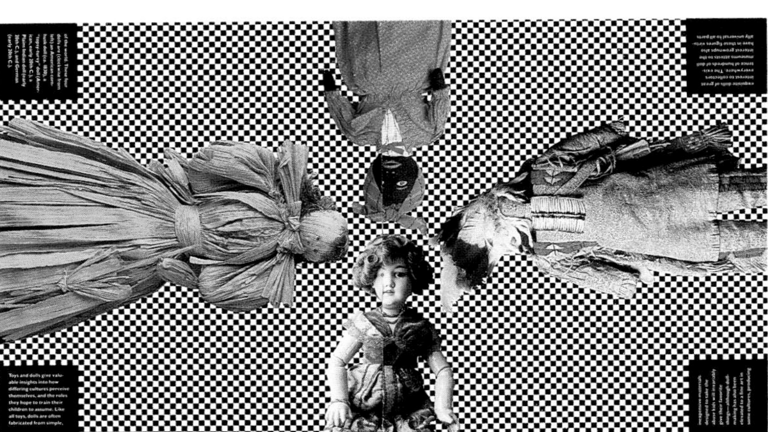

G R A N T S P A I D I N 1 9 8 7

PROJECTS OF HISTORIC INTEREST

Cabrillo College, Aptos, California
Support for program to research the history of the native American and Spanish colonial era in Santa Cruz County using as a focus the activities of the Franciscan Mission. The research will provide the basis for the State Department of Parks and Recreation's interpretation of the Santa Cruz Mission Historical Park and provide data for Santa Cruz County Office of Education in developing curriculum on local heritage and for the bicentennial celebration of the founding of Santa Cruz Mission in 1791.
$7,500

Center for Southern Folklore, Memphis, Tennessee
First installment of three-year grant totalling $30,000 to organization dedicated to increasing awareness of the cultural and historical heritage of the South.
$10,000

Colonial Williamsburg Foundation, Williamsburg, Virginia
Third installment of a four-year grant totalling $100,000 to assist in the interpretative program at Williamsburg to explore and document the development of a thoroughly American legal system under English colonial rule. This grant will focus on the historic courthouse of 1770 at Williamsburg and will include architectural, historical and decorative arts research.
$25,000

Desert Research Institute, Reno, Nevada
General support of archaeological project at Arroyo Cuervo in New Mexico. The project, which has been ongoing for approximately 20 years, is developing evidence which will allow scientists to understand how Arroyo Cuervo's occupants evolved from small bands of hunting and plant gathering nomads 7,000 years ago to the first village dwellers whose descendants are today's Pueblo Indians.
$15,000

East Bay Negro Historical Society, Inc., Oakland, California
Second installment of a three-year grant totalling $30,000 to assist in the transition of the Society from a purely volunteer operation to a professionally staffed organization. The Society has accumulated archives and, in addition to its many educational programs throughout the East Bay, provides resource material for researchers of historical matters relating to the Black communities of the East Bay.
$10,000

Galveston Historical Foundation, Galveston, Texas
Second installment of a three-year grant totalling $50,000 for the archaeological project at Ashton Villa, an 1859 house museum of the Historical Foundation. The project will unearth several feet of filled dirt used during the grade raising of Galveston following the great 1900 hurricane. Old foundations, stairways, cisterns and artifacts will be excavated and interpreted.
$20,000

Hangtown's Gold Bug Park, Placerville, California
Grant to assist in the preparation of the master plan, design and implementation program for the historical and cultural interpretation of Hangtown's Gold Bug Mine.
$10,000

Historic Deerfield, Inc., Deerfield, Massachusetts
Grant, to match NEH funds, for an archaeological and documentary study of land use in the village of Deerfield, Massachusetts. The project will explore archaeological and documentary resources and present preliminary studies of landscape change in the village of Deerfield to support the accurate reinstallation of museum buildings and their environments and to inform the public of the living patterns and material culture of the Connecticut Valley from settlement to urbanization.
$15,000

Hoghton Tower Preservation Trust, Hoghton, Lancashire, England
Grant to support development of educational programs and interpretation schemes at historic English house.
$15,000

ICCROM, Rome, Italy
First installment of two-year grant totalling $40,000 to assist in the training of African conservators and museum technicians. The program will include conservation courses on textiles, wooden objects and collections and techniques applicable to African artifacts. In addition to courses given in Rome, seminars and other programs will be held in African countries.
$20,000

Institute of Early American History and Culture, Williamsburg, Virginia
First installment of three-year grant totalling $45,000 to assist in program of conferences, research and publications on colonial and revolutionary American history and culture.
$15,000

International Council on Monuments and Sites (U.S.), Washington, D.C.
Final installment of a four-year grant totalling $40,000 to assist in the preparation of the 1987 General Assembly of the International Council on Monuments and Sites held in Washington, D.C.
$10,000

Marshall Media Arts Center, Marshall, California
Grant to support historic preservation program in Nevada County, California, including oral histories, cataloguing documents, collecting and copying letters, photographs and documents of pioneer families as well as preservation and restoration of Gold Rush era cemeteries and preparation of education programs.
$5,000

Montana Historical Society, Helena, Montana
Grant to support photo documentation of murals painted during the 1930's under WPA programs in six Montana post offices.
$5,000

Mt. Vernon Ladies Association, Mt. Vernon, Virginia
Final installment of a four-year grant totalling $100,000 for archaeological research at George Washington's Mt. Vernon estate. This comprehensive study assisted in the planning of future restoration and reconstruction projects as well as educational programs. The survey identified existing foundations, building sites, garden plans, walls, wells, cisterns and roads.
$25,000

32

Sisterhood Is Global Institute, New York, New York
Grant to a project to handle emergency support movements for individual women who have been censored, jailed, tortured, exiled or otherwise persecuted for activities on behalf of female human rights.
$10,000

Third World Movement Against the Exploitation of Women, Manila, Philippines
Grant to this international organization of women from 50 countries working to stop female sexual slavery (prostitution and trafficking in women) through a series of educational activities including a newsletter, speaking engagements, conferences and collaboration with other international agencies; for a program on military prostitution in the Philippines which collaborates with chaplains in the U.S. military bases to increase male awareness of the harmfulness of "recreational" prostitution.
$10,000

University of Hawaii Foundation, Honolulu, Hawaii
(Grant cancelled due to inability to carry out project. Grant amount refunded in 1988.)
$10,000

TOTAL $142,500

PERFORMING ARTS

American Conservatory Theatre, San Francisco, California
Grant for general support.
$5,000

Berkeley Repertory Theatre, Berkeley, California
Grant to assist in acquisition of sound equipment and to support sound design for 1987 productions.
$10,000

Bilingual Foundation of the Arts, Los Angeles, California
Grant in suport of the completion of a new Hispanic-American opera with music by Ian Krouse entitled, "Lorca, Child of the Moon." Designed to be performed by smaller ensembles (such as at colleges and in regional opera settings), the work gives American audiences an introduction to the work of the great Spanish poet and playwright, Federico Garcia Lorca.
$5,000

Black Repertory Theatre, Berkeley, California
Grant to community oriented theatre which produces plays by black playwrights.
$2,000

California Theatre Council, Los Angeles, California
Grant to support annual conference for California theatre professionals, held at Stanford University.
$3,000

Consortium Recordings, Inc., Los Angeles, California
Grant in support of a compact disc recording of the chamber music of the composer Ernst Toch (1887-1964) whose centennial is being celebrated by UCLA with a number of special concerts, scholarly programs and lectures, films and other activities relating to Toch's life and times. The recording project was a part of the UCLA festivities.
$4,000

Dance Perspectives Foundation, New York, New York
Second installment of a two-year $20,000 grant in support of the completion of editorial preparation for the five volume *International Encyclopedia of Dance* which is scheduled to be published in 1988.
$10,000

Eureka Theatre, San Francisco, California
Grant to support partial salary of development director as well as the Individual Donor Campaign.
$6,750

Ferndale Repertory Theatre, Ferndale, California
Grant for salary supplements.
$1,250

Friends of Olympia Station, Inc. (Tandy Beal and Company), Santa Cruz, California
One of the three participants in the Foundation's Institutional Stabilization Program for Performing Arts grantees. Despite excellence in artistic quality and the ever-increasing renown of its artistic director, Tandy Beal, this company has had a difficult time fundraising because of its location away from a major metropolitan center. Thus, this company created a subsidiary profit-making venture (a coffeehouse) located in Santa Cruz to help to provide a steady source of operating funds. Our support was earmarked for development of the coffeehouse venture.
$50,000

GroveMont Theatre, Monterey, California
Grant to theatre company which produces a full season, including an annual free festival in the historic section of Monterey's waterfront. The festival includes several outdoor performances at the Custom House Plaza. This grant provided salary support to the general manager and artistic director.
$5,000

Kronos Performing Arts Association, San Francisco, California
Founded in 1973, the Kronos Quartet has specialized in the music of the 20th century, and has grown to be among the most highly acclaimed of the world's contemporary music performance specialists. Their continued organizational growth depends upon the ability of their staff to effectively manage their complex travel and booking arrangements. This grant assisted them with the purchase of a microcomputer system.
$5,000

Life On The Water, San Francisco, California
Grant to support partial underwriting for Leonard Pitt's *Not For Real.*
$3,000

Magic Theatre, San Francisco, California
Grant to support artistic and production salaries and fees for the 20th Anniversary Season.
$10,000

National Conference on Piano Pedagogy, Princeton, New Jersey
The National Conference on Piano Pedagogy provides a forum for discussion and training for piano teachers. They hold a conference at a major university site biennially, and this grant supported publishing the proceedings of their 1987 conference at the University of Michigan.
$3,500

The New Conservatory Children's Theatre Company and School, San Francisco, California
Grant to support a radio and print media campaign to increase enrollment and visibility of the school within the community.
$3,000

Oakland Ballet Company, Oakland, California
First installment of a three-year grant totalling $40,000 for the Oakland Ballet's Twentieth Anniversary Campaign to create The L. J. Skaggs and Mary C. Skaggs Foundation Choreographers Fund. This fund will assist with the underwriting of expenses associated with bringing to Oakland guest choreographers from around the world.
$12,000

Oakland Ensemble Theatre, Oakland, California
General support for company dedicated to multicultural issues.
$5,000

East Bay Community Foundation (East Bay Dance Series), Oakland, California
General operating support grant to a series of dance performances, utilizing the 325-seat Laney College Theatre, one of the finest in the Bay Area for dance. The 1987 series featured 27 different companies in 30 performances over a ten-week period, introducing East Bay audiences to local dance companies featuring widely divergent dance styles.
$5,000

One Act Theatre Company, San Francisco, California
General support.
$5,000

Oregon Shakespearean Festival, Ashland, Oregon
Grant to support company's 1987 production of *"Master Harold"... and the boys* by Athol Fugard.
$10,000

Philharmonia Baroque Orchestra, Berkeley, California
One of three participants in the Foundation's Institutional Stabilization Program for Performing Arts grantees. This $50,000 grant has been added to last year's $50,000 subvention and was placed in a fund functioning as an endowment for the orchestra, beginning the implementation of a plan to build towards a more stable funding base as the orchestra grows.
$50,000

Pickle Family Circus, San Francisco, California
Grant to support the Sponsor Liaison Project, designed to increase earned income to both the circus and sponsoring organizations.
$5,000

Pocket Opera, San Francisco, California
One of three participants in the Foundation's Institutional Stabilization Program for Performing Arts Grantees. As Pocket Opera continues to plan for the future, the need for a permanent home for the company has become paramount. Funds from the Foundation were placed in a special fund to support conversion of a movie theatre into a small non-profit performing space, the Waterfront Theatre.
$50,000

Sacramento Theatre Company, Sacramento, California
Grant to theatre company serving central Northern California for an audience development project under the direction of marketing consultant, Stephen Dunn, and production support for Eugene O'Neill's *A Moon For The Misbegotten.*
$10,000

San Francisco Ballet Association, San Francisco, California
Grant in support of the annual Student Showcase of the San Francisco Ballet School. Each year all 250 Professional Division students perform in the Opera House, with appearances by some of the younger children as well. This provides a stimulating performance experience to dance students, and also provides dancers within the main company a chance at choreography, an opportunity few of them are ever afforded elsewhere.
$10,000

San Francisco Early Music Society (MusicSources: A Public Center For Historically Informed Performance), San Francisco, California
General support grant to MusicSources Center. Created by well- known early music

56

Front cover: Ball toss game, France, late 19th–early 20th C., France (top and bottom). Left and right: Hand puppets, Western Europe. With exaggerated characteristics, each puppet represents a personality from the popular literature of the time. Performances included Shakespearean plays, political commentary, Biblical themes as well as the ever-popular "Punch and Judy" dramas.

Inside back cover: To the folk artist, very often "more is more"—this woven carrying cloth from Oaxaca (probably Huave, ca. 1950), has every square inch covered with an exuberant celebration of bird and animal life. A closer look shows that as in nature, no two of the figures are exactly alike.

CLIENT:
L.J. SKAGGS AND MARY C. SKAGGS FOUNDATION

DESIGN FIRM:
VANDERBYL DESIGN

ART DIRECTOR:
MICHAEL VANDERBYL

DESIGNER:
MICHAEL VANDERBYL

PHOTOGRAPHERS:
VARIOUS

WRITER:
JILLIAN STEINER SANDROCK

PRODUCTION MANAGER:
LINDA ANDERSON

TYPOGRAPHER:
ON LINE

PAPER SELECTION:
QUINTESSENCE AND SPECKLETONE

PRINTER:
GEORGE RICE & SONS

NUMBER OF PAGES:
56

SIZE:
8 1/2" X 9 1/2"

TYPE SELECTION:
GILL SANS

JILLIAN STEINER SANDROCK, ASSISTANT SECRETARY, PROGRAM DIRECTOR, THE L.J. SKAGGS AND MARY C. SKAGGS FOUNDATION, OAKLAND, CALIFORNIA

I had written the main essay in the annual report, which discussed the importance of multi-cultural influences on the future of art, including specifically folk art. In the annual report, we wanted to show many of the works indicated in the essay, an interplay showing demographics, impact and changing influences in our society. Our designer, Michael Vanderbyl, has an esthetic that is pared down and lean, but for this he pushed the decorative, busy look so evocative of folk art. The borders he used as a graphic device, for instance, are different on every page. His design unified it all. The response to this annual report for 1987 was fabulous. We felt that it was important that this report be beautiful, and also important that the report be read.

MICHAEL VANDERBYL, VANDERBYL DESIGN, SAN FRANCISCO, CALIFORNIA

The Skaggs Foundation is a non-profit organization and the annual report is the only report done all year. This concentrates on the area of grants, and on start-up, non-profit groups. The foundation deals with art with a little "a"–people's art, art as part of the community. The visuals we used in the annual report were from an international folk art museum in Sante Fe. These were colorful and bright and created visual excitement. We didn't want this to look Swiss; it had to be the furthest thing from minimal. It was active, with designs on top of designs.

JILLIAN STEINER SANDROCK, ASSISTANT SECRETARY, PROGRAM DIRECTOR, THE L.J. SKAGGS AND MARY C. SKAGGS FOUNDATION, OAKLAND, KALIFORNIEN

In meinem Text für den Jahresbericht ging es um die Bedeutung der Einflüsse verschiedener Kulturen auf die Kunst, ganz besonders auf die Volkskunst. Im Bericht wollten wir viele der von mir erwähnten Arbeiten zeigen und die demographischen Besonderheiten und Veränderungen unserer Gesellschaft verdeutlichen. Unser Designer, Michael Vanderbyl, setzt normalerweise sparsame Mittel ein, hier aber entschied er sich für das Dekorative, Lebendige, das bezeichnend für Volkskunst ist. Die als graphisches Element verwendeten Umrahmungen sind auf jeder Seite verschieden, verbinden sich aber zu einem einheitlichen Bild. Die Reaktionen auf den Jahresbericht waren phantastisch. Uns war es wichtig, dass dieser Bericht gut aussieht und dass er gelesen wird.

MICHAEL VANDERBYL, VANDERBYL DESIGN, SAN FRANCISCO, KALIFORNIEN

Die Skaggs Foundation ist eine Stiftung, und der Jahresbericht ist der einzige Geschäftsbericht innerhalb des Jahres. Im Mittelpunkt stehen Subventionen und Non-Profit-Gruppen. Die Stiftung befasst sich mit Kunst, d.h. mit Volkskunst, Kunst als Teil der Gesellschaft. Die im Jahresbericht verwendeten visuellen Elemente stammen aus dem Museum für Volkskunst in Santa Fe. Sie sind farbenfroh, leuchtend und ansprechend. Wir wollten keinen Schweizer Stil, keine Reduzierung auf das Minimum. Das Zusammenspiel mit dem Design hat funktioniert.

JILLIAN STEINER SANDROCK, ASSISTANT SECRETARY, PROGRAM DIRECTOR, THE L.J. SKAGGS AND MARY C. SKAGGS FOUNDATION, OAKLAND, CALIFORNIE

J'ai rédigé pour ce rapport annuel le texte principal traitant de l'importance que les influences pluriculturelles revêtent pour l'avenir de l'art, y compris les arts populaires. Nous avons voulu présenter dans le rapport un grand nombre des œuvres mentionnées en faisant autant de témoins des tendances démographiques et des transformations qui affectent notre société. Notre designer, Michael Vanderbyl, a pour une fois délaissé son esthétique dépouillée en faveur d'un style décoratif et animé représentatif de l'art populaire. Ainsi, la bordure utilisée comme élément graphique varie de page en page. Pourtant, cette disparité est unifiée au sein de son design. L'echo qu'a rencontré ce rapport annuel pour 1987 est proprement fabuleux.

MICHAEL VANDERBYL, VANDERBYL DESIGN, SAN FRANCISCO, CALIFORNIE

La Fondation Skaggs est une organisation sans but lucratif dont le rapport annuel est le seul document de gestion publié au cours de l'année. L'accent est mis sur les subsides accordés et sur les groupes sans but lucratif. La Fondation œuvre dans le domaine de l'art du peuple, l'art en tant que vécu communautaire. Nous devons les illustrations au musée international de l'art populaire de Santa Fé. Cette imagerie haute en couleur est propre à stimuler l'imagination visuelle. Nous n'avons pas voulu d'un look suisse et nous sommes situés à l'antipode de tout minimalime.

Southwestern Bell Foundation
1987 Annual Report

Message From the President

Our work would be easy if the Foundation could just send money to everybody who needed it. But there isn't enough for everyone and that fact became increasingly clear during 1987. Once again, we had a record number of requests, while our funding level remained constant: $11.9 million for more than 2,000 organizations.

When there's so much to be done, and not enough resources to do it all, you tend to take a bigger interest in what happens to every dollar you dispatch. Is it being used in the best way, to accomplish the most good?

All through 1987 we worked hard to get the right answers to those questions. We tried to put our money into projects that not only would meet a particular need but also help call attention to issues that were just coming into their own. While our interests are many, adult literacy was one of those issues. So were programs for children, pre-collegiate public education and taking the arts to the people.

We believe our dollars worked harder in these areas in two ways: first, by helping both up-and-coming and major nonprofit agencies make a difference in the areas they know best; and second, by calling attention to the issues themselves.

The agencies we assisted in 1987 got to know us not just as check writers but, we hope, as partners in helping solve the most deserving problems. In this way, our project funding activities spoke well for the direction we have set for our overall grants program. And that has made 1987 a year of great progress for the Southwestern Bell Foundation.

Gerald D. Blatherwick

Gerald D. Blatherwick
Chairman of the Board and President

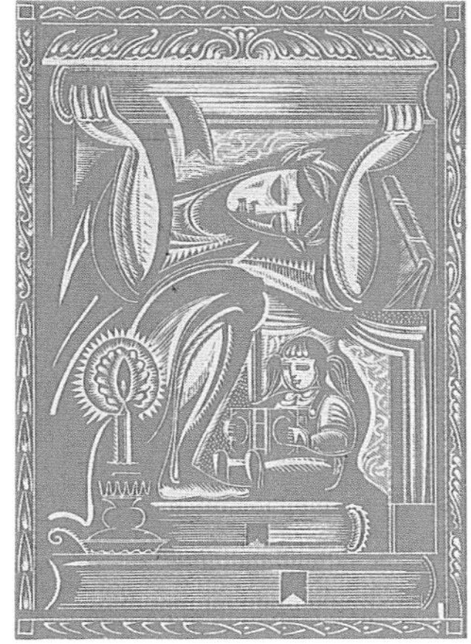

Initiatives in Pre-collegiate Public Education

Evidence suggests the quality of public education in America is failing. This comes at a time when the Information Age is causing the world to shrink and competition is increasing in world economies. No issue potentially affects the long-term economic and social future of the nation more than the quality of our public education system.

We must be able to think and express ourselves, be aware of our history and culture and the history and culture of others, and be unafraid of science and mathematics. And, in a country of diverse traditions, we are bound together by a sense of shared values, largely taught through the public education system.

Southwestern Bell Corporation is a major communications company that relies on informed employees and customers and depends on an informed public. The Foundation's choice of public education as a target issue is clear.

However, dollars alone can't solve the problem. The issues are complex. We can only make an impact by focusing our resources on a few carefully chosen pieces of the overall issue. Our aim is to at least influence the public debate. The public consensus emerging from this debate can and will lead to basic changes in public education.

We are convinced that the keys to improving education lie in the quality of the teachers, their freedom to teach and the degree to which parents work with them to encourage student discipline and study.

In 1987, the Foundation made several grants affecting public education. They include:

· A grant to the Coalition of Essential Schools at Brown University, headed by Dr. Theodore R. Sizer. The Coalition works to strengthen student learning by restructuring schools and giving greater authority to teachers as professionals. The grant will permit more information about the work of the Coalition to reach state governments, policymakers and other interested parties.

· A grant to the Rand Corporation's Center for the Study of the Teaching Profession, headed by Dr. Arthur Wise. The grant will underwrite a publication for general distribution summarizing several of the Center's studies dealing with the teaching profession.

· A grant to the Center for Educational Renewal, headed by Dr. John Goodlad, to partially underwrite efforts to redesign teacher education programs.

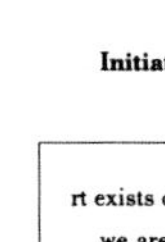

· A grant to Harvard University's Graduate School of Education to partially underwrite the Shared Leadership Program. This program is designed to reorient the traditional public school administrative structure by bringing teachers into the decision-making process.

"School reform must be both a political and a pedological effort — change within schools and, concurrently, change in the organizational and community context in which they exist. Both must proceed carefully in tandem."

Theodore R. Sizer
Chairman
Education Department
Brown University

Initiatives in Arts Outreach

Art exists only when there is an audience to appreciate it. In our initiatives, we are making art a reality for more people – young and old.

Our aim is to seek out and support nontraditional methods of bringing cultural activities to more people in more places. The programs we support span the spectrum: arts and crafts for children, traveling exhibits, touring symphonies and performing arts facilities.

Among the arts outreach activities undertaken in 1987:

· Foundation funding helped a local black history exhibit go on national tour. The funding allowed an exhibit by the Arkansas Endowment for the Humanities to travel to more than 70 sites, including many cities outside the state. The exhibit focused on the development of blacks in Arkansas.

· The Foundation also continued its support of the Arkansas Arts Center's Traveling Artmobile. The Artmobile, a gallery installed in a 40-foot tractor trailer, travels throughout rural Arkansas, exhibiting original works of art from the Arts Center's permanent collection. An artist/educator travels with the Artmobile, conducting tours, workshops and giving lectures about the exhibition.

· Music lovers in Moberly, Kirksville and St. Joseph, Mo. and Topeka, Kan., were the first audiences to hear the Saint Louis Symphony Orchestra when it began the National Endowment for the Arts/Southwestern Bell Foundation Regional Orchestra Tour last fall. Eleven more communities hosted performances by the Saint Louis and Houston symphony orchestras in 1988. This public/private partnership supported appearances by these world-class symphonies in towns that might not otherwise have been able to afford them.

· A "Hands Out to Children" program in Austin, Texas, gives many young people their first hands-on experiences in arts and crafts by taking the arts to shopping malls. Once curiosity is piqued, children and their parents learn more by visiting the young people's cultural outreach programs at the Laguna Gloria Arts Museum.

· The second year of the Kansas Arts Excellence Program brought the arts close to thousands of Kansans. Foundation funding supports the program, which helps underwrite the local performing arts and art education projects in Kansas communities that otherwise could not afford them.

· In Oklahoma, students looking for a career in the arts soon will have a new, permanent area for their summer arts training. The Foundation is helping underwrite new facilities at Quartz Mountain State Park that will support the Summer Arts Institute. Each summer at the Institute, young talent in the state will attend training sessions conducted by arts professionals.

"People who've never gone into a gallery, who've never had the sense of importance of the arts and visiting museums, now have access through the Arkansas Arts Center's Artmobile. With it, we can go places and reach people who've never before had the opportunity to see what the Arts Center has to offer."

Carolyn Staley
Director
State Services
The Arkansas Arts Center

The Foundation addresses many current needs of the community, but we do it with an eye on the future. Programs that can help prevent larger problems tomorrow or pay larger dividends are one way we can multiply our Foundation efforts.

Grants to education are good examples. So are projects involving children who face great risks in their lives.

Broken homes, drug abuse and other childhood traumas are present day realities. It never may be possible to eradicate these social ills. But we can support initiatives that offer greater opportunity to children at a time when encouragement and direction could prevent wasted lives.

These are a few of the 1987 grants for children at risk:

· A multi-year commitment to TARGET, a national organization that fights drug abuse among high school and junior high students. Established by the National Federation of High School Associations, TARGET provides training for teachers as well as material to be used when educating students on the dangers of drugs. The Foundation's grant was used to establish and staff a toll-free number to the organization's Resource Center. Schools and students from across the country now have immediate access to information on drug prevention programs.

· In Houston, the Foundation continues to support an outreach program encouraging Hispanic youth to join the Boy Scouts. This project has increased the number of Hispanics in Scouting in the Houston area from 1,600 in 1982 to more than 10,000 today. It has been shown that involvement in Scouting influences young people to stay in school and stay away from trouble. Foundation funds have been used to support the staffing of the outreach project, purchase uniforms and pay for camping fees for disadvantaged youth.

"Scouting is giving these kids a way to cope with the streets. They're learning discipline, respect and to be self-sufficient. They wouldn't have this opportunity without Scouting."

Joe Ramirez, Director Hispanic Scouting Sam Houston Area Council

· A grant to the Edgewood Children's Center in St. Louis is being used to expand therapy services and student centers. Edgewood is a residence for children with severe emotional disturbances. The home provides extensive individual, group, and family therapies and activities. In-patient as well as out-patient treatment allows a greater number of children to receive help.

· Foundation support for the Hugh O'Brian Youth Foundation also continued in 1987. HOBY brings together high school sophomores in leadership seminars around the country. Leading professionals in business, education, and the arts contribute their time and expertise to share ideas and concerns with these students. In 1988, Southwestern Bell Foundation will be a major underwriter for the nationwide Youth Leadership Conference to be held in St. Louis. The conference will bring together 10th graders from around the country to share in the HOBY experience.

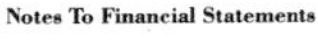

1. Summary of Significant Accounting Policies — Southwestern Bell Foundation ("Foundation") was incorporated in November 1984 under the laws of the State of Missouri. The Foundation was organized exclusively for charitable, scientific, literary and educational purposes, including for such purposes, the making of distributions to organizations that qualify as exempt organizations under Section 501(c)(3) of the Internal Revenue Code.

The accompanying financial statements are prepared on the accrual basis.

Long-term investments are stated at market value. The market value of investments traded on national securities exchanges or the over-the-counter market is based on published quotations. The market value of nonpublicly traded investments is determined by the investment trustee.

Other long-term assets primarily represent the Foundation's investment in a limited partnership. This investment is not publicly traded and is stated at cost.

Purchases and sales of long-term investments are recorded as of the trade date. Realized gains and losses on sales of long-term investments are determined on the basis of average cost.

Interest income is recognized as earned on the accrual basis. Dividend income is recognized on the ex-dividend date.

In accordance with the policy of stating long-term investments at market value, net unrealized appreciation or depreciation is reflected in the statement of changes in fund balance.

Grants authorized by the Board of Directors of the Foundation for payment in future years are subject to subsequent review and approval and are, therefore, recognized as expenses when paid.

2. Administrative Expenses — All administrative expenses of the Foundation, including investment trustee fees, are paid by Southwestern Bell Corporation and have not been recorded in the financial statements of the Foundation.

3. Federal Excise Tax — In accordance with the applicable provisions of the Internal Revenue Code, the Foundation is subject to and has provided a 2 percent excise tax on net investment income.

The Internal Revenue Code requires certain minimum distributions be made in accordance with a specific formula. At December 31, 1987 and 1986, the Foundation had distributed in excess of the required minimum.

4. Long-Term Investment Transactions — A summary of realized and unrealized gains or losses on long-term investments is as follows.

Realized gain on long-term investments sold:	1987	1986
Proceeds	$14,791,769	$5,965,622
Cost	13,232,019	5,143,618
	$ 1,559,750	$ 822,004

Unrealized gain (loss) on long-term investments held:	1987	1986
End of year	$ (2,394,714)	$ 233,195
Beginning of year	233,195	—
	$ (2,627,909)	$ 233,195

5. Commitments — The Board of Directors of the Foundation had approved, as of December 31, 1987, grants amounting to $6,557,000. Such grants are subject to the satisfaction by the intended recipients of prior conditions before payment. The commitments outstanding at December 31, 1987, are scheduled for payment as follows.

Year	Amount
1988	$2,727,000
1989	2,061,000
1990	1,282,000
1991	442,000
1992	45,000
	$6,557,000

The Board of Directors
Southwestern Bell Foundation

We have examined the accompanying balance sheets of Southwestern Bell Foundation at December 31, 1987 and 1986, and the related statements of changes in fund balance for the years then ended. Our examinations were made in accordance with generally accepted auditing standards and, accordingly, included such tests of the accounting records and such other auditing procedures as we considered necessary in the circumstances.

In our opinion, the financial statements mentioned above present fairly the financial position of Southwestern Bell Foundation at December 31, 1987 and 1986, and the results of its operations for the years then ended, in conformity with generally accepted accounting principles applied on a consistent basis during the period.

Arthur Young & Company

Arthur Young & Company
St. Louis, Missouri
March 8, 1988

CLIENT:
SOUTHWESTERN BELL CORPORATION

DESIGN FIRM:
HAWTHORNE/WOLFE

ART DIRECTOR:
DOUGLAS WOLFE

DESIGNER:
BUCK SMITH

ILLUSTRATOR:
STEPHEN ALCORN

WRITER:
JAMIE ANDERSON

PRODUCTION MANAGER:
KATE GORDON

TYPOGRAPHER:
COMPOSING ROOM

PAPER SELECTION:
MOHAWK SUPERFINE 100LB

PAPER MANUFACTURER:
MOHAWK

PRINTER:
GULF PRINTING

NUMBER OF PAGES:
24 PLUS COVER

SIZE:
7 5/8" X 11 3/4"

TYPE SELECTION:
BODONI ANTIQUA

CHARLES O. DERIEMER, EXECUTIVE DIRECTOR, SOUTHWESTERN BELL FOUNDATION, ST. LOUIS, MISSOURI

The Southwestern Bell Foundation was two years old in 1987 and this is its second annual report. The main intention of the report was to outline the Foundation's philosophy for awarding $12 million to over 2,000 non-profit organizations. The 1987 annual report featured four programs: adult literacy, programs for disadvantaged children, pre-college public education, and provision for cultural activity. The audience for the annual report includes key management employees, community leaders, other corporate foundations and organizations seeking grants. We feel the annual report did report well on what we did, and why we did it, especially in the use of the illustrations.

DOUGLAS WOLF, HAWTHORNE/WOLFE, ST. LOUIS, MISSOURI

Southwestern Bell Foundation's annual report announces how the organization gives its money away. We were required to use photographs provided to us, which we did, but the key to the success of this annual report was the selection of Stephen Alcorn as the illustrator. His literary, bookplate-style linocuts symbolized each of the four programs supported by the foundation. This annual report also had a soft image due to the use of muted colors and black text printed on uncoated, acid-free paper.

CHARLES O. DERIEMER, EXECUTIVE DIRECTOR, SOUTHWESTERN BELL FOUNDATION, ST. LOUIS, MISSOURI

Die Southwestern Bell Foundation war 1987 zwei Jahre alt, und dies war der zweite Jahresbericht. Er sollte vor allem über die Subventionen in Höhe von insgesamt $ 12 Millionen informieren, die diese Stiftung über 2000 gemeinnützigen Unternehmen gewährt. Es wurden vier Programme in folgenden Bereichen vorgestellt: Analphabetismus bei Erwachsenen, benachteiligte Kinder, Schulbildung und Kultur. Die Empfänger des Jahresberichtes sind Kaderangestellte, Verwaltungsbeamte, Stiftungen und Organisationen, die Subventionen benötigen. Der Jahresbericht informiert besonders dank der Illustrationen ausgezeichnet über unsere Aktivitäten.

DOUGLAS WOLFE, HAWTHORNE/WOLFE, ST. LOUIS, MISSOURI

Der Jahresbericht der Southwestern Bell Foundation gibt Auskunft darüber, wie diese Stiftung ihre Subventionen verteilt. Wir verwendeten die uns zur Verfügung gestellten Photos, das Besondere sind aber die literarischen, an Buchillustrationen erinnernden Linolschnitte von Stephen Alcorn. Sie symbolisierten jeden der vier von der Stiftung unterstützten Bereiche. Dieser Jahresbericht wirkt dank der gedämpften Farben und des ungestrichenen, säurefreien Papiers sanft und weich.

CHARLES O. DERIEMER, EXECUTIVE DIRECTOR, SOUTHWESTERN BELL FOUNDATION, ST. LOUIS, MISSOURI

En 1987, la Southwestern Bell Foundation bouclait son deuxième exercice. Le rapport annuel avait pour tâche de mettre en vedette la philosophie de la Fondation présidant à la distribution de 12 millions de dollars à plus de 2000 organisations sans but lucratif. A cet effet, le rapport détaille quatre programmes différents: l'alphabétisation des adultes, l'aide à l'enfance défavorisée, la promotion de l'enseignement secondaire public et celle des activités culturelles. Ce rapport annuel est destiné aux cadres d'entreprises, aux responsables politiques et sociaux, à d'autres fondations, ainsi qu'aux organisations sollicitant des subsides. Le rapport a parfaitement rempli son rôle.

DOUGLAS WOLFE, HAWTHORNE/WOLFE, ST. LOUIS, MISSOURI

Le rapport annuel de la Southwestern Bell Foundation énumère les récipiendaires des dons distribués par la société. Nous avons utilisé les photos fournies par le client. Pourtant ce sont les linogravures littéraires de Stephen Alcorn dans le style des ex-libris symbolisant chacun des quatre programmes subventionnés par la Fondation qui en ont fait un succès. Nous avons en outre adouci l'aspect physique du rapport en employant des couleurs mates et du papier non couché sans acide.

3Com Corporation 1987 Annual Report

Corporate Profile

3Com Corporation designs, manufactures, markets and supports workgroup computing systems for network-based, graphics-intensive applications. The company sells its products worldwide through value-added dealers, vertical-application resellers and computer manufacturers for resale to end users. The Company was incorporated in 1979 and completed its initial public offering of Common Stock in March 1984. Its stock is traded on the NASDAQ National Market System under the symbol COMS.

About the cover:

Increasingly, growing businesses are looking to networks of desktop PCs to improve the productivity of their office-based workforces. This year's annual report explains the industry trends driving the growth and acceptance of these workgroup systems. Increased productivity through workgroup systems is the key to enhancing 3Com's customers' ability to compete.

Financial Highlights

(dollars in thousands, except per share data)	Years Ended May 31 1987	1986	Increase (Decrease)
Sales	$110,377	$63,992	72%
Operating income	20,294	12,149	67%
Net income	11,146	6,681	67%
Net income per share	.76	.48	58%
Total assets	$88,679	$41,722	113%
Working capital	68,461	28,351	141%
Long-term obligations	174	717	(76%)
Retained earnings	24,119	12,973	86%
Shareholders' equity	76,352	32,710	133%
Number of employees	552	372	48%

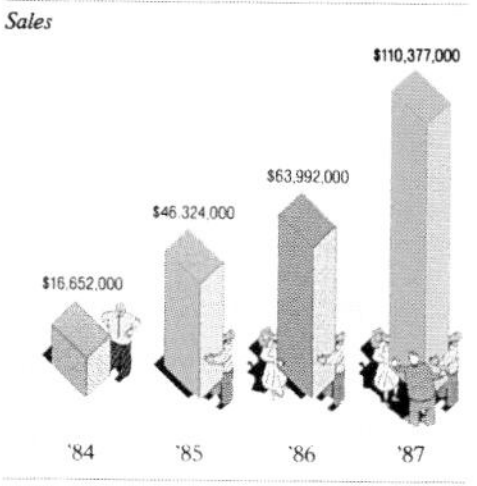

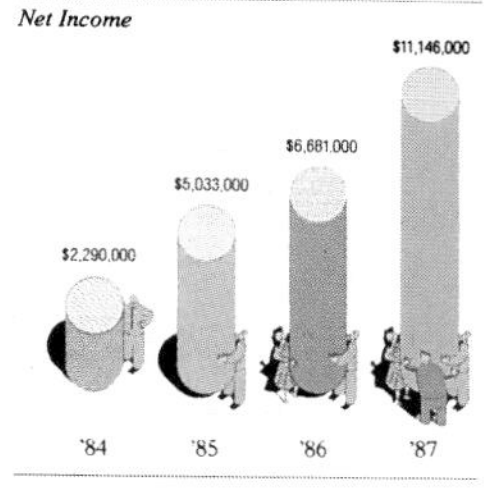

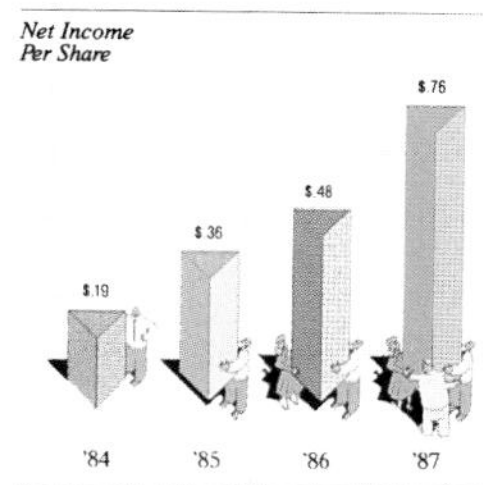

To Our Shareholders:

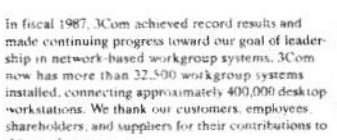

In fiscal 1987, 3Com achieved record results and made continuing progress toward our goal of leadership in network-based workgroup systems. 3Com now has more than 32,500 workgroup systems installed, connecting approximately 400,000 desktop workstations. We thank our customers, employees, shareholders, and suppliers for their contributions to this year's success.

3Com reached record levels in orders, sales, and net income in fiscal 1987. Orders were $111.0 million, up 68% from last year. Sales increased 72% over last year to $110.4 million. Net income was $11.1 million ($.76 per share), up 67% from the previous year. In addition to a second equity offering of 1.38 million shares, which netted the company $30.4 million, 3Com generated $3.9 million of positive cash flow during the year. The company finished fiscal 1987 with a record return on equity of 26.8%. 3Com has never been in a more sound financial position.

Market Trends The computer industry is discovering its next frontier and beginning a new era of growth. 3Com customers are increasingly looking to networks of personal computers (PCs) to gain dramatic improvements in the productivity of their office-based work force to compete more effectively worldwide. For the previous 4-5 years, the workgroup systems market has been in the development phase. This market's growth phase is now beginning, will continue for the next 4-5 years, and is forecast by industry experts to achieve a 50% compound annual growth rate. This growth is primarily being driven by the recognition that people in business do not work alone, the growing importance of industry standards and open system platforms, and the increasing availability of network-based application software. Additionally, customer success stories are beginning to abound, inspiring others to install workgroup systems.

Customers Achieving customer satisfaction second to none and marketing our products through value-added reseller channels of distribution continue as the cornerstones of our marketing strategy. During 1987, customers purchased more than 12,800 3Com workgroup systems. We continued to improve the quality and reliability of 3Com products. Warranty costs were less than 0.5% of sales, well below industry averages. The 3Server workgroup server product line achieved a mean time between failure of more than 7 years, well above industry averages. We certified 250 3Wizards in our new, advanced technical consulting program for workgroup systems engineering specialists. To provide increased technical support to our resellers and their customers, 3Com opened training and systems engineering centers in Santa Clara (Calif.), Dallas, Chicago, Rockville (Md.), and New York. We expanded our product training courses and graduated more than 3,725 3Com workgroup systems specialists.

We continue to see evidence that competent resellers, including value-added dealers (VADs) and vertical-application resellers (VARs), have the infrastructure to best serve the reported 7.1 million workgroups in both large and small companies. In 1987, we were pleased to add Tandy and NYNEX as authorized resellers of 3Com workgroup systems. Businessland continued as our largest dollar volume reseller, and resellers as a group represented 76% of the company's sales. In 1987, sales of 3Com products to original equipment manufacturers such as Hewlett-Packard, Xerox, Sun Microsystems, and Apollo Computers increased by 28% and represented 23% of 3Com's sales. International, which grew sales by 197%, was 3Com's fastest growing geographical market segment in 1987 and represented 24% of sales.

New Products We believe a continuous stream of innovative, high-quality new products is essential for 3Com to achieve its growth goal of at least 50% per year over the next 3-4 years. In 1987, we invested $9.3 million (8.4% of sales) in R&D and, to support our workgroup systems' focus, more than 60% of our engineers were involved in software developments. 3Com brought 9 new products to market this past year, which both expanded our workgroup systems offerings and enhanced our existing product lines. Among the new products were the 3Station, 3Com's first netstation optimized for use in a network-based workgroup system, which was awarded PC Magazine's coveted *Editors' Choice* award; 3Server3, our high-performance workgroup server; new EtherLink and TokenLink network adapters to allow customers to integrate general purpose PCs into 3Com systems, and the first Ethernet adapters for Apple's new Macintosh II; and enhancements to our 3+ network operating software, including the only capability available for internetworking popular third-party application software programs. 3+ celebrated its first anniversary, was recognized by Computerworld as the best networking software program of 1986, and was also awarded PC Magazine's prestigious *Editors' Choice* award.

In fiscal 1988, we plan to focus our R&D efforts on products that will differentiate our workgroup systems and gain competitive advantages based on four key features: (1) open architecture to support multivendor solutions, (2) ease of everything, (3) increased connectivity, and (4) a price performance range of application-compatible systems.

3Com People 3Com's ability to attract and retain capable and motivated people continues to be our number one critical success factor. Our organizational strategy emphasizes small, entrepreneurial teams of people operating with a great deal of independence, and we stress equity as our principal form of incentive for company performance. 3Com people increased their productivity to $238,000 in sales per person from the previous year's $203,000, and this was accomplished while increasing our work force from 372 people to 552 people at year end. We further strengthened our organization with the integration of sales, marketing, and customer service and promoted John Marman to lead this new division as Senior Vice President, Sales, Marketing & Services. We were also pleased that Jerry Dusa joined 3Com as Vice President, North American Field Operations.

Outlook for 1988 and Beyond We are the most optimistic and upbeat about 3Com's prospects for the future since becoming a public company in March 1984. In fiscal 1988, the benefit from lower corporate tax rates will be used to increase investments in new product developments and marketing to achieve four primary objectives: (1) exceed $165 million in orders, (2) continue to enhance customer satisfaction, (3) launch 10 new products and expand our markets, and (4) strengthen our competitive market position.

Looking ahead, there are four major trends driving the growth phase of the workgroup systems market: (1) downsizing computer platforms, (2) requirement for ease of everything, (3) desire for improved computer communication compatibility, and (4) convergence on and acceptance of industry standards. Workgroup systems are the progeny of these trends and are the key to enhanced productivity for growing businesses in the 1990s. As such, 3Com's mission has never been more clear—*lead in network-based workgroup systems that enhance our customers' ability to compete.* The pages that follow expound on how these trends are impacting business and review 3Com's participation in the workgroup systems market.

With our ambition for continued growth and market leadership, we are diligently working to better serve our customers, build a stronger company, manage for return on equity sufficient to fund our growth, and implement our vision of the evolving computing industry. Thank you for your interest and continuing support.

L. William Krause
President and Chief Executive Officer

Robert M. Metcalfe
Chairman of the Board

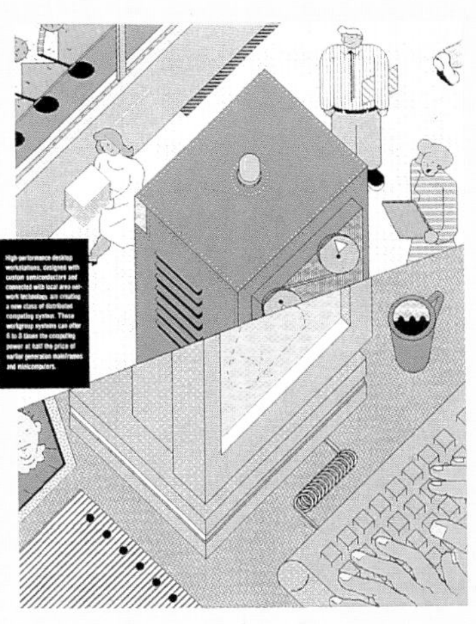

Downsizing Computer Platforms

3Com has contributed to the increasing momentum of the workgroup computing marketplace with the introduction of 3System, our first network-based workgroup system. A typical 3System consists of 3+, our network operating software providing minicomputer-like functionality to the workgroup, 3Server workgroup servers which are optimized for network applications, and 3Stations, our high performance networkstations with built-in graphics. 3System, based on an open architecture and using industry standards, uniquely permits the integration of IBM® PCs and compatibles and Apple Macintosh workstations with Ethernet, Token Ring and AppleTalk networks. This workgroup system interconnectivity and compatibility is achieved with 3Com's broad range of network adapters.

The proliferation of powerful desktop workstations like 3Station provides an unprecedented opportunity for new, network-based, graphics-intensive application software programs. In fact, many of these programs are tailored specifically for those applications that are inherently workgroup activities—activities such as publishing, decision support, communications, and computer-aided design and engineering.

To ensure that end customers have the best available solutions to their workgroup application needs, 3Com is building partnerships with leading software companies to develop, certify and support new application programs. To date, we have established relationships with more than 250 software companies, including such industry leaders as Adobe, Aldus, Ashton-Tate, Lotus, Microsoft and Software Publishing, and have tested many of their application programs with 3System.

"New hardware platforms are creating [illegible] for a new generation of network-based, graphics-intensive application software that dramatically improves the productivity of people working together in workgroups. Our ability to improve the way we do business is limited only by our imaginations."

Fred Gibbons, President
Software Publishing Corporation

One of 3Com's hallmarks is its strict adherence to industry standards. Standards expand engineering opportunities. Quality manufacturers and software developers readily expand their offerings knowing there will be a market for their products. And customers gain the flexibility to choose among a wealth of creative computing alternatives while protecting their investments against obsolescence and rapid technological change.

Our unswerving focus on standards creates a win/win situation for both 3Com and end customers. We can continually take advantage of the breadth of computer technology to provide the most current, state-of-the-art systems relatively easily, quickly and inexpensively. Standards also allow 3Com customers to interconnect their PCs, Macintosh workstations and 3Stations, permitting the valuable and transparent interchange of information through all levels of the corporation.

Our end customers are confident that their investments in 3Com systems are always guaranteed. They know we will provide an efficient and cost-effective expansion and/or upgrade path from their original 3Com system to our latest workgroup platform. For example, 3Com and Microsoft Corporation are co-developing the Microsoft OS/2 LAN Manager, the networked version of the new OS/2 multi-tasking operating system software. As application software developers increase their offerings to include new OS/2-based programs, 3Com customers will be able to take full advantage of these applications and the increased computing power of new OS/2-based servers and workstations, which will be easily and inexpensively integrated into their current 3Systems.

"Industry standards are the driving force behind the explosion of desktop workstations and the thousands of application software programs that run on them. Standards are providing the essential infrastructure for continued growth in what 3Com refers to as the Third Computing Millenium."

Bill Gates, *Chairman*
Microsoft Corporation

10

Convergence on Industry Standards

11

CLIENT:
3COM CORPORATION

DESIGN FIRM:
FRAZIER DESIGN/ MARILYN FRIEDMAN

ART DIRECTOR:
CRAIG FRAZIER

DESIGNERS:
CRAIG FRAZIER, DEBORAH HAGEMANN

PHOTOGRAPHER:
JOCK MCDONALD

ILLUSTRATOR:
JOHN HERSEY

WRITER:
BARBARA SHAPIRO

TYPOGRAPHER:
DISPLAY LETTERING + COPY

PAPER SELECTION:
VINTAGE DULL 100 LB COVER, CARNIVAL OFFSET 70 LB TEXT

PAPER MANUFACTURER:
POTLATCH, CHAMPION

PRINTER:
GRAPHIC ARTS CENTER

NUMBER OF PAGES:
24

SIZE:
81/2" X 11"

TYPE SELECTION:
TIMES ROMAN

BARBARA SHAPIRO, MANAGER, INVESTOR RELATIONS, 3COM CORPORATION, SANTA CLARA, CALIFORNIA

We like designers who like to brainstorm, so we piled them up with documents before we sat down to have a meeting on our 1987 annual report. Our company is concerned with computer networking; the 3Com stands for computer communication compatibility. We chose industry trends as our theme, and we decided on four of these. We featured macro-trends in the visual illustrations, and micro-trends in our editorial copy. It is hard to photograph a trend, so we decided on illustrations. These were done on a Macintosh computer, and they all featured people. The response we had was favorable, especially because the report made technology interesting.

CRAIG FRAZIER, FRAZIER DESIGN, SAN FRANCISCO, CALIFORNIA

In this annual report we needed to show what 3Com does: they manufacture networking systems. We had the objective of featuring what the company developed, how it was defined, why it was doing so well, and why it would continue to do well. There were a lot of things to say. As a vehicle for work group systems within the company, we decided on Macintosh-generated illustrations for ideas that would be hard to articulate. The company wanted to show people working, so we decided to tell the story via cartoon. These were done by John Hersey as high-style editorial cartoons. Everybody loves cartoons.With cartoons, you can take a complex subject and make it simple. These achieved the result that we wanted.

BARBARA SHAPIRO, MANAGER, INVESTOR RELATIONS, 3COM CORPORATION, SANTA CLARA, KALIFORNIEN

Wir mögen Designer, die ihren Kopf gebrauchen. Deshalb überhäuften wir sie mit Unterlagen, bevor wir unseren Jahresbericht für 1987 mit ihnen besprachen. Unsere Firma befasst sich mit der Vernetzung von Computern; 3Com steht für Computer-Kompatibilität. Als Thema wählten wir die Trends in der Industrie. Wir konzentrierten uns auf vier Bereiche. Macro-Trends wurden in den Illustrationen, Micro-Trends im Text behandelt. Ein Trend lässt sich schlecht photographieren, deshalb entschieden wir uns für Illustrationen, die mit einem Macintosh gemacht wurden. Alle zeigten Leute. Der Bericht kam gut an, weil Technologie interessant darstellt war.

CRAIG FRAZIER, FRAZIER DESIGN, SAN FRANCISCO, KALIFORNIEN

In diesem Jahresbericht sollte gezeigt werden, was 3Com macht: sie stellen Vernetzungssysteme her. Wir wollten zeigen, was die Firma entwickelt hat, warum die Geschäfte so gut gingen und warum sie sich weiterhin gut entwickeln werden. Als Ausdrucksmittel für Gruppenarbeit innerhalb der Firma wählten wir mit einem Macintosh hergestellte Illustrationen, um Ideen darzustellen, die man schwer in Worte fassen kann. Da wir Leute bei der Arbeit zeigen sollten, beschlossen wir, die Geschichte durch einen Cartoon zu erzählen. John Hersey machte sie im Stil redaktioneller Cartoons. Jeder mag Cartoons. Man kann mit ihrer Hilfe ein komplexes Thema einfach darstellen. Das ist uns gelungen.

BARBARA SHAPIRO, MANAGER, INVESTOR RELATIONS, 3COM CORPORATION, SANTA CLARA, CALIFORNIE

Nous aimons les styliciens qui s'adonnent au brainstorming. Nous les avons submergés de documents avant de définir la présentation de notre rapport annuel pour 1987. Notre société s'occupe de réseaux informatiques; 3Com signifie «computer communication compatibility». Nous avons choisi pour thème quatre orientations majeures de notre branche. L'illustration a mis en évidence les macro-tendances, le texte les micro-orientations. Nous avons choisi l'illustration, comme elle se prête mieux à la représentation de tendances de développement que la photo. Réalisées sur Mac., elles mettent toutes des personnes en scène. Nous avons eu des réactions de lecteurs favorables.

CRAIG FRAZIER, FRAZIER DESIGN, SAN FRANCISCO, CALIFORNIE

Il fallait montrer dans ce rapport annuel ce que 3Com réalise dans le domaine industriel, on y fabrique des réseaux informatiques. Nous avions pour tâche de référencer les produits mis au point, les raisons de son succès et le pourquoi des perspectives brillantes. Comme véhicule des systèmes de travail en groupe, nous avons opté pour des illustrations assistées par Mac. permettant de mieux exprimer des idées difficiles à présenter autrement. L'entreprise souhaitait montrer son personnel au travail, ce qui nous a amenés à recourir à la B.D. C'est John Hersey qui s'en est chargé dans le style de magazine élaboré. Au moyen d'une B.D., on peut exposer simplement des sujets assez complexes.

Times Mirror

1987 Annual Report

"The Times Mirror Company
is committed to gathering and disseminating
the information that people need to live,
work and govern themselves in a free society.

We will strive to do so with the highest standards
of accuracy, fairness, quality
and timeliness."

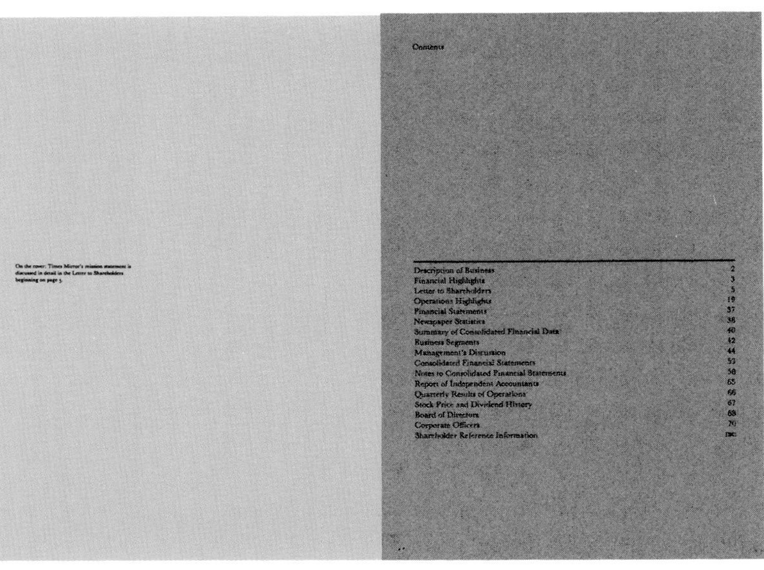

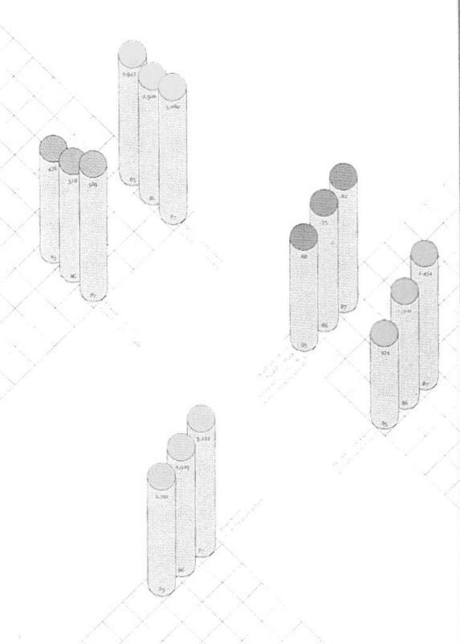

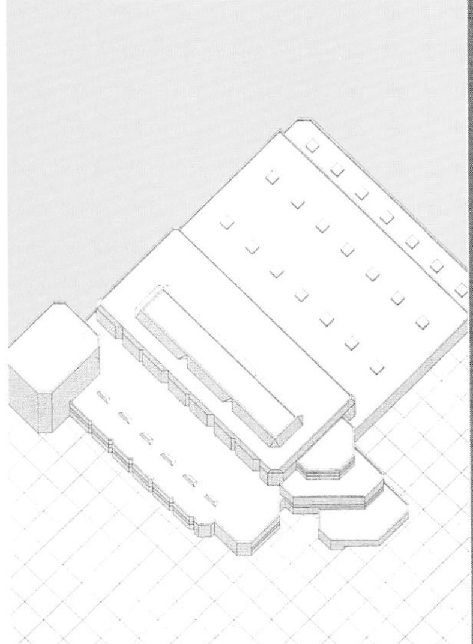

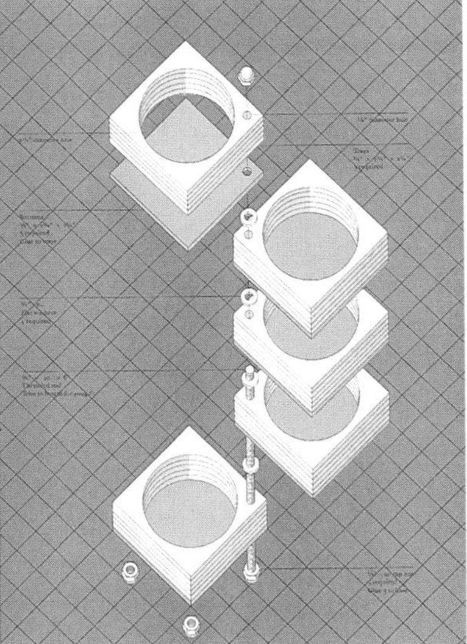

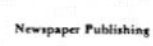

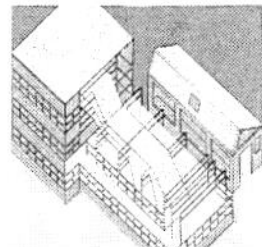

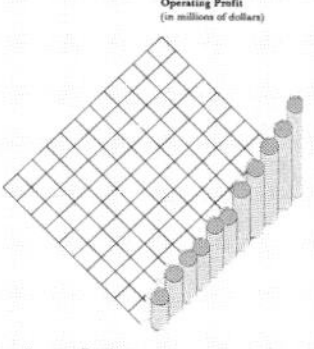

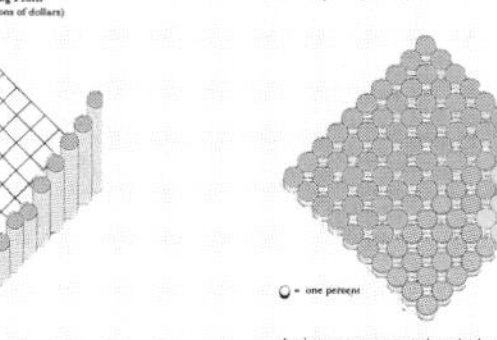

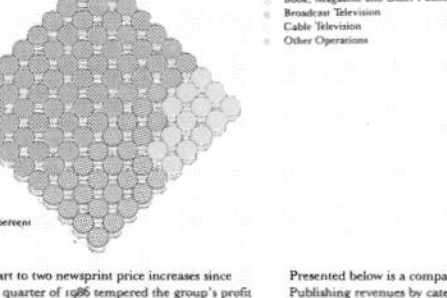

Quarterly Results of Operations (Unaudited)

A summary of the unaudited quarterly results of operations follows (in thousands of dollars, except for per share amounts):

1987 Quarters Ended	March 29	June 28	Sept. 27	Dec. 31
Revenues				
Operating revenues	$702,812	$772,451	$765,260	$839,061
Other income	12,943	20,996	16,994	24,054
	715,755	793,447	782,254	863,115
Costs and expenses				
Cost of sales	388,658	415,164	432,644	433,822
Selling, administrative and general expenses	206,166	212,890	203,312	272,493
Interest expense	13,319	12,992	12,581	13,739
	608,143	641,046	648,537	720,054
Income before loss on sale of assets and income taxes	107,612	152,401	133,717	143,061
Loss on sale of assets				(41,451)
Income before income taxes	107,612	152,401	133,717	101,610
Income taxes	49,426	69,400	63,117	46,906
Net income	$ 58,186	$ 83,001	$ 70,600	$ 54,704
Earnings per share	$.45	$.64	$.55	$.42

1986 Quarters Ended	March 30	June 29	Sept. 28	Dec. 31
Revenues				
Operating revenues	$689,775	$740,845	$686,275	$803,415
Other income	4,984	8,065	11,428	3,349
	694,759	748,910	697,703	806,764
Costs and expenses				
Cost of sales	393,638	412,726	388,696	428,291
Selling, administrative and general expenses	202,279	198,351	187,124	219,207
Interest expense	15,377	15,073	14,939	14,353
	611,294	626,150	590,759	661,851
Income before gain on sales of assets and income taxes	83,465	122,760	106,944	144,913
Gain on sales of assets		175,097	17,429	29,624
Income before income taxes	83,465	297,857	124,373	174,537
Income taxes	40,342	106,194	50,398	75,213
Net income	$ 43,123	$191,663	$ 73,975	$ 99,324
Earnings per share	$.33	$1.48	$.58	$.77

66

Times Mirror Stock Price and Dividend History

The Series A common stock of the company is traded principally on the New York Stock Exchange. The ticker symbol is TMC. The number of shareholders of record of the company's common stock at December 31, 1987, was 5,323.

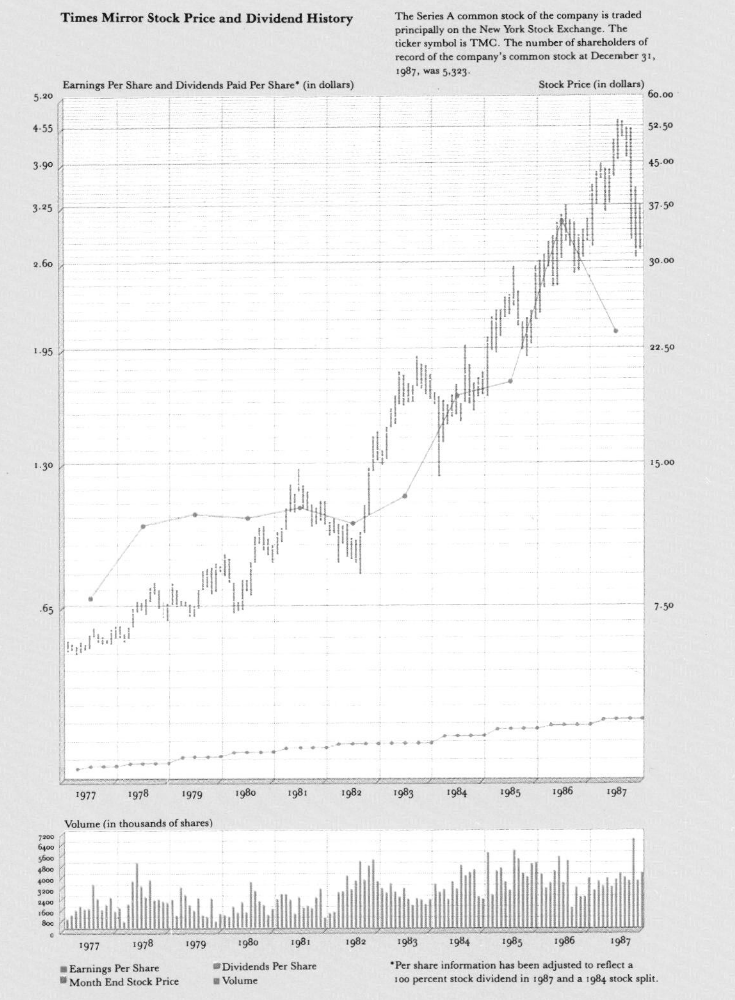

*Per share information has been adjusted to reflect a 100 percent stock dividend in 1987 and a 1984 stock split.

67

CLIENT:
THE TIMES MIRROR COMPANY

DESIGN FIRM:
ROBERT MILES RUNYAN & ASSOCIATES

ART DIRECTOR:
JIM BERTÉ

DESIGNER:
JIM BERTÉ

ILLUSTRATOR:
PAUL BICE

WRITER:
BONNIE CHAIKIND

TYPOGRAPHER:
COMPOSITION TYPE

PRINTER:
GEORGE RICE & SONS

NUMBER OF PAGES:
70 PLUS COVER

SIZE:
8" X 11 1/4"

TYPE SELECTION:
BASKERVILLE

BONNIE CHAIKIND, MANAGER OF CORPORATE COMMUNICATIONS, THE TIMES MIRROR COMPANY, LOS ANGELES, CALIFORNIA

The 1987 Times Mirror annual report highlighted the successful asset redeployment and restructuring program completed by the company. Of particular importance was the newly formulated mission statement, which was featured on the cover. We wanted a hard-working book for a hard-working company and the design was a graphic representation of that. It was different than what had come before. We felt this report was a success and achieved the purpose.

JIM BERTÉ, ROBERT MILES RUNYAN & ASSOCIATES, PLAYA DEL REY, CALIFORNIA

The Times Mirror Company decided that it would be better served in its annual report if it had graphics rather than photographs in the design. We needed boldly graphic charts and we started using diagrams to depict the theory of the company's business structure. This was a six-color job, and we intermixed the colors, since the information illustrated was so important to the impact of the book. Of course, the cover itself is a graphic interpretation of the company's mission statement. We found that financial people liked this annual report a lot.

BONNIE CHAIKIND, MANAGER OF CORPORATE COMMUNICATIONS, THE TIMES MIRROR COMPANY, LOS ANGELES, KALIFORNIEN

Im Mittelpunkt des Jahresberichtes 1987 von Times Mirror standen erfolgreiche Investitionen und die Umstrukturierung der Firma. Besonders wichtig war die neue Firmenpolitik, die auf dem Umschlag zum Ausdruck gebracht wird. Wir wollten einen Bericht, der nach harter Arbeit, aussieht und die graphische Gestaltung entsprach diesem Anliegen. Sie war anders als bisher. Wir fanden, dass der Bericht ein Erfolg war und unseren Bedürfnissen entsprach.

JIM BERTÉ, ROBERT MILES RUNYAN & ASSOCIATES, PLAYA DEL REY, KALIFORNIEN

Die Times Mirror Company fand, dass sich graphische Elemente am besten für ihren Jahresbericht eignen würden. Wir brauchten aussagekräftige Darstellungen, deshalb setzten wir Diagramme für die Erläuterung der Firmenstruktur ein. Wir verwendeten sechs Farben und mischten sie, weil die so vermittelten Informationen von grosser Bedeutung für die Wirkung des Berichtes waren. Natürlich ist der Umschlag eine graphische Interpretation des Selbstverständnisses der Firma. Besonders bei den Finanzexperten kam der Bericht gut an.

BONNIE CHAIKIND, MANAGER OF CORPORATE COMMUNICATIONS, THE TIMES MIRROR COMPANY, LOS ANGELES, CALIFORNIE

Le rapport annuel de Times Mirror pour 1987 a mis en évidence le redéploiement réussi des actifs et le programme de restructuration mis en œuvre par notre société. Une importance particulière revenait à la nouvelle formulation de la politique de l'entreprise, mise en exergue sur la couverture même. Il nous fallait unouvrage d'aspect laborieux pour une société où tout le monde travaille dur. Le design en a été une représentation fidèle. Ce rapport été une réussite.

JIM BERTÉ, ROBERT MILES RUNYAN & ASSOCIATES, PLAYA DEL REY, CALIFORNIE

La Times Mirror Company a estimé que dans son rapport annuel pour 1987, elle serait mieux servie par des représentations graphiques. Il nous fallait des graphiques audacieux que nous avons utilisés pour décrire la structuration de l'entreprise. Il s'agissait d'un travail en six couleurs que nous avons employées pour la présentation graphique d'informations qui étaient très importantes pour le succès du rapport. Bien entendu, la couverture interprète graphiquement la mission formulée par l'entreprise. Ce rapport a été bien reçu par les experts financiers.

PARTNERS FOR THE LONG RIDE
ANNUAL REPORT 1987
USWEST
FACT BOOK AND
STATISTICAL SUMMARY 1987
USWEST

Financial Highlights
(Dollars in millions, except per share amounts)

	1987	Percent Change	1986	Percent Change	1985	Percent Change	1984
CONSOLIDATED FINANCIAL DATA							
Sales of services and products	$8,445	1.6	$8,308	6.3	$7,813	7.3	$7,280
Income from operations	1,996	2.5	1,947	(2.3)	1,993	5.2	1,893
Net income	1,006	8.9	924	(0.2)	926	4.4	887
Total assets	$19,095	1.9	$18,747	4.3	$17,975	5.6	$17,017
Long-term borrowings	4,949	0.8	4,909	3.7	4,733	(2.5)	4,855
Common shareowners' equity	7,456	2.4	7,279	4.8	6,944	4.5	6,648
Earnings per share	$5.31	9.3	$4.86	0.4	$4.84	4.8	$4.62
Dividends per share	3.28	7.9	3.04	6.3	2.86	5.9	2.70
Return on shareowners' equity	13.5%	3.8	13.0%	(4.4)	13.6%	(0.7)	13.7%
Debt to capital ratio	41.2%	(0.7)	41.5%	(2.8)	42.7%	0.5	42.5%
Capital expenditures	$1,908	(16.4)	$2,282	9.2	$2,089	17.8	$1,774
OTHER SELECTED DATA							
Employees	68,523	(1.2)	69,375	(1.2)	70,202	(0.8)	70,765
Weighted average shares outstanding (000's)	189,513	(0.3)	190,135	(0.6)	191,196	(0.4)	192,034
Number of shareowners	1,049,625		1,082,710		1,156,186		1,219,863
Network access lines in service (000's)	11,613	2.5	11,332	1.5	11,167	2.7	10,871

We're fortunate to have the foundation of our business in the West. Traditional industries such as petroleum, agriculture, forest products, and minerals have lagged, but are beginning to recover. And the Census Bureau predicts our region will have one of the nation's fastest-growing populations.

Further, the economy of the West is becoming increasingly diversified. In Nebraska, telemarketing firms have added $100 million a year to the state's economy. Minnesota is home not only to the World Series Champion Twins, but also to 17 Fortune 500 firms. In Oregon and Washington, new data management firms are being formed and others are expanding. New Mexico's high-tech research labs are growing. Arizona's population and economy are among the fastest growing in the United States.

Richard D. McCormick, President

What's more, there is a renewed commitment to education throughout the West, a commitment we're proud to share. We announced a five-year, $20 million program to support all levels of education in our 14-state region. The program includes a fellowship to recognize excellence in teaching.

A federal court ruling gives promise that we will be allowed to have a greater opportunity to market the resources of our network. It will allow us and others to take the first steps to bringing the Information Age to America.

We are building on the foundation of our three Bell telephone companies a diversified group of businesses that helps prepare us for an emerging information economy.

We are proud of the diversity not only of our companies, but also of our employees. Women and minorities make up a growing percentage of our work force–at all levels. We believe that using the talents of *all* people helps us compete.

Our vision is to be a leader in the information industry. On the pages that follow, we report our strategies and our progress. In the months and years that follow, we will continue to become a more effective competitor by emphasizing the importance of people and technology and ideas.

JACK A. MACALLISTER   RICHARD D. MCCORMICK

The Future is Calling. In the 1960s a technological revolution began to change the way America lives and works. Over time, it led to personal computers, automated teller machines, cellular phones, the merging of voice and data technology. It changed the way we communicate. Yet it is a revolution just begun.

Part of the satisfaction of working alongside someone is learning how to be a good partner. When a goal is pursued by two, it's easier to reach.

U S WEST, which was created when this revolution helped bring about the breakup of the Bell System, has set out to be a leader in the information industry. It's an industry of thousands of products and services that help people communicate, make decisions, and manage time and resources.

Our leadership in this industry depends on our understanding the needs of our customers. Everything we do must stand the test of whether it meets the needs of customers today and prepares us to meet their needs of tomorrow.

Some time ago, we set down four strategies to guide us:

1. We will be a lean, effective organization. We're providing better service to more customers more efficiently.

Customers of our Bell telephone companies say our service is good and getting better. In our research, more than 90 percent say they are satisfied with our service.

Our Bell companies have nearly 13,000 fewer employees than four years ago, yet serve one million more customer lines.

During 1987, we invested $1.6 billion in new equipment to maintain and improve service to our 11.6 million telephone customer lines. Included were nearly 24,000 miles of new fiber optic cable and more than 100 new digital switching centers.

2. We will focus on the needs of our customers. "Historically, a market was a *place*, where roads crossed, rivers crossed: merchants and caravans stopped en route, farmers brought their food, artisans their skills," Professor Daniel Bell of Harvard University observed. "In the new economy this is no longer true."

In a new community development near Phoenix, Mountain Bell has set up a shared-tenant communications system allowing a single vendor to provide telephone service, alarm security and energy-use monitoring to 12,000 homes.

Like most corporations, U S WEST has been organized around the products it sells and the places it serves. Today, however, we have a new look based on a new definition of a market: not a place, but people with similar needs.

Thus we began to form market units to meet the overall communications needs of specific groups of customers.

6

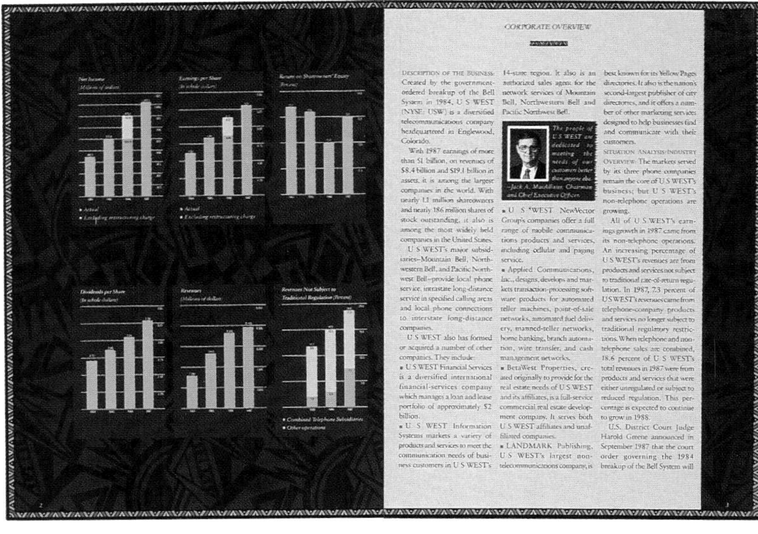

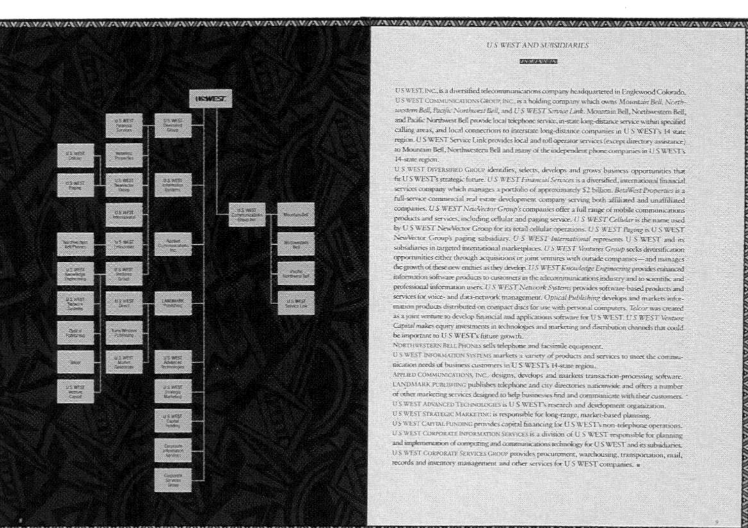

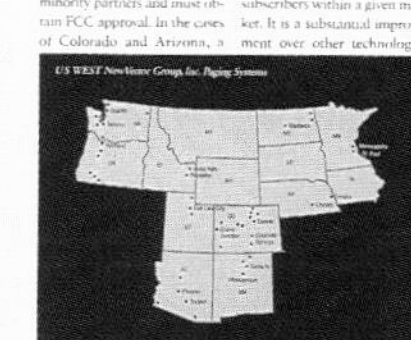

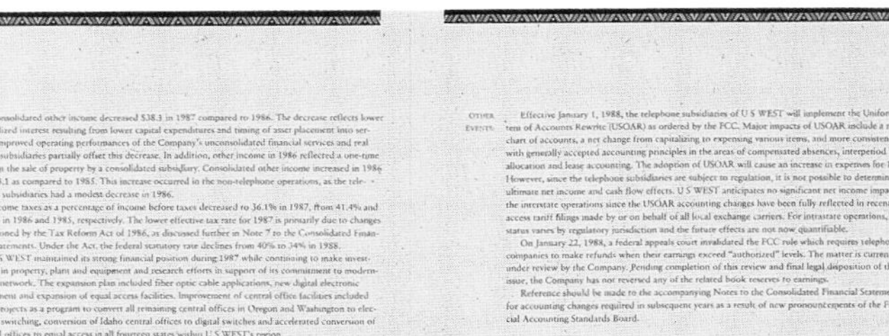

CLIENT:
US West

DESIGN FIRM:
The Duffy Design Group

ART DIRECTOR:
Sharon Werner

DESIGNERS:
Sharon Werner, Haley Johnson

PHOTOGRAPHERS:
Tom Berthiaume, Arthur Meyerson, Dan Weaks, Tom Tracy

PRODUCTION MANAGER:
Peg Layer

TYPOGRAPHER:
Typeshooters

PAPER SELECTION:
Warren Lustro Cream, Speckletone

PAPER MANUFACTURER:
Warren, French Paper Co.

PRINTER:
Williamson Printing Co.

NUMBER OF PAGES:
96

SIZE:
8" x 11"

TYPE SELECTION:
Sabon

JERRY BROWN, DIRECTOR OF FINANCIAL COMMUNICATIONS, US WEST, ENGLEWOOD, COLORADO

In the 1987 US West annual report, we used the theme of "partners for the long ride" because we had started a major effort to look at ways we could serve our customers better. The company had evolved out of the Bell Telephone system, and we were more competitve, and more customer-oriented. Now we were looking at how we could best serve our customers. We did two books. Since we have one million shareholders, we consciously kept the annual report relatively brief. We also had a companion fact book and summary, which gave descriptions necessary for financial analysts. These were both designed for an audience who would pay attention to the warm and somewhat soft, out-of-the-ordinary design.

SHARON WERNER, THE DUFFY DESIGN GROUP, MINNEAPOLIS, MINNESOTA

US West's corporate positioning had been created by Fallon McElligott, the company's advertising firm, and it stressed the attributes of the West. Earlier annual reports had shown images of the old West, and in 1987, US West wanted to move more toward the New West, since the company is in telecommunications and competes with cutting-edge technology. So we kept the Western theme, and we mixed a high-tech and low-tech contrast in the design. We showed the Western theme, but indicated that the company was concerned with today and the future.

JERRY BROWN, DIRECTOR OF FINANCIAL COMMUNICATIONS, US WEST, ENGLEWOOD, COLORADO

Das Thema für den Geschäftsbericht 1987 hiess «Partner auf dem langen Weg», weil wir uns sehr bemüht hatten, den Kundendienst zu verbessern. Die Firma hatte sich aus der Bell Telephone-Gruppe entwickelt, und wir waren konkurrenzfähiger und serviceorientierter geworden. Wir machten zwei Berichte. Da wir eine Million Aktionäre haben, fassten wir uns im Jahresbericht bewusst relativ knapp. Wir hatten daneben einen Bericht mit Fakten über das Unternehmen und eine Zusammenfassung der Informationen, die für die Finanzanalytiker notwendig waren. Beide waren für ein Publikum gestaltet, das sich von einem ungewöhnlichen Design angesprochen fühlt, das menschliche Wärme ausstrahlt.

SHARON WERNER, THE DUFFY DESIGN GROUP, MINNEAPOLIS, MINNESOTA

Die Werbeagentur der Firma, Fallon McElligott, hatte US West als eine Firma aus dem Westen positioniert. In früheren Jahresberichten wurden Bilder des alten Westens gezeigt, aber 1987 wollte US West auf den neuen Westen eingehen, weil die Firma sich mit Telekommunikation befasst und es dabei um hochentwickelte Technologien geht. Wir blieben deshalb beim Thema, arbeiteten aber bei der Gestaltung mit dem Kontrast von fortschrittlicher und rudimentärer Technologie. Dabei wurde betont, dass es der Firma um die Gegenwart und die Zukunft geht.

JERRY BROWN, DIRECTOR OF FINANCIAL COMMUNICATIONS, US WEST, ENGLEWOOD, COLORADO

Le rapport annuel d'US West pour 1987 est centré sur le thème des «partenaires au long cours». La société s'est développée à partir du système téléphonique Bell en accentuant l'aspect concurrentiel et l'orientation en fonction des besoins des consommateurs. Nous avons cherché à leur rendre vraiment service en préparant deux ouvrages. Le premier, destiné à un million d'actionnaires, constitue le rapport annuel proprement dit, réduit à l'essentiel. Dans le second ouvrage, nous avons réuni la documentation et les faits et descriptions utiles pour les analystes financiers. Le design est spécifiquement conçu pour sortir de l'ordinaire et transmettre une optique personnalisée de chaleur.

SHARON WERNER, THE DUFFY DESIGN GROUP, MINNEAPOLIS, MINNESOTA

US West doit son positionnement institutionnel à Fallon McElligott, l'entreprise chargée de la publicité du groupe, qui mettait l'accent sur les attributs de l'Ouest américain. C'est ainsi que les rapports annuels précédents étaient illustrés de vues historiques de l'Ouest. Pour 1987, US West a voulu mettre en évidence l'Ouest moderne, adapté à son profil d'entreprise spécialisée dans les télécommunications et engagée dans la compétition de haute technologie. Nous avons donc gardé le thème de l'Ouest tout en mixant un contraste high et low-tech .

VORWERK GESCHÄFTS BERICHT 1987

VORWERK

Darf ein Geschäftsbericht Rätsel aufgeben? Natürlich nicht. In diesem Band über das 104. Geschäftsjahr gibt es – anders als für Dürers Grübler vor dem magischen Zahlenquadrat – nichts zu deuteln. Die Zahlen sprechen für sich und schaffen Spielraum für das neue Jahresmotto unserer Firmengruppe: „Offen sein für neue Ideen".

In den Geschäftsberichten hat dieser Geist schon Tradition. Neben Rechenschaftsbericht und Zahlenwerk hat immer ein begleitendes Thema Anregungen vermittelt oder zu Vergnüglichem angestiftet.

In diesem Jahresband werden bei der Berichterstattung Rätsel aufgegeben. Eine kleine Kulturgeschichte der Formen, wie sie sich Hintersinn, Bluff oder Spaß am Spielerischen in Jahrhunderten schufen, wird im Folgenden ausgebreitet.

Inhalt

Alle Rätsel, die diesen Geschäftsbericht am Rande begleiten, sind eine kleine Herausforderung für kreative Minuten. Sie sind allesamt zu raten. Etliche Einzellösungen (Seite 44) machen sogar im Zusammenhang Sinn – am Ende ergeben sie einen wegweisenden Spruch.

Die allerletzte Seite ist den Ungeduldigen oder Selbstzweiflern vorbehalten. Sie (ver)birgt die Lösung.

Sie sind älter als die Sage vom Minotauros, dem Ungeheuer, das im Gängegewirr des Palastes von Knossos auf Kreta seine Menschenopfer verlangte. Das Labyrinth bekam hier zwar seinen Namen (nach der kretischen Doppelaxt „labrys"), aber die Ägypter hatten den Kretern mit gigantischen labyrinthischen Grabanlagen den Weg gewiesen. Aus der Lust an Spiralen und Mäandern und der Notwendigkeit, „taktische", leicht zu verteidigende irrwegige Palastzugänge zu bauen, erneuerte sich in allen Völkern und Generationen immer wieder die Kenntnis um das eindeutige Symbol: Der Weg verstellt das Ziel, aber der kreative Nachvollzug der verborgenen Struktur „erlöst".

So wurden Labyrinthe beliebte „Devisen", als Wahlsprüche für Zuversicht und Geduld (wie hier als Motto des Sekretärs Karls V. in Neapel). Königin Christina von Schweden wählte zum Labyrinth-Symbol den Spruch: „Das Schicksal wird einen Weg finden."

In Kirchen galten Labyrinthe im Pflaster als „Chemin de Jérusalem" und ersparten, wenn Büßer sie kniefällig durchmaßen, die Pilgerfahrt ins Heilige Land.

Doch bald wurden Labyrinthe zu „Irrgärten" und schönstem, säkularen Spaß: Stein- und Rasenlabyrinth amüsierten, und Gärtner heckten diesen Zeitvertreib gegen höfische Langeweile aus. Lange galt die Bauregel, daß der Weg zum Rendezvous oder späten Déjeuner im Herzen des Labyrinths immer rechtsherum zu führen habe. Noch der Verwirr-Garten des Hampton Court Palace bei London, das bekannteste aller englischen Heckenlabyrinthe und das älteste dazu (angelegt 1690) läßt sich auf diese sichere Weise begehen. Bis zum Zentrum aber sind es dennoch 750 Meter Kieswege. Wer viermal die Regel verletzt, die Hecke nur rechterhand zu haben, kommt schneller ans Ziel. Wie?

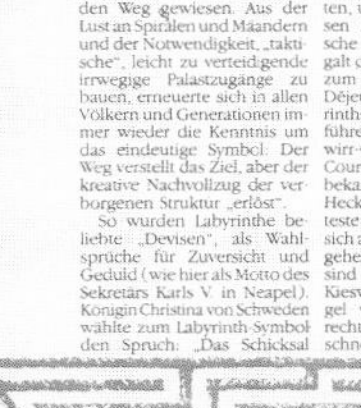

Unternehmen der Vorwerk-Gruppe

Dem Stammhaus Vorwerk & Co. sind folgende Gesellschaften angeschlossen:

	Kapital		unmittelbare oder mittelbare Beteiligung der Obergesellschaft
1. Inländische Unternehmen			
1.1 In den Konzernabschluß einbezogen:			
Vorwerk & Co. Elektrowerke KG, Wuppertal	DM	25.000.000	100 %
Vorwerk & Co. Thermomix GmbH, Wuppertal	DM	50.000	100 %
Vorwerk & Co. Teppich-Beteiligungsgesellschaft mbH, Wuppertal	DM	100.000	100 %
Vorwerk & Co. Teppichwerke KG, Wuppertal	DM	30.000.000	100 %
OKA Teppichwerke GmbH, Hameln	DM	15.000.000	100 %
Vorwerk & Co. Möbelstoff-Beteiligungsgesellschaft mbH, Wuppertal	DM	50.000	100 %
Vorwerk & Co. Möbelstoffwerke GmbH & Co. KG, Wuppertal	DM	5.500.000	100 %
Türk & Kneitz GmbH, Kulmbach	DM	100.000	95 %
ZEDA Beteiligungsgesellschaft mbH, Wuppertal	DM	50.000	100 %
ZEDA Gesellschaft für Datenverarbeitung und EDV-Beratung mbH & Co., Wuppertal	DM	200.000	100 %

7

Unternehmensbereich Elektro

bau begriffen und noch nicht bundesweit tätig; ihr Umsatz ist im Außenumsatz der Vorwerk & Co. Elektrowerke KG einbegriffen.

Der Kundendienst der Vorwerk & Co. Elektrowerke KG beschäftigte im Berichtsjahr 274 Kundendiensttechniker. Für Service- und Reparaturleistungen wurden 1987 20,9 Millionen DM abgerechnet.

Vorwerk ist das einzige bedeutende Unternehmen auf dem Sektor Raumpflegegeräte, welches die Geräte in der Wohnung des Kunden repariert. Eine 1987 durchgeführte Befragung bei 1.314 Vorwerk-Kunden ergab eine hohe Zufriedenheit mit dieser Art der Reparatur. Sehr zufrieden waren die Kunden auch mit der Qualität der Reparatur und der pünktlichen Einhaltung der Termine.

Zum Bilanzstichtag beschäftigte die Vorwerk & Co. Elektrowerke KG 2.873 Mitarbeiter (ohne Außendienst).

Wir haben nach den Zahlen der ersten vier Monate des laufenden Jahres Grund anzunehmen, daß das Jahr 1988 einen weiteren Zuwachs bei Raumpflegegeräten bringen wird. Auch für das Küchengeschäft der Vorwerk & Co. Elektrowerke KG wird aufgrund der deutlich höheren Auftragseingänge und des hohen Auftragsbestandes zum Jahresende 1987 wieder ein deutlicher Zuwachs für das neue Geschäftsjahr erwartet. Die Vorwerk & Co. Thermomix GmbH hat eine erneute Verdoppelung ihres Jahresumsatzes geplant.

Im Ausland vertreiben unsere Gesellschaften das Vorwerk-Raumpflegeprogramm und den bei der Semco in Frankreich hergestellten „Thermomix", jedoch keine Einbauküchen.

Insgesamt verbesserten die im Unternehmensbereich Elektro tätigen Auslandsgesellschaften ihre Außenumsätze im Berichtsjahr um 7,7 Prozent auf zusammen 447,6 Millionen DM nach 415,7 Millionen DM im Vorjahr.

Die seit Jahren erfolgreichste Auslandsgesellschaft ist die vor 50 Jahren 1938 gegründete Folletto S.r.l. mit Sitz in Mailand. Der Name „Folletto" (die Übersetzung des deutschen Wortes „Kobold") ist in Italien gleichbedeutend mit Staubsauger. Der Marktgeltung und dem damit einhergehenden sehr hohen Marktanteil entsprechend fiel zum Jubiläumsjahr der Geschäftsabschluß 1987 aus. Er erbrachte bei einer Steigerung um 20 Prozent gegenüber dem Vorjahr mit 255,2 Millionen DM einen erfreulichen Rekordumsatz. Die ebenfalls auf dem italienischen Markt tätige Contempora S.r.l., die dort den „Thermomix" im Direktvertriebssystem verkauft, unterschritt ihren Vorjahresumsatz um 7,2 Prozent und erzielte 14,2 Millionen DM Verkaufserlöse. Das Geschäft der Vorwerk USA Inc. wurde weiter planmäßig auf 16,3 (35,5) Millionen DM zurückgeführt. Auf diesem nach wie vor aussichtsreichen Markt wird ein Neuaufbau angestrebt, was aber weitere Umstrukturierungen im Vertriebssystem erfordert. Eine starke Marktstellung besitzen dagegen unsere Vertriebsgesellschaften in Österreich und Spanien. Die Vorwerk Austria Ges.m.b.H. (Hard) ist seit Jahren wachstumstragend und verbesserte ihren Jahresumsatz 1987 erneut um 4 Prozent auf 57,7 Millionen DM. Der Vorwerk España S.A. gelang sogar eine Umsatzausweitung von 36,9 Prozent auf 21,5 Millionen DM. In Frankreich, wo überwiegend der Thermomix vertrieben wird, wurden 1987 43,0 Millionen DM umgesetzt – 5,9 Prozent mehr als im Vorjahr. Von den kleinen, noch nicht so lange bestehenden Gesellschaften erzielten die Vorwerk Nippon K.K. (Tokio) 9,5 Millionen und die Vorwerk U.K. Ltd. 5,1 Millionen DM (plus 6,3 %) Umsatzerlöse. Gerade bei der englischen Gesellschaft zeigen die Zahlen der letzten Monate einen sprunghaften Anstieg.

Das Vexieren, wörtlich „das Quälen", also das Necken und Irreführen, ist ein menschliches Grundbedürfnis. Der Manierismus hatte es mit Allegorien und Emblemata auf die Spitze getrieben, nach der Barockzeit aber amüsierte man sich verständlicher. Es entstand eine eigene Gattung rätselhafter Graphiken, deren perspektivische Verzerrungen scheinbar unverständliche Bilder lieferten. Der Spruch im Kreis ist nach bester Vexiermanier nur Buchstabe für Buchstabe um den Stern herum zu entziffern. Ein verzerrender Kunstgriff schuf „Anamorphosen" (gesetzmäßige Verzerrungen), die ein Betrachter erst mit Hilfe von konvex auflösenden spiegelnden Zylindern oder durch extremes Schräghalten des Blattes erkennen konnte. Nicht selten wurden verzerrte Pikanterien auf diese Weise zu eindeutigen Illustrationen. Daß dieser ganz flach von links betrachtete Geiger nur ein Knie ausstreckt, ist dagegen höchst harmlos. ...

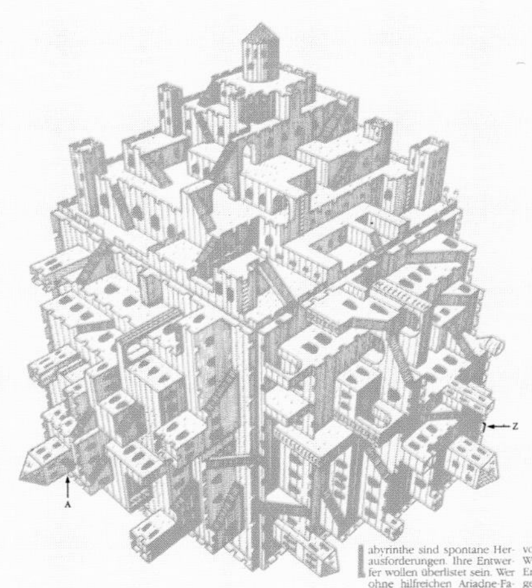

Labyrinthe sind spontane Herausforderungen. Ihre Entwerfer wollen überlistet sein. Wer ohne hilfreichen Ariadne-Faden ans Ziel kommt, hat den Labyrinth-Designer auf seinem eigenen Terrain besiegt.

Ein harmloses Gartenlabyrinth nicht zu durchwandern, wäre schon eingestandene Niederlage. Aber längst sind wir viel weiter: Computer helfen, schlichte Grundrisse zu komplizieren oder in andere Perspektiven oder neue Dimensionen zu verformen. Je überraschender die verschlungene Wegführung, desto reizvoller wird es, spontan den Winkelzügen des Labyrinth-Entwerfers mit dem Zeigefinger (Profis nehmen angespitzte Streichhölzer) auf die Schliche zu kommen.

Hier gilt es, die „Burg im Raum" (Castle in Space) bei der Ein-Punkt-Fahne (unten A) zu betreten und nur über Treppen und Terrassen (nicht auf Mauern) zur Zwei-Punkt-Fahne (rechts) zu gelangen. Jede der drei Burgebenen hat ihre Wege und Terrassen mit einem Übergang zur nächsten.

Um wieviele Ecken führt der verschlungene Weg?

Unternehmen der Vorwerk-Gruppe

Hygienic Service Gebäudereinigung und Gebäudedienste KG, Wuppertal	DM	2.500.000	95 %
Hygienic Service Gebäudereinigung Betriebs-KG, Wuppertal	DM	1.000.000	48,45 %
Clift-Fertigbau Verwaltungs-GmbH, Wuppertal	DM	50.000	100 %
Clift-Fertigbau GmbH & Co. KG, Wuppertal	DM	237.350	100 %
Vorwerk & Co. Interholding GmbH, Wuppertal	DM	6.000.000	100 %
1.2 Nicht in den Konzernabschluß einbezogen:			
AKF Kreditbank Beteiligungsgesellschaft mbH., Wuppertal	DM	100.000	72 %
AKF Kreditbank GmbH & Co., Wuppertal	DM	7.500.000	71,4 %
AKF Leasing Beteiligungsgesellschaft mbH., Wuppertal	DM	50.000	71,4 %
AKF Leasing GmbH & Co., Wuppertal	DM	1.000.000	71,4 %
2. Ausländische Unternehmen			
Vorwerk International AG. Wollerau/Schweiz	CHF	5.000.000	100 %
Vorwerk France S. A. Marly-le-Roi (Paris)/Frankreich	FRF	3.000.000	100 %
Société Electro-Mécanique et Compagnie «Semco» S. A. Cloyes/Frankreich	FRF	2.620.600	80 %
Société Anonyme des Immeubles Vorwerk «SADIV» Marly-le-Roi (Paris)/Frankreich	FRF	2.100.000	100 %
Interservice France S. A. Marly-le-Roi (Paris)/Frankreich	FRF	250.000	100 %

9

Konzernbilanz zum 31. Dezember 1987

Aktiva		1987 DM
A. Anlagevermögen		
I. Immaterielle Vermögensgegenstände		
Konzessionen, gewerbliche Schutzrechte und ähnliche Rechte und Werte, sowie Lizenzen an solchen Rechten und Werten		224.444
II. Sachanlagen		
1. Grundstücke, grundstücksgleiche Rechte und Bauten, einschließlich der Bauten auf fremden Grundstücken		26.541.601
2. Technische Anlagen und Maschinen		22.314.435
3. Andere Anlagen, Betriebs- und Geschäftsausstattung		13.227.821
4. Geleistete Anzahlungen und Anlagen im Bau		4.210.992
		66.294.849
III. Finanzanlagen		
1. Anteile an verbundenen Unternehmen		7.536.210
2. Beteiligungen		6.633.179
3. Wertpapiere des Anlagevermögens		18.000
4. Sonstige Ausleihungen		2.444.814
		16.632.203
Anlagevermögen		83.151.496
B. Unterschiedsbetrag aus der Erstkonsolidierung		1.244.374
C. Umlaufvermögen		
I. Vorräte		
1. Roh-, Hilfs- und Betriebsstoffe		22.164.683
2. Unfertige Erzeugnisse, unfertige Leistungen		12.859.249
3. Fertige Erzeugnisse und Waren		30.609.105
4. Geleistete Anzahlungen		5.666
		65.638.703
II. Forderungen und sonstige Vermögensgegenstände		
1. Forderungen aus Lieferungen und Leistungen;		83.010.353
davon mit einer Restlaufzeit von mehr als einem Jahr:	DM 5.131.927	
2. Forderungen gegen verbundene Unternehmen		7.369.831
3. Forderungen gegen Unternehmen, mit denen ein Beteiligungsverhältnis besteht		41.322
4. Sonstige Vermögensgegenstände		54.697.256
davon mit einer Restlaufzeit von mehr als einem Jahr:	DM 4.435.548	
		145.118.762
III. Wertpapiere		
Sonstige Wertpapiere		84.462.798
IV. Schecks, Kassenbestand, Bundesbank- und Postgiroguthaben, Guthaben bei Kreditinstituten		158.006.852
Umlaufvermögen		453.227.115
D. Rechnungsabgrenzungsposten		684.337
		538.307.322

36

Passiva		1987 DM
A. Eigenkapital		221.168.000
B. Ausgleichsposten für Anteile in Fremdbesitz		
1. an Kapital und Rücklagen		449.939
2. an Gewinn		987.415
		1.437.354
C. Sonderposten mit Rücklageanteil gem. §§ 6b, 7c und 52 Abs. 5 EStG		15.783.029
D. Rückstellungen		
1. Rückstellungen für Pensionen und ähnliche Verpflichtungen		142.962.203
2. Steuerrückstellungen		8.776.149
3. sonstige Rückstellungen		43.095.991
		194.834.343
E. Verbindlichkeiten		
1. Verbindlichkeiten gegenüber Kreditinstituten;		20.000.000
davon mit einer Restlaufzeit bis zu einem Jahr:	DM 5.000.000	
2. Erhaltene Anzahlungen auf Bestellungen;		4.438.915
davon mit einer Restlaufzeit bis zu einem Jahr:	DM 4.438.915	
3. Verbindlichkeiten aus Lieferungen und Leistungen;		16.646.183
davon mit einer Restlaufzeit bis zu einem Jahr:	DM 16.646.183	
4. Verbindlichkeiten aus der Annahme gezogener Wechsel und der Ausstellung eigener Wechsel;		16.000.000
davon mit einer Restlaufzeit bis zu einem Jahr:	DM 16.000.000	
5. Verbindlichkeiten gegenüber verbundenen Unternehmen;		734.206
davon mit einer Restlaufzeit bis zu einem Jahr:	DM 734.206	
6. Sonstige Verbindlichkeiten;		44.024.840
davon aus Steuern:	DM 8.448.922	
davon im Rahmen der sozialen Sicherheit:	DM 4.481.342	
davon mit einer Restlaufzeit bis zu einem Jahr:	DM 44.024.840	
		101.844.144
F. Rechnungsabgrenzungsposten		3.240.452
Haftungsverhältnisse		
1. Verbindlichkeiten aus der Begebung und Übertragung von Wechseln;	DM 3.811.557	
2. Verbindlichkeiten aus Bürgschaften	DM 320.000	
3. Verbindlichkeiten aus Gewährleistungsverträgen	DM 1	
		538.307.322

37

Neue Rätselgattungen sind höchst selten. Aber mit der Designerschrift für die Flüssigkeitskristallanzeigen in den Taschenrechnern für jedermann gelang Rätselmachern ein neuer „Dreh": Über Kopf werden die Null und alle Ziffern (bis auf die 6) „sprechend": 0, 1, 2, 3, 4, 5, 7, 8 und 9 werden, andersherum betrachtet, zu O, I, Z, E, h, S, L, B, G. Damit konnten schon Volksschüler dem Lehrer vorrechnen, was 1.470.663x5 ergibt: Andersherum gelesen nämlich SIE ESEL! Und Manager rechneten sich abseits der Konferenzen vor, wer „einerseits" 7.708.918 Mark verdiene, könne „andererseits" nur BIG BOSS sein. Seit 1983 findet die „Frankfurter Allgemeine Zeitung" in einer Tüftelkolumne ihres Magazins Woche für Woche deutsche und englische Wörter, die sich mit Ziffern darstellen und amüsant ineinander „umrechnen" lassen. Und ein Ende dieses „Kopfrechnens" ist nicht abzusehen, seit sie auch das Hawaiianische Wörterbuch zu Rate ziehen: hO'OLi (oder 17.004), erfuhr die Öffentlichkeit auf diese Weise heißt andersherum natürlich – „to make happy"...

Das ganze Rätsel löst sich höchst amüsant, wenn man bereit ist, alle Hinweise auf Rechenoperationen wortwörtlich zu nehmen und auszuführen. Damit werden Ziffern zu Buchstaben und ganzen Wörtern:

„Artikel-Nr. 39.138 war also der Teppichboden in BEIGE. 3mal hatte die Marketing-Abteilung einen Relaunch-Versuch unternommen. Ohne (–)3 Präsentationen kam sie nicht aus, 6300 waren für einen Farbpsychologen ausgegeben (–) worden. Sein Gutachten stand zwar wie eine Eins, aber 1 Abstrich (–) mußte auch er machen: Der Umsatz betrug nach wie vor nur 1/10. Da gab das Unternehmen 1762 Mark für Design-Studenten aus (–). Was diese lieferten, sah im Quadrat (!) gut aus, 6.067 gingen für eine Musterproduktion vom Etat ab (–) und endlich war die neue Farbe auch der Marketing-Abteilung recht. Wie hieß die neue Farbe?"

BEI 6E

SI EESEL

Konzern-Gewinn- und Verlustrechnung

Vom 1. Januar bis zum 31. Dezember 1987

		1987 DM
1. Außenumsatzerlöse (brutto)		947.901.116
abzüglich Umsatzsteuer		100.359.494
		847.541.622
2. Bestandsveränderung der Erzeugnisse und noch nicht abgerechneten Leistungen		+ 14.539.571
3. Andere aktivierte Eigenleistungen		995.410
4. Gesamtleistung		863.076.603
5. Sonstige betriebliche Erträge;		35.350.701
davon aus der Auflösung von Sonderposten mit Rücklageanteil:	DM 8.909.220	
6. Materialaufwand:		
a) Aufwendungen für Roh-, Hilfs- und Betriebsstoffe und für bezogene Waren		254.712.726
b) Aufwendungen für bezogene Leistungen		6.874.086
		261.586.812
7. Rohertrag		636.840.492
8. Personalaufwand:		
a) Löhne und Gehälter		207.647.869
b) Soziale Abgaben und Aufwendungen für Altersversorgung und für Unterstützung;		43.504.515
davon für Altersversorgung:	DM 13.087.425	
		251.152.384
9. Abschreibungen auf immaterielle Vermögensgegenstände des Anlagevermögens und Sachanlagen		28.647.314
10. Erträge aus Beteiligungen;		2.963.057
davon aus verbundenen Unternehmen:	DM 1.352.739	
11. Erträge aus anderen Wertpapieren und Ausleihungen des Finanzanlagevermögens;		57.230
davon aus verbundenen Unternehmen:	DM –	
12. Sonstige Zinsen und ähnliche Erträge;		20.228.427
davon aus verbundenen Unternehmen:	DM 545.020	
13. Abschreibungen auf Finanzanlagen und auf Wertpapiere des Umlaufvermögens		4.409.493
14. Zinsen und ähnliche Aufwendungen;		2.148.615
davon an verbundene Unternehmen:	DM 36.551	
15. Sammelposition:		
Sonstige betriebliche Aufwendungen, Steuern und Jahresüberschuß;		373.731.400
davon Einstellungen in Sonderposten mit Rücklageanteil:	DM 725.820	
		–

41

CLIENT:
VORWERK & CO.

DESIGNER:
HERMANN MICHELS

WRITERS:
*MANFRED PIWINGER,
UDO PINI*

MANFRED PIWINGER, DIRECTOR OF PUBLIC RELATIONS, VORWERK & CO., WUPPERTAL, WEST GERMANY

In the past five years, we have searched for a way to show the special quality of this family business, which produces various kinds of electrical appliances, carpeting, and upholstery. In this annual report, we feel we have come close to portraying visually the philosophy of our company. We decided on "riddles" as the subject, since they evoke fantasy, creativity and a kind of logic. We also intended to capture the feeling of our company in this annual report. We wanted to indicate cheerfulness, calmness, and strength. We did this through artwork, which we thought conveyed these emotions. We have received a variety of comments on this report including that it was an esthetic pleasure to look at, and that it was interesting and entertaining.

MANFRED PIWINGER, LEITER DES RESSORTS ÖFFENTLICHKEITSARBEIT, VORWERK & CO., WUPPERTAL, BRD

In den vergangenen fünf Jahren haben wir nach einem Weg gesucht, um die Individualität eines Familienunternehmens auszudrücken, das elektrische Geräte, Spannteppiche und Möbelstoffe herstellt sowie verschiedene Dienstleistungen anbietet. Wir entschieden uns für Rätsel, denn sie verlangen Phantasie, Kreativität und logisches Denken. Wir wollten einen Geschäftsbericht, der etwas von der inneren Stimmung nach draussen trägt, Heiterkeit und Gelassenheit als Stärke unseres Unternehmes. Dank der künstlerischen Gestaltung gelang es, dies zum Ausdruck zu bringen. Das Echo auf diesen Bericht war aussergewöhnlich, die häufigsten Äusserungen waren, dass der Bericht ein ästhetisches Vergnügen, interessant und unterhaltend sei.

MANFRED PIWINGER, DIRECTEUR DES RELATIONS PUBLIQUES, VORWERK & CO., WUPPERTAL, RFA

Ces cinq dernières années, nous avons cherché le moyen approprié pour mettre en valeur les qualités de cette entreprise familiale qui produit différents appareils électriques, ainsi que des tapis de sol et des tissus d'ameublement. Comme thème, nous avons choisi des «énigmes» évoquant la fantaisie et la créativité en même temps qu'une certaine logique. Nous avons aussi cherché à restituer l'ambiance propre à Vorwerk, faite de bonne humeur et de force tranquille. Les compositions artistiques utilisées nous paraissent propres à traduire ces émotions. Ce rapport annuel nous a valu des commentaires intéressants affirmant par exemple qu'il suscitait à l'examen un réel plaisir esthétique, qu'il était à la fois intéressant et distrayant.

WARNER COMMUNICATIONS, INC.

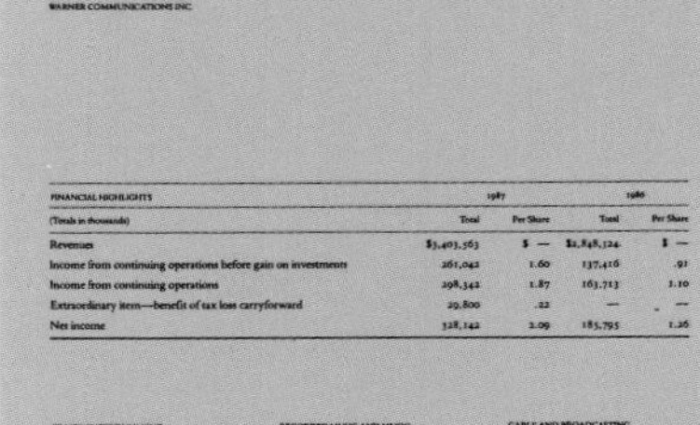

The company that is today Warner Communications publicly traded its stock for the first time on June 19, 1962. Five years later, WCI became involved in the entertainment business when its founder, Steven J. Ross, took the initial steps that ultimately shaped an entertainment industry giant. That year, the company acquired Ashley Famous Agency, Inc., an international talent agency based in Los Angeles, and National Periodical Publications, publisher of DC Comics and Mad magazine. ❖ In 1969, a decisive move was made as the company acquired Warner-Seven Arts, comprised of the Warner Bros. motion picture studio and the Warner Bros., Reprise, and Atlantic record companies. In 1970, Warner Communications Inc. was officially formed. ❖ Over the years, each of WCI's core operations—Filmed Entertainment, Recorded Music, and Cable—has proved to be among the most innovative and profitable in its field.

In 1980, Warner Amex, a joint venture between WCI and American Express, launched the first of several cable television networks that would have an explosive impact on the cable industry. The first channel was *Nickelodeon*, a service devoted to high quality programming for children and teenagers. A second network was launched on August 1, 1981: *MTV: Music Television.* MTV offered a radical new form of entertainment: music videos, 24-hours-a-day. ❖ In 1976, WCI created Warner Cosmetics with famed fashion designer Ralph Lauren. The company launched four new fragrances under the Lauren name: *Lauren* and *Tuxedo* for women, and *Polo* and *Chaps* for men. In 1982, a new women's fragrance, *Vanderbilt*, was developed in conjunction with well-known designer Gloria Vanderbilt. ❖ In 1984-85, when the decision was made to restructure WCI focusing on its roots in the entertainment business, Atari, Warner Cosmetics, and WCI's cable programming interests were sold. The three businesses, all essentially start-up operations just a few years before, brought WCI more than $800 million in cash and marketable securities.

CONSOLIDATED STATEMENT OF OPERATIONS

Years ended December 31 (Thousands, except per share amounts)	1987	1986	1985
Operating revenues	$3,403,563	$2,848,324	$2,234,891
Operating costs and expenses:			
Cost of revenues	2,412,599	2,043,477	1,608,553
Selling, general and administrative expenses	542,964	454,579	348,687
Total operating costs and expenses	2,955,563	2,498,056	1,957,240
Total operating income	448,000	350,268	277,651
Unallocated income (expenses):			
Corporate general and administrative	(49,377)	(38,092)	(33,547)
Interest and other, net	(20,211)	(54,560)	(64,438)
Gain on investments, net	40,330	39,797	222,639
Total unallocated income (expenses)	(29,258)	(52,855)	124,654
Income from continuing operations before income taxes	418,742	297,413	402,305
Provision for income taxes	120,400	133,700	207,000
Income from continuing operations	298,342	163,713	195,305
Gain from discontinued operations, net of income taxes	—	22,082	—
Income before extraordinary item	298,342	185,795	195,305
Extraordinary item—benefit of tax loss carryforward	29,800	—	—
Net income	328,142	185,795	195,305
Less preferred dividend requirements	37,297	14,856	2,991
Net income applicable to common and dilutive common equivalent shares	$ 290,845	$ 170,939	$ 192,314
Per share amounts:			
Income from continuing operations	$1.87	$1.10	$1.43
Income before extraordinary item	$1.87	$1.26	$1.43
Extraordinary item	$ .22	$ —	$ —
Net income	$2.09	$1.26	$1.43
Average number of common and dilutive common equivalent shares outstanding	139,464	135,766	134,061

See accompanying notes to consolidated financial statements and summary of significant accounting policies.

34

CONSOLIDATED STATEMENT OF CASH FLOWS

Years ended December 31 (Thousands)	1987	1986	1985
Operating Activities:			
Net income	$328,142	$185,795	$195,305
Adjustments for noncash and nonoperating items:			
Depreciation and amortization	142,424	118,233	23,676
Gain on investments, net	(40,330)	(39,797)	(222,639)
Gain from discontinued operations	—	(22,082)	—
Equity-method accounting	24,172	(4,297)	14,946
Changes in related balance sheet accounts:			
Accounts and notes receivable	(159,504)	(66,562)	(156,851)
Inventories	(65,133)	(80,208)	(3,936)
Accounts payable and accrued expenses	189,398	85,771	38,817
Other balance sheet changes	(15,005)	45,337	(25,517)
Excess of provision for income taxes over net payments for income taxes	35,324	61,615	180,191
Cash provided by operations	439,488	283,805	43,992
Investing Activities:			
Capital expenditures	(164,775)	(153,759)	(19,459)
Acquisition of Chappell in 1987 and 50% of Warner Cable in 1986 (a)	(122,839)	(393,050)	—
Cash balances of acquired companies	14,793	73,615	—
Proceeds from the sale of MTV and S/TMC	—	326,203	123,852
Proceeds from sale of other investments, including investments in operations discontinued in 1984	26,648	122,762	209,535
Decrease (increase) in marketable securities	68,355	(196,596)	(4,202)
Other investments	(39,677)	(6,809)	(30,110)
Cash (used) provided by investing activities	(217,495)	(227,634)	279,616
Financing and Capital Activities:			
Issuance of Series A preferred stock	—	484,402	—
Reduction of debt	(87,129)	(390,749)	(330,091)
Payment of dividends	(91,455)	(48,113)	(7,363)
Other	11,929	17,446	65,818
Cash (used) provided by financing and capital activities	(166,655)	62,986	(271,636)
Increase in cash and cash equivalents	$ 55,338	$119,157	$ 51,972

(a) The principal noncash effects of the 1987 Chappell acquisition on WCI's balance sheet include the following increases in account balances: receivables—$57,813,000; other assets—$279,571,000; accounts payable and accrued expenses—$161,948,000; and, to record the Series A preferred shares issued, shareholders' equity—$77,556,000. The principal noncash effects of the 1986 Amexco transaction include the following increases in account balances: receivables—$367,239,000; property, plant and equipment—$585,920,000; other assets—$152,190,000; long-term debt—$405,213,000; and accounts payable and accrued expenses—$174,956,000; and a reduction in investments of $203,256,000.

See accompanying notes to consolidated financial statements and summary of significant accounting policies.

35

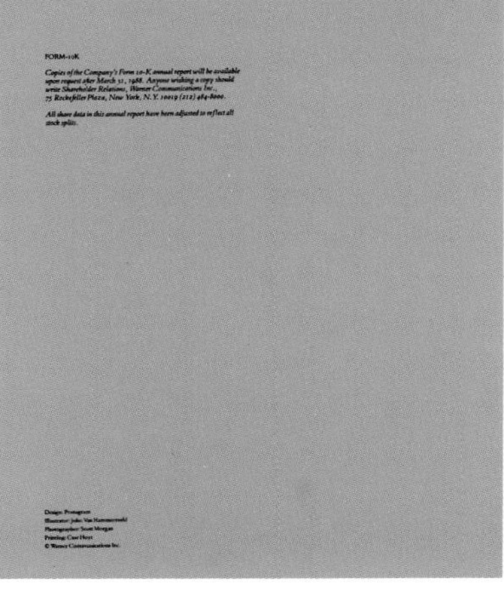

CLIENT:
WARNER COMMUNICATIONS INC.

DESIGN FIRM:
PENTAGRAM DESIGN

ART DIRECTORS:
PETER HARRISON, HAROLD BURCH

DESIGNERS:
HAROLD BURCH, PETER HARRISON

PHOTOGRAPHER:
SCOTT MORGAN

ILLUSTRATOR:
JOHN VAN HAMMERSVELD

LES EDWARDS, DIRECTOR OF CORPORATE COMMUNICATIONS, WARNER COMMUNICATIONS INC., NEW YORK, NEW YORK

One of the main purposes of the 1987 Warner annual report was to commemorate 25 years of Warner Communications. For this concept we needed a visual sensibility; we wanted to convey in a visual sense the excitement of our company and the entertainment industry. We wanted to project the energy of this business in a tasteful and esthetic way, documenting the years through our performing artists and films. Peter Harrison and Harold Burch of Pentagram and I worked very closely together. We collaborated on all of the ideas. The resulting annual report was received ecstatically in-house. We managed to show our company's history in a risk-taking way. Warner Communications does not follow the crowd in its products, and neither does this annual report in its presentation. This annual report has the effect of a coffee table book. When people see it, they reach to pick it up and look at it.

LES EDWARDS, DIRECTOR OF CORPORATE COMMUNICATIONS, WARNER COMMUNICATIONS INC., NEW YORK, NEW YORK

Eines der Hauptthemen des Warner Geschäftsberichtes für 1987 war das 25jährige Bestehen der Warner Communications. Für dieses Konzept brauchten wir eine starke visuelle Aussage; wir wollten so das Aufregende an unserem Geschäft und an der Unterhaltungsindustrie zeigen. Wir wollten die Dynamik dieser Branche projizieren, indem wir die Jahre mit Hilfe unserer darstellenden Künstler und unserer Filme dokumentierten. Peter Harrison und Herold Burch von Pentagram arbeiteten eng mit mir zusammen. Der fertige Bericht wurde in unserem Hause begeistert aufgenommen. Es ist uns gelungen, die Geschichte unserer Firma auf ganz mutige Art darzustellen... Warner Brothers schwimmt nicht mit der Masse, was die Produkte angeht, und das gilt auch für die Präsentation des Jahresberichtes. Dieser Jahresbericht wird von jederman gern in die Hand genommen.

LES EDWARDS, DIRECTOR OF CORPORATE COMMUNICATIONS, WARNER COMMUNICATIONS, INC., NEW YORK

L'un des objectifs principaux du rapport annuel de Warner pour 1987 était de commémorer le 25e anniversaire de Warner Communications. A ce concept, il fallait une sensibilité visuelle particulière, car nous souhaitions transposer au plan visuel l'enthousiasme que cet événement suscitait au sein de l'entreprise et de l'industrie des spectacles. Nous entendions projeter l'énergie de cette branche à travers nos acteurs et actrices et nos films. Peter Harrison et Harold Burch de Pentagram m'ont fait bénéficier de leur coopération continue. Le rapport annuel qui en est résulté a été accueilli avec enthousiasme dans la maison. Nous avons tenté de retracer de manière quelque peu hasardeuse l'histoire de notre société. Warner Communications n'adopte pas le goût du vulgaire dans ses productions; la présentation adoptée pour le rapport annuel ne déroge pas à la règle. Ce rapport annuel est un succès.

PETER HARRISON, PENTAGRAM DESIGN, NEW YORK, NEW YORK

The brief we received from Warner Communications for the 1987 report was to recall the major events of the 25 year period of the company's history in an entertaining way. We cast about for ideas to present a serious topic with energy and wit. One idea came to mind thinking of old movie theaters and the posters that were put up; which eventually wore away, leaving layer upon layer of posters. Using this graphic part of entertainment captured by torn paper became a basic idea. We then decided on the illustrator John Van Hammersveld and used him for the illustrations and carried this look of torn paper into the border designs. We introduced world events into the report to put the Warner historic moments into context. We made icons of these events, resulting in an eclectic scrapbook feeling. The cover grew out of the inside content. We continued with the idea of torn paper and within this collage background, numbers were introduced emphasizing the sense of all those years. We presented significant events in a significant way in this company's annual report.

PETER HARRISON, PENTAGRAM DESIGN, NEW YORK, NEW YORK

Im Zusammenhang mit der Gestaltung des Jahresberichtes für 1987 wurden wir von Warner Communications beauftragt, die Hauptereignisse der Firmengeschichte der vergangenen 25 Jahre auf unterhaltsame Art darzustellen. Wir präsentierten einige Ideen, wie man ein ernstes Thema lebendig und humorvoll darstellen kann. Wir dachten unter anderem an die alten Kinos und die Plakate, die immer wieder abnutzten und überklebt wurden. Die Darstellung dieses graphischen Aspekts der Unterhaltungsindustrie durch abgerissenes Papier wurde zur Grundidee. John Van Hammersveld machte die Illustrationen. Wir griffen weltbewegende Ereignisse auf und brachten sie in Zusammenhang mit den Ereignissen bei Warner, so dass eine Art eklektisches Notizbuch entstand. Der Umschlag ergab sich aus dem Inhalt. Wir blieben bei der Idee des zerfetzten Papiers, und auf dem Hintergrund dieser Collage wurden Zahlen eingesetzt, um all die Jahre darzustellen. Wir präsentierten in diesem Jahresbericht bedeutende Ereignisse auf angemessene Art.

PETER HARRISON, PENTAGRAM DESIGN, NEW YORK, NEW YORK

Les instructions de Warner Communications pour le rapport annuel 1987 précisaient l'évocation divertissante des grands événements qui ont constellé le quart de siècle écoulé dans la maison. Nous avons testé les idées propres à présenter un sujet sérieux sous un jour dynamique et spirituel. L'une de ces idées avait trait aux vieux cinémas d'antan et aux affiches qu'on y placardait l'une sur l'autre. C'est ainsi qu'est née l'idée de base de l'aspect graphique du spectacle représenté par du papier déchiré. Nous avons ensuite fait appel à l'illustrateur John Van Hammersveld. Les événements jalonnant l'histoire de Warner ont été mis en parallèle avec les événements de l'Histoire tout court. Nous en avons fait des icônes, donnant à l'ensemble l'aspect d'un album de coupures de presse éclectiques. La couverture est née des pages intérieures. Reprenant l'idée du papier déchiré, nous avons obtenu un collage comme arrière-plan des chiffres soulignant l'importance des années passées en revue. Dans ce rapport annuel, nous avons présenté des événements significatifs sous une forme significative.

W C R S

centre are partners within the Group rather than servants of the master. But we want, indeed expect, to be the best. Thus we reward and promote outstanding performance. And make changes if our performance is lacking. We also avoid the filtering layers of staff that so often seem to discourage or screen out entrepreneurial ideas and creativity.

We believe that every business in the Group must always be trying to improve. Whatever the sector, whatever the continent, our businesses all strive to be the best where it matters most, the "best in local market."

Building by adding value

Finally, as a Group we are committed to identifying added value before we make an acquisition – defining exactly what extra benefits the Group can bring to the new company, expressing our determination to make it a conspicuously better business. That is why, unlike other highly acquisitive groups, you will also see changes within the businesses we acquire. This is not a simple matter of cross-referral, valuable though this is, but a commitment by us and our partners to develop and improve the skills brought to bear on our clients' businesses.

For example, the merger of Della Femina, Travisano and HBM/Creamer in New York has been much publicised but additionally we have made several smaller acquisitions to strengthen our existing businesses. We have spun off Creamer Dickson Basford and Heller Breene. We have started several new ventures; we have attracted considerable new talent to the leadership of our various operations; and have underpinned such changes with the necessary systems modifications to promote better control, while encouraging risk-taking and initiative. The benefits of these changes are evident in the continuing organic growth and enhanced reputations of our businesses.

The winning streak

Not only is our strategy a winning strategy, but we have a unique blend of management talent and other values within the Group that will keep us ahead of the competition. These values – of creative excellence balanced by pillars of business management, entrepreneurship, commitment to innovation, and a willingness to act boldly and rapidly – are demonstrated in the review of operations contained in the body of this document.

Boldness and leadership have transformed your company since I last reported to you. But do not think that the Group stops here. The pace in the current year promises to be every bit as hectic.

Whilst the globalisation of many business sectors is accelerating (and ours is no exception), we see little evidence that this will lead to the full-scale globalisation of the advertising message. Consequently, there is little purpose in recreating the conventional branch office network proliferated by the American multinational agencies in the 1960s. We have instead opted for internationalisation based on a federal structure – with each of our agencies pursuing a "best in local market" positioning and at the same time offering the benefits of network co-ordination for those international clients who seek it.

WCRS MATHEWS MARCANTONIO

Two years ago the agency adopted as its five-year goal the ambition to become a top 10 UK agency. It is well on the way to meeting this objective. According to Campaign, the advertising industry magazine, it is now ranked number 14 in terms of UK billings, following an increase in new business last year of £25 million. Perhaps more important it continues to be rated highly in independent research for its reputation. In the most recent study available the agency was nominated by prospective clients as the one they were most likely to consider in the event of an account review.

New team at the top

In an eventful year perhaps the most important single development was the appointment of Roger Mathews as Managing Director WCRS Mathews Marcantonio together with the creation of a new management structure within the agency as part of the wider Group reorganisation. His appointment last November was well received and under his direction the agency is continuing to attract new clients, among the most recent being the £6 million a year McVitie's account for United Biscuits, and the £5 million account for Laura Ashley.

We also scored highly with existing clients. The launch of the new BMW 7 series was a great success and the car quickly built up a nine-month waiting list. The campaign brought the agency gold awards for both press and television advertising. A rare achievement.

The agency also gained recognition for its campaign for Carling Black Label, the UK's best selling lager. It is an indication of its continued creative excellence that, in what is a very crowded market, the Carling television advertising has been recognised as the most recalled and best regarded lager campaign in the United Kingdom.

The Media Department continues to flourish as clients use our central buying services to place their media spend. Our buying power in this area is now so considerable that we are in a position to negotiate first-class prices for our clients, and would rank as one of the top six firms in the sector if we were independent.

The federation idea at work

An early encouraging sign of the benefits to come from the cross-referral of business between Britain and the Group's agencies in other parts of the world came when WCRS Mathews Marcantonio was appointed to handle Sheraton throughout Europe. In a parallel development, The Ball Partnership in Australia was also appointed by Sheraton and additionally BMW, a long-standing London client.

The agency continued to win awards and attract widespread recognition for its creative excellence. Once again we did exceptionally well in both the Campaign Press Awards, and in the British Television Advertising Awards, winning "golds" and "silvers". Such recognition brings a definite business benefit, in addition to the satisfaction and pride it naturally gives to those responsible. It helps us attract major new clients and be an attractive employer to many of the most talented people in British advertising. And that of course in turn helps us attract more business.

Since the year end we have been very fortunate in securing the outstanding talent of Alfredo Marcantonio who joined us as Executive Creative Director and Joint Deputy Chairman of the now renamed agency – WCRS Mathews Marcantonio. Alfredo spent four years at Collett Dickenson Pearce, and six at Lowe Howard-Spink where he built one of the most successful and admired creative departments in London.

FCO

Activity at FCO has been no less exciting. FCO joined the Group in the summer of 1986, and our intention was to develop it as a second major creative force in the UK which would enable the Group as a whole to resolve client conflicts.

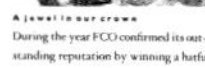

A jewel in our crown

During the year FCO confirmed its outstanding reputation by winning a hatful

Roger Mathews WCRS Mathews Marcantonio. Richard French FCO

The last three years have witnessed unparalleled growth in the market for design services. Greater consideration is now being given to the role of design in the development of corporate and brand identities – particularly in the light of escalating media costs.

The design opportunity

For an increasing number of clients design is no longer perceived as a fragmented series of projects whose goal is simply to make things look attractive. Design is now an integral part of the business system itself; its task is to create a substantial, consistent image that shines through virtually every form of visual communication about a product or service – be it the creation of a corporate identity or the design of a retail outlet. Because we believe that the type of expertise necessary to produce outstanding work will differ by design discipline, our strategy for the design group entails bringing together consultancies with specialist skills and creating the framework within which they can work in parallel.

Our design business so far consists of four companies in three countries with an income of £7 million.

SAUNDERS DESIGN

Saunders Design, acquired in September 1986, specialises in the design of commercial interiors – including retail stores, offices and exhibitions. Recent clients

include Stylo Barratt, Trusthouse Forte, Argyll Foods, Sketchley and Sears. Saunders Design has improved its trading performance substantially.

In October it was appointed by Bentalls to develop and implement the concept for a new 200,000 sq.ft. department store in Kingston-on-Thames. This is part of a £120 million project which will open in 1989.

It was commissioned by Hamleys to relaunch the legendary toy store in Regent Street, London, and to supervise the design and development of several regional branches. This contract was won against fierce competition from other design groups.

The year also saw Saunders Design working in Hong Kong, where the consultancy has been commissioned to redevelop the Watsons drugstore chain.

SIEBERT/HEAD

In January 1987 WCRS bought Siebert/Head with immediately encouraging results. Founded in London in 1972 by Ed Siebert and Richard Head, it was the first consultancy outside America to establish package design as a specialist skill. Since then it has positioned itself, outside the US, as the leading specialist package design consultancy, with clients in 17 countries.

Siebert/Head successfully marries creative skills with a highly analytical approach. As a result, its already impressive core client list, which includes Procter & Gamble, RHM Foods and Mars, has expanded with the recent addition of Van den Berghs, Batchelors and United Biscuits.

Pack redesign developed by Siebert/Head was recently the fulcrum of a major relaunch of the McDougalls brand of flours and food mixes. It designed the logo, wrapper, cereal box and display carton for Tracker, the successful new gran-

ola bar from Mars Confectionery, and also created a dynamic new container shape for Duckhams QXR and Hypergrade motor oil.

HELLER BREENE

In the United States the graphics-based design group acquired with the purchase of HBM/Creamer Boston was relaunched as Heller Breene under the inspired leadership of Cheryl Heller. Cheryl has already established a national reputation by winning more than 300 local and national awards for her work, and the agency is now the largest design company in the North East.

Its specialist skill is the creation of high-quality printed communications for clients whose visual image is of crucial importance. Boosted by the addition during the year of Maslow, Gold & Roths-

child's design interests, turnover has grown rapidly to £2.5 million. Its client list includes the highly successful athletic footwear company, Reebok International, Reed & Barton, S D Warren (a division of Scott Paper Company) and Bank of Boston.

LUNN DYER

WCRS has also recently acquired the Lunn Dyer Group, a Sydney-based design company. Lunn Dyer, whose clients include Qantas, BHP, Sheraton and Rosemount Wines, are Australia's leading corporate identity designers and will spearhead our design growth in the Pacific Basin.

David Saunders Saunders Design. **John Braddell** The WCRS Group. **Cheryl Heller**, Heller Breene. **Richard Head** Siebert/Head

The WCRS Group plc: Cross-servicing

We work for the following clients in two or more service divisions

	Advertising	Public relations	Design	Other
Alcos	■	■		
Allied Signal	■	■		■
American Brands	■	■		
Bank of Boston	■		■	■
BASF Systems	■		■	■
BHP	■		■	■
Booker Health	■	■		
Colgate	■	■		
Digital	■		■	
Dow Chemical	■		■	■
Duckhams	■		■	■
Guinness	■	■		
G D Searle	■	■		
Hercules	■	■		■
Hershey	■			■
Mars		■	■	
McDonald's	■	■		
Nestlé	■	■		
Procter & Gamble		■	■	
Qantas	■	■	■	
Qualcast	■	■		
Reebok	■		■	■
RHM Foods	■		■	
Rémy Martin	■			■
Schering-Plough	■	■		
Sheraton Hotels	■	■	■	■
Stanley Tools	■		■	
St Ivel		■		■
Tambrands		■	■	
Tetra Pak	■	■		
Thomson Travel	■	■		
United Biscuits	■		■	■

26 CROSS-SERVICING

We work for the following clients in two or more geographical areas

	UK	US	Pacific Basin
BASF	■	■	
BMW	■		■
Bristol-Myers		■	■
Dow Chemical		■	■
Hayes	■	■	
Laura Ashley	■	■	■
Procter & Gamble	■	■	

The WCRS Group: creative awards

Andrew Rutherford The WCRS Group

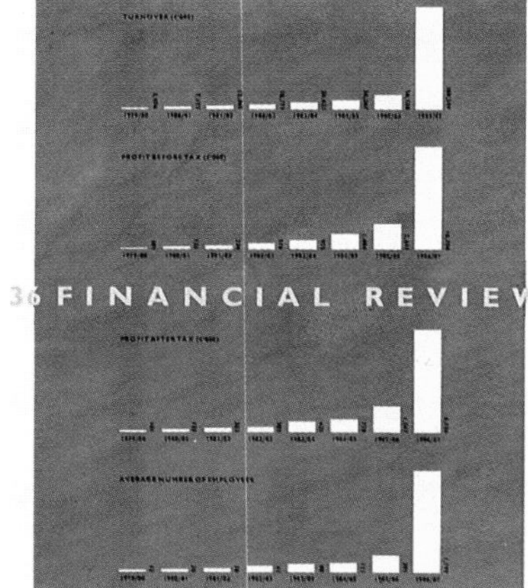

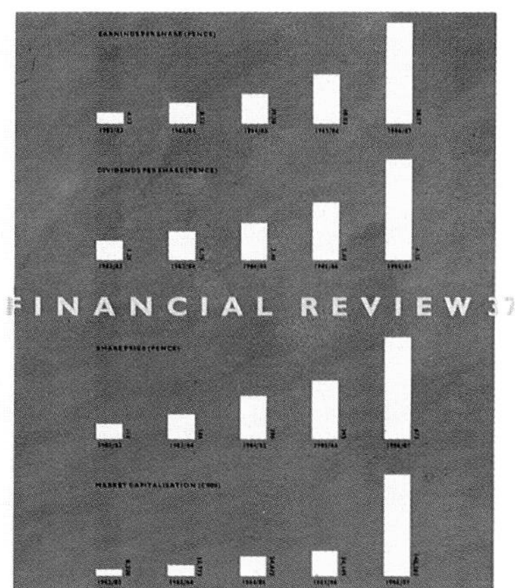

Notes forming part of the financial statements

1 POST BALANCE SHEET EVENTS

Since the year end the following events have taken place:

i On 12 June 1987 the Group completed the acquisition of The Ball Partnership, a network of advertising and direct response companies operating in the Pacific Basin.

The consideration for the acquisition was as follows:

a the sum of US$10,383,000 in cash.

b the allotment and issue of 123,570 Ordinary shares.

c the issue of a debenture constituting the WCRS unlisted non-interest bearing convertible secured loan stock 1992 in nominal amount of sterling equivalent to US$2,450,000 (for which one of the vendors subscribed US$1,000,000) convertible into Ordinary shares at a price of 630p per share, as to 50% within the conversion period following 30 June 1990 and 50% within the conversion period following 30 June 1992 dependent on achieving profit targets within those periods.

d the sum of US$918,378 paid to one of the vendors to discharge certain Promissory Notes given by The Ball Partnership.

ii On 29 May 1987 the authorised share capital was increased from £4,700,000 to £5,300,000 by the creation of 6,000,000 Ordinary shares of 10p each. In addition approximately £28,400,000 net of expenses was raised by way of a rights issue to shareholders of 5,140,154 Ordinary shares, in the proportion of 1 Ordinary share of 10p for every 4 Ordinary shares of 10p previously held and 5.1875 Ordinary shares of 10p for every 100 Convertible Preference shares of 10p previously held.

By special resolution passed on 29 May 1987, in order to preserve the distributable reserves of the Group, and subject to confirmation by the Court, approval was given for the reduction of the share premium account (which has been augmented by approximately £28,100,000 as a result of the rights issue) by £29,550,000. An equivalent amount was transferred to the credit of reserves to be used for writing off goodwill on acquisitions. With effect from the close of business on 24 July 1987, each of the authorised and issued Ordinary shares of 10p each of the Company were subdivided into 2 Ordinary shares of 5p each, to increase their marketability.

The effect of events **i** and **ii** above on the consolidated balance sheet at 30 April 1987 is illustrated on page 45.

iii On 25 June 1987 the Group acquired the business and certain assets of Garland Stewart & Roache Pty. Limited, a consumer advertising agency based in Sydney, Australia. The consideration for the acquisition is a maximum of A$5,000,000 payable as follows:

a A$1,272,098 on account of the goodwill of the business satisfied at completion by the issue of 46,143 Ordinary shares and the payment of A$572,444.

b the issue of 1,319 Ordinary shares on account of the value of the fixed assets.

c as to the balance of the value of the goodwill, by the issue of Ordinary shares at the then market price in five equal instalments on the five consequent anniversaries of the completion date.

d as to the balance of the value of the fixed assets, by the issue of Ordinary shares at the then market price when the value of those assets has been calculated.

e additional consideration satisfied by the issue of Ordinary shares at the then market price (but, in the event of exceptional growth, in part at the completion price) dependent on the post-tax profits of the Sydney agency in the five years ending 30 April 1992.

iv On 29 June 1987 the Group acquired Lunn Dyer & Associates Pty. Limited, an Australian company based in Sydney and the design business previously conducted by that company as trustee of the Lunn Dyer & Associates Unit Trust, for the following aggregate consideration:

a the sum of A$1,390,015 paid in cash on completion.

b additional consideration of up to A$3,060,000 payable in cash or Ordinary shares at the then market price at the option of the vendors in four tranches dependent on the pre-tax profits of the company in the four years ending 30 April 1991.

v On 1 July 1987 the Group acquired Robert A Becker, Inc., a US medical agency, for consideration as follows:

a the sum of US$8,000,000 paid in cash on completion.

b additional consideration of up to US$12,000,000 in five tranches dependent on the pre-tax profits of the company in the five years ending 30 April 1992.

c If all the profit targets of Becker are met the Group will pay a further US$1,250,000 to be used for the benefit of the employees of the company.

44 NOTES

Notes forming part of the financial statements

Pro forma consolidated balance sheet showing effect of acquisition of The Ball Partnership, rights issue and reduction of share premium account

	30 April 1987 (as adjusted)	30 April 1987
Fixed assets	**£000**	**£000**
Tangible assets	10,621	10,131
Investments	733	733
	11,354	10,864
Current assets		
Work in progress	999	799
Motor vehicle fleet	1,689	1,689
Debtors	57,087	51,733
Investments	124	8
Cash at bank and in hand	31,477	9,328
	91,376	63,557
Creditors		
Amounts falling due within one year	69,608	63,406
Net current assets	21,768	151
Total assets less current liabilities	33,122	11,015
Creditors		
Amounts falling due after more than one year	12,383	10,496
Provisions for liabilities and charges	438	438
Minority interests	3	3
	20,298	78
Capital and reserves		
Called-up share capital	4,044	3,518
Share premium account	563	1,405
Goodwill reserve	—	(10,808)
Special reserve*	9,728	—
Profit and loss account	5,963	5,963
	20,298	78

*The special reserve represents the excess of the share premium account reduction over goodwill and will be used to write off goodwill arising on future acquisitions.

NOTES 45

CLIENT:
WCRS GROUP PLC

DESIGN FIRM:
TATHAM PEARCE LTD.

ART DIRECTORS:
AMANDA TATHAM,
GILL DAVIES

DESIGNERS:
GILL DAVIES,
TRACEY GARNHAM

PHOTOGRAPHER:
JIM SIMMONS

ILLUSTRATOR:
GILL DAVIES

WRITER:
WCRS

TYPOGRAPHERS:
GILL DAVIES,
TRACEY GARNHAM

PAPER SELECTION:
PATRILUX MATT,
ANTIQUE SNOW WHITE

PAPER MANUFACTURER:
ISTD FINE PAPER,
GF SMITH

PRINTER:
WESTERHAM PRESS

NUMBER OF PAGES:
60 PLUS COVER

SIZE:
247 X 307 MM

TYPE SELECTION:
GILL SANS, BASKERVILLE

ADELE BISS, DIRECTOR OF THE WCRS GROUP PLC, LONDON, ENGLAND

The WCRS Group Annual Report and Accounts 1987 had to show the tremendous growth of the organization through 1986, which for WCRS, was phenomenal. We then needed to focus on the various new aspects of the company, which had burgeoned to include advertising, public relations, and design. We wanted to feature our new ventures. The 1987 annual report functioned as an introduction to our diverse divisions and as a portfolio of the company's work.

GILL DAVIES, TATHAM PEARCE LTD., LONDON, ENGLAND

For the 1987 WCRS annual report, we wanted to show the personalities of the various people the firm had joined up with and to emphasize that WCRS has offices in England, the United States, and elsewhere internationally. Many of these people are very famous in their fields, like Alan Pascoe, the British athlete. We wanted to indicate what these people did, and to indicate that these were the staffs of the individual companies, and also part of the entire WCRS group. The cover, we decided, should be plain, since so much was going on inside in the photographs. This annual report went down very well. It had a large format, was unconventional, and it had a lot of impact.

ADELE BISS, DIRECTOR DER WCRS GROUP PLC, LONDON, ENGLAND

Der Jahresbericht der WCRS-Gruppe für 1987 sollte das enorme Wachstum des Unternehmens im Jahre 1986 dokumentieren, das für WCRS phänomenal war. Wir mussten dabei die vielen neuen Aktivitäten unserer Firma berücksichtigen, zu denen jetzt auch Werbung, Public Relations und Design gehören. Wir wollten über unsere neuen Unternehmungen berichten. Der Jahresbericht für 1987 bietet einen Überblick über die verschiedenen Geschäftsbereiche von WCRS.

GILL DAVIES, TATHAM PEARCE LTD., LONDON, ENGLAND

Im WCRS-Geschäftsbericht für 1987 wollten wir die Persönlichkeit verschiedener Leute zum Ausdruck bringen, die jetzt für die Firma arbeiten. Gleichzeitig sollte hervorgehoben werden, dass WCRS Büros in England, USA und anderen Orten der Welt hat. Viele dieser Leute sind auf ihren Gebieten sehr berühmt, wie z.B. der britische Athlet Alan Pascoe. Wir wollten zeigen, was diese Leute machen, dass sie Teil der Belegschaft der einzelnen Firmen und gleichzeitig der ganzen WCRS-Gruppe sind. Der Umschlag sollte unserer Auffassung nach schlicht sein, weil auf den Photos im Inhalt des Berichts soviel passiert. Der Jahresbericht wurde gut aufgenommen.

ADELE BISS, DIRECTOR, WCRS GROUP PLC, LONDRES, GRANDE-BRETAGNE

Le rapport annuel du WCRS Group pour 1987 devait faire état de l'extraordinaire croissance que notre organisation a connue au cours de l'année 1986. Il fallait aussi mettre en lumière les divers aspects nouveau du group entré en force dans les secteurs de la publicité, des relations publiques et du design, d'où de nouvelles perspectives alléchantes. Le rapport annuel 1987 a ainsi servi à présenter nos diverses divisions. Il a été agrémenté d'un choix des travaux exécuté chez WCRS.

GILL DAVIES, TATHAM PEARCE LTD., LONDRES, GRANDE-BRETAGNE

Dans le rapport annuel 1987 de WCRS, nous avons voulu présenter diverses personnalités associées à cette entreprise et souligner son caractère international en montrant ses bureaux en Amérique et ailleurs. Nos portraits concernent des personnalités célèbres dans leur domaine, telles qu'Alan Pascoe, l'athlète britannique. Nous avons fait état de leurs activités et de leur rôle au sein de sociétés membres du groupe WCRS. Nous avons opté pour une couverture d'autant plus simple que l'illustration photo intérieure est surabondante. Ce rapport annuel a très bien été accueilli. Son grand format et son caractère peu conventionnel ont contribué à son impact.

A OF METROPOLITAN CHICA

YMCA OF METROPOLITAN CHICAGO

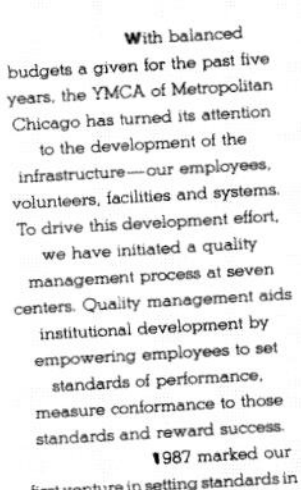

With balanced budgets a given for the past five years, the YMCA of Metropolitan Chicago has turned its attention to the development of the infrastructure—our employees, volunteers, facilities and systems. To drive this development effort, we have initiated a quality management process at seven centers. Quality management aids institutional development by empowering employees to set standards of performance, measure conformance to those standards and reward success.

1987 marked our first venture in setting standards in the program area. The Program Development Committee of the Board of Managers grouped our many programs into six identifiable categories—the core program areas that represent the essence of the YMCA. Technical committees of dedicated Y program staff then created standards for delivery of several program offerings within these core areas.

The following pages explain the six core program areas. As you review them, keep in mind that every YMCA in our association will soon offer at least one program from each of the six areas as appropriate for the community it serves. We will then use the core program areas to communicate the YMCA's image in a simple and straightforward way.

Our thanks to the hundreds of staff and volunteers who continue to facilitate our movement toward providing caring, quality service to children and families.

1

2

CHILD CARE

At the YMCA, we believe that high quality, affordable child care is crucial for today's families. Our programs support the healthy maturation of children from ages 3 to 13 while their parents are at work, school or job training. 3

Child care is distinct from other children's programs because it involves a long-term, comprehensive commitment. Pre-school children, for instance, are with us for up to ten hours a day, and many grow with us year after year.

Our child care core program area encompasses three programs: licensed pre-school and school-age child care and summer day camp. 1987 saw growth and improvement in all these areas. Our Day Camp Task Force developed, implemented and monitored standards for this important summer program offered at 24 centers. In the area of licensed programs, we served over 1300 children, up 120 slots from last year. We opened new Head Start programs at Pilsen and Logan Square. And we began adopting High/Scope, a highly respected pre-school curriculum model.

The YMCA of Metropolitan Chicago is truly a leader in child care, with 12 sites in the city and suburbs. But with a waiting list of over 700, we must continue to expand our offerings and advance the standards of excellence in this critical service that enriches family life.

SPORTS AND RECREATION

The sports and recreation core area encompasses many of our most solidly established and popular programs. It includes all skill development classes, organized sports, unstructured recreational activities and youth resident camping. Within this category we served over 100,000 people last year.

Strengthened by national YMCA standards and backed by training, programs such as youth progressive swim and progressive gymnastics have been taking children from fundamentals to mastery for almost 50 years. Our youth resident camps teach a wide range of skills in a setting away from home. They also provide outdoor education to hundreds of school children.

In addition to teaching skills, we also organize leagues and tournaments and provide unstructured playing time. "Play," according to one source, "is whatever you give yourself to completely." The many adults who join in pick-up basketball games and compete in handball leagues would agree.

As we develop standards and improve our offerings, we will pay special attention to 14- to 18-year olds and those over 55. Since program represents the way the YMCA carries out its mission in the community, we are committed to finding better ways of serving people of all ages.

FAMILY LIFE

The YMCA was created in the 19th century to assist young men—transient, single young men—as they moved from farms to cities. When they married and became family men, the YMCA responded to their new service needs. From these beginnings, we have become the premiere family institution. 7

Family life is the core area containing programs specifically designed for families or parents in which family interaction is the primary focus.

By a large percentage, most of our families participate in parent-tot gym and swim classes. Last year we served close to 85,000 people by strengthening the parent-child bond as the child explores water and land environments.

Indian Guides and Princesses involve a one-on-one relationship between a parent and child in the context of the American Indian tradition. Children range from ages 5 to 13 and enjoy a precious commodity—special time alone with mom or dad. Over 2,000 people benefit from this companionship.

The YMCA also offers family camping, both at family Camp Nawakwa and in special sessions at our other camps. In addition, most of our centers hold open recreation time, giving family members the freedom to play together.

As we assess our offerings in this area, we plan to design new program models for single-parent and other non-traditional family units.

LEADERSHIP DEVELOPMENT

11

Are leaders born or made? At the YMCA we believe that leadership can be taught through activities and modeled through the behavior of teachers. For this reason, many of our leadership programs are apprenticeships—close and extended contact between student and mentor.

We define this core program area as those organized activities and programs that have the primary purpose of increasing the ability of an individual to be an effective leader. Our target age group is teens and pre-teens.

YMCA Leader's Clubs assemble young people for the purpose of learning teaching skills, strengthening values and putting both to use in the service of others. In the process of volunteering at the Y, Leaders learn self-respect and responsible decision-making.

Our Counselor-In-Training (CIT) program is a two-year apprenticeship at resident camp. CITs receive training in camp skills and safety. By living in cabins with children and assisting counselors, they also learn group dynamics and develop responsibility for others.

Youth And Government gives students hands-on experience in the democratic process. Both the state and city programs combine education and government simulation to help teens grow into the leadership positions they role-play.

As we work further in this area, we will plan programs to assist in the development of our many adult volunteers.

FINANCIAL RESULTS

18

SUMMARY FINANCIAL INFORMATION
(as of 6/30/87, 6/30/86, 6/30/85 and for the fiscal years then ended)

Balance Sheet

	6/30/87	6/30/86	6/30/85
Current Assets	$ 3,036,000	$ 3,883,000	$ 2,422,000
Investments	18,221,000	14,482,000	11,506,000
Property and Other Assets	37,974,000	38,280,000	42,986,000
Total Assets	$59,231,000	$56,645,000	$56,914,000
Current Liabilities	$ 7,076,000	$ 7,543,000	$12,338,000
Long Term Debt and Other Liabilities	8,194,000	9,143,000	9,725,000
Total Liabilities	15,270,000	16,686,000	22,063,000
Fund Balances	43,961,000	39,959,000	34,851,000
Total Liabilities and Fund Balances	$59,231,000	$56,645,000	56,914,000

OPERATING FUND RESULTS

	1987	1986	1985
Support	$12,594,000	$11,706,000	$10,286,000
Revenue	21,900,000	21,874,000	21,770,000
Total	34,494,000	33,580,000	32,056,000
Expenses:			
Program Services	30,253,000	30,023,000	28,070,000
Supporting Services	4,642,000	4,302,000	4,391,000
Total	34,895,000	34,325,000	32,461,000
Interest and Dividend Income	1,849,000	2,043,000	2,035,000
Excess Operating Funds	$ 1,448,000	$ 1,298,000	$ 1,630,000

NON-OPERATING

Capital Contributions	$ 1,964,000	$ 1,277,000	$ 1,377,000
Capital Reinvestment:			
Capital Expenditures	1,715,000	1,694,000	2,184,000
Repayment of Indebtedness	$ 1,065,000	$ 984,000	$ 946,000

The audited financial statements together with the auditor's report thereon, are available upon written request to Mr. Leonard A. Hollenbeck, Vice President/Chief Financial Officer.

PROGRAM PARTICIPATION

TOTAL NUMBER OF ENROLLED PARTICIPANTS BY PROGRAM CLASSIFICATION AND AGE GROUP 19

Program Classification	Age Group					
	0-5	6-13	14-18	19-54	55+	Total
Health Enhancement	—	11,350	1,381	47,619	3,748	64,098
Aquatics	—	25,122	606	9,552	2,878	38,158
Sports and Recreation	28,940	25,893	7,175	19,401	6,310	87,719
Camping	—	12,154	1,284	8,573	215	22,226
Education and Training	—	5,028	1,571	5,014	131	11,744
Leadership Development	—	1,278	961	—	—	2,239
Family Life	18,159	25,831	3,695	36,697	1,396	85,778
Child Care	16,558	13,342	—	—	—	29,900
Social Development	1,217	1,549	3,588	4,166	4,078	14,598
Total	64,874	121,547	20,261	131,022	18,756	356,460

OTHER COMMUNITY RELATED SERVICE

Community groups assisted	53
Total occupancy nights in YMCA facilities	668,007

TOTAL NUMBER OF MEMBERS SERVED IN FISCAL YEAR 1987

	Youth		Adult		Grand Total
	Male	Female	Male	Female	Male & Female
Chicago centers	13,892	10,204	23,093	20,128	67,317
Suburban centers	15,267	13,551	36,140	30,666	95,624
Total	29,159	23,755	59,233	50,794	162,941

CLIENT:
YMCA OF METROPOLITAN CHICAGO

DESIGN FIRM:
SAMATA ASSOCIATES

ART DIRECTORS:
PAT AND GREG SAMATA

DESIGNER:
PAT SAMATA

PHOTOGRAPHER:
MARK JOSEPH

WRITER:
PATRICE BOYER

PATRICE BOYER, DIRECTOR OF MARKETING AND COMMUNICATION, YMCA OF METROPOLITAN CHICAGO, CHICAGO, ILLINOIS

The theme of our 1987 annual report was our core programs, which are umbrella categories for the areas of work we do. We needed a way of presenting these categories to the public, which is hard to convey. For example, we have social services and job training programs as well as the usual sports and recreation programs. Pat and Greg Samata found a way of depicting them through the use of colors, and we used photographs of real people who use the YMCAs. We have been working with the Samatas since 1983. Then, we needed an annual report to make a big splash; now, we have a scaled-down version. Even so, the Samatas have made the commitment to keep the annual report looking wonderful.

PATRICE BOYER, DIRECTOR OF MARKETING AND COMMUNICATION, YMCA OF METROPOLITAN CHICAGO, CHICAGO, ILLINOIS

Den thematische Schwerpunkt unseres Jahresberichtes für 1987 bildeten unsere Hauptprogramme. Wir suchten nach einer Möglichkeit, dem Publikum unsere Arbeitsbereiche zu verdeutlichen, was nicht einfach ist. Wir haben z.B. Sozialdienste und Ausbildungsprogramme neben den üblichen Sport- und Freizeitprogrammen. Pat und Greg Samata lösten die Aufgabe durch Kennzeichnung der Kategorien mit Farben und Photos von Leuten, die die YMCAs benutzen. Wir arbeiten seit 1983 mit den Samatas zusammen. Damals brauchten wir einen sensationellen Bericht, jetzt haben wir eine zurückhaltendere Version. Trotzdem ist es den Samatas gelungen, einen sehr schönen Bericht herzustellen.

PATRICE BOYER, DIRECTOR OF MARKETING AND COMMUNICATION, YMCA OF METROPOLITAN CHICAGO, CHICAGO, ILLINOIS

Le sujet de notre rapport annuel pour 1987 était l'ensemble de nos programmes-clefs dont chacun recouvre l'un des domaines où nous travaillons. Il fallait trouver moyen de présenter ces catégories au public, ce qui n'est pas chose facile. Nous avons par exemple des services sociaux et de formation professionnelle aussi bien que les programmes de sport et de loisirs habituels. Pat et Greg Samata ont su les décrire par le biais de couleurs, en employant les photos d'usagers réels de l'YMCA. Nous travaillons avec les Samata depuis 1983. A l'époque, on avait besoin d'un rapport-choc. Cette fois-ci, l'échelle était plus modeste, et pourtant les Samata ont su donner une présentation merveilleuse à notre rapport.

PAT SAMATA, GREG SAMATA, SAMATA ASSOCIATES, DUNDEE, ILLINOIS

For the 1987 YMCA annual report, we were dealing with the core programs of the YMCA in a unique way. We had to feature programs, for example, which the Y runs for seniors, and child care. We decided to use large letters, and to have one person symbolize or represent each program. Then we had these people jumping out of the letter forms. The YMCA gives us a lot of leeway, so we develop the concept and theme with the staff, and then we develop our ideas on how to portray these.

PAT SAMATA, GREG SAMATA, SAMATA ASSOCIATES, DUNDEE, ILLINOIS

Beim Jahresbericht 1987 für den YMCA haben wir die Hauptprogramme des YMCA auf ganz ungewöhnliche Art dargestellt. Dazu gehörten z.B. Programme für Senioren und Kinder. Wir entschieden uns für grosse Buchstaben. Jedes Programm wurde durch eine Person dargestellt, die aus den Buchstaben heraussprang. Der YMCA gibt uns einen grossen Spielraum; wir besprachen das Konzept und Thema mit den Mitarbeitern. Auf dieser Basis entwickelten wir unsere Ideen.

PAT SAMATA, GREG SAMATA, SAMATA ASSOCIATES, DUNDEE, ILLINOIS

Pour le rapport annuel 1987 de l'YMCA, nous avons traité ces programmes-clefs de manière inhabituelle. Il nous fallait par exemple illustrer des activités pour le 3e âge et pour les petits. Nous avons décidé d'avoir recours à des grosses lettres et de représenter chaque programme par une seule personne typée, que nous avons fait jaillir de chaque lettre. L'YMCA nous accorde une large liberté de manœvre. Nous avons développé le concept et le thème avec l'équipe YMCA.

ANNUAL REPORT DESIGN

GESTALTUNG VON JAHRESBERICHTEN

DESIGN DES RAPPORTS ANNUELS

IMMUNEX CORPORATION

IMMUNEX 1988 ANNUAL REPORT

FINANCIAL HIGHLIGHTS

Immunex Corporation

Selected Financial Data

	1988	1987	1986	1985	1984
Revenues	$22,234,444	$15,703,964	$ 9,481,872	$ 3,226,830	$ 3,471,139
Net income (loss)	657,300	(175,488)	(1,413,268)	(4,441,768)	(2,464,497)
Net loss per common share	(.01)	(.02)	(.20)	(.75)	(.42)
Total assets	95,176,780	73,641,296	72,661,382	12,707,934	17,293,048
Long-term debt, including current portion	43,216,201	42,595,381	42,185,907	1,416,396	1,765,330
Stockholders' equity	48,223,591	28,265,290	28,259,268	10,879,173	15,145,148

Research Revenues ($ in millions)

1988	15.4
1987	10.0
1986	6.2
1985	2.4
1984	2.2

Research Expenses ($ in millions)

1988	13.7
1987	9.5
1986	7.8
1985	6.5
1984	4.8

Stockholders' Equity ($ in millions)

1988	48.2
1987	28.3
1986	28.3
1985	10.9
1984	15.1

Working Capital ($ in millions)

1988	63.2
1987	57.4
1986	60.9
1985	7.3
1984	11.2

LETTER TO OUR STOCKHOLDERS

Immunex looks a lot more like the company we have always envisioned than it did a year ago. We have reorganized the corporation and signed significant new agreements with Eastman Kodak. These are not the kinds of developments that make big headlines–or make big impressions on Wall Street–but they have moved the company in a direction we all want to go.

I'm not suggesting that 1988 was what coaches often dismiss as "a building year." Far from it. During the past year, we:

• began clinical testing of three new products, IL-4, IL-3 and IL-1, giving us a total of six products in the clinic;

• started up our new manufacturing plant, working up from laboratory to pilot scale the production of GM-CSF, IL-2, IL-3, IL-4 and G-CSF;

• started preclinical testing of IL-7 and the IL-1 receptor, our discovery and cloning of which were described in 1988 issues of *Science* and *Nature*;

• saw the testing for approval of IL-2 completed (tests of IL-2 in combination with alpha interferon will continue and tests in combination with IL-4 are planned).

We expect Hoffmann-La Roche, our partner in the development of IL-2, and Behringwerke AG of West Germany, our partner in the development of GM-CSF, to file this year with the FDA for approval to market those products.

We were pleased to see Ajinomoto receive a broad U.S. patent last April for recombinant IL-2. Our partner, Hoffmann-La Roche, has a right to all non-Asian marketing of IL-2 under Ajinomoto's patents. Roche subsequently agreed with Cetus, which also holds IL-2 patents, to cross-license each other's products. The Cetus-Roche agreement should prevent a fight over U.S. patents. Under our own agreements with Roche, Immunex is entitled to royalties on both Roche and Cetus sales of IL-2.

During 1988, we also built our cash reserve to $64.9 million. Our revenues exceeded our research costs for the third straight year. Our net loss per share was only one cent. (We'll have to absorb the costs of expanded research before we see revenues from IL-2 or GM-CSF, so look for somewhat higher losses per share in 1989 and 1990.)

Normally, all this might have stirred some interest in the press and on Wall Street, but during most of 1988, media and investor enthusiasm for biotechnology was at a low ebb. Interest has lagged ever since the stock market crash of October 1987. People were further disillusioned by Genentech's well-publicized troubles with the clot-dissolving drug TPA. In terms of immediate sales, TPA was very successful. In terms of public perception, it was disappointing. The whole industry has suffered.

Probably our most exciting development of 1988 was the signing of new agreements with Eastman Kodak. As you know, in 1986, Immunex and Kodak agreed to establish a joint venture, build a pilot manufacturing plant, and have Immunex search Kodak's extensive library of organic compounds for small molecules that mimicked or inhibited the action of lymphokines.

One 1988 agreement with Kodak takes the creation of new products a long step further. It sets up a process of "rational drug design" that works like this: Immunex scientists isolate a lymphokine gene, produce a recombinant product, and send the product to Kodak; Kodak chemists then crystallize the lymphokine, make a three-dimensional model of the molecule, and try to mimic its active site as a small organic molecule; Immunex takes the new organic compound back to the laboratory and tests its effects. Organics may be the next generation of lymphokine therapeutics; as smaller molecules, they may have fewer side effects than the proteins we develop in our labs, and unlike proteins, which must be injected, they may be given orally. They hold out the promise of much broader markets. Immunex has U.S. marketing rights for any product developed by the "rational" process.

The Kodak agreements also call for joint development of protease inhibitors. Proteases are enzymes which act on proteins. They play crucial roles in the maturation of several viruses, in mediating some of the undesirable aspects of inflammation, and in the tissue destruction seen in a number of degenerative diseases.

Finally, Kodak paid $20 million for shares of Immunex convertible preferred stock. Fifteen million went into our working capital. Five million was used to acquire Kodak's share of the pilot manufacturing plant. Kodak now has a stake in Immunex, and therefore in seeing that our collaboration

Discovery is not simply stumbling on to the unknown. It stems from both broad-based and specific, targeted research. At Immunex, discovery is a result of wide-ranging, biologically-oriented investigation into various functional properties of the immune system and pursuit of the molecular mechanisms behind them.

Widmer

Michael Widmer
Senior Staff Scientist
Immunology

Dirk Anderson
Research Associate
Molecular Biology

TOO SMALL TO BE SEEN UNAIDED, A SUCCESSFUL DISCOVERY IS OFTEN DETECTED BY THE BANDS ON A GEL. INTERPRETING SUCH EVIDENCE AND WHAT IT COULD MEAN FOR TREATING A DISEASE REQUIRES IMAGINATION. WHEN SUCCESS IS EVENTUALLY MEASURED BY VIALS SHIPPED AND PATIENTS TREATED, IMAGINATIVE DISCOVERIES WILL HAVE PLAYED A VITAL ROLE.

• *Discovery*
• *Rational Drug Design*
• *Development*
• *Manufacturing*
• *Clinical Affairs*
• *Corporate Development*

Greater emphasis is being directed towards development as our future products progress through clinical trials and approach the marketplace. Our current efforts are focused on optimization of purification processes for manufacturing and detailed characterization studies.

Klinke

Helmut Sassenfeld
Director
Process Development

Ralph Klinke
Research Associate
Process Development

VALIDATING THE REPRODUCIBILITY OF A PRODUCT IS AN IMPORTANT FACTOR IN SUCCESSFULLY MANUFACTURING PROTEINS. COMPARING CHROMATOGRAPHS OR PEPTIDE MAPS, AS SHOWN, IS A QUALITY CONTROL MEASURE WHICH DEMONSTRATES THAT PREPARATIONS FROM SUCCESSIVE PRODUCTION RUNS ARE IDENTICAL.

• *Discovery*
• *Rational Drug Design*
• *Development*
• *Manufacturing*
• *Clinical Affairs*
• *Corporate Development*

Immunex now has the facilities to manufacture lymphokines at a commercial scale under controlled conditions. Our team of manufacturing specialists is working closely with the Process Development Group in R&D and the Regulatory Affairs Department to scale up the current processes into operations suitable for production.

Grassam

Bogdan Dzsurzynski
Director
Regulatory Affairs

Peter Grassam
Vice President
Immunex
Manufacturing
Corporation

David Urdal
Vice President
Immunex R&D
Corporation

IN ITS FIRST SIX MONTHS OF OPERATION, THE PILOT PLANT PRODUCED INITIAL RUNS OF FIVE DIFFERENT LYMPHOKINE PRODUCTS. ALREADY IN 1989, MANUFACTURING HAS ORDERS FROM COLLABORATORS FOR CLINICAL TRIAL QUANTITIES OF GM-CSF, IL-3, IL-4, G-CSF, AND IL-1. IMMUNEX WILL ALSO USE IL-1 IN ITS OWN TRIALS.

• *Discovery*
• *Rational Drug Design*
• *Development*
• *Manufacturing*
• *Clinical Affairs*
• *Corporate Development*

A priority in 1988 was to secure quality preclinical data on IL-1 as a wound healing agent. Once the IND is approved, Immunex will begin clinical testing of its first proprietary product. This is an important step, and one Immunex looks forward to with confidence.

Sinkule

Cindy Jacobs
Staff Scientist
Immunology

Joseph Sinkule
Assistant Director
Clinical Research

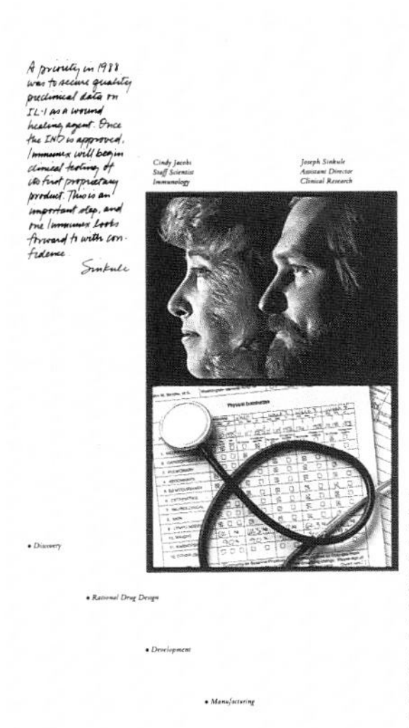

THE CLINICAL TRIALS DEPARTMENT AT IMMUNEX HAS BEEN STAFFED SINCE 1987, MANAGING AND ASSISTING WITH A NUMBER OF COLLABORATORS' CLINICAL TRIALS. THIS VALUABLE EXPERIENCE HAS AIDED IN BUILDING UP IMMUNEX'S OWN CLINICAL PROGRAM, AND WILL BE USED WHEN TESTING OF PROPRIETARY PRODUCTS BEGINS IN 1989.

• *Discovery*
• *Rational Drug Design*
• *Development*
• *Manufacturing*
• *Clinical Affairs*
• *Corporate Development*

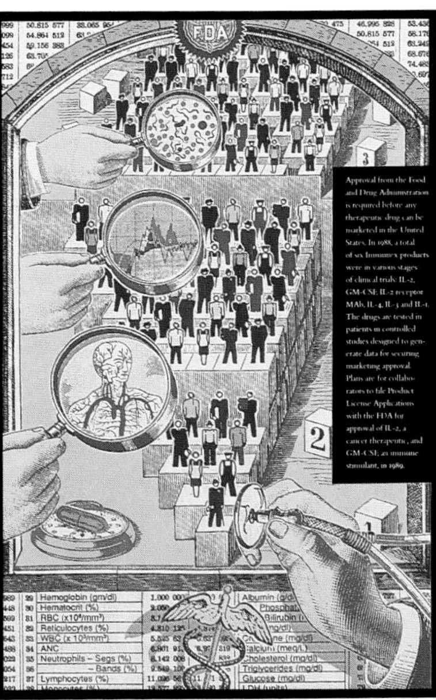

Immunex finished 1988 with six products in clinical testing. In addition, the company began manufacturing at its Seattle pilot plant, concluded major new agreements with Kodak, created new subsidiaries for research and manufacturing, and began preclinical testing of its newly discovered IL-7 and its newly cloned receptor for IL-1.

Immunex's collaborative partners in the development of IL-2 and GM-CSF, Hoffmann-La Roche and Behringwerke AG, both expect to apply this year for FDA licenses to market the products. Licensing normally takes 12 to 24 months.

Clinical tests directed toward initial FDA approval of IL-2 were completed in 1988. It has been tested both alone and in conjunction with lymphokine-activated killer cells (LAK). It is also being tested in combination with alpha interferon. In these regimens, IL-2 has shown promise as a therapeutic agent against some melanomas and renal cell carcinomas. It has been possible to lower the dose, which has in turn reduced side effects of the drug that posed an early problem. Eventually, using IL-2 in combination with IL-4 may permit still lower doses, and reduce side effects even further.

The Immunex-Roche proprietary position on IL-2 has become stronger. Ajinomoto received a broad U.S. patent for recombinant IL-2 in April; Roche has a right to all non-Asian manufacturing and marketing of IL-2 under Ajinomoto patents. In addition, Cetus, which also holds IL-2 patents, and Roche agreed to cross-license each other's products. Under Immunex's agreements with Roche, the company is entitled to royalties on any IL-2 that Roche or Cetus sells. Immunex also has an option from Roche to manufacture up to 25 percent of the IL-2 for the North American market.

GM-CSF, which stimulates production of infection-fighting macrophages and granulocytes, may be useful for cancer patients whose immune systems have been depleted by radiation or chemotherapy, cancer patients who have undergone bone marrow transplants, and people who suffer from inherited white blood cell disorders; it may also be useful for patients with AIDS. Immunex believes that it and Behringwerke AG have a substantial lead in the commercial development of GM-CSF. Immunex and Behringwerke currently run one of the biopharmaceutical industry's broadest programs for the development of colony stimulating factors (CSFs) in general. Under a 1984 agreement, Behringwerke will test, manufacture, and market any CSFs that Immunex develops. Immunex has an option to manufacture up to one-third of each CSF for the North American market. Discussions begun last year with Behringwerke give Immunex a reasonable expectation that it will be able to manufacture 100 percent of the GM-CSF for North America.

Immunex has helped manage American clinical testing for GM-CSF since February 1987, and has manufactured all GM-CSF for those tests. Now, it is producing the GM-CSF in its Seattle manufacturing plant, which began operating last spring. This year, Immunex expects the plant not only to make all the GM-CSF the company needs for U.S. testing but also to start stockpiling GM-CSF for Behringwerke's future commercial sales.

In addition, the new manufacturing plant is expected to produce G-CSF, IL-1, IL-3 and IL-4 for clinical tests.

Three of those lymphokines entered clinical testing in 1988. All are being tested on cancer patients. IL-4, which stimulates the production of B and T cells, is being used as a direct cancer therapy. IL-3 is being given after radiation or chemotherapy, to accelerate the immune system's recovery. It stimulates the production of white blood cells, and early evidence indicates it stimulates the production of platelets. Collaborators on IL-3 and IL-4 are Behringwerke AG and Sterling Drug (Kodak), respectively.

IL-1 is being given to cancer patients in a Phase I safety study. Once the safety study is completed, plans are to administer IL-1 immediately after radiation or chemotherapy, to limit damage to the bone marrow. Immunex is collaborating with Syntex on this particular use of IL-1. The company will investigate other uses on its own. Immunex plans to file this year an Investigational New Drug application for permission to begin clinical testing of IL-1

Products Under Development	*Preclinical*	*Drug Master File*	*Clinical Testing Phases* I	I/II	III	*On Market*
Interleukin-2					•	
GM-CSF					•	
IL-2 receptor MAb				•		
Interleukin-4			•			
Interleukin-3			•			
G-CSF		•				
Interleukin-1 (radioprotectant)			•			
Interleukin-1 (wound healing)		•				
Interleukin-1 (vaccine adjuvant)		•				
Interleukin-7	•					
IL-1 receptor	•					
Flag® Kit (protein purification system)						•

as an aid to wound healing. Initial tests will focus on hospitalized patients with decubitus ulcers. IL-1 as a wound healing agent is the first product for which Immunex will have total control of clinical testing and marketing.

Immunex's sixth product in clinical testing, IL-2R MAb, is a monoclonal antibody specific to the IL-2 receptor. It is being developed in partnership with Becton-Dickinson.

Two entirely new products, IL-7 and the receptor for IL-1, the cloning of which were announced early last year, have entered preclinical testing. Both are being tested in mice. Preclinical testing normally takes about one year. IL-7 stimulates the development of precursors of both B and T cells. The IL-1 receptor might be used in the treatment of rheumatoid arthritis and other autoimmune diseases. Excess IL-1 in the body has been implicated as a contributing factor in inflammation and tissue destruction associated with rheumatoid arthritis, multiple sclerosis, diabetes,

MANAGEMENT'S DISCUSSION AND ANALYSIS OF FINANCIAL CONDITION AND RESULTS OF OPERATION

Immunex Corporation

Liquidity and Capital Resources

The Company continued to maintain a high level of liquidity and substantial working capital in 1988. Cash and marketable securities at December 31, 1988 increased to $64.9 million from $59.2 million at December 31, 1987. Working capital amounted to $63.2 million at December 31, 1988, compared to $57.4 million at December 31, 1987. The Company's strong financial position primarily resulted from a series of equity financings and one convertible debenture offering, aggregating $93.6 million, beginning with the Company's initial public offering in 1983.

The $5.7 million net increase in cash and marketable securities in 1988 was principally the result of an issuance of Series A Cumulative Convertible Preferred Stock to Eastman Kodak Company ("Kodak") for $20 million and positive cash flow from operations of $1.5 million, partially offset by capital investments. Significant capital investments were capital contributions of $4.4 million to Immunology Ventures (the "Joint Venture"), the Company's partnership with Kodak, expenditures of $5.2 million for continued expansion of the Company's research and administrative facilities, and the $4.7 million purchase of Kodak's interest in the pilot-scale manufacturing facility. The Company's purchase from Kodak occurred after an equal distribution of the Joint Venture's net manufacturing assets to its partners.

The Company's capital contributions to the Joint Venture are expected to increase in the coming years as a result of changes which occurred in 1988. In May, the research activities of the Joint Venture were significantly expanded by adding new programs, primarily in the areas of Rational Drug Design and Protease Inhibitors. The Company agreed to fund 50% of the costs related to these new projects in cash. In return for its investment, the Company will receive exclusive rights to develop and market in the United States any products resulting from the new programs. In 1989, the Company plans to invest $3.8 million of cash in the Joint Venture.

Investments in property, plant and equipment are expected to be significant in the coming years as the Company continues to expand its capabilities. In 1989, the Company expects to spend $4.9 million toward further expansion and equipping of its research facilities, which will be funded with equipment lease financing and working capital. The Company believes that this expansion should result in facilities which are adequate to support the levels of research planned for the next five years. A full-scale manufacturing plant will be required in the future, the timing of which will depend on the demand for products and the ultimate yields achieved on products manufactured in the pilot-scale facility. The cost of such a facility will be significant and, ideally, will be financed with a combination of working capital and long-term financing.

The Company's corporate strategy includes greater emphasis on proprietary research activities and a program to seek out acquisitions of products complementary to its current product portfolio. The extent of success in these areas, along with the degree of competition in technical developments, the time and cost of obtaining governmental approval of the Company's products, and the degree of market acceptance of those products, once approved, are all factors that will influence the Company's future capital requirements. However, the Company forecasts that existing funds will be sufficient to finance planned operations and capital requirements over the next several years.

Results of Operations

The Company earned $0.7 million for the year ended December 31, 1988, following declining losses in the years ended December 31, 1986 and 1987 of $1.4 million and $0.2 million, respectively. The calculation of earnings per common share resulted in a loss of $.01 per share in 1988, because earnings per common share reflect the deduction of preferred stock dividends from net income.

The steady improvement in the Company's earnings over the three years ended December 31, 1988 resulted primarily from increases in the amount of research payments received from collaborative partners which were greater than the increases in total research and development expense. This trend is expected to reverse in 1989 as the Company pursues its strategy of emphasizing proprietary research projects. Accordingly, operating losses, which could approach the levels experienced on a per share basis in years prior to 1986, are anticipated until significant royalty and manufacturing income is received from sales of the Company's therapeutic products.

Revenue under collaborative agreements was $15.4 million in 1988, a 54% increase over 1987 and a 148% increase over 1986. The increases resulted principally from higher levels of preclinical research activity under collaborative agreements with corporate partners and the Joint Venture, and greater involvement in managing the clinical trials of GM-CSF. Product sales and royalties increased over the three years, growing from $0.4 million in 1986 to $1.8 million in 1988, reflecting increasing sales of products to collaborators for use in clinical trials. Interest income increased in 1987 and 1988 due to a rising level of funds available for investment, a result of the previously mentioned issuance of preferred stock in 1988 and the convertible debenture and common stock offerings in 1986.

Total expenses were $21.8 million in 1988, increasing by $6.3 million from 1987 to 1988 and by $4.6 million from 1986 to 1987. Research and development expense was the largest component of the 1988 increase, growing by $4.3 million. The increase resulted primarily from additions to scientific staff necessary to accomplish the expanded objectives of the Joint Venture and other collaborative research projects, and the cost of operating the pilot-scale manufacturing facility, initially for process development purposes. General and administrative expenses also increased substantially in 1988 as a result of personnel additions needed to effectively manage the Company's growth and increasing complexity. The major elements of the 1987 expense increase were increased interest expense related to the convertible bond and moderate growth in research and development activities.

Since the Joint Venture's formation in 1986, the Company's losses from the Joint Venture have been minimized by its contributions of technology in lieu of cash aggregating $8.3 million, and milestone revenues of $9.2 million earned by the Joint Venture for the sale of Interleukin-4 and Interleukin-7 product rights to Kodak. No further contributions of technology are planned, and further milestone revenues may or may not be earned by the Joint Venture. This, together with the Company's decision to pursue new areas of Joint Venture research, should result in greater losses from the Joint Venture beginning in 1989. The extent of such losses will depend on the success of the Joint Venture's research efforts.

CLIENT:
IMMUNEX CORPORATION

DESIGN FIRM:
PENTAGRAM DESIGN

ART DIRECTOR:
KIT HINRICHS

DESIGNERS:
KIT HINRICHS,
BELLE HOW

PHOTOGRAPHER:
STEVE FIREBAUGH

ILLUSTRATORS:
WILSON MCLEAN,
JACK UNRUH, ED LINDLOF,
DOUG FRASER,
JOHN CRAIG,
DAVE STEVENSON

WRITER:
VALOREE DOWELL

TYPOGRAPHER:
REARDON & KREBS

PAPER SELECTION:
STARWHITE TIARA VICKSBURG,
QUINTESSENCE GLOSS

PAPER MANUFACTURER:
SIMPSON PAPER, POTLATCH PAPER

PRINTER:
GRAPHIC ARTS CENTER

NUMBER OF PAGES:
32 PLUS COVER

SIZE:
7 3/4" X 12"

TYPE SELECTION:
BEMBO

VALOREE DOWELL, DIRECTOR OF COMMUNICATIONS, IMMUNEX CORPORATION, SEATTLE, WASHINGTON

For the Immunex 1988 annual report, we wanted to feature the separate parts of the organization coming to work together as a whole. Each of the units, each small group is focused on the same kind of work. And, of course, our goal was to portray this, and to show the units also working closely together. The portraits of the Immunex staff in this report are very unusual. And the artwork in general generated a lot of comment. The 1988 annual report achieved its objective in fitting together this overall look at the company. The annual report conveyed Immunex as a creative and innovative company.

KIT HINRICHS, PENTAGRAM DESIGN, SAN FRANCISCO, CALIFORNIA

For the Immunex 1988 annual report, we were just proceeding in this evolutionary process. We had told the story before, but this time the annual report talked specifically about the people in the company. This is a refinenment, since conceptually this report is not different. Graphically, we show each unit of the company interrelated. On the cover, we wanted to show that the whole was greater than its parts. Of course, we design our books from the inside out. We gave each of the illustrators working on one of the inside illustrations the same photograph to do his version of the cover face. Each built his own interpretation of the face, and then we transformed them into this cover. We had a very positive response; this report received a lot of attention.

VALOREE DOWELL, DIRECTOR OF COMMUNICATIONS, IMMUNEX CORPORATION, SEATTLE, WASHINGTON

Im Immunex-Geschäftsbericht für 1988 wollten wir die verschiedenen Bereiche des Unternehmens und ihre Zusammenarbeit beschreiben. Die Tätigkeit jeder Betriebseinheit, jeder kleinen Gruppe, ist auf das gleiche Ziel ausgerichtet. Die für diesen Bericht gewählten Porträts der Immunex-Mitarbeiter sind sehr ungewöhnlich. Die gesamte Gestaltung rief ein beachtliches Echo hervor. Im Jahresbericht 1988 ist es gelungen, die einzelnen Teile zu einem Gesamtbild zusammenzufügen. Immunex erscheint hier als ein kreatives, innovatives und aufstrebendes Unternehmen.

KIT HINRICHS, PENTAGRAM DESIGN, SAN FRANCISCO, KALIFORNIEN

Im Jahresbericht 1988 für Immunex ging es für uns um eine Weiterverfolgung des Entwicklungsprozesses. Wir hatten die Geschichte bereits erzählt, aber in diesem Jahr ist im Geschäftsbericht besonders von den Mitarbeitern die Rede. Hier geht es um Feinheiten, am Konzept wurde nichts geändert. Graphisch stellten wir die enge Verbindung der einzelnen Betriebseinheiten dar. Auf dem Umschlag wollten wir zeigen, dass das Ganze grösser als seine Teile ist. Wir gaben jedem der mit den Illustrationen für den Inhalt Beauftragten das gleiche Photo. Nachdem jeder seine Version des Gesichtes auf dem Umschlag kreiert hatte, machten wir aus allen diesen Umschlag. Das Echo auf den Bericht war beachtlich und sehr positiv.

VALOREE DOWELL, DIRECTOR OF COMMUNICATIONS, IMMUNEX CORPORATION, SEATTLE, WASHINGTON

Pour le rapport annuel 1988 d'Immunex, nous avons voulu présenter les différentes parties de l'organisation et leur intégration dans l'action commune. Chaque unité, chaque petit groupe poursuit le même genre de travaux. Les portraits des collaborateurs d'Immunex dans ce rapport sont très inhabituels. Et le design en général a suscité bien des commentaires. Notre rapport annuel pour 1988 a atteint ses objectifs en assemblant les éléments de cette présentation globale de notre entreprise et en faisant comprendre qu'Immunex est une société créative, novatrice, leader de sa spécialité.

KIT HINRICHS, PENTAGRAM DESIGN, SAN FRANCISCO, CALIFORNIE

Pour le rapport 1988 d'Immunex, nous avons continué à déployer l'image de la société. Alors que précédemment nous en avions fait l'historique, ce rapport s'est attaché spécifiquement à parler des gens qui y travaillent. Il s'agit là d'un affinement du concept resté inchangé. Au plan graphique, nous montrons les interrelations unissant les différentes unités de recherche. La couverture interprète cet adage que le tout est plus grand que la somme des ses parties. A chacun des illustrateurs travaillant sur ces pages, nous avons confié la même photo pour qu'il en tire sa version du visage de la couverture. Nous avons ensuite utilisé ces différentes interprétations individuelles pour faire la couverture. Les réactions à ce rapport annuel sont très positives.

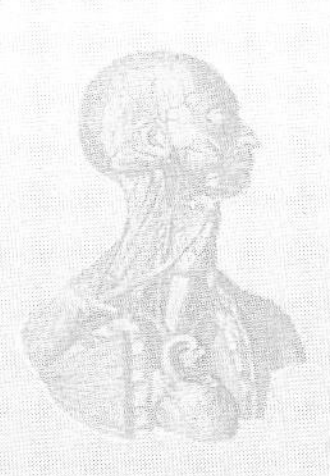

Special Report: Cardiac Support Devices

To Our Shareholders:

Fiscal 1988 was most eventful for ABIOMED. We reached several major milestones in the development of cardiac assist devices and can report major achievements for our other products, particularly the dental probe and the medical laser system. It was also the year in which we saw income from the sale of our products begin to make a meaningful contribution to our revenue stream.

With this report, our first as a public company, I would like to welcome our new shareholders. The $12 million you have provided is being used to advance the development of our products. This report is designed to give you a clear idea of our products, our goals for the coming year, and a sense of our corporate philosophy and strategy.

Cardiac Assist Devices

ABIOMED was founded because we saw a market for innovative, cost effective medical devices. Foremost among these was the cardiac assist market where, in our opinion, recent technological advances had not been optimally applied. To date, our technical staff has positioned ABIOMED to become a leader in the emerging cardiac assist market. Spin-off technology has also been produced which is applicable to a broad range of medical products that ABIOMED believes to be socially and economically valuable.

"This report is designed to give you, our shareholders, a clear idea of where our products stand, our goals for the coming year, and a sense of our corporate philosophy and strategy."

BVS™ System 5000

Our BVS™ bi-ventricular support system is currently being sold for clinical use in Europe and is in clinical trials in Canada and the United States. The BVS™ is an external cardiac system that temporarily assumes the blood pumping function of the heart for patients after open heart surgery, for patients with severe heart failure, or for patients awaiting a heart transplant.

"ABIOMED was founded because we saw a market for innovative, cost-effective medical devices."

ICS™ System 8000

We are presently completing all necessary testing activities to submit an application to the FDA to begin clinical trials in the US of our ICS™ System 8000 intra-arterial cardiac support pump. When threaded through a leg artery into position outside the left ventricle, the ICS™ is designed to assist the pumping action of the heart, stabilizing patients in heart failure and protecting the heart until corrective procedures such as angioplasty or bypass surgery can be undertaken.

Extensive bench and animal tests have demonstrated that the ICS provides significantly greater assist than currently available, non-surgical devices. Upon receipt of FDA approval, we plan to start clinical testing later this year.

Permanent Cardiac Support

Our research towards fully implantable artificial heart pumps continued to make progress during the year. The National Institutes of Health (NIH) estimate that between 17,000 and 35,000 such systems will be needed annually because of the limited supply of human donor hearts. To answer this need, ABIOMED is developing a left ventricular assist system (VAS), and a total artificial heart (TAH), both of which share common technology but address different technical issues and patient populations.

The VAS is in a more advanced stage of development. It permanently assists, but does not replace, a patient's left heart. The VAS is currently undergoing pre-clinical testing in collaboration with the Massachusetts General Hospital under a $5.4 million NIH contract awarded in 1984.

Financial Results

Sales of ABIOMED products reached $407,103 in the fiscal year, up from $157,476 in the previous 12 months. Although this amount equals only about eight percent of our total revenues, it is a clear indication of the commercial acceptance of our products.

We have now sold BVS™ systems to hospitals in six European countries. Based on the continued expansion of this market, as well as the sales of the disposable blood pumps to this installed base, we expect to be able to substantially offset the completion of funding from our R&D limited partnership with revenues from product sales in the coming year.

Due primarily to our public offering, we have ended the year with over $13 million in working capital. We expect these funds to be sufficient to complete the clinical testing and bring our BVS™ and ICS™ products to market.

If we continue to progress according to plan, we should have two products, the BVS™ and the dental probe, awaiting US regulatory approval at fiscal year end, and a third, the ICS™, completing the initial phase of clinical trials. However, the accuracy of such forecasts can be greatly affected by the unknowns of clinical testing. We expect the current year to be one of expanding product sales and the year after to be one in which sales of our products become our primary source of revenue.

David Lederman

David M. Lederman
Chief Executive Officer

May 31, 1988

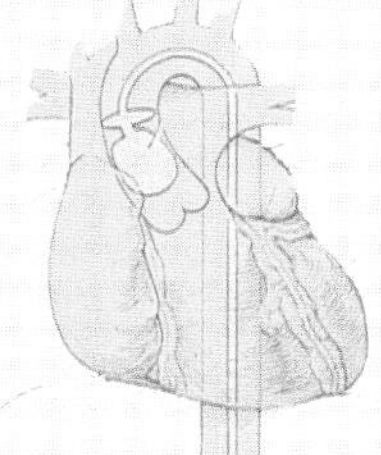

Temporary Non-Surgical Cardiac Support

A minimally invasive cardiac assist device under development at ABIOMED is the non-surgical, intra-arterial cardiac support system (ICS™). The ICS™, once threaded through a leg artery to a position in the aorta outside of the heart, can provide a significant boost to help the natural heart. A primary advantage of the ICS™ is that it is designed to be quickly inserted without open chest surgery.

ABIOMED researchers have shown in preclinical studies that its *Intra-Arterial Cardiac Support System 8000™* is a superior method of aiding a failing heart than presently used intra-aortic balloon pumps, a technology developed nearly 20 years ago. ABIOMED's development team is now performing the tests and evaluations necessary for submission to the Food and Drug Administration for approval to start human trials.

The non-surgical intra-arterial cardiac support system was designed by ABIOMED to assist a failing heart during an acute attack, allowing it to recover. Clinical trials are expected to start this year.

ABIOMED's biventricular cardiac assist system can temporarily assume the total blood pumping function of the human heart. It is currently being used with heart patients in Europe, and undergoing trials in selected clinical centers in the United States and Canada.

Temporary Surgical Cardiac Support

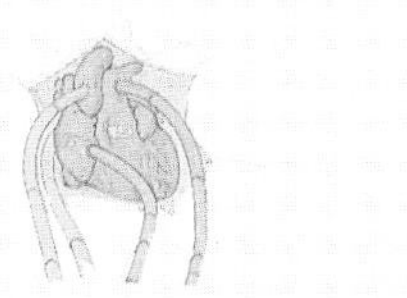

Permanent Cardiac Support

Permanent, fully implantable, left heart assist devices and total artificial hearts under development at ABIOMED share blood contacting components with the company's temporary cardiac assist systems.

The Company has funded operations chiefly by research and development contracts with the Partnership, government contracts and grants, and the proceeds from the sale of its common stock. At the end of fiscal 1988, the Company had received the entire $6.8 million payable under its contract with the Partnership and had loaned the Partnership approximately $440,000 to continue development of the BVS™ and the ICS™ systems. The Company expects that it will loan the Partnership about $350,000 per quarter until development and clinical trials of those products are complete. These loans would be repayable out of amounts due the Partnership if the Company chooses to exercise its license or purchase options on either the BVS™ or ICS™. The Company is expensing these loan amounts as additional research and development because repayment is dependent upon the receipt of future royalties, which are uncertain.

The Company currently has an inventory valued at $554,000 and expects to make significant expenditures to establish product inventory over the next several years as marketing activity expands. The Company has available a $1.5 million unsecured line of credit from a bank which was unused by March 31, 1988.

Management expects that it will have to make significant expenditures over the next several years to support the commercialization of the Company's products. Management believes that these and other anticipated capital needs for at least the next two years can be met by current cash reserves, interest income thereon, and internally generated funds.

Report of Independent Public Accountants

To ABIOMED, Inc.:

We have examined the consolidated balance sheets of ABIOMED, Inc. (a Delaware corporation) and subsidiaries as of March 31, 1987 and 1988 and the related consolidated statements of operations, stockholders' investment and cash flows for each of the three years in the period ended March 31, 1988. Our examinations were made in accordance with generally accepted auditing standards and, accordingly, included such tests of the accounting records and such other auditing procedures as we considered necessary in the circumstances.

In our opinion, the financial statements referred to above present fairly the financial position of ABIOMED, Inc. and subsidiaries as of March 31, 1987 and 1988 and the results of their operations and cash flows for each of the three years in the period ended March 31, 1988, in conformity with generally accepted accounting principles applied on a consistent basis.

Arthur Andersen & Co

Boston, Massachusetts
May 23, 1988

ABIOMED, Inc. and Subsidiaries — Consolidated Balance Sheets

	March 31, 1987	March 31, 1988
Assets		
Current Assets:		
Cash and short-term investments (Note 1)	$2,430,527	$13,255,147
Accounts receivable	218,611	515,616
Inventories (Note 1)	433,505	553,989
Unbilled costs and fees on contracts (Note 1)	330,491	–
Prepaid expenses	36,245	90,892
Total current assets	$3,449,379	$14,415,644
Property and Equipment, at cost (Note 1):		
Machinery and equipment	$ 509,770	$ 662,591
Furniture and fixtures	54,803	56,305
Leasehold improvements	46,266	64,044
	$ 610,839	$ 782,940
Less – Accumulated depreciation and amortization	339,845	513,169
	$ 270,994	$ 269,771
Investment in Limited Partnership (Note 9)	$ 28,945	$ 10,664
	$3,749,318	$14,696,079
Liabilities and Stockholders' Investment		
Current Liabilities:		
Accounts payable	$ 331,419	$ 429,364
Accrued expenses (Note 11)	475,613	619,440
Deferred partnership contract profit (Note 9)	542,701	–
Billings in excess of contract revenue (Note 1)	39,995	140,396
Total current liabilities	$1,389,728	$ 1,189,200
Commitments (Note 6)		
Stockholders' Investment (Notes 2, 7, 8 and 9):		
Class A Convertible Preferred Stock, $.01 par value – Authorized – 150,000 shares at March 31, 1987 and none at March 31, 1988; Issued and outstanding – 150,000 shares at March 31, 1987 and none at March 31, 1988	$ 1,500	$ –
Class B Preferred Stock, $.01 par value – Authorized – 1,000,000 shares; Issued and outstanding – none	–	–
Common Stock, $.01 par value – Authorized – 10,000,000 shares; Issued and outstanding – 960,750 shares at March 31, 1987 and 2,304,750 shares at March 31, 1988	9,608	23,048
Common Stock, Class A, $.01 par value – Authorized – 2,346,000 shares; Issued and outstanding – 2,040,000 shares at March 31, 1987 and 2,346,000 shares at March 31, 1988	20,400	23,460
Additional paid-in capital	2,887,599	14,609,763
Accumulated deficit	(559,517)	(1,149,392)
Total stockholders' investment	$2,359,590	$13,506,879
	$3,749,318	$14,696,079

The accompanying notes are an integral part of these consolidated financial statements.

CLIENT:
ABIOMED, INC.

DESIGN FIRM:
WEYMOUTH DESIGN

ART DIRECTOR:
MICHAEL WEYMOUTH

DESIGNERS:
TOM LAIDLAW,
CORY FANELLI

PHOTOGRAPHER:
MICHAEL WEYMOUTH

ILLUSTRATOR:
HARRIET GREENFIELD

TYPOGRAPHER:
ACME

PAPER SELECTION:
BRIGHTWATER, KARMA

PAPER MANUFACTURER:
CURTIS, POTLATCH

PRINTER:
ACME

NUMBER OF PAGES:
32 PLUS COVER

DAVID M. LEDERMAN, CHIEF EXECUTIVE OFFICER, ABIOMED, INC. DANVERS, MASSACHUSETTS

For the 1988 Abiomed annual report, we wanted to emphasize that our products were now in the clinical phase. The company is in transition from research and development to clinical practice, with products that address important medical needs, like the cardiac support devices featured in the special section in this report. The design of this report we thought to be outstanding. Our audience responded positively to this on all counts, and we have been complimented on its quality.

MICHAEL WEYMOUTH, WEYMOUTH DESIGN, INC., BOSTON, MASSACHUSETTS

The 1988 Abiomed annual report was the very first one for this relatively new company, which makes health-care devices. Since this is a small startup company, this annual report was the only document that explains what the company is all about. this is truly a biomedical company, and we needed to show that this company had viable products right away. This is not a static business. We used black-and-white photography. We showed items bottom lit and top lit. These photographs were not executed in an ordinary way, and the resulting annual report worked well for Abiomed. Devid Lederman, The Chief Executive Officer, was effusive in his reaction to this report. We didn't want to show a utilitarian product, but a special product. This annual report doesn't reek of money, but it does show how we utilize graphic enhancement qualities to achieve an elegant effect.

DAVID M. LEDERMAN, CHIEF EXECUTIVE OFFICE, ABIOMED, INC., DANVERS, MASSACHUSETTS

Im Jahresbericht 1988 für Abiomed wollten wir sagen, dass unsere Produkte jetzt in der klinischen Versuchsphase sind. Nach der Entwicklungs- und Testphase geht es jetzt um die klinische Anwendung bedeutender Produkte wie z.B. Herzschrittmacher, denen ein besonderes Kapitel gewidmet ist. Wir finden die Gestaltung des Berichts hervorragend. Unser Publikum hat in jeder Hinsicht positiv auf den Jahresbericht reagiert, wobei besonders die Qualität gelobt wurde.

MICHAEL WEYMOUTH, WEYMOUTH DESIGN, INC., BOSTON, MASSACHUSETTS

Der Jahresbericht 1988 war der erste für diese relativ junge Firma, die medizinische Geräte herstellt. Da die Firma klein angefangen hat, war dieser Jahresbericht das einzige Dokument, das über das Unternehmen Auskunft gibt. Es handelt sich um eine biochemische Firma, und wir mussten deutlich machen, dass sie bereits brauchbare Produkte hat. Wir verwendeten Schwarzweiss-Photos, wobei wir die Gegenstände mal von unten und mal von oben beleuchteten. Die Aufnahmen sind aussergewöhnlich, und der Jahresbericht erfüllte seine Aufgabe insgesamt sehr gut. David Lederman, der Geschäftsführer, war vollkommen begeistert. Wir wollten aus einem Industrieprodukt ein besonderes Produkt machen. Dieser Jahresbericht sieht nicht nach Geld aus, aber dank der graphischen Gestaltung wirkt er ansprechend und anspruchsvoll.

DAVID M. LEDERMAN, CHIEF EXECUTIVE OFFICER, ABIOMED, INC., DANVERS MASSACHUSETTS

Dans le rapport annuel d'Abiomed pour 1988, nous avons voulu souligner le fait que nos produits en sont à la phase d'essais cliniques. Après la phase de recherche et de développement, il s'agit maintenant de soumettre à l'appréciation clinique des produits qui répondent à des besoins fondamentaux, tels les appareils stabilisateurs du rythme cardiaque. Nous estimons qu'au plan du design ce document a bénéficié d'une conception tout à fait remarquable. Nos lecteurs ont réagi favorablement.

MICHAEL WEYMOUTH, WEYMOUTH DESIGN, INC., BOSTON, MASSACHUSETTS

Le rapport annuel d'Abiomed pour 1988 a couvert le premier exercice de cette société de fondation récente vouée à la production d'appareillages médicaux. Comme il s'agit d'une petite société nouvelle venue sur le marché, ce rapport annuel était le seul document expliquant la démarche de l'entreprise. Nous avons donc dû montrer que cette société biomédicale disposait de produits parfaitement viables. Il fallait éviter une présentation statique. Nous avons opté pour des photos noir et blanc, en éclairant les produits par le haut et par le bas de manière insolite. Le résultat a été très apprécié. David Lederman, le directeur général, s'est montré particulièrement enthousiaste. Nous n'entendions pas présenter un produit utilitaire, mais mettre en évidence un produit spécial. Ce rapport annuel ne sent pas l'argent; son élégance est due à des moyens graphiques.

Annual Report 1988

Letter to Shareholders

By any measure, fiscal 1988 was an extraordinary year in the securities business. Prices and volume exhibited extreme volatility, investor sentiment varied from euphoria to despair and operating systems withstood the pressures from new volume thresholds. We are pleased to report to you that Bear Stearns weathered this test and emerged stronger than ever. The company is meeting new challenges and is taking advantage of opportunities as they arise. Fiscal 1988 was a year

CONTINUED INSIDE

Memos from the Chairman
1978–1988

BEAR
STEARNS

1978
1982
1985
1988

From the time of its founding in 1923, to
1978, Bear Stearns changed from a small commission house to an important factor in the secu-
ities industry and expanded into many areas, in-
ling those that risked capital. The driving force
that growth and expansion was Cy Lewis,
med leadership of the firm in 1936. On
April 26, 1978, he suffered a massive stroke and
died two days later; so we started our fiscal year on

CONTINUED INSIDE

CONTINUED FROM THE COVER

where the merits of our managerial philosophy were confirmed.

- We enter a business only after careful consideration of its profit potential. Our constant goal is return.
- We try to thoroughly understand the businesses we are in, with systems in place to monitor and control risk.
- We are in a number of securities-related businesses, which create diversity in earnings sources to mitigate a downturn in any one difficult market.

Net income for the challenging year ended April 30, 1988 was $142.9 million, a 17.5% decrease from $173.1 million for fiscal 1987. Earnings per share were $1.56 compared to $2.02 last year.

Our deliberate growth and ongoing cost control program in strong years allowed us to selectively expand during fiscal 1988. We added the capacity necessary for future growth, completing the relocation of our New York headquarters to 245 Park Avenue, and our data processing center to Whippany, New Jersey. At a time of industry consolidation, we have the confidence and the resources to hire new, productive talent.

Growth and positioning for expansion are made possible by the solid contributions from the five major areas that drive the firm.

Investment Banking continued to increase in stature. Building on innovation and sales and trading strengths, Bear Stearns broadened its capabilities in 1988 with the addition of the Latin American Corporate Finance and the Receivables-Based Financing Groups.

Institutional Equities expanded its research capabilities and established a full-time link with the Investment Banking Division to organize and coordinate equity and convertible offerings.

Fixed Income maintained Bear Stearns' position as one of the largest trading houses in government, municipal, mortgage-backed and corporate securities, strong in market making, as well as having one of the largest distribution salesforces on Wall Street.

Individual Investor Services, despite a downturn in this business, continues to offer to its sophisticated client base high-quality products with emphasis on close attention to investors' particular needs.

Correspondent Clearing now serves more than 750 clients.

Bear Stearns is very grateful to, and would like to add special thanks to our operating and administrative staff. Their dedication and professionalism through the tumultuous markets of last October made us particularly proud of everyone in that area.

Since the end of our fiscal year, the company has made the following changes: On May 2, 1988, the Office of the President, in which both E. John Rosenwald, Jr. and James E. Cayne had served since Bear Stearns became a public company in 1985, was eliminated. Mr. Rosenwald was elected vice chairman and Mr. Cayne was elected president of the public company and the broker-dealer subsidiary.

In addition, in order to report our quarterly earnings on a consistent basis with the majority of firms in the securities industry, the company has changed its fiscal year end to June 30 from April 30. The change will be effective with the new fiscal year, and the first full quarter of fiscal 1989 will be the three-month period ending September 30, 1988.

The events of the past year reinforce the constant need to anticipate and respond to changing conditions. As part of this effort, we have always recognized the importance of monitoring and controlling expenses. This year's annual report is an illustration of this principle. In fact, we have saved a page by printing this letter on the cover.

July 1, 1988

Alan C. Greenberg
Chairman and
Chief Executive Officer

James E. Cayne
President

FINANCIAL HIGHLIGHTS

In thousands, except share data	The Bear Stearns Companies Inc.				Bear, Stearns & Co. (A Partnership)		
	Fiscal Year Ended April 30, 1988	Fiscal Year Ended April 30, 1987	Fiscal Year Ended April 30, 1986 (Pro forma)	October 29, 1985 through April 30, 1986	May 1, 1985 through October 28, 1985	Fiscal Year Ended April 30, 1985	Fiscal Year Ended April 30, 1984
OPERATING RESULTS							
Revenues	$ 1,887,908	$ 1,774,003	$ 1,409,882	$ 860,655	$ 549,227	$ 960,871	$ 795,861
Net income of Partnership[1]					92,033	168,725	162,817
Income before provision for income taxes and extraordinary item	201,255	329,125	226,546	157,118	*	*	*
Income before extraordinary item	142,884	176,473	131,711	89,474	*	*	*
Net income	142,884	173,134	131,711	89,474	*	*	*
Earnings per share[2]	1.56	2.02	1.55	1.06	*	*	*
Cash dividends declared per common share	.485	.45	.20	.20	*	*	*
	April 30, 1988	April 30, 1987	April 30, 1986		October 28, 1985	April 30, 1985	April 30, 1984
FINANCIAL POSITION							
Total assets	$ 32,170,841	$ 25,247,152	$ 26,939,440		$ 28,177,023	$ 23,918,090	$ 17,953,428
Subordinated indebtedness and long-term debt	385,854	386,830	298,000		162,500	167,325	133,325
Partners' capital					378,000	350,000	302,000
Stockholders' equity	1,024,686	938,221	651,435		*	*	*
Book value per common share	10.43	9.27	7.66		*	*	*

* Information is not applicable for the predecessor partnership.
[1] Represents information for the Company and the Partnership on a pro forma basis for the fiscal year ended April 30, 1986. See Note 2 of Notes to Consolidated Financial Statements.
[2] Results for the Partnership are not fully comparable with those of the Company. See Note 2 of Notes to Consolidated Financial Statements.
[3] See Note 11 of Notes to Consolidated Financial Statements.

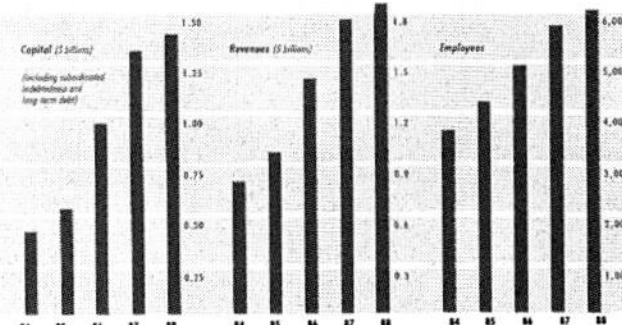

INVESTMENT BANKING

Building off innovation backed by trading and distribution strength, our investment banking business continued to gain in stature in fiscal 1988. In underwriting rankings over the past three years, Bear Stearns has moved from 14th to 9th position. In fiscal 1988, 39 companies included Bear Stearns in the bulge bracket.

Our growth can also be measured by the size of the financings we are called upon to undertake, by our product breadth and innovation and by the repeat business we attract. Last year, the Federal National Mortgage Association relied on Bear Stearns for over $3 billion in financings. We broadened our product line to include medium-term note programs and created an innovative currency investment tool–Currency Exchange Warrants. In fiscal 1988, Ford Motor Credit Company called on us for the sixth time.

Our Mergers and Acquisitions Group also showed strong growth in fiscal 1988, demonstrating its ability to shift focus with changes in the markets as well as in the regulatory environment.

But the ultimate measure is our expanding client list which now includes American Express Credit Corporation, Carnival Cruise Lines, Inc., Carolco Pictures Inc., CITICORP, Emerson Electric Co., General Electric Capital Corporation, General Motors Acceptance Corporation, International Controls Corp., J.P. Morgan & Co. Incorporated, Mark IV Industries Inc., PepsiCo, Inc., Rorer Group, Inc., Sequa Corporation, Student Loan Marketing Association, TRINOVA Corporation and USLIFE Corporation.

Corporate Finance/Capital Markets
Public Offerings:
Debt: U.S. dollar and foreign currency denominated; Fixed and floating rate; Straight and convertible; Medium-term notes.
Equity: Initial, primary and secondary offerings; Domestic common stock; American depositary receipts (ADRs); Floating and fixed rate preferred stock; Convertible and adjustable rate preferred stock.
Currency Exchange Warrants.
Private placements:
Equity and debt securities denominated in U.S. dollars; Leveraged buyouts; Leveraged recapitalizations; Secondary private placements; Master limited partnerships.
Structured asset/liability transactions.
Risk management:
Interest rate and exchange rate; Hedging strategies and techniques.
Interest rate and currency swaps.
Asset-backed financing.
Project financing:
Equity; Long-and intermediate-term debt; Government agency-guaranteed debt.
Latin American Corporate Finance:
Corporate finance transactions. Less developed country asset trading. Debt-for-equity conversions.

Financial Advisory
Recapitalizations. Debt/equity repurchases. Dividend policy advice. Valuation of businesses, securities and assets. Fairness opinions. Corporate cash management. Aftermarket services. Asset restructuring consulting. Rating agency presentations. Financial policy and long-range financial planning. Analysis of specific financing alternatives. Advice on government-related financial matters. Repurchases of common stock. Debt and asset sales.

Financial Restructuring
Out of court workouts. Chapter 11 reorganization. Credit restructure and reorganization. Debt/equity exchange offers. Acquisitions of troubled companies. Expert testimony on valuations and financial matters. Secondary placement of problem loans.

Leveraged Buyout Investments
Acquisition of operating companies in conjunction with management and other professional investors.

Mergers and Acquisitions
Asset redeployment: Spin-offs; Recapitalizations; Divestitures. Buyer advisory. Exclusive sales. Financial fairness opinions. International transactions: Europe, Far East, Latin America. Leveraged buyouts. Merchant banking/principal commitments. Proxy/consent advice and solicitation. Strategic financial counseling. Structure and valuation. Takeover defense. Transaction initiation.

Public Finance
Public offerings and private placements of taxable and tax-exempt securities.
Negotiated and competitive underwritings:
Airports. Education. Federal asset sales. Financial advisory services. General obligation bonds. Health care. Housing. Industrial development. Infrastructure development. Municipal leasing. Pollution control. Project financing. Resource recovery. Transportation systems. Water systems.

Real Estate
Real estate investment banking services:
Corporate asset redeployment and realizations. Real estate investment trusts and master limited partnerships. Private placements: Institutional debt and equity; Retail "Reg D" equity offerings. Financial advice and strategy for real estate users and owners. Mergers and acquisitions/disposition valuations and strategies.
Real estate financings:
Construction and mini-perm loans; Permanent and standby mortgages; Participating debt and joint venture equity; Sale/lease-back transactions.
Investment property acquisitions and sales:
Advisory services. Acquisition and disposition brokerage.
Principal investments and joint ventures.
Asset-backed financings: Energy; leasing; corporate fixed assets.

Specialized Industry Coverage
Communications; Energy; Entertainment; Health care; Natural resources/oil; Project finance; Utilities.

2

INSTITUTIONAL EQUITIES

Previous investment in the institutional equities business at Bear Stearns was realized in fiscal 1988 in the form of market share gains. We increased that investment by selective additions to our sales, research and trading staff. We improved and expanded trading systems, introduced new products and created a dedicated team to coordinate the marketing of equity offerings initiated by our investment banking team.

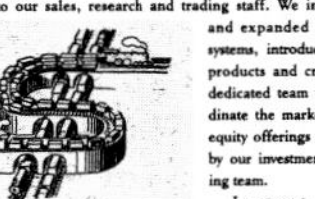

Investment research is critical to a successful institutional equity business. During the year, we added new analysts and again broadened our industry coverage and established new groups to cover the important technology and telecommunications industries.

Utilizing our experience and expertise in evaluating, investing and trading in risk arbitrage situations, we have successfully marketed a risk arbitrage research product to major institutional investors. We believe it is without comparison.

Equities
Listed U.S. and international equity securities; Over-the-counter securities; Convertible securities; Listed and over-the-counter options; Warrants and rights; Canadian equities: U.S. and Canadian dollar denominated; Restricted stock transactions; Corporate repurchase programs; Syndicated equity; Direct equity placements; Registered and nonregistered secondary offerings; Spe-

CONTINUED

3

CONSOLIDATED STATEMENTS OF INCOME

The Bear Stearns Companies Inc.

In thousands, except share data

	Fiscal Year Ended April 30, 1988	Fiscal Year Ended April 30, 1987	Fiscal Year Ended April 30, 1986 (Pro Forma)	October 29, 1985 through April 30, 1986
REVENUES				
Commissions	$ 404,017	$ 349,700	$ 261,956	$ 156,034
Principal transactions	386,107	406,623	361,521	236,251
Investment banking	242,983	289,922	200,621	121,875
Interest and dividends	846,378	720,728	583,440	344,588
Other income	8,423	7,030	2,344	1,907
Total revenues	1,887,908	1,774,003	1,409,882	860,655
EXPENSES				
Employee compensation and benefits	613,373	628,997	492,208	305,133
Interest	668,053	549,998	464,136	273,110
Floor brokerage, exchange and clearance fees	52,857	42,965	43,168	25,017
Communications	46,581	45,759	35,383	18,966
Occupancy	47,867	31,821	26,077	13,969
Advertising and market development	30,511	27,641	22,679	12,961
Data processing and equipment	31,395	26,614	22,558	12,848
Provision for doubtful accounts	52,731			
Other expenses	143,285	91,083	77,127	41,533
Total expenses	1,686,653	1,444,878	1,183,336	703,537
INCOME BEFORE PROVISION FOR INCOME TAXES AND EXTRAORDINARY ITEM	201,255	329,125	226,546	157,118
Provision for income taxes	58,371	152,652	94,835	67,644
INCOME BEFORE EXTRAORDINARY ITEM	142,884	176,473	131,711	89,474
Extraordinary item: loss from in-substance defeasance of debt (net of income tax benefit)		(3,339)		
NET INCOME	$ 142,884	$ 173,134	$ 131,711	$ 89,474
Earnings per share:				
Income before extraordinary item	$ 1.56	$ 2.06	$ 1.55	$ 1.06
Extraordinary item		(.04)		
EARNINGS PER SHARE	$ 1.56	$ 2.02	$ 1.55	$ 1.06
WEIGHTED AVERAGE SHARES OUTSTANDING	84,850,041	84,908,858	84,908,858	84,498,955

See Notes to Consolidated Financial Statements.

12

CONSOLIDATED STATEMENTS OF FINANCIAL CONDITION

The Bear Stearns Companies Inc.

In thousands, except share data

	April 30, 1988	April 30, 1987
ASSETS		
Cash and cash equivalents	$ 491,153	$ 17,722
Cash and securities deposited with clearing organizations or segregated in compliance with Federal regulations	971,494	427,838
Securities purchased under agreements to resell	11,870,389	8,494,070
Receivable from brokers, dealers and others	6,296,400	2,806,407
Receivable from customers, net of allowances of $35,276 in 1988 and $6,737 in 1987	3,219,925	4,216,308
Marketable securities and commodities owned—at market value:		
United States Government and agency securities	6,373,019	5,342,204
State and municipal	114,490	300,928
Corporate equity securities	816,502	2,468,729
Corporate debt securities	657,701	447,827
Other	825,004	360,876
Furniture, equipment and leasehold improvements, net of accumulated depreciation and amortization of $62,382 in 1988 and $55,382 in 1987	172,150	67,070
Other assets	362,614	297,173
Total Assets	$ 32,170,841	$ 25,247,152
LIABILITIES AND STOCKHOLDERS' EQUITY		
Short-term borrowings	$ 1,261,682	$ 916,767
Drafts payable	235,914	267,217
Securities sold under agreements to repurchase	14,130,270	11,012,106
Payable to brokers, dealers and others	3,950,381	2,086,602
Payable to customers	4,342,189	4,282,911
Marketable securities and commodities sold, but not yet purchased—at market value:		
United States Government and agency securities	3,836,796	2,788,012
State and municipal	7,424	28,596
Corporate equity securities	2,255,361	1,855,667
Corporate debt securities	201,892	59,011
Other	97,918	84,562
Accrued employee compensation and benefits	186,096	199,601
Other liabilities and accrued expenses	228,714	210,976
Deferred income taxes payable	25,664	130,073
	30,760,301	23,922,101
Commitments and contingencies		
Long-term borrowings	385,854	386,830
STOCKHOLDERS' EQUITY		
Preferred stock, $1.00 par value; 10,000,000 shares authorized:		
Adjustable Rate Cumulative Preferred Stock, Series A–$50 liquidation preference; 3,000,000 shares issued	150,000	150,000
Cumulative Convertible Preferred Stock–$100 liquidation preference; 327,335 shares and 525,000 shares issued and outstanding in 1988 and 1987, respectively	32,734	52,500
Common stock, $1.00 par value; 200,000,000 shares authorized; 81,653,696 shares and 79,787,383 shares issued in 1988 and 1987, respectively	81,654	79,787
Paid-in capital	620,943	604,541
Retained earnings	150,956	61,094
	1,036,287	947,922
Less: Deferred compensation	(2,730)	(9,701)
Treasury stock, at cost -		
Adjustable Rate Cumulative Preferred Stock, Series A–180,000 shares in 1988	(7,380)	
Common stock–150,000 shares in 1988	(1,491)	
Total Stockholders' Equity	1,024,686	938,221
Total Liabilities and Stockholders' Equity	$ 32,170,841	$ 25,247,152

See Notes to Consolidated Financial Statements.

13

Memo

BEAR STEARNS

To All General & Limited Partners Date October 5, 1978

CC

From Alan C. Greenberg

Subject

Bear Stearns is moving forward at an accelerated rate and everybody is contributing. It is absolutely essential for us to be able to talk to our partners at all times. All of us are entitled to eat lunch, play golf and go on vacation. But, you must leave word with your secretary or associates where you can be reached at all times. Decisions have to be made and your input can be important!

I conducted a study of the 200 firms that have disappeared from Wall Street over the last few years and I discovered that 62.349% went out of business because the important people did not leave word where they went when they left their desk if even for 10 minutes.

That idiocy will not occur here.

Memo

BEAR STEARNS

To All General & Limited Partners Date March 13, 1979

CC

From Alan C. Greenberg

Subject

The Executive Committee last night approved a group of people that will be asked to become Limited Partners of Bear, Stearns & Co., subject to the approval of the other General Partners. You will be receiving this list shortly.

Carl Holstrom has just informed me that we have signed a $12 million long-term loan agreement with a major insurance company. This will replace our loan with the First National Bank of Chicago. The implications and the actual dollar savings of this agreement are of tremendous importance to Bear, Stearns & Co.

I also just received the P and L results for February and in my opinion, they were great. These three items will be covered in detail at the Partners' Meeting on March 19th.

The developments at Bear Stearns certainly seem to be positive and as a result, we will, of course, intensify our surveillance of all positions and expenses. You know how I feel about the dangers of overconfidence.

It certainly looks like we have a dynamic future in store as long as we remember the words of the famous philosopher, Haimchinkel Malintz Anaynikal, "thou will do well in commerce as long as thou does not believe thine own odor is perfume."

CONTINUED FROM THE COVER

May 1, 1978 without the man who was credited with having made Bear Stearns what it then was. It was the prevalent thought on Wall Street that without Cy Lewis, Bear Stearns would fade away like nomads in the night. Those skeptics overlooked one of Cy's main attributes. He encouraged and promoted young people as fast as they warranted it. He left a group that could and *did* carry on.

As the new chief executive officer, I knew I needed help to implement policies that had been running through my mind for some time. It was at this point that I met Haimchinkel Malintz Anaynikal, the dean of business philosophers, who immediately became my mentor and advisor. Through memos to my associates, I communicated his wisdom and ideas about how best to strengthen our bottom line.

These memos cover the ten years from May 1978 to May 1988. They may give you some idea of our growth and the fun we had participating in the further building of Bear Stearns. Although they seem to have been written in jest, I can assure you that the points I was trying to make in these communications were things I believed in very strongly and still do. There are many ways to run and build a firm. I used those memos to express my philosophies, and, in our case, I think they worked.

Alan C. Greenberg
Chairman and
Chief Executive Officer
June 1, 1988

"Thou will do well in commerce as long as thou does not believe thine own odor is perfume."

CONTENTS

Memo

BEAR STEARNS

TO: Managing Directors
Associate Directors

DATE: June 18, 1987

FROM: Alan C. Greenberg

The more you read about our competitor's problems, the more you realize what a job our people did in the month of April.

The media is consistent. They seem to only print negatives about Bear Stearns. Our earnings for the year and quarter ending April 30, 1987 were given to the newspapers, and we stressed in our release that the month of April was plenty volatile, but we did fine.

It is hard not to get upset when you see our stock behave as it has, but I can assure you that if our record continues, our multiple will increase dramatically. My guarantee may not mean much, but Haimchinkel Malintz Anaynikal agrees, and that does mean something.

If we continue to earn 50% on our equity (pre-tax), some MBA will recognize us, and then we may even sell at nine times earnings.

We are doing great! Just keep it up and leave the price of the stock to me.

Memo

BEAR STEARNS

To ALL MANAGING DIRECTORS Date July 13, 1987

From THE EXECUTIVE COMMITTEE CC

Subject COST CONTROL AND OVERALL EFFICIENCY

Bear Stearns has recently announced a record year - a period during which some of the majors in our industry had problems in certain areas that affected adversely their P&L. We may be entitled to some degreee of pride in our performance, but certainly not smug self satisfaction.

While our cost/revenue ratios appear to be reasonably satisfactory, now is the time to pause and remind ourselves that:

1) We have expanded rapidly, adding 800 employees during FY 1987 alone;

2) The move to 245 Park Avenue will increase significantly our fixed expenses;

3) Our industry is cyclical, and we are in the midst of the longest bull market in history;

4) A sharp downturn could be painful if we are not lean and mean;

5) Many of us get paid primarily out of bonus pool profits; and,

6) Inevitably fat creeps in with expansion and prosperity.

Consequently, we want all Managing Directors to begin critically examining their areas. Here is a list of some of the things you should be reviewing:

A. Your work force

1. Who is not sufficiently productive?

2. Who should be replaced?

3. Who should be eliminated and need not be replaced?

4. Before hiring anyone new, ask whether your existing staff can be assigned additional responsibilities.

5. Do you have employees performing functions that are duplicating those performed in other departments, such as Accounting or Data Processing?

continued...

CLIENT:
BEAR STEARNS

DESIGN FIRM:
ROSS CULBERT HOLLAND & LAVERY

ART DIRECTOR:
PETER ROSS

DESIGNERS:
PETER ROSS, LAURA BENJAMIN

ILLUSTRATOR:
DAVID SUTE

WRITER:
BEAR STEARNS

PRODUCTION MANAGER:
PETER ROSS

TYPOGRAPHER:
TYPOGRAPHIC IMAGES

PAPER SELECTION:
TAPESTRY

PAPER MANUFACTURER:
HOPPER PAPER CO.

PRINTER:
L.P. THEBAULT

NUMBER OF PAGES:
32 PLUS COVER

SIZE:
8 1/2" X 11"

TYPE SELECTION:
CLOISTER

HANNAH SECHRIST, ASSOCIATE DIRECTOR OF INVESTOR RELATIONS, BEAR STEARNS & CO. INC., NEW YORK, NEW YORK

This annual report was a reflection of October 19, 1987 and the securities industry. People were scared. Bear Stearns is high in the industry, and we had had a profitable quarter; had made significant amounts. However, part of the message was to be that we were frugal; we had a non-glitzy, non-glossy annual report. We also wanted to show that we didn't lose money. We chose as the overiding image the machine, as in all engines go and the trains came in. We wanted to show and to emphasize the strength of Bear Stearns: We control the bottom line. No space was wasted on the cover, since we began the letter to the shareholders there. This was a simple, well-designed, and easy-to-read annual report. The audience got the message quickly–this was a bare-bones book.

PETER ROSS AND DEBBIE HOLLAND, ROSS, CULBERT, HOLLAND & LAVERY, INC., NEW YORK, NEW YORK

This annual report was prepared in the year after the 1987 crash, and the client wanted to reinforce the idea of active cost control. For the shareholders, the annual report was supposed to look economical, and we followed that theme. We used uncoated paper, no color processing. Then we used a brilliant illustrator, classic typography, and it was a nice little report that was well-received. The illustrations done by David Suter incorporate the trains and engines for each of the five profit centers, and the emphasis is that these are people-driven, people with their shoulders to the grindstone. This report is not splashy, but it is also not dreary. Ironically, it wasn't particularly cheap, since the cost was in the concept and in the execution. Along with this, done in the same style, are the collected memos from the Chairman; a companion booklet that also emphasized frugality.

HANNAH SECHRIST, ASSOCIATE DIRECTOR OF INVESTOR RELATIONS, BEAR STEARNS & CO. INC., NEW YORK, NEW YORK

Dieser Jahresbericht ist ein Spiegelbild des 19. Oktobers 1987 und des Wertpapiermarktes. Die Leute hatten Angst. Bear Stears ist führend im Handel mit Wertpapieren, und wir hatten in dem Quartal Gewinn gemacht, und zwar beträchtliche Summen. Ein Teil der Botschaft war jedoch, dass wir sparsam sind, deshalb wollten wir einen schlichten Jahresbericht, ohne Glanz und Glimmer. Wir wollten auch zeigen, dass wir kein Geld verloren hatten. Als zentrales Bildthema wählten wir Maschinen: Züge. Wir wollten Bear Stearns Stärke zeigen: Wir kontrollieren die Basis. Auf dem Umschlag wurde kein Platz verschwendet, wir begannen hier mit dem Brief an die Aktionäre. Die Publikum verstand die Botschaft sofort... es war ein auf das Notwendigste beschränkter Bericht.

PETER ROSS, DEBBIE HOLLAND, ROSS, CULBERT HOLLAND & LAVERY, INC., NEW YORK, NEW YORK

Dieser Jahresbericht entstand 1988, dem Jahr nach dem Crash, und der Kunde wollte aktive Kostenkontrolle zum Hauptthema machen. Für die Aktionäre sollte der Jahresbericht sparsam aussehen - wir folgten diesem Konzept. Wir benutzten ungestrichenes Papier und verzichteten auf Farben. Wir engagierten einen brillanten Illustrator und verwendeten klassische Typographie. Das Ergebnis war ein ansprechender, kleiner Bericht, der guten Anklang fand. Die Illustrationen von David Suter zeigen Lokomotiven für jeden der fünf Gewinnbereiche Der Bericht ist nicht spritzig, aber er ist auch nicht langweilig. Ironischerweise war er nicht besonders billig, das Konzept, nicht die Ausführung, verursachte die Kosten. Im gleichen Stil wurden die gesammelten Memoranden des Vorsitzenden veröffentlicht, in denen es ebenfalls um Sparsamkeit geht.

HANNAH SECHRIST, ASSOCIATE DIRECTOR OF INVESTOR RELATIONS, BEAR STEARNS & CO. INC., NEW YORK, NEW YORK

Ce rapport annuel a reflété les événements du 19 octobre 1987 et le choc boursier. Les gens avaient pris peur. Bear Stearns occupe une place importante dans la branche financière et nous venions d'enregistrer des résultats trimestriels très satisfaisants. Ce qui ne nous a pas empêché de produire un rapport annuel simple, dépourvu d'ostentation. Nous avions aussi à cœur de montrer que nous n'avions pas perdu d'argent. L'image qui s'est imposée alors est celle de la machine, de la locomotive, du train. Nous voulions démontrer la force de Bear Stearns, celle d'avoir des résultats financiers parfaitement contrôlés. Nous n'avons pas sacrifié d'espace à la couverture, puisque la lettre aux actionnaires y débute. Ca a été un rapport annuel sans fioritures, bien conçu, facile à lire.

PETER ROSS, DEBBIE HOLLAND, ROSS, CULBERT, HOLLAND & LAVERY, INC., NEW YORK, NEW YORK

Ce rapport annuel a été préparé l'année d'après le krach de 1987, et le client désirait souligner tout spécialement l'idée du contrôle efficace des coûts. Le rapport devait se présenter aux yeux des actionnaires sous un jour économique. Nous avons employé du papier non couché et avons renoncé à la couleur. Avec l'aide d'un brillant illustrateur et une typo classique, ça a donné un gentil petit rapport, qui a été très bien accueilli. Les illustrations de David Suter comportent des trains et locomotives pour chacun des cinq centres de profit. Si ce rapport ne fait pas d'étincelles, il n'est pas non plus ennuyeux. Comble de l'ironie, il n'a même pas été très bon marché, étant donné le coût de la conception et de l'exécution. Dans le même style, nous avons produit un recueil des mémos du P.-D.G., où l'accent est également mis sur la frugalité.

chili's
GRILL & BAR
ANNUAL REPORT
88

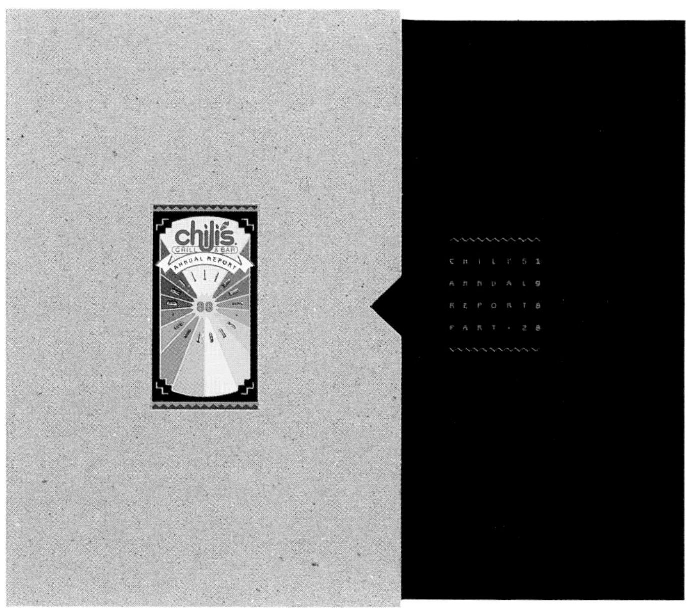

C O N T E N T S

F I N A N C I A L H I G H L I G H T S

(IN THOUSANDS, EXCEPT PER SHARE AMOUNTS)	YEAR ENDED JUNE 30,		
	1988	1987	1986
Income Statement Data:			
Revenues	$218,298	$177,236	$123,738
Cost of Sales	61,744	50,930	34,525
Operating Expenses	115,055	91,895	65,349
General and Administrative	12,933	10,171	7,924
Depreciation and Amortization	13,373	11,165	7,839
Interest Expense	3,405	2,179	1,342
Other, Net	(615)	(378)	(156)
Total Costs and Expenses	205,895	165,962	116,823
Income Before Provision for Income Taxes and Cumulative Effect of an Accounting Change	12,403	11,274	6,915
Provision for Income Taxes	4,269	4,788	1,944
Income Before Cumulative Effect of an Accounting Change	8,134	6,486	4,971
Cumulative Effect of an Accounting Change	600	—	—
Net Income	$ 8,734	$ 6,486	$ 4,971
Per Share Amounts:			
Income Before Cumulative Effect of an Accounting Change	$ 1.35	$ 1.11	$ .88
Cumulative Effect of an Accounting Change	.10	—	—
Net Income	$ 1.45	$ 1.11	$ .88
Weighted Average Shares Outstanding	6,023	5,829	5,630

1

T O O U R S T O C K H O L D E R S

For rapidly expanding and evolving enterprises to be successful, the passing of significant milestones becomes almost a matter of routine. Critical goals are reached; new goals are established, and the growth goes on. Many times, however, these companies fail to evolve, and become distant memories because they did not adapt their strategies to address the changing competitive environment they faced each day.

For Chili's, because we are so close to our customers on a daily basis, growth and evolution go hand in hand. Consequently, as the customer base we serve has broadened and changed, Chili's has expanded and changed.

Evolution is a major part of our culture. This year, for example, we introduced a new menu design, new menu items, and improved our restaurant design. The changes helped enhance Chili's uniqueness and personality, further strengthening our leadership role and competitive advantage in a rapidly changing industry.

In last year's annual report, we outlined our goals for fiscal 1988 and are pleased to report on our progress toward meeting those objectives.

Our first objective was to open 20-23 new Company operated restaurants. In fact, we opened 21 restaurants during the year, and the more recently opened new units have set performance records for both the highest opening day and opening week sales. We continued to deploy our new unit resources in focused market-penetration clusters around the United States, concentrating our development in areas where we can optimize leverage and efficiency in our advertising and promotional programs. This strategy also helps us achieve significant economies of scale in supervision, purchasing, and real estate, and makes effective use of our reputation and customer image. At present, 101 of our 146 restaurants are supported by television advertising.

We intended to maintain our return on unleveraged capital of at least 25% and are proud to have exceeded that rate again in fiscal 1988.

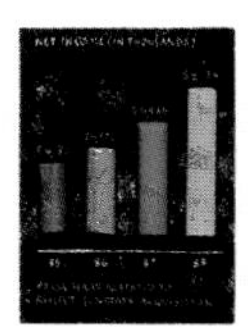

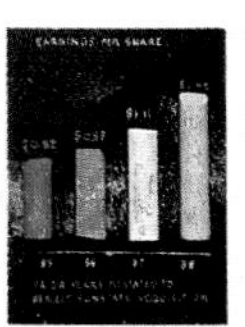

2

We are again counting on the unique skills of our team members to meet our objectives for the coming year. Our first goal is to increase our average unit volume to $2.1 million. This will be accomplished through our focused sales-building programs that include advertising, promotions and product merchandising efforts.

We expect to add 20-23 new Company units and 12-15 joint venture and franchise units this fiscal year in existing and new markets, selecting sites that give us the optimum characteristics needed to effectively compete for the consumers' business. We plan to add restaurants in the new states of New York, Oregon, Washington, and Alabama, together with further developing the clustered concentrations of units in established markets. Total system revenue should exceed $325 million by June, 1989.

More than ever, we value the association we have with our customers, and plan to remain their preferred choice for a casual, fun, high-value dining experience. We also wish to thank our loyal and dedicated employees. Without them this excellent year, plus past years and the years to come, would not and could not be possible.

Sincerely,

Norman Brinker
Chairman of the Board
Chief Executive Officer

Ronald A. McDougall
President
Chief Operating Officer

5

S E L E C T E D F I N A N C I A L D A T A

(IN THOUSANDS, EXCEPT PER SHARE AMOUNTS)	YEAR ENDED JUNE 30,				
	1988	1987	1986	1985	1984
Income Statement Data:					
Revenues	$218,298	$177,236	$123,738	$ 76,858	$ 43,816
Cost of Sales	61,744	50,930	34,525	21,060	11,442
Operating Expenses	115,055	91,895	65,349	39,497	21,710
General and Administrative	12,933	10,171	7,924	6,186	5,198
Depreciation and Amortization	13,373	11,165	7,839	3,394	2,056
Interest Expense	3,405	2,179	1,342	962	905
Other, Net	(615)	(378)	(156)	(188)	(104)
Total Costs and Expenses	205,895	165,962	116,823	70,911	41,207
Income Before Provision for Income Taxes and Cumulative Effect of an Accounting Change	12,403	11,274	6,915	5,947	2,609
Provision for Income Taxes	4,269	4,788	1,944	1,767	795
Income Before Cumulative Effect of an Accounting Change	8,134	6,486	4,971	4,180	1,814
Cumulative Effect of an Accounting Change	600	—	—	—	—
Net Income	$ 8,734	$ 6,486	$ 4,971	$ 4,180	$ 1,814
Per Share Amounts:					
Income Before Cumulative Effect of an Accounting Change	$ 1.35	$ 1.11	$ .88	$ .82	$ .41
Cumulative Effect of an Accounting Change	.10	—	—	—	—
Net Income	$ 1.45	$ 1.11	$ .88	$ .82	$ .41
Weighted Average Shares Outstanding	6,023	5,829	5,630	5,114	4,382
Balance Sheet Data (end of period):					
Working Capital	$ 4,537	$ 25,685	$ 437	$ 1,372	$ (129)
Total Assets	127,303	111,311	69,472	47,322	23,282
Long-Term Debt	48,482	48,735	19,573	15,994	5,444
Stockholders' Equity	60,297	48,996	39,072	23,707	12,951
Number of Company-Operated Restaurants Open at End of Period	119	98	78	53	30

6

CONSOLIDATED BALANCE SHEETS

(THOUSANDS OF DOLLARS, EXCEPT PER SHARE AMOUNTS)

	June 30, 1988	June 30, 1987
Assets		
Current assets:		
Cash and cash equivalents	$ 5,621	$ 2,958
Short-term investments (note 3)	1,700	24,100
Accounts receivable	4,950	4,031
Federal income taxes receivable	1,364	—
Assets held for sale and leaseback	1,588	2,448
Inventories	3,046	2,665
Prepaid expenses	4,792	3,063
Total current assets	23,061	39,265
Property and equipment, at cost (notes 6 and 9):		
Land	7,612	3,180
Buildings and leasehold improvements	56,291	42,060
Furniture and equipment	41,723	31,333
Construction-in-progress	2,946	5,194
	108,572	81,767
Less accumulated depreciation and amortization	29,322	18,821
Net property and equipment	79,250	62,946
Other assets:		
Deferred costs	6,385	4,368
Investment in joint ventures, at equity (note 4)	4,012	3,154
Long-term marketable securities (note 3)	12,811	—
Other	1,784	1,578
	24,992	9,100
	$127,303	$111,311
Liabilities and Stockholders' Equity		
Current liabilities:		
Current installments of long-term debt (notes 6 and 9)	$ 275	$ 320
Accounts payable	5,958	7,533
Accrued liabilities (note 5)	11,050	5,727
Deferred income taxes (note 7)	1,241	—
Total current liabilities	18,524	13,580
Long-term debt, less current installments (notes 6 and 9)	43,147	43,322
Deferred income taxes (note 7)	5,143	5,204
Deferred gain on sale and leaseback	182	209
Other liabilities	10	—
Commitments (note 9)		
Stockholders' equity (note 8):		
Preferred stock—authorized 1,000,000 shares of $1.00 par value each; no shares issued	—	—
Common stock—authorized 20,000,000 shares of $.10 par value each; 5,912,341 and 5,775,561 shares issued and outstanding in 1988 and 1987, respectively	592	578
Additional paid-in capital	33,732	29,979
Unrealized loss on marketable securities (note 3)	(1,200)	—
Retained earnings	27,173	18,439
Total stockholders' equity	60,297	48,996
	$127,303	$111,311

SEE ACCOMPANYING NOTES TO CONSOLIDATED FINANCIAL STATEMENTS.

11

CONSOLIDATED STATEMENTS OF INCOME

(THOUSANDS OF DOLLARS, EXCEPT PER SHARE AMOUNTS)

	Year ended June 30, 1988	1987	1986
Revenues	$ 218,298	$ 177,236	$ 123,738
Costs and expenses:			
Cost of sales	61,744	50,930	34,525
Operating expenses (note 9)	115,055	91,895	65,349
General and administrative	12,933	10,171	7,924
Depreciation and amortization	13,373	11,165	7,839
Interest expense	3,405	2,179	1,342
Other, net (note 3)	(615)	(378)	(156)
Total costs and expenses	205,895	165,962	116,823
Income before provision for income taxes and cumulative effect of an accounting change	12,403	11,274	6,915
Provision for income taxes (note 7):			
Current	2,489	3,526	455
Deferred	1,780	1,262	1,489
	4,269	4,788	1,944
Income before cumulative effect of an accounting change	8,134	6,486	4,971
Cumulative effect of an accounting change (note 7)	600	—	—
Net income	$ 8,734	$ 6,486	$ 4,971
Per share amounts:			
Income before cumulative effect of an accounting change	$ 1.35	$ 1.11	$ .88
Cumulative effect of an accounting change	.10	—	—
Net income	$ 1.45	$ 1.11	$ .88
Weighted average shares outstanding	6,023,000	5,829,000	5,630,000

SEE ACCOMPANYING NOTES TO CONSOLIDATED FINANCIAL STATEMENTS.

12

NOTES TO CONSOLIDATED FINANCIAL STATEMENTS

1. Significant Accounting Policies

(A) BASIS OF PRESENTATION

The financial statements include the accounts of Chili's, Inc., a Delaware corporation (the "Company") and all wholly-owned subsidiaries. All significant intercompany accounts and transactions have been eliminated in consolidation.

(B) CASH AND CASH EQUIVALENTS

The Company's policy is to invest cash in excess of operating requirements in income producing investments. Cash equivalents at June 30, 1988 included commercial paper, variable rate demand notes and money market accounts. At June 30, 1987, cash equivalents included certificates of deposit and money market accounts.

(C) INVENTORIES

Inventories, which consist of food, beverages and supplies, are stated at the lower of cost (first-in, first-out method) or market.

(D) PROPERTY AND EQUIPMENT

Buildings and leasehold improvements are amortized by the straight-line method over the lesser of the life of the lease including renewal options or the estimated useful lives of the assets, which range from 5 to 30 years.

Furniture and equipment are depreciated by the straight-line method over the estimated useful lives of the assets, which range from 3 to 7 years.

(E) DEFERRED COSTS

The costs of selecting new sites and of hiring and training personnel relating to new restaurants are capitalized and amortized over the restaurants' first 24 months of operations. Deferred costs related to a projected site subsequently determined to be unsatisfactory and general site selection costs which cannot be identified with a specific restaurant are charged to operations currently.

(F) CAPITALIZATION OF INTEREST

The amounts of interest cost capitalized during the construction period of restaurants for the years ended June 30, 1988, 1987 and 1986 were $350,000, $287,000 and $297,000, respectively.

(G) NET INCOME PER SHARE

Net Income Per Share is based on the weighted average number of shares outstanding during the year increased by common equivalent shares (stock options and warrants) determined using the treasury stock method. For the years ended June 30, 1988 and 1987, the Company's 6¾% Convertible Subordinated Debenture issue was anti-dilutive and therefore not included in the computation of primary or fully diluted net income per share. There is no significant additional dilution for fully diluted net income per share.

(H) RECLASSIFICATIONS

Certain amounts in previously issued financial statements have been reclassified to conform to the 1988 presentation.

2. Business Combinations

On January 16, 1987, the Company acquired Sunstate Restaurant Corporation ("Sunstate"), the Company's joint venture partner in the ownership and operation of Chili's restaurants in Florida and Georgia. The transaction was effected through the exchange of 400,535 newly issued shares of the Company's Common Stock, $.10 par value, for all of the issued and outstanding Common and Preferred Stock of Sunstate. The merger has been treated as a pooling of interests and, accordingly, the consolidated financial statements and notes thereto have been restated to include the accounts and operating results of Sunstate for the periods presented.

Revenues, Net Income and Net Income Per Share combined for the six months ended December 31, 1986 and the year ended June 30, 1986 are as follows (thousands of dollars, except per share amounts):

	Six months ended December 31, 1986 (Unaudited)	Year ended June 30, 1986
Revenues:		
Chili's	$72,154	$106,990
Sunstate	1,101	1,234
Adjustments(*)	10,773	15,514
Combined	$84,028	$123,738
Net income:		
Chili's	$ 2,835	$ 4,799
Sunstate	289	172
Combined	$ 3,124	$ 4,971
Net income per share:		
Chili's	$ .53	$ .92
Sunstate	$ —	$ —
Combined	$ .55	$ .88

(*) Adjustments to reflect: 1) Net Revenues of the Chili's/Sunstate Joint Venture, 2) Elimination of equity in earnings of the Chili's/Sunstate Joint Venture, 3) Elimination of transactions between Chili's and Sunstate.

15

In July, 1987, CBS Development Company ("CBS"), a wholly-owned subsidiary of the Company, acquired Border Stop-Lemmon, Ltd., the trademark "Border Stop" (the "Mark"), the system for operating Mexican style, fast food restaurants under the Mark, an existing restaurant located in Dallas, Texas and certain other real and personal property (together "Border Stop"). The transaction was accounted for as a purchase, and the consolidated statement of income for the year ended June 30, 1988 includes the results of operations from the purchase date. All of these assets were acquired in exchange for 71,174 newly issued shares of the Company's common stock and $200,000 in cash. The assets acquired are included in the consolidated financial statements at a cost of $2,700,000, allocated on the basis of fair values at the acquisition date.

The consolidated results of operations on a pro forma basis as though Border Stop had been acquired on July 1, 1985 are not presented as the results do not differ materially from the results as presented.

The Mark acquired in the purchase is recorded as a deferred cost and is being amortized on a straight-line basis over an estimated life of 30 years.

3. Marketable Securities

Marketable securities include equity securities, notes, and bonds. Securities which the Company intends to hold for a limited period are classified as short-term investments. These securities are held primarily for their interest or dividend yields and are carried at cost, which approximates market. Other marketable securities are classified as long-term investments and are carried at the lower of aggregate cost or market.

Realized gains and losses are determined on a specific identification basis. Realized gains from investment activity of $254,000 are included in Other, Net for the year ended June 30, 1988. No realized gains were recognized in the prior two years.

At June 30, 1988 the aggregate cost of the long-term investment portfolio exceeded its aggregate market value by $1,200,000 and a valuation allowance for unrealized losses has been established to reduce Stockholders' Equity by this amount.

During fiscal 1988, the Company transferred certain marketable securities from its short-term to its long-term investment portfolio resulting in a charge to operations included in Other, Net for the year ended June 30, 1988 of $566,000. Other realized losses of $254,000 resulting from the sale of securities and $806,000 resulting from recognition of permanent decline in market value on certain securities for the year ended June 30, 1988 are included in Other, Net. There were no other realized losses incurred in the prior two year periods.

The Company earned $1,587,000, $378,000, and $156,000 in dividends and interest income for the years ended June 30, 1988, 1987, and 1986, respectively.

4. Investment in Joint Ventures

The Company has entered into two joint ventures which operate Chili's restaurants. The Company has a 50% interest in each of the joint ventures and accounts for its interest on the equity method.

On August 28, 1987, CBS entered into a joint venture agreement with Taco Cabana International, Inc. to develop, own, operate and/or franchise Taco Cabana restaurants in selected markets. Under the terms of the agreement, CBS agreed to contribute the Border Stop restaurant, additional capital and management services in return for an ownership interest in the joint venture.

5. Accrued Liabilities

Accrued liabilities consist of the following:

(Thousands of dollars)	June 30, 1988	1987
Sales tax	$ 1,080	$ 714
Rent	1,868	1,259
Insurance	2,987	153
Payroll	3,101	1,764
Other	2,205	1,835
	$11,050	$5,727

6. Long-term Debt

Long-term debt consists of the following:

(Thousands of dollars)	June 30, 1988	1987
Mortgage notes payable	$ 380	$ 377
Obligations under capital leases (note 9)	8,021	8,232
6¾% Convertible Subordinated Debentures	35,000	35,000
Other	21	33
	43,422	43,642
Less current installments of long-term debt	275	320
	$43,147	$43,322

16

CHILI'S OFFICERS

Norman Brinker

Ron McDougall

Jim Parish

Creed Ford III

Doug Bates

Doug Brooks

Lane Cardwell

Ken Dennis

Doug Lanham

John Miller

Mike Nahkunst

Russell Owens

Ed Palms

Debra Smithart

Richard Spellman

John Titus

21

CLIENT:
CHILI'S INC.

DESIGN FIRM:
RICHARDS BROCK MILLER MITCHELL & ASSOCIATES

ART DIRECTOR:
BRIAN BOYD

DESIGNER:
BRIAN BOYD

PHOTOGRAPHER:
ROBERT LATORRE

ILLUSTRATOR:
REAGAN DUNNICK

WRITER:
KEVIN ORLIN JOHNSON

KENNETH D. DENNIS, VICE PRESIDENT, MARKETING, CHILI'S INC., DALLAS, TEXAS

We felt that our annual report should show Chili's accomplishments. We think of ourselves as professional, successful, with a sense of fun and flair. We are different and distinct, and we take pride in that. We are good, and creative in what we do. We talked about that in our round-table meeting with the Richards Group, and this theme was taken over by Brian Boyd. He went berserk, and he produced this creative and very distinctive annual report. We get to see the evolution of the year. The sense of fun we wanted is pictorially depicted with the character of Johnny Chili Seed. We've had tremendous response to this. It was noticed, saved, and enjoyed. It was exciting, but it also presented facts.

KENNETH D. DENNIS, VICE PRESIDENT, MARKETING, CHILI'S INC. DALLAS, TEXAS

Wir fanden, dass der Jahresbericht zeigen sollte, was Chili erreicht hat. Wir betrachten uns als professionell, erfolgreich, mit einem Quentchen Spass, mit Flair. Darüber sprachen wir bei unserem Roundtable-Treffen mit der Richards-Gruppe, und das Thema wurde von Brian Boyd umgesetzt. Er produzierte dann diesen einfallsreichen, sehr speziellen Jahresbericht. Darin wird die Entwicklung des vergangenen Jahres präsentiert. Die Illustrationen mit dem Typen Johnny Chili Seed sorgen für den Spass, den wir uns gewünscht hatten. Es gab ein enormes Echo. Der Bericht erweckte Aufmerksamkeit, er wurde aufgehoben und geschätzt. Er war anregend, zeigte aber auch Tatsachen auf und informierte.

KENNETH D. DAVIS, VICE PRESIDENT, MARKETING, CHILI'S INC., DALLAS, TEXAS

Nous estimions que notre rapport annuel devait exposer les réalisations de Chili's. Nous nous considérons comme une entreprise faisant preuve de professionalisme et connaissant le succès, dont les actions dénotent un certain sens de l'humour et du flair. C'est ce que nous avons expliqué en rencontrant l'équipe de Richards, et ce thème a été repris par Brian Boyd. Il nous a livré un rapport annuel créatif très spécial. On y voit la marche des affaires au courant de l'année. L'humour trouve son compte dans le personnage de Johnny Chili Seed. On a eu des réactions extraordinaires de la part des lecteurs qui ont remarqué, gardé, aimé ce rapport qui s'est avéré stimulant, objectif et riche en informations.

BRIAN BOYD, RICHARDS, BROCK, MILLER, MITCHELL & ASSOCIATES/THE RICHARDS GROUP, DALLAS, TEXAS

The main theme presented in Chili's 1988 annual report is basically the controlled growth of the company, so we wanted to talk about growth and show how well they are doing. We had a great meeting with Chili's, and we came up with this unique format. We thought that the company might have some concerns over this foldout with both sides presenting different information, and were prepared to go back to the drawing board. But they said "Let's do it." We think this reflects the restaurant very well. They were pleased from the business standpoint, and with the message about the company's growth treated illustratively. The format broke ground and broke the rules. We got responses to this annual report quickly, and people had wonderful things to say about the concept and the book itself.

BRIAN BOYD, RICHARDS, BROCK, MILLER, MITCHELL & ASSOCIATES/THE RICHARDS GROUP, DALLAS, TEXAS

Das Hauptthema des Jahresberichtes 1988 von Chili's ist im wesentlichen das kontrollierte Wachstum der Firma. Wir wollten also über Wachstum sprechen und zeigen, wie gut sich die Firma entwickelt hat. Wir hatten ein ausgezeichnetes Gespräch mit Chili's und kamen dann auf die Idee, dieses besondere Format zu verwenden. Wir erwarteten, dass der Kunde einige Zweifel wegen der Ausleger mit verschiedenen Informationen auf den beiden Seiten haben würde. Aber sie sagten: «In Ordnung.» Wir glauben, dass das Restaurant hier sehr gut charakterisiert wurde. Der Kunde war sehr zufrieden, ganz besonders mit den Illustrationen. Mit dem Format begaben wir uns auf Neuland, es verstiess gegen alle Regeln. Die Reaktionen auf diesen Bericht waren ausgezeichnet.

BRIAN BOYD, RICHARDS, BROCK, MILLER, MITCHELL & ASSOCIATES/THE RICHARDS GROUP, DALLAS, TEXAS

Le thème principal dont s'inspire le rapport annuel de Chili's pour 1988 est en fait la croissance contrôlée de l'entreprise. Nous avons donc voulu parler de cette croissance et en montrer les résultats convaincants. On a fait une grande réunion avec Chili's. On proposait ce format exceptionnel et on pensait que l'entreprise aurait quelque difficulté à accepter un encart dépliant dont les deux volets présentaient des informations différentes, mais on nous a simplement dit: «Allez-y.» A notre avis, c'est typique de ce restaurant. Au plan affaires, ils ont été satisfaits et de la transposition illustrative du thème de la croissance de l'entreprise et du format qui dérogeait aux règles du genre et qui a fait école. Les réactions à ce rapport ont été rapides à venir, et les gens nous ont fait des commentaires superbes.

THE FLUOROCARBON COMPANY

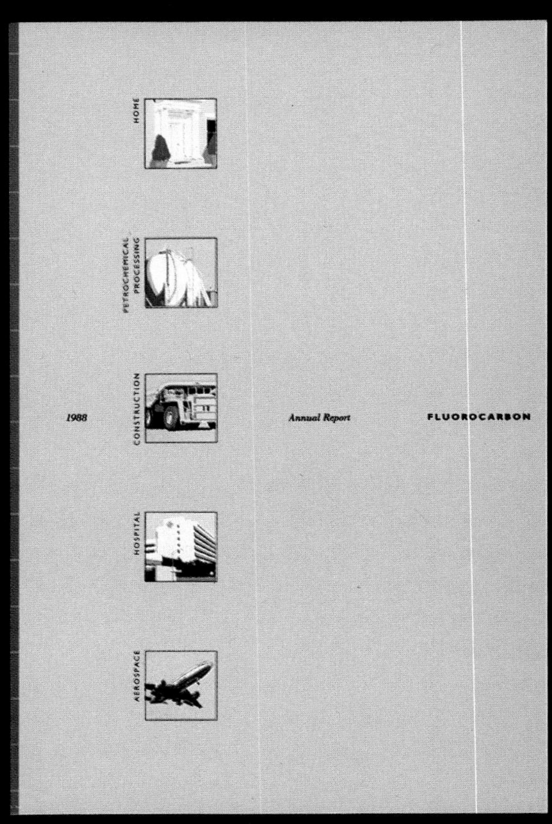

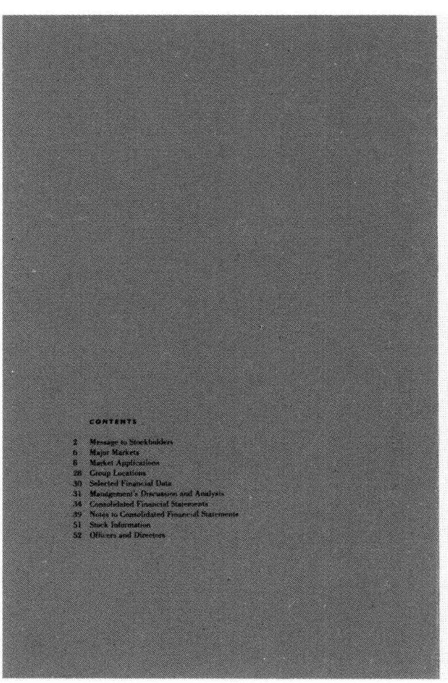

CONTENTS

HIGHLIGHTS

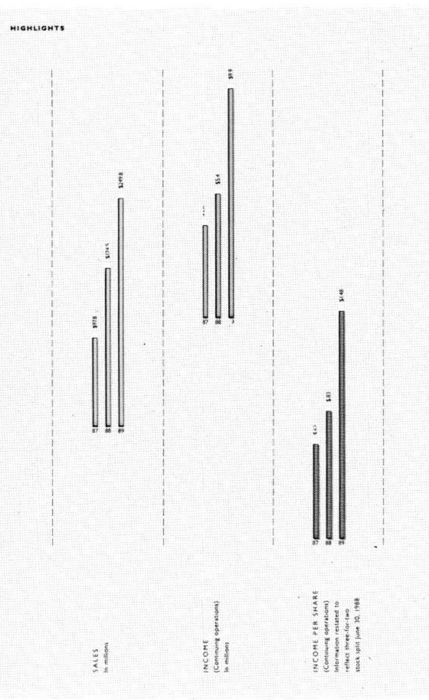

TO OUR STOCKHOLDERS

We don't know what to talk about first. So many great things happened to us this past year. But the number one main event was our record performance with sales up 43% and earnings from continuing operations up 81% over last year. Earnings before taxes were $6 million over our business plan, and we thought our business plan was ambitious. The industrial economy was good all year and we are delighted that we were able to benefit from it.

All four of our groups prospered. Engineered Products had a trade sales increase of 40% and a profit increase of 6% over last year; Advanced Polymers sales were up 13%, profits up 34%; Fluid Sealing sales up 22%, profits up 28%. Sales for the Samuel Moore Group were up 19% and profits rose 53% on an annualized basis.

Our other big news at year-end was the acquisition of Dixon Industries, Bunnell Plastics, and CHR Industries for $86 million in cash. Here we go—betting the farm again. Last time we bet the farm, it was in Ohio with the

Samuel Moore Group in 1987. This time it's in New England and South Jersey with the group of companies we purchased from Bundy Corporation. The way the crops have come in at Samuel Moore, we may use the same kind of cultivation at Bundy.

The sequence of events was unreal and almost made us sure that the purchase was per-ordained. We signed a new line of credit with our banks on November 25, 1988, providing us with, among other things, a $100 million war chest for acquisitions. Within 30 days of that date the three Fluorocarbon-related businesses of Bundy came on the market. Talk about kids on Christmas Eve—there we were with $100 million in our hands looking at three companies we knew well, fit our business plan perfectly and that we were dying to buy—and all that stood in our way were investment bankers, lawyers, and a couple of dozen other people who were interested in buying all or part of the package. Anyway, it all worked out. We are thrilled. The folks in the three businesses seem to be thrilled. The banks are thrilled. Our competitors are not thrilled.

We will talk about product and people fit in future reports—and it's incredible. But let's talk now about debt and leverage. Even with our good earnings, we now have more debt than we like or are comfortable with. So the watchword around here is "Reduce the debt." It is the number one priority of everyone. We have some very innovative programs already under way, and you will be surprised at how much we pay off loans in the next 12 to 18 months.

Our new year is starting strong and at this early date the year looks just fine. Quarter-by-quarter comparisons are going to be challenging, however, and will keep us scrambling to increase earnings while covering the interest and acquisition costs. Our historical businesses, including Samuel Moore, are doing a great job of contributing profits; so, if the economy stays at present levels, scrambling or not, we will have another excellent year.

A part of our business we don't mention often is our foreign sales; both products manufactured in this country and shipped overseas (old military term—now called off-shore), and products made in our foreign plants. A couple of years ago these sales accounted for about 7% of our total sales. Last year

that figure was about 14%, and very profitable. We plan to continue our penetration of these foreign markets—our products are competitive from a price standpoint, and our quality can compete with anyone. American quality is still tops.

We know we are a difficult company to understand—so many plants, products, markets. In this report we have tried to present to you some of our typical applications in five of our major markets. Our objectives continue to be to manufacture as many products as possible from high performance polymer-based materials to serve all industrial markets in this country and all over the world.

Are we going to top last year? We're not sure, but we are sure going to try. Please stay with us. We hope we don't know what to talk about first, next year, too.

J. Michael Hagan
President

Peter Churm
Chairman

MAJOR MARKETS

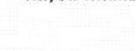

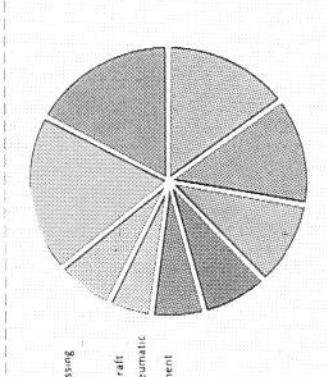

- 19% Chemical Processing
- 17% Auto/Truck
- 15% Aerospace/Aircraft
- 13% Hydraulic & Pneumatic
- 10% Machine Equipment
- 8% Construction
- 6% Electronic
- 5% Utilities
- 7% Other

MARKET APPLICATIONS

Fluorocarbon is a major supplier to many different markets, and we've picked five to highlight in this year's annual report. Applications in the home, petrochemical, construction, medical and aircraft/aerospace industries were selected since these are typical places where you'd be likely to come across our products.

Airports and aerospace applications are veritable showcases for Fluorocarbon components. We have parts in the aircraft, in the ground service equipment, in the airport buildings, and more. Here's a quick run-down:

The terminal has Fluorocarbon silicone rubber glazing on its windows for enduring good looks and effective sealing from the elements. Its radar equipment, also subjected to severe conditions from harsh weather, needs a special seal on the critical joint where it rotates. Fluorocarbon fills the bill with a special low-friction design that holds up in heavy use, even in Arctic temperatures.

Naturally, ground loading equipment also takes a beating by operating out of doors for long hours. That's why original equipment manufacturers and airport maintenance crews have come to rely on rugged push-pull controls designed and built by Fluorocarbon.

Taking to the air, our spring-energized Teflon seals are specified in passenger comfort systems to provide heating and air conditioning services. We also supply custom air conditioning ducts and panel insulation that resist high heat and flames to promote passenger safety.

Our airborne applications extend to military service and especially into space. For the space shuttle, Fluorocarbon supplies spring-energized seals used in the main engine plumbing, propellent systems, space suits, and dozens of additional places.

Airports and aerospace applications are veritable showcases for Fluorocarbon components. We have parts in the aircraft, in the ground service equipment, in the airport buildings, and more. Here's a quick run-down:

The terminal has Fluorocarbon silicone rubber glazing on its windows for enduring good looks and effective sealing from the elements. Its radar equipment, also subjected to severe conditions from harsh weather, needs a special seal on the critical joint where it rotates. Fluorocarbon fills the bill with a special low-friction design that holds up in heavy use, even in Arctic temperatures.

Naturally, ground loading equipment also takes a beating by operating out of doors for long hours. That's why original equipment manufacturers and airport maintenance crews have come to rely on rugged push-pull controls designed and built by Fluorocarbon.

Taking to the air, our spring-energized Teflon seals are specified in passenger comfort systems to provide heating and air conditioning services. We also supply custom air conditioning ducts and panel insulation that resist high heat and flames to promote passenger safety.

Our airborne applications extend to military service and especially into space. For the space shuttle, Fluorocarbon supplies spring-energized seals used in the main engine plumbing, propellent systems, space suits, and dozens of additional places.

24

LOCATIONS

Fluid Sealing Group

Mechanical Seal Division
Los Alamitos, California 90720
213.594.0941
Spring Energized Teflon Seals

Components Division
Columbia, South Carolina
29209
803.783.1880
Metallic O-Rings, C-Rings & Rotary Lip Seals

Metallic Gasket Division
Houston, Texas 77049
713.458.5830
Spiral Wound & Heat Exchanger Metallic Gaskets

Fluorocarbon Seals NV/SA
Antwerpen, Belgium
3.830.0080

Grover Piston Ring Division
Milwaukee, Wisconsin 53215
414.384.9472
Metallic & Polyurethane Piston Rings & Hydraulic Cylinder Components

Universal Seal
Bancroft, Ontario
Canada KOL 1CO
613.332.3182

Minneapolis Division
Eden Prairie, Minnesota 55344
612.941.5474
Rubber O-Rings

Industrial Electronic Rubber Division
Twinsburg, Ohio 44087
216.425.7121
Custom Precision Molding of Fluoroelastomers

Industrial Electronic Rubber Division
Liverpool, Pennsylvania 17045
717.444.3715
Custom Precision Molding of Fluoroelastomers

Advanced Polymers Group

Anaheim Division
Anaheim, California 92803
714.772.7920
Plastic Fabrication & Compressor Components

Fluid Handling Division
Anaheim, California 92803
714.772.3000
Fluid Handling Components, Pumps, Valves, Tubes & Fittings

Chicago Division
Mundelein, Illinois 60060
312.949.0850
Automatic Compression Molding & Machining

Ohio Division
Dover, Ohio 44622
216.878.5521
Molding & Fabrication

Structural Bearings Division
Athens, Texas 75751
214.675.8571
Elastomeric Bearings & Fluorogold Slide Bearings

Reeves Rubber Division
Albertville, Alabama 35950
205.878.6810
Compression & Injection Molding, Extruding & Splicing

Dixon Division
Bristol, Rhode Island 02809
401.253.2000
Engineered Components, Sheet, Film & Bearings

NTN-Rulon Industries Co., Ltd.
Tokyo, Japan
03.494.2851

Samuel Moore Group

Dekoron Division
Aurora, Ohio 44202
216.562.9111
Plastic & Metallic Tubing, Plenum Cable, Irradiated Wire, Temperature Control Products

Dekoron Division
Mt. Pleasant, Texas 75455
214.572.3475
Thermoplastic Wire

Felsted Division
Holmesville, Ohio 44633
216.279.3711
Cables, Control Cables, Levers, Control Systems

Synflex Division
Mantua, Ohio 44255
216.274.3171
Hydraulic Hose, Specialty Hose, Bundles, Truck Tubing

Synflex Division
Aurora, Ohio 44202
216.562.9111
Assembled Products, Paint & Hydraulic Hose

Samuel Moore Europe S.A.
Gembloux, Belgium
81.612.985

Felsted U.K.
Peterborough PE6 9HQ
England
778.348.111

Bunnell Plastics Division
Mickelton, New Jersey 08056
Engineered Plastic Extrusions & Fabrication

Bunnell Plastics Division
Osoir La Ferriere, France
33.01.64.40.10.44

Engineered Products Group

Seattle Division
Seattle, Washington 98118
206.723.5600
Custom Fabrication, Composite Laminates, Polyimide Foam & Materials Testing

Seattle Division
Kent, Washington 98032
206.723.5600
Urethane & Polyimide Foam

Sunnyvale Division
Sunnyvale, California 94089
408.734.4711
Silicone Rubber Molding & Extruding

Flo-Med Division
Fremont, California 94539
415.651.2022
Silicone Rubber Molded & Extruded Medical Products

Plastic & Rubber Products Division
Houston, Texas 77041
713.466.4365
Filtration Products & Custom Molding

Fo-Mac Division
Tulsa, Oklahoma 74106
918.425.5524
Molding & Bonding of Rubber & Plastic

Reynolds & Taylor Division
Santa Ana, California 92705
714.540.4850
Fabrication of Advanced Composites & High Performance Plastics

CHR Division
New Haven, Connecticut 06509
203.777.3631
Pressure Sensitive Tapes, Solid & Sponge Silicone Rubber

CHR/T&F Division
Rolling Meadows, Illinois
60008
312.392.8090
Teflon Coated Fabrics

CHR Europe B.V.
Wierden, Holland
31.5496.5953

SELECTED FINANCIAL DATA

In thousands except share and per share amounts	February 4 1989	1988	1987	1986	Years ended January 31 1985
Net sales	$249,847	$174,513	$97,782	$103,957	$94,165
Cost of sales	177,324	124,533	68,623	71,424	65,832
Gross profit	72,523	49,980	29,159	32,533	28,333
Selling, general and administrative expenses	50,845	35,351	21,656	21,416	18,473
Other income, net	(2,392)	(1,657)	(2,799)	(1,748)	(1,166)
Interest expense	6,566	5,716	2,046	1,795	1,683
Income from continuing operations before taxes	17,504	10,570	8,256	11,070	9,343
Taxes based on income	7,648	5,127	4,210	5,505	4,611
Income from continuing operations	9,856	5,443	4,046	5,565	4,732
Discontinued operations:					
Income from discontinued operations (net of taxes)	—	—	—	286	378
Gain (loss) on sale of discontinued operations (net of taxes)	—	(1,030)	—	260	—
Extraordinary gain (net of taxes)	—	—	—	—	608
Net income	$ 9,856	$ 4,413	$ 4,046	$ 6,111	$ 5,718
Income per share:					
Primary:					
Continuing operations	$ 1.48	$ .83	$ .62	$ .85	$ .73
Discontinued operations	—	—	—	.04	.06
Gain (loss) on sale of discontinued operations	—	(.16)	—	.04	—
Extraordinary gain	—	—	—	—	.09
Net income	$ 1.48	$ .67	$ .62	$ .93	$ .88
Fully diluted:					
Continuing operations	$ 1.29	$ .77	$ .60		
Loss on sale of discontinued operations	—	(.12)	—		
Net income	$ 1.29	$ .65	$ .60		
Average number of common shares and equivalents outstanding:					
Primary	6,665,997	6,548,806	6,528,360	6,543,126	6,499,641
Fully diluted	8,535,568	8,417,387	8,397,003		
Cash dividends per share	$ .20	$ .19	$ .19	$ .17	$ .13
At year end:					
Total assets	$167,441	$165,456	$81,695	$ 81,613	$65,432
Total long-term obligations	$ 69,104	$ 85,796	$25,136	$ 25,543	$13,190

MANAGEMENT'S DISCUSSION AND ANALYSIS OF FINANCIAL CONDITION AND RESULTS OF OPERATIONS

Fluorocarbon

Three years ended February 4, 1989 and January 31, 1988 and 1987

RESULTS OF OPERATIONS

Sales increased 43% in fiscal 1989 (19% when removing the effect of acquisitions) compared to fiscal 1988. The growth in sales reflects volume increases in all groups, the acquisition of the Samuel Moore Group in May 1987, and the acquisition of the Reynolds & Taylor division in July 1988, (accounting for 66% and 6%, respectively, of the sales increase). On an annualized basis, the Samuel Moore Group sales volume in 1989 increased by 20% over 1988. Sales increased 78% in fiscal 1988 (12% when removing the effect of acquisitions) compared to fiscal 1987. The growth in sales reflects volume increases and the inclusion of the Samuel Moore Group (which accounted for 83% of the sales increase).

Cost of sales as a percentage of sales decreased from 71.4% in 1988 to 71.0% in 1989. The improvement is due to a 3% increase in gross profit percentage for the Samuel Moore Group resulting from a reduction in fixed manufacturing cost as a percentage of sales. The improvement for the Samuel Moore Group was offset by a reduction of 4% in gross profit percentage for the Engineered Products Group attributable to competitive price reduction on composite products, and an unusually large sale of tooling which has a lower profit percentage. Cost of sales as a percentage of sales increased from 70.2% in 1987 to 71.4% in 1988. The adverse change in gross profit percentage was entirely due to the acquisition of the Samuel Moore Group which experienced a lower gross profit percentage relative to other operations of the Company.

Selling, general and administrative expenses as a percentage of sales have remained static for fiscal 1989 and 1988 at 20% as compared to 22% for 1987. Total selling, general and administrative expenses increased 44% and 63% in fiscal 1989 and 1988, respectively, over the prior year due to the net effect of acquisitions and divestitures. In addition, general and administrative expenses for 1989 include increased management incentive compensation and retirement benefits, as well as a fourth quarter provision for the Main Office relocation and property tax liabilities.

Other income in 1989 includes the pretax gain of $1,841,000 realized on the sale of the 50% joint venture interest in Nitta-Moore. The gain was partially offset by a fourth quarter reserve for costs related to the disposition of certain assets. The decrease in other income for 1988 and 1987 was primarily due to the reduction in interest income from short-term cash equivalent investments made with the excess proceeds from the subordinated debenture offering in late 1986. The excess cash was used in fiscal 1988 for the Samuel Moore acquisition.

Interest expense increased 15% in fiscal 1989 due to a general rise in the borrowing rate, the effect of the Samuel Moore acquisition debt for the full year and the write-off of loan fees related to the Company's previous bank line of credit, which was replaced with a new line in the fourth quarter. The significant increase in interest expense in fiscal 1988 over 1987 was due to the debt incurred for the purchase of the Samuel Moore Group in May 1987.

The Company's effective tax rate in fiscal 1989 was 43.7% compared to 48.5% and 51.0% in fiscal years 1988 and 1987, respectively. The primary reason for the decline in 1989 is due to the decline in the federal tax rate and rise in income level which reduces the effect of non-deductible expenses.

9. SELECTED QUARTERLY CONSOLIDATED FINANCIAL DATA *(unaudited)*

In thousands except per share data	*Net Sales*	*Gross Profit*	*Income from Continuing Operations*	*Loss on Sale of Discontinued Operations*	*Net Income*	*Primary Income Per Share from Continuing Operations*	*Primary Loss Per Share on Sale of Discontinued Operations*	*Primary Net Income Per Share*	*Fully Diluted Net Income Per Share*
Year ended February 4, 1989									
1st Quarter	$60,476	$17,012	$3,054	$ —	$3,054	$.46	$ —	$.46	$.39
2nd Quarter	60,212	17,493	2,523	—	2,523	.38	—	.38	.33
3rd Quarter	63,564	18,200	2,522	—	2,522	.38	—	.38	.33
4th Quarter	65,595	19,818	1,757	—	1,757	.26	—	.26	.24
Year ended January 31, 1988									
1st Quarter	$27,382	$ 8,957	$1,307	$ —	$1,307	$.20	$ —	$.20	$.19
2nd Quarter	43,999	12,344	1,319	—	1,319	.20	—	.20	.19
3rd Quarter	52,178	14,676	1,487	—	1,487	.23	—	.23	.21
4th Quarter	50,954	14,003	1,330	(1,030)	300	.20	(.16)	.04	—

Included in the fourth quarter of fiscal year 1989 were costs related to the disposition of certain assets, the relocation of the Main Office, increased liability for property taxes, and the write-off of loan fees related to the Company's previous bank line of credit which was replaced with a new line in the fourth quarter.

10. SEGMENT INFORMATION

The Company manufactures and sells products in four business segments: Engineered Products, Advanced Polymers, Fluid Sealing and Samuel Moore. During the past year the Company restructured its operating groups into segments which the Company believes more accurately combine complementary and similar products both in the materials used in each segment and the technology and processes employed in the manufacturing of each group's products. The financial information presented in the Notes has been restated for all years presented to reflect this restructuring.

Engineered Products—The molding and extrusion of rubber, silicone-rubber, specially formulated elastomeric compounds of composites into a wide variety of products.

Advanced Polymer Products—The processing, fabrication and sale of products manufactured from high performance plastics, primarily those generically known as the fluorocarbon family of plastics.

Fluid Sealing Products—The design, development, and manufacture of sealing devices.

Samuel Moore Group—The manufacture of wire and cable products, tubing, hose, and push-pull cable and control systems.

In thousands	*Engineered Products Group*	*Advanced Polymers Group*	*Fluid Sealing Group*	*Samuel Moore Group*	*Corporate and Other*	*Adjustments and Eliminations*	*Consolidated*
February 4, 1989							
Sales to outside customers	$40,861	$43,254	$54,560	$111,172	$ —	$ —	$249,847
Intercompany sales	174	3,304	962	1,111	—	(5,551)	—
Total sales	$41,035	$46,558	$55,522	$112,283	$ —	$(5,551)	$249,847
Operating profit	$ 3,928	$ 6,655	$ 9,448	$ 11,183	$ —	$ —	$ 31,214
General corporate and other expense					(7,181)		(7,181)
Interest expense					(6,529)		(6,529)
Income before taxes based on income							$ 17,504
Identifiable assets at February 4, 1989	$28,721	$21,175	$32,902	$ 72,070	$12,573	$ —	$167,441
Depreciation and amortization	$ 1,466	$ 1,501	$ 2,012	$ 4,317	$ 538	$ —	$ 9,834
Additions to plant and equipment	$ 724	$ 1,160	$ 1,964	$ 2,269	$ 61	$ —	$ 6,178
January 31, 1988							
Sales to outside customers	$29,279	$38,299	$44,548	$ 62,387	$ —	$ —	$174,513
Intercompany sales	192	2,950	586	1,048	—	(4,776)	—
Total sales	$29,471	$41,249	$45,134	$ 63,435	$ —	$(4,776)	$174,513
Operating profit	$ 3,705	$ 4,950	$ 7,354	$ 4,871	$ —	$ —	$ 20,880
General corporate and other expense					(4,594)		(4,594)
Interest expense					(5,716)		(5,716)
Income before taxes based on income							$ 10,570
Identifiable assets at January 31, 1988	$16,065	$20,565	$26,854	$ 88,878	$13,094	$ —	$165,456
Depreciation and amortization	$ 1,055	$ 1,435	$ 1,950	$ 2,808	$ 331	$ —	$ 7,579
Additions to plant and equipment	$ 877	$ 1,299	$ 853	$ 1,118	$ 162	$ —	$ 4,309
January 31, 1987							
Sales to outside customers	$25,040	$31,955	$40,787	$ —	$ —	$ —	$ 97,782
Intercompany sales	40	1,961	591	—	—	(2,592)	—
Total sales	$25,080	$33,916	$41,378	$ —	$ —	$(2,592)	$ 97,782
Operating profit	$ 1,955	$ 4,470	$ 5,643	$ —	$ —	$ —	$ 12,068
General corporate and other expense					(1,766)		(1,766)
Interest expense					(2,046)		(2,046)
Income before taxes based on income							$ 8,256
Identifiable assets at January 31, 1987	$13,730	$19,952	$26,340	$ —	$21,673	$ —	$ 81,695
Depreciation and amortization	$ 991	$ 1,346	$ 1,855	$ —	$ 316	$ —	$ 4,508
Additions to plant and equipment	$ 936	$ 3,152	$ 1,496	$ —	$ 615	$ —	$ 6,199

Operating profit is total revenue less operating expenses. Identifiable assets are those assets of the Company that are identified to the four classes of similar products. Corporate assets are principally cash and cash equivalents, notes receivable, and fixed assets at the Company headquarters. Corporate expenses are primarily comprised of general and administrative expenses with adjustments to operating groups for profit in inventory, pricing reserves and interest income, which are normally carried at the Company headquarters.

11. CONTINGENCIES

The Company is currently involved in litigation arising in the normal course of business. Management of the Company is of the opinion that such litigation will have no material effect on the Company's consolidated financial position or results of operations.

CLIENT:
THE FLUOROCARBON COMPANY

DESIGN FIRM:
THE JEFFERIES ASSOCIATION

ART DIRECTOR:
RON JEFFERIES

DESIGNER:
SUSAN GARLAND

ILLUSTRATOR:
DENNIS MUKAI

WRITER:
RON BISSELL

TYPOGRAPHER:
CAPCO

PAPER SELECTION:
REFLECTIONS GLOSS

PAPER MANUFACTURER:
POTLATCH

PRINTER:
LITHOGRAPHIX

NUMBER OF PAGES:
52

SIZE:
7 3/4" X 11 7/8"

TYPE SELECTION:
*BODONI BOOK,
GILL SANS BOLD*

RON BISSELL, DIRECTOR OF COMMUNICATIONS, THE FLUOROCARBON COMPANY, LAGUNA NIGUEL, CALIFORNIA

Because of Fluorocarbon's many products and capabilities, the company had become difficult to understand at first glance, especially for the investment community and potential stockholders.The company specifically wanted investor relations targeted in the 1988 annual report.The report was to be a communication and an educational tool for the investment community. The designer accomplished this very well through the use of five illustrations that depict our services and products, which Fluorocarbon provides to major markets. The response has proven the design to have been effective in accomplishing our goals.

RON BISSELL, DIRECTOR OF COMMUNICATIONS, THE FLUOROCARBON COMPANY, LAGUNA NIGUEL, KALIFORNIEN

Angesichts der zahlreichen Produkte und Leistungen von Fluorocarbon war es besonders für die Investoren und potentiellen Aktionäre schwierig geworden, die Firma auf einen Blick zu erfassen. Der Jahresbericht für 1988 sollte als Kommunikationsmittel dienen und besonders Investoren ansprechen und zu ihrer Aufklärung beitragen. Dem Designer gelang dies ausgezeichnet durch den Einsatz von fünf Illustrationen, in welchen Dienstleistungen und Produkte von Fluorocarbon in seinen wichtigsten Märkten dargestellt sind. Die Reaktionen der Zielgruppe zeigen, dass dank des Designs unsere Ziele erreicht wurden.

RON BISSELL, DIRECTOR OF COMMUNICATIONS, THE FLUOROCARBON COMPANY, LAGUNA NIGUEL, CALIFORNIE

La multiplication des produits et capacités de Fluorocarbon ne permet guère la compréhension immédiate de ses activités, surtout si l'on est investisseur et actionnaire potentiel. Pour son rapport annuel 1988, la société souhaitait cibler plus particulièrement ses relations avec les investisseurs en faisant de son rapport annuel un support de la communication et un outil d'instruction à leur service. Le designer s'en est acquitté à la perfection en utilisant cinq illustrations-clefs décrivant les services et produits Fluorocarbon. La réaction des lecteurs a démontré l'efficacité du design et son utilité pour la réalisation de nos objectifs.

RON JEFFRIES, THE JEFFRIES ASSOCIATION, LOS ANGELES, CALIFORNIA

Fluorocarbon makes parts, which are not seen or identified with the final product. The intention of the annual report in 1988 was to show the world that Fluorocarbon parts are in products which affect everyone. These products had to be recognizable to the average person. For this, we wanted to create artwork that illustrated the company in a special way. We used illustrations by Dennis Mukai to highlight five specific markets, and then we used vellum overlays to give information while keeping the integrity of the illustrations. We heard that the company loved it, and that shareholders and investors commented that they understood the relationships in many areas of the firm's work from this report.

RON JEFFRIES, THE JEFFRIES ASSOCIATION, LOS ANGELES, KALIFORNIEN

Fluorocarbon stellt Teile her, die beim Endprodukt erkennbar sind. Aufgabe des Jahresberichtes für 1988 war es, der Welt zu zeigen, dass Fluorocarbons Erzeugnisse für Produkte verwendet werden, die jeden angehen. Diese Produkte sollten dem Durchschnittsleser nähergebracht werden. Die Illustrationen von Dennis Mukai beziehen sich auf fünf spezifische Märkte. Die dazugehörigen Informationen wurden auf Transparentpapier gedruckt, um den Gesamteindruck der Illustrationen nicht zu beeinträchtigen. Wir hörten, dass der Kunde begeistert war und dass Aktionäre wie Investoren sagten, dass dieser Bericht zum besseren Verständnis der Zusammenhänge auf vielen Gebieten der Firmenarbeit geführt habe.

RON JEFFRIES, THE JEFFRIES ASSOCIATION, LOS ANGELES, CALIFORNIE

Fluorocarbon fabrique des pièces qui ne se reconnaissent pas sur le produit fini. L'intention du rapport annuel pour 1988, c'était d'apporter au monde entier la démonstration de l'ubiquité des pièces Fluorocarbon dans les objets de consommation journalière. Ces produits devaient être aisément identifiables. Les illustrations de Dennis Mukai sont focalisées sur cinq marchés distincts, avec superposition d'informations essentielles sur vélin de manière à ne pas nuire à l'intégrité de l'illustration sous-jacente. Nous avons appris que notre client en a été très satisfait et que les actionnaires et investisseurs ont été séduits par la clarification graphique des interactivités au sein de l'entreprise.

THE GROWTH IN enrollment and the beginning of coeducation at Goucher in the fall of 1987 helped set the stage for the college's emergence into a second century of excellence and a new era of achievement. Members of the Goucher community played leading roles in the changing scene.

Goucher College 1988 Annual Report

Setting the Stage

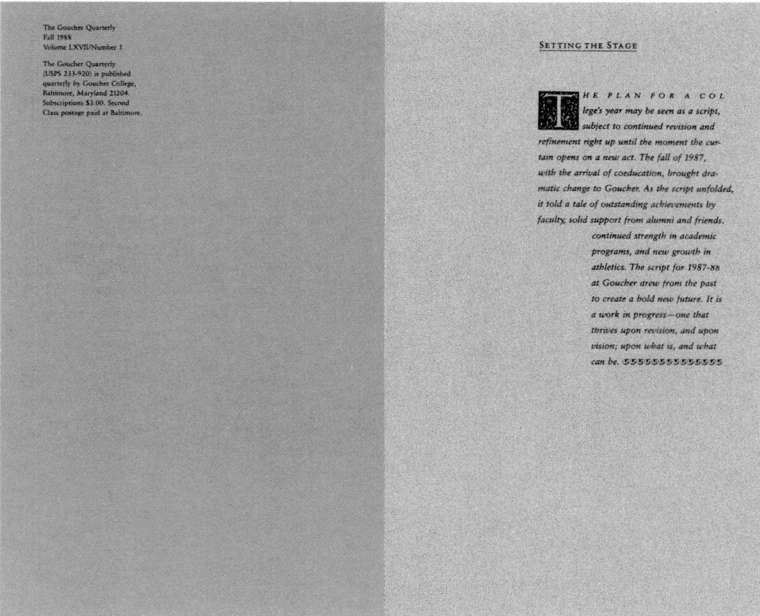

The Goucher Quarterly
Fall 1988
Volume LXVII/Number 1.

The Goucher Quarterly (USPS 233-920) is published quarterly by Goucher College, Baltimore, Maryland 21204. Subscriptions $3.00. Second Class postage paid at Baltimore.

Setting the Stage

The plan for a college's year may be seen as a script, subject to continued revision and refinement right up until the moment the curtain opens on a new act. The fall of 1987, with the arrival of coeducation, brought dramatic change to Goucher. As the script unfolded, it told a tale of outstanding achievements by faculty, solid support from alumni and friends, continued strength in academic programs, and new growth in athletics. The script for 1987-88 at Goucher drew from the past to create a bold new future. It is a work in progress—one that thrives upon revision, and upon vision; upon what is, and what can be.

President's Letter

"All the world's a stage, and all the men and women merely players."

William Shakespeare, As You Like It, Act II, Scene VII

A college campus sometimes seems to be one big stage—a stage that accommodates many plays with numerous acts and scenes, a constantly changing cast of characters, and rich and varied sets. For the first 101 years of Goucher's history, the student roles were all filled by women. In the fall of 1987 we witnessed a dramatic change with the arrival of the first coeducational freshman class—the largest in almost two decades. This growth in enrollment, along with new initiatives in academics, student life, finance and planning, admissions, and advancement, set the stage for Goucher's emergence as an academically rigorous, intellectually stimulating, and lively coeducational campus.

This year was a stellar one for faculty, to the benefit of the college overall and of our students. Academic programs also shone brightly. The Decker and Hughes Field Politics Centers continued to expand, while a new International Technology and Media Center prepared for its debut. Intercollegiate athletics for both men and women grew in size, strength, and quality. Leadership training and development matured into an integral part of the co-curricular program and also moved into the academic realm.

During the past year, planning was done for two new campus buildings: a sports and recreation center and the Robert and Jane Meyerhoff Arts Center. Trustees, staff members, and students on the Buildings and Grounds Committee of the board painstakingly reviewed plans and contained costs. Meanwhile, the Steering Committee of the Campaign for Expanding Excellence: Arts and Athletics, under the leadership of Fern Karesh Hurst '68, and co-vice-chairs Douglas W. Dodge and Martha Howell Eck '60, made an impressive start toward its goal of raising $9.8 million. The state of Maryland provided much needed—and much appreciated—support for the arts center with a $1.4 million grant.

The Admissions Office had barely taken its bows for recruiting the class of '91 when it was back on the road again, working hard to bring in another outstanding cast for the fall of 1988. Alumni, as always, played a strong supporting role in the admissions effort, and students also began to assume significant parts in the recruitment process. The Goucher Alumni Association undertook the first reorganization in its 94-year history.

It was, on the whole, an extraordinarily exciting and promising year. The ghosts of Goucher past haunted our stage in a decidedly friendly manner. The past informed our present and inspired our future. We've prepared for our new role as we begin our second hundred-year run. Let the curtain rise.

Rhoda M. Dorsey
Dr. Rhoda M. Dorsey
President, Goucher College

"My soul, sit thou a patient looker-on;
Judge not the play before the play is done:
Her plot hath many changes; every day
Speaks a new scene; the last act crowns the play."

Francis Quarles, Epigram. Respice Finem

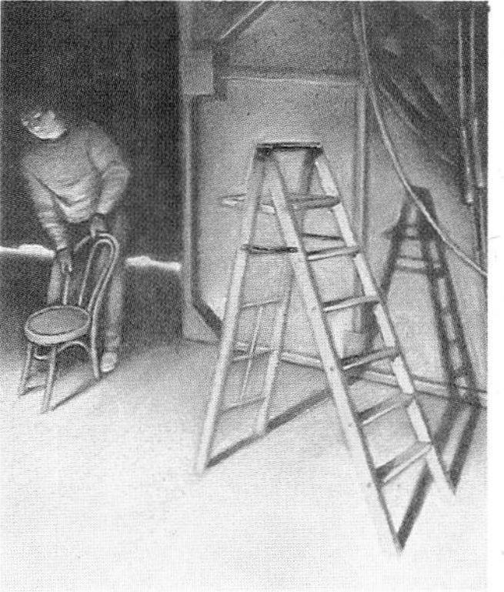

The arrival of a large and well-qualified first coeducational class in 1987 helped set the stage for a stellar season.

Another Opening

In the fall of 1987, the Goucher College freshman class broke records. The class of 1991, numbering 290, was the largest since 1970. With an 11 percent male enrollment, it was also the first coeducational freshman class. Size and coeducation weren't the only distinguishing factors. Average SAT scores were up, and there were more valedictorians, National Merit Scholars, and National Honor Society members. By the end of the 1987-88 academic year, the college had completed a second successful season of recruiting highly qualified men and women, with men accounting for 23 percent of the fall 1988 entering class. In the view of Goucher's admissions officers, alumni, and student volunteers, the stage has indeed been set for a continued long and successful run. Under the direction of Dean of Admissions and Financial Aid Barbara Fritze and Admissions Director Lee Seraydarian, the college strengthened its regional approach to recruitment. "Each counselor is responsible for a different specific region of the country. He or she follows the students from that region through the admissions process. The counselor is an advocate for the student within the overall program," explains Ms. Seraydarian. The fact that each counselor has an assigned territory increases his or her specialized knowledge of that area and its students.

The Alumni Admissions Representative Program also focused on a regional approach, with more than 350 alumni volunteers attending college fairs, holding parties for prospective students, and making phone calls in their areas.

Current students have become more involved in the admissions process, too, through the new Student Admissions Representative Program. Headed by Deborah Harris '88, an English/Spanish major, the SAR program is a formal network of more than 100 students who serve as tour guides, liaisons with their high schools, hosts for special events, and callers to prospective students.

"Student enthusiasm is high," says Ms. Harris. "We even have several volunteers for Saturday tours. I think more students are getting involved because the level of excitement about the college has increased."

Enthusiasm is also growing among prospective students. "Many of the men I interviewed two years ago were concerned and even skeptical about a newly coeducational college," says Admissions Counselor Scott Greatorex. "Now, I don't get many questions about the composition of the student body. Students are much more interested in the academic program, internships, facilities, sports, and location."

High school guidance counselors have become more receptive to the change at Goucher. "I haven't had any trouble getting appointments at boys' schools this year," notes Mr. Greatorex. "We're being asked by counselors to make visits," adds Associate Director Mary Brune. "Transition doesn't seem to be an issue any more."

Goucher's newest students seem to be more widely travelled, more politically and socially aware, and more interested in the core curriculum, say the admissions counselors. "Interviews with prospective students are more philosophical, and students know more about Goucher," adds Mr. Greatorex. "They are coming to Goucher because this is exactly what they want. In fact, many parents tell me that Goucher has everything they would have wanted as an undergraduate."

Deborah Harris, who found out about Goucher both from a computer search in her high school guidance office and a family friend who was an alumna, isn't surprised that the good news about Goucher is spreading. "There's so much here that you can take and run with—academically, socially, intellectually. The atmosphere and opportunities are so varied, with so much to explore. I can't imagine being anyplace else."

Plans for a new studio and theatre arts building and sports and recreation center are part of the changing scene.

"On no other stage are the scenes shifted with a swiftness so like magic as on the great stage of history when once the hour strikes."

Edward Bellamy, Looking Backward, Author's postscript

Bright Stars

"Teaching at an undergraduate college is a good way to get at the essentials of history."

Dr. Jean Baker
Professor of History

Star power can ignite a classroom, attract admiration from afar, and light up the deepest recesses of the intellect. Although a faculty star may not have his or her name in lights, a stellar classroom performance can have a long-reaching effect on students. During the past year, several Goucher faculty members received recognition for work both within and outside the classroom. "Our faculty's scholarship benefits them and the entire campus community," comments Academic Dean and Vice President Gerald Duff. "It's been an excellent and productive year for the faculty."

One of the brightest lights reaching beyond the campus was cast by Jean Baker, a 1961 Goucher graduate and professor of history on the Elizabeth Conolly Todd Foundation. Dr. Baker's penetrating study Mary Todd Lincoln: A Biography received favorable reviews by such publications as the New York Times and Washington Post and was a Book-of-the-Month Club alternate and History Book-of-the-Month Club selection. In addition, Dr. Baker spent the fall 1987 semester on sabbatical teaching at Harvard University, where she was profiled in the Crimson as the first woman to teach at the full professorial rank in American history in Harvard's 350 years.

For Dr. Baker, teaching at Goucher carries equal weight with her research. In fact, she says, it even enhances her scholarship. "Teaching at an undergraduate college is a good way to get at the essentials of history," she notes. "Our students ask the core kinds of questions that force you to deal with issues logically . . . they are interested in the past from a different perspective than graduate students. For example, many of the students I taught at Harvard had read more widely, but they were more concerned about specific areas and issues."

Goucher's emphasis on the role of women influenced her, too, Dr. Baker says. "I approached the subject of Mary Todd Lincoln with far more sensitivity to feminist issues."

There were other Goucher authors who received wide recognition during the past year. Zero DB and Other Stories, a collection of short stories by Madison Smartt Bell, lecturer in English, was published to critical acclaim by the New York Times and others. Dr. Vassily Aksyonov, writer-in-residence, published a witty account of his experiences as a Soviet emigre in the United States, including teaching at Goucher. His In Search of Melancholy Baby received laudatory reviews and made him a sought-after guest on talk shows around the nation, including Good Morning America. Gary Edgerton, chair and associate professor of communication, edited Film and the Arts in Symbiosis, a resource guide on the relationships between motion pictures and other communication arts.

In the sciences, George Delahunty, associate professor of biological sciences, received a $50,000 grant from the National Institutes of Health for his research on insulin-like growth factors in non-mammalian vertebrates. Edward Worteck, assistant professor of art and communication, was one of only four Maryland artists chosen for the first Maryland Invitational Exhibition. His photographs were displayed at the Baltimore Museum of Art. For the 17th year in a row, Robert Hall Lewis, professor of music, received an award for his compositions from the American

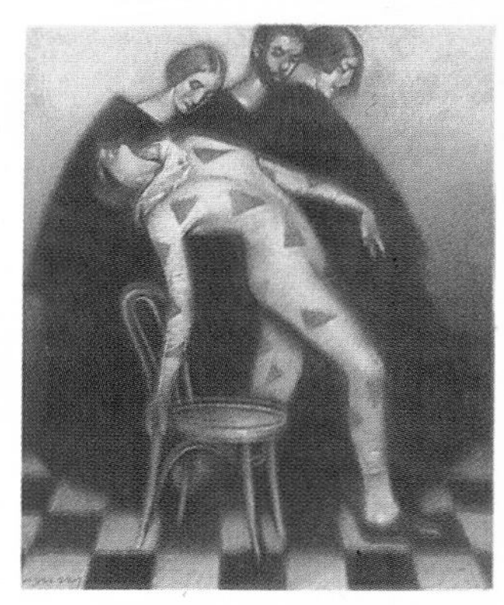

SUPPORT FROM FRIENDS GAVE THE EDGE FOR SUCCESS IN ACADEMICS, IN ADMISSIONS, AND IN FUND RAISING FOR 1987-88.

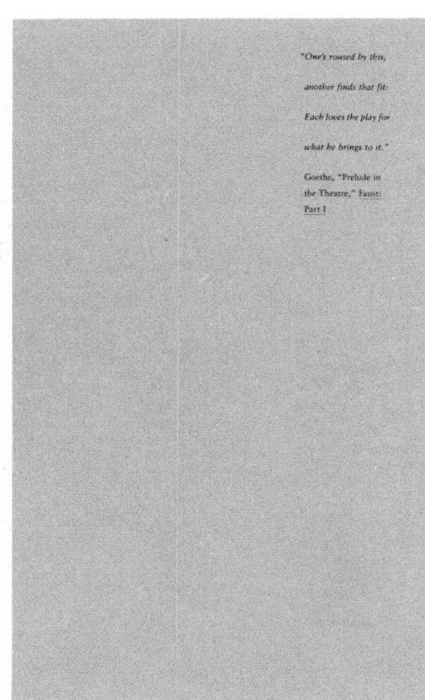

"One's roused by this,

another finds that fit:

Each loves the play for

what he brings to it."

Goethe, "Prelude in the Theatre," Faust: Part I

Summary of Voluntary Support Gifts Through Development Office

	1983-84	1984-85	1985-86	1986-87	1987-88
Capital Campaigns	$1,160,982	$ 972,757	$ 304,521	$ 43,961	$ --
Expanding Excellence: Arts and Athletics Campaign	--	--	--	--	887,139
Restricted Funds, Endowment and Plant	1,265,007	1,526,043	2,155,840	1,706,169	1,314,056
Annual Giving Operating Funds	783,003	1,395,391	987,107	1,031,816	1,071,039
Total	$3,208,992	$3,894,191	$3,447,468	$2,781,946	$3,272,234

Nº 26.

Endowment and Similar Funds Market Value

1988	$54,663,791
1987	$54,109,945
1986	$50,244,394
1985	$40,892,650.
1984	$33,472,464

Nº 27.

The Financial Report 1987-88

STATEMENT OF CURRENT REVENUES AND EXPENDITURES YEARS ENDED JUNE 30, 1987 AND 1988

REVENUES	1988	1987
Student Tuition and Fees	$ 7,866,919	$ 6,609,142
Government Grants	1,004,105	1,041,265
Endowment Income	3,113,321	2,747,732
Gifts	1,328,656	2,006,410
Other Sources	525,724	595,663
Auxiliary Enterprises	3,711,377	3,159,926
Total Revenues	$17,550,102	$16,160,138

EXPENDITURES AND MANDATORY TRANSFERS	1988	1987
Instruction and Research	$ 5,450,292	$ 4,784,183
General Administration	765,949	762,820
General Institutional	2,642,602	2,399,462
Student Services	1,463,773	1,466,761
Student Aid	1,963,729	1,682,169
Library	511,534	457,221
Physical Plant	1,772,226	1,439,200
Auxiliary Enterprises	2,568,486	2,308,520
Mandatory Transfers	195,153	198,624
Total Expenditures and Mandatory Transfer	$17,333,744	$15,498,960
Excess of Revenues over Expenditures Prior to Non-Mandatory Transfers	$ 216,358	$ 661,178
Non-Mandatory Transfers (to)/from Other Funds	(177,986)	(637,074)
Net Surplus (Deficit)	38,372	24,104

Nº 28.

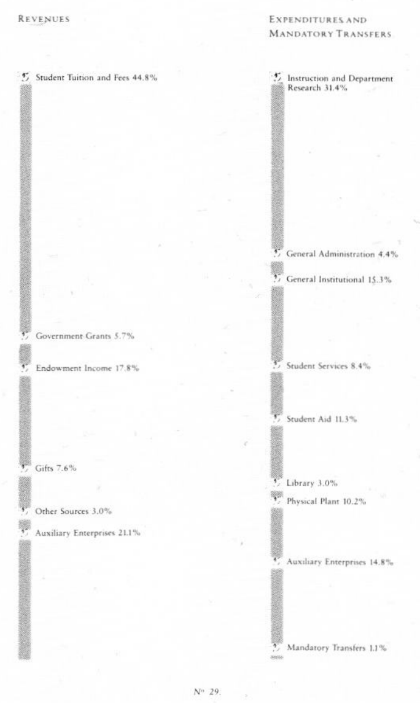

Annual Class Report

CLASS	ALUMNI FUND REPRESENTATIVE	AMOUNT	DONORS	PARTICIPATION
1912	--------------------	$ 250.00	1	N.A.
1913	--------------------	600.00	1	N.A.
1914	--------------------	200.00	2	N.A.
1915	--------------------	----	--	----
1916	--------------------	1,050.00	4	N.A.
1917	Irene Rice Robb	1,200.00	11	79%
1918	--------------------	870.00	7	32%
1919	A. Grace Hamilton	14,975.00	16	59%
1920	Carrie B. Josselyn	63,493.88	21	57%
1921	Gladys Tebbs Bills	23,755.00	38	48%
1922	--------------------	2,935.00	19	31%
1923	Louise Dallett Darlington	13,352.50	42	56%
1924	Virginia W. Duval	8,479.00	47	48%
1925	Margaret E. Keen	11,047.50	47	46%
1926	Gertrude Damerel Nordling	25,775.00	74	59%
1927	Sarah H. Ackler	15,690.44	50	44%
1928	Jane Bisbee	33,516.20	83	71%
1929	Dorothy M. Taylor	25,483.76	75	52%
1930	Mary Crum Fox	13,728.00	93	66%
1931	Margaret C. Taylor	15,235.06	85	50%
1932	Jessie Richardson Kratzer	11,056.00	75	59%
1933	Adelaide Forbush Fowler	20,677.75	86	62%
1934	Florence Eisen Fineman	24,364.48	88	62%
1935	Charlotte Cassell Thom	11,604.50	78	58%
1936	Leah Baach Tannenbaum	11,333.75	57	45%
1937	Ruth Stone Burchard	10,222.50	72	73%
1938	Mignon Mackensen Bieber	26,482.62	92	78%
1939	Naomi Zeller Miller	23,240.00	96	63%
1940	Adelaide Mason Comstock	8,381.00	80	54%
1941	Margaret Krausz Olson	10,200.00	76	56%
1942	Betty Chinn Smith	6,836.00	75	62%
1943	Brice Black Bramman	12,194.06	54	52%
1944	Eleanor Brown Jones	10,511.25	48	39%
1945	Jennie Ann Gray	12,835.00	64	58%
1946	Patricia Falconer Weldon	14,085.00	71	58%
1947	Hilda Cohen Fisher	6,395.00	68	55%
1948	Elaine Knorr Gompf	13,940.49	87	59%
1949	Betty Silverstein Spear	11,756.50	72	55%
1950	Margaret Wilson Jones	6,786.50	83	49%

Nº 34.

CLASS	ALUMNI FUND REPRESENTATIVE	AMOUNT	DONORS	PARTICIPATION
1951	Jean Schwartz Bernstein	$23,699.00	96	48%
1952	Helen Manos Karkazis	10,555.19	88	46%
1953	Robin Donaldson Strahan	11,897.15	99	67%
1954	Connie Rice Russell	8,755.00	80	58%
1955	Beverly Heuschober Winter	14,314.63	57	46%
1956	Beth Cheney Desmond	10,908.70	74	54%
1957	Emily Chase Weaver	10,358.38	81	51%
1958	Debby Richards Berman	15,510.06	99	60%
1959	Leslie Noll Kayne	10,135.00	78	51%
1960	Betsy Land Jedlicka	10,365.00	95	56%
1961	Gretchen Kalb Scherping	15,060.75	82	45%
1962	Taylor Freeman Sader	10,105.00	81	42%
1963	Nancy Overbagh Brett	18,260.00	107	55%
1964	Caroline Potter Normann	12,848.00	87	49%
1965	Peggy Spence Gunn	9,605.00	82	45%
1966	Lorraine L. Brown	18,525.00	113	51%
1967	Debby Sody Wahl	13,974.39	97	49%
1968	Gretchen Lundgren Lewis	28,836.99	143	53%
1969	Nancy Hemstreet Eaton	12,263.50	90	44%
1970	Marty McClintock Sippel	6,785.00	73	36%
1971	Marjory Watts Hopper	7,655.00	86	37%
1972	Suzanne Berry Maurer	10,486.00	63	26%
1973	Jacqueline Greenberg	13,187.50	86	38%
1974	Debra E. Shore	11,150.00	67	25%
1975	Odile Zientek Tyler	8,670.00	44	20%
1976	Kathleen C. Barna	6,570.00	61	26%
1977	Valerie A. Lippmann	3,945.00	49	23%
1978	Katherine E. Healy	5,311.54	52	23%
1979	Debbi Oresman Kasper	2,570.00	30	14%
1980	Maria Sabol Richard	2,085.00	40	21%
1981	Katya Bennett O'Leary	3,500.00	52	23%
1982	Hilary V. Greene	1,289.88	37	15%
1983	Lisa Kolman Cunninghis	2,219.49	49	20%
1984	Emily Susan Vaill	1,145.00	25	17%
1985	Paula S. Gabbert	535.00	22	13%
1986	Michelle Brettschneider Levin	663.73	21	10%
1987	Naomi G. Penney	460.00	24	11%
1988	--------------------	644.52	64	47%

Nº 35.

CLIENT:
GOUCHER COLLEGE

DESIGN FIRM:
RUTKA WEADOCK DESIGN

ART DIRECTOR:
KATE BERGQUIST

DESIGNER:
KATE BERGQUIST

PHOTOGRAPHER:
BARRY HOLNIKER

ILLUSTRATOR:
GARY KELLEY

WRITER:
JUDITH PHAIR

TYPOGRAPHER:
THE TYPE HOUSE

PAPER SELECTION:
80LB JERSEY,
80LB SUPERFINE

PAPER MANUFACTURER:
CURTIS, MOHAWK

PRINTER:
E. JOHN SCHMITZ
& SONS, INC.

NUMBER OF PAGES:
48 PLUS COVER

SIZE:
5 1/2" X 9"

TYPE SELECTION:
SABON, SABON ITALIC

JUDITH T. PHAIR, VICE-PRESIDENT FOR PUBLIC RELATIONS, GOUCHER COLLEGE, BALTIMORE, MARYLAND

For our second year of transition at Goucher College, where we had enormous changes when we went co-ed, we chose the theme of "setting the stage" because we wanted to address the whole issue of stability and our future in our 1988 annual report. We thought of taking the college year as a script, stressing that there is constant revision until the curtain opens. We wanted to show our significant achievements as a high-quality liberal arts institution. The script book became the design device suggested by the designer, and he also suggested using illustration, which we had not done in this way before. That was greeted with some skepticism, but the designer convinced us that this would add the right tone and an elegance to the book. We had a wonderful response and the report, which was tied-in to our fundraising for an arts and theater building.

JUDITH T. PHAIR, VICE-PRESIDENT FOR PUBLIC RELATIONS, GOUCHER COLLEGE, BALTIMORE, MARYLAND

Im zweiten Jahr der durch die Umwandlung in eine gemischte Schule bedingten Übergangsphase am Goucher College entschieden wir uns für das Thema «Aufbau der Bühne». Wir wollten das Schuljahr als Skript nehmen und hervorheben, dass es konstante Verbesserungen geben würde, bis sich der Vorhang hebt. Wir wollten unsere wichtigsten Leistungen als erstklassiges, liberales Kunstinstitut zeigen. Das Skript wurde gemäss Vorschlag des Designers zum Gestaltungselement. Ausserdem schlug er eine besondere Art der Illustration vor, die mit einer gewissen Skepsis aufgenommen wurde, doch er überzeugte uns, dass wir damit den richtigen Ton treffen würden. Das Echo auf den Bericht war ausgezeichnet, und er erwies sich bei unseren Bemühungen um Spenden für ein neues Kunst- und Theatergebäude als sehr nützlich.

JUDITH T.PHAIR, VICE-PRESIDENT FOR PUBLIC RELATIONS, GOUCHER COLLEGE, BALTIMORE, MARYLAND

Pour la deuxième année de la transformation de Goucher College en établissement d'enseignement mixte, nous avons choisi le thème «plantons le décor», afin de traiter de la question de la stabilisation et de l'avenir du Collège. Les événements de l'année écoulée nous ont servi de scénario. Nous avons voulu présenter les réalisations significatives qui font de notre Collège une institution vouée à l'enseignement de très haut niveau. Le scénario est devenu le pivot du design. Le designer a aussi suggéré l'emploi d'illustrations d'une manière spéciale. Nous avons été sceptiques au début, puis nous nous sommes laissé convaincre. Les réactions des lecteurs ont été époustouflantes, et le rapport nous a été utile pour mettre en route une campagne de collecte de fonds en vue de l'adjonction d'un bâtiment destiné aux arts et au théatre.

ANTHONY RUTKA, RUTKA WEADOCK DESIGN, BALTIMORE, MARYLAND

When the college suggested the theme of "setting the stage," we ran with it. We decided on a script book, and then the copy fell into place. With the theater as part of the concept, we could use the idea of role, role model, mentor...We decided on illustration because we felt photography would not be appropriate to carry the theme. We do use small portraits in the book, but the Gary Kelley illustrations capture the sense of theater we had hoped to indicate. The small-sized format was either considered smashing, or it was thought to be too avant-garde. We do think that the audience more and more appreciates these annual reports.

ANTHONY RUTKA, RUTKA WEADOCK DESIGN, BALTIMORE, MARYLAND

Mit dem vom College vorgeschlagenen Thema - «Aufbau der Bühne» - waren wir sofort einverstanden. Wir entschieden uns für ein Skript und fanden damit eine Lösung für die Textgestaltung. Mit dem Theater als Teil des Konzepts konnten wir die Idee der Rolle, des Rollenmusters, des Mentors verwenden... Wir wählten Illustrationen, weil wir fanden, dass Photographie nicht zum Thema passt. Wir benutzten zwar kleine Porträtaufnahmen, aber es sind die Illustrationen von Gary Kelley, die genau die gewünschte Theateratmosphäre herstellen. Einige fanden das kleine Format umwerfend, andere empfanden es als zu gewagt.

ANTHONY RUTKA, RUTKA WEADOCK DESIGN, BALTIMORE, MARYLAND

Lorsque le collège a opté pour le thème «plantons le décor», nous avons marché tout de suite en proposant d'écrire un scénario dont le texte fut vite trouvé. Avec le théâtre pour concept, nous avons utilisé l'idée de rôle, de modèle de rôle, de metteur en scène... Nous avons donné la préférence à l'illustration, estimant que la photo serait moins porteuse du thème choisi. Nous avons bien eu recours à de petits portraits dans le corps de l'ouvrage, mais les illustrations de Gary Kelley restituent ce sens du théâtre que nous avions en vue. Le petit format a paru assommant au lecteurs, ou bien alors trop avant-gardiste.

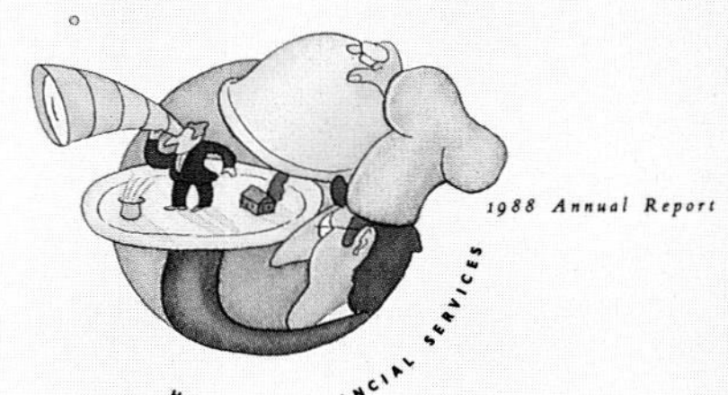
1988 Annual Report
HORIZON FINANCIAL SERVICES

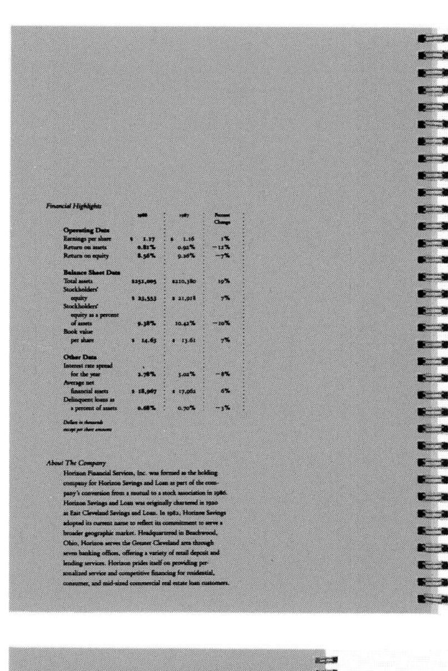

Financial Highlights

	1988	1987	Percent Change
Operating Data			
Earnings per share	$ 1.17	$ 1.16	1%
Return on assets	0.81%	0.92%	−12%
Return on equity	8.56%	9.26%	−7%
Balance Sheet Data			
Total assets	$251,005	$210,380	19%
Stockholders' equity	$ 23,553	$ 21,918	7%
Stockholders' equity as a percent of assets	9.38%	10.42%	−10%
Book value per share	$ 14.63	$ 13.61	7%
Other Data			
Interest rate spread for the year	2.78%	3.02%	−8%
Average net financial assets	$ 18,967	$ 17,962	6%
Delinquent loans as a percent of assets	0.68%	0.70%	−3%

Dollars in thousands except per share amounts

About The Company

Horizon Financial Services, Inc. was formed as the holding company for Horizon Savings and Loan as part of the company's conversion from a mutual to a stock association in 1986. Horizon Savings and Loan was originally chartered in 1920 as East Cleveland Savings and Loan. In 1982, Horizon Savings adopted its current name to reflect its commitment to serve a broader geographic market. Headquartered in Beachwood, Ohio, Horizon serves the Greater Cleveland area through seven banking offices, offering a variety of retail deposit and lending services. Horizon prides itself on providing personalized service and competitive financing for residential, consumer, and mid-sized commercial real estate loan customers.

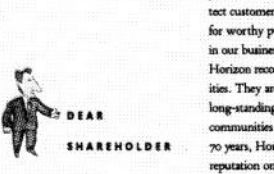

DEAR SHAREHOLDER

The public places its trust in us as a provider of financial services. To protect customer deposits. To make loans for worthy purposes. To be prudent in our business practices. We at Horizon recognize these responsibilities. They are essential to preserving long-standing relationships with the communities we serve. For nearly 70 years, Horizon has built its reputation on the principles of safety and soundness. Today, those same principles distinguish Horizon from its competitors.

Additionally, as a public company, we are ever mindful that the interests of our shareholders must be well served. In our view, that is best done by enhancing the long-term value of the company. Because of our past performance and financial strength, Horizon is optimistic about its future in the Greater Cleveland market. We are positioned to take advantage of growth opportunities as they arise — but only when they are consistent with sound business practices and long-range goals. As this annual report illustrates, our plans to increase returns to shareholders are still unfolding.

Recap of 1988

Like other thrifts, Horizon faced a number of challenges in 1988. Despite suboptimal conditions, earnings rose for the fourth consecutive year. Net income was $1.17 per share versus $1.16 per share in 1987.

Several factors negatively affected earnings last year. Rising interest rates, which are always a hazard for the industry, reduced profitability. Furthermore, the spread between short-term and long-term interest rates narrowed. Because thrifts typically "borrow short and lend long," profit margins declined as the spread narrowed. New accounting regulations also required us to defer a portion of loan fee income to future periods. This change reduced 1988 earnings significantly; however, these deferred fees will boost income in subsequent years.

Earnings were aided by some positive events. Horizon's 1988 effective federal income tax rate dropped to 30% from 36% in 1987, so more of our income went to the bottom line. Also contributing to earnings was our planned growth of nearly 20%, which brought our assets to $250 million at year-end.

Unlike many competitors whose growth is constrained by inadequate capital levels, our expansion is more than adequately supported by a

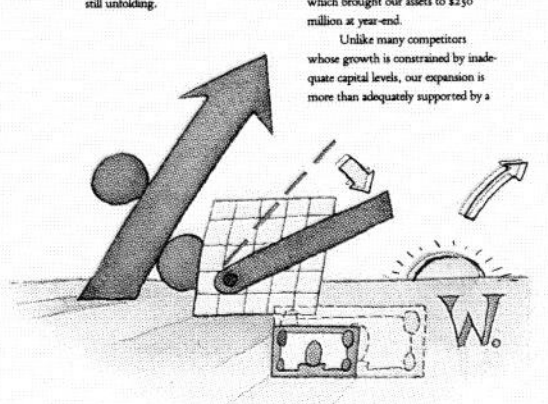

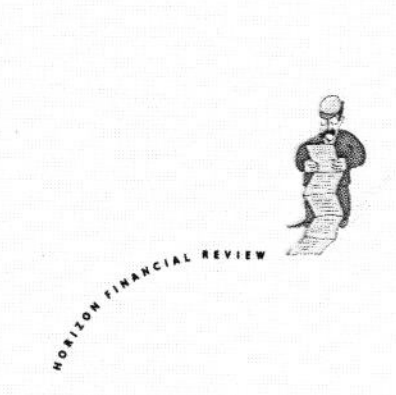

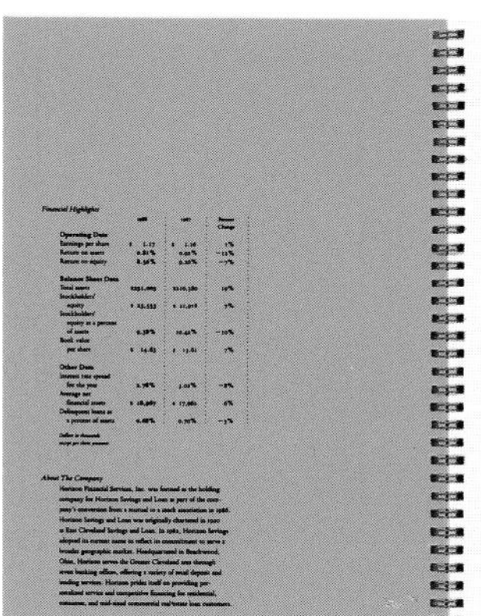

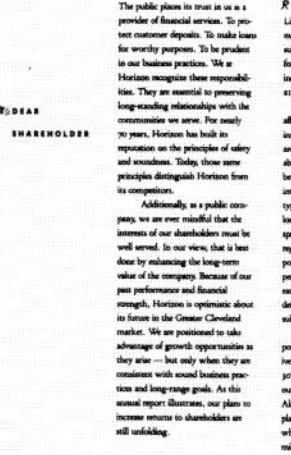

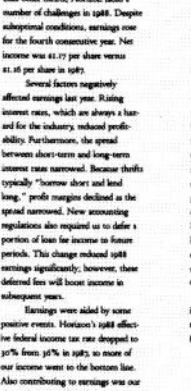

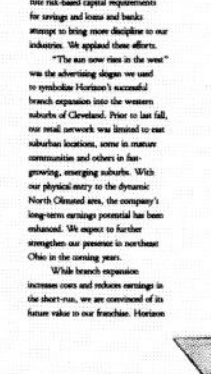

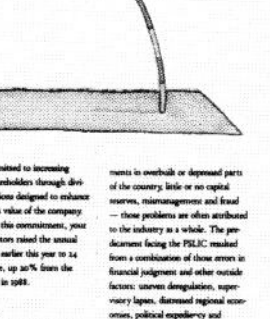

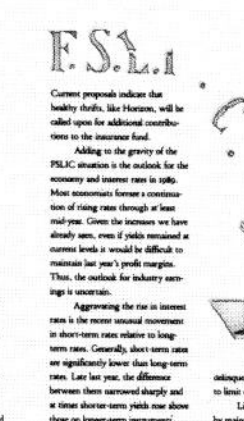

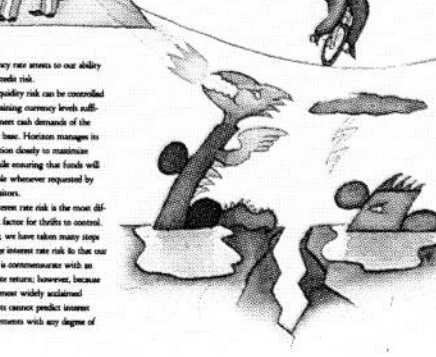

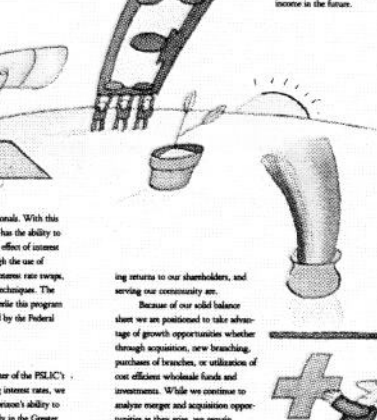

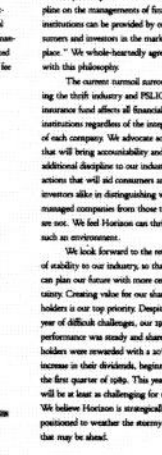

SELECTED CONSOLIDATED FINANCIAL DATA

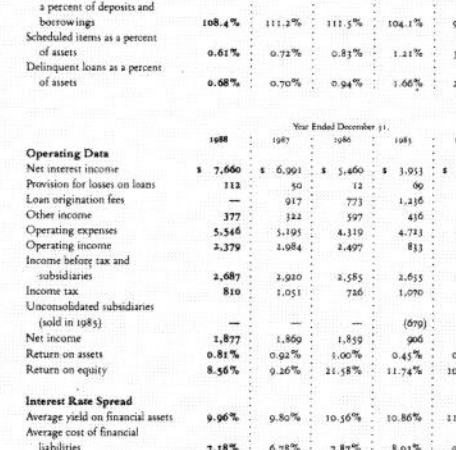

FINANCIAL REVIEW:

Yield/Cost Analysis

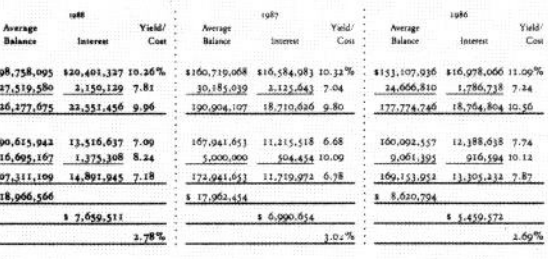

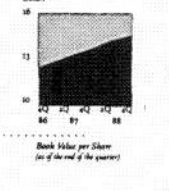

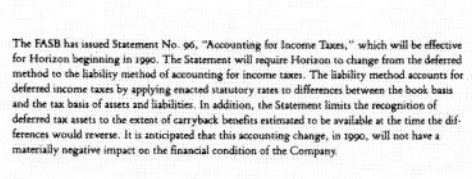

Interest Rate Sensitivity

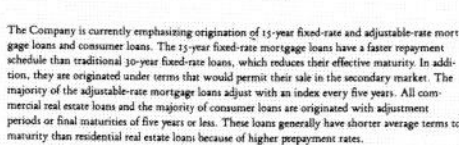

CONSOLIDATED BALANCE SHEETS

	Notes	December 31, 1988	1987
Assets			
Financial assets:			
Loans receivable	2,7	**$220,239,790**	$176,133,000
Investment securities	3	**10,362,113**	17,546,042
Cash investments	3	**10,661,010**	7,909,378
Investments required by law	3	**1,497,900**	1,362,900
Total financial assets		**242,760,813**	202,951,320
Real estate in development		**2,058,971**	2,125,637
Real estate acquired in settlement of loans	4	**197,898**	523,206
Premises and equipment	5	**2,739,177**	2,767,983
Cash and demand deposits		**1,131,477**	692,225
Other assets		**2,116,484**	1,319,437
		$251,004,820	$210,379,808
Liabilities and Stockholders' Equity			
Deposits	6	**$200,211,692**	$177,565,840
Borrowed funds	7	**23,689,408**	5,000,000
Other liabilities		**3,550,425**	5,896,053
Total liabilities		**227,451,525**	188,461,893
Stockholders' equity:	10,11		
Preferred stock — $0.01 par value. 2,000,000 shares authorized; none issued		**—**	—
Common stock — $1 par value. 7,000,000 shares authorized; 1,610,000 shares issued		**1,610,000**	1,610,000
Paid-in capital		**8,037,000**	8,037,000
Retained earnings, substantially restricted		**13,906,295**	12,270,915
Total stockholders' equity		**23,553,295**	21,917,915
		$251,004,820	$210,379,808

The accompanying notes are an integral part of these statements.

CONSOLIDATED STATEMENTS OF INCOME

	Notes	Year ended December 31, 1988	1987	1986
Interest income:				
Loans		**$20,401,327**	$16,584,983	$16,978,066
Investment securities and cash investments		**2,014,819**	2,005,243	1,649,325
Investments required by law		**135,310**	120,400	137,413
Total interest income		**22,551,456**	18,710,626	18,764,804
Interest expense:				
Deposits		**13,516,637**	11,215,518	12,388,638
Borrowings		**1,375,308**	504,454	916,594
Total interest expense		**14,891,945**	11,719,972	13,305,232
Net interest income		**7,659,511**	6,990,654	5,459,572
Provision for losses on loans	2	**111,655**	50,466	12,401
Net interest income after provision for losses on loans		**7,547,856**	6,940,188	5,447,171
Other income:				
Loan origination fees	1	**—**	917,075	772,658
Other fees and income, net		**377,140**	321,583	596,728
Total other income		**377,140**	1,238,658	1,369,386
Operating expenses:				
Compensation and benefits	12	**2,551,407**	2,460,889	2,200,553
Equipment and data processing services		**602,491**	544,004	502,145
Office occupancy		**408,156**	347,247	403,122
Federal deposit insurance		**352,530**	344,905	334,501
State franchise tax		**302,643**	279,056	124,101
Marketing		**251,371**	174,669	86,106
Other		**1,077,205**	1,044,413	668,853
Total operating expenses		**5,545,803**	5,195,183	4,319,381
Operating income		**2,379,193**	2,983,663	2,497,176
Gain on sale of loans		**153,951**	133,387	—
Gain on sale of investments		**153,736**	—	—
Gain on loans held for sale		**—**	—	87,418
Loss on FSLIC write-off		**—**	(196,752)	—
Income before income taxes		**2,686,880**	2,920,298	2,584,594
Income tax expense (benefit):	8			
Current		**955,000**	1,170,000	452,400
Deferred		**(145,000)**	(119,000)	273,600
Total income tax expense		**810,000**	1,051,000	726,000
Net income		**$ 1,876,880**	$ 1,869,298	$ 1,858,594
Net income per share	1	**$1.17**	$1.16	$0.24

The accompanying notes are an integral part of these statements.

16

17

REPORT OF MANAGEMENT

INDEPENDENT AUDITORS' REPORT

BOARD OF DIRECTORS

SENIOR OFFICERS

CORPORATE OFFICE

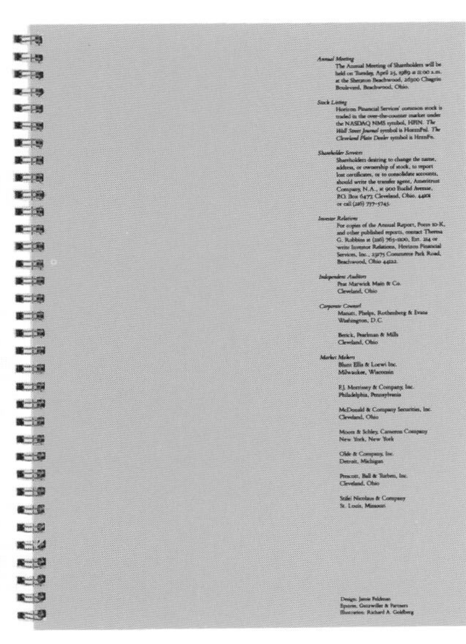

CLIENT:
HORIZON FINANCIAL SERVICES

DESIGN FIRM:
JAMIE FELDMAN, EPSTEIN/GUTZWILLER & PARTNERS

ART DIRECTOR:
JAMIE FELDMAN

DESIGNER:
JAMIE FELDMAN

ILLUSTRATOR:
RICHARD A. GOLDBERG

WRITER:
TERRY ROBBINS

TYPOGRAPHER:
T.S.I. TYPESETTING, INC.

PAPER SELECTION:
KROMEKOTE 2000, GLENEAGLE, LOE CREAM DULL

PAPER MANUFACTURER:
CHAMPION, BOWATERS U.K., WARREN

PRINTER:
AUSTIN

NUMBER OF PAGES:
30 PLUS COVER

SIZE:
8 1/4" X 11 3/4"

TYPE SELECTION:
BEMBO

TERRY ROBBINS, FIRST VICE-PRESIDENT, HORIZON FINANCIAL SERVICES, BEACHWOOD, OHIO

Horizon is small in an industry with big players, and the financial industry had lots of press during the previous year. What we wanted to do in the 1988 annual report was to address the problems inherent in the industry head-on. We wanted to state that we were not part of these problems. Our message was that we could hurdle any problem. The annual report was intended to build confidence, and to look at the long-run. This message, we felt, was needed specifically on the cover. With our designer, we chose an illustrator who could combine these concepts in a cover image, i.e. the future on a service platter. This came after Jamie Feldman, with whom we had worked before, helped us to find an illustrator we were comfortable with. Then we wrote the report's opening letter, sent the illustrator the draft, and the illustrations came from this. We had a favorable response to this book, and we were glad we got people to look at us through this annual report.

TERRY ROBBINS, FIRST VICE-PRESIDENT, HORIZON FINANCIAL SERVICES, BEACHWOOD, OHIO

Horizon ist klein im Vergleich zu den Mitbewerbern in der Finanzbranche, die im vergangenen Jahr viel Presse hatten. Im Jahresbericht für 1988 wollten wir die Probleme der Branche direkt angehen. Wir wollten festhalten, dass wir selbst kein Problem haben, das wir nicht lösen können. Der Jahresbericht sollte Vertrauen aufbauen und auf die Zukunft ausgerichtet sein. Dies sollte vor allem auf dem Umschlag zum Ausdruck kommen. Zusammen mit unserem Designer Jamie Feldman entschieden wir uns für einen Illustrator, der in der Lage war, diese Konzepte in einem Umschlagbild umzusetzen, d.h. wir wollten, dass die Zukunft auf einem Tablett serviert wird. Dann schrieben wir den Einführungsbrief des Berichtes, schickten dem Illustrator den Entwurf und erhielten daraufhin seine Illustrationen. Die Reaktionen auf den Bericht waren positiv, und wir sind froh, dass die Leute uns durch diesen Jahresbericht kennenlernen.

TERRY ROBBINS, FIRST VICE-PRESIDENT, HORIZON FINANCIAL SERVICES, BEACHWOOD, OHIO

Horizon occupe une petite place au sein d'une industrie où les gros joueurs donnent le ton, et ces institutions financières ont un peu trop fait la Une des journaux l'année passée. Par conséquent, nous avons voulu faire état, en toute franchise, des problèmes inhérents à la branche dans notre rapport annuel pour 1988, en indiquant que nous n'étions pas partie prenante en ce qui concernait ces problèmes. Notre message a consisté à affirmer que nous étions en mesure de venir à bout de toute contingence. Ce rapport entendait susciter la confiance et envisager le long terme. C'est ce qui devait être dit à notre avis dès la couverture. En accord avec notre designer Jamie Feldman, nous avons choisi un illustrateur capable de combiner ces concepts en une image de couverture sous forme de l'avenir présenté sur un plateau. Nous avons enregistré des réactions favorables à ce rapport et sommes heureux d'avoir amené le public à nous voir sous l'angle de ce document.

JAMIE FELDMAN, EPSTEIN, GUTZWILLER & PARTNERS, CLEVELAND, OHIO

We started with the theme of serving the community for the 1988 annual report for Horizon Financial Services. The cover illustration, done by Richard A. Goldberg, included the chef representing service, and on the platter we included a house, because the firm deals in home equity, along with a man looking into the future through a telescope. Next we moved to a letter to the shareholders. Here the illustrations were done to parallel the ideas in the text, including rising interest rates, problems relating to the "thrift industry," and a forecast for 1989. The illustrations were really good, and hit on the main themes effectively. We picked up some of the artwork done for this letter as spot illustrations for the rest of the report. The client was happy with the results and the annual report.

JAMIE FELDMAN, EPSTEIN, GUTZWILLER & PARTNERS, CLEVELAND, OHIO

Das Ausgangsthema des Jahresberichtes für 1988 hiess Dienstleistung. Auf der Umschlagillustration von Richard A. Goldberg ist deshalb ein Chef de Service zu sehen, auf dem Tablett ein Haus (das Unternehmen befasst sich mit der Finanzierung von Immobilien) und schliesslich ein Mann, der in die Zukunft blickt. Als nächstes ging es um den Aktionärsbrief. Hier sollten die Illustrationen den Text unterstützen, in dem es u.a. um Zinsen, um mit der «Spar- Branche» verbundene Probleme und die Aussichten für 1989 geht. Die Illustrationen sind gelungen und bringen die Hauptanliegen ausgezeichnet zum Ausdruck. Wir benutzten einige der Illustrationen auch als Blickfang auf den übrigen Seiten. Der Kunde war glücklich mit dieser Lösung.

JAMIE FELDMAN, EPSTEIN, GUTZWILLER & PARTNERS, CLEVELAND, OHIO

Pour le rapport annuel 1988 de Horizon Financial Services, nous avons commencé par le thème du service à la communauté. L'illustration de couverture réalisée par Richard A. Goldberg symbolise ce service par un chef de cuisine. La maison sur le plateau signale que l'entreprise est spécialisée dans les prêts hypothécaires; l'autre personnage a les yeux fixés sur l'avenir. Nous nous sommes ensuite occupés de la Lettre aux actionnaires, en interprétant dans les illustrations les données du texte relatives à la hausse des taux d'intérêt, aux problèmes de l'épargne et de la prévoyance et aux prévisions pour l'année 1989. Les illustrations sont de qualité; elles traitent avec efficacité les sujets proposés. Certaines illustrations de la Lettre ont été reprises dans le rapport même. Le client était satisfait.

KEMPER REINSURANCE
Kemper Reinsurance Company Annual Report 1988

In the life of an individual or a company, twenty years is a period long enough for substantial changes, but short enough for memory to maintain a grip on the threads of continuity that link past to present.

Despite gyrating markets, the twenty years since the foundation of Kemper Reinsurance Company have seen significant growth coupled with a remarkable stability in personnel and principles of operation.

Kemper Re was started in 1969 with an infusion of $10 million in capital and surplus from its parent, Kemper Corporation. By 1984 its stockholder's equity had grown to $125 million, and another $100 million was added to take advantage of striking opportunities in the marketplace. At year end 1988, Kemper Re's stockholder's equity was $365 million.

Net written premiums were just $18 million in 1969. In 1988, they were $309 million. Over the twenty years of its existence, the total annual rate of return to its parent, based on growth in book value and dividends paid, was 19.5%.

This growth was attained against a backdrop of profound change in an industry where competition was intense, but the critical element of trust in business relationships embodied in the "handshake" approach to resolving issues and problems was equally strong. Expanding and surprising notions of liability, the emergence of a truly international economy, and the entrance of new forces into all kinds of financial services, including reinsurance, shook the business to its core. Nor could the industry escape being affected to some degree by the intensifying cycle of the primary insurance business, with every succeeding peak and valley more extreme than its predecessor.

That Kemper Re has flourished in this difficult period is due to the skill of its personnel and the consistency of their approach.

Highlights

Premiums Assumed*	$ 346 million	− 31.2%
Net Premiums Written	309 million	− 20.6%
Assets	1,270 million	− 1.5%
Operating Earnings	53 million	+ 4.7%
Stockholder's Equity	365 million	+ 16.1%

*Professional reinsurance premium

Net Premiums Written

1988	− 20.6%	308,883
1987	− 21.4%	388,800
1986	+ 35.3%	494,932
1985	+ 54.9%	365,676
1984	+ 37.1%	236,095

(Amounts In Thousands)

Assets

1988	− 1.5%	1,269,918
1987	+ 7.5%	1,288,803
1986	+ 34.9%	1,198,641
1985	+ 29.6%	888,436
1984	+ 11.1%	685,282

(Amounts In Thousands)

Operating Earnings

1988	+ 4.7%	52,896
1987	+ 95.0%	50,532
1986	+332.0%	25,908
1985	+ 63.6%	5,997
1984	+ 80.1%	3,665

(Amounts In Thousands)

Stockholder's Equity

1988	+ 16.1%	364,792
1987	+ 15.9%	314,310
1986	+ 45.1%	271,245
1985	+ 49.9%	187,001
1984	− 8.7%	124,733

(Amounts In Thousands)

CHAIRMAN AND CEO *Kemper Re's very positive outlook on the future is supported by its demonstrated ability to deal constructively with a wide array of issues and challenges over the last twenty years. Kemper Re's successful growth has been shaped and guided by a management team and staff with clear commitment and a high degree of continuity and stability. This has been the key to the success of the enterprise as a whole. There can be no question that real opportunities lie ahead for a company which enjoys as many fundamental strengths as Kemper Re.* DAVID B. MATHIS

CHAIRMAN'S LETTER For the third consecutive year, Kemper Reinsurance Company posted record operating earnings in 1988. Lower sales during the year reflected our determination to maintain high underwriting standards in the face of a softening market and declining demand. Also contributing to our success was the absence of major insured catastrophes involving reinsurance and the on-going benefits of our continued careful control of expenses.

Operating earnings in 1988 were $52.9 million versus $50.5 million in 1987, an increase of 4.7 percent. Sales declined 20.6 percent from $388.8 million in 1987 to $308.9 million in 1988. Earnings in 1988 include a "fresh start" benefit of $6.5 million due to the Tax Reform Act of 1986, compared to $13.8 million in 1987. It's worth noting that if these "Fresh Start" benefits were disregarded, the 1988 operating earnings would represent a 26 percent increase over the level of the previous year.

While it is gratifying that our strategies are working to produce excellent profits, our planning for the future must include a careful analysis of the causes of the decline in sales, which is a function of the reinsurance cycle.

WHERE WE ARE IN THE CYCLE In reinsurance, cycles are re-occurring but not necessarily regular. Externalities such as interest rate levels, natural catastrophes, rapid technological innovation, political change and new concepts of liability bend and twist the trajectory of the cycle. On a more fundamental level, the cycle is driven by the inability of buyers and sellers to react in the precisely right way to these variables. It seems there is always overreaction in one direction or the other.

President And COO

Donald R. Smith

Notes to Consolidated Financial Statements (amounts in thousands)

Securities

Investment in Unconsolidated Companies

Reinsurance

Transactions With Affiliates

Notes to Consolidated Financial Statements (amounts in thousands)

Cash Flow Information

Statutory Capital and Surplus

Report of Independent Public Accountants

The Board of Directors and Stockholder
Kemper Reinsurance Company:

KPMG Peat Marwick

Chicago, Illinois
March 14, 1989

Consolidated Statement of Income (amounts in thousands)

Kemper Reinsurance Company and Subsidiaries

	Year ended December 31 1988	1987
Underwriting operations:		
Net premiums earned	$320,926	$411,861
Losses and adjusting expenses incurred	262,302	345,921
Amortized insurance acquisition costs	56,289	73,510
Other operating costs and expenses	8,357	4,994
Total losses and expenses incurred	326,948	424,425
Net underwriting loss	(6,022)	(12,564)
Net investment income	68,359	64,676
Operating gain before federal and foreign income tax and equity in net operating earnings of unconsolidated companies	62,337	52,112
Federal and foreign income tax (benefit):		
Current	11,434	19,456
Deferred	(1,758)	(17,455)
Total federal and foreign income tax	9,676	2,001
Operating earnings before equity in net operating earnings of unconsolidated companies	52,661	50,111
Equity in net operating earnings of unconsolidated companies	235	421
Operating earnings	52,896	50,532
Realized investment gain, net of federal and foreign income tax	1,173	11,352
Net income	$ 54,069	$ 61,884

Consolidated Statement of Stockholder's Equity (amounts in thousands)

	Year ended December 31 1988	1987
Common stock, at beginning and end of year	$ 3,350	$ 3,350
Additional paid in capital, at beginning and end of year	109,700	109,700
Unrealized loss on foreign currency translations, beginning of year	(2,474)	(2,447)
Unrealized loss on foreign currency translations during year, net of federal income tax	(194)	(27)
End of year	(2,668)	(2,474)
Unrealized gain (loss) on investments, beginning of year	(4,365)	8,263
Unrealized gain (loss) on investments during year, net of federal income tax	7,997	(12,628)
End of year	3,632	(4,365)
Retained earnings, beginning of year	208,099	152,379
Operating earnings	52,896	50,532
Realized investment gain, net of federal and foreign income tax	1,173	11,352
Cash dividends to stockholder	(11,390)	(6,164)
End of year	250,778	208,099
Total stockholder's equity	$364,792	$314,310

See accompanying notes to consolidated financial statements.

Consolidated Statement of Cash Flows (amounts in thousands)

Kemper Reinsurance Company and Subsidiaries

	Year ended December 31 1988	1987
Cash flows from operating activities:		
Net income	$ 54,069	$ 61,884
Change in non-cash items:		
Liability for losses and adjusting expenses	(60,098)	84,426
Unearned premiums	(10,334)	(22,694)
Loss balances payable	(3,241)	7,178
Funds held for others	933	(2,976)
Accounts payable and other liabilities	6,986	(5,723)
Federal and foreign income tax balances	(4,877)	(20,934)
Net premium balances receivable	(1,888)	(3,820)
Deferred insurance acquisition costs	1,861	5,940
Funds held by reinsured companies	(1,471)	(21,434)
Accrued investment income	1,130	(2,953)
Accounts receivable and other assets	(3,984)	8,684
Reinsurance recoverable on paid losses	(9,975)	683
Other, net	(428)	(63)
Net cash provided from (used in) operating activities	(31,317)	88,198
Cash flows from investing activities:		
Cash from invesment sold or matured, excluding realized gain or loss:		
Fixed maturities	240,784	325,856
Equity securities	95,485	50,836
Short-term investments	988,954	648,597
Cost of investments purchased:		
Fixed maturities	(170,297)	(334,122)
Equity securities	(111,664)	(149,902)
Short-term investments	(975,173)	(626,872)
Mortgage loans	(1,716)	(2,525)
Investment in unconsolidated companies	(5,103)	1,313
Other, net	(9,228)	9,811
Net cash provided from (used in) investing activities	52,042	(77,008)
Dividends paid to stockholder	(11,390)	(6,164)
Net increase in cash	9,335	5,026
Cash, beginning of year	26,451	21,425
Cash, end of year	$ 35,786	$ 26,451

See accompanying notes to consolidated financial statements.

CLIENT:
KEMPER REINSURANCE

DESIGN FIRM:
SAMATA ASSOCIATES

ART DIRECTOR:
GREG SAMATA

DESIGNER:
GREG SAMATA

PHOTOGRAPHER:
BOB TOLCHIN

COPYWRITER:
ANNE SHARP

TYPOGRAPHER:
TYPOGRAPHIC RESOURCE

PAPER SELECTION:
KROMEKOTE, CARDIGAN LAMBSWOOL

PAPER MANUFACTURER:
CHAMPION, HOPPER

PRINTER:
ROHNER PRINTING

NUMBER OF PAGES:
26 PLUS COVER

SIZE:
8" X 11 1/2"

TYPE SELECTION:
JANSEN ANTIQUE, ENGLISH SCRIPT

CHARLES JOHANNS, VICE-PRESIDENT, KEMPER CORPORATION, CHICAGO, ILLINOIS

The Kemper Reinsurance annual report for 1988 celebrated the company's 20 years in business. For us, it was important to show how far the company had come in 20 years. Of course we needed to show the financial data, but we also wanted to feature the management of the company as a way to comment on the industry. We have a certain stature in this marketplace, and in our 20 years, we have become one of the top ten in this industry. The annual report demonstrated this fact very effectively, and the response we received from our audience was favorable.

CHARLES JOHANNS, VICE-PRESIDENT, KEMPER CORPORATION, CHICAGO, ILLINOIS

Im Jahresbericht 1988 der Kemper Reinsurance wurde das 20jährige Firmenbestehen gefeiert. Uns war es wichtig zu zeigen, wie weit es die Firma in 20 Jahren gebracht hatte. Natürlich mussten wir die Finanzdaten aufführen, aber wir wollten auch das Management des Unternehmens zeigen und mit seiner Hilfe die Entwicklung der Branche kommentieren. In den 20 Jahren unseres Bestehens sind wir zu einer der Top-Ten-Firmen der Branche geworden. Der Jahresbericht zeigte dies sehr wirkungsvoll, und das Echo unseres Publikums war positiv.

CHARLES JOHANNS, VICE-PRÉSIDENT, KEMPER CORPORATION, CHICAGO, ILLINOIS

Le rapport annuel de Kemper Reinsurance pour 1988 commémore les 20 années d'existence de notre société. Il nous a semblé important de retracer les progrès accomplis dans ces deux décennies. Il nous fallait bien sûr exhiber les résultats financiers; pourtant nous désirions aussi présenter la direction de l'entreprise à travers des commentaires sur la branche de la réassurance. Nous avons accédé en l'espace de 20 ans au peloton de tête des dix plus grands réassureurs. Ce rapport annuel en a apporté une démonstration efficace, et la réaction du public a été favorable.

PAT SAMATA AND GREG SAMATA, SAMATA ASSOCIATES, DUNDEE, ILLINOIS

The Kemper Reinsurance annual report was based on the company's 20th year, and we featured six of the people in the company. These people provided statements of how the industry had changed over the years. With these clients, we tend to have a lot of leeway, and once these spokespersons had been decided on, we made a presentation, and finalized the design. We used a classic typographic solution. For the section on the company executives, we combined script with classic type. For the cover we chose gold and to continue this as a design element, we put the gold around the photographs. On the cover we only indicated the anniversary with roman numerals. We wanted to keep this report a symbolic recreation of the company and its image.

PAT SAMATA UND GREG SAMATA, SAMATA ASSOCIATES, DUNDEE, ILLINOIS

Thema des Jahresberichtes der Kemper Reinsurance (Rückversicherung) sollte das 20jährige Bestehen sein. Wir stellten sechs Mitarbeiter vor. Diese Leute äusserten sich zu den Veränderungen in der Branche. Dieser Kunde lässt uns normalerweise viel Spielraum. Wir entschieden uns für eine klassische typographische Lösung. Für das Kapitel über das Firmenkader kombinierten wir Handschrift mit klassischer Typographie. Für den Umschlag wählten wir Gold und verwendeten dies auch im Inhalt als Design-Element für die Einrahmung der Photos. Auf dem Umschlag zeigten wir eine römische Zwanzig als Hinweis auf das Jubiläum. Wir wollten, dass der Jahresbericht zum Symbol für die Firma wird, und wir wollten Klasse zeigen.

PAT SAMATA ET GREG SAMATA, SAMATA ASSOCIATES, DUNDEE, ILLINOIS

Le rapport annuel de Kemper Reinsurance était basé sur le 20e anniversaire de la société. Nous avons braqué les feux de la rampe sur six personnes représentatives de Kemper, qui ont évoqué les transformations de l'industrie. Ce client nous garantit une grande liberté d'action. Nous avons adopté une solution typographique de type classique. Pour le chapitre consacré aux dirigeants de l'entreprise, nous avons combiné typo classique et écriture. L'or de la couverture se prolonge comme élément de design dans les bordures des photos. La couverture ne porte que l'anniversaire en chiffres romains. Nous avons voulu préserver le B.C.B.G. à ce rapport en nous contentant de lui conférer un caractère symboliquement distrayant.

L I N C O L N   B A N C O R P

LINCOLN BANCORP

1988 ANNUAL REPORT

1988

proved to be another milestone year in the history of the Company. With earnings virtually doubling over 1987 and shareholder value increasing by 174%, we have securely established our presence in Southern California and the investment community.

LINCOLN BANCORP

THE YEAR IN BRIEF

Lincoln Bancorp is a bank holding company which was incorporated under the laws of the state of California on September 3, 1981. The Company's subsidiary, Lincoln National Bank, opened for business on April 14, 1982, and by December 31, 1988 the company had grown to over $416 million in assets. The Bank currently provides a wide range of commercial banking services with a special emphasis on commercial lending to small and medium-sized business, and professional and high net-worth individuals. The Bank attributes its growth and profitability to its ability to custom tailor traditional banking products to its customers' unique needs and the Bank's responsiveness in providing such services.

	1988	*1987*	*% Change*
Revenue from Earning Assets	$ 25,854,277	$ 18,206,175	42.0%
Net Interest Income	19,249,994	12,681,705	51.7%
Net Income	4,190,405	2,116,360	98.0%
Net Income per Share	1.36	0.93	46.2%
Total Assets	416,131,563	300,895,552	38.3%
Total Deposits	390,172,984	279,653,814	39.5%
Loans, Net	194,662,084	145,480,364	33.8%
Shareholders' Equity	24,515,839	20,249,507	21.1%

Net Income
Dollars in thousands
84 | *781*
85 | *1,022*
86 | *1,401*
87 | *2,116*
88 | *4,190*

Earnings Per Share
Dollars
84 | *0.51*
85 | *0.62*
86 | *0.78*
87 | *0.93*
88 | *1.36*

Total Assets
Dollars in millions
84 | *125.0*
85 | *155.3*
86 | *242.0*
87 | *300.9*
88 | *416.1*

| 1

DEAR FELLOW SHAREHOLDER

For 1988, Lincoln Bancorp, through its subsidiary Lincoln National Bank, enjoyed the most successful year in its history. Net income for 1988 reached a historical high of $4.2 million – virtually doubling that posted for 1987. Total assets reached a historical high of $416.1 million, advancing 38.3% over last year.

The year also proved to be a milestone for the value of our investment, with the Company's stock closing 1988 at $15.625 per share. This performance represented appreciation of 174% over 1987's close of $5.712 per share. Coupled with annual volume of 1.9 million shares, our stock proves to be a valued and liquid investment. So much so that Lincoln Bancorp stock was ranked thirteenth among *Fortune* magazine's one hundred best performing stocks for 1988.

Since organizing in 1982, a large part of our perennial success has been guided by the dynamic, vibrant and diverse economy of the Greater Los Angeles metropolitan area. This year's annual report, therefore, is focused on showcasing that environment. This environment has been the cornerstone of our success and is the foundation upon which future growth and profitability will be built.

Greater Los Angeles, with a population of 13.8 million and producing $310 billion of goods and services, is one of the most dynamic and fertile economies in the world. This helped boost net income for 1988 to $4.2 million and represented a 98.0% increase over 1987. Earnings per share of $1.36, were 46.2% greater, roughly half the rate of increase in total income. This was the result of a full year of 1 million additional shares outstanding.

Net interest income advanced by 51.8% over 1987 to close the year at $19.2 million, with margins increasing to 7.14%. This performance was driven by a 32.2% increase in earning assets, which ended 1988 at $313.7 million. Net loans, our primary earning asset, grew by 33.9% or $50.0 million. Of this advance, $24.1 million comprised growth in our commercial loan portfolio. The remainder was derived from our mortgage banking division, established in the first half of the year. The division's objective is to underwrite real estate mortgage loans for subsequent resale in the secondary market, while earning origination and servicing income thereon. During the year, $39.6 million in loans were originated and sold.

Additionally, the superlative quality of our loan portfolio improved. Net loan losses represented only 0.19% of period end loans compared to 0.42% in 1987. These results kept us well ahead of industry norms.

Return on average assets in 1988 also made a healthy gain over last year, advancing to 1.35% versus 0.91% and demonstrating increased economies and more efficient asset utilization. Net results for 1988 also yielded a return of 18.8% on our equity, surpassing the 13.8% in 1987 by 5%.

On the deposit side, Lincoln enjoyed a growth rate of 39.5% amounting to $110.5 million ending the year at $390.2 million. A substantial portion of this growth was in low cost demand deposits, which advanced by $93.7 million and accounted for 63.1% of total

2 |

deposits. This ratio of demand to total deposits compares favorably to the 54.5% in 1987. Stressing growth in this low-cost source of funds, Lincoln continues to enjoy above average returns on its earning assets.

Our performance for 1988 advanced shareholders' equity to $24.5 million representing $9.02 per share compared to $7.88 per share a year ago. Furthermore, our equity to asset ratio ended 1988 at 5.9% while regulatory capital stood at $27.7 million and represented 6.6% of total assets. This, coupled with the high quality of our asset base has earned the Company both an "A" Quality Rating and "Premier Performing Bank" for 1988 from the prestigious Findley Reports of California Banks – a rating which we have been given each of our six full years of our existence.

In the coming year, we will continue to build the value of our investment through prudent management of our assets and lending practices, coupled with continued expansion of the local economy. We look forward to keeping you apprised of our progress and, on behalf of the board of directors, officers and staff, we thank you for your confidence and support.

Steven C. Good
Chairman of the Board

John J. Keating
President and
Chief Executive Officer

| 3

SERVICE BUSINESSES

Driven by consistent per capita income gains, service businesses have emerged as the fastest growing segment of the economy. Lincoln Bancorp expects to reap the benefit through similar gains in per share income.

Fernando Valley. Without a heavy investment in non-earning assets and fewer employees, we are able to enjoy a higher asset base and a higher ratio of operating income per employee than other banks of similar size.

Given its high concentration of economic resources such as availability of labor, capital, quality higher education, transportation facilities and strong business support services, the economic foundation and future outlook of the region and Lincoln Bancorp is promising. Consequently we would like to highlight four segments of the economy, which represent a cross section of our customer base.

Service Businesses The largest sector of the region's economy, forming a substantial portion of Lincoln's customer base, is represented by service businesses. Included in this economic sector are such non-goods producing industries as retail establishments, wholesalers, financial services, insurance, real estate and transportation, as well as the traditionally defined service businesses such as computer/data processing, legal, accounting and health care.

One out of every three persons in the area are employed by service businesses, which sustained a 67% growth rate during the current decade and employs 1.8 million people. The progress of the service industries in Los Angeles largely depends on the expansion of the population and growth of the general business base as a whole. Generally, prospects for service businesses are expected to follow past trends, benefiting from rising household incomes as a large segment of the population progresses towards its peak earning years. Secondly, it is important to realize that services have traditionally functioned as a stabilizing influence in the local economy. While not entirely insulating the area from cyclical swings, the broad foundation of service businesses adds resilience to the economy. Paralleling this, the large and diverse number of service businesses in Lincoln's customer base will also add resilience to the Company's asset quality and earning capacity.

Greater L.A.
Per Capita Income
Dollars
84 | *15,100*
85 | *16,100*
86 | *17,000*
87 | *18,000*
88 | *19,200*

With increasing amounts of personal income, the region's economy has seen significant growth in services. Lincoln's growth in per share earnings have mirrored this. In 1984, per capita income for the metropolitan area was $15,100 and advanced to $19,200 for 1988. Reflecting the positive move in personal income, earnings per share for the Company ended 1988 at $1.36 compared to $0.51 posted for 1984. The region's rising affluence translates into continued growth in the services sector and consequently Lincoln Bancorp's loan and deposit base have advanced in similar fashion.

Lincoln Bancorp
Earnings Per Share
Dollars
84 | *0.51*
85 | *0.62*
86 | *0.78*
87 | *0.93*
88 | *1.36*

Consumer Goods The overall buying power of the area has shown continued growth and strength. Integral to this strength is growth in the population coupled with increasing affluence. In terms of population, the Greater Los Angeles area ranks second only to that of Greater New York and strong population gains have been a prominent feature of the area over the past four decades. Consumer spending capacity is based on a high level of total personal income. On a per capita basis the area's income is 15%

6 | 7

EXPORTS AND INTERNATIONAL TRADE

The perennial growth of international commerce passing through the local customs district has made Los Angeles a leading financial center with the second largest pool of cash deposits in the nation.

L.A. Customs District Value of Trade Flows
Dollars in Billions
84 | 49.6
85 | 63.8
86 | 68.5
87 | 77.6
88 | 90.0

L.A. County Total Bank & Savings Deposits
Dollars in Billions
84 | 125.6
85 | 135.9
86 | 145.2
87 | 153.9
88 | 164.2

Lincoln Bancorp Deposits
Dollars in Millions
84 | 111.8
85 | 143.7
86 | 229.6
87 | 279.7
88 | 390.2

Volume of deposits in financial institutions is a major indicator and beneficiary of trade activity. In 1986, Los Angeles county was third nationally in terms of bank deposits with $68.6 billion, behind Chicago and New York, with $70.6 billion and $173.3 billion, respectively. In terms of savings and loan deposits, Los Angeles was by far number one with $82.1 billion in 1987 compared to that of Chicago with $36.5 billion. Combining bank deposits with savings gives Los Angeles the second largest pools of cash deposits in the nation. It is this pool of cash resources that enables financial institutions such as Lincoln Bancorp, to finance the area's general businesses expansion.

The overall growth in the local deposit base, largely the result of international trade expansion, has filtered through to Lincoln. Combined bank and savings deposits for the area grew at an average rate of 7.68% from $125.6 billion in 1984 to $164.2 billion in 1988. Lincoln Bancorp's deposit resources for the same period, however, exceeded the region's average growth rate by over eightfold, advancing from $111.8 million in 1984 to $390.2 million in 1988.

The business potential of the region, both domestic and foreign, has not gone unnoticed by financial institutions. Most major U.S. banks have established a Los Angeles operation. Many of course are positioning themselves for 1991, when the California market opens to out of state banks. Foreign institutions also have a presence in the area, with 117 having local operations. Additionally major investment banking houses have either opened an operation in Los Angeles or augmented already existing operations.

The region's attractiveness as a focal point of international commerce is undeniable based on its location, size, industry mix and income levels of its residents. As a world marketplace, it is very attractive to importers and as a source of necessary goods, it is poised to fulfill many export needs of the future. The continued success of international commerce will not only serve to further enhance the general quality of the area's economic base, but also serve to keep Los Angeles as hub for the financial services sector.

Looking Ahead In the coming years, Lincoln Bancorp will continue to reap the benefits from the anticipated expansion of the fertile economic climate of Greater Los Angeles. Continuing to focus on serving middle market businesses in the area, we will steadily increase shareholder value. We continue to focus on internal growth coupled with searching for a potential merger or acquisition. Through this, we will achieve a size of $500 million to $1 billion with a substantial presence in the area and economies of scale to effectively compete with other institutions entering the marketplace.

CONSOLIDATED STATEMENTS OF FINANCIAL CONDITION

Lincoln Bancorp and Subsidiary

December 31,	*1988*	*1987*
Assets		
Cash and due from banks (Note 2)	$ 97,913,668	$ 58,801,321
Time deposits with other financial institutions	15,264,000	26,056,181
Investment securities (market value of $32,651,502 and $27,719,150 in 1988 and 1987, respectively)(Note 3)	33,453,378	28,108,179
Federal funds sold	61,350,000	37,546,000
Loans, net (Notes 4 and 5)	194,662,084	145,480,364
Bankers' acceptances	8,948,036	—
Premises and equipment, net (Note 6)	1,947,834	1,487,240
Accrued interest receivable and other assets	2,592,563	3,416,267
	$416,131,563	$300,895,552
Liabilities and Shareholders' Equity		
Deposits:		
Demand deposits	$246,126,865	$152,396,787
Savings deposits	94,485,665	83,926,038
Time deposits under $100,000	5,024,671	4,395,896
Time deposits of $100,000 or more	44,535,783	38,935,093
Total deposits	390,172,984	279,653,814
Accrued interest payable and other liabilities	1,442,740	992,231
Total liabilities	391,615,724	280,646,045
Commitments and Contingencies (Notes 6 and 9)		
Shareholders' equity (Note 8):		
Preferred stock, no par value:		
Authorized — 10,000,000 shares		
No shares issued or outstanding in 1988 or 1987	—	—
Common stock, no par value:		
Authorized — 20,000,000 shares		
Issued and outstanding — 2,718,306 in 1988 and 2,569,013 in 1987	17,118,536	15,948,423
Retained earnings	7,397,303	4,301,084
Total shareholders' equity	24,515,839	20,249,507
	$416,131,563	$300,895,552

The accompanying notes are an integral part of these statements.

CONSOLIDATED STATEMENTS OF INCOME

Lincoln Bancorp and Subsidiary

For the years ended December 31,	*1988*	*1987*	*1986*
Revenue from earning assets:			
Interest and fees on loans	$19,425,239	$12,991,430	$10,241,353
Interest on investment securities (Note 3)	1,994,421	1,570,928	1,697,878
Interest on time deposits with other financial institutions	1,506,742	960,657	495,333
Interest on federal funds sold	2,804,777	2,683,160	992,994
Interest on bankers' acceptances	123,098	—	24,363
Total revenue from earning assets	25,854,277	18,206,175	13,451,921
Cost of funds:			
Interest on savings deposits	3,693,370	3,095,481	2,646,457
Interest on time deposits under $100,000	274,060	254,662	275,668
Interest on time deposits of $100,000 or more	2,636,853	2,133,077	1,969,943
Interest on short term borrowings	—	—	7,400
Interest on capital note	—	41,250	92,021
Total cost of funds	6,604,283	5,524,470	4,991,489
Net revenue from earning assets before provision for loan losses	19,249,994	12,681,705	8,460,432
Provision for loan losses (Note 4)	1,250,300	1,233,000	855,000
Net revenue from earning assets	17,999,694	11,448,705	7,605,432
Other operating revenue:			
Gain on sale of mortgage loans	619,147	—	—
Service charges	519,706	520,973	464,105
Other fees and charges	345,517	452,588	330,959
Gain on sale of investment securities (before taxes of $13,719, $22,145 and $237,452 in 1988, 1987 and 1986, respectively)	30,729	47,486	457,309
Total other operating revenue	1,515,099	1,021,047	1,252,373
Other operating expenses:			
Salaries and related benefits	5,097,257	3,740,298	2,985,948
Occupancy expense (Note 6)	846,747	636,691	612,250
Other operating expenses (Note 10)	6,329,484	4,349,703	2,985,395
Total operating expenses	12,273,488	8,726,692	6,583,593
Income before provision for income taxes	7,241,305	3,743,060	2,274,212
Provision for income taxes (Note 7)	3,050,900	1,626,700	872,900
Net income	$ 4,190,405	$ 2,116,360	$ 1,401,312
Earnings per common and common equivalent share (Note 1)	$1.41	$0.93	$0.78
Fully diluted earnings per share (Note 1)	$1.36	$0.93	$0.78

The accompanying notes are an integral part of these statements.

9. Commitments and contingencies —

At December 31, 1988 and 1987, the Bank had the following commitments and contingent liabilities:

	1988	*1987*
Standby letters of credit	$ 4,821,721	$ 2,400,677
Loan commitments	7,745,000	8,829,575
Undisbursed loans	48,950,627	39,653,027

Loan commitments are generally made for no more than 30 days. If rates are quoted, they are stated in relation to the prime rate. The Company does not anticipate any losses as a result of these commitments.

In the normal course of business the Company occasionally becomes a party to litigation. In the opinion of management, pending or threatened litigation involving the Company will have no material adverse effect upon its financial condition.

In November of 1988, the Bank established a revolving line of credit with a correspondent in the amount of $20,000,000. This credit facility was established to counter potential liquidity shortfalls between the time mortgage loans are funded and sold to third parties. Draw downs on the facility carry a rate of interest equal to the weekly average closing federal funds rate plus 122 basis points and are collateralized by the Bank's mortgage loans held for resale. For maintaining this facility, the Bank is charged a fee of 1/8 of 1% per annum on the unused portion. During 1988 and through the date of this report, no draw downs were made.

10. Other operating expenses —

Other operating expenses included the following:

	Year ended December 31,		
	1988	*1987*	*1986*
Data processing for customers	$2,169,528	$1,421,133	$ 844,964
Director and advisory fees	283,000	277,167	239,500
Legal fees	320,664	216,230	171,859
Messenger services	440,490	338,304	225,535
Selling expenses — mortgage loans	295,469	—	—
Other data processing fees	292,636	191,947	177,786
Other	2,527,697	1,904,922	1,325,751
	$6,329,484	$4,349,703	$2,985,395

11. Condensed financial information of Lincoln Bancorp —

At December 31, 1988 and 1987, the condensed unconsolidated balance sheets of the Company are as follows:

Balance Sheets	*December 31,*	
	1988	*1987*
Cash	$ 288,872	$ 235,301
Investment in Lincoln National Bank	24,226,967	20,014,206
Total assets	$24,515,839	$20,249,507
Shareholders' equity	24,515,839	20,249,507
Total liabilities and shareholders' equity	$24,515,839	$20,249,507

For the years ended December 31, 1988, 1987 and 1986, the condensed unconsolidated statements of income of the Company are as follows:

Statements of Income	*1988*	*1987*	*1986*
Equity in undistributed earnings of the Bank	$4,207,761	$2,123,245	$1,402,373
Operating expenses	17,356	6,885	1,061
Net income	$4,190,405	$2,116,360	$1,401,312

Under National banking law, the Bank is limited in its ability to declare dividends to the Company to the total of its net income for the year, combined with its retained net income for the preceding two years less any required transfers to surplus. The effect of this law is to limit the dividends the Bank may declare at December 31, 1988 to approximately $5,509,000.

Under Federal Reserve regulations, the Bank is also limited in the amount it may loan to the Company, unless such loans are collateralized by specific obligations. At December 31, 1988 the maximum amount available for transfer from the Bank to the Company in the form of loans was approximately $288,800.

To the Shareholders and the Board of Directors of Lincoln Bancorp and Subsidiary:

We have audited the accompanying consolidated statements of financial condition of Lincoln Bancorp (a California corporation) and subsidiary (the Company) as of December 31, 1988 and 1987, and the related consolidated statements of income and changes in shareholders' equity for the three years ended December 31, 1988, cash flows for the year ended December 31, 1988 and changes in financial condition for the two years ended December 31, 1987. These financial statements are the responsibility of the Company's management. Our responsibility is to express an opinion on these financial statements based upon our audits.

We conducted our audits in accordance with generally accepted auditing standards. These standards require that we plan and perform the audit to obtain reasonable assurance about whether the financial statements are free of material misstatement. An audit includes examining, on a test basis, evidence supporting the amounts and disclosures in the financial statements. An audit also includes assessing the accounting principles used and significant estimates made by management, as well as evaluating the overall financial statement presentation. We believe that our audits provide a reasonable basis for our opinion.

In our opinion, the financial statements referred to above present fairly, in all material respects, the financial condition of Lincoln Bancorp and subsidiary as of December 31, 1988 and 1987, the results of their operations for the three years then ended, their cash flows for the year ended December 31, 1988 and the changes in their financial condition for each of the two years ended December 31, 1987, in conformity with generally accepted accounting principles.

As discussed in Note 1 to the financial statements, the Company, as required by generally accepted accounting principles, has presented a consolidated statement of cash flows for the year ended December 31, 1988, in place of a statement of changes in financial condition.

Los Angeles, California
January 20, 1989

Arthur Andersen & Co.

CLIENT:
LINCOLN BANCORP

DESIGN FIRM:
BESSER JOSEPH

ART DIRECTORS:
DOUGLAS JOSEPH,
RIK BESSER

DESIGNER:
DOUGLAS JOSEPH

ILLUSTRATOR:
DOUG FRASER

WRITER:
LINCOLN BANCORP

TYPOGRAPHER:
COMPOSTION TYPE

PAPER SELECTION:
TWEED WEAVE, REFLECTIONS

PAPER MANUFACTURER:
CURTIS, CONSOLIDATED

PRINTER:
GEORGE RICE & SONS

NUMBER OF PAGES:
28 PLUS COVER

TYPE SELECTION:
BASKERVILLE #2

ROBERT J. VECCI, CHIEF FINANCIAL OFFICER, LINCOLN BANCORP, ENCINO, CALIFORNIA

Our main objective for our 1988 annual report was, of course, to communicate to our shareholders and investors. But we especially wanted to convey how diverse and vibrant the Los Angeles economy is. We wanted the annual report not on ourselves, but on L.A. We didn't want a typical annual report in which we pat outselves on the back because we had done well, or beat ourselves up because we hadn't. We also didn't want to show just the usual sea, sand and sun airbrushed look of California. We wanted to get away from that image and stress that Los Angeles is the largest manufacturing city in the state, that the customs service here deals with vast amounts of goods and services. We felt that with our management team, the company would have done well anywhere, so we wanted to feature Los Angeles because of this market's economic vitality. This report was well-received, and it was exactly what we wanted.

ROBERT J. VECCI, CHIEF FINANCIAL OFFICER, LINCOLN BANCORP, ENCINO, KALIFORNIEN

Mit dem Jahresbericht für 1988 wollten wir uns vor allem an die Aktionäre und Investoren wenden. Wir wollten zeigen, wie vielseitig und dynamisch die Wirtschaft in Los Angeles ist. Der Jahresbericht sollte nicht uns, sondern Los Angeles gewidmet sein. Wir wollten keinen typischen Jahresbericht, in dem wir uns selbst wegen unserer guten Leistungen auf die Schulter klopfen oder wegen schlechter Leistungen bezichtigen. Wir wollten auch nicht das übliche Meer-Sand-Sonne-Bild von Kalifornien zeigen. Wir wollten vielmehr hervorheben, dass Los Angeles die grösste Industriestadt in Kalifornien ist mit einer grossen Menge von Waren und Dienstleistungen. Wir sind überzeugt, dass die Firma mit ihrer Geschäftsführung überall gut funktioniert hätte und wollten deshalb Los Angeles wegen der wirtschaftlichen Vitalität der Stadt in den Mittelpunkt stellen. Das Echo auf den Bericht war gut, und er entsprach unseren Vorstellungen.

ROBERT J. VECCI, CHIEF FINANCIAL OFFICER, LINCOLN BANCORP. ENCINO, CALIFORNIE

Le but principal dans notre rapport annuel pour 1988 était l'information due à nos actionnaires et aux investisseurs, mais nous avons aussi voulu donner une idée du caractère dynamique et diversifié de l'économie de Los Angeles. Le rapport devait donc être centré non pas sur nous-mêmes, mais sur Los Angeles. Nous ne voulions pas de rapport annuel type où l'on se congratule bruyamment au vue des résultats financiers ou bat son mea culpa. Nous ne voulions pas non plus présenter une image type de la Californie, avec ses plages de sable, son soleil et la mer. On voulait s'en écarter pour mettre en évidence que Los Angeles est la plus grosse agglomération industrielle de l'Etat, avec d'énormes volumes de biens et services. Avec son équipe dirigeante, notre société aurait connu la réussite n'importe où. D'où les projecteurs braqués sur Los Angeles et sa vitalité économique. Le rapport a été bien accueilli, et c'est bien ce que nous voulions.

DOUGLAS JOSEPH, BESSER JOSEPH PARTNERS, SANTA MONICA, CALIFORNIA

We were told to show in this annual report how Lincoln Bancorp fit into the Southern California economy and how they established their success here. The initial thoughts included having photographs of the industries in the area. We subsequently decided that illustrations could capture the image of the Southern California economy, especially as this was interpreted by Douglas Fraser. Lincoln Bancorp is not a consumer bank, but a commercial bank, providing personalized services to high net worth individuals and small businesses. This annual report became Lincoln Bancorp's calling card to the financial community.

DOUGLAS JOSEPH, BESSER JOSEPH PARTNERS, SANTA MONICA, KALIFORNIEN

Wir sollten in diesem Jahresbericht die Rolle von Lincoln Bancorp in der Wirtschaft Südkaliforniens und die Gründe für ihren Erfolg zeigen. Wir dachten zuerst an Photos von Industriebetrieben in dieser Gegend, doch dann beschlossen wir, dass Illustrationen sich für die Darstellung der Wirtschaft Südkaliforniens besser eignen würden, besonders die von Douglas Fraser. Lincoln Bancorp ist eine Handelsbank, die Einzelpersonen mit grossem Vermögen und kleinen Unternehmen individuellen Service bietet. Dieser Jahresbericht wurde Lincoln Bancorps Visitenkarte in der Finanzwelt.

DOUGLAS JOSEPH, BESSER JOSEPH PARTNERS, SANTA MONICA, CALIFORNIE

On nous a demandé de montrer comment Lincoln Bancorp s'insère dans l'économie sud-californienne et comment cette banque a assuré son succès. Les idées remuées au départ incluaient la photo des industries de la région. Puis nous avons décidé que l'image de l'économie de la Californie du Sud serait mieux rendue par les illustrations, de Douglas Fraser. Lincoln Bancorp n'est pas une banque de dépôt, mais une banque d'affaires qui met ses services spécialisés à la disposition d'individus avec de moyens considérables. Ce rapport annuel est devenu la carte de visite de Lincoln Bancorp auprès de la communauté financière.

ONAL MEDICAL ENTERPRIS

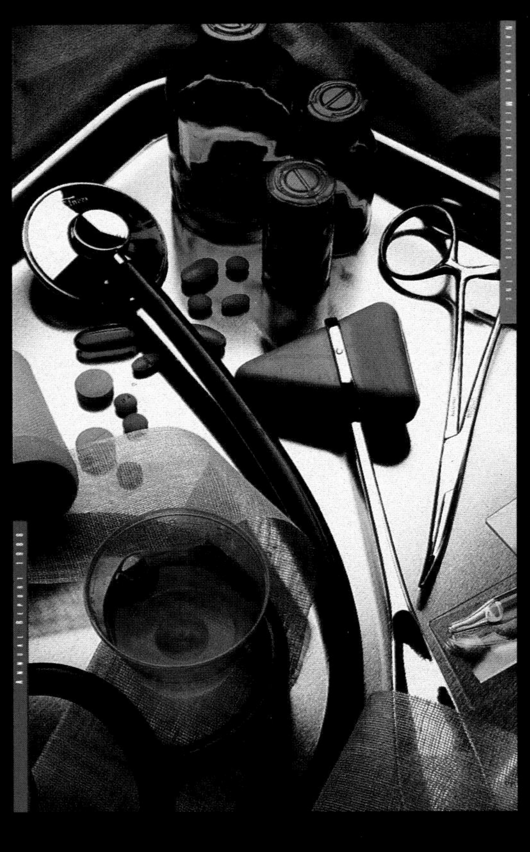

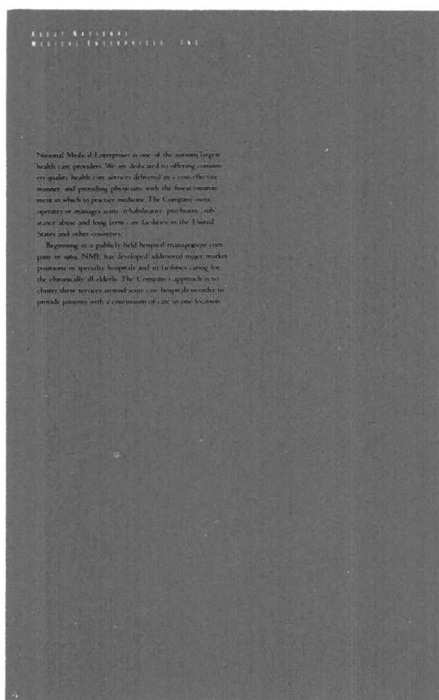

Highlights

		Years Ended May 31, 1988	1987	% Change
Financial Summary	Net Operating Revenues	$3,202,000,000	$2,881,000,000	+11%
	Income from Continuing Operations	$ 170,000,000	$ 140,000,000	+21%
	Earnings Per Share from Continuing Operations:			
	Primary	$2.29	$1.84	+24%
	Fully Diluted	$2.09	$1.68	+24%
	Total Assets	$3,507,000,000	$3,434,000,000	+ 2%
	Stockholders' Equity	$ 962,000,000	$ 925,000,000	+ 4%
	Selected Ratios (after tax):			
	Net Profit Margin	5.3%	4.9%	
	Return on Assets	5.0%	4.2%	
	Return on Equity	17.9%	14.7%	

		Years Ended May 31, 1988	1987	% Change
Facilities Owned or Operated (Domestic and International) at Fiscal Year-End	Acute Care Hospitals	41	43	− 5%
	Beds	7,359	7,514	− 2%
	Psychiatric Hospitals and Substance Abuse Facilities	62	59	+ 5%
	Beds	4,864	4,342	+12%
	Rehabilitation Hospitals	21	18	+17%
	Beds	1,933	1,659	+17%
	Long Term Care Facilities	376	383	− 2%
	Beds	45,088	46,554	− 3%
	Total Facilities	500	503	− 1%
	Total Beds	59,244	60,069	− 1%

Hospital Group

The successful operation of acute care hospitals requires a number of ingredients: dedicated people, an excellent physical plant, the latest medical technology and access to capital. NME provides all of these. Rather than taking a cookie cutter approach to facility management, we place a premium on hospital managers who are sensitive to the needs of the community and physicians, and entrepreneurial enough to fill those needs. We've simplified our decision-making process so our administrators can execute their plans as quickly as possible.

Michael H. Focht, Sr.
President and Chief Executive Officer Hospital Group

Q *Has the Hospital Group completed its restructuring?*

A The restructuring is substantially completed. However, we will be consolidating the acute services of two hospitals into nearby facilities and converting the remaining buildings to specialty use. Over time, a few other hospitals may be converted or sold. We are currently constructing two new facilities in California: the private teaching hospital for the School of Medicine at the University of Southern California and the San Ramon Valley Community Hospital Medical Center.

Q *What is the Hospital Group doing in response to the nursing shortage?*

A First of all, we're paying nurses more. Second, in order to cut down the use of expensive contract labor, we've developed a new system of delivering care which we call the Care Giver System. The system moves away from the traditional "primary care" approach requiring an all-registered nurse staff, to a team approach making use of registered nurses, licensed practical nurses and nurse assistants. Care Giver enables them to provide more efficient, cost-effective care to the patients along with more hours of bedside care. The new system has also simplified documentation and improved communications among medical personnel. By reducing stress and increasing job satisfaction, NME's Care Giver System is aiding in both recruitment and retention of nurses.

Q *What has the Hospital Group done to improve market share for individual hospitals?*

A The Group has followed two strategies: one is to develop services that either fill a niche, such as obstetrics or cardiac catheterization, or develop services that position the hospital as the exclusive provider of services such as open heart surgery. The second strategy is to recruit physicians with existing practices. This enables the NME facility to increase its market share very quickly without creating competition for loyal physicians already on staff.

Q *Does the Hospital Group have any special programs to attract physicians to NME hospitals?*

A We've developed and executed a joint venture of an entire acute care hospital and executed several service specific joint ventures such as cardiac catheterization laboratories. We also provide practice enhancement opportunities for our staff physicians, ranging from seminars for their business office managers to practice evaluation by outside consultants.

Q *What steps has the Hospital Group taken to create a working environment that will attract and hold physicians?*

A Recognizing that physicians still direct the vast majority of all patient admissions, our hospital administrators endeavor to be responsive to physicians' feedback. We give them access to facilities that offer the most up-to-date equipment, a responsive staff, impeccable standards of cleanliness and the availability of amenities for their patients.

The Hospital Group has expanded the Physicians Advisory Board, which consists of physicians who practice at our facilities and provide us with insight about the future direction of medicine. These physicians make suggestions for refining current hospital services, as well as recommendations for equipment selection, design and construction of new units, and market opportunities.

Q *Does the Hospital Group plan to continue adding specialty units to its acute care hospitals?*

A We will continue analyzing opportunities to convert unused acute care beds for specialty use. Currently there are 14 chemical dependency units, nine psychiatric units and four rehab units located within our acute care facilities, almost all of which are managed by NME's Specialty Hospital Group. These programs have been very successful in filling market niches and providing previously unavailable services to the communities our hospitals serve.

Q *How is the Hospital Group addressing the reduction in Medicare reimbursement?*

A The trend in Medicare reimbursement will continue to have negative consequences for hospitals. Without adequate payment, some hospitals won't be able to maintain their physical plants or stay up-to-date with new technology and will have to close. The cost of treating a patient is growing at double-digit rates, as the severity of illness increases, new technology becomes available for diagnosis and therapy, and labor shortages worsen. At the same time, payment rates for Medicare patients have increased at less than two percent per year, in spite of prior promises that payment rates would keep abreast of the hospital "market basket." This means that profit margins on Medicare business are expected to decline again next year. The Hospital Group is responding by deferring or eliminating non-essential expenses, cutting costs and organizing grass roots political action campaigns to bring this problem to the attention of Congress.

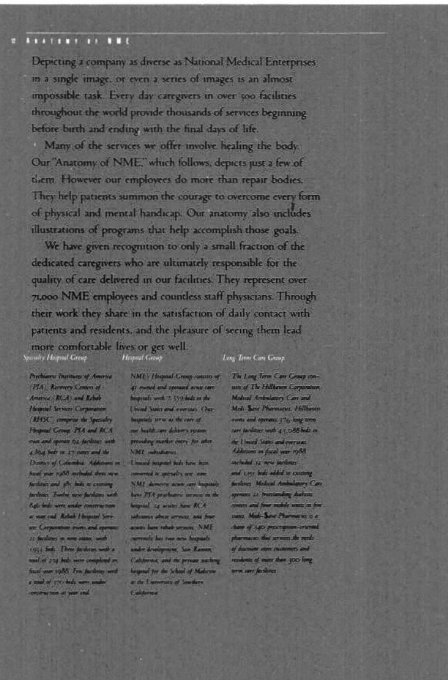

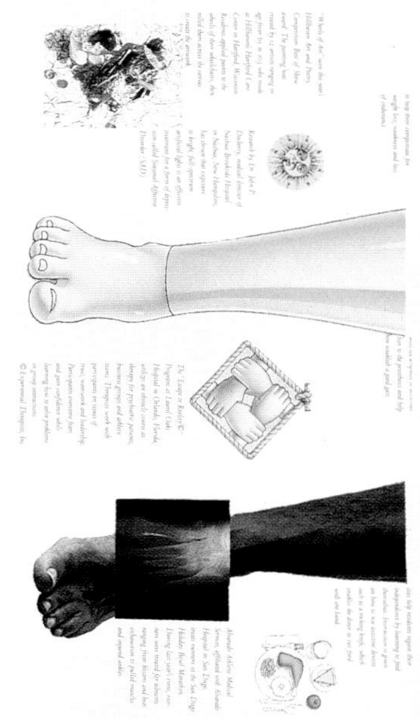

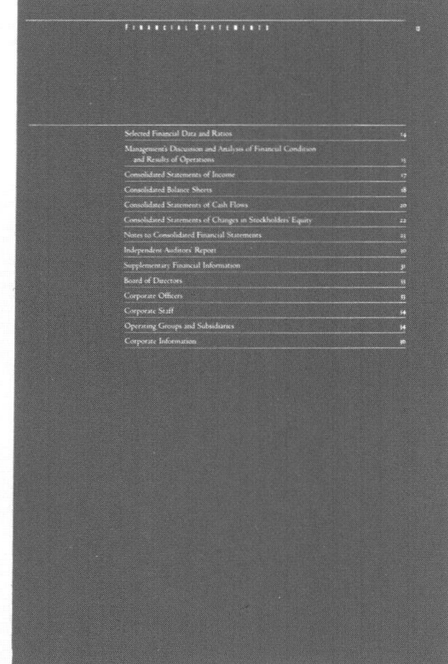

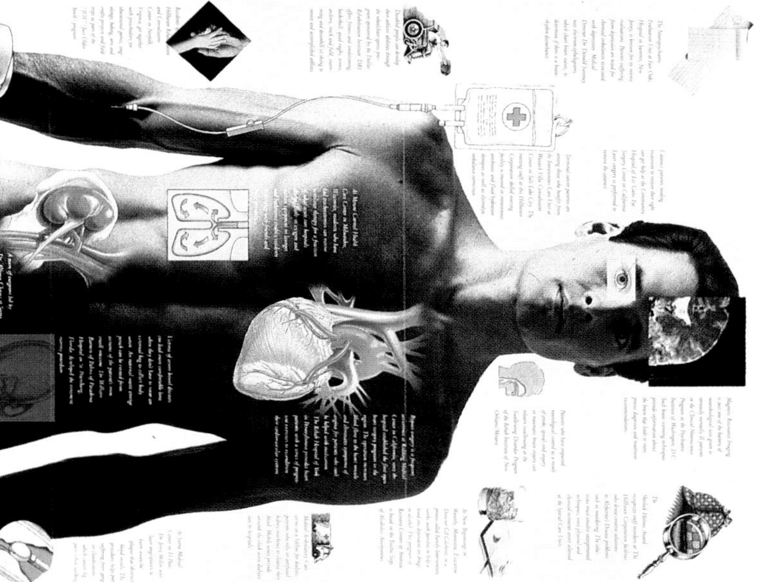

Selected Financial Data and Ratios

National Medical Enterprises, Inc. and Subsidiaries

(dollar amounts, except per share amounts, are expressed in millions)

		Years Ended May 31, 1988*	1987*	1986*	1985	1984
Operating Results	Net operating revenues	$3,202	$2,881	$2,577	$2,191	$1,756
	Total costs and expenses	2,944	2,625	2,389	1,954	1,575
	Operating income from continuing operations	258	256	188	237	181
	Investment earnings	26	23	22	25	25
	Income from continuing operations before income taxes	284	279	210	262	206
	Taxes on income from continuing operations	114	139	94	118	91
	Income from continuing operations	$ 170	$ 140	$ 116	$ 144	$ 115
	Earnings per share from continuing operations:					
	Primary	$ 2.29	$ 1.84	$ 1.48	$ 1.88	$ 1.54
	Fully diluted	$ 2.09	$ 1.68	$ 1.45	$ 1.85	$ 1.52
	Cash dividends per share	$ 0.63	$ 0.59	$ 0.55	$ 0.50	$ 0.43
Balance Sheet Data	Total assets	$3,507	$3,434	$3,296	$2,877	$2,310
	Long-term debt, including convertible debentures	1,517	1,487	1,375	1,260	980
	Stockholders' equity	962**	925**	1,010	940	793
	Book value per share	$13.11	$12.47	$12.83	$12.18	$10.55
Ratios	Pretax margin***	8.9%	9.7%	8.1%	12.0%	11.7%
	Working capital ratios:					
	Acid test****	1.38/1.0	1.29/1.0	1.25/1.0	1.58/1.0	1.36/1.0
	Current ratio	1.57/1.0	1.53/1.0	1.43/1.0	1.79/1.0	1.58/1.0
	Debt/equity ratio	1.58/1.0**	1.61/1.0**	1.36/1.0	1.34/1.0	1.23/1.0
	Return on assets, after tax***	5.0%	4.2%	3.8%	5.6%	5.4%
	Return on equity, after tax***	17.9%	14.7%	11.9%	16.6%	15.7%
	Interest expense coverage***	3.1	3.3	2.9	3.6	3.7

* *1988 and 1987 operating results were affected by the Tax Reform Act of 1986. Operating results for 1986 are after restructuring charges of $24 included in continuing operations.*

** *1988 and 1987 stockholders' equity reflect the repurchase of common stock.*

*** *Based on continuing operations.*

**** *Excludes inventories and prepaid expenses from current assets.*

Management's Discussion and Analysis of Financial Condition and Results of Operations

Results of Operations

During the past two years the Company's operations have been restructured into three operating groups: the General Hospital Group, the Specialty Hospital Group and the Long Term Care Group. Income from these continuing operations before taxes increased $4,538,000 in 1988. Operating profits before interest expense and gains on sales of facilities increased 3% in 1988, reflecting a $46,426,000 (or 41%) increase from specialty hospitals (psychiatric, rehabilitative and substance abuse), a $3,548,000 (or 2%) decline from general hospitals and a $32,211,000 (or 42%) decline from long term care facilities. The decline in long term care operating profits was due primarily to increases in labor, workers' compensation and other operating costs exceeding increases in Medicaid reimbursements.

The Company's net operating revenues from continuing operations increased by $321,070,000 (or 11%) during fiscal 1988 and by $303,659,000 (or 12%) during 1987. Facilities acquired or new facilities placed in service during the year accounted for $27,675,000 (or 9%) of the 1988 increase and $105,121,000 (or 35%) of the increase in 1987.

The General Hospital Group provided 41% of the Company's total net operating revenues in 1988, 44% in 1987, and 51% in 1986. Net operating revenues were $1,323,219,000 in 1988, $1,273,535,000 in 1987, and $1,312,700,000 in 1986.

General hospital net patient revenues for domestic facilities were $1,211,383,000 in 1988, $1,133,392,000 in 1987, and $1,146,864,000 in 1986. Although the Company disposed of two hospitals in 1988, its net patient revenues increased in 1988 by 7% over 1987. Contributing to this change were increases for the hospitals operated in both years of 8% in outpatient visits and 2% in patient days. The principal reason for the net patient revenue decline in 1987 was the completion of the sales of nine hospitals during the year. Increases in inpatient and outpatient prices, intensity of services, and allowances and discounts from established billing rates also affect net patient revenues between years.

Allowances and discounts from established billing rates increased in each of these three years and may continue to rise because payments from government programs and certain private group health plans continue to be substantially less than established hospital billing rates. In an effort to increase admissions, the Company has been offering discounts to a number of private payor groups.

As a result of the disposals of nine facilities in 1987 and two facilities in 1988, the General Hospital Group is better positioned to maximize its returns in the current operating environment. In 1988, of the 36 domestic acute care hospitals operating for a full year in both 1988 and 1987, 26 had increases in outpatient visits, 20 had increases in admissions and 20 had increases in patient days. Future inpatient utilization will be affected by continuing payor pressures to maximize outpatient and alternative health care delivery services for less acutely ill patients.

The Specialty Hospital Group, which includes psychiatric hospitals, rehabilitation hospitals and substance abuse treatment facilities, had $854,098,000 in net operating revenues in 1988, or 27% of the Company's total. Revenues in 1987 and 1986 were $614,465,000 (or 21%) and $432,791,000 (or 17%), respectively, of total net operating revenues in each year. Of the $239,633,000 increase in 1988, $20,550,000 was from six facilities placed in service during the year. Facilities acquired or placed in service in 1987 accounted for $46,028,000 of the $181,674,000 increase over 1986. Also contributing to additional revenues in 1988 over 1987 were increases of 24% in patient days and 24% in admissions, higher rates, and the full-year revenue effect from additional and expanded facilities placed in service in fiscal 1987. Allowances and discounts from established billing rates for this group are expected to increase because of payor payment limitations.

The Long Term Care Group, which includes long term care facilities, retail pharmacies and dialysis treatment centers, provided 32% of net operating revenues in 1988,

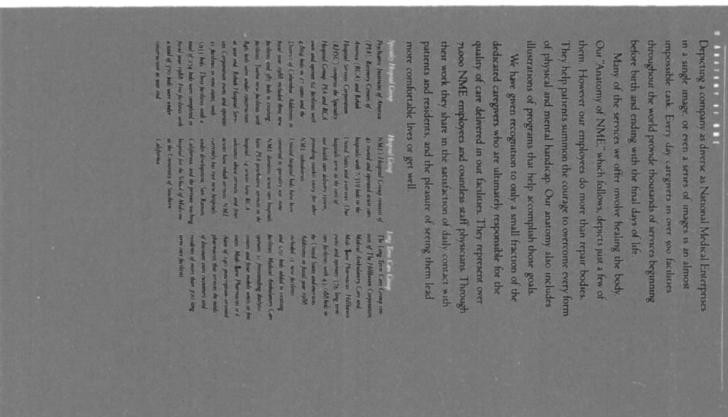

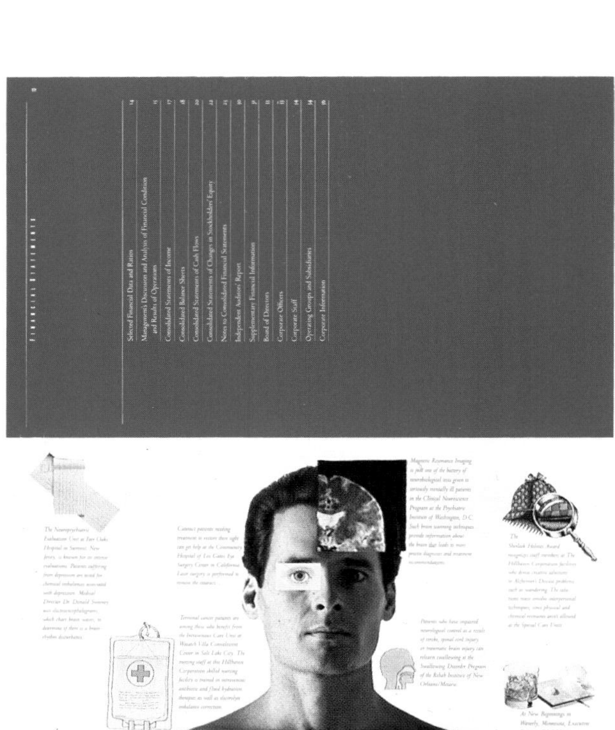

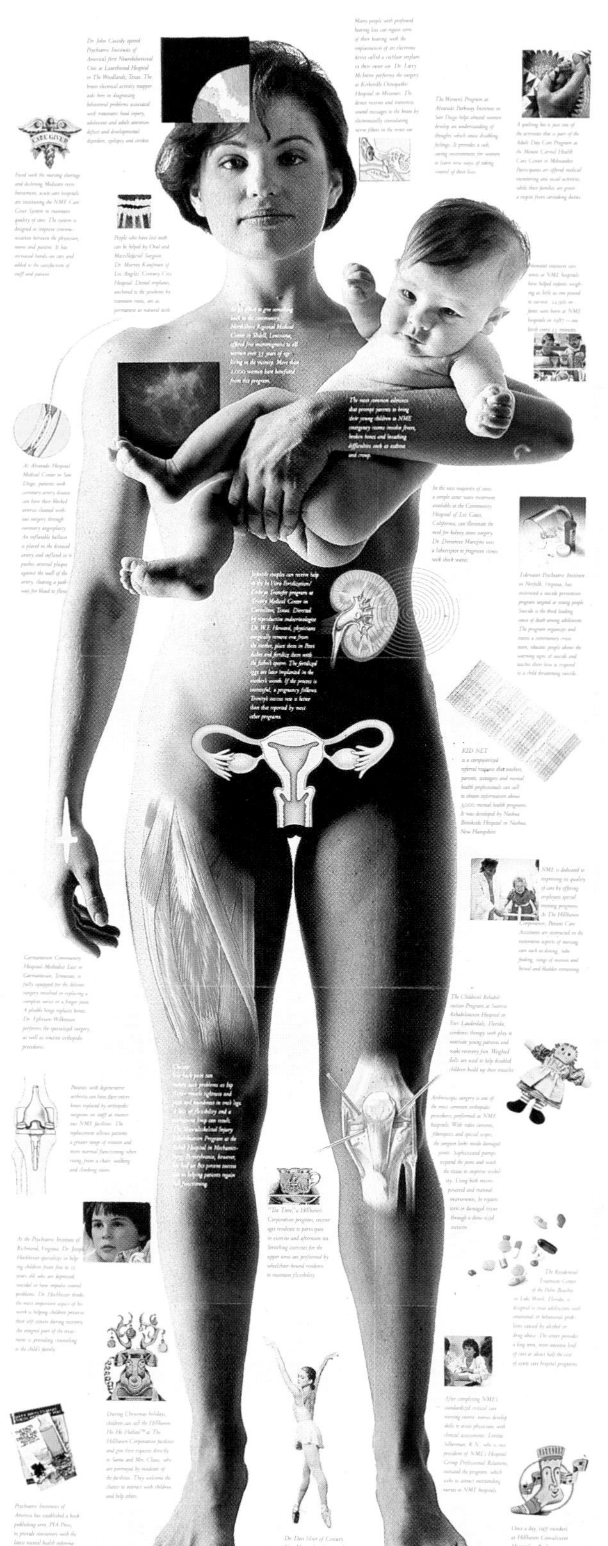

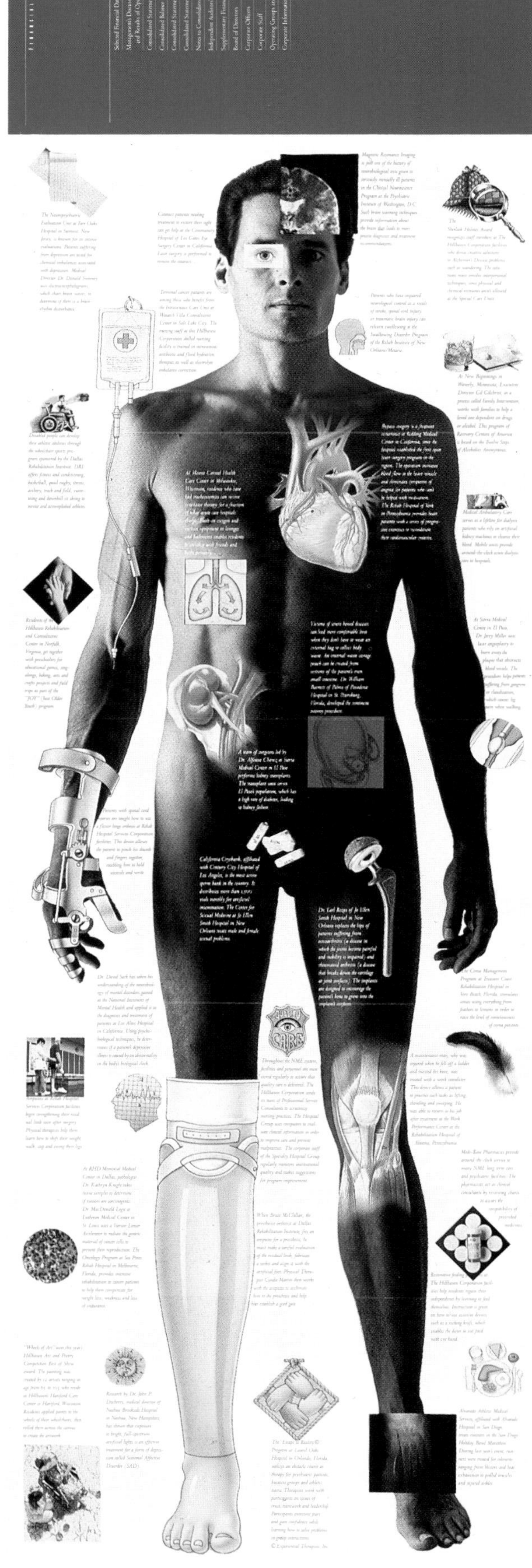

CLIENT:
NATIONAL MEDICAL ENTERPRISES

DESIGN FIRM:
PENTAGRAM

ART DIRECTOR:
KIT HINRICHS

DESIGNERS:
KIT HINRICHS,
KAREN BOONE

PHOTOGRAPHERS:
MICHELE CLEMENT,
TERRY HEFFERNAN,
JEFF CORWIN

ILLUSTRATORS:
VINCE PEREZ,
JUSTIN CARROLL,
TIM LEWIS

WRITER:
TIIU LUK

TIIU LUCK, PROJECT MANAGER, WRITER, AND MADELAINE KING, CORPORATE DESIGN DIRECTOR, NATIONAL MEDICAL ENTERPRISES INC., LOS ANGELES, CALIFORNIA

This company offers services that fill 500 or so categories in hospitals. At first, we had no idea of how to show this since even listing all of these services can be tedious. We must have done six presentations of the concept, which were based on showing the services rather than explaining them. Kit Hinrichs gets all the credit for coming up with giving the anatomy of National Medical Enterprises from head to toe by having fold-out pages of a woman's body and a man's body. The blurbs written to go with these are compact and to the point. Everyone was pleased about how the finished report turned out, because it was intriguing and thought-provoking. Nothing like this had been seen in the health industry.

TIIU LUCK, PROJECT MANAGER, AUTOR UND MADELAINE KING, CORPORATE DESIGN DIRECTOR, NATIONAL MEDICAL ENTERPRISES INC., LOS ANGELES, KALIFORNIEN

Die Firma bietet Dienstleistungen an, die ca. 500 Bereiche in Spitälern betreffen. Anfangs hatten wir keine Vorstellung, wie wir dies zeigen könnten, da selbst die Auflistung aller dieser Dienste mühsam sein kann. Wir sahen, glaube ich, sechs Präsentationen des Konzepts, das auf einer Darstellung anstelle einer Erklärung der Dienstleistungen aufbaut. Es war Kit Hinrichs Idee, die Anatomie der National Medical Enterprises von Kopf bis Fuss durch einen Frauenkörper und einen Männerkörper auf Auslegerseiten darzustellen. Die dazugehörigen Informationen sind knapp und präzise. Der fertige Bericht gefiel jedem. Auf dem Gesundheitssektor ist bisher nichts Vergleichbares produziert worden.

TIIU LUCK, PROJECT MANAGER, WRITER ET MADELEINE KING, CORPORATE DESIGN DIRECTOR, NATIONAL MEDICAL ENTERPRISES INC., LOS ANGELES, CALIFORNIE

Cette société offre un éventail de services recourant quelque 500 catégories prévues dans la gestion hospitalière. Nous ne savions pas au départ comment mettre cela en évidence, puisqu'une simple liste aurait été fastidieuse. Six projects differérents se sont succédés, avec pour idée de montrer les services plutôt que de les décrire. C'est à Kit Hinrichs que revient toute le mérite d'avoir présenté l'anatomie de National Medical Enterprises, de la tête aux pieds, au moyen de pages dépliantes avec un corps d'homme et un corps de femme. Les textes assortis sont denses et précis. Tout le monde s'est déclaré enchanté du rapport une fois terminé. On n'avait jamais rien vue de tel dans l'industrie de la santé.

KIT HINRICHS, PENTAGRAM DESIGN, SAN FRANCISCO, CALIFORNIA

National Medical Enterprises is a hospital group that does everything from drug-rehabilitation to long-term care. It was important to somehow show all the facilities. A synergism does exist between acute care, long-term care, psychiatric care. We needed to show that variety of services, that head-to-foot care. So we decided to take the body itself, male and female, and use these as the centerfolds. We wanted to show quality. We wanted to give the company the real look of confidence we work for on behalf of our clients.

KIT HINRICHS, PENTAGRAM DESIGN, SAN FRANCISCO, KALIFORNIEN

Die National Medical Enterprises sind eine Spitalgruppe, die alles von Drogenentziehungskuren bis zur langfristigen Krankenpflege bietet. Es war wichtig, das ganze Spektrum zu zeigen. Zwischen der Behandlung akuter, chronischer und psychischer Leiden besteht durchaus ein Synergismus. Wir mussten die Vielfalt der Dienstleistungen zeigen, Behandlungen von Kopf bis Fuss. Deshalb beschlossen wir, den Körper selbst einzusetzen, einen männlichen und einen weiblichen, und zwar auf Auslegerseiten.

KIT HINRICHS, PENTAGRAM DESIGN, SAN FRANCISCO, CALIFORNIE

National Medical Enterprises est un groupe hospitalier aux multiples activités allant de la réhabilitation des drogués aux soins continus aux malades chroniques. Il importait de mettre en image cette polyvalence des services. Il existe une synergie entre les soins à court terme, les soins à long terme et les soins psychiatriques. Nous avons décidé d'illustrer cette variété de services, qui embrasse le patient tout entier, de la tête aux pieds. C'est ce qui nous a amenés à faire porter la démonstration sur le corps même.

P R I M E   C A B L E

There are two things to know if you're going to succeed in the cable business. The first is you must deliver good pictures. The second is you must answer the telephone. One is a matter of science, the other a matter of service. Both have to do with taking care of the customer.

Taking care of customers has made Prime Cable one of the most successful multi-system cable television operators in the history of the cable industry.

Robert W. Hughes, Chairman and CEO. Entered the cable industry in 1968.

"Consumers have been telling us the same things for years.

They want quality, they want variety, and they want it on their television sets in their homes.

That's why cable's grown from serving a quarter of America's television households

to over half and why it will grow even more in the future.

We're seeing a video revolution in this country and it's a long, long way from over."

Taking Care Of Business

Consumer demand has made cable television possible. Management has made Prime Cable good at satisfying the demand. Our track record, both as a company and management team, is a history of success based upon the fundamentals of attention to detail, financial analysis, and motivated employees.

Assembled over the years by Bob Hughes, the management team is distinguished by its experience in the cable industry, a diversity of skills, its philosophy, and its continuity. The senior members have worked together, on average, for a decade. We know the industry as well as anyone, from financing to franchising, acquisition, consumer research, government and consumer relations, and operations. Direct experience in a variety of cable systems in all kinds of communities–urban, suburban, rural–has given us a knowledge of what works and what doesn't, of when to overhaul a system and when to fine tune it.

If our skills and our experience as a team are diverse, our operating philosophy is unified. We believe strongly in keeping our promises and in communicating our intentions clearly and candidly from the outset. It's our responsibility to know what's possible, reasonable, and fair in our business and to run our cable systems based on those conditions. We have a reputation for delivering consistently on clearly defined promises to customers, municipal authorities, financial backers, and employees. We guard this reputation carefully because we know it's our future.

Much of our success stems from the emphasis we place on motivating employees throughout the ranks of Prime. We make sure we have the right people in the right jobs. They're provided with stringent fiscal and procedural policies. They're given responsibility. And they're made accountable.

The result is good management at all levels, not just among the policymakers in the home office. Actually, there isn't a home office in the usual sense at Prime. Certainly, senior management develops performance goals and an operating plan to meet them for each system we acquire. But, since the individual cable system's management has to make it work, we always involve system managers in the plan. We use sound management fundamentals. We tailor the plan to the individual system. And we monitor performance. What we don't do is stifle initiative.

In an industry that's seen its share of volatility, Prime and our predecessors have 20 years of internal stability and economic growth. Good management is the reason.

(Left to right) David Justice, Treasurer;
William P. Glasgow, Vice President, Finance;
and Shirley C. Gambone, Controller.

C. Ronald Dorchester, Senior Vice President, Operations. Entered the cable industry in 1973.

"In every cable system we've been associated with,

we've significantly increased the subscriber base. There's a simple explanation for this:

We understand the business for what it is, a service business. Our job is to train

and motivate our employees to do everything it takes to keep customers happy–

from good pictures to the right kind of attention.

That's the only way we can expect to be invited back every month."

Jerry D. Lindauer, Senior Vice President, Corporate Development. Entered the cable industry in 1977.

"We've been in this industry for a long time and we plan to be in it a lot longer.

We'd like the people we want to do business with to want to do business with us.

That's why we place so much importance on making

our intentions clear at the outset to everyone we're associated with–employees, customers,

municipalities, the financial community–and on delivering

on the commitments we've made to them."

Northwest Harris County, Texas

Also in 1986, Income Fund I acquired the cable television system serving Northwest Harris County, Texas (the "Northwest Harris County System"). This system encompasses several subdivisions of suburban Houston, Texas. The Northwest Harris County System has benefitted from the economies of scale achieved due to its proximity to the Ft. Bend System. Office procedures were instituted that eliminated several positions in the sales and accounting departments. Also, significant amounts of time and money were invested in sales efforts that focused on improving basic subscriber penetration. During 1987, cash flow grew from $2.5 million to $3.2 million, an increase of 30%.

	At Acquisition December 1986	*As of December 1987*	*Annual Growth Rate*
Subscribers	14,678	15,744	7.3%
Annual Revenues	$6,255,000*	$6,214,000	(0.7)
Annual Cash Flow	$2,483,000*	$3,233,000	30.2

*Estimate

In July 1988, Income Fund I became fully invested when it bought the cable television systems serving approximately 20,000 subscribers in Valparaiso and LaPorte, Indiana (the "Indiana Systems"). These are well built and well operated systems with high basic subscriber penetration and high operating margins. The Management Team's strategy, therefore, will be to increase basic and pay television subscribers.

Prime Cable Growth Partners, L.P.

In 1987, PVI formed Growth Fund, a $47 million fund, as its primary vehicle for acquisition of growth-oriented cable systems.

In 1988, Growth Fund and PVI together acquired a 19.4% interest in the Atlanta System. Also in 1988, Growth Fund acquired a 66.6% interest in the Ft. Bend System, which is also partially owned by PVI. The proceeds from the sale of new limited partnership interests in the Ft. Bend System were used to purchase three systems in the Houston metropolitan area as described under "Ft. Bend, Texas." Growth Fund currently has approximately $11.9 million remaining to invest.

Summary Of Returns To Investors

Year of Investment		*Amount of Investment*	*Internal Rate of Return*
Realized Investments			
Communications Properties, Inc.[a]			
1968	Common Stock	$ 250,000	31%
1973	Common Stock	3,188,000	19
Prime Cable Corp.[b]			
1979	Common Stock	525,000	69
	Units:		
	Preferred Stock and Convertible Subordinated Debentures	1,000,000	29
	Convertible Subordinated Debentures	615,000	48
	Preferred Stock with Warrants	3,000,000	28
1980	Units:		
	Common Stock, Preferred Stock, and Convertible Debentures	5,780,000	29
1981	Preferred Stock	16,000,000	22
1982	Common Stock	1,000,000	23
	Subordinated Debentures with Warrants	40,000,000	21
	Convertible Subordinated Notes	10,000,000	27
1983	Limited Partnership Units of the Atlanta System	48,000,000	21
1985	Common Stock and Preferred Stock of Prime Cable of Maryland, Inc.	14,500,000	52
Unrealized Investments			
Prime Venture I[c]			
1985	Preferred Stock	$20,875,000	30%

(a) In addition to common stock, CPI had multiple debt offerings which carried warrants.
(b) Assumes sale of Prime Cable of Maryland, Inc. (Prince George's County, MD) will close in 1988.
(c) The 30% internal rate of return shown is based upon estimates assuming that all assets currently held by PVI are liquidated at the end of 1988.

Communities Served By Communications Properties, Inc. & Prime Cable Corp. & Those Currently Owned By Prime Venture I, Inc.

Arkansas
Jacksonville
North Little Rock

Connecticut
Hartford
East Hartford
West Hartford
Windsor
Simsbury
Bloomfield Hills
Meriden
Southington
Cheshire

Georgia
*Atlanta**

Illinois
Springfield

Indiana
Lafayette
*LaPorte**
*Valparaiso**

Kentucky
Ashland
Hopkinsville
Louisville

Maryland
Annapolis and Anne Arundel County
Lexington Park and St. Mary's County
Prince Georges County and municipalities (14)

Massachusetts
Amherst
Greenfield
Millers Falls
Turners Falls
Shelburne
Haverhill
Grove Land
Marlborough
Palmer
Ware
Pelham

Nevada
*Las Vegas**
North Las Vegas
Henderson
Boulder
Clark County

New Jersey
Brick Township
Hoboken
Union City
West New York
North Bergen
Weehauken
Point Pleasant
Princeton

New York
Suburban Buffalo (14 communities)

North Carolina
*Chapel Hill**
Orange County
Durham County
*Hickory**
Maiden
Catawba County

Ohio
Cambridge
Coshocton
Defiance
Wauseon
Napoleon
Dover
Irontown
Lisbon
Logan
New Philadelphia
Newark
Newcomerstown
Salem
Strasburg
Sugar Creek
Toronto
Empire
Stratton
Waverly
Greenfield

Pennsylvania
Beaver Falls
South Philadelphia (City of)
Upper Darby
Washington
Williamsport

Texas
Cedar Creek Lake Area
Del Rio
Gladewater
*Humble**
Northeast Harris County
Atascocita
Channelview
The Highlands
*Katy**
Kerrville
Marlin
Marshall
Midland
*Northwest Harris County**
*Pasadena**
LaPorte
Deer Park
Portland
*Sugar Land**
Richmond
Needville
Ft. Bend County
Texarkana
Uvalde

Virginia
Ft. Belvoir
Leesburg
Quantico USMC
Town of Quantico
Town of Dumfries
Prince William County

West Virginia
Weirton

Wyoming
Jackson Hole
Teton County

**Systems Currently Owned*

CLIENT:
PRIME CABLE

DESIGN FIRM:
LOWELL WILLIAMS DESIGN

ART DIRECTOR:
LOWELL WILLIAMS

DESIGNERS:
BILL CARSON,
CINDY WHITE

PHOTOGRAPHERS:
ARTHUR MEYERSON,
MIKE HART

WRITER:
JOANN STONE

PRODUCTION MANAGER:
BILL CARSON

TYPOGRAPHER:
ONEWORKS

PAPER SELECTION:
VINTAGE, CARNIVAL

PAPER MANUFACTURER:
POTLATCH, CHAMPION

PRINTER:
GROVER

NUMBER OF PAGES:
52

SIZE:
7 3/4" X 12 1/4"

TYPE SELECTION:
TIMES, HELVETICA

GREGORY S. MARCHBANKS, PRESIDENT, PRIME CABLE, AUSTIN, TEXAS

Prime Cable is a private company. For this report, we had three major targets: prospective investors, municipal authorities in areas where we hoped to expand, and our new employees. This was a nervous time for us. We were moving into new markets, acquiring cable companies, and we wanted to show how service-oriented and fair-minded we are to insure acceptance and a smooth transition. When Lowell Williams Design gave its first major presentation to us, we embraced it wholeheartedly, from the cover right on through. The officers were interviewed extensively, in part to convey that we are, in fact, good guys, but also to show that we have a lot of history in an industry that's still fairly young. We were photographed in our offices to give a personal touch to the brochure and in the field to empahsize that we really do take care of the customer. The whole process was very fast and efficient, but also thorough We were very comfortable with this report.

GREGORY S. MARCHBANKS, PRESIDENT, PRIME CABLE, AUSTIN, TEXAS

Prime Cable ist ein privates Unternehmen, und mit diesem Bericht richten wir uns speziell an zukünftige Investoren, an die für uns im Zusammenhang mit Expansionsplänen wichtigen städtischen Behörden und an neue Mitarbeiter. Wir waren dabei, einen neuen Markt zu erobern, und wir brauchten ein positives Image, was im Kabelgeschäft nicht immer einfach ist. Als Lowell Williams Design bei uns die erste wichtige Präsentation machte, waren wir von der Idee begeistert. Der Umschlag war rot, und das gewählte Archiv-Photo zeigte einen Kabelmonteur bei der Arbeit. Die Mitarbeiter unserer Firma wurden ausgiebig befragt, da wir zeigen wollten, welche Leute für uns arbeiten. Es wurde in unseren Büros photographiert, hinzu kamen dann noch Aufnahmen, die unsere Arbeiter draussen in ihren Einsatzgebieten zeigen. Lowell engagierte dafür einen ausgezeichneten Photographen, der sehr professionel arbeitete. Wir waren sehr zufrieden.

GREGORY S. MARCHBANKS, PRESIDENT, PRIME CABLE, AUSTIN, TEXAS

Prime Cable est une entreprise privée dont le rapport s'adresse à trois cibles différentes: les investisseurs potentiels, les municipalités des régions retenues pour des implantations futures, et nos nouveaux collaborateurs. Comme nous nous aventurions sur un nouveau marché, cette période a été éprouvante. Il fallait trouver moyen de nous présenter sous un jour avenant en dérogeant à l'image pas toujours très brillante de l'industrie du câble. Lorsque Lowell Williams Design nous a soumis le premier jet de son projet, nous y avons immédiatement souscrit. La couverture était rouge, la photo-type montrait un monteur de lignes au travail. Des interviews exhaustives ont été recueillies auprès des cadres supérieurs de notre société que nous entendions présenter au public et à notre personnel, d'où les photos prises dans leurs bureaux. Nous avons ensuite fait procéder à des prises de vues sur le terrain pour montrer nos hommes au travail. Ce rapport nous a emplis de satisfaction; on l'a tous aimé.

LOWELL WILLIAMS, LOWELL WILLIAMS DESIGN, INC., HOUSTON, TEXAS

Prime Cable is one of the most successful television cable television companies in the industry. In a business that can be very flashy, they wanted a corporate, big-business image, because that's the way they are. We let photography show not only their very elegant, corporate offices but also that they had service staff and equipment–that there was more to them than promotional gimmicks. We also separated information so the book could be printed with financail information for investors and without it for the other audience. The only stock photo was the cover. We'd used it in an early presentation simply to convey the tone we wanted, and they fell in love with it. We couldn't have asked for a better client. They gave us the help we asked for and then let us do our job.

LOWELL WILLIAMS, LOWELL WILLIAMS DESIGN, INC., HOUSTON, TEXAS

Prime Cable ist eine der erfolgreichsten Fernsehkabelfirmen. Es ging darum, sich gegenüber zukünftigen Investoren als effizientes Grossunternehmen und gleichzeitig gegenüber dem übrigen Publikum als serviceorientierte, leistungsfähige Firma darzustellen. Wir fanden, dass wir mit Hilfe von Photos deutlich machen konnten, dass diese Firma Mitarbeiter, Ausrüstung und das notwendige Material hat, um ihre Aufgabe zu erfüllen und dass wir auf Werbegags verzichten können. Wir wollten eine richtig sympathische Gruppe von führenden Mitarbeitern zeigen. Wir bereiteten einen roten Umschlagentwurf mit einem Archiv-Photo vor, das der Firmenleitung so gut gefiel, dass alle anderen Versionen keine Chance hatten.

LOWELL WILLIAMS, LOWELL WILLIAMS DESIGN, INC., HOUSTON, TEXAS

Prime Cable est l'une des entreprises de câbles de télé-distribution les plus prospères de la branche. Son souci était de présenter une image institutionnelle évoquant le big business aux investisseurs potentiels et de souligner son professionnalisme et l'étendue de ses services aux yeux de divers publics. Nous avons pensé démontrer par la photo que cette société disposait du personnel, des équipements et des matériels nécessaires pour remplir son rôle autrement que par des artifices de promotion. Nous avons voulu mettre en scène un groupe de cadres supérieurs sympathiques. Notre première maquette dont la couverture rouge s'ornait d'une photo d'archives correspondait exactement à ce que voulait le client. Pas de chance pour d'autres photos.

MORTGAGE INVESTMENT CORPO

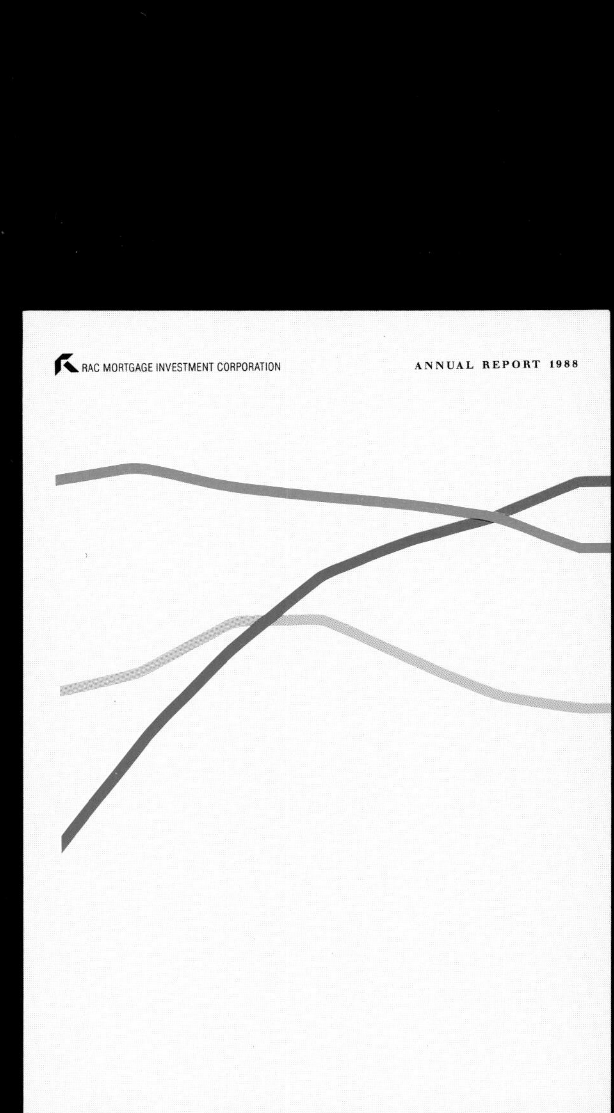

COMPANY PROFILE

1988 SUMMARY OF QUARTERLY RESULTS AND SELECTED FINANCIAL DATA

(unaudited)
(amounts in thousands except share data)

	Feb. 18 to Mar. 31	April 1 to June 30	July 1 to Sept. 30	Oct. 1 to Dec. 31	Feb. 18 to Dec. 31
Operating results:					
Total revenues	$ 8,275	$ 19,825	$ 20,273	$ 24,385	$72,758
Net interest income	2,175	3,357	3,482	4,336	13,348
Net income	1,311	3,664(1)	2,959	2,231	10,165
Net income per share (2)	0.16	0.45	0.36	0.16	1.02
Cash dividends declared per share	0.20	0.40	0.40	0.34	1.34
Selected balance sheet data (at period end):					
Total assets	$725,938	$771,322	$905,445	$1,100,402	
CMO bonds, net	628,843	635,276	699,127	676,407	
Shareholders' equity	77,572	76,027	130,046	129,656	
Average shareholders' equity (during period)	77,572	76,800	77,654	130,775	
Other information:					
Average LIBOR (3)	6.80%	7.32%	8.20%	8.89%	
Average ten-year treasury yield	8.33%	8.91%	9.10%	8.96%	

(1) Includes $1,218 gain on sale of residual interests
(2) Computed on weighted average shares outstanding during period; therefore, the sum of the quarterly per share income results is not equal to the per share income for the total period
(3) Average during each quarter of the one-month London Inter-Bank Offered Rate (LIBOR)

During 1988, RAC Mortgage completed two public offerings of the shares of the Company's common stock, raising more than $150 million in equity, and declared dividends of $1.34 per share. These dividends represent an annualized return of 15.1 percent upon the shares purchased in the initial offering on February 18, 1988, at a price of $10 per share. However, as the foregoing chart illustrates, the net income per share declined as short-term interest rates increased through the year. Accordingly, the Company reduced the dividend payment rate in the fourth quarter of 1988, and again in the first quarter of 1989.

RAC Mortgage fully invested its shareholders' equity in a portfolio of mortgage loans, mortgage securities and residual interests in CMOs collateralized by mortgage loans and mortgage securities. During 1988, RAC Mortgage purchased more than $92 million of mortgage loans through its daily mortgage loan purchase program. RAC Mortgage took advantage of an opportunity to sell in June two residual interests it had purchased in February, for a profit of $1.2 million. Also in 1988, RAC Mortgage generated $880,000 in fee income relating principally to commitments to purchase residual interests on a contingent basis.

The lines on the cover represent the returns from various mortgage assets in RAC Mortgage's portfolio in certain interest rate environments, starting with short-term rates of 9.25 percent. The green line on the graph to the right shows the blended return from these mortgage assets. Each type of mortgage asset is more fully described in this report at the color tab that corresponds to the line on the cover.

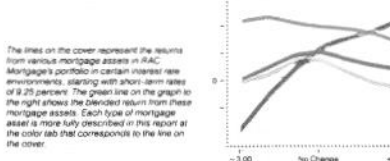

FIXED-RATE RESIDUALS

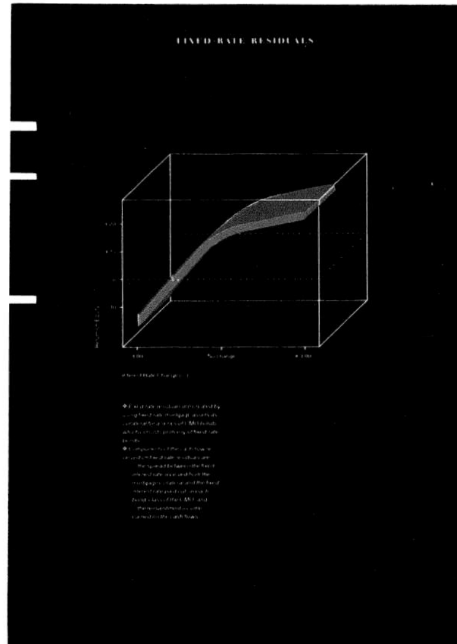

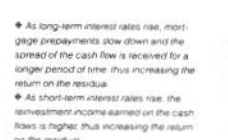

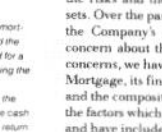

To Our Shareholders:

During its first year in operation, RAC Mortgage Investment Corporation ("RAC Mortgage" or "the Company") experienced both the risks and the rewards related to its investments in mortgage assets. Over the past six months, we have received many inquiries about the Company's investments and strategies. Many have expressed concern about the recent reductions in the dividend. To meet these concerns, we have included in this annual report a discussion of RAC Mortgage, its financial position and liquidity, its investment strategies, and the composition and risks of its portfolio. Also, we have explained the factors which affect the returns on each type of asset in the portfolio and have included graphs which illustrate the anticipated yields from those assets in the interest rate environment of year-end 1988 and in various alternative interest rate environments.

The Company's strategy is to invest in mortgage loans and mortgage securities which will enable it to return to its shareholders a 12 to 15 percent yield based on the original $10.00 share price. Through 1988 we maintained this yield. However, because of an inverted yield curve, a factor which is explained more fully in the following pages, we have not been able to sustain this level during the early part of 1989.

RAC Mortgage's earnings are sensitive to changes in interest rates. We structured the portfolio to perform best in normal interest rate environments, not in today's unusual inverted rate environment. This structuring should enable the Company to improve results when interest rates return to more normal relationships. To further protect our shareholders' investments, we have been conservative in the level of our borrowings and have protected the returns in 1989 from still higher short-term rates.

RAC Mortgage's financial position and strategies are sound, and its capital position and liquidity have been maintained. As we enter the second quarter of 1989, RAC Mortgage and its management are confident that the Company is well positioned to withstand the current unusual interest rate environment and to improve results in a more favorable rate environment.

Sincerely,

Thomas H. Potts
President

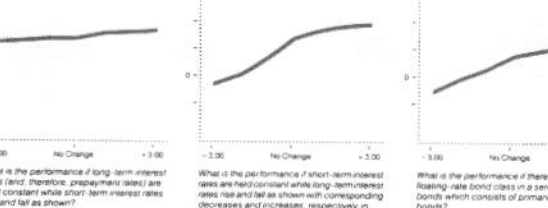

FLOATING-RATE RESIDUALS

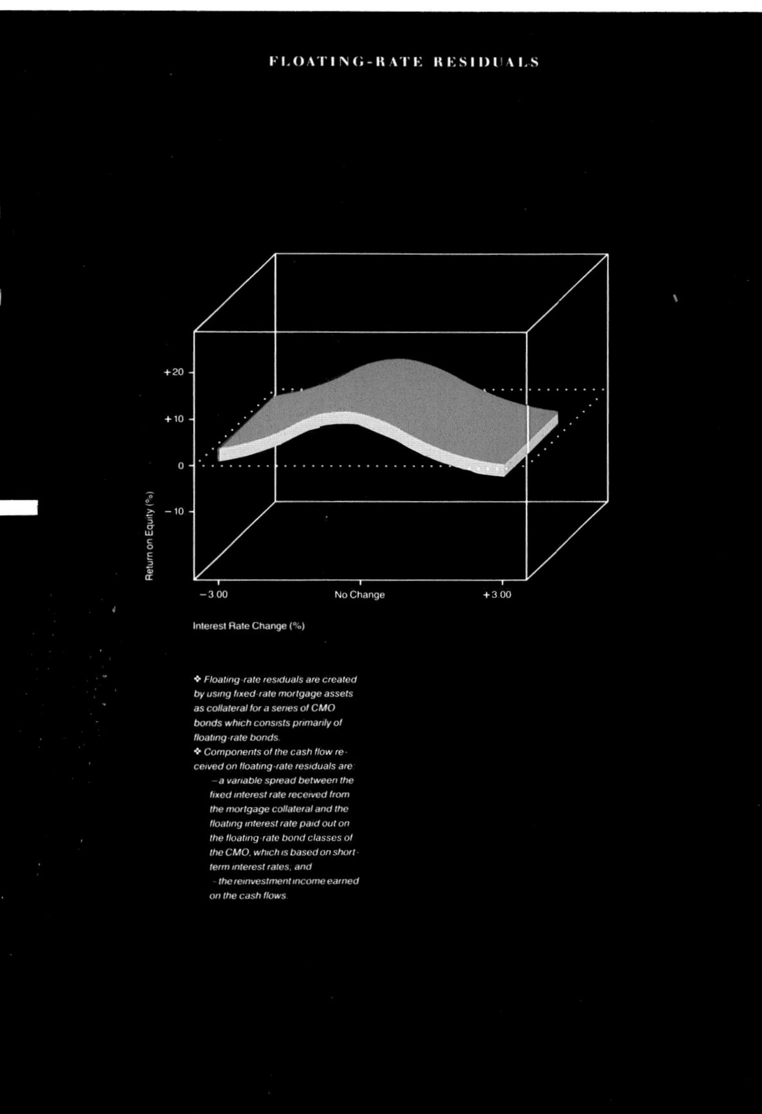

❖ Floating-rate residuals are created by using fixed-rate mortgage assets as collateral for a series of CMO bonds which consists primarily of floating-rate bonds.
❖ Components of the cash flow received on floating-rate residuals are:
– a variable spread between the fixed interest rate received from the mortgage collateral and the floating interest rate paid out on the floating-rate bond classes of the CMO, which is based on short-term interest rates, and
– the reinvestment income earned on the cash flows.

❖ As short-term interest rates rise (i) the primary effect is a decrease in the variable spread as more of the fixed cash flow from the CMO mortgage assets is used to pay the higher interest on the floating-rate CMO bonds, thus diminishing the return on the residual, and (ii) a second, though less important effect, is higher reinvestment income earned on the cash flow prior to its distribution to the residual holder, thus mitigating partially the decline in the return on the residual.
❖ As long-term interest rates rise, mortgage prepayments slow down and the variable spread portion of the cash flow is received for a longer period of time, thus increasing the return on the residual.
❖ The graph to the left assumes long-term and short-term interest rates move together.
❖ The left and middle graphs below illustrate the extreme sensitivity of these residuals to changes in both short-term interest rates and long-term interest rates (which influence the rate of prepayments on the underlying mortgages).
❖ Over the past six months, short-term interest rates have increased without a compensating change in long-term interest rates. Thus the current return profile (left) is very different from a typical profile at the time of purchase (below right).
❖ Approximately 60 percent of the Company's residual portfolio consists of floating-rate residuals.

and the related borrowings are explained in the graphs included in this annual report.

It is important to note that even when short-term rates are quite high, there is a cap on the interest paid on floating-rate CMO bonds. Although the cash flows from floating-rate residuals may cease, the floating-rate CMO bonds are supported fully by the underlying mortgage collateral. Therefore, RAC Mortgage will not have to invest additional amounts to support the payments on the bonds. Should short-term rates drop from current levels, there will be a substantial recovery in the return on such floating-rate residuals as the spread widens between the cash received from the fixed-rate assets and the cash paid on the floating-rate bonds.

Because the borrowings supporting RAC Mortgage's portfolio are affected by both short-term and long-term interest rates, RAC Mortgage's earnings and dividends will vary as short-term rates change relative to long-term rates. When long-term rates rise, there usually is a slow-down in mortgage prepayments which extends cash flow on mortgage assets and thereby increases the return on the residuals. When short-term interest rates rise and long-term interest rates are stable, there is no increase in the return from slower prepayments to counterbalance the higher costs of floating-rate CMO bond classes and borrowings tied to short-term interest rates. Short-term interest rates usually are lower than long-term interest rates. However, since late 1988, short-term interest rates have increased while long-term interest rates have remained stable, and now short-term interest rates are higher than long-term interest rates. When short-term rates are higher than long-term rates, the interest rate environment is described as an inverted yield curve. This inversion of the yield curve has had and will continue to have a negative effect on RAC Mortgage's earnings. Further inversion of the yield curve could cause a further reduction in earnings.

In order to increase the stability of the yield on the portfolio, RAC Mortgage has attempted to balance the portfolio to protect the yield when short- and long-term rates move together. In addition, RAC Mortgage has sold a limited number of financial futures contracts to provide a degree of protection against further increases in short-term rates in 1989. The performance of these futures contracts is described in the graph entitled "Hedging of Short-Term Interest Rates."

What is the performance if long-term interest rates (and, therefore, prepayment rates) are held constant while short-term interest rates rise and fall as shown?

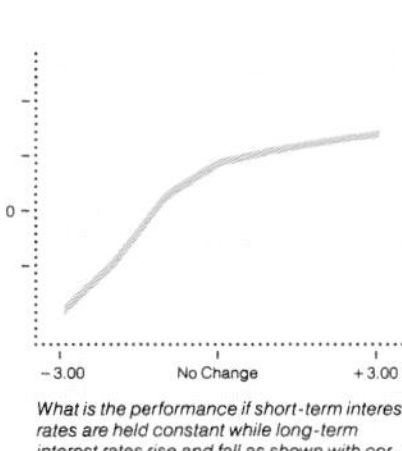

What is the performance if short-term interest rates are held constant while long-term interest rates rise and fall as shown with corresponding decreases and increases, respectively, in prepayment rates?

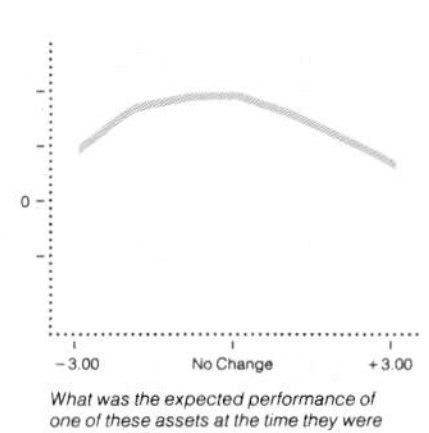

What was the expected performance of one of these assets at the time they were purchased?

7

ARM SECURITIES/SYNTHETIC RESIDUALS

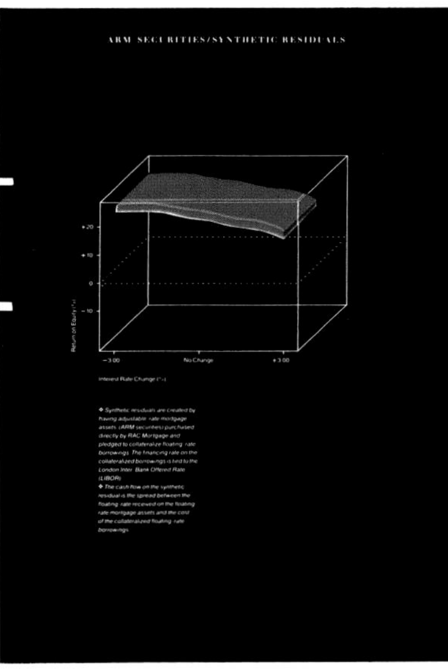

Portfolio Description

The Company's portfolio consists of mortgage loans and mortgage securities, as well as residual interests in collateralized mortgage obligations (CMOs) which are backed by mortgage loans and securities. Each of these asset groups combines a mortgage-related asset with various forms of borrowings.

Mortgage loans are purchased by the Company through its daily mortgage loan purchase program. RAC Mortgage purchased more than $92 million of single-family residential mortgage loans during 1988 and provides a secondary market conduit for mortgage loans for more than 90 mortgage originators. RAC Mortgage pledged these loans to collateralize two series of CMOs and retained the residual interests from these CMOs. Because the market for mortgage loans is less efficient than the market for mortgage securities, RAC Mortgage can create these residual interests in CMOs backed by its mortgage loans at higher yields than the yields on residual interests in CMOs backed by mortgage securities.

The Company purchased approximately $250 million of adjustable-rate mortgage (ARM) securities during 1988. When combined with short-term borrowings, these ARM securities create a "synthetic residual." The Company's net investment in such synthetic residuals is approximately $20 million.

The balance of the Company's portfolio is invested in residual interests. During 1988, RAC Mortgage invested (i) $51 million in fixed-rate residuals, which are fixed-rate assets supported primarily by fixed-rate CMO bonds, and (ii) $81 million in floating-rate residuals, which are fixed-rate assets supported primarily by floating-rate CMO bonds.

R: Residual Interest

A-D: Regular Bond Classes

As illustrated in the chart to the right, a residual interest in a CMO is the excess of the cash flow received from the mortgage assets over the amounts paid on the CMO bonds. This excess cash flow is represented by the green strip at the top of the chart. The yellow bars represent the amounts paid to the bondholders. Both prepayment rates on the mortgage collateral and the interest rates paid to the bondholders will affect the value of, and return on, the residual interest over time.

The characteristics of the mortgage assets and of the borrowings against those assets determine the respective returns of RAC Mortgage's investments. The effects of the relationships between the assets

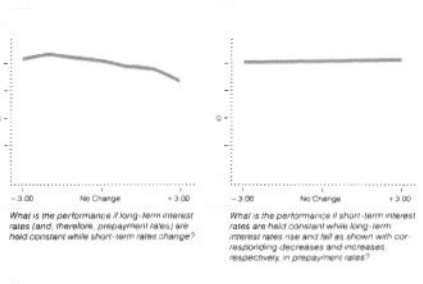

What is the performance if long-term interest rates (and, therefore, prepayment rates) are held constant while short-term rates change?

What is the performance if short-term interest rates are held constant while long-term interest rates rise and fall as shown with corresponding decreases and increases, respectively, in prepayment rates?

CONSOLIDATED STATEMENT OF CASH FLOWS

RAC Mortgage Investment Corporation
For the year ended December 31, 1988
(amounts in thousands)

Cash flows from operating activities:	
Net income	$10,165
Adjustments to reconcile net income to net cash provided by operating activities:	
Amortization of financing and organizational costs	141
Amortization of discounts on collateralized mortgage obligations	75
Amortization of discounts and premiums on mortgage loans and securities	(474)
Gain on sale of residual interests	(1,218)
Valuation adjustment—residual interest	1,287
Net increase in other assets and other payables	(3,154)
Increase in net interest accruals	1,085
Net cash provided by operating activities	7,907
Cash flows from investing activities:	
Proceeds from sale of mortgage loans	3,507
Proceeds from sale of residual interests	40,116
Principal reduction in mortgage loans and securities	47,321
Principal reduction in residual interests	6,505
Purchase of mortgage loans and securities, net of assumed collateralized mortgage obligations of $665,666	(347,866)
Purchase of residual interests	(157,436)
Net increase in funds held by trustees	(12,775)
Net cash from (used for) investing activities	(420,628)
Cash flows from financing activities:	
Proceeds from repurchase agreements and notes payable, net of repayments	281,010
Proceeds from issuance of collateralized mortgage obligations	53,500
Proceeds from public offerings of common stock	152,605
Dividends paid	(11,524)
Reductions in collateralized mortgage obligations	(42,634)
Net cash provided by financing activities	412,755
Net increase in cash	34
Cash at beginning of year	1
Cash at end of year	$ 35
Supplemental disclosures of cash flow information—cash paid for interest	$54,563

See accompanying notes to consolidated financial statements.

NOTES TO CONSOLIDATED FINANCIAL STATEMENTS

RAC Mortgage Investment Corporation
December 31, 1988
(amounts in thousands except share data)

Note 1
The Company

RAC Mortgage Investment Corporation (the "Company") was incorporated in Virginia on December 18, 1987, as a wholly owned subsidiary of Ryland Mortgage Company ("Ryland Mortgage"), which is a wholly owned subsidiary of The Ryland Group, Inc. At incorporation, 100 shares of the Company's common stock were issued to Ryland Mortgage at $10 per share. On February 18, 1988, the Company issued 2,700,000 shares of its common stock at $10 per share in the Company's initial public offering. In addition, on that date, the Company sold directly to Ryland Mortgage 300,000 shares of the Company's common stock at $9.30 per share, the initial public offering price net of underwriting discounts and commissions. As part of the initial public offering on March 18, 1988, the Company issued an additional 200,000 shares of its common stock at $10 per share in connection with the exercise of an over-allotment option by the underwriters of the Company's initial public offering. On September 30, 1988, the Company issued an additional 6,000,000 shares of its common stock at $9.75 per share. As part of this second offering, on October 31, 1988, the Company issued an additional 250,000 shares of its common stock at $9.75 per share in connection with the exercise of an over-allotment option by the underwriters of the Company's second public offering.

The Company's sole activities through December 31, 1987, consisted of the organization and start-up of the Company. The Company commenced operations on February 18, 1988, in connection with its initial public offering.

The Company has entered into a Management Agreement (the "Management Agreement") with Ryland Acceptance Corporation (the "Manager"), a wholly owned subsidiary of Ryland Mortgage (see note 9).

Note 2
Summary of Significant Accounting Policies

Basis of presentation

The consolidated financial statements include the accounts of the Company and its wholly owned subsidiary, RMIC Finance Co., and the accounts of RMIC Finance Co.'s wholly owned subsidiary, N.D. Holding Co. All significant intercompany balances and transactions have been eliminated in consolidation. Included in the consolidated balance sheet of the Company at December 31, 1988, are assets of $55,999 and liabilities of $52,984 held by RMIC Finance Co., and assets of $531,095 and liabilities of $518,541 held by N.D. Holding Co. Both of these companies are limited-purpose finance subsidiaries. These assets secure collateralized mortgage obligations ("CMO bonds") (see notes 3 and 5).

Federal income taxes

The Company will elect to be taxed as a real estate investment trust under the Internal Revenue Code. As a result, the Company generally will not be subject to federal income taxation at the corporate level to the extent it distributes annually at least 95 percent of its taxable income to its shareholders and complies with certain other requirements. The Company has met its distribution requirements for 1988 and, accordingly, no provision has been made for income taxes in the accompanying consolidated financial statements.

Real estate investments

Mortgage loans and securities are carried at their outstanding principal balances, plus any premium and net of any discount.

Residual interests represent the right to receive the excess of (i) the cash flow from the collateral pledged to secure CMO bonds, together with any reinvestment income thereon over (ii) the amount required for debt service payments on the CMO bonds, together with related administrative expenses.

CMO bonds and reinvestment earnings thereon are intended to be sufficient to make timely payments of interest on each series and to retire each class of such series by its stated maturity. Each series of bonds is subject to redemption according to specific terms of the respective indentures.

Mortgage loans and securities with an aggregate outstanding principal balance of $680,606 and funds of $12,775 collateralizing the CMO bonds are held by banks as trustees. Principal and interest payments on the mortgage loans and securities are received and retained by the trustees in collection accounts and together with reinvestment earnings thereon are used to make principal and interest payments on each series of CMO bonds pursuant to terms of the indentures.

Note 6
Repurchase Agreements and Notes Payable

As of December 31, 1988, the Company had entered into various repurchase agreements for total borrowings of $249,833. Of these borrowings, $227,564 had a weighted average annual rate of 10.52 percent, was due within thirty days and was secured by certain adjustable-rate mortgage certificates with an aggregate carrying value of $246,014 and market value of $247,079. The Company had also entered into various repurchase agreements for borrowings of $22,269 at a weighted average annual rate of 10.17 percent, due within thirty days and secured by certain residual interests with an aggregate carrying value of $46,930.

In April 1988, the Company entered into a warehousing credit and security agreement with a commercial bank for $100,000. The agreement has a term of one year. Amounts borrowed under this agreement bear interest at either a fixed- or floating-rate, are due on demand and are collateralized by a portion of the Company's mortgage loans not subject to CMO indebtedness. The Company may increase the line of credit up to $150,000 by giving thirty days notice to the bank. At December 31, 1988, the Company had borrowed $28,380 under the line of credit at an interest rate of 10.29 percent per annum and had pledged mortgage loans with an aggregate principal balance of $32,410 as collateral.

In June 1988, the Company entered into a credit agreement with a commercial bank for $25,000. The agreement can be terminated either with one hundred eighty days notice by the bank or sixty days notice by the Company. Amounts borrowed under this agreement bear interest at a fixed- or floating-rate, are due on demand and are secured by a portion of the Company's residual interests. On July 20, 1988, this agreement was amended to increase the credit available to the Company to $50,000. At December 31, 1988, the Company had pledged residual interests with an aggregate carrying value of $23,390 as collateral under this agreement and had outstanding borrowings of $2,797 under the line of credit at an interest rate of 11.0 percent per annum.

Note 7
Dividends

A dividend of $.11 per common share was declared December 19, 1988, payable on or about January 10, 1989, to stockholders of record on January 3, 1989. During 1988, the Company paid dividends of $11,524 ($1.23 per share) consisting of $10,405 ($1.11 per share) of ordinary income and $1,119 ($.12 per share) of capital gains. A dividend of $.08 per common share was declared January 19, 1989, payable on or about February 10, 1989, to stockholders of record on January 31, 1989.

Note 8
Stock Option Plan

The Company has adopted a stock option plan as a means of providing incentive compensation to the Manager. The stock option plan provides for the issuance to the Manager of options to purchase up to 410,000 shares of the Company's common stock at a price not less than the fair market value of the common stock at the time the option

is granted. The stock option plan also provides for dividend equivalent rights which permit the optionholder to obtain additional shares of common stock based upon formulae set forth in the stock option plan.

On February 8, 1988, the Company granted to the Manager options to acquire 405,000 shares of common stock at an exercise price of $10 per share. One-fifth of the options are exercisable annually beginning on February 8, 1989, and the options terminate on February 7, 1998.

Note 9
Other Matters

The Company has entered into a Management Agreement with the Manager under which the Manager advises the Company on various facets of its business and manages its day-to-day operations, subject to the supervision of the Company's Board of Directors. The Manager receives a base management fee and incentive compensation based upon certain specific levels of performance. These fees for the year ended December 31, 1988, amounted to $1,486, consisting of $464 of base management fee and $1,022 of incentive compensation.

In addition to the management fees, the Company paid to the Manager $165 for operating the Company's mortgage loan purchase program. The Company paid to the Manager $250 in connection with the start-up of the Company and $336 in administration fees on CMO bonds.

In the ordinary course of the Manager's business, its affiliates issue and administer CMO bonds. In the ordinary course of the Company's business, it acquires residual interests, including residual interests from various underwriters in which the underlying CMO bonds were issued by an affiliate of the Manager. During the year ended December 31, 1988, the Company acquired $101,140 of such residual interests and $548,635 principal balance of mortgage loans and securities subject to debt represented by CMO bonds issued and administered by affiliates of the Manager.

The Company has purchased residual interests from underwriters which do business with the Manager and its affiliates. During 1988, the Manager received $9,228 of aggregate issuance fees and an affiliate of the Manager earned $2,050 of administration fees from these underwriters, relative to all CMO bonds issued and administered by affiliates of the Manager, including CMO bonds in which the Company has no interest.

As of December 31, 1988, mortgage loans with an aggregate outstanding balance of $8,965 were serviced by an affiliate of the Manager. As of December 31, 1988, mortgage loans with an aggregate outstanding balance of $90,575 were serviced under a master servicing agreement by an affiliate of the Manager. Servicing fees were $57 during 1988.

In July 1988, the Company pledged $55,000 of mortgage loans as collateral for a CMO bond series issued by an affiliate of the Manager. In connection with the issuance of the CMO bonds, the Company received cash and issued a note payable of approximately $53,500.

Note 10
Subsequent Event

In January 1989, the Company committed to sell $50,000 of mortgage loans as collateral for a series of CMO bonds issued by an affiliate of the Manager on January 26, 1989. In connection with the issuance of this series of CMO bonds, the Company received cash and a residual interest with an approximate value of $629.

INDEPENDENT AUDITORS' REPORT

The Board of Directors
RAC Mortgage Investment Corporation:

We have audited the accompanying consolidated balance sheet of RAC Mortgage Investment Corporation and subsidiaries as of December 31, 1988, and the related consolidated statements of operations, shareholders' equity and cash flows for the year then ended. These consolidated financial statements are the responsibility of the Company's management. Our responsibility is to express an opinion on these consolidated financial statements based on our audit.

We conducted our audit in accordance with generally accepted auditing standards. Those standards require that we plan and perform the audit to obtain reasonable assurance about whether the financial statements are free of material misstatement. An audit includes examining, on a test basis, evidence supporting the amounts and disclosures in the financial statements. An audit also includes assessing the accounting principles used and significant estimates made by management, as well as evaluating the overall financial statement presentation. We believe that our audit provides a reasonable basis for our opinion.

In our opinion, the consolidated financial statements referred to above present fairly, in all material respects, the financial position of RAC Mortgage Investment Corporation and subsidiaries at December 31, 1988, and the results of their operations and their cash flows for the year then ended in conformity with generally accepted accounting principles.

PEAT MARWICK MAIN & CO.

Baltimore, Maryland
February 6, 1989

OFFICERS AND DIRECTORS

RAC Mortgage Investment Corporation

Officers

Thomas H. Potts
President

J. Sidney Davenport
Executive Vice President

Michael J. Sonnenfeld
Senior Vice President

Lynn M. Kells
Treasurer and Secretary

Officers (from left): Michael J. Sonnenfeld, J. Sidney Davenport, Lynn M. Kells, Thomas H. Potts

Directors

J. Sidney Davenport
Vice President
The Ryland Group, Inc.
Senior Vice President
Ryland Mortgage Company

Richard C. Levine
General Partner

Thomas H. Potts
Treasurer
The Ryland Group, Inc.
Vice President
Ryland Mortgage Company
Executive Vice President
Ryland Acceptance Corporation

Paul S. Reid
President and Chief Executive Officer
American Home Funding Corporation

Donald B. Axden
President
Johnson Mortgage Company

Directors (from left): Paul S. Reid, J. Sidney Davenport, Donald B. Axden, Thomas H. Potts. Not pictured: Richard C. Levine

CLIENT:
RAC MORTGAGE INVESTMENT CORPORATION

DESIGN FIRM:
PENELOPE STYGAR

ART DIRECTOR:
JAMES A. STYGAR

DESIGNER:
KRISTIN SEEBERGER

WRITER:
MICHAEL SONNENFELD

PRODUCTION MANAGER:
SHANNON SCARVEY

TYPOGRAPHER:
RIDDICK

PAPER SELECTION:
GOLDEN CASK DULL

PAPER MANUFACTURER:
KANZAKI

PRINTER:
WASHBURN PRESS

NUMBER OF PAGES:
24 PLUS COVER

SIZE:
8" X 11 1/2"

TYPE SELECTION:
BEMBO

SHERYL KURLAND, PUBLIC RELATIONS MANAGER, RAC MORTGAGE INVESTMENT CORPORATION, COLUMBIA, MARYLAND

The goal of our first annual report was to portray, illustrate, and explain the complex interest-rate relationship, and how a portfolio is directed by these figures. We had a committee of people working on the content of the report, including all of these complex and detailed figures. The Stygar Group managed to graphically convey this difficult information. We were satisfied with the report, especially since the information included would have been so complicated to follow without the graphic treatment.

PENELOPE STYGAR, STYGAR GROUP, INC. RICHMOND, VIRGINIA

For the RAC Mortgage Investment Corporation's first annual report, our greatest objective was to somehow find a way to clearly explain how their assets were invested. We needed a graphic device to show how the investments behaved in a complex financial structure with three types of assets. We chose color coding and simple graphs. We didn't want to use anything more complex, but the opportunity allowed us to also take a simple line and create a three-dimensional situation for the internal graphs. We needed to educate the investor, and we had a good reading on the response.

SHERYL KURLAND, PUBLIC RELATIONS MANAGER, RAC MORTGAGE INVESTMENT CORPORATION, COLUMBIA, MARYLAND

Ziel unseres ersten Jahresberichtes war die Darstellung der komplexen Zinssatzverhältnisse und ihres Einflusses auf bestimmte Geschäftsbereiche. Bei uns arbeitete ein Komitee am Inhalt des Berichtes, einschliesslich all der Zahlenangaben. Der Stygar-Gruppe ist es gelungen, diese komplexe Information graphisch darzustellen. Wir waren mit dem Bericht sehr zufrieden, besonders weil die darin enthaltenen Informationen ohne graphische Unterstützung sehr schwer verständlich gewesen wären.

PENELOPE STYGAR, STYGAR GROUP, INC., RICHMOND, VIRGINIA

Beim ersten Jahresbericht der RAC Mortgage Investment Corporation wollten wir darstellen, wie ihre Vermögenswerte investiert wurden. Wir brauchten ein graphisches Mittel, um zeigen zu können, wie sich ihre Investitionen innerhalb einer komplexen Finanzstruktur mit drei Arten von Vermögenswerten verhalten haben. Wir verwendeten eine Farbkodierung und einfache graphische Darstellungen. Anstelle von komplexeren Diagrammen verwendeten wir eine einfache Linie mit dreidimensionaler Wirkung. Die Reaktionen zeigten, dass der Bericht gelesen wurde.

SHERYL KURLAND, PUBLIC RELATIONS MANAGER, RAC MORTGAGE INVESTMENT CORPORATION, COLUMBIA, MARYLAND

Le but de notre premier rapport annuel était de décrire, d'illustrer et d'expliquer la réalité complexe qui gouverne les taux d'intérêt, et la manière dont ces chiffres dictent la constitution d'un portefeuille. Un comité s'est penché sur le contenu du rapport, y compris tous les chiffres y relatifs. Le Stygar Group a réussi à mettre cette somme d'informations sous une forme graphique attrayante. Ce rapport nous a satisfaits d'autant plus que l'information qui y est réunie aurait eu du mal à être assimilée sans son traitement graphique.

PENELOPE STYGAR, STYGAR GROUP, INC., RICHMOND, VIRGINIE

Pour le premier rapport annuel de la RAC Mortage Investment Corporation, nous avons considéré comme notre tâche essentielle de trouver moyen d'expliquer avec clarté la manière dont ses avoirs sont investis. Nous avions besoin d'un procédé graphique permettant de montrer le comportement de ces investissements au sein d'une structure financière complexe, sur la base de trois types d'actifs. Nous avons opté pour un code couleur et des graphiques simples. Nous avons évité le recours à des éléments sophistiqués. Il nous fallait instruire l'investisseur, et les réactions confirment que nous avons réussi.

THE REECE CORPORATION

On the cover and throughout this report are shown the end results of Reece products — high-quality dress and leisure wear which is bought and worn by men, women and children around the world.

For 108 years Reece has been a leading manufacturer, distributor and lessor of specialized machinery, related products and services to the worldwide clothing industry. Reece is known to apparel makers around the world for its automation of the manufacture of dress and leisure clothing for men, women and children.

Reece machines produce buttonholes, feed and sew buttons and other types of sewn fasteners, cut and stitch pockets, button shirts, bag finished garments, perform short stitching operations and blindstitch and serge many different garment parts. Reece also sells Japanese-made equipment in North and Latin America, which performs many operations in the garment assembly process. Various other products including shirt folding, specialized stitching, spreading and pressing equipment are distributed in local markets by the Company's European operations.

Reece has facilities in key locations to serve the needs of a changing international marketplace. Manufacturing facilities are located in Fall River, Massachusetts U.S.A.; Gorham, Maine U.S.A.; and Leiden, The Netherlands. Sales and service of products in the United States are directed by offices in Stantonsburg, North Carolina; Los Angeles, California; Dallas, Texas; and Bordentown, New Jersey and by a distribution center in Stantonsburg, North Carolina.

The Corporation also has a distribution center in Leiden, The Netherlands; sales and service operations in Canada, France, Hong Kong, India, West Germany, and the United Kingdom. An office in Miami, Florida U.S.A. directs Latin American marketing activities. Garment manufacturing centers in other areas of the world are covered by more than 50 independent distributors and dealers who both market and service products.

1

Financial Highlights

Dollars in thousands except per share amounts	1988	1987	1986
Total revenues	$59,570	$56,978	$55,281
Income before taxes	3,028	2,405	1,311
Net income	2,018	1,625	1,011
Net income per common share	.79	.64	.40

To Our Stockholders:

1988 was a year of continued progress financially and operationally. As shown in the table, revenues rose and reached the highest levels in the Company's history, just under $60 million. Earnings increased 24 percent, and the fourth quarter marked the 12th consecutive period of year-to-year earnings improvement. A complete summary, discussion and analysis of our financial results are included in this annual report beginning on page 13.

eece supplies an extensive range of specialized apparel manufacturing machinery, offering customers a variety of prices and features. Through product innovations and enhancements, such as those in our new lockstitch buttonhole machine and new pocket welting equipment, we help our customers improve productivity and keep pace with the changing demands of the apparel industry.

While the financial performance is gratifying, it tells only part of the story. The year saw continued improvement in virtually all facets of our operations, positioning us well for the years ahead. We also embarked on some exciting new activities which should benefit us in our mature markets.

2

Revenues and earnings rose as a result of higher pricing, more favorable product mix, and other factors, but unit orders for Reece-brand products actually declined slightly in 1988. Total orders for new and reconditioned machines were eight percent below the 1987 level as softness in demand developed in the U.S. market and our international markets grew more slowly than in prior years. It should be noted, however, that except for 1987, 1988 unit orders were higher than in any other year in the 80s.

eece has strategic marketing relationships with key overseas companies, strengthening its global growth opportunities. Our agreement with Aisin Seiki of Japan allows us to distribute Toyota-brand apparel equipment and market the TSS just-in-time sewn products manufacturing system in North and Latin America, renewing growth in the mature U.S. and Canadian markets.

Continuing Strength Abroad

Despite some slowing in growth, international orders were still four percent ahead of 1987's very strong levels, with most markets showing year-to-year gains. The greatest rise was registered in the Far East where orders grew 50 percent over 1987's level. Our Far East operation began serving the Hong Kong market directly in 1988 while maintaining its distributor network, an effort which yielded a significant sales improvement. At the same time the competitiveness of our U.S.-made products in such markets as Japan, Taiwan, South Korea and Singapore resulted in sharply higher sales, despite more aggressive dollar pricing which improved margins. We expect continued strength in this market as apparel-making shifts from established Far East sources to such developing areas as the Peoples Republic of China, the Philippines, Indonesia and Fiji.

Sharply lower sales of Reece's French subsidiary caused European orders in total to decline year-to-year. The domestic French apparel industry has been severely hurt by reduced consumer confidence and imports from low-wage countries. In addition, several unusually large orders received in 1987 from the French export market did not repeat in 1988.

5

The German company saw sharply higher demand in 1988, while unit sales in the United Kingdom dropped only marginally. Both markets were helped by the increased technical competitiveness of new product offerings and more favorable costs.

Unit sales in Latin America continued to rise both as a result of continued improvement in distribution and the sustained strength of the Caribbean market, a major exporter of apparel to the United States. As U.S. import restrictions threatened the Asian apparel industry in 1988, a number of Far East exporters started or expanded Caribbean production of apparel, further helping that region's machine demand.

The growth in Latin American and Far Eastern markets partly offset, and was in many ways responsible for, the continued decline in demand in the United States. U.S. demand had improved earlier in the year but then dropped sharply. However, we had an exceptionally strong fall trade exhibition which buoyed year-end shipments.

While imports of apparel to the U.S. have slowed, increased domestic production has not immediately translated into capital investment because of the availability of surplus capacity. In addition, the important U.S. jeans market has suffered from changing consumer tastes and overcapacity.

New Products Boost Growth

The introduction of several new products in 1988 aided unit sales in all markets. Our updated Series 32 chainstitch (non-bobbin) pocket welting machine was universally well received, and we are now increasing deliveries of the advanced, programmable lockstitch Series 48. The units, along with other pocket welting models, give Reece the broadest line in the highly competitive industry, offering a variety of price and feature levels.

In the eyelet-end buttonhole area, we introduced an enhanced Series 104 machine and demonstrated a prototype unit with electronic motor and controls. The latter unit, now on field test, provides increased reliability, flexibility and quieter operation, while the enhanced version offers performance improvements.

We also introduced a new automated bagging system which allows packaging of multiple garments in a single container to minimize theft, aid production control, and reduce customer

handling and distribution costs. The machine, currently made in Germany by the Wilfried Pavel Company, will eventually be produced at our Gorham, Maine U.S.A. plant from German and locally made and sourced components.

We also penetrated the shirt market with sales of our Mitchell line of buttonfeeders and related products, acquired at the end of 1987. Mitchell unit sales increased over historical levels, and only now are we introducing this line internationally. In addition, late in the year we introduced the AutoButtoner, a new shirt buttoner which speeds and eases a tedious finishing operation often subject to work-related injuries. The AutoButtoner is now being shipped to customers and has been the subject of keen industry interest. Later this year we shall begin international marketing of the unit.

uring 1988, sales reached the highest level in our Company's history and the fourth quarter marked our 12th consecutive quarter of year-to-year earnings improvement. As a reflection of this financial strength, the Company reinstated payment of dividends in 1988.

Our sales to the shirt market also will benefit from availability of the new S4 lockstitch buttonhole machine. This year will see increased shipments of the product and overseas placements. We expect the S4 to gain a solid foothold in this large market with its offer of high buttonhole quality, productivity advantages, and simplicity.

While the availability of these products will bolster short-term sales and competitiveness, we are aggressively pursuing future models and diversified product lines. In 1989 we expect to spend 25 percent more on research and development than was spent in 1988.

Marketing With Global Partners

Aside from our own internal efforts, we have established marketing relationships with a number of companies on product distribution and rights to equipment in development. Perhaps the most significant such relationship was the agreement last fall with Aisin Seiki of Japan. The agreement calls for distribution of Aisin's Toyota-brand apparel equipment in North

and Latin America. The high-quality Toyota machines broaden our offerings and, when coupled with our sales of Yamato-brand machines, give Reece nearly a full line in North America.

More importantly, Reece and Aisin will be marketing in North America and appropriate areas of Latin America Aisin's just-in-time (JIT) system for the sewn products industry. Based on the Toyota production system, the JIT process provides manufacturers with improved quality, flexibility, worker satisfaction and productivity, while reducing work-in-process, inventories and lead times.

eece continued its investment in its own plants in flexible manufacturing and just-in-time assembly during the year, enhancing cost efficiencies and productivity in our key business units. In 1989, this program will be expanded at the U.S. and Dutch plants.

Introduced in Japan in the late 1970s and successfully installed in some 300 different locations both within and outside Japan, the system offers opportunities for increased competitiveness by U.S. manufacturers. Since we announced the Reece-Aisin relationship last fall, we have encountered strong interest by U.S. manufacturers in the system and are now in active discussions on implementation. Sales of Toyota-brand machines are also accelerating.

The system, known as TSS (Toyota Sewing Management System), will help improve our domestic U.S. business as placements begin later in 1989. Moreover, TSS is opening up new markets beyond apparel such as health products, seat covers and furniture. Aisin and Reece also agreed to include Reece machines in TSS systems worldwide, jointly develop additional industrial sewing equipment and review marketing relationships in other regions.

Cost Efficiencies and Productivity Gains

Last year also saw continued progress in our restructuring efforts. With the softer U.S. demand, we further consolidated distribution and sales organizations. We also combined the

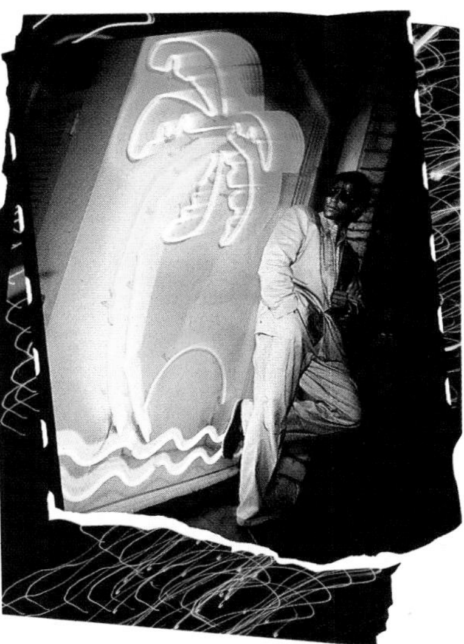

Quarterly Financial Information (Unaudited) — *The Reece Corporation*

Below is a summary of selected quarterly financial information for fiscal years 1988 and 1987 (dollars in thousands except per share amounts):

	Quarter First	Second	Third	Fourth	Year
Fiscal Year 1988					
Revenues:					
Machine and parts sales	$13,071	$13,962	$11,044	$14,338	$52,415
Rental, service and finance income	1,922	1,893	1,756	1,584	7,155
Total revenues	14,993	15,855	12,800	15,922	59,570
Costs and Expenses:					
Cost of sales	8,425	8,915	6,659	9,046	33,045
Operating expenses	5,684	5,711	5,496	5,332	22,223
Interest expense, net	320	321	283	273	1,197
Foreign exchange (gains) losses, net	77	15	25	(47)	70
Other (income) expense, net	29	5	3	(30)	7
Total costs and expenses	14,535	14,967	12,466	14,574	56,542
Income Before Provision for Income Taxes	458	888	334	1,348	3,028
Provision for Income Taxes	151	293	110	456	1,010
Net Income	$ 307	$ 595	$ 224	$ 892	$ 2,018
Net Income per Common Share	$ .12	$ .23	$ .09	$ .35	$ .79
Dividends Declared per Common Share	$ .05	$ .05	$ .05	$ .05	$ .20
Number of Shares Used in Computing Net Income per Common Share (000's)	2,542	2,548	2,549	2,552	2,549
Stock Price:					
High	$ 12½	$ 12¾	$ 12¼	$ 12⅞	$ 12⅞
Low	9⅜	10¾	11½	11⅝	9⅜
Fiscal Year 1987					
Revenues:					
Machine and parts sales	$11,126	$12,318	$11,803	$13,574	$48,821
Rental, service and finance income	2,082	2,045	1,927	2,103	8,157
Total revenues	13,208	14,363	13,730	15,677	56,978
Costs and Expenses:					
Cost of sales	7,398	7,890	7,684	8,829	31,801
Operating expenses	5,111	5,371	5,217	5,678	21,377
Interest expense, net	334	357	385	413	1,489
Foreign exchange (gains) losses, net	(54)	40	97	(123)	(40)
Other (income) expense, net	12	(54)	51	(63)	(54)
Total costs and expenses	12,801	13,604	13,434	14,734	54,573
Income Before Provision for Income Taxes	407	759	296	943	2,405
Provision for Income Taxes	134	251	97	298	780
Net Income	$ 273	$ 508	$ 199	$ 645	$ 1,625
Net Income per Common Share	$ .11	$ .20	$ .08	$ .25	$ .64
Dividends Declared per Common Share	$ —	$ —	$ —	$ —	$ —
Number of Shares Used in Computing Net Income per Common Share (000's)	2,532	2,545	2,556	2,543	2,545
Stock Price:					
High	$ 11⅝	$ 13	$ 15	$ 16	$ 16
Low	9⅛	11⅛	12	8¼	8¼

Consolidated Statements of Operations — *The Reece Corporation*
Fiscal Years 1988, 1987 and 1986

(Dollars in thousands except per share amounts)	Fiscal Year 1988	1987	1986
Revenues:			
Machine and parts sales	$52,415	$48,821	$45,994
Rental, service and finance income	7,155	8,157	9,287
Total revenues	59,570	56,978	55,281
Costs and Expenses:			
Cost of sales	33,045	31,801	31,775
Selling, rental and service expenses	17,881	17,169	15,390
General and administrative expenses	2,857	2,865	3,604
Product development and engineering expenses	1,485	1,343	1,479
Interest expense	1,321	1,538	1,747
Interest income	(124)	(49)	(53)
Foreign exchange (gains) losses, net	70	(40)	357
Other (income) expense, net (Note 11)	7	(54)	(329)
Total costs and expenses	56,542	54,573	53,970
Income Before Provision for Income Taxes	3,028	2,405	1,311
Provision for Income Taxes (Notes 2 and 6)	1,010	780	300
Net Income	$ 2,018	$ 1,625	$ 1,011
Net Income per Common Share (Note 2)	$ .79	$ .64	$ .40
Dividends Declared per Common Share	$ .20	$ —	$ —

Consolidated Statements of Stockholders' Equity
Fiscal Years 1988, 1987 and 1986

(Dollars in thousands)	Common Stock Issued at Par Value	Capital in Excess of Par Value	Retained Earnings	Cumulative Effects of Translation	Treasury Stock	Total Stockholders' Equity
Balance at December 28, 1985	$2,888	$2,686	$32,386	$(2,786)	$(3,732)	$31,442
Net income for 1986	—	—	1,011	—	—	1,011
Exercise of stock options	—	(54)	—	—	173	119
Translation adjustment	—	—	—	2,224	—	2,224
Balance at January 3, 1987	2,888	2,632	33,397	(562)	(3,559)	34,796
Net income for 1987	—	—	1,625	—	—	1,625
Exercise of stock options	—	(43)	—	—	139	96
Translation adjustment	—	—	—	2,897	—	2,897
Balance at January 2, 1988	2,888	2,589	35,022	2,335	(3,420)	39,414
Net income for 1988	—	—	2,018	—	—	2,018
Exercise of stock options	—	(87)	—	—	114	27
Translation adjustment	—	—	—	(1,362)	—	(1,362)
Payment of dividends on common stock	—	—	(502)	—	—	(502)
Balance at December 31, 1988	$2,888	$2,502	$36,538	$ 973	$(3,306)	$39,595

See notes to consolidated financial statements.

CLIENT:
REECE CORPORATION

DESIGN FIRM:
WEYMOUTH DESIGN

ART DIRECTOR:
TOM LAIDLAW

DESIGNER:
CORY FANELLI

PHOTOGRAPHERS:
MICHAEL WEYMOUTH, GEORGE SIMIAN

WRITER:
LEONARD EGAN

TYPOGRAPHER:
DANIELS

PAPER SELECTION:
REFLECTIONS, CONFETTI

PAPER MANUFACTURER:
CONSOLIDATED, LINWEAVE

PRINTER:
DANIELS

NUMBER OF PAGES:
36

DONALD BLOM, VICE PRESIDENT, FINANCE AND ADMINISTRATION AND CHIEF FINANCIAL OFFICER, THE REECE CORPORATION, WALTHAM, MASSACHUSETTS

The theme for The Reece Corporation's 1988 annual report was a portrayal of the final products done on our machines. We make sewing machines for the clothing industry, and each of the photographs features garments that our machines were used to make. We also wanted to have the annual report be representative of the different parts of the world where we are increasing our sales of equipment. The annual report showed all styles of apparel with this international flair. The company liked it since it was different and eye-catching. For some of our audience, it may have been a little oblique, because they asked why we didn't show our machines.

DONALD BLOM, VICE PRESIDENT, FINANCE AND ADMINISTRATION AND CHIEF FINANCIAL OFFICER, THE REECE CORPORATION, WALTHAM, MASSACHUSETTS

Thema für den Jahresbericht 1988 der Reece Corporation war die Darstellung der Endprodukte, die mit unseren Maschinen hergestellt werden. Wir machen Nähmaschinen für die Bekleidungsindustrie, und jede der Aufnahmen zeigt Kleidung, die auf unseren Maschinen hergestellt wurde. Wir wollten ausserdem, dass der Annual Report die verschiedenen Regionen der Welt berücksichtigt, in denen wir unsere Verkäufe gesteigert haben. Die im Jahresbericht gezeigten Kleidungsstile haben dieses internationale Flair. Unsere Firma war damit sehr zufrieden, weil es etwas Neues ist und ins Auge fällt. Für einige war dies vielleicht ein bisschen zu ungewöhnlich.

DONALD BLOM, VICE-PRESIDENT, FINANCE AND ADMINISTRATION AND CHIEF FINANCIAL OFFICER, THE REECE CORPORATION, WALTHAM, MASSACHUSETTS

Le thème du rapport annuel 1988 de la Reece Corporation était l'illustration des produits finis que nous réalisons sur nos machines. Nous fabriquons des machines à coudre pour l'industrie de l'habillement; or, chacune des photos du rapport présente un vêtement réalisé sur l'une de nos machines spécialisées. Nous voulions aussi donner une idée des différentes parties du monde où nous augmentons notre chiffre d'affaires. Le rapport a donc présenté tous ces styles de vêtement en les situant au plan international. La société a applaudi à ce rapport annuel parce qu'il était différent et qu'il accrochait l'attention. Il a néanmoins déconcerté certains de nos clients.

MICHAEL WEYMOUTH, WEYMOUTH DESIGN, BOSTON, MASSACHUSETTS

For the Reece Corporation 1988 annual report, we wanted to show that the company had changed management and had a new marketing and promotional thrust. We wanted to show their creative muscle, and to make a fashion statement, since the company's machines were used to create apparel all over the world. We put together layout boards, and we decided on this dynamic route to go with photographs, shot by two photographers, using location shots. The cover, for example, was done in Amsterdam with flash and ambient light. We also incorporated the look of neon into the design of the pages by using neon letters graphically in the text as initial caps. When we used these in four-color, we had to add a varnish. These created an excitement on the type pages. The chemistry created in this annual report was good. The company liked it a lot.

MICHAEL WEYMOUTH, WEYMOUTH DESIGN, BOSTON, MASSACHUSETTS

Im Jahresbericht 1988 der Reece Corporation wollten wir zeigen, dass es einen Wechsel in der Geschäftsleitung gegeben hatte und damit eine neue Marketing- und Werbepolitik. Wir wollten ihre kreative Seite zeigen und entschieden uns deshalb für Mode, denn die Maschinen der Firma werden überall in der Welt für die Herstellung von Kleidung eingesetzt. Wir machten ein Layout und beschlossen, die an Ort und Stelle entstandenen Aufnahmen von zwei Photographen zu verwenden. Der Umschlag zum Beispiel wurde in Amsterdam mit Blitzlicht und Strassenlicht gemacht. Wir übernahmen den Neon-Look auch im Design der Seiten, indem wir Neon-Buchstaben als Initialen des Textes verwendeten. Dadurch wurde auf den Textseiten eine gewisse Spannung erreicht. Die erzielte Stimmung ist sehr gut. Die Firma war sehr zufrieden.

MICHAEL WEYMOUTH, WEYMOUTH DESIGN, BOSTON, MASSACHUSETTS

Pour le rapport annuel 1988 de la Reece Corporation, nous avons voulu montrer que la société avait renouvelé ses organes dirigeants et faisait montre d'un dynamisme nouveau en matière de marketing et de promotion des ventes. Il fallait également souligner son potentiel créatif et délivrer un message de mode puisque les machines fabriquées par Reece servent à réaliser des vêtements aux quatre coins de la planète. Nous avons préparé nos maquettes et avons recruté deux photographes qui ont réalisé des prises de vues dynamiques sur les sites mêmes. C'est ainsi que la couverture a été faite à Amsterdam, au flash et sous éclairage ambiant. Nous avons aussi incorporé le néon dans le design des pages en utilisant des lettres néon pour en faire au plan graphique les capitales initiales. Le tout a animé les pages de texte. La société s'en est montrée enchantée.

REEVES

COMMUNICATIONS

CORPORATION

1988

ANNUAL

REPORT

Fiscal Years Ended June 30 (in millions, except amounts per share)	1988	1987	1986
Net sales and revenues from continuing operations	$105.5	$ 70.6	$ 92.0
Income from continuing operations	6.0	5.7	11.3
(Loss) from discontinued operations	–	–	(7.2)
Income from extraordinary item	2.3	.7	.9
Net income	8.3	6.4	5.0
Income (loss) per share			
Continuing operations	.47	.45	.89
Discontinued operations	–	–	(.57)
Extraordinary item	.18	.06	.07
Net income per share	$ .65	$ .51	$ .39
Total assets	$154.0	$139.8	$121.6
Shareholders' equity	$ 62.5	$ 54.0	$ 47.0

Reeves Communications Corporation creates, develops, and produces entertainment for television. It licenses these programs to network television, to the syndication market, to cable television, and to foreign markets. Reeves also provides television production and other communications services and facilities for the entertainment industry and corporate clients.

We are pleased to report that Fiscal 1988 was the third consecutive year of earnings growth for Reeves. More importantly, we believe that 1988 marks a significant breakthrough for Reeves with regard to the scope of the television programming which we have produced. Net income increased to $8,326,000 or $.65 per share, from $6,423,000 or $.51 per share, in 1987. Revenues increased from $70,575,000, in Fiscal 1987, to $105,530,000. This higher level of revenues reflects the recognition of a large initial syndication sale of 100 episodes of "Kate & Allie", our highly successful on-going television series. October 1988, marked the first showing of "Kate & Allie" in syndication. We are delighted to report that the rating success achieved in its initial outings on the CBS Television Network has carried over into the syndication marketplace. Of course, "Kate & Allie" continues on CBS in prime-time with new episodes reflecting the network's renewal for the 1988-89 season.

THE AWARD-WINNING "KATE & ALLIE", STARRING SUSAN SAINT JAMES AND JANE CURTIN, IS NOW IN ITS SIXTH ORIGINAL SEASON ON CBS WHILE THE 100 COMPLETED EPISODES RUN IN SYNDICATION.

This year the series will feature new and exciting developments–including Allie's (Jane Curtin) wedding! Reeves has established itself as a major supplier of network prime-time television programming with particular emphasis on comedy series such as "Kate & Allie" and "Gimme A Break" (which ran on NBC for six years). In recognition of this expertise, we currently have firm commitments for three new series. Production has begun on "A Doc's Life" for CBS which will air early in 1989 with an initial order of six episodes. We have begun the development of two new series ordered by ABC–each with an initial commitment of thirteen episodes. The first will be created and produced by Michael Leeson (a creator of "The Cosby Show") and the other is being developed by Mike Nichols. Another successful arena for Reeves has been the development and production of reality-based programming. Among our past accomplishments are the series, "In Search of...", "That's Incredible!", "Those Amazing Animals", and network national syndication for the 1989-90 television season. Another arena of great potential for Reeves is that of advertiser-supported programming. We have recently formed a new division to capitalize on the clearly aggressive programming role being played by advertisers and marketers. The new division will concentrate primarily on the areas of basic cable, first-run syndication, international barter, and home video. We have now developed a significantly enhanced capability for foreign distribution in what is becoming an increasingly important marketplace. We will aggressively seek to acquire product from third parties to distribute together with our own library, which is expanding in size and increasing in value. We expect significant financial benefits to accrue from our foreign distribution. We continue to take great pride in our creative team which is capable of developing and producing a variety of television programming to meet the changing needs of the television industry.

AFTER SIX YEARS ON THE NBC TELEVISION NETWORK, THE 137 EPISODES OF THE HIT COMEDY SERIES "GIMME A BREAK", STARRING NELL CARTER, ARE NOW RUNNING IN SYNDICATION.

"ON TRIAL", A DAILY HALF-HOUR SHOW UTILIZING ACTUAL COURTROOM TAPE AND "LIFE'S MOST EMBARRASSING MOMENTS", A WEEKLY HALF-HOUR SPECIAL, MARK REEVES' INITIAL INVOLVEMENT IN FIRST-RUN SYNDICATION.

We are confident that our ability to identify and respond to the opportunities that present themselves in this ever-changing marketplace will assure that Reeves continues as a successful producer of television programming in future years. We would like to express our appreciation to all of the members of the Reeves organization for their outstanding effort. Sincerely, November 20, 1988

MARVIN H. GREEN, JR.	MERRILL GRANT
CHAIRMAN OF THE BOARD AND CHIEF EXECUTIVE OFFICER	PRESIDENT AND CHIEF OPERATING OFFICER

Management's Discussion and Analysis of Financial Condition and Results of Operations.

The following discussion reviews the operations and financial position of the continuing operations of Reeves Communications Corporation (RCC). The discontinued direct marketing operations are discussed in Note 2 of the Notes to Consolidated Financial Statements.

Liquidity and Capital Resources

Working Capital

The following table sets out the working capital (current assets less current liabilities) and the working capital ratio (current assets to current liabilities).

As at June 30 ($000's)	1988	1987	1986	1985	1984
Working capital	$33,293	$27,214	$14,391	$ 4,680	$13,164
Working capital ratio	2.7:1	2.2:1	1.6:1	1.2:1	1.8:1

Television production is in large part funded by the three major networks. It is not until these productions are released for foreign and domestic syndication that they begin to add to RCC's working capital. In 1988, the working capital increase came primarily from the syndication of the series "Kate and Allie". In 1987, the working capital increase was primarily the result of long-term syndication receivables which became current. In 1986, working capital increases came primarily from the syndication of the series "Gimme A Break", from the receipt of distribution advances and from the sales of production and post-production facilities. Most of these funds were used to reduce long-term debt.

Leverage

The following table shows the percentage of long term debt to equity and the number of times the existing interest charge is covered by earnings:

	1988	1987	1986	1985	1984
Long-term debt to equity	51%	65%	66%	146%	68%
Income before interest and taxes to interest expense	2.8	2.4	5.0	1.5	4.6

RCC's debt to equity percentage declined in 1988 principally due to collections of syndication receivables which were used to reduce long term debt. The debt to equity percentage declined significantly in 1986 as funds provided by continuing operations, including distribution advances, combined with proceeds from disposals of assets enabled the Company to reduce long-term debt substantially.

Profitability

	1988	1987	1986	1985	1984
Return on equity plus long-term debt	6%	6%	14%	2%	5%
Return on equity	10%	11%	24%	5%	9%
Return on sales	6%	8%	12%	3%	11%

Profitability percentages declined slightly in 1988 as a greater number of programs were delivered without anticipated future syndication revenues. Profitability percentages increased in 1986 but declined in 1987 primarily due to higher revenues generating better profit margins from the initial syndication of "Gimme A Break" in 1986.

Results of Operations

A five year summary of sales and operating income for the continuing operations follows:

($000's)	1988	1987	1986	1985	1984
Net sales and revenues	$105,530	$70,575	$92,010	$73,202	$27,654
Operating income	10,329	6,795	13,858	3,625	11,634

Revenues in 1988 include the initial syndication sales of 100 episodes from the series "Kate & Allie" and the syndication of the last 25 episodes from the series "Gimme A Break". Revenues in 1987 include results of the syndication of 24 episodes from "Gimme A Break", as compared to the series' initial syndication sales of 88 episodes included in 1986. In addition, 1987 operating income included a fourth quarter provision of $800,000 for potentially uncollectible accounts receivable from syndication sales.

Interest

The following table shows interest expense and average interest rate for the past five years:

($000's)	1988	1987	1986	1985	1984
Interest	$ 4,730	$ 4,740	$ 3,173	$ 3,360	$ 2,842
Average interest rate on borrowed funds	9.4%	8.9%	9.3%	11.9%	12.4%

Interest expense remained substantially unchanged in 1988 as the benefit of lower borrowings was offset by higher rates. Interest expense increased in 1987 primarily as a result of recording imputed interest applicable to distribution advances. Interest rates were lower during 1986 and long-term obligations were substantially reduced with funds provided by distribution advances and proceeds from the sales of production and post production facilities. The effects of these reductions were largely offset by interest applicable to debt which had been part of discontinued operations in prior years.

Income Taxes

The effective tax rate over the last five years is as follows:

	1988	1987	1986	1985	1984
Effective tax rate	30%	15%	11%	(45%)	18%

The effective rate increased in 1988 despite the drop in the federal statutory rate (from 46% to 34%) as the Tax Reform Act of 1986 substantially reduced the availability of investment tax credits and carryforwards. The Financial Accounting Standards Board has issued a statement which will change the accounting for income taxes effective for fiscal years beginning after December 15, 1988. The Company does not expect the adoption of this pronouncement to have a material effect on its financial position. Low effective rates in 1987 and 1986 were due to the utilization of investment tax credits. The benefit in 1985 was primarily the result of the reversal of deferred tax credits due to net operating losses.

Consolidated Statements of Income

Years Ended June 30 (in thousands, except per share amounts)	1988	1987	1986
Net sales and revenues	$105,530	$ 70,575	$ 92,010
Costs and expenses:			
Cost of sales	84,636	53,060	67,811
Selling, general and administrative expenses	10,065	9,591	10,119
Provision for doubtful accounts	500	1,127	222
	95,201	63,780	78,152
Operating income	10,329	6,795	13,858
Other income (expense):			
Interest (expense), net	(1,602)	(246)	(1,136)
Other	(86)	123	(15)
	(1,688)	(123)	(1,151)
Income from continuing operations before income taxes	8,641	6,672	12,707
Provision for income taxes	2,601	969	1,398
Income from continuing operations	6,040	5,703	11,309
(Loss) from discontinued operations	–	–	(7,200)
Income before extraordinary item	6,040	5,703	4,109
Extraordinary item–tax benefit resulting from utilization of net operating loss carryforward	2,286	720	851
Net income	$ 8,326	$ 6,423	$ 4,960
Continuing operations	$ 0.47	$ 0.45	$ 0.89
Discontinued operations	0.00	0.00	(0.57)
Extraordinary item	0.18	0.06	0.07
Net income per share	$ 0.65	$ 0.51	$ 0.39

Consolidated Statements of Retained Earnings/Deficit

Years Ended June 30 (in thousands)	1988	1987	1986
Balance at beginning of year	$ (6,876)	$ (13,299)	$(18,259)
Net income	8,326	6,423	4,960
Balance at end of year	$ 1,450	$ (6,876)	$(13,299)

See accompanying notes to consolidated financial statements.

Directors and Officers

Directors

Marvin H. Green, Jr.
Chairman of the Board,
and Chief Executive Officer

Henry D. Clarke, Jr.
Chairman and
Chief Executive Officer
Clabir Corporation

Anthony A. Greener
Managing Director of
United Distillers Group

H.R. Hoyt
Founder of H.R. Hoyt Inc.

Jeanne Hoyt Olinger
President of H.R. Hoyt, Inc.

Wendell M. Smith
President and
Chief Executive Officer
Baldwin Technology Corporation

Coen Solleveld
Former President of the
International Federation
of Phonogram and Videogram
Producers
Former President and
Chief Executive Officer
of the Polygram Group

Officers

Marvin H. Green, Jr.
Chairman of the Board,
and Chief Executive Officer

Merrill Grant
President and
Chief Operating Officer

William A. Wetzel
Executive Vice President
Chief Administrative Officer,
Secretary

Richard S. Reisberg
Senior Vice President

Simon Lazowsky
Vice President
Controller

Transfer Agent

Harris Trust Company
of New York
110 William Street
New York, NY 10038

Auditors

Peat Marwick Main & Co.
345 Park Avenue
New York, NY 10154

Counsel

Coudert Brothers
200 Park Avenue
New York, NY 10166

Form 10-K

Form 10-K, filed with the Securities and Exchange Commission, is available without charge upon written request to Reeves Communications Corporation.

Reeves
Communications
Corporation
Executive Offices

708 Third Avenue
New York, NY 10017
212 573-8600

Special thanks to Arnold L. Chase and the American Museum of the Moving Image for allowing Reeves Communications Corporation to photograph the Philco Predicta Tandem 1959 (page 2) and RCA Victor 1959 (page 3) television sets for this annual report.

Design: Frankfurt Gips Balkind/NY
Photography: Paul Stevens, Televisions
Michael Melford, Executives

CLIENT:
REEVES COMMUNICATIONS CORPORATION

DESIGN FIRM:
FRANKFURT GIPS BALKIND

ART DIRECTOR:
AUBREY BALKIND

DESIGNER:
DAVID SUH

PHOTOGRAPHERS:
PAUL STEVENS, MICHAEL MELFORD

WRITER:
REEVES COMMUNICATIONS CORPORATION

TYPOGRAPHER:
FRANKFURT GIPS BALKIND

PAPER SELECTION:
PAGEANTRY WHITE VELLUM 80LB

PAPER MANUFACTURER:
CHAMPION

PRINTER:
LEBANON VALLEY OFFSET

NUMBER OF PAGES:
24 PLUS COVER

WILLIAM A. WETZEL, EXECUTIVE VICE-PRESIDENT, CHIEF ADMINISTRATIVE OFFICER, SECRETARY, REEVES COMMUNICATIONS CORPORATION, NEW YORK, NEW YORK

For our 1988 annual report, we had one main objective: To demonstrate that Reeves Communications was a serious and important player in television and production. The company had gone through an evolution, and we wanted to show the basic corporation here with substantive, completed projects, and our future. We're very pleased with the design work of Frankfurt Gips Balkind, because this theme was captured in the annual report while capturing a sense of the historical changes in television and highlighting shots from our shows. The response we had to this annual report was positive.

AUBREY BALKIND, FRANKFURT GIPS BALKIND, NEW YORK, NEW YORK

Reeves Communications Corporation had streamlined its business. They wanted to show the company as not as glitzy as it had been. We usually can do what we like creatively, and we devised our concept around television sets–these relate to everybody. Much of the company's business revolves around situation comedies for television, so we featured these productions, and we interspersed text on these programs in a contrasting color throughout the type treatment of the message to the shareholders. This report is understandable; it gets its message across easily.

WILLIAM A. WETZEL, EXECUTIVE VICE-PRESIDENT, CHIEF ADMINISTRATIVE OFFICER, SECRETARY, REEVES COMMUNICATIONS CORPORATION, NEW YORK, NEW YORK

Beim Geschäftsbericht für 1988 ging es um ein Hauptanliegen: zu zeigen, dass Reeves Communications ein seriöser und wichtiger Fernsehproduzent ist. Das Unternehmen war gestrafft worden, und wir wollten im Bericht die Basis sowie die wichtigsten fertigen Produktionen und die Zukunftspläne zeigen. Wir waren mit der Arbeit von Frankfurt Gips Balkind sehr zufrieden, weil das Thema im Geschäftsbericht zum Ausdruck kommt, wie auch die historischen Veränderungen auf dem Gebiet des Fernsehens und weil Aufnahmen unserer Shows gezeigt werden. Die Reaktionen waren positiv.

AUBREY BALKIND, FRANKFURT GIPS BALKIND, NEW YORK, NEW YORK

Reeves Communications Corporation hatte rationalisiert. Sie wollten zeigen, dass die Firma nicht mehr so glamourös wie einst ist. Unser Konzept basierte auf TV-Geräten, weil jeder damit etwas anfangen kann. Viele der TV-Produktionen der Firma haben mit Situationskomik zu tun, wir zeigten deshalb etwas aus ihren Produktionen, und in der Botschaft an die Aktionäre wurden in einer Kontrastfarbe immer wieder auf Produktionen bezogene Texte eingestreut. Dieser Bericht ist leicht verständlich, und die Botschaft kommt gut zum Ausdruck.

WILLIAM A. WETZEL, EXECUTIVE VICE-PRESIDENT, CHIEF ADMINISTRATIVE OFFICER, SECRETARY, REEVES COMMUNICATIONS CORPORATION, NEW YORK, NEW YORK

Pour notre rapport annuel 1988, nous avions un objectif principal en vue: démontrer que Reeves Communications joue un rôle sérieux et important dans le domaine de la télévision et de la production. La société avait évolué, et nous entendions présenter ses activités de base à travers d'importants projets achevés tout en ouvrant des perspectives sur l'avenir. Nous aimons bien la manière de Frankfurt Gips Balkind qui ont su incarner ce thème dans le rapport annuel et rendre compte de l'évolution historique de la télévision à travers des photos choisies de nos émissions. Les réactions étaient positives.

AUBREY BALKIND, FRANKFURT GIPS BALKIND, NEW YORK, NEW YORK

La Reeves Communications Corporation a rationalisé ses opérations, d'où le besoin de débarrasser l'entreprise de son image clinquante du passé. Nous avons situé sur l'axe central de notre conception ces postes de télévision qui sont si familiers au grand nombre. La plus grande partie des activités de la société est consacrée aux comédies de situation pour la TV. Nous avons donc mis en vedette ces productions en y entremêlant des commentaires en couleurs contrastantes tout au long du message adressé aux actionnaires. Le message a passé aisément.

RHODE · ISLAND · SCHOOL · OF · DESIGN

ANNUAL
REPORT
AND
DONOR
LISTING
1987–88

RHODE · ISLAND · SCHOOL · OF · DESIGN

RHODE · ISLAND · SCHOOL · OF · DESIGN

RHODE · ISLAND · SCHOOL · OF · DESIGN

RHODE ISLAND SCHOOL OF DESIGN

USPS 075-040
Volume 75 Number 3 December 1988
Issues of *Rhode Island School of Design* are published five times a year in September, October, December, March, and August by the Office of Publications, Rhode Island School of Design, Two College Street, Providence, Rhode Island 02903.

Postmaster: Please send address changes to the Development Office, Rhode Island School of Design, Two College Street, Providence, Rhode Island 02903

Editor: Thomas C. Pautler

Printing: Cogens Printing Services, Inc.

Paper: Strathmore Americana, Warren Lustro Dull.

Creative Direction: Tyler Smith ('66)
Tyler Smith is an art director and graphic designer in Providence. He has won numerous national and international graphic design awards, including a gold and silver medal from the New York Art Director's Club. Feature articles on his work have appeared in *Communication Arts, Art Direction, Photo/Design* and *Print* Magazines.

Illustration: Emily Lisker ('86)
Emily Lisker is an illustrator living in Providence. A 1986 RISD graduate in painting, her illustrations have appeared in *The Boston Globe, The Kansas City Star, The Providence Journal, Rhode Island Monthly, Psychology Today* and *Print's Regional Design Annual.*

PREFACE

Leadership is essential to progress. The fact of RISD's steady growth and fiscal stability is certain testimony to the leadership of President Thomas F. Schutte during his first five years at this institution.

This publication highlights the accomplishments of President Schutte and is a tribute to all those who have given their time and treasure in support of RISD.

CONTENTS

A NEW SPIRIT

Shortly after his arrival at RISD in late summer of 1983, Thomas F. Schutte began the practice of taking several meals each week at the Metcalf Refectory. RISD students were amazed that the College's new president would immediately make himself so visible and accessible. On these occasions, he listened attentively to student viewpoints and concerns, gaining a deeper understanding of the opportunities and problems he would encounter as the institution's sixth president. Recognizing that RISD's most important resources were its students and its faculty, he began meeting on a regular basis with faculty, staff, and with alumni as well. This eagerness to listen and respond heralded the new president's role as a communicator and conciliator who would bring together and involve all members of the RISD community. For an institution previously fractured by confrontation and conflict, this approach represented a new spirit. Five years later, Tom Schutte continues to impress believers and skeptics alike with his considered approach to problem solving, balanced by an exuberance in embracing new ideas and making things happen.

From his early planning sessions with groups throughout the RISD community, Tom Schutte constructed a lengthy agenda of major issues and challenges: explore new ways to reach, communicate with, and involve faculty; energize the fund raising programs for the College and Museum; set priorities for new construction and expansion of academic areas, student residences, and the Museum of Art; strengthen and broaden the institution's investment and endowment activities; simultaneously soothe and invigorate a largely uninvolved alumni constituency; visit and assess the European Honors Program in Rome; experiment with new ways to recruit students, with emphasis on minorities. Maintain traditions; create new ones. Reach out. Restore. Renew. Stretch. Solve. Mediate. Energize.

Space and Facilities

Responding to RISD's chronic shortage of academic and student residence space, Tom Schutte moved quickly to win trustee approval of building renovation and construction projects totalling $17.2 million. At the board's December 1984 meeting, plans were approved for a complex that would consolidate four buildings (two of them historic) located between Canal and North Main Streets, restored and updated to yield 54,400 net square feet of space. To be called the Design Center, it would house the departments of graphic design, photography, and graduate studies, in addition to headquarters for Continuing Education, the academic computer center, galleries for the exhibition of student work, and a gleaming new book and supply store. The second major project included provisions for additional student housing, dining, social, and work spaces — together forming a quadrangle-type enclosure and constructed in and around the existing residence/refectory complex bounded by Angell, Benefit, and Waterman Streets. Construction for the new Design Center, designed by Ellenzweig, Moore and Associates and constructed by Gilbane Company, and the Residence Life complex, designed by William D. Warner and built by the

Dimeo Construction Company, was completed in late 1986. Many individuals, corporations, and foundations supported these important campus projects through major gifts to RISD: Fleet National Bank, the Koffler Family Foundation, Kresge Foundation, June Rockwell Levy Foundation, the Metcalf Family, Ocean State Charitable Trust, Old Stone Charitable Foundation, Pew Memorial Trust, Prince Charitable Trusts, Providence Journal Company, Rhode Island Foundation, and James and Gloria Winston.

The final project to be completed in the residence complex was the Catanzaro Student Center, funded by Robert and Marjorie Catanzaro, which formally opened on September 16, 1988 with a school-wide celebration. Ingeniously created from space under the Refectory, the interior, designed by architecture professor James Barnes, includes spaces for club meetings, dance and aerobics, weightlifting, and music practice in soundproof surroundings. Furniture was provided by a gift from the Class of 1988. The student newspaper, *The RISD Voice*, pronounced the center an instant success "especially after dinner and on weekends... [not] just for the weights or the dance floor... [but] to study in the quiet of the main hall."

In addition, renovations had begun on Benson Hall to transform the former home of the photography department into a state-of-the-art printmaking facility with 3,000 square feet of additional space and a special HVAC system to improve ventilation.

With added beauty and enhanced security as its goals, a 10-year program was begun in 1986 to improve campus grounds, upgrade lighting and illumination, and unify campus building signage. Participating in the project were Associate Professor Michael Everett and Everett Associates, Associate Professor Colgate Searle (of Searle & Searle), and part-time faculty member Sara Bradford. Trees donated by the Class of 1986 were planted on Benefit and Prospect Streets, and the entire Residence Life complex was landscaped. New lighting was installed and a campus-wide signage system designed by Malcolm Grear Associates helped to unify RISD's 41 campus buildings.

Toward Better Planning

In August of 1986, Tom Schutte announced the formation of a Strategic Planning Committee — comprising students, faculty, administrators, and trustees — charged with producing a comprehensive series of recommendations on RISD's goals, priorities, and direction. A planning model was adopted that consisted of five phases conceived as consecutive stages of the process: research, analysis, community review, decision making and implementation, and evaluation. By August 1988, the 13-member committee had created a 31-page "interim" report, incorporating the first four stages with observations and suggestions on governance, academic organization, curriculum, financial development, faculty, students, human resources, physical plant and equipment, the Museum, continuing education, and community involvement. The fifth stage would continue indefinitely and become integrated into the management and governance structure of the College. A final report is due to be issued by early 1989.

Calling it "a significant step in RISD's long-range educational space planning and a reflection of the school's commitment to the downtown Providence community," President Schutte announced, on March 31, 1988, that RISD had acquired the Providence-Washington Insurance Company's huge headquarters building on North Main Street between Waterman and Steeple Streets. RISD paid $8.2 million for the 40-year-old structure and then immediately leased it back to the insurance company for a five-year term. Within this time, RISD will complete an overall campus space plan that will include specific use and adaptation of the building's approximately 89,000 gross square feet of space. The purchase was financed through asset reallocation of RISD's endowment, converting some of the portfolio's securities to real estate. The net lease to the insurance company will yield a favorable income return to RISD's endowment. Looking ahead to the renaissance of the Providence waterfront, board chairman Sidney F. Greenwald noted that this provides a cornerstone for future planning: "As the Providence River relocation proceeds, the campus will form an attractive, vibrant, and functioning area along the river from Market House to the south, to Providence-Washington on the north. This will reenforce the school's presence in the area of the new Capital Center and River Relocation projects now underway in the downtown area."

A Challenge From Washington

"We're on a roll... the NEA has extraordinary confidence in RISD as the leading art and design school in the country." The September 10, 1986 edition of the *Providence Journal* was quoting President Schutte in its announcement that RISD had been awarded a $1-million "challenge grant" from the National Endowment for the Arts (NEA) in Washington —the largest grant ever awarded to a school of art and design. "Such grants," explained U.S. Senator Claiborne Pell, who had proposed the legislation to create the NEA, "are special... they are given only once a year after the most intensive review, and are given only to institutions of the highest artistic caliber." The grant would establish a $4-million cash reserve fund, income from which would go toward stipends and grants for faculty research, travel, and commission work; to bring expert critics to campus; and to provide scholarships for minority students. The provisions of the grant stipulated that RISD must raise three additional dollars for every NEA dollar it received — with a deadline of June 30, 1990.

Further Enrichment and Support

Two particularly sensitive issues were addressed during the summer of 1988: supplementary financial support for faculty projects, and funding for student scholarships. By early October, Tom Schutte had announced that the Finance Committee had authorized the establishment of RISD's first endowed Faculty Development Fund, for $300,000. The interest income from this permanent endowment will be restricted solely to the funding of professional development projects for faculty and Museum curators. He also announced the approval of a new $500,000 scholarship trust fund, interest from which would go toward additional student scholarships.

More and Better Students

While RISD's distinctive attributes have always enabled it to attract exceptional student talent, in each year's applicant pool, the school's fortunes in this vital area continue to improve. For each of the past five years, student applications have increased in quality and quantity, and the acceptance rate stands at a record low figure of just 30 percent of applications received. Approximately 31 percent of the freshmen admitted in 1988 came from outside New England, compared with 24.5 percent in 1983. RISD's student body is both more national and more international than ever before, including students from 49 states and 48 countries. To maintain a stable enrollment, Tom Schutte significantly reduced the growth rate of the student body, limiting to 150 the number of students added to overall yearly enrollment during the last six years — a 1.4 percent yearly growth rate.

Students Who Care

Student activities in recent years have reflected an increasing concern for community involvement on their part, with participation ranging from class projects wherein students assist homeless political refugees, to the design and creation of architectural models for the proposed Providence convention center. Student concerns about tuition increases prompted dialogues with administration and faculty relative to the factors behind those costs. This motivated students to participate as callers in alumni phonathons that were held to raise funds for student financial aid.

Alumni Growth

During the October 1986 Alumni Reunion Weekend, President Schutte presided at the reading of a proclamation dedicating the structure at 52 Angell Street (originally the Judson Blake House) as the RISD Alumni House, recognizing the tremendous growth and influence of RISD's enormously accomplished alumni constituency. This "dedicated space" on campus would, the president added, officially acknowledge the alumni role and presence — both on-campus and off. Although currently serving as the College's designated alumni headquarters, the facility will eventually undergo renovation and repair. Future plans call for office space, a meeting and conference room, and a gallery for exhibition of alumni work.

When not on the Providence campus, Tom Schutte could most likely be found visiting alumni groups around the country. This year's round of receptions occurred as part of the $1-million Alumni Challenge Campaign, with visits to Seattle, San Francisco, Los Angeles, Atlanta, New York, Washington, and Chicago.

Other alumni milestones included a major exhibit of alumni work, *44 Alumni*, which appeared in the Museum's main gallery during the fall and winter of 1985 — the first show in the Museum's history dedicated exclusively to RISD alumni. Alumni auctions continued to raise money for student scholarships, with total proceeds of approximately $28,000 generated from events held in May of 1986 and October of 1988. These auctions were enhanced by works donated through the generosity of such alumni as Eric Javits ('78), Adrienne Kornstein ('79), Nicole Miller ('73), Steven Branfman ('75), Geoffrey Pagen ('75), Donald Friedlich ('82), Dale Chihuly ('68), and Elizabeth Pannell ('81), to name just a few.

1986 exhibition *Eden of America, Rhode Island Landscapes 1820–1920* in late winter of that year. While critics raved, thousands of visitors lined up to see impressive canvases that featured scenes of Newport coastlines, crashing breakers at Narragansett, and a winding path at Sakonnet Point, among many others. Edward M. Bannister, George Bellows, William Glackens, Childe Hassam, and John LaFarge were among those artists whose works appeared in the show.

In January of this year, Museum Director Frank Robinson expressed his gratitude to Fleet National Bank for its sponsorship of *1900 to Now: Modern Art from Rhode Island Collections*, an exhibition comprising examples of the major aesthetic movements of the past 87 years. The exhibition included paintings, sculpture, prints, drawings, photographs, costumes and textiles, and decorative arts — 290 works by over 250 artists.

Reaching for yet a larger audience, the Museum was able to share many of its riches with viewers in New York City this past summer, through the generosity of the IBM Corporation. On view at the IBM Gallery of Science and Art on Madison Avenue was the exhibition, *Highlights from the Collection of the Museum of Art, Rhode Island School of Design* (July 5 through September 10). Attendance figures for this attraction set a record for an art exhibit at the gallery, with a final count of over 110,000 visitors in just 10 weeks. Works from the Museum's permanent collection of 18th, 19th, and 20th century painting and sculpture were on view.

A Focus on Positive Change

Despite the substantial innovations and advances that have marked Tom Schutte's five years at RISD, he would be the first to point out that much remains to be done: increase alumni involvement, reduce faculty course loads, "fine tune" the institution's administrative structure, proceed with planning for a new Museum wing to accommodate additional galleries and storage spaces, oversee a systematic review of the curriculum, pursue new courses of funding for student scholarship assistance and faculty projects. These are challenges, however, that this president obviously relishes, knowing that RISD has grown in strength and resources under his leadership and is in a solid position to confront — and control — its future. ☐

FUND RAISING REPORT 1987–1988

The most outstanding achievements of 1987–1988 were in the area of annual support. The College Annual Fund exceeded its goal, raising $280,653 — an 18 percent increase in one year. The growth came both in the number of donors (243 more alumni and 285 more parents) and in the size of gifts. This is particularly encouraging since increased annual support is an essential part of RISD's continuing strength. Rhode Island School of Design will need at least $1,000,000 per year in annual gifts by 1995 in order to adequately support operating needs.

The Museum Annual Giving Program also achieved a new record of gift support — $411,969 — a nine-percent increase over 1986–87. Important elements of this growth include the special fund raiser "Eat Your Art Out Again," which raised over $22,000; and the Collectors' Club, which increased both the number and size of donations to add nearly $17,000 in new and increased gifts.

The Museum was also the recipient of a very generous bequest from former Providence resident Donald Mabey, as well as numerous grants for catalogs and exhibits. The Institute for Museum Services renewed its support for the Museum of Art, adding $75,000 to the total grants received.

As of June 30, gifts and pledges toward the National Endowment for the Arts challenge grant total $1,646,039. RISD must raise an additional $1,353,961 before June 30, 1990 in order to secure the million-dollar trust fund pledged by the NEA. Meeting that goal will be our top priority in the year ahead. When established, the fund will support student scholarships, faculty development, visiting scholars and critics, and graduate assistantships. Rhode Island School of Design is the first and only school of its kind to receive a million-dollar NEA challenge grant.

Corporate support has also been extremely important during the past year and holds great promise for the future. Fleet National Bank made a generous contribution to underwrite a major Museum show, *1900 to Now: Modern Art from Rhode Island Collections*, resulting in a very successful collaboration of two of Rhode Island's leading institutions, Fleet and RISD. IBM also collaborated with the Museum of Art to produce an exceptionally well-received show in its Gallery of Science and Art in New York City. *Eighteenth to Twentieth Century European and American Painting and Sculpture: Highlights from the Collection of the Museum of Art* was visited by over 110,000 people during its ten-week engagement. IBM also underwrote production of a new Museum Handbook.

It is extremely gratifying for RISD to receive the recognition and appreciation implied by this generous support. We, in turn, are grateful to our many donors and volunteers for their willingness to invest in RISD. With your help we can aspire to do even more.

Sidney F. Greenwald
Chairman, Board of Trustees

GIFTS AND GRANTS

Gifts for Annual Operations	1987	**1988**
College Fund	$ 238,518	**$ 280,653**
Museum Annual Giving Program	377,456	**411,969**
Museum — Government Grants	136,890	**67,660**
Gifts for Special Purposes	541,482	**445,378**
Subtotal, Annual Operations	1,294,346	**1,205,660**
Gifts to Endowment and Capital Projects	2,728,520	**899,963**
Total	$ 4,022,866	**$ 2,105,623**

CAPITAL CAMPAIGN

Anonymous
A. T. Cross Company
Alcas Cutlery Corporation
Amica Mutual Insurance Comany
Amtrol, Inc.
Jorge R. Anchondo & Meredith Nemirov de Anchondo
Ms. Deirdre B. Anderson
Mrs. Ann H. Armstrong
Ms. Joan M. Arnaud
Mrs. Peter Aspinwall
Mrs. James Azzinaro
B. A. Ballou & Co Inc.
Mrs. Martin J. Badoian
Bank of New England/Old Colony
Ms. Sarah A. Barker
Mr. & Mrs. Alan Barnett
Ms. Merle L. Barnett
Mrs. Martha Bartsch
Ms. Elizabeth M. Bass
Mr. & Mrs. James L. Beckner
Mr. Anthony C. Belluschi
Mrs. William C. Belvin
Mrs. Greene Benton Jr.
Mrs. Suzanne C. Bird
Mrs. Davis B. Bliss
Mr. & Mrs. Noah O. Blosser
Mr. & Mrs. Norman J. Bolotow
Bonnell Design Associates, Inc.
Ms. Patricia Bouley
Mr. & Mrs. Arnie Braeski
Ms. Linda R. Brenner
Dr. Marvin W. Bromberg
Mrs. Avery Rogers Brooke
Mr. Harry Brown
Ms. Lois B. Bryant
Mr. & Mrs. J. Scott Burns
Mrs. Marilyn A. Cafarelli
Mr. David M. Calver
Mr. & Mrs. John A. Campbell
Carbone Smolan Associates
Ms. Suzanne O. Carlson
Ms. Lynn Edith Casey
Mr. & Mrs. Robert S. Catanzaro
Mary Dexter Chafee Fund
Mr. David R. Chapman
Mr. & Mrs. Samuel N. Chase
Mr. & Mrs. Bernard Chaus
Citizens Bank
Ms. Lucy Commoner
Mr. Philip Cook
Mr. & Mrs. Gary C. Cooke
Mr. & Mrs. Donald J. Currie
Mr. & Mrs. Joseph D'Errico
Daedalus Design
Mr. & Mrs. John D. Dale, Jr.
Ms. Jean E. Davis
Ms. Caroline DeCesare
Ms. Pamela M. DeSpain
Mr. Raymond H. Dearden
Deblois Oil Company
Mr. Robert L. Demichiell, Jr.
Mr. & Mrs. Robert deVito
Ms. Nina T. Dillof
Mr. & Mrs. James M. Dillon
Ms. Margaret Dressel
E-M Associates, Inc.
Mr. & Mrs. Robert L. Edsall
Mrs. Bonnie S. Eiber
Mrs. E. William Ewers
Mr. & Mrs. Bayard Ewing
Mr. & Mrs. Gene Federico
Fiduciary Trust International
Mr. & Mrs. Carl T. Finkbeiner
Mr. William R. Firth
Fleet National Bank
Ms. Michelle P. Forrester
Foundation of Jewish Philanthropies
Ms. Miriam K. Fredenthal & Ms. Ruth A. Fredenthal
Mr. & Mrs. Peter B. Freeman
Mr. John E. Garstka
Mr. Henry A. Gentille
Mr. & Mrs. Bernard Gewirz
Gilbane Building Company
Mrs. Robert Gilbert
Mr. John Lodge Gillespie
Mr. Milton Glaser
Ms. Allois Anne Glasser
Mr. & Mrs. Robert H.I. Goddard
Mr. & Mrs. Sidney F. Greenwald
Mr. & Mrs. Michael F. Gregorio
Mr. Louis Grieco
Ms. Marjorie Guido
Mr. Philip B. Hackbarth
Mr. & Mrs. Stanley E. Hall
Mr. & Mrs. Edward O. Handy
Ms. Jessica Hart
Mr. Clayton R. Hasser
Hazel Siegel Corporation
Ms. Dorothy Hebden-Heath
The Estate of Eta Hentz
Ms. Elizabeth W. Hirsch
Ms. Margo Hoff
Mr. & Mrs. Frank C. Hooper
The Hope Foundation
Hope Charitable Foundation
Mr. & Mrs. Kenneth Hunnibell
Igarashi Studio
Rev. & Mrs. James L. Johnson & Family
Phyllis Kimball Johnstone
Mr. & Mrs. Doug Kanz
Mr. Stephen J. Karakashian
Mr. & Mrs. Toshihiro Katayama
Mr. Robert A. Keeler
Keith Muller Limited
Kenney Manufacturing Company
Ms. Moon Hye Kim
Knight Foundation
Ms. Barbara Knutson
Koffler Family Foundation
Mr. & Mrs. Philip Kretz
Mr. & Mrs. Harold Leavitt
Mrs. Martha E. Leone
Mr. Richard S. Levine
J Rockwell Levy Foundation
Ms. Laura S. Lienhard
Mr. Frederick Lippitt
Ms. Helen R. Litt
Mr. & Mrs. Mark D. Litt
Little Family Foundation
Mrs. William S. Lynch
Ms. Diane Lyon
Sonya Mackintosh
Miss Chiaki Maki
Ms. Kaori Maki
Mr. Bruce W. Manwaring
Ms. Alice A. Marcoux
Ms. Ruth Massey
Mrs. Mary Massucco
Mr. & Mrs. Frank Mauran
Mr. Roger R. Mayer
Mr. Alexander T. McBride, III
Mrs. Marilyn M. Meardon
Medical Economics Co., Inc.
Mr. James N. Miho
Tomoko J. Miho
Mrs. Geoffrey H. Moore
Mr. & Mrs. Richard Moore
Mr. & Mrs. Carlos Morales Sr.
Mr. George S. Morfogen
Ms. Miranda L. Morris
Ms. Mary J. Murphy
Ms. Constance A. Mussells
Mr. Patrick J. Nagle
Narragansett Electric Company
Mrs. Dorothy M. Nelson
Mr. Daniel E. Nerney
Mr. Dana M. Newbrook
Dr. & Mrs. Robert C. Northcutt
Ocean State Charities Trust
Old Stone Bank
Ms. Ann S. Orth
Dr. & Mrs. David N. Orth
Mrs. John J. Orth
Mr. & Mrs. George T. Osterkamp
Mrs. Susan H. Packard
Mrs. Carr Payne
Mr. Gordon F. Peers
Ms. Christine Pellicano
Mr. & Mrs. Alan S. Perry
Mr. & Mrs. Herrick R. Peterson
Ms. Marion E. Prilook
Print and Design Inc.
Ms. Julie H. Proshek

Providence Art Club
Mr. & Mrs. M. E. Pulitzer
RISD Faculty Association
Polo Ralph Lauren Corporation
Carolyn Ray Inc.
Mr. Glenn C. Reeves
Ress Family Foundation
The Rhode Island Foundation
Richard Danne & Associates Inc.
Mr. John David Ridge
Mr. & Mrs. Donald Roach
Mr. & Mrs. David E. Roche
Mr. Roger E. Roche
Mr. George B. Rome
Mr. & Mrs. Charles E. Rossbach
Mrs. Joel Rotman
Mr. & Mrs. Leonard Rumpler
Mrs. Carol Ryan
Ms. Pamela Scheinman
Scheuer Tapestry Studio, Inc.
Mrs. Cynthia Schira
Mr. Harry Schmitke
Ms. Madeline Schwartz
Ms. Virginia Schwarz
Mr. & Mrs. Bernard R. Schweid
Mr. & Mrs. Henry D. Sharpe, Jr.
Ms. Beverly S. Shichtman
Ms. Roberta R. Shortlidge
Mr. Dean Silvers & Marlen Hecht
Mr. Scot Simon
Ms. Lenore Singerman
Ms. Margaret Howe Sloan
Mr. Edward P. Smith
Ms. Joyce R. Smith
Mr. & Mrs. Larry S. Socea
Ms. Donna M. Solecki
Ms. Dorothy Sonday
Mr. Milton F. Sonday, Jr.
Mrs. Mary O. Sowinski
Mrs. Nancy Sprague
Surdna Foundation
Mr. & Mrs. Alfred Tagtmeier
Mr. & Mrs. C. George Taylor
Tennessee Repertory Theatre
Ms. Susan A. Tharp
Mr. & Mrs. Michael O. Thorner
Edwardo Tiscornia & Maia Bilbao
Ms. Naomi Whiting Towner
Mr. & Mrs. Robert F. Troiano
Mr. & Mrs. George Tschemy
Ms. Maria Tulokas
Ms. Stephanie Urdang
Vanderbilt University
Vector Marketing Corporation
Vignelli Associates
Barbara D. Wagner
Ms. Beatrice G. Wagner
Wendy Walsh
Walter Henry Freygang Foundation
Ms. Esther C. Weiner
Mr. & Mrs. Harlan Weisman
Mr. John A. White
Ms. R. Linda Wichtel
Mr. & Mrs. David W. Wiley, Jr.
Mrs. Jesse E. Wills
Mr. & Mrs. J. M. Wilson
Mr. W. Don Woollings
Mr. Wilbur E. Yoder
Ms. Ada Yonenaka
Mr. Thomas R. Zito
Ms. Jennifer Zitron
Miss Nelle I. Znamierowski
Robert Zukerman & Jan Moseman

David A. Riley
Dorothy Dodworth Scullin
David Seccombe
Nancy Reutti Segerberg
Lloyd P. Shapleigh, Jr.
James P. Shattuck, Jr.
Alfred T. Sisson
Gerald F. Small
John B. Smith
William Sola
Jane Loring Straight
Marcus Thompson
Robert O. Thornton
Patricia Owen Van Dusen
Pamela Huse Wallace
Stuart A. Warshaw
Phyllis Weissblatt Wertenteil
James Y. Whittier
Nancy Davis Wood
Josephine Cole Wright
John P. Zerega

Andrew L. Alger
Ann Morton Bannister
Robert E. Barry
Mary Mills Belmore
Mary Crowley Brooks
Metje Cappon Butler
Dorothy J. Chase
Sarah Winlock Chase
Jay R. Cross
Carl R. Daley
Louis DeFusco
Shirley Dadisman Drasher
Dorothy Christian Durudogan
Jon E. Ericson
Edward Ferreira
John Flori
Ruth Goodwin Folta
Constance Kuhl Francis
Lucian A. Geraci, Jr.
Eugene Giancarlo
Johnson L. Gibbs
Carol Bradford Hamilton
James H.P. Hamilton
James Lyman Hamilton
Barbara Booth Hazard
Philip A. Hodge
Dorothy Weeks Hovey
Edward T. Howell
Robert Jones
Robert P. Keating
Ellsworth H. Kent
Michael Kosubinsky
Alfred Kozar
Virginia Woods Kuhl
Joyce King LaForce
Robert LaForce
Harriette Sibley Lusty
William R. Marley
Robert P. McKenna
John W. Moses
Ruth Quigley Mullaney
Arthur P. O'Sullivan
Walter F. Pasieka
Cynthia Crawford Patriquin
Judith Cotter Rayner
James B. Rieck
Joan Rappoport Rogers
Russell R. Santora
Dawn Malven Senftleber
Frederick Senftleber
Peggy Boyd Sharpe
Herman D. J. Spiegel
John H. Squadra
Richard P. Swallow
John A. Topoleski
Arthur R. Turner, Jr.
Margery Hagenbuch Waggoner
Anthony A. Waring
Sunny Bertrand Warner
Euphemia Hunter Weber
Noel E. Weber
Ray B. Wheeler
William Wightman
Patricia Avery Wilcox
Cecily Hazard Zerega

Edward J. Adams
Carol J. Bancroft
John G. Bozarth
Angelo M. Calitri
John J. Coughlin
William M. Curtis
Frank DeMattos
John A. DiStefano
Lillian Machado Dickson
Jean Caldwell Donkin
Louise Munson Dunn

Rhoda Zarrow Friedman
Wendy Morris Gash
Robert Giuliani
Charles L. Goslin
Robert F. Hammerquist
Frances Lee Heminway
Elizabeth Flynn Hodge
Frank Iafrate
Michael Keselica, Jr.
Isabel Anderson Konradi
Frederic J. Licht
Richard G. Marsden
Marilyn Hardy McKenna
Donald H. Pinckney
Leah Lancaster Richardson
George V. Rickel
Stanley Rosen
Lester S. Rutt
Robert J. Soforenko
Eugenie Stiehler Spratt
Ann-Martha Bernstein Stanzler
Clifford Stead, Jr.
Thomas Thomasian
Mimi Barteau Turner
Peterfield Turpin
Hercules A. Volpe
J. Edwin Warren
Sheila Barney Welch
Gretchen Wessels

Lois Haley Ballard
Joan Thornley Booth
Theodore S. Burr
Jack L. Bursack
Blanche Rondina Coyne
Lorraine Sanderson Dimeo
Robert Donelly
Allan S. Downing
Sally Somers Eaton
Nancy Anderson Etani
Herman Freedman
Patricia Downey Garry
Charles Gaudet
Carole Wilhelm Geyer
Natalie A. Hay
Mary Melikian Haynes
Letitia Meinhold James
Elizabeth Hamer Keane
Sebastian L. LaBella
Martin V. Maloney
Roland L. Marchand
Carolyn Hayes McCarthy
William C. McDade
Carol Huntle McKeon
Glenn W. Monigle
Theodore L. Newberg
Janis Parker
Cornelius C. Richard, Jr.
William E. Rusterholz
Carol Fookes Ryder
Richard C. Schuman
Helene Silver Schwartz
Nancy Fishbein Sher
Betty Welker Stroh
E. Elliot Terzian
Richard A. Tougas
Wallace A. Underwood
Alfred S. Venditto
William M. Wagner
Phyllis Lanin Way
Judith Brownstein Zlotsky

Edith J. Allard
Raymond P. Alvarez
Harold P. Ashton, Jr.
Joyce Gray Baker
Edwin H. Benz
Ronald C. Binks
Leslie Rogers Blum
Clarice Davis Booth
Jean Thompson Bravin
Yvonne Jacquette Burckhardt
Elayne Schwartzman Canter
Eugene J. Caramante
Nancy Cutting Coveney
Georgianna Fulkerson Decoster
Sylvio de Rouin
Anthony V. DiStefano
Peter W. Drake
James E. Farrington
John J. Feroce
Alan D. Grover
Joseph D. Hopkins
Sally Nielsen Hough
Gretchen Kiehn Irving
Rachel Sweeny Kennedy

Edward J. Maffeo
James C. Markarian
Roberta Thibaudeau Masse
Martha Stickney Matthews
Diane Beehler Moore
Harold E. North
Joan Barney Rosengren
Theodore A. Sande
Barbara Hyde Scalo
Cynthia Jones Schira
Nancy Fatzinger Schumann
Walter Schwaner, Jr.
Daniel Shea
Joanne Egan Shea
Mary Ann Clegg Smith
Judith Kaufman Steinberg
Richard M. Stoughton
Muriel Hulbert Thomas
Victor G. Zacksher
Rita Derjue Zimmerman

Janet Novick Albert
Helen Flanders Anderton
Frances V. Antupit
Patricia Murphy Aubin
Marjorie Olson Barstow
Gaetano Bazzano
Richard E. Beasley
Roland J. Belhumeur
Robert Black
Guy R. Blais
Judith C. Bray
William M. Brigden
Jane Hill Burns
Judith Hindley Cadieux
Nancy Holmes Calise
Dolores Rosa Campbell
Judith Singer Caro
Lawrence E. Charity
Jeremiah Clarke, Jr.
Donald R. Conlon
Rino Conti
Allan H. Copeland
Rosaire A. Cournoyer
Robert R. Demers
Nancy Harrison Devita
Robert R. Dion
Ina Larson Donnan
Marge Dunlap
Patricia Knowlton Durham
Joan E. Forbes
Sylvia Klanian Forti
Seymour Glantz
Lucy Forkner Greene
Michel G. Griffiths
Robert S. Gumley
Dorothy Hebden-Heath
Edward J. Hill
Fay Bailey Jones
Elisa Tufenkjian Khachian
Lynne MacCubrey Khambaty
Francis Klay, Jr.
Suzanne Sperry Klay
Arthur M. Love, Jr.
Vanghel T. Lupu
Joseph P. Mallozzi
Constance Rychlik Maloney
George T. Mellekas
Daniel E. Morris
Judith Wasson Motta
James V. Murphy
Gretchen Clapp Orr
George J. Perry
Rotraut A. Postler
Cynthia Cohen Ross-Feig
Donald J. Roy
Richard H. Russell
Robert J. Russett
Richard A. Schira
Harry Spruyt
Ellen Sulides
Ruth Grout Vaill
Mitchell Waian
Haze B. Warner
Jeanne McAlice Warren
Mette Arup Watt
Janet Hershey Woolman

Judith Greene Albert
Donald F. Allen
Vincent C. Amore
Dale La Plante Anderson
Fred R. Angier, Jr.
Robert A. Ayotte
Roberta Hopkins Ayotte
David C. Bailey, Jr.
Thomas R. Beaudet
Sara Sidore Berman
Gabrielle Camaroe Black
Paul Bookbinder
Gardner R. Bradbury
Edgar I. Broadhead, Jr.
Constance Bartolini Cook
Joan Hopkins Coughlin
Marjorie Djerf Cristadoro
John Dalton
Barbara Goldenberg Davis
Marina Dognin Del Sesto
Donna Romano DeMello
Marjorie Foss Dente
Donn P. Devita
Janice Kennedy Doctor
Alan P. Dodge
Robert M. Eichinger
Leana Lanning Fay
Patricia Goss Fry
Lee C. Griffin
David I. Grist
Joseph M. Gwozdz
Ruth Sanek Haft
Russell E. Harrison
Beverly Moore Hoffsis
Nancy Sickles Horch
C. Linda Dutra Hunnibell
Kenneth Hunnibell
Janet Shaw Juenger
David F. Kelley
Rosemary Kennett
Pauline Scheck Ladd
Maryanna Fuller Langlois
Robert W. Lepper
Frank A. Lukasik
Stanley Mack
Reta Axelrod Masters
Joseph H. McCusker
Jacqueline Bean Melissas
Ralph A. Muscatiello
Roberta Rohrbach Ohliger
Alexander S. Oliver
Manuela Yona Paul
Leandre A. Poisson
Sandra Griffiths Rigney
Martin G. Rothman
Ursula Miskolczy Rowan
Terry A. Rutledge
Theresa Carbo Shattuck
Diane Damrell Shumway
Judith Greenberg Spitzer
Frances Sherwood Stevenson
Carol Russo Stufano
Carol L. Swope
Joan V. Traverso
Margot Trout
Lawrence Voyer
Paul M. Warner
Mary Soule Webb
Bernice Augustsson Williams
Sandra South Wilson
Karol Bowker Wyckoff

Robert D. Alberetti
Norma Moore Allison
Claude J. Almand
Barbara Olins Alpert
William K. Anderson
Fred M. Baker, Jr.
Carol Allen Bloomquist
Mall Timusk Blumfeld
Elizabeth Kvaratzkhelia Booth
Janet Mongeau Bruno
Richard H. Casale
James H. Caswell, Jr.
Jean Burgess Cook
Robert L. Cronin
Raymond DeCesare
Lawrence DeHart
Johanna Demetrakas
Edward DeZabala
Glenda Hazen Ducharme
Sarah Saloomey Fink
David R. Flaharty
Kathleen Behre Fletcher
Peter W. Floodman
John R. Frazier, Jr.
Dorothy Platt Frederick
A. Corwin Frost
Rosalie Halsey Frost
Joseph Furtado
W. Chris Gorman
Eugene P. Gregan
Janice Reynolds Grover
Richard S. Halpert
Judith Borden Honeywood
Phyllis Rothstein Huggett
Brian T. Kirkpatrick
Linna Kendall Kite
Joan Strauss Kleeman
Lois White Leveillee
Joan Matter Longobardi
Kenneth Longtemps
Joy MacConnell
Robert Marculewicz
Earl R. Marsh, Jr.
Carol Hesse Marsland
Richard Masse
Ann Higgins McCutcheon
Marcia Fleishman Moger
Leslie Moore
Janet A. Newberg
Linda Dean Paradee
Kenneth C. Potter
Dorothy A. Rhodes
Beatrice Turek Robinson
Esteruth Feldman Rumpler
Thomas J. Ryan
Millicent DeFeo Sloan
Sandra Stroud Snow
Katherine King Sozanski
Roxanne Russell Stosur
William E. Talley, Jr.
Linda Krutchkoff Thompson
Benjamin F. Wheeler
Vida Merriken Wheeler
Jonathan Willetts
Anthony J. Woidyla, Jr.

Penelope Price Ackley
Manuel Andrade
Maurice R. Antaya
Elliott I. Barowitz

Phyllis Bartlett
Robert F. Bateman
Ruth Furgiuele Benson
Richard A. Brazil
Marilyn Glazier Brierley
Celia Malkin Brown
Merrill P. Budlong, Jr.
Judith Nesbit Burgess
June E. Capstack
Leslie Shuster Carter
Robert A. Cipriani
Michael A. Cousins
Edward K. Cunard
Marjorie Zucker Del Rossi
Richard W. Derviss
Martin E. Donnelly, Jr.
Caroline Sullivan Ellingwood
John C. Ellingwood
Karel Greenblatt Gertsacov
Phyllis Croll Goodblatt
Donald E. Gove
Patricia Barlow Healey
Charles Hildebrand
Dorothea Behr Hildebrand
Wendy Ingram
Joanna Miller Jacobus
Marshall B. Johnson
Shirley Nicholson Joyce
James H. Kay, III
William Kite, Jr.
William W. Lane
Lorraine Kaufman Levan
James O. Lincoln
Carole Stein Ludwig
Richard D. Ludwig
Sydney Hall Maddox
Nancy Brooks Marculewicz
Amy Hodge Martin
Helga Jorgenson McCallum
Thomas McCallum
Martin G. Myers
Nikolai Nechipurenko
Dale Peraner Osterle
William J. Ouellette
David A. Presbrey
Nancy Austin Reed
Worden G. Robinson
Ellen Schimelman
Richard B. Shanklin
Jane Lewis Snerson
James A. Spillman
William E. Sydlowski
Samuel Wang
Carol Ann Dooley Westfall
Jonathan Wetzel
Charles F. Wheeler
Robert C. White
Eunice Straight Whiting
Jean Prignano Winslow
Wilmot D. Winslow
Philip S. Winsor
Richard M. Wolfman

David A. Abercrombie
Sandra Dryden Angle
Ronald F. Arnholm
Natalie Bigelow Babson
Hans H. Bauer
Carol Forer Belt
William H. Bocook
Paul A. Burkhardt, Jr.
Joseph A. Capostagno
Moira McCarthy Cumming
Nancy Nickerson Decesare
Robert DeVito
Andrew S. Dragat
Kenneth B. Dresser, Jr.
Evelyn Fogg Dunbar
Laurent Dupont
Wallace N. Farnum
Helga P. Freund
Irene Cunin Glaser
J. Paul Guertin
George L. Horton
Donald C. Hughlett
David M. Itchkawich
Whitney L. Lane
Donald R. Lavallee
Herbert M. Libby
Roslyn Dephoure Martin
Anthony Miles
Lucy Webb Millsaps
Brenda E. Minisci
William Morrison
Frank J. Olney
Samuel A. Otis, Jr.
Ann Barbour Parks
Albert A. Pointe
Armand Renaud, Jr.
Dolores Henninger Richter
George J. Rogers
C. Richard Sheeran
Peter M. Smith
Susan Smith-Hunter
Sue Benner Sugahara
James H. Sullivan, III
Muriel Burbank Townsend
Ronald H. Vandenberg
Rene Villeneuve
Marilyn Hughes Woodworth

David R. Chapman
Raymond Coburn
Domenick De Santis
Judith Turner DeVito
Paula N. Dubrow
Robert J. Francisco
Richard W. Gores
Victoria Dudley Hirsch
Femn Carlson Hubbard
Sara Dunham Hutchinson
Flo Sheldon Kerr
Susan Bird Kittredge
Anthony E. Kurneta
Diane Martineau Leathers
Palmina Wolf Lipani
Georgette Pereir Macafee
Roger R. Mayer
Jacob R. Myers
Janet A. Pinsonneault
Harry Schmitke
Erica Lavine Swadley
Deborah Hoyt Taylor
Dorothy C. Westby
David N. White
John H. Williams
Robert J. Wood

Mary Cannell Andrews
Sylvia Harding Appleton
Sandra Bolotin Bassow
Eric W. Bennett
Donald H. Berg
Donald J. Binkley
Curtis Blanchard
Elizabeth Shank Blanchard
Clark Brennan
Kathie Bunnell
Sandra Bellem Campbell
Eleanor Morris Caponigro
Joseph A. Cirillo
Gail Andrews Crimmins
Natalie Steeves DiCostanzo
William H. Ewen, Jr.
Richard A. Fishman
Judith Bowering Funkhouser
Charlotte Schley Garedo
Anthony L. Gelardi
Louis P. Gelinas
Israel Goldberg
Antonia Pisciotta Goldmark
David B. Gray
Harleston J. Hall, Jr.
Mervyn S. Hammatt
Alan E. Hubbard
Sue Anne Cleaves Johnson
John C. Karrasch
Steven C. Kellogg
John F. Kramer
Barbara Tolen Lapin
Bernard J. Lombardi
Elaine Mendolia Longtemps
David E. Luce
Suellen Libby MacStravic
Carolyn Voigt McCoy
Paul J. McKenna
Anne Armstrong Meyer
Carolyn A. Mills
Virginia Hughes Morrison
John Muhlhausen
Victoria Kilbourn Munson
Elizabeth Nelson
Leon I. Nigrosh
Melody Trowbridge Ojala
Daniel W. Packard
John G. Parrillo
Susan Wilcock Patrick
Sarah Wardrobe Peel
Marjorie E. Probst
Nancy Smith Prout
Kenneth R. Rich
Denis R. Samson
Michael W. Sand
Roberta Alpern Schwartz
William R. Searle
Dinah Maxwell Smith
William O. Smith
Joshua M. Sprague
Jane E. Sterrett
Peterene Sweistis Stanhope
Peter G. Thompson
Jan W. Wampler
Helen Webber
Raymond L. Webster, Jr.

Laurence Appleton
Jotham W. Bailey
Margaret Fitzgerald Bailey
Betsy Leslie Bean
Arthur G. Beckenstein
Flavia Pantaleoni Blechinger
Ellen Lyle Bradley
Stewart H. Brecher
Philip M. Briggs
Elizabeth Sommers Busch
Daniel R. Cahill
Judith F. Gardner Coburn
Nancy Smullen Crasco
James L. Crowell
Peter B. Devries
Rachel G. Doane
Valerie Urban Dohrenwend
Paul Donham, Jr.
Elizabeth Vaughan Drake
Mary Spater Drummond
Jane Hasbrouck Duncan
Lorellie Stubbs Durocher
Eric G. Engstrom
David R. Estey
Susan Grabber Falk
Sandra Lounsbury Foose
Thomas C. Funk
Barbara Perkins Gaffron
Peter E. Gaffron

Alan D. Gamache
Brenda Sullivan Geishecker
Margaret Worthington Gilson
Elizabeth G. Ginsberg
Diana Rantoul Harrison
Ronald H. Hatcher
William B. Hellmuth
Joan Kokkins Herron
Sherrill Edwards Hunnibell
Susan Prendergast Kendrot
Carrie Talvy Klehr
Nicholas J. Krenitsky
Laura Smith Lynch
Martha T. Mackey
Patricia White Maka
James I. Meyer
Jan Thomas Michael
Hiroshi Murata
Nancy Silvia Murata
Stuart J. Murphy
Pauline Majka Parrillo
Karen Eisin Pellaton
Marcia Gebhard Pennington
Nancy C. Reeser
Sibyl Selldorff Rubottom
Ronald D. Russo
R. Scott Samuel
Ellen Riley Schneider
Ellen Schwarzbek
Patricia Brown Selbert
Barbara Feinberg Shafer
Carolyn Coleman Sieffert
Elaine Moore Sinowitz
Siegfried Snyder
Susan Myerhoff Stapleford
Howard C. Sussel
Nancy Hollingsworth Taplin
Louis W. Taschner
Mary Feder Taschner
Nancy Terry Tulloh
Selby L. Turner, Jr.
Sharon DuPont Tyler
Ronald Wilczek
Carolina Y. C. Woo
Marion Bernstein Alexandri
Doris Danesi Anderson
Gregory R. Atkinson
James B. Baker
Martha Tyson Ballantine
Nancy Crossley Blank
Brenda Bonick-Davis
Richard A. Bonney
Melville Grant Boyd
Richard Canavan, III
Steven W. Caney
Wendy Hertz Caputo
Stephanie Woodberry Clayton
David J. Crabbe
H. Kenneth Crasco
Nancy Smullen Crasco
Virginia Dubrucq
Lloyd G. Dyson, Jr.
Isabelle Baer Famiglietti
Martha C. Farnsworth
Priscilla Burr Foley
Wilfrid Gates, Jr.
Kenneth J. Gaulin
Richard H. Gobeille
Richard W. Gove
Joan H. Gramatte
Ann Funnell Graves
Sidney Graves, Jr.
Abigail S. Hadley
William R. Hammer
Dorothy Marsh Haney
Suzanne Amy Henricksen
Ann Cole John
David A. Joy
Richard Kendrot
Frank W. Kibbe, Jr.
Stuart R. Kipperman
Andrew W. Kramer
Paul H. Langmuir
Robert D. Lasus
Robert S. Leathers
Frances Telen Leventhal
Stephen G. Maka
Dianne L. Martin
Donald McKendry
Glenda Wilcox Milewski
John C. Navilliat
Robert H. Oppenheim
Richard M. Pantano
John E. Paquette
John G. Parsons
Michael A. Pasquale
Charles N. Peck
David O. Pressier
Diane Miller Price
J. Timothy Prout
Nancy Smith Prout
Susan McSweeney Ross
Irene Fontaine Ruth
John W. Saalfield
Catherine DiTommaso Schmitz
Arthur G. Selbert
Mary Shaffer
Richard Shnitzler
Booth Simpson
Linda Robinson Sokolowski
William Stanhope
Charlotte Staub
Allan H. Stecker
Eleanore Dixon Stecker
Allan B. Strauss
Judith Walsh Szymanski
Judy Dougan Thomas
Bernard L. Vining
David P. Weindel
Margaret Wells
Marilyn Miller Wilbur
Ruth Byers Wilcox
George M. Woolsey

Diane E. Aeschliman
Bruce B. Anderson
Elizabeth Moreton Anderson
Judith Maddock Anderson
Elaine Anthony
Barbara L. Bell
Helen Risom Belluschi
Anthony C. Belluschi
Judith Kruger Bromley
Peter B. Corbridge
Nicolette Ausschnitt Crisman
Marsha Zackler Dowshen
Joyce R. Dunn
Michelle Eagle-Krauss
Joan Pollins Feldman
Charlotte Leveton Foreman
Douglas A. Fraser
Nancy J. Friedman
Judith Sherburne Gates
Judy Sue Goodwin-Sturges
Stephanie Finberg Graham
Marjorie H. Greenhut
Samuel L. Guiffre
Peter D. Haney
Cheryl Sickler Hennecy
R. Kring Herbert
Stanley C. Hutchinson
David W. Johnsen
Lawrence A. Kahn
George E. Kauffman
David F. Kaufholz
Chester P. Keefe, II
Jill Politzer Krach
Maija Krustans-Slesers
John Lazarowski, Jr.
Elizabeth Grammer Marshall
Philip J. Marshall
Boyd C. Mefferd
Jonna D. Meyler
Jay Michaels
Karen Canner Moss
William J. Nemey
Sandra Cullen Nippes
Charles R. Nyberg
Emily L. Marrone O'Brien
Leigh F. Palmer
Phyllis Gay Palmer
Geoffrey B. Piece
Samuel F. Posey
Nancy Barron Roy
Raymond Sauer
Ann Wheeler Saunderson
Roger Schlaifer
William A. Shank
W. Tyler Smith
Alexandra E. Sonneborn
Beverly Dickson Spitzer
Sarah Brown Stabler
M. Lucy Wade Stern
Harold S. Sweet
Pamela Boyd Tobey
Philip E. Tobey
Marilyn Avery Turner
Jill Gibbons Tyler
Julie L. Wagner
Elizabeth G. Wahle
Sonya Gurewitsch Walton-Teter
Patricia Wilkie Warwick
Daniel C. Wills
Henry R. Wolf
Judith Wolfe
Karen Slawsby Zechel

Donna Sutton Almquist
Ingrid Petersen Apgar
Diana Minisci Appleton
Charlene D. Davis Batey
Karlyn Atkinson Berg
Nadine Ingerman Berkowsky
Paul R. Blakeslee
Isabel Bodor Brown
Dean C. Cail
Deborah S. Casdin
Peter A. Chamberlain
Margaret McCallister Choteborsky
Catherine J. Collishaw
Linda S. Connor
Beatrice Main Dalsass
Carla Hall Danes
Katherine A. DeSousa
Caroline McKenney Dickinson
Mary Ann Dubis Dulude
Derek M. Durst
Willoughby Elliott
Charlotte Forsythe
Mollie Gibbons
Graham Gund
Robert Haig, Jr.
Bunny Harvey

CLIENT:
RHODE ISLAND SCHOOL OF DESIGN

DESIGN FIRM:
TYLER SMITH

ART DIRECTOR:
TYLER SMITH

DESIGNER:
TYLER SMITH

ILLUSTRATOR:
EMILY LISKER

WRITER:
CATHERINE CONNOVER

PRODUCTION MANAGER:
JOSEPH COHEN

TYPOGRAPHER:
COGENS PRESS

PAPER SELECTION:
AMERICANA, LOE (DULL CREAM)

PAPER MANUFACTURER:
STRATHMORE, WARREN

PRINTER:
COGENS PRESS

NUMBER OF PAGES:
48

SIZE:
6" x 6"

TYPE SELECTION:
GILL SANS SERIF

THOMAS C. PAULTER, DIRECTOR OF PUBLICATIONS, RHODE ISLAND SCHOOL OF DESIGN, PROVIDENCE, RHODE ISLAND

The primary purpose of our annual report each year is the formal closing of the financial year, and the thanking (in print) of all who gave to the school. We have a museum, for example, and people donate art work and money, even real estate to this.We have our alumni fund, along with the donors to the museum, and the annual report lists all of these acknowledgements. We've been doing this for the past three years. The annual report doesn't have to look like anything else; it doesn't need continuity. We have had in the past slick and corporate-looking annual reports. When we asked an alumnus, Tyler Smith, to do the 1987-88 edition, he wanted to give it a warmth and an artistic intimacy. So he did that with a small book. This goes to many people and 90 per cent of the audience was wildly enthusiastic and complimentary about this annual report.

THOMAS C. PAULTER, DIRECTOR OF PUBLICATIONS, RHODE ISLAND SCHOOL OF DESIGN, PROVIDENCE, RHODE ISLAND

Hauptgrund für unseren jährlichen Geschäftsbericht ist der Abschluss des Finanzjahres und der Dank (in gedruckter Form) an alle, die die Schule unterstützten. Wir haben zum Beispiel ein Museum, und manche Leute stiften Kunst oder Geld, manchmal sogar Immobilien. Ausserdem haben wir den von ehemaligen Studenten gestifteten Fond, und im Jahresbericht werden alle diese Gönner erwähnt. Wir haben das in den letzten drei Jahren so gemacht. Der Jahresbericht muss keine bestimmte Form haben, wir brauchen keine einheitliche Linie. Wir baten einen Absolventen der Schule, Tyler Smith, den Bericht für 1987/88 zu gestalten. Er dachte an eine intime, künstlerische Atmosphäre. Dies verwirklichte er in einem kleinformatigen Bericht. Viele Leute haben diesen Jahresbericht bekommen, und 90 Prozent sind vollkommen begeistert.

THOMAS C. PAULTER, DIRECTOR OF PUBLICATIONS, RHODE ISLAND SCHOOL OF DESIGN, PROVIDENCE, RHODE ISLAND

Tous les ans, notre rapport annuel a pour objectif principal la clôture de l'exercice financier, à quoi s'ajoutent les remerciements dus à tous les généreux donateurs. C'est ainsi que nous avons un musée pour lequel les gens nous font don d'œuvres d'art et d'espèces, voire de valeurs immobilières. Nous avons notre fonds d'anciens étudiants, ainsi qu'un fonds recueillant les dons pour le musée, et notre rapport en fait dûment mention. Dans le passé, nous avons fait réaliser des rapports bien léchés superbement objectifs. Lorsque nous avons invité un ancien étudiant, Tyler Smith, à préparer celui de 1987/88, il a préfére lui conférer un caractère chaleureux et artistiquement intimiste. C'est ce qu'il a réussi à travers ce petit volume. Notre rapport atteint un public nombreux; le 90% s'est déclaré enthousiaste, et nous avons été couverts d'éloges.

TYLER SMITH, TYLER SMITH DESIGN, PROVIDENCE, RHODE ISLAND

Many of the previous annual reports for the Rhode Island School of Design had featured photography. What we did was different. We wanted to represent what the school was about, the spirit of the school. Another RISD alumnus, Emily Lisker, did the illustrations, which were glimpses of the school. We had a small budget, so we decided to work with a small press and we had this tiny size, but the feeling was that of a hand-done, crafted thing. It seemed personal, as if it were one of a kind. It provided an intimate look at the Rhode Island School of Design. We wanted to break rules; we wanted this to look like it came froman art school.

TYLER SMITH, TYLER SMITH DESIGN, PROVIDENCE, RHODE ISLAND

In vielen der bisherigen Jahresberichte der Rhode Island School of Design dominierte die Photographie. Wir machten etwas ganz anderes. Wir wollten den Geist dieser Schule vermitteln. Emily Lisker, ebenfalls ehemalige Studentin der Schule, machte die Illustrationen, die Einblick in das Schulleben geben. Wir hatten ein bescheidenes Budget und beschlossen deshalb, mit einer kleinen Druckpresse zu arbeiten. Der Bericht wirkt persönlich, wie ein Einzelstück. Man bekommt einen guten Einblick in die Schule. Wir wollten Regeln brechen; wir wollten, dass dieser Jahresbericht so aussieht wie der Bericht einer Kunstschule.

TYLER SMITH, TYLER SMITH DESIGN, PROVIDENCE, RHODE ISLAND

La plupart des rapports annuels précédents de la Rhode Island School of Design étaient basés sur la photo. Nous avons procédé autrement en essayant de montrer l'esprit qui y prévaut. Une ancienne étudiante de la RISD, Emily Lisker, a créé les illustrations qui donnent une idée des activités de l'établissement. Nous disposions d'un petit budget, d'où le petit format, mais aussi l'impression d'un travail cousu main et personnalisé comme s'il s'agissait d'un exemplaire unique. On y trouve une relation intimiste de ce qui se passe à l'école. Nous avons voulu outrepasser les règles et faire comprendre ce que peut produire une école d'art.

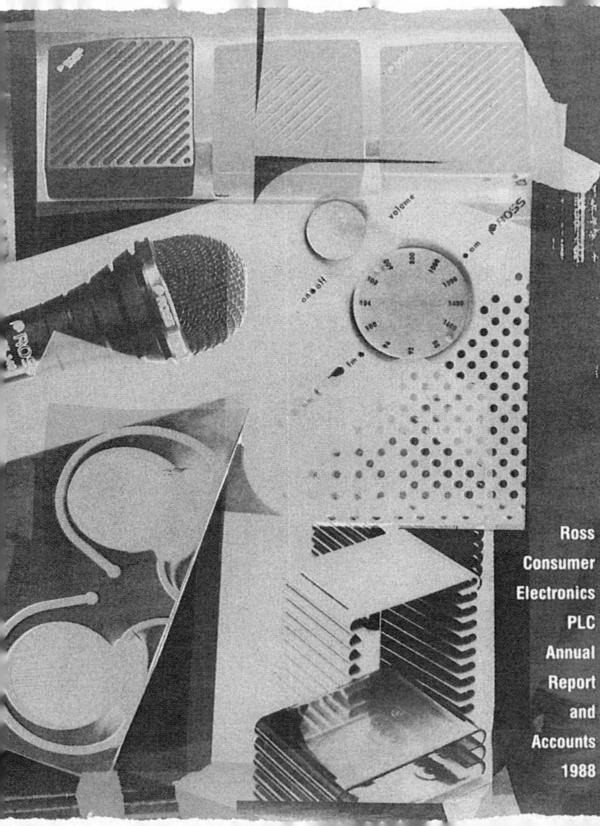
ROSS
volume
on/off
ROSS
Ross
Consumer
Electronics
PLC
Annual
Report
and
Accounts
1988

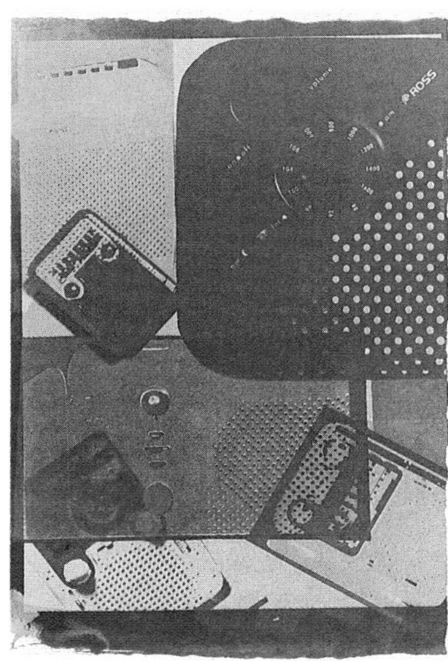

Ross Consumer Electronics PLC Annual Report and Accounts 1988

The Group's overall objectives are to:

Maximise returns to its shareholders by the continued improvement of prospects and profitability

Expand the Group's activities both organically and by acquisitions which meet closely defined investment parameters

Strengthen consumer association of the Ross brand name with innovative design, high quality and value for money

ROSS

Directors and Advisers

Directors
(Chairman) R I L Marks
A C Murphy
M T Carr
S P Genis
P J Owens ACA
(Non-executive) T N Clarke
(Non-executive) L G Marks

Company Secretary and Registered Office
P J Owens ACA
8 Baker Street
London W1M 1DA

Auditors
Stoy Hayward
8 Baker Street
London W1M 1DA

Stockbrokers
Smith New Court Agency Limited
Chetwynd House
24 St Swithin's Lane
London EC4N 8AT

Solicitors
Binks Stern and Partners
Queens House
55/56 Lincoln's Inn Fields
London WC2A 3LT

Registrars and Transfer Office
Close Registrars Limited
803 High Road
Leyton
London E10 7AA

Bankers
National Westminster Bank PLC
208 Piccadilly
London W1A 2DG

Financial Highlights

for the year ended 31 March 1988

1987 £000	1988 £000	
3,983	**4,263**	Turnover
589	**635**	
30	**2**	Other income
619	**637**	Operating profit
109	**102**	Interest payable
510	**535**	Profit before taxation
152	**134**	Taxation
358	**401**	
—	**153**	Dividends paid and proposed
358	**248**	
9.4p	**9.5p**	Earnings per ordinary share

Financial Calendar

22 September 1988	Annual General Meeting 1988
23 September 1988	Final ordinary dividend for 1988
January 1989	Interim report for the six months to 30 September 1988
February 1989	Interim ordinary dividend for 1989
July 1989	Preliminary announcement of results for 1989

Our commitment to quality, design and style, has enabled Ross to retain its position as UK market leader whilst increasing its share of the market.

Chairman's Statement I am pleased to present our first annual results as a public company. The year to 31 March 1988 was one of great significance: it saw our flotation on the Unlisted Securities Market in June 1987, the move to new premises and our continued commitment to product development. Three main reasons, however, prevented us from achieving the full result we anticipated:

1 The Christmas trading period was below expectations because the High Street electrical retailers experienced difficult trading conditions. Indications to date suggest this is unlikely to be repeated in 1988/9.

2 Certain products, in particular the British micro speaker range, were delayed in reaching the market. These products, which are now available in stores, are expected to make a significant contribution in the current period.

3 The non-recurring expenses of the move to White City were at least £30,000 higher than anticipated. These costs have been fully absorbed during the period and the improved facilities will meet the increasing demands from the market place.

Nevertheless, turnover increased from £4.0 million to £4.3 million and operating profits, after adjustment for the non-recurring relocation expenses, improved by some 13.0%. The Directors are recommending a final dividend of 2.3p net per ordinary share to make a total of 3.5p net for the year.

Business Development Investment in the future has been fundamental to the Group's strategy. During the year substantial expenditure has been incurred in relation to the introduction of new designs for the headphone range and on the development of new products, such as our cordless headphone system, which will reach the market later in the current year. Our commitment to quality, design and style, has enabled Ross to retain its position as UK market leader whilst

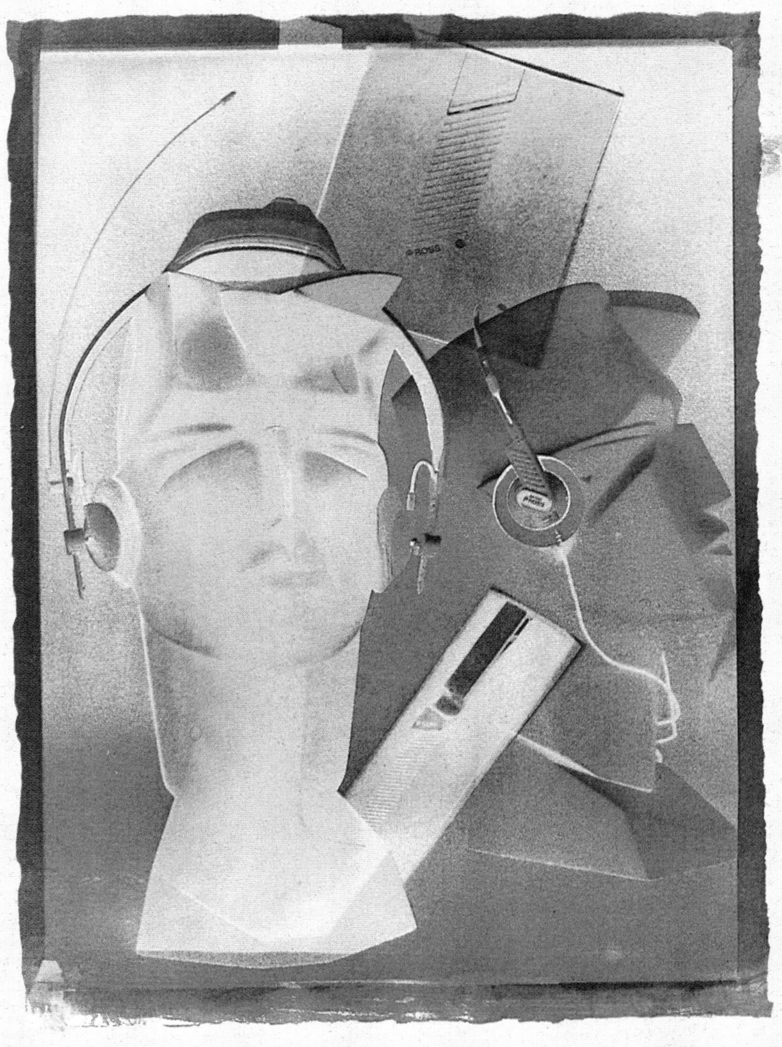

Notice of Annual General Meeting

Notice is hereby given that the Annual General Meeting of Ross Consumer Electronics PLC will be held at Film House, Wardour Street, London W1 at 10.30 am on Thursday 22 September 1988 for the following purposes:

As ordinary business

1 To receive the directors' report and accounts for the year ended 31 March 1988.

2 To declare a final dividend.

3 To re-elect Mr A C Murphy as a director.

4 To re-elect Mr M T Carr as a director.

5 To re-elect Mr P J Owens as a director.

6 To re-appoint Stoy Hayward as auditors and to authorise the directors to fix their remuneration.

By Order of the Board 25 August 1988
P J Owens **Company Secretary**

Notes

1 A member entitled to attend and vote at the above meeting may appoint a proxy or proxies to attend and on a poll to vote on his behalf. A form of proxy is enclosed which, if used, must reach the registrars of the Company, Close Registrars Limited, 803 High Road, Leyton, London E10 7AA, not less than forty eight hours before the time appointed for the holding of the meeting.

2 There will be available for inspection at Binks Stern and Partners, Queens House, 55/56 Lincolns Inn Fields, London WC2A 3LT during normal hours on any weekday (Saturday and public holidays excepted) from the date of this notice until the date of the meeting and at the place of the meeting from not less than fifteen minutes before the meeting to its conclusion:

I The register of directors' interests in the shares of the Company;

II Copies of directors' contracts of service.

Designed and Produced by Michael Peters Literature Limited

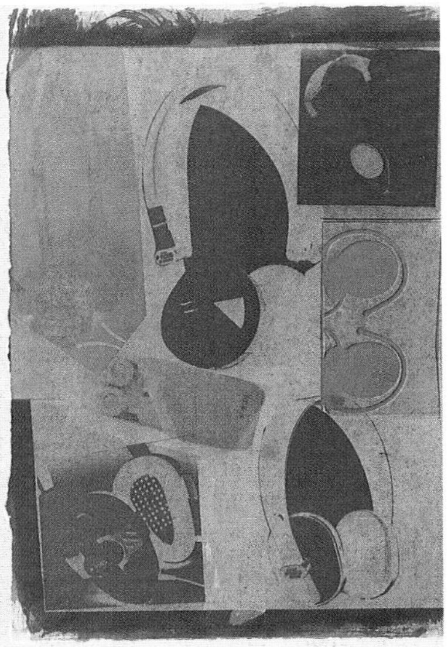

Group Profit and Loss Account

for the year ended 31 March 1988

1987 £000	1988 £000	
3,983	**4,263**	Turnover[2]
		Increase in stocks of finished goods and
360	**612**	work in progress
4,343	**4,875**	
3,754	**4,240**	Operating charges[3]
589	**635**	
30	**2**	Other income
619	**637**	Operating profit[5]
109	**102**	Interest payable[6]
		Profit on ordinary activities
510	**535**	before taxation
152	**134**	Taxation on profits from ordinary activities[7]
358	**401**	Profit on ordinary activities after taxation[8]
—	**153**	Dividends[9]
358	**248**	Retained profit for the year
9.4p	**9.5p**	Earnings per ordinary share[10]

Group Balance Sheet

at 31 March 1988

1987 £000	1987 £000	1988 £000	1988 £000	
				Fixed assets
	239		**423**	Intangible assets[11]
	228		**342**	Tangible assets[12]
	467		**765**	
				Current assets
1,249		**1,861**		Stocks[14]
779		**1,208**		Debtors[15]
30		**37**		Investments[16]
2,058		**3,106**		
				Creditors
				Amounts falling due within
1,322		**1,761**		one year[17]
	736		**1,345**	*Net current assets*
	1,203		**2,110**	*Total assets less current liabilities*
				Creditors
				Amounts falling due after
57		**21**		more than one year[18]
				Provisions for liabilities
48		**20**		and charges[19]
	105		**41**	
	1,098		**2,069**	
				Capital and reserves
	58		**438**	Called up share capital[20]
	—		**665**	Share premium account[21]
	13		**13**	Capital redemption reserve[22]
	1,027		**953**	Profit and loss account[23]
	1,098		**2,069**	

These Accounts were approved by the Board on 25 August 1988

R I L Marks **Director**
P J Owens **Director**

Balance Sheet

at 31 March 1988

1987 £000	1987 £000	1988 £000	1988 £000	
				Fixed assets
	84		**113**	Intangible assets[11]
	228		**342**	Tangible assets[12]
	9		**9**	Investments[13]
	321		**464**	
				Current assets
939		**1,291**		Stocks[14]
943		**1,840**		Debtors[15]
30		**37**		Investments[16]
1,912		**3,168**		
				Creditors
1,097		**1,581**		Amounts falling due within one year[17]
	815		**1,587**	Net current assets
	1,136		**2,051**	Total assets less current liabilities
				Creditors
				Amounts falling due after
57		**21**		more than one year[18]
38		**—**		Provisions for liabilities and charges[19]
	95		**21**	
	1,041		**2,030**	
				Capital and reserves
	58		**438**	Called up share capital[20]
	—		**665**	Share premium account[21]
	13		**13**	Capital redemption reserve[22]
	970		**914**	Profit and loss account[23]
	1,041		**2,030**	

These Accounts were approved by the Board on 25 August 1988

R I L Marks **Director**
P J Owens **Director**

Group Statement of Source and Application of Funds

for the year ended 31 March 1988

1987 £000	1987 £000	1988 £000	1988 £000	
				Source of funds
				Profit on ordinary activities
	510		**535**	before taxation
				Adjustment for items not
				involving the movement of funds:
80		**80**		Depreciation and amortisation
(11)		**4**		Loss/(profit) on sale of fixed assets
	69		**84**	
	579		**619**	Total generated from operations
				Funds from other sources
57		**723**		Issue of shares
—		**47**		Sale of fixed assets
	57		**770**	
	636		**1,389**	
				Application of funds
114		**215**		Purchase of fixed assets
194		**105**		Taxation paid
25		**25**		Repayment of bank loan
4		**7**		Purchase of listed investments
222		**214**		Deferred development expenditure
—		**52**		Dividends paid
	559		**618**	
	77		**771**	
				Increase/(decrease) in working capital
360		**612**		Stock
86		**429**		Debtors
(52)		**24**		Creditors
	394		**1,065**	
	(317)		**(294)**	Movement in net liquid funds

CLIENT:
ROSS CONSUMER ELECTRONICS

DESIGN FIRM:
MICHAEL PETERS LITERATURE

ART DIRECTOR:
JACKIE VICARY

DESIGNER:
SARAH DAVIES

PHOTOGRAPHER:
CHRISTINA RENDINA

ILLUSTRATOR:
CHRISTINA RENDINA

PRODUCTION MANAGER:
ADRIAN SLEEMAN

TYPOGRAPHER:
SARAH DAVIES

PAPER SELECTION:
GAINSBOROUGH

PAPER MANUFACTURER:
SIMPSONS

PRINTER:
FINANCIAL AND GENERAL

NUMBER OF PAGES:
24 PLUS COVER

TYPE SELECTION:
HELVETICA, TIMES

ROSS MARKS, MANAGING DIRECTOR, ROSS CONSUMER ELECTRONICS PLC, LONDON, ENGLAND

This is our first annual report as a public company and we wanted to create the right impression for our shareholders. We are a small public company, and we felt that the City didn't understand us, so in this annual report, we needed to have it express who we are. This was the basis of what we wanted our designer to do for us. The rest came from Michael Peters, who told me what one tried to achieve in an annual report, and what impression one could make. We wanted to show, for instance, that we were more than just a UK company. The annual report did give the right impression, and did meet our brief of introducing us to the City. Our designers made us conscious of design and how to use it. We did have mixed reactions from the City, perhaps because the City doesn't understand companies like ours.

ROSS MARKS, MANAGING DIRECTOR, ROSS CONSUMER ELECTRONICS PLC, LONDON, ENGLAND

Dies war unser erster Jahresbericht als öffentliche Firma, und wir wollten, dass unsere Aktionäre den richtigen Eindruck von uns bekommen. Wir sind eine kleine Firma und wir hatten das Gefühl, dass wir im Banken- und Börsenviertel nicht richtig eingeschätzt werden. Deshalb wollten wir in diesem Jahresbericht zeigen, wer wir sind. Das war unser Hauptanliegen an unseren Designer. Der Rest kam von Michael Peters, der mir sagte, worum es in einem Jahresbericht geht und welchen Eindruck man machen kann. Wir wollten zum Beispiel zeigen, dass wir mehr als nur ein britisches Unternehmen sind. Der Jahresbericht gab genau den richtigen Eindruck von uns und entsprach unserem Wunsch, besser in der Londoner Finanzwelt eingeführt zu werden. Unsere Designer überzeugten uns von der Wichtigkeit der Gestaltung.

ROSS MARKS, MANAGING DIRECTOR, ROSS CONSUMER ELECTRONICS PLC, LONDRES, GRANDE-BRETAGNE

C'est le premier rapport annuel que nous publions depuis notre ouverture au public, et il nous fallait créer une impression satisfaisante pour nos actionnaires. Nous sommes une petite entreprise encore inconnue du monde financière de Londres, d'où la nécessité d'annoncer la couleur dans ce rapport annuel. C'est donc sur cette base que s'est définie la mission du designer. Le reste a été l'affaire de Michael Peters qui m'a expliqué ce que l'on tente communément de réaliser à travers un rapport annuel et quelle impression peut s'en dégager. Nous voulions par exemple montrer que nous étions bien plus qu'une simple entreprise britannique. L'ouvrage achevé a crée l'impression adéquate et satisfait notre besoin de communication avec la communauté financière. Nos designers nous ont fait prendre le pouls de la stylique .

JACKIE VICARY, MICHAEL PETERS LITERATURE, THE MICHAEL PETERS GROUP, LONDON, ENGLAND

This was Ross Consumer Electronics' first year as a public company, and its first year on the Unlisted Securities Market. The Michael Peters Group had done packaging and developing of the product range for Ross Consumer Electronics, so it was logical that we would do the company's first annual report. We had a limited budget, but we wanted to make this report innovative. So we got Christina Rendina to do the photographs, and once she shoots, she then washes color over the photographic paper creating this dramatic effect. This made the visual treatment unusual. Then we chose special paper that was sympathetic to the images. Our type choice was in keeping with the style of the client–bold and confident. The client felt this fulfilled his brief, and we had a generally good response on this annual report.

JACKIE VICARY, MICHAEL PETERS LITERATURE, THE MICHAEL PETERS GROUP, LONDON, ENGLAND

Dies war das erste Jahr von Ross Consumer Electronics als öffentliche Gesellschaft und das erste Jahr, in dem die Aktien ausserbörslich gehandelt wurden. Die Michael Peters Group hatte für Ross Consumer Electronics eine Produktreihe und Verpackungen entwickelt; es war also logisch, dass wir auch den ersten Jahresbericht für die Firma machten. Das Budget war beschränkt, aber wir wollten trotzdem einen innovativen Bericht machen. Wir engagierten Christina Rendina für die Aufnahmen. Als die Aufnahmen fertig waren, verteilte sie Farbe über das Photopapier und erreichte damit einen ganz dramatischen Effekt. Wir wählten ein besonderes Papier, das ausgezeichnet zu den Illustrationen passte. Die Wahl der Schrift entsprach dem Stil des Kunden - mutig und zuversichtlich. Der Kunde war mit dem Bericht zufrieden.

JACKIE VICARY, MICHAEL PETERS LITERATURE, THE MICHAEL PETERS GROUP, LONDRES, GRANDE-BRETAGNE

Il s'agissait du premier exercice bouclé par Ross Consumer Electronics depuis son ouverture à l'actionnariat. Le Michael Peters Group ayant réalisé les emballages et le développement de la gamme de produits pour Ross Consumer Electronics, il était logique de nous confier la présentation du premier rapport annuel. Malgré le budget limité, nous entendions faire quelque chose d'insolite. Nous avons donc chargé Christina Rendina de réaliser les photos qu'elle a ensuite passées à la couleur pour en rehausser l'intérêt. Puis nous avons opté pour un papier de qualité spéciale en accord avec nos images. La typo est assortie au style de l'entreprise, respirant l'audace et l'assurance. Le client a estimé que notre mission était bien remplie, et nous avons enregistré des réactions généralement encourageantes .

SAN FRANCISCO INTERNATIONAL AIRPORT

THE YEAR IN REVIEW

The successful completion of several large projects at San Francisco International Airport distinguished Fiscal Year 1987/88. The Airport finished its $512 million Modernization and Renovation Program with the completion of Boarding Area C in June 1988. The Modernization and Renovation Program was successfully completed under budget, as well as on schedule, and with minimum disruption to the traveling public.

The Modernization and Renovation Program included the construction of the North Terminal in 1979, the completion of the 7,000-space garage in 1981, and the modernization of the South Terminal. In addition, the old Central Terminal was renovated and reopened in 1983 as the International Terminal.

4

In Fiscal Year 1987/88, work was also completed on the new Airport roadway interchange with the adjacent Highway 101 and Interstate 380. A project of the California State Department of Transportation, the new roadway system has dramatically reduced traffic congestion.

The Airport also completed 43 other construction projects in Fiscal Year 1987/88. These projects were designed to maintain the Airport's infrastructure and to improve Airport safety and efficiency. Runways and taxiways were resurfaced and strengthened, roads were repaired, and utility and lighting systems were improved.

As the Terminal Modernization and Renovation Program was being completed, staff started work on a new Airport Master Plan to guide the development of the Airport over the next twenty years. The first Master Plan working paper, which included forecasts of Airport activity, was released in July 1987. The second working paper, which provides specific facility and land use recommendations, was released in September 1988. The Airport is continually seeking to balance the often conflicting interests of its neighboring communities, Airport tenants, and the traveling public. As air travel grows and world trade increases, San Francisco International Airport is preparing for the future.

In Fiscal Year 1987/88 the Airport continued to make significant improvements in offering a variety of services of the highest quality to the traveling public. New exhibition areas, shops and eating and drinking facilities were opened in the South Terminal. Among airports nationwide, San Francisco International Airport is recognized as a leader in providing high quality services to the air traveler.

Japan

There are over 1,400 direct flights annually from San Francisco to Japan. The Airport is an important gateway to the Far East, handling 46% of all passenger traffic between the West Coast and Japan.

5

SAFETY AND NOISE CONTROL

Safety has been of paramount concern as air traffic has grown. The Airport's safety and emergency preparedness program is unequaled in the nation. The prestigious Aviation Safety Institute Award has been bestowed on San Francisco International Airport for nine consecutive years, in recognition of "the best airport/community safety program in North America."

As a part of its safety program, the Airport conducts three unscheduled safety drills a month. Major disaster drills are periodically conducted in cooperation with neighboring communities and the Airport Medical Clinic, which is equipped with the latest in medical technology and emergency life support systems. The Airport's two fire stations also maintain a rescue boat and a staff of scuba divers for emergencies in the San Francisco Bay.

8

The Airport has established a sophisticated communications center which is recognized as a prototype for emergency management systems throughout the nation, with a mobile communications command post available for aircraft emergencies and natural disasters. The communications center also handles messages for the traveling public. Every day, dispatchers handle over 3,000 calls from the Airport's white courtesy telephones.

◆

Even as the importance of the Airport to international travel and trade grows, the Airport continues to respond to the needs of its surrounding communities. An issue of great concern is aircraft noise. The Airport has established twenty-four noise monitoring stations and the most sophisticated noise monitoring and evaluation system in the country. In the latest count, 4,221 homes were in the 65dB CNEL contour area. This is significantly less than the June 30, 1988 goal of 7,000 homes, as established by the Community Roundtable. The Community Roundtable consists of representatives from nine neighboring cities and San Francisco and meets on a regular basis to review the Airport's noise mitigation efforts.

The San Francisco Airports Commission is sensitive to the concern and needs of the Airport's neighboring communities. In January of 1988, the Commission promulgated a noise regulation program to phase out noisy older aircraft from the Airport. Under this program, by 1999 at least 75% of all aircraft using the Airport will be of the newer, quieter Stage 3 type.

Mexico

The Airport's acclaimed Exhibition Program featured 61 unique exhibits during the year. One of the most popular was "Mexican Folk Art," displaying 500 contemporary and historic folk artifacts from Mexico.

9

12

The Airport makes a tremendous contribution to the Bay Area economy, creating over 31,000 jobs at the Airport and another 151,000 throughout the Bay Area. Altogether, these workers earn over $4.1 billion annually. Businesses dependent on the Airport generate $8.3 billion annually in revenues. As well, over $1.1 billion in local, State, and Federal taxes are raised annually because of the Airport.

The Airport has made substantial outreach efforts to include small, minority, and women-owned firms in the business opportunities at the Airport. Today, 24 concessions are owned and operated by such firms. Last year, 73 contracts were awarded to minority and women-owned businesses accounting for $9.6 million, or 79% of the total dollar amount awarded.

◆

Although owned and operated by the City and County of San Francisco, the Airport receives no support from the City's General Fund. The Airport is run as a successful business enterprise, and actually contributes over $9 million annually to the City's General Fund. This represents an annual dividend of $12 to each San Francisco resident.

The Airport's revenue sources are highly diversified. The largest single Airport tenant accounted for only 17% of total revenues. No other tenant accounted for more than 7% of total revenues. Over the last decade, Airport revenues have grown 350% through sound financial and operational management.

Since 1981, the Airport has reduced airline landing fees more than 57%. San Francisco now has the third lowest landing fee among major airports in the U.S.

The Airport has increased staff only 5% since 1981 although passenger volume has grown 40% and public area square footage has increased 65%. In 1980 dollars, operating cost per enplaned passenger has actually decreased from $3.71 to $3.49. This was accomplished despite the issuance of $218 million in new bonds since 1981 to finance the completion of the Terminal Modernization and Renovation Program.

The Airport's sound financial performance is supported by Standard & Poor's continued A+ and Moody's A1 ratings of the Airport's bonds. Few major airports in the United States have received bond ratings this high. A high revenue bond coverage ratio of 1.9 also underscores the Airport's continued strong financial strength.

Australia

Sydney is San Francisco's "sister city." Once weeks away by sailing ship, the land "down under" is connected to the Bay Area by over 400 direct flights each year from San Francisco International Airport.

13

16

Statement of Income

	Years Ended June 30 1988	1987
Operating Revenues:		
Aviation	$ 58,420,084	$ 59,870,439
Concessions	64,459,746	60,362,313
Net sales and services	3,085,332	3,053,975
Total Operating Revenues	125,965,162	123,286,727
Operating Expenses:		
Operations	27,962,482	26,269,376
Maintenance	33,617,642	29,743,021
Administrative	12,095,173	13,786,749
Depreciation	20,764,098	16,492,086
Total Operating Expenses	94,439,395	86,291,232
Operating Income	31,525,767	36,995,495
Other Income (Expense):		
Interest income	16,117,755	15,564,244
Interest expense	(20,238,177)	(16,648,096)
Non-operating income	69,469	1,369,268
Loss on disposal of property, plant and equipment	(1,879,854)	(1,179,131)
Total Other Income (Expense)	(5,930,807)	(893,715)
Income Before Operating Transfer	25,594,960	36,101,780
Operating Transfer to the City and County of San Francisco	(10,304,251)	(9,048,709)
Net Income	$ 15,290,709	$ 27,053,071

The accompanying notes are an integral part of this statement.

Statement of Equity

	Years Ended June 30 1988	1987
Contributed Capital:		
Beginning of year	$102,937,572	$ 91,918,114
Federal government grants	2,695,012	11,019,458
End of Year	105,632,584	102,937,572
Retained Earnings:		
Beginning of year	251,127,857	224,074,786
Net income	15,290,709	27,053,071
End of Year	266,418,566	251,127,857
Equity at End of Year	$372,051,150	$354,065,429

The accompanying notes are an integral part of this statement.

17

Statement of Changes in Financial Position

	Years Ended June 30 1988	1987
Sources of Funds:		
Operations:		
Net Income	$15,290,709	$27,053,071
Expenses not using working capital:		
Depreciation	20,764,098	16,492,086
Amortization	326,920	342,740
Loss on disposal of property, plant and equipment	1,879,854	1,179,131
Total from Operations	38,261,581	45,067,028
Decrease in restricted assets	24,216,294	27,683,059
Contributed capital—federal grants	2,695,012	11,019,458
Cash proceeds from disposal of equipment	18,595	
Total Sources of Funds	65,191,482	83,769,545
Uses of Funds:		
Acquisition of property, plant, and equipment	38,135,713	51,738,360
Reduction of bonded debt	9,250,000	8,795,000
Decrease in payables from restricted assets	2,985,700	1,078,882
Total Uses of Funds	50,371,413	61,612,242
Increase in Working Capital	$14,820,069	$22,157,303
Working Capital Increase (Decrease) by Component:		
Cash	$27,485,488	$26,862,678
Accounts receivable	(1,022,918)	2,545,086
Accrued interest	522,165	(617,019)
Federal grants receivable	(1,573,311)	15,989
Receivable from City and County of San Francisco		(136,531)
Other	28,408	130,927
Current maturities of bonded debt	(455,000)	(400,000)
Accounts payable	(618,082)	184,832
Claims payable	(197,106)	(3,205,610)
Accrued bond interest payable	113,658	107,525
Accrued payroll and related costs	(767,154)	(300,981)
Payable to City and County of San Francisco	3,248,723	(115,717)
Rent collected in advance and other	(828,337)	166,063
Aviation revenue collected in advance	(11,116,465)	(3,079,939)
Increase in Working Capital	$14,820,069	$22,157,303

The accompanying notes are an integral part of this statement.

Notes to Financial Statements

Note 1

Significant Accounting Policies:

Organization
San Francisco International Airport ("Airport") is an enterprise fund of the City and County of San Francisco ("City"). A five-member Airports Commission is responsible for its operation, development, and maintenance. Commission members are appointed by the City's Mayor for terms of four years. The Airport is an integral part of the City, and the accompanying financial statements are included as a component in the City's Comprehensive Annual Financial Report.

CLIENT:
SAN FRANCISCO INTERNATIONAL AIRPORT

DESIGN FIRM:
MORLA DESIGN

ART DIRECTOR:
JENNIFER MORLA

DESIGNERS:
JENNIFER MORLA, MARIANNE MITTEN

PHOTOGRAPHER:
PAUL FRANZ-MOORE

WRITER:
LEO FERMIN

PRODUCTION MANAGER:
MICHELLE MITCHELL

TYPOGRAPHER:
MERCURY TYPOGRAPHY

PAPER SELECTION:
KASHMIR 80LB, SHASTA GLOSS 80LB

PAPER MANUFACTURER:
SIMPSON PAPER COMPANY

PRINTER:
MASTERCRAFT PRESS

NUMBER OF PAGES:
24

SIZE:
8" X 12"

TYPE SELECTION:
BODONI, FUTURA ULTRABOLD

JOHN MARTIN, ASSISTANT DEPUTY DIRECTOR OF AIRPORTS, SAN FRANCISCO, CALIFORNIA

In 1988, the San Francisco International Airport decided on a "Connecting the World" theme. We wanted to show the link between the San Francisco airport and the places the airport served. Of course, we also wanted to feature San Francisco and the Bay Area as exciting and attractive to visitors. Jennifer Morla did a good theme tie-in. There are large photographs indicating countries and cities. The venues featured in the report have direct, non-stop flights from our airport. We wanted a visually exciting report and we have that. A lot of people called asking for this report, and it is different from annual reports for other airports. This annual report projects an image that is important for this airport to have.

JOHN MARTIN, ASSISTANT DEPUTY DIRECTOR OF AIRPORTS, SAN FRANCISCO, KALIFORNIEN

«Die Länder der Welt verbinden» war das zentrale Thema, das der International Airport San Francisco für den Jahresbericht 1988 gewählt hatte. Wir wollten die Verbindung zwischen dem Flughafen von San Francisco und den Orten zeigen, die von hier aus angeflogen werden. Jennifer Morla gelang eine gute Interpretation des Themas. Grosse Photos zeigen Länder und Städte. Die im Bericht gezeigten Destinationen sind alle durch Direktflüge von San Francisco aus zu erreichen. Wir haben einen visuell attraktiven Bericht bekommen. Viele Leute haben uns angerufen, um diesen Bericht zu erhalten. Er unterscheidet sich sehr deutlich von den Jahresberichten anderer Flughäfen, und er vermittelt genau das richtige Image.

JOHN MARTIN, ASSISTANT DEPUTY DIRECTOR OF AIRPORTS, SAN FRANCISCO, CALIFORNIE

«Mettre en communication le monde entier», tel était le thème à traiter. Nous avons voulu montrer les liens unissant l'aéroport de San Francisco et les destinations desservies. Nous avons bien entendu aussi eu à cœur de mettre en vedette la ville de San Francisco et sa baie. Jennifer Morla a parfaitement saisi le thème, avec les photos de pays et de villes. Les destinations illustrées dans le rapport sont toutes reliées à notre aéroport par des vols directs sans escale. Nous voulions un rapport annuel attrayant sur le plan visuel, et nous l'avons eu. Un tas de gens nous ont appelés pour obtenir le rapport, qui tranche nettement sur ce que produisent les autres aéroports. Notre rapport annuel projette une image importante pour nos besoins spécifiques.

JENNIFER MORLA, MORLA DESIGN, SAN FRANCISCO, CALIFORNIA

San Francisco International Airport wanted an annual report that could express a theme relating to its services. Flying at the moment is no longer considered wonderful, and airport annual reports usually feature the airport and airplanes, or the history of the airport with archival photography. Of course, the airport is part of the city, so there was only a limited budget, but we wanted to show "connecting the world" by indicating destinations that were part of the airport service. This was done through a series of photographs in which the items were quintessential to the places they represented. We also wanted to show San Francisco as a destination, and this is used on the cover, which features a map, telling details, and a feeling of the city along with the baggage claim tags that were created as a graphic device. We also used these individually to introduce each section. We were determined to capture the romance of travel.

JENNIFER MORLA, MORLA DESIGN, SAN FRANCISCO, KALIFORNIEN

Die Flughafenverwaltung wollte, dass in diesem Jahresbericht die Dienstleistungen angesprochen werden. Im Moment wird Fliegen nicht mehr als Vergnügen angesehen, und im allgemeinen werden in den Jahresberichten der Flughafen und Flugzeuge gezeigt. Natürlich ist der Flughafen in städtischem Besitz, was einen kleinen Werbe-Etat bedeutete, aber auf der anderen Seite wollten wir entsprechend dem Thema die vom Flughafen bedienten Destinationen zeigen. Dies geschah durch eine Reihe von Aufnahmen, die typisch für die jeweiligen Orte sind. Wir wollten auch San Francisco als Anflugsziel darstellen und wählten dafür den Umschlag, auf dem eine Karte zu sehen ist, die ein Gefühl dieser Stadt vermittelt. Gepäckscheine dienten dabei als graphische Gestaltungselemente und auch einzeln als Einführungen zu den verschiedenen Kapiteln. Wir wollten etwas von der Romantik des Reisens einfangen.

JENNIFER MORLA, MORLA DESIGN, SAN FRANCISCO, CALIFORNIE

L'Aéroport international de San Francisco souhaitait disposer d'un rapport annuel basé sur un thème qui mettrait en vedette les services offerts. Les vols n'étant aujourd'hui plus considérés comme quelque chose d'extraordinaire, les rapports annuels des aéroports mettent généralement en évidence les structures aéroportuaires, leur histoire, et les avions. L'aéroport étant géré par la municipalité, le budget alloué était modeste. Nous avons voulu illustrer le thème de la «mise en communication du monde entier» par des destinations desservies par l'aéroport de San Francisco. C'est à quoi ont servi une série de photos centrées sur les caractéristiques typiques des villes choisie. Nous avons fait illustrer la couverture par un plan, pour donner un feeling pour l'ambiance de la ville, sans oublier les étiquettes de bagages que nous avons utilisées comme rappel graphique. Nous avons cherché à faire ressentir l'aspect romanesque qui s'attache aux voyages.

FRIDAY'S

FRIDAY'S

T G I Friday's Inc.

1988 Annual Report

Your Just Desserts for a Great Year!

TGI Friday's Inc. had a great year in 1988! And your continued loyalty and support played a big part. We encourage all of our shareholders to be regular Friday's customers. The next time you visit, use this coupon for a free dessert of your choice. Our treat, your pleasure.

Richard E. Rivera
President and
Chief Executive Officer

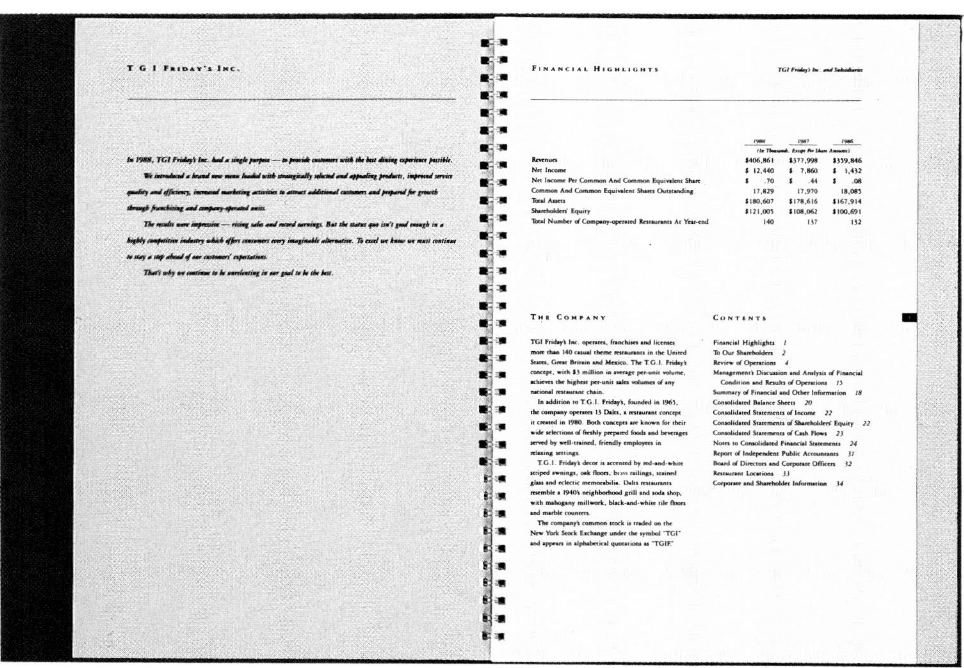

T G I Friday's Inc.

In 1988, TGI Friday's Inc. had a single purpose — to provide customers with the best dining experience possible.

We introduced a brand new menu loaded with strategically selected and appealing products, improved service quality and efficiency, increased marketing activities to attract additional customers and prepared for growth through franchising and company-operated units.

The results were impressive — rising sales and record earnings. But the status quo isn't good enough in a highly competitive industry which offers consumers every imaginable alternative. To excel we know we must continue to stay a step ahead of our customers' expectations.

That's why we continue to be unrelenting in our goal to be the best.

Financial Highlights

TGI Friday's Inc. and Subsidiaries

	1988	1987	1986
	(In Thousands, Except Per Share Amounts)		
Revenues	$406,861	$377,998	$359,846
Net Income	$ 12,440	$ 7,860	$ 1,432
Net Income Per Common And Common Equivalent Share	$ .70	$ .44	$ .08
Common And Common Equivalent Shares Outstanding	17,829	17,970	18,085
Total Assets	$180,607	$178,616	$167,914
Shareholders' Equity	$121,005	$108,062	$100,691
Total Number of Company-operated Restaurants At Year-end	140	137	132

The Company

TGI Friday's Inc. operates, franchises and licenses more than 140 casual theme restaurants in the United States, Great Britain and Mexico. The T.G.I. Friday's concept, with $3 million in average per-unit volume, achieves the highest per-unit sales volumes of any national restaurant chain.

In addition to T.G.I. Friday's, founded in 1965, the company operates 13 Dalts, a restaurant concept it created in 1980. Both concepts are known for their wide selections of freshly prepared foods and beverages served by well-trained, friendly employees in relaxing settings.

T.G.I. Friday's decor is accented by red-and-white striped awnings, oak floors, brass railings, stained glass and eclectic memorabilia. Dalts restaurants resemble a 1940's neighborhood grill and soda shop, with mahogany millwork, black-and-white tile floors and marble counters.

The company's common stock is traded on the New York Stock Exchange under the symbol "TGI" and appears in alphabetical quotations as "TGIF."

Contents

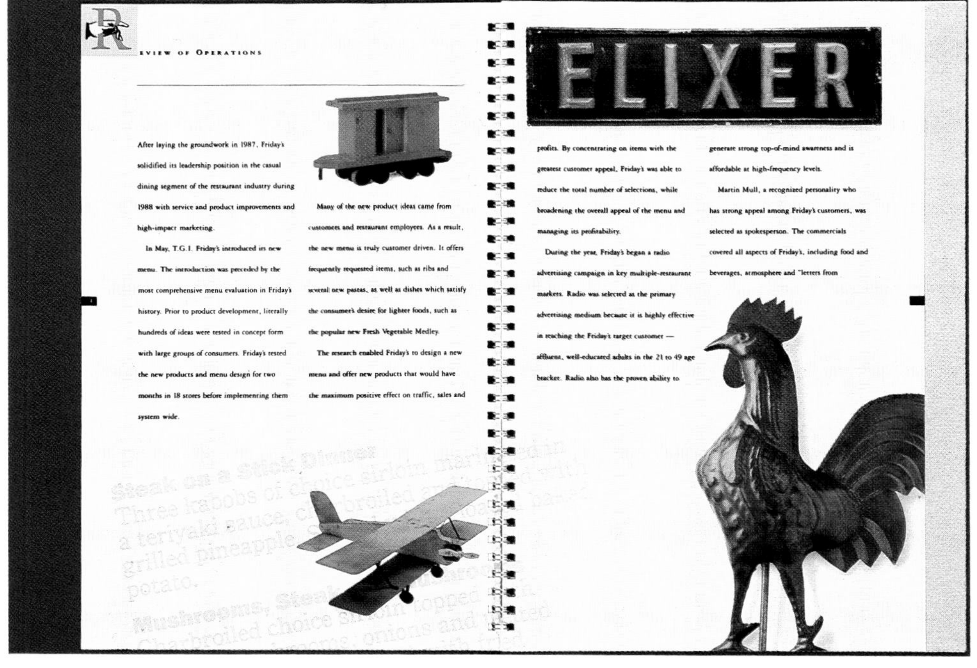

Review of Operations

After laying the groundwork in 1987, Friday's solidified its leadership position in the casual dining segment of the restaurant industry during 1988 with service and product improvements and high-impact marketing.

In May, T.G.I. Friday's introduced its new menu. The introduction was preceded by the most comprehensive menu evaluation in Friday's history. Prior to product development, literally hundreds of ideas were tested in concept form with large groups of consumers. Friday's tested the new products and menu design for two months in 18 stores before implementing them system wide.

Many of the new product ideas came from customers and restaurant employees. As a result, the new menu is truly customer driven. It offers frequently requested items, such as ribs and several new pastas, as well as dishes which satisfy the consumer's desire for lighter foods, such as the popular new Fresh Vegetable Medley.

The research enabled Friday's to design a new menu and offer new products that would have the maximum positive effect on traffic, sales and

profits. By concentrating on items with the greatest customer appeal, Friday's was able to reduce the total number of selections, while broadening the overall appeal of the menu and managing its profitability.

During the year, Friday's began a radio advertising campaign in key multiple-restaurant markets. Radio was selected as the primary advertising medium because it is highly effective in reaching the Friday's target customer — affluent, well-educated adults in the 21 to 49 age bracket. Radio also has the proven ability to generate strong top-of-mind awareness and is affordable at high-frequency levels.

Martin Mull, a recognized personality who has strong appeal among Friday's customers, was selected as spokesperson. The commercials covered all aspects of Friday's, including food and beverages, atmosphere and "letters from

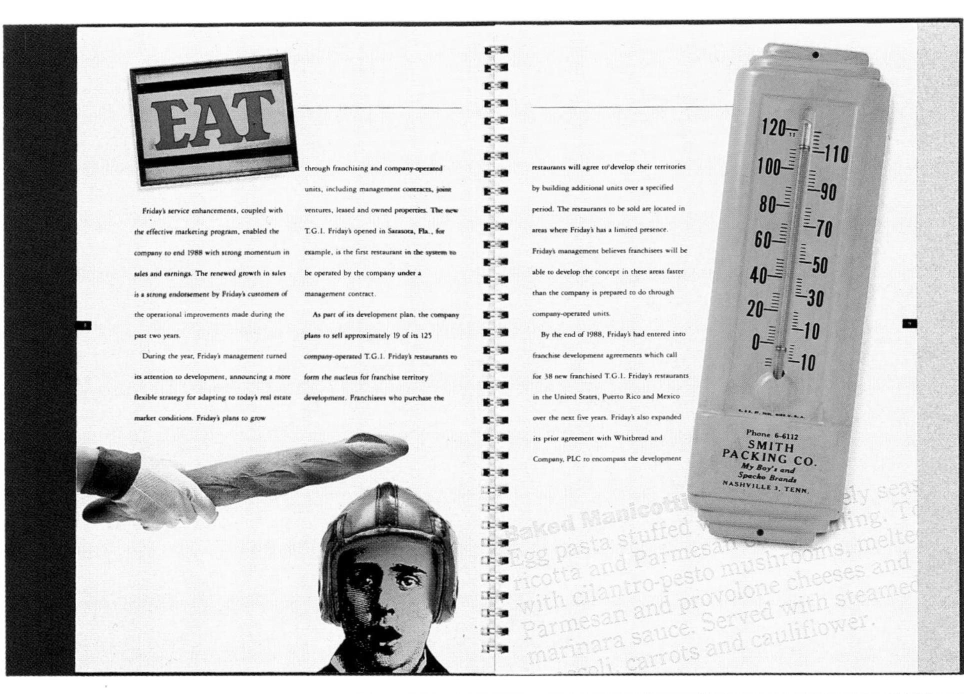

Friday's service enhancements, coupled with the effective marketing program, enabled the company to end 1988 with strong momentum in sales and earnings. The renewed growth in sales is a strong endorsement by Friday's customers of the operational improvements made during the past two years.

During the year, Friday's management turned its attention to development, announcing a more flexible strategy for adapting to today's real estate market conditions. Friday's plans to grow through franchising and company-operated units, including management contracts, joint ventures, leased and owned properties. The new T.G.I. Friday's opened in Sarasota, Fla., for example, is the first restaurant in the system to be operated by the company under a management contract.

As part of its development plan, the company plans to sell approximately 19 of its 125 company-operated T.G.I. Friday's restaurants to form the nucleus for franchise territory development. Franchisees who purchase the restaurants will agree to develop their territories by building additional units over a specified period. The restaurants to be sold are located in areas where Friday's has a limited presence. Friday's management believes franchisees will be able to develop the concept in these areas faster than the company is prepared to do through company-operated units.

By the end of 1988, Friday's had entered into franchise development agreements which call for 38 new franchised T.G.I. Friday's restaurants in the United States, Puerto Rico and Mexico over the next five years. Friday's also expanded its prior agreement with Whitbread and Company, PLC to encompass the development

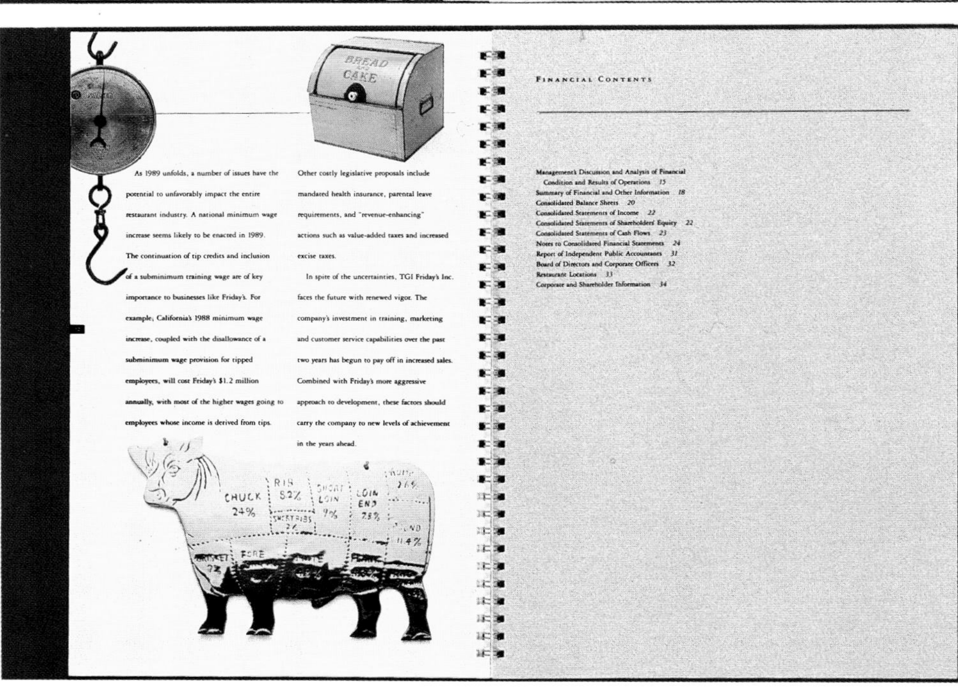

As 1989 unfolds, a number of issues have the potential to unfavorably impact the entire restaurant industry. A national minimum wage increase seems likely to be enacted in 1989. The continuation of tip credits and inclusion of a subminimum training wage are of key importance to businesses like Friday's. For example, California's 1988 minimum wage increase, coupled with the disallowance of a subminimum wage provision for tipped employees, will cost Friday's $1.2 million annually, with most of the higher wages going to employees whose income is derived from tips.

Other costly legislative proposals include mandated health insurance, parental leave requirements, and "revenue-enhancing" actions such as value-added taxes and increased excise taxes.

In spite of the uncertainties, TGI Friday's Inc. faces the future with renewed vigor. The company's investment in training, marketing and customer service capabilities over the past two years has begun to pay off in increased sales. Combined with Friday's more aggressive approach to development, these factors should carry the company to new levels of achievement in the years ahead.

Financial Contents

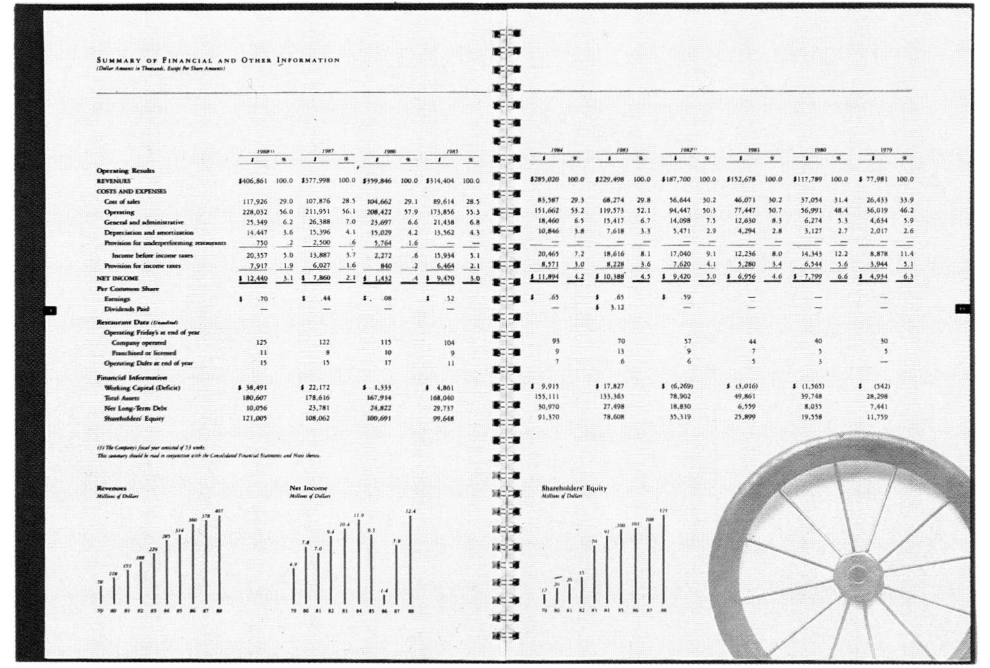

Summary of Financial and Other Information
(Dollar Amounts in Thousands, Except Per Share Amounts)

	1988(1) $	%	1987 $	%	1986 $	%	1985 $	%
Operating Results								
REVENUES	$406,861	100.0	$377,998	100.0	$359,846	100.0	$314,404	100.0
COSTS AND EXPENSES								
Cost of sales	117,926	29.0	107,876	28.5	104,662	29.1	89,614	28.5
Operating	228,032	56.0	211,951	56.1	208,422	57.9	173,856	55.3
General and administrative	25,349	6.2	26,388	7.0	23,697	6.6	21,438	6.8
Depreciation and amortization	14,447	3.6	15,396	4.1	15,029	4.2	13,562	4.3
Provision for underperforming restaurants	750	.2	2,500	.6	5,764	1.6	—	—
Income before income taxes	20,357	5.0	13,887	3.7	2,272	.6	15,934	5.1
Provision for income taxes	7,917	1.9	6,027	1.6	840	.2	6,464	2.1
NET INCOME	$ 12,440	3.1	$ 7,860	2.1	$ 1,432	.4	$ 9,470	3.0
Per Common Share								
Earnings	$ .70		$ .44		$ .08		$ .52	
Dividends Paid	—		—		—		—	
Restaurant Data *(Unaudited)*								
Operating Friday's at end of year								
Company operated	125		122		115		104	
Franchised or licensed	11		8		10		9	
Operating Dalts at end of year	15		15		17		11	
Financial Information								
Working Capital (Deficit)	$ 38,491		$ 22,172		$ 1,333		$ 4,861	
Total Assets	180,607		178,616		167,914		168,040	
Net Long-Term Debt	10,056		23,781		24,822		29,737	
Shareholders' Equity	121,005		108,062		100,691		99,648	

	1984 $	%	1983 $	%	1982(1) $	%	1981 $	%	1980 $	%	1979 $	%
Operating Results												
REVENUES	$285,020	100.0	$229,498	100.0	$187,700	100.0	$152,678	100.0	$117,789	100.0	$ 77,981	100.0
COSTS AND EXPENSES												
Cost of sales	83,587	29.3	68,274	29.8	56,644	30.2	46,071	30.2	37,054	31.4	26,433	33.9
Operating	151,662	53.2	119,573	52.1	94,447	50.3	77,447	50.7	56,991	48.4	36,019	46.2
General and administrative	18,460	6.5	15,417	6.7	14,098	7.5	12,630	8.3	6,274	5.3	4,634	5.9
Depreciation and amortization	10,846	3.8	7,618	3.3	5,471	2.9	4,294	2.8	3,127	2.7	2,017	2.6
Provision for underperforming restaurants	—	—	—	—	—	—	—	—	—	—	—	—
Income before income taxes	20,465	7.2	18,616	8.1	17,040	9.1	12,236	8.0	14,343	12.2	8,878	11.4
Provision for income taxes	8,571	3.0	8,228	3.6	7,620	4.1	5,280	3.4	6,544	5.6	3,944	5.1
NET INCOME	$ 11,894	4.2	$ 10,388	4.5	$ 9,420	5.0	$ 6,956	4.6	$ 7,799	6.6	$ 4,934	6.3
Per Common Share												
Earnings	$ .65		$ .65		$ .59		—		—		—	
Dividends Paid	—		$ 3.12		—		—		—		—	
Restaurant Data *(Unaudited)*												
Operating Friday's at end of year												
Company operated	93		70		57		44		40		30	
Franchised or licensed	9		13		9		7		5		5	
Operating Dalts at end of year	7		6		6		5		3		—	
Financial Information												
Working Capital (Deficit)	$ 9,915		$ 17,827		$ (6,269)		$ (3,016)		$ (1,565)		$ (542)	
Total Assets	155,111		133,363		78,902		49,861		39,748		28,298	
Net Long-Term Debt	30,970		27,498		18,830		6,559		8,035		7,441	
Shareholders' Equity	91,370		78,608		35,319		25,899		19,558		11,759	

(1) The Company's fiscal year consisted of 53 weeks.
This summary should be read in conjunction with the Consolidated Financial Statements and Notes thereto.

CLIENT:
T.G.I. FRIDAY'S INC.

DESIGN FIRM:
HARRISON SIMMONS

ART DIRECTOR:
RICK GAVOS

DESIGNERS:
MIKE CASEBOLT, LINDY GROOMS

PHOTOGRAPHER:
JIM OLVERA

WRITER:
C. PHARR & CO.

PRODUCTION MANAGER:
REBECCA KLUSTNER

TYPOGRAPHER:
SOUTHWEST TYPOGRAPHICS

PAPER SELECTION:
88LB TETON COVER PLUS, 100LB SIGNATURE GLOSS, 70LB GAINSBOROUGH, 70LB TETON TEXT

PAPER MANUFACTURER:
SIMPSON, MEAD

PRINTER:
WILLIAMSON PRESS, DALLAS

NUMBER OF PAGES:
34

SIZE:
12 1/2" X 8 3/4"

TYPE SELECTION:
GARAMOND

MIKIE CASEBOLT, DESIGNER, T.G.I.FRIDAY'S, INC., DALLAS, TEXAS

What we wanted at T.G.I. Friday's was to play off Friday's menu in the 1988 annual report. We wanted the blue cover and cream-colored paper, so that the annual report would capture in some way the feeling of the restaurants. It had been a good year, stable, positive, growing, so we thought we could use the elements that made up aspects of the restaurant and incorporate these in the annual report. We brought in Rick Gavos, and we talked about using the menu, since food is the essence of Friday's. The restaurants also have antiques as part of their decor. We even have a warehouse in Nashville filled with antiques that we use. Rick helped us by bringing a critical eye to the annual report. We deal with these elements every day. We liked his use of enlarged type taken from the menu and the insertion of the antiques within the design, and the capturing of the feeling of the menu. It has been our most requested annual report so far.

MIKIE CASEBOLT, DESIGNER, T.G.I.FRIDAY'S, INC., DALLAS, TEXAS

Im Mittelpunkt des Jahresberichts für 1988 sollte die Menu-Karte stehen. Wir entschieden uns für den blauen Umschlag und das cremefarbene Papier, um etwas von der Atmosphäre des Restaurants im Jahresbericht wiederzugeben. Wir hatten ein gutes Jahr hinter uns, stabil, positiv, mit wachsendem Erfolg und kamen deshalb auf die Idee, verschiedene Elemente, die für das Restaurant bezeichnend sind, im Jahresbericht zu benutzen. Wir engagierten Rick Gavos und diskutierten die Idee der Speisekarte. Zu den Ausstattungen der Restaurants gehören auch Antiquitäten, die wir aus unserem zentralen Lager in Nashville holten. Rick spielte bei unseren Plänen für den Jahresbericht den Kritiker. Seine visuellen Elemente sind uns vertraut. Uns gefiel die vom Menu entlehnte vergrösserte Typographie, der Einbezug der Antiquitäten und die Stimmung, die den Menus entspricht. Dies ist bisher der am meisten gefragte Jahresbericht.

MIKIE CASEBOLT, DESIGNER, T.G.I. FRIDAY'S, INC., DALLAS, TEXAS

Ce qu'on a voulu faire chez T.G.I. Friday's, c'est axer le rapport annuel 1988 sur le menu de nos restaurants, d'où le bleu de la couverture et le papier crème qui tentent de recréer l'atmosphère de restaurant. L'année a été bonne, stable, positive et profitable, ce qui nous a amenés à incorporer dans notre rapport annuel divers éléments visuels propres aux restaurants. Nous avons fait appel à Rick Gavos et avons discuté de l'évocation du menu. Des meubles d'époque sont intégrés au décor de nos restaurants; nous les puisons aux stocks d'un entrepôt central que nous avons à Nashville. Rick nous a aidés à considérer ce rapport d'un œil critique. Ses éléments visuels nous sont familiers. Nous avons particulièrement aimé les caractères de menus agrandis et l'inclusion de meubles d'époques dans le design, ainsi que l'évocation de l'ambiance crée par les menus. A ce jour, c'est le rapport annuel qui nous a été le plus demandé.

RICK GAVOS, ART DIRECTOR, HARRISON SIMMONS, DALLAS, TEXAS

There wasn't going to be a specific message in Friday's 1988 annual report. It had been a good year, and we were going to use a restaurant theme including featuring the antiques the restaurants are decorated with. We wanted to show that going to Friday's was fun. We chose some type from the menus and basically created photocopied art; we placed memorabilia on every spread. Then we matched the colors for the cover and the inside pages to the menu colors. We did an innovative wire binding and two trims (one for the the opening section, one for the financials) and we placed this in a dark blue configured cover to hide the wire and make it look more like the menu.

RICK GAVOS, ART DIRECTOR, HARRISON SIMMONS, DALLAS, TEXAS

In dem Jahresbericht 1988 für Friday's ging es um keine spezielle Botschaft. Es war ein gutes Jahr gewesen, und wir hatten uns für das Restaurant-Thema entschieden, wobei die zur Ausstattung gehörenden Antiquitäten miteinbezogen werden sollten. Wir wollten zeigen, dass ein Besuch bei Friday's ein Vergnügen ist. Wir wählten eine Schriftart, die auf den Menus verwendet wird und stimmten die Farben für den Umschlag und den Inhalt auf die tatsächlichen Speisekarten ab. Wir benutzten eine spezielle Drahtbindung. Zwei schmalere Seiten dienen als Auftakt zum Textteil und zum Finanzteil. Ein Umschlag in Dunkelblau verdeckt den Draht, so dass der Bericht wie ein Menu wirkt.

RICK GAVOS, ART DIRECTOR, HARRISON SIMMONS, DALLAS, TEXAS

Le rapport annuel de Friday's pour 1988 ne comportait pas de message spécifique à interpréter. L'année avait été bonne, et nous allions utiliser un sujet de restaurant mettant en vedette les meubles d'époque qui font partie de la décoration. Nous avons voulu montrer que c'était un plaisir d'aller dîner chez Friday's. Nous avons sélectionné certains caractères des menus et puis nous avons assorti les couleurs de la couverture et des pages intérieurs à celles des menus. Nous avons procédé à un brochage novateur au fil métallique en rognant le chapitre initial et la section financière et en plaçant le tout dans une couverture bleu foncé qui cache le fil et évoque l'aspect d'un menu.

1988 Annual Report

TIME INC.

By the mid-1990s, the media and entertainment industry will consist of a handful of vertically integrated, worldwide giants. Time Inc. will be one of them...

FINANCIAL HIGHLIGHTS *(in millions except per share amounts)*	Time Incorporated and Subsidiaries 1988	1987
Revenues	$4,507	$4,195
Operating income	653	582
Net income	289	250
Earnings per share	$ 5.01	$ 4.18
Total assets	$4,913	$4,424
Working capital	416	427
Long-term debt	1,485	1,118
Shareholders' equity	1,350	1,248
Return on year-end equity	21.3%	20.0%
Long-term debt as a percentage of capitalization	52.2%	47.3%
Shares outstanding at December 31	56.7	57.8

To Our Shareholders Since the environment we find ourselves in is so unusual, so filled with change and turmoil, we've decided to start where we normally leave off: with the shape of things to come.

It is the middle of the next decade. The media and entertainment industry has been radically reconfigured from what it was just five or six years before. As a result of mergers, acquisitions and joint ventures undertaken to achieve the size necessary to compete in the international marketplace, there is now a limited number of global giants.

VISION

Whether American or European or Asian, all of these companies have a common denominator. They are vertically integrated: that is, large enough to create, market and disseminate their products worldwide, and smart enough to amortize costs across as many distribution outlets as possible.

Time Inc. is one of them.

The net effect will be to encourage the forces already at work in the current round of mergers and acquisitions. Since the new Administration pledges continuity with the old, we don't foresee any urgent attempt to slow the process down. To the contrary, with foreign interests buying more and more of our domestic assets, Congress may be receptive to legislative changes that put American industry in a stronger competitive position.

CREATIVITY

In the areas that concern Time Inc. most, we expect regulatory changes that will permit networks to own cable systems, and to own and syndicate their productions. This will make those networks, cable operations, cable networks and film/entertainment companies attractive targets for acquisition, merger and joint venture

Every player in the media/entertainment business – at least every smart one – will be trying to build vertically integrated enterprises that can compete in the new reality of the global marketplace. To master the scope of this challenge and to achieve the necessary economies of scale, companies will have to grow dramatically in size.

As a result, Time Inc.'s future depends on its ability to achieve two goals: first, to become vertically integrated in the entertainment business; second, to expand aggressively outside this country.

We have no doubt Time Inc. will meet these goals.

$289 million, up 16 percent, and earnings per share rose 20 percent to $5.01.

We're proud that for the second year in a row Time Inc.'s operations turned in a record performance. We believe these results reflect our commitment to excellence and the consumer loyalty that this commitment has earned us. But being proud doesn't make us presumptuous. Tastes change, and we have to anticipate those changes. Each of our franchises must be constantly renewed and reinvigorated, sometimes reinvented, always rethought, continually made to give added value to our customers.

COMPETITION

Time Inc. Magazines is a case in point. In 1988, *Time* and *People* underwent extensive redesign. We also added four new titles to our list. Our magazines are among the best known in the world, but what isn't so well known is how aggressively we've expanded. We published eight magazines at the beginning of the decade. We now publish 24.

For the future, we're excited about the momentum Time Inc. Magazines is building, especially the partnerships and joint ventures that are giving us access to new markets and new advertisers. These include our purchase of a half-interest in Whittle Communications, as well as our international ventures with companies like Hachette, Mondadori and Seibu.

Ask people what they associate with Time Inc., and the first response will probably be the quality of our editorial product. That's true as far as it goes,

Every smart player in the media and entertainment business will try to compete in the new global marketplace. To do so and achieve the necessary economies of scale, companies will have to grow dramatically.

COMMITMENT

but it doesn't go nearly far enough. We are a company composed of unique strengths. All of our franchises currently rank first or second in their categories.

In programming, for example, we possess the preeminent pay-TV franchise: Home Box Office. It is a brand name with almost universal recognition. In 1988 HBO strengthened its reputation as the best programmer in cable television – some would say in television, period. Along with its sister pay service, *Cinemax*, *HBO* won 37 ACE Awards. Home Box Office also won the Golden ACE for General Excellence, and cable TV's first Emmy Awards.

We are the country's largest and most effective direct marketer of print and programming, but as strong as we are, we're always seeking ways to improve our performance. In early 1989, we united Time-Life Books and Book-of-the-Month Club under a new management umbrella, Time Inc. Books Direct, that will allow us to realize economies of scale in marketing and distribution.

We see potential for the dramatic expansion of all our businesses through internal growth and acquisitions. American Television and Communications, our cable arm, has successfully pursued both. ATC's basic cable subscribers have increased for 26 consecutive months, and the company has also made some strategically important acquisitions.

"We are in the idea business." We not only strive to benefit our shareholders and serve our customers, we also expect to make a significant contribution to public discourse.

In judging the worth of potential acquisitions, the aim has never been merely to make our cable business big. In all our businesses, we have the same standard. We want a high return on our investment. If a deal offers us a major strategic benefit, we won't be as rigid on the return requirements. But the benefit must be there.

There is no secret to Time Inc.'s success or to our confidence in the Company's future. But in Time Incers we have an asset that, if not hidden, is perhaps sometimes undervalued by those outside this Company. Time Inc.'s core strength is its people. Their work is the essence of everything we produce, and their loyalty is as much to an idea as to an institution: to the independence that allows them the full use of their talent and creativity.

We know that the time ahead will be full of unanticipated events and unexpected outcomes. But to a large degree the future we described at the beginning of this Letter is already here. The evolution of a global economy is fact, not fantasy, and so is Time Inc.'s place in it.

Time Inc. will be one of the media and entertainment giants of the 21st Century. More important, the enduring commitment of this Company will remain what it has always been: to make a significant contribution to public discourse, to stand for something, to make a difference.

J. RICHARD MUNRO
Chairman and Chief Executive Officer

N.J. NICHOLAS JR
President and Chief Operating Officer

"There is no secret to Time Inc.'s success or to our confidence in this Company's future. Our core strength is our people. Their work is the essence of everything we produce.

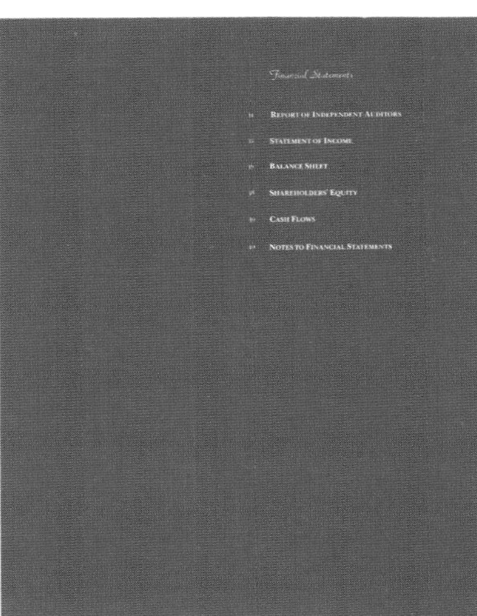

Financial Statements

CLIENT:
TIME INC.

DESIGN FIRM:
FRANKFURT GIPS BALKIND

ART DIRECTOR:
KENT HUNTER

DESIGNER:
KENT HUNTER

PHOTOGRAPHERS:
MARK JENKINSON, WILLIAM -DUKE

ILLUSTRATORS:
VARIOUS

WRITER:
TIME INC.

TYPOGRAPHER:
FRANKFURT GIPS BALKIND, JCH GRAPHICS

PAPER SELECTION:
CENTURA DULL, TETON IVORY, TETON HEATHER

PAPER MANUFACTURER:
CONSOLIDATED, SIMPSON

PRINTER:
L.P. THEBAULT

NUMBER OF PAGES:
48 PLUS COVER

LOUIS J. SLOVINSKY, VICE-PRESIDENT OF CORPORATE COMMUNICATIONS, TIME WARNER INC., NEW YORK, NEW YORK

For the Time, Inc. 1988 annual report, we decided on our strategic vision late in the year. Then we worked on it with Frankfurt Gips Balkind, who understand our company. There wasn't a lot of time, but our management analyst's presentation articulated the firm's vision of the 1990s and beyond. The bulk of the stockholders had not yet been exposed to this thinking. It was a daring notion. The annual report had to contain a letter, a review of the operations, and the financial statements. The letter had a message; the annual report had to reduce these abstract concepts to concrete illustrations. The illustrations were all developed by different artists, who captured the sense of our future through editorial-looking illustrations. We had also used stylized photography to reflect the past year. The annual report proved, of course, to be critical. It had an important role in our new departure for the company. We also had a happy ending, since we then acquired Warner.

LOUIS J. SLOVINSKY, VICE-PRESIDENT OF CORPORATE COMMUNICATIONS, TIME WARNER INC., NEW YORK, NEW YORK

Die Strategie für den Jahresbericht 1988 von Time Inc. wurde gegen Ende des Jahres festgelegt. Dann setzten wir uns mit Frankfurt Gips Balkind zusammen, die mit unserem Unternehmen vertraut sind. Es lag eine klare Formulierung der Zukunftspläne der Geschäftsführung für die 90er Jahre und sogar darüberhinaus vor. Die meisten Aktionäre waren damit noch nicht vertraut, und das war eine unangenehme Vorstellung. Der Jahresbericht musste einen Brief enthalten, einen Rückblick auf den Geschäftsgang und die Finanzdaten. Im Jahresbericht mussten diese abstrakten Konzepte in konkrete Illustrationen umgesetzt werden. Sie wurden von verschiedenen Künstlern kreiert, Bilder der Zukunft im Stil von redaktionellen Illustrationen. Ausserdem verwendeten wir stilisierte Photos, um das vergangene Jahr zu illustrieren. Der Bericht spielte eine wichtige Rolle für das neue Konzept. Es gab schliesslich ein gutes Ende, da wir Warner übernehmen konnten.

LOUIS J. SLOVINSKY, VICE-PRESIDENT OF CORPORATE COMMUNICATIONS, TIME WARNER INC., NEW YORK, NEW YORK

Pour le rapport annuel 1988 de Time, Inc., nous avons opté pour une vision stratégique déterminée en fin d'année. Puis nous y avons travaillé avec Frankfurt Gips Balkind, qui comprennent nos objectifs. Il ne nous restait que peu de temps, d'autant plus que l'analyste attaché à notre direction avait rédigé un text évoquant la décennie 1990 et le siècle nouveau - notion qui n'était pas encore familière à la majorité de nos actionnaires. Le rapport annuel devait comporter une lettre, un sommaire des opérations et les résultats financiers. Le rapport annuel devait réduire ces concepts abstraits à des illustrations concrètes. Ces dernières ont été confiées à différents artistes qui ont adopté le style éditorial pour leurs images de l'avenir. Nous avons aussi eu recours à des photos stylisées pour évoquer les événements de l'année écoulée. Bien entendu, ce rapport venait à un moment décisif, puisqu;il a joué un rôle important dans la transition qui a mené à l'acquisition de Warner.

AUBREY BALKIND, FRANKFURT GIPS BALKIND, NEW YORK, NEW YORK

In a normal annual report we expect to cover a lot of topics, but for this Time Inc. annual report, we had to deal with the future of the company. It was the centerpiece of the report. We had six key words–and these words led to six illustrations of great diversity. These appeared as part of spreads that also contained vision statements relating to the words. Along with this new vision of the company, we used big photographs with a historical feeling to them to convey what had happened in the past year. As a graphic device, we used a frame on the pages to tie the book together. This annual report presented many levels of information. Luckily, the client loved it.

AUBREY BALKIND, FRANKFURT GIPS BALKIND, NEW YORK, NEW YORK

In einem normalen Jahresbericht müssen allgemein viele Themen behandelt werden, aber in diesem Geschäftsbericht für Time Inc. ging es um die Zukunft der Firma. Wir hatten sechs Schlüsselbegriffe - und diese Begriffe führten zu sechs Illustrationen in den verschiedensten Auffassungen. Auf diesen Seiten wurden auch entsprechende Äusserungen über die Zukunftspläne aufgeführt. Daneben wurde das Geschehen im vergangenen Jahr anhand von grossen, historisch wirkenden Photos dargestellt. Die Einrahmungen der Seiten dienten als verbindendes graphisches Element. Es ging um viele Informationsebenen. Der Kunde war sehr zufrieden.

AUBREY BALKIND, FRANKFURT GIPS BALKIND, NEW YORK, NEW YORK

Dans un rapport annuel courant, nous nous attendons à traiter toute une série de sujets. Dans ce rapport annuel pour Time Inc., nous n'en avons eu qu'un: l'avenir de la société. Les six mots-clefs choisis ont été transposée en six illustrations. Sur les doubles pages qui les reproduisent, on trouve également des messages verbaux. Parallèlement à ces projections sur l'avenir de l'entreprise, nous avons utilisé des photos au grand format à caractère historique pour rendre compte des opérations de l'année passée en revue. Au plan graphique, nous avons utilisé le cadrage des pages pour assurer l'homogénéité de l'ouvrage. Ce rapport annuel étage l'information sur plusieurs niveaux.

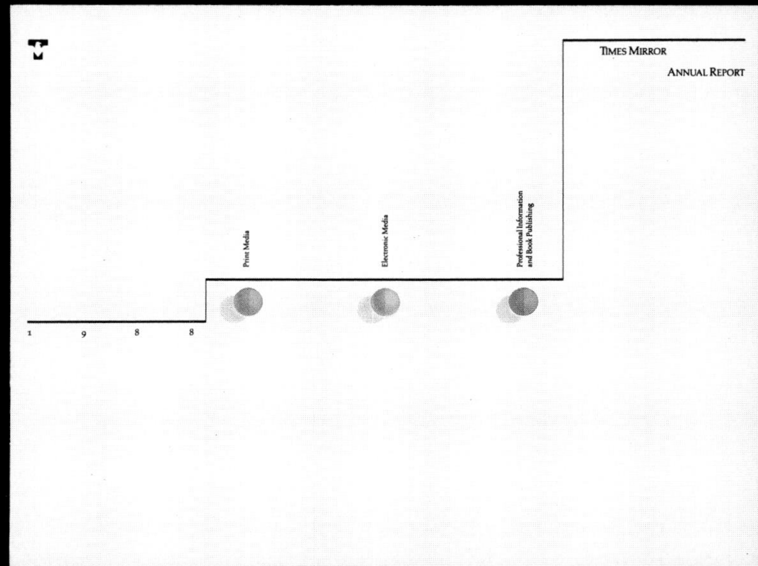
TIMES MIRROR
ANNUAL REPORT
Print Media
Electronic Media
Professional Information and Book Publishing
1 9 8 8

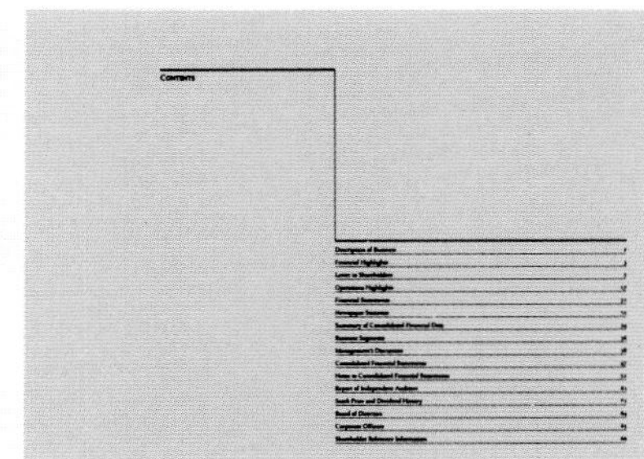

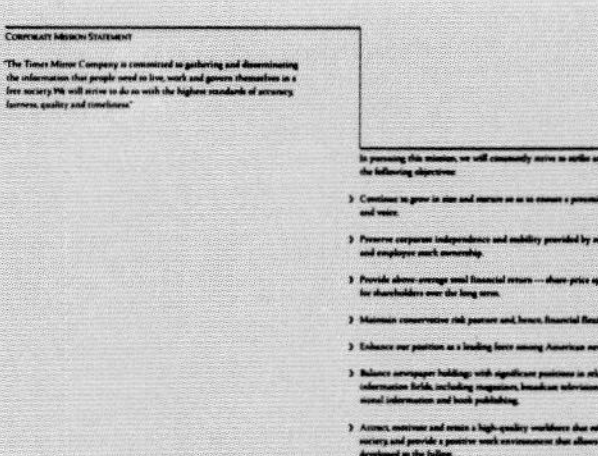

1983 Areas of Business

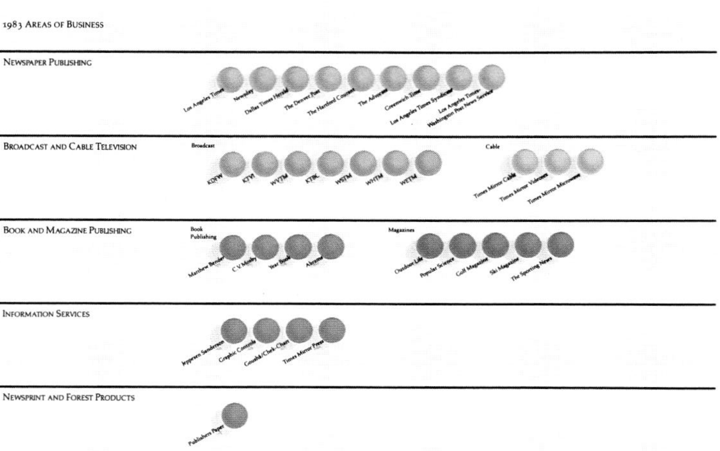

Newspaper Publishing

Los Angeles Times · Newsday · Dallas Times Herald · The Denver Post · The Hartford Courant · The Advocate · Greenwich Time · Los Angeles Times Syndicate · Los Angeles Times-Washington Post News Service

Broadcast and Cable Television

Broadcast: KDFW · KTVI · WVTM · KTBC · WSTM · WHTM · WETM

Cable: Times Mirror Cable · Times Mirror Videotex · Times Mirror Microwave

Book and Magazine Publishing

Book Publishing: Matthew Bender · C.V. Mosby · Year Book · Abrams

Magazines: Outdoor Life · Popular Science · Golf Magazine · Ski Magazine · The Sporting News

Information Services

Jeppesen Sanderson · Graphic Controls · Coustha/Chek-Chart · Times Mirror Press

Newsprint and Forest Products

Publishers Paper

Art and Graphic Products

M. Grumbacher · Chartpak · Plan Hold

6

Current Areas of Business

Print Media

Newspaper Publishing: Los Angeles Times · Newsday and New York Newsday · The Baltimore Sun Newspapers · The Hartford Courant · The Morning Call · The Advocate · Greenwich Time · Los Angeles Times Syndicate · Los Angeles Times-Washington Post News Service

Field & Stream · Popular Science · Outdoor Life · Home Mechanix · Golf Magazine · Ski Magazine · Skiing · Salt Water SPORTSMAN · Yachting · The Sporting News · Sports inc. The Sports Business Weekly · Broadcasting · National Journal

Electronic Media

Broadcast Television: KDFW · KTVI · WVTM · KTBC

Cable Television: Times Mirror Cable

Professional Information and Book Publishing

Matthew Bender · C.V. Mosby · Year Book · Richard D. Irwin · Jeppesen Sanderson · Learning International · Zenger-Miller · Mirror Systems · Abrams

7

Share of Revenues by Business Segment

Times Mirror's operations are concentrated in three core areas: print media (newspapers and magazines), electronic media (broadcast and cable television), and professional information and book publishing. For current financial reporting purposes, the company uses the business segments shown in the charts on this page, with the exception of Newsprint and Forest Products.

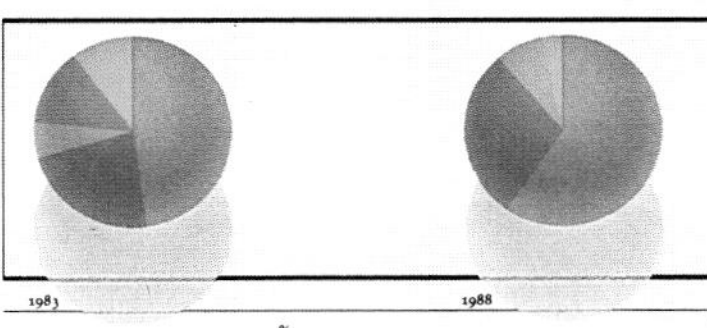

1983	%	1988	%
Newspaper Publishing	48	Newspaper Publishing	60
Book, Magazine & Other Publishing	18	Book, Magazine & Other Publishing	26
Broadcast Television	4	Broadcast Television	3
Cable Television	6	Cable Television	8
Newsprint and Forest Products	13	Newsprint and Forest Products	—
Corporate and Other	11	Corporate and Other	3

Operating Profit by Business Segment

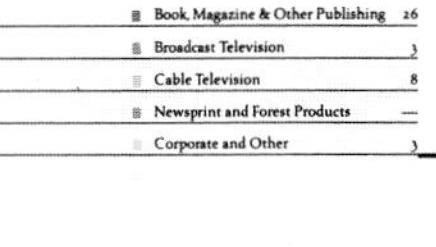

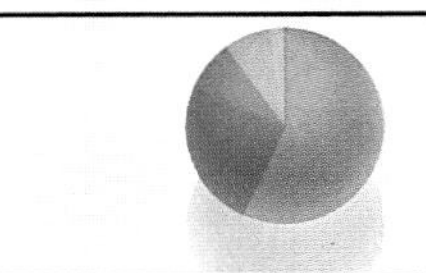

1983	%	1988	%
Newspaper Publishing	59	Newspaper Publishing	58
Book, Magazine & Other Publishing	23	Book, Magazine & Other Publishing	24
Broadcast Television	17	Broadcast Television	8
Cable Television	4	Cable Television	8
Newsprint and Forest Products	(2)	Newsprint and Forest Products	—
Corporate and Other	(1)	Corporate and Other	2

More than 25 percent of our revenues was derived from cable television and professional publishing. In a year when growth in advertising revenues was depressed, the results of these operations, whose revenues are not advertising driven, increased significantly. These increases did not, however, fully offset the 21 percent decline in operating profit from newspaper publishing, magazines and broadcast television.

While our newspapers struggled hard to overcome the problem of soft advertising revenues and unusually high newsprint price increases, as noted above, we pushed forward with strategic programs designed to enhance our growth prospects and meet competitive challenges. Total payments for capital programs for the company reached $301.6 million in 1988, compared with $246.5 million in 1987. More than $229 million was spent in 1988 on continuing expansion and modernization programs at our newspapers, reflecting the fact that the largest share of our capital spending currently is related to our newspapers. Total capital spending on these important production improvements will reach $1 billion over a 14-year period, beginning with the expansion programs at the *Los Angeles Times* and *Newsday* in 1979 and extending to the scheduled completion in 1992 of programs currently under way. The benefits of these investments will soon become evident and will continue for years to come.

Development projects at the *Los Angeles Times* relate to the core product as well as to separate editions of *The Times* in Orange County, the San Fernando Valley and elsewhere within the newspaper's large and rapidly growing market area. An integral part of these product, marketing and service improvements is the greatly enhanced production capabilities to be derived from *The Times'* press project begun in 1987. Construction of the paper's new, downtown 650,000-square-foot Olympic Plant proceeded on schedule and on budget in 1988. Installation of the first Colorliner presses has begun, and initial production runs will commence later this year with completion of the entire plant expected in 1990. Work will begin this year on the San Fernando and Orange County phases of the press project, which will be completed in 1992.

The Times exceeded $1 billion in revenues for the first time in 1988. Twelve-month average circulation achieved record levels of 1,127,117 daily and 1,409,092 on Sunday. Advertising revenues increased by 4 percent, as *The Times* once again led all U.S. newspapers in total advertising linage, as it has since 1955. *The Times* faces strong challenges from other successful newspapers in various parts of Southern California—competition that we intend to counter aggressively with all the resources and skills required to do so.

Our second largest newspaper, *Newsday*, enjoyed another year of dynamic circulation growth as *New York Newsday* achieved circulation records in 1988. Total 12-month average *Newsday* circulation exceeded 679,000 daily, moving the newspaper into sixth place among U.S. dailies. Development cost of *New York Newsday* remains substantial but was slightly less in 1988 than in 1987. The acceptance of this edition remains a high priority and one of our most promising long-term initiatives.

At the same time, *Newsday* is strengthening its basic Long Island franchise and adding to its production capabilities at its Melville headquarters. A ninth 10-unit press went into production in 1988, and installation of a 10th press is scheduled to be completed late in 1989. New inserting systems will effectively double capacity on each press. The first of these inserting systems will come on line in 1990.

9

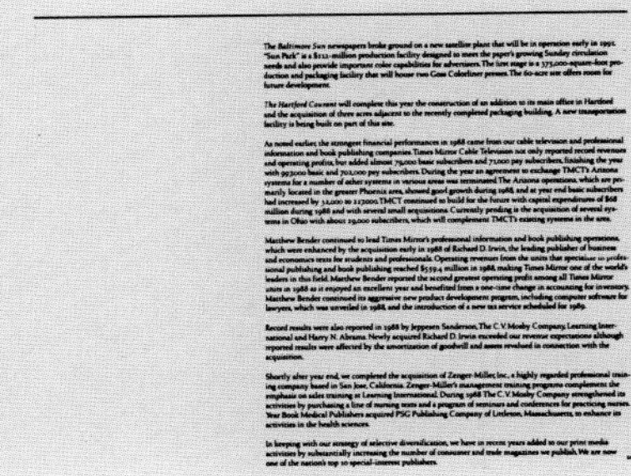

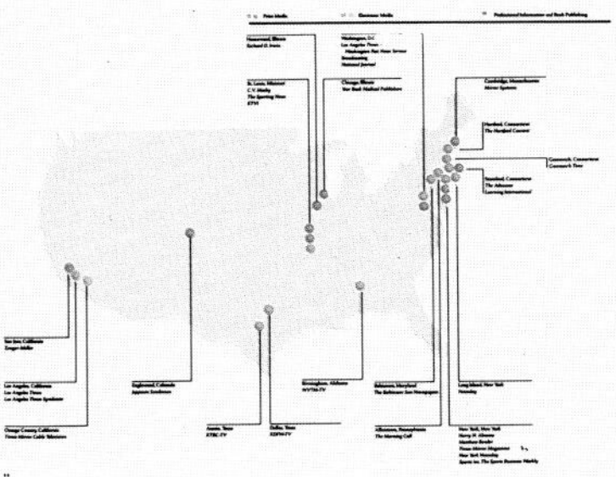

Note D – Dispositions	During 1988 the company sold certain assets of Times Mirror Press to GTE Directories Corporation for approximately $33,000,000 and also sold more than 171,000 acres of timberlands for approximately $85,811,000. These sales resulted in an aggregate gain of $58,880,000 before income taxes and $39,969,000 (31 cents per share) after applicable income taxes.

During 1987 the company completed its sale of *The Denver Post* to an affiliate of the Media News Group. The company received $25,000,000 in cash and long-term notes with a face value of $70,000,000. The company also sold more than 94,000 acres of timberlands for approximately $63,000,000. These sales resulted in a loss of $29,225,000 before income taxes and $15,801,000 (12 cents per share) after applicable income tax benefits.

During 1986 the company sold Times Mirror Microwave Communications Company, television stations WHTM-TV, Harrisburg, Pennsylvania; WSTM-TV, Syracuse, New York; and WETM-TV, Elmira, New York; its interest in Community Cable TV of Las Vegas, Nevada; The Times Herald Printing Company; The H.M. Goushā Company; and Graphic Controls Corporation. These sales resulted in an aggregate gain of $222,150,000 before income taxes and $170,087,000 ($1.32 per share) after applicable income taxes. Proceeds from the sale of Graphic Controls included preferred stock, some of which has voting rights.

The effect of these dispositions has been presented in the Statements of Consolidated Income as "Gain (Loss) on sales of assets."

Note E – Interest Expense

For the years ended December 31, 1988, 1987 and 1986, interest expense of $69,237,000, $59,496,000 and $64,993,000, respectively, was incurred; $11,520,000, $6,865,000 and $5,251,000 of which was capitalized.

Note F – Inventories

Inventories consist of the following (in thousands):

	1988	1987	1986
Newsprint and paper	$ 58,892	$ 48,456	$ 51,393
Books and other finished products	57,027	47,744	52,363
Work-in-process	25,525	10,341	10,066
Raw materials	3,445	3,015	2,552
	$144,889	$109,556	$116,374

Inventories determined on the last-in, first-out method were $53,971,000, $44,775,000 and $59,668,000 at December 31, 1988, 1987 and 1986, respectively, and would have been higher by $20,121,000 in 1988, $17,848,000 in 1987 and $15,429,000 in 1986 had the first-in, first-out method (which approximates current cost) been used exclusively.

Note G – Timber-Cutting Contracts

Subsidiaries of the company have entered into a number of timber-cutting contracts, which will expire at various times through 1991, with the federal government and the state of Oregon. Some of the contracts require the company to harvest and pay for timber at prices that exceed the current market value of such timber. Improvements in the economy and the construction industry may result in increased timber prices, thereby eliminating or substantially mitigating the company's economic exposure under the contracts. The company anticipates that losses, if any, on its timber contracts would not have a significant effect on the company's earnings in any single year and, in the aggregate, would not have a material adverse effect on its financial position at any date.

Note H – Income Taxes

The company reports certain income and expense items in different years for financial and tax reporting purposes. Deferred income taxes have been provided with respect to such items that are related principally to accelerated depreciation, the cutting of timber, pension income or expense, magazine subscription expenses, deferred compensation, installment sales and book returns.

The Financial Accounting Standards Board issued Statements of Financial Accounting Standards No. 96, "Accounting for Income Taxes" (SFAS 96), and No. 100, "Accounting for Income Taxes—Deferral of the Effective Date of SFAS 96." Companies are required to adopt the new method of accounting for income taxes no later than 1990. The company has not determined when it will adopt SFAS 96 or whether it will restate prior-year financial statements. This adoption is not expected to have an adverse effect on the financial position of the company.

54

Income tax expense consists of the following (in thousands):

	1988	1987	1986
Current			
Federal	$133,069	$135,909	$163,880
State	41,458	39,325	42,561
Foreign	9,608	9,539	9,713
Deferred			
Federal	21,715	38,510	49,646
State	4,382	5,566	6,347
	$210,232	$228,849	$272,147

Deferred income tax expense resulted from the following (in thousands):

	1988	1987	1986
Accelerated depreciation	$ 15,904	$ 18,028	$ 21,845
Pension	18,209	22,296	30,913
Other	(8,016)	3,752	3,235
	$ 26,097	$ 44,076	$ 55,993

Income tax expense differs from the amount computed by applying the federal statutory rate to income before income taxes. This difference is reconciled as follows (in thousands):

	1988	1987	1986
34% of pretax income (40% in 1987 and 46% in 1986)	$184,309	$198,136	$312,907
State and local income taxes, net of federal effect	30,254	26,935	26,410
Goodwill amortization not deductible for tax purposes	8,152	8,513	6,802
Effect from income taxed at capital gains rates principally related to the sales of assets and the cutting of timber		(1,511)	(31,927)
Investment tax credit	(2,038)	(5,049)	(10,933)
Difference in basis on sales of assets			(23,756)
Other	(10,445)	1,825	(7,356)
	$210,232	$228,849	$272,147

Note I – Long-Term Debt

Long-term debt consists of the following (in thousands):

	December 31, 1988	December 31, 1987
Commercial paper effectively due in 1991 with average interest rates of 9.37% in 1988 and 7.73% in 1987	$ 93,315	$278,973
8% Notes due December 15, 1996	100,000	100,000
8¼% Notes due April 1, 1996	100,000	100,000
8⅜% Notes due March 1, 1991, net of unamortized discount	99,946	99,921
8⅞% Notes due February 1, 1998, net of unamortized discount	99,727	
8⅞% Notes due January 1, 1993, net of unamortized discount	99,660	
10% Notes due December 30, 1990	55,000	55,000
10% Notes due August 15, 1990, net of unamortized discount	99,756	99,606
Guaranteed bank loans of Employee Stock Ownership Plan	109,900	121,800
Others maturing through 2000 with interest rates from 5% to 15%	19,600	22,488
	$876,904	$877,788

55

Stock Price and Dividend History

The Series A common stock of the company is traded on the New York Stock Exchange. The ticker symbol is TMC. The number of shareholders of record of the company's common stock at December 31, 1988, was 5,461.

*Per share information has been adjusted to reflect a 100 percent stock dividend in 1987 and a 1984 stock split.

62

Stock Price and Dividend History

Earnings Per Share*

Month End Stock Price

Dividends Per Share*

Volume

78 79 80 81 82 83 84 85 86 87 88

CLIENT:
THE TIMES MIRROR COMPANY

DESIGN FIRM:
ROBERT MILES RUNYAN & ASSOCIATES

ART DIRECTOR:
JIM BERTÉ

DESIGNER:
JIM BERTÉ

PHOTOGRAPHER:
CYNTHIA MOORE

ILLUSTRATOR:
PAUL BICE

WRITER:
BONNIE CHAIKIND

TYPOGRAPHER:
COMPOSITION TYPE

PRINTER:
GEORGE RICE & SONS

NUMBER OF PAGES:
66 PLUS COVER

SIZE:
8 1/2" X 11"

TYPE SELECTION:
ALDUS

BONNIE CHAIKIND, MANAGER OF CORPORATE COMMUNICATION, THE TIMES MIRROR COMPANY, LOS ANGELES, CALIFORNIA

In the Times Mirror 1988 annual report, we wanted to stress our recently completed restructuring program. Our company was now divied into three distinct areas of business. We wanted the Chairman's introduction to be incorporated into the graphics, and Jim Berté introduced the idea of spheres, which became the device to make the new structure clear. We had a color-coded map with spheres to show the concentration of growth in each area. We discovered that this logically followed the use of the charts that had been introduced in the 1987 annual report. We found that through a graphic representation people were reacting to the way information was depicted, the way they could see things clearly on paper. For the 1988 annual report, the graphics were further honed to indicate the new core area of the business.

BONNIE CHAIKIND, MANAGER OF CORPORATE COMMUNICATION. THE TIMES MIRROR COMPANY, LOS ANGELES, KALIFORNIEN

Im Times Mirror Jahresbericht 1988 wollten wir das kürzlich abgeschlossene Umstrukturierungsprogramm in den Mittelpunk stellen. Unsere Firma wurde in drei klar abgegrenzte Geschäftsbereiche aufgeteilt. Die Einleitung des Geschäftsführers sollte graphisch unterstützt werden, und Jim Berté hatte die Idee mit den Kugeln, mit deren Hilfe die neue Struktur verdeutlicht werden sollte. Anhand einer farbkodierten Karte und der Kugeln zeigten wir das konsolidierte Wachstum in jedem Bereich. Wir betrachteten dies als die logische Fortsetzung der im Bericht für 1987 verwendeten Diagramme. Wir stellten fest, dass die graphische Darstellung der Informationen die Leute ansprach. Im Bericht für 1988 wurden Graphiken zudem für die Darstellung der neuen Hauptgeschäftsbereiche eingesetzt.

BONNIE CHAIKIND, MANAGER OF CORPORATE COMMUNICATIONS, THE TIMES MIRROR COMPANY, LOS ANGELES, CALIFORNIE

Dans le rapport annuel de Times Mirror pour 1988, nous souhaitions faire ressortir l'achèvement de notre programme de restructuration selon trois axes principaux de l'entreprise. Nous désirions faire bénéficier l'introduction de notre P.-D.G. du traitement graphique par Jim Berté, qui a eu l'idée des sphères pour clarifier la nouvelle structure. Dans chacun des trois secteurs d'activité, la concentration de la croissance est indiquée par ces billes sur une carte codée couleur. Pour nous, c'était la suite logique des graphiques introduits dans notre rapport annuel pour 1987. La représentation graphique permet de mieux décoder l'information donnée. Pour le rapport annuel 1988, les graphiques déjà utilisés ont été affinés afin de distinguer clairement les nouveaux secteurs-clefs de nos activités.

JIM BERTÉ, ROBERT MILES RUNYAN & ASSOCIATES, PLAYA DEL REY, CALIFORNIA

The 1988 Times Mirror annual report was a big book for a big client that is conservative by nature. For this year, we created geometrically shaped charts. Also, it was important to show the organization after the restructuring of the company. We had to find a way of doing a second annual report with charts and graphics without repeating ourselves. The solution was obviously to focus on the changes and switch to a horizontal format for this one.

JIM BERTÉ, ROBERT MILES RUNYAN & ASSOCIATES, PLAYA DEL REY, KALIFORNIEN

Der Jahresbericht von Times Mirror für 1988 war ein grosser Bericht für einen grossen Kunden, der von Natur aus konservativ ist. Dieses Mal benutzten wir geometrische Tabellen. Es war wichtig, die Firma nach der Umstrukturierung darzustellen. Wir überlegten, wie wir den Bericht mit Tabellen und Diagrammen gestalten konnten, ohne uns zu wiederholen. Die Lösung war das Einkreisen der Veränderungen und das Querformat.

JIM BERTÉ, ROBERT MILES RUNYAN & ASSOCIATES, PLAYA DEL REY, CALIFORNIE

Le rapport annuel de Times Mirror pour 1988 était un gros ouvrage pour un gros client traditionnellement conservateur. Cette fois, nous avons utilisés des graphiques géométriques. Il était essentiel de bien mettre en images l'organisation après la restructuration du groupe. Il fallait réaliser des tableaux et des graphiques sans pourtant nous répéter. La solution consistait à mettre en relief les changements et de choisir un format horizontal.

TRACE PRODUCTS

TRACE PRODUCTS ANNUAL REPORT 1988

*"We are committed
to fully understanding
our customers' needs,
providing them with
the right solutions,
and ensuring their
ongoing satisfaction."*

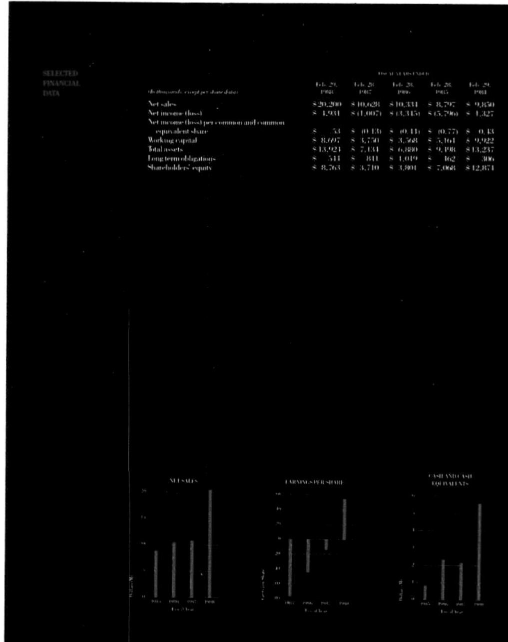

SELECTED FINANCIAL DATA

(In thousands, except per share data)	Feb. 29, 1988	Feb. 28, 1987	Feb. 28, 1986	Feb. 28, 1985	Feb. 29, 1984
Net sales	$20,200	$10,628	$10,334	$ 8,797	$ 9,850
Net income (loss)	$ 4,931	$(1,007)	$(3,345)	$(5,796)	$ 1,327
Net income (loss) per common and common equivalent share	$ .53	$ (0.13)	$ (0.44)	$ (0.77)	$ 0.43
Working capital	$ 8,697	$ 3,750	$ 3,568	$ 5,161	$ 9,922
Total assets	$13,924	$ 7,134	$ 6,880	$ 9,498	$13,237
Long term obligations	$ 544	$ 841	$ 1,019	$ 462	$ 306
Shareholders' equity	$ 8,763	$ 3,710	$ 3,801	$ 7,068	$12,874

T race Products is the world's leading manufacturer of equipment for duplicating digital information on the most widely distributed magnetic media—3½" diskettes, 5¼" diskettes and ¼" tape.

Software publishers from the largest to the smallest, together with other corporations which distribute information on diskettes, form the market and Trace's broad product line of diskette duplication systems, tape duplication systems, and high-speed diskette autoloaders reflects their customers' diverse needs with regard to performance and capacity.

The January 1987 merger of the two industry-leading manufacturers, Formaster Corporation and Magnetic Designs Holding Corporation (formed in 1981 and 1984, respectively) created Formaster Magnetic Designs. The new entity changed its name to Trace Products in June 1987.

"We couldn't have accomplished these results without the remarkable enthusiasm and dedication of our employees. Our people from Formaster and Magnetic Designs, our new management team, our new employees in every department—everyone deserves congratulations."

DENNIS P. McDONNELL
President and Chief Executive Officer

TO OUR SHAREHOLDERS:

A t the onset of fiscal 1988, our new management team embarked on a challenging program designed to transform Trace into a profit-producing company. We are pleased to report that the results of this program have exceeded our goals in nearly every respect.

For the year, Trace Products increased sales 90% to $20.2 million. Net income was $4.9 million, a vast improvement over 1987's $1 million loss. Our 27% pre-tax profit margin is a gratifying validation of our expense-containment and revenue-growth strategies. Not incidentally, our efforts have resulted in an increase in cash from $2 million to $5.6 million during the same period.

In keeping with Trace's continued aggressive emphasis on shareholder value, we achieved a return on shareholders' equity of 131%. (The computer industry averages about 12%.) And, at $200,000 per employee, our revenue per employee is nearly double the industry norm—a positive reflection on the dedication of all of our Trace people.

Several developments in the marketplace had a positive impact on our business: IBM announced standardization on 3½" flexible disk drives for its entire personal computer line. Among software manufacturers, the practice of including both 3½" and 5¼" diskettes in every package has been gaining prominence. And, at the same time, actual unit volume in the software industry increased dramatically.

In last year's annual report, we made a commitment to profitability on a long-term, sustained basis. To achieve this, we expanded our focus beyond growing revenue levels and identified two additional values and key result areas as crucial to the achievement of lasting success: investment in future growth through focused marketing and research-and-development efforts; and recognition that our success is predicated on the success of our customers and their perception of our contribution to that success.

Thus a significantly increased research and development investment during the second half of the year has already begun strengthening Trace's product line, and customers have been responsive. Our GhostWriter systems, introduced in July, represent the foundation for the most advanced, low-cost duplication system in the industry today. We are excited about the demand for medium-to-low volume systems which this product family is addressing.

Trace's new management team (l. to r.) Al Sadler, Craig McHugh, Kevin McDonnell, Paul Chesterman, Bill Bollinger, Dennis McDonnell and Georgette Pearis.

"I like talking to my customers. I like to make each of them feel like my only customer, make them feel special. We are here to help."

CHI TRAN
Customer Service

Note 1. The Company

Trace Products is engaged in the development, manufacture, marketing and servicing of computer-based systems used to format, duplicate and verify digitally recorded information on magnetic media such as floppy diskettes and 1/4" computer tape cartridges, and its business falls exclusively within one industry segment.

No single customer accounted for 10% or more of sales in each of the three fiscal years ended February 29, 1988.

Note 2. Significant Accounting Policies

Principles of Consolidation: The consolidated financial statements of the Company include the accounts of the Company and its wholly-owned subsidiaries, after elimination of all significant intercompany accounts and transactions.

Inventories: Inventories are stated at the lower of standard cost (which approximates actual cost determined by the first-in, first-out method) or market.

Depreciation and Amortization: Depreciation of property and equipment is computed using the straight-line method over their estimated useful lives, which range from three to five years.

Revenue Recognition: The Company recognizes revenue from the sale of its systems upon shipment to customers. Service revenues are recognized ratably over the contractual period or as services are provided.

Foreign Currency Translation: The Company has determined the functional currency of its United Kingdom subsidiary to be the U.S. dollar. Accordingly, the monetary assets and liabilities of this subsidiary are translated into U.S. dollars at current exchange rates and certain other assets (primarily inventory) are translated at historical rates. Sales and expenses are translated at average exchange rates, except for those expenses which relate to assets translated at historical exchange rates. All gains and losses from foreign currency transactions are included in results of operations.

Earnings Per Common Share: Net income per share in 1988 is based on the weighted average common and common equivalent shares (stock options and preferred stock) outstanding. Net income per share on a fully diluted basis is the same as net income per share. There were no common share equivalents used in the determination of per share amounts in the two fiscal years ended February 28, 1987, inasmuch as their inclusion would have been anti-dilutive.

Recent Accounting Pronouncements: The Financial Accounting Standards Board recently released Statements of Financial Accounting Standards No. 95, *Statement of Cash Flows* and No. 96, *Accounting for Income Taxes.* Statements No. 95 and No. 96 are effective for fiscal year 1989 and 1990, respectively. The Company has elected not to adopt the provisions of either statement in 1988. See Note 7 for a discussion of the effects on the financial statements had the Company adopted Statement No. 96.

Note 3. Acquisition of Magnetic Designs Holding Corporation

On January 23, 1987, Magnetic Designs Holding Corporation ("MDC") was merged with and into Formaster Corporation and the combined company was named Formaster Magnetic Designs Corporation. Formaster Magnetic Designs Corporation was subsequently renamed Trace Products. Each outstanding share of MDC stock was converted into approximately .7964 shares of Formaster Common Stock, so that the holders of all classes of MDC stock collectively received 4,010,413 shares of Formaster Common Stock. The merger has been accounted for as a pooling of interests and the consolidated financial statements have been restated accordingly. MDC's financial data have been combined with Formaster using twelve-month periods ended March 31. A reconciliation of consolidated net revenues and net loss, as originally reported and as restated, for the year ended February 28, 1986 is as follows:

(in thousands)	
Net revenues:	
As originally reported	$ 7,388
MDC	2,946
As restated	$10,334
Net loss:	
As originally reported	$ 3,227
MDC	118
As restated	$ 3,345

The separate net revenues and net income for MDC through January 23, 1987 (effective date of merger), included in the consolidated financial statements for the year ended February 28, 1987, are $3,943,000 and $138,000, respectively.

Note 4. Consolidated Balance Sheet Detail

(in thousands)	1988	1987
Inventories:		
Purchased parts	$ 1,017	$ 682
Work-in-process	1,070	631
Finished goods	1,111	293
	$ 3,198	$ 1,606
Property and equipment:		
Machinery and equipment	$ 1,707	$ 1,609
Furniture and fixtures	567	541
	2,274	2,150
Less accumulated depreciation and amortization	(1,713)	(1,441)
	$ 561	$ 709

Note 5. Long-Term Liabilities

Long-term liabilities consist of the following:

(in thousands)	1988	1987
Accrued rent expense	$ 55	$ 29
Deferred compensation	—	143
Deferred income taxes	—	22
Long-term debenture	722	825
Capital leases	46	117
Other	—	2
	823	1,138
Less current portion	(279)	(297)
	$ 544	$ 841

In September 1985, the Company entered into a long-term debt arrangement with its landlord for $753,000 which allowed it to relocate into a smaller, less expensive headquarters facility, better suited to its needs. The debt arrangement is a debenture which is convertible into common stock of the Company during the term of the debenture (after March 1, 1987) at the option of the debenture holder. The conversion price is $4.00 per share on the outstanding balance of the debenture. The debenture bears interest at the rate of 10% per annum and all future borrowings or issuances of securities of the Company in excess of $1 million require approval of the majority of the debenture holders. Future payments under the terms of the debenture call for principal and interest payments as follows:

(in thousands)	
Fiscal year ended:	
February 28, 1989	$ 272
February 28, 1990	379
February 28, 1991	193
	844
Less amount representing interest	(122)
	$ 722

Interest expense for each of three years ended February 29, 1988 was $105,000, $102,000 and $7,000, respectively.

The Shareholders and Board of Directors of Trace Products

We have examined the consolidated balance sheets of Trace Products (formerly Formaster Magnetic Designs Corporation) as of February 29, 1988 and February 28, 1987, and the related consolidated statements of operations, shareholders' equity and changes in financial position for each of the three fiscal years in the period ended February 29, 1988. Our examinations were made in accordance with generally accepted auditing standards and, accordingly, included such tests of the accounting records and such other auditing procedures as we considered necessary in the circumstances.

In our opinion, the financial statements referred to above present fairly the financial position of Trace Products as of February 29, 1988 and February 28, 1987, and the results of its operations and changes in its financial position for each of the three fiscal years in the period ended February 29, 1988, in conformity with generally accepted accounting principles applied on a consistent basis.

Coopers & Lybrand

Coopers & Lybrand
San Jose, California
April 1, 1988

Common stock of Trace Products is traded on the over-the-counter market by members of the National Association of Securities Dealers, Inc., under the trading symbol TRCE (or the former symbol FMSR). Share prices between March 1, 1986 and February 29, 1988, by fiscal quarter were:

	BID	
	HIGH	LOW
Quarter ended:		
May 31, 1986	1¾	1¼
August 31, 1986	1¼	1⅛
November 30, 1986	1¼	1
February 28, 1987	1⅛	1
May 31, 1987	1½	⅞
August 31, 1987	1 9/16	1⅜
November 30, 1987	1¼	1
February 29, 1988	1⅞	1⅛

The quotations represent inter-dealer quotations, without retail markups, markdowns or commissions, and may not represent actual transactions.

On February 29, 1988, there were approximately 333 holders of record of the Company's common stock. The Company has not paid dividends on common stock since its incorporation, and management anticipates the Company will continue to retain earnings for use in its business. The Company's borrowing agreements restrict the payment of cash dividends.

CORPORATE DATA

DIRECTORS AND OFFICERS

Dennis P. McDonnell
President, Chief Executive Officer and Director

Bill Bollinger
Vice President—International Sales

Paul J. Chesterman
Vice President—Finance, Chief Financial Officer and Secretary

Kevin J. McDonnell
Vice President—Engineering and Director

Craig L. McHugh
Vice President—Sales

Georgette Psaris
Vice President—Marketing

Al Sadler
Vice President—Operations

Lester E. Thompson
Chairman of the Board

SEC FORM 10-K

A copy of the Company's annual report to the Securities and Exchange Commission on Form 10-K is available without charge on written request to: Paul J. Chesterman, Vice President—Finance and Chief Financial Officer, Trace Products, 2190 Bering Drive, San Jose, CA 95131.

LEGAL COUNSEL

Pillsbury, Madison & Sutro
San Jose, California

INDEPENDENT ACCOUNTANTS

Coopers & Lybrand
San Jose, California

TRANSFER AGENT AND REGISTRAR

Bank of America N.T. & S.A.
55 Hawthorne Street
San Francisco, CA 94105

CORPORATE HEADQUARTERS

2190 Bering Drive
San Jose, California 95131
(408)435-7800 Telex: 466462

EUROPEAN OFFICE

Trace U.K.
Spring Valley Business Centre
Porters Wood, St. Albans
Herts, AL36PP, England
Telex: 265259

CLIENT:
TRACE PRODUCTS

DESIGN FIRM:
LAUREN SMITH DESIGN

ART DIRECTOR:
LAUREN SMITH

DESIGNER:
LAUREN SMITH

PHOTOGRAPHER:
MEL LINDSTROM

WRITER:
TED COOPER

TYPOGRAPHER:
2-TYPE

PAPER SELECTION:
REFLECTIONS

PAPER MANUFACTURER:
CONSOLIDATED

PRINTER:
HOUSE OF PRINTING

NUMBER OF PAGES:
36

SIZE:
8 1/2" X 11"

TYPE SELECTION:
BODONI

DENNIS P. MCDONNELL, PRESIDENT AND CHIEF EXECUTIVE OFFICER, TRACE PRODUCTS, SAN JOSE, CALIFORNIA

Trace Products manufactures equipment for duplicating digital information, so software publishers are the prime clients. This company had been formed after completing a merger, and it was important for us to convey to our customers and our stockholders that this was a new, vibrant company founded on teams of people, including the new management team. There were other things we wanted to show, such as a new outlook on the company's part that was much brighter, and that we expected a superior financial response. Because we are a conservative and honest company, we expected profitability and success. We were very pleased with this 1988 annual report because it got all these things across with a strong emphasis on quality. It is a classy piece which hit our message dead on.

LAUREN SMITH, LAUREN SMITH DESIGN, SAN JOSE, CALIFORNIA

The messages we had to convey in the Trace Products annual report were numerous. This company had just gone through a merger and became a bigger company. We had to show this new image and we had to make a departure from previous annual reports stylistically. The main theme, aside from the new company, was the management team. The company was really completing a very good year, and this came from the dedication of these people. So we emphasized that with large portraits. We interviewed a lot of people and got statements, and we had secondary themes, which were woven through, with points being made about quality control and global marketing. We wanted to give the impression of a new vision. The cover was deliberately understated with a quote from the president set in type as the only design element. We wanted to create a sense of surprise and we were whispering the message on the cover.

DENNIS P. MCDONNELL, PRESIDENT AND CHIEF EXECUTIVE OFFICER, TRACE PRODUCTS, SAN JOSE, KALIFORNIEN

Trace Products stellt Geräte für das Kopieren digitaler Information her, unsere Hauptkunden sind Software-Hersteller. Die Firma ging aus einer Fusion hervor, und es war uns wichtig, unseren Kunden und Aktionären das Bild eines neuen, dynamischen Unternehmens zu vermitteln, das auf Team-Arbeit aufbaut, und zwar auch in der Geschäftsführung. Ausserdem wollten wir zeigen, dass die Aussichten nach der Fusion viel positiver sind. Als konservative und vertrauenswürdige Firma durften wir auf einen guten Geschäftsgang und Erfolg hoffen. Wir sind mit dem Jahresbericht für 1988 sehr zufrieden, weil alle diese Dinge zum Ausdruck kommen und ganz besonderes Gewicht auf Qualität gelegt wurde. Es ist ein klassischer Bericht, der genau unserer Botschaft entspricht.

LAUREN SMITH, LAUREN SMITH DESIGN, SAN JOSE, KALIFORNIEN

Im Jahresbericht für Trace Products sollten zahlreiche Aspekte berücksichtigt werden. Die Firma hatte kürzlich fusioniert und war entsprechend gewachsen. Wir mussten das neue Image unterstreichen und uns deutlich vom Stil der bisherigen Jahresberichte absetzen. Das Hauptthema war, neben der neuen Gesellschaft, das Management Team. Die Firma hatte ein wirklich gutes Jahr hinter sich, und das war auf die Leistungen dieser Leute zurückzuführen. Also entschlossen wir uns für grossformatige Porträts. Wir interviewten viele Leute und bekamen Aussagen, in denen auch andere Themen angesprochen wurden, wie Qualitätskontrolle und ein globales Marketing. Wir wollten eine ganz neue Einstellung zeigen. Der Umschlag war bewusst zurückhaltend, mit dem Zitat des Direktors als einzigem Gestaltungselement. Wir wollten Spannung erzeugen, und auf dem Umschlag die Botschaft nur flüstern.

DENNIS P. MCDONNELL, PRESIDENT AND CHIEF EXECUTIVE OFFICER, TRACE PRODUCTS, SAN JOSÉ, CALIFORNIE

Trace Products fabrique des équipements de duplication d'informations digitales, avec pour principaux clients les éditeurs de logiciels. Notre société ayant résulté d'une fusion d'entreprises, il importait de faire comprendre à nos clients et à nos actionnaires qu'il s'agit d'une société nouvelle et dynamique portée à bout de bras par des équipes dévouées et une équipe dirigeante nouvelle. Bien sûr, d'autres sujets nous tenaient encore à cœur, ainsi les perspectives bien plus favorables. En tant qu'entreprise conservatrice et honnête, nous sommes assurés du succès et de la profitabilité de nos opérations. Ce rapport nous a donné toute satisfaction du fait que tous ces éléments s'y retrouvent avec l'accent sur la qualité. C'est un document qui traduit à la perfection notre message.

LAUREN SMITH, LAUREN SMITH DESIGN, SAN JOSÉ, CALIFORNIE

Dans le rapport annuel de Trace Products, il fallait faire place à toute une série de messages. Cette société venait de s'agrandir à la suite d'une fusion d'entreprises. Il fallait donc faire état de cette image nouvelle et changer le style des rapports annuels précédents. Le second sujet à mettre en valeur était la composition de la nouvelle équipe dirigeante. L'année écoulée avait été très bonne, ce qui était dû au dévouement de la direction. C'est ce que nous avons souligné à travers des portraits développés. Nous avons interviewé un tas de gens ; en plus, des thèmes secondaires apparaissent ça et là en contrepoint, tels le contrôle de la qualité et la dimension globale du marketing. Nous avons voulu créer l'impression d'une vision neuve des choses. Pour la couverture, nous avons adopté un profil bas, avec pour seul élément de design une citation du président. Nous avons réduit le message en couverture à un simple murmure.

1988 ANNUAL REPORT

TRENWICK

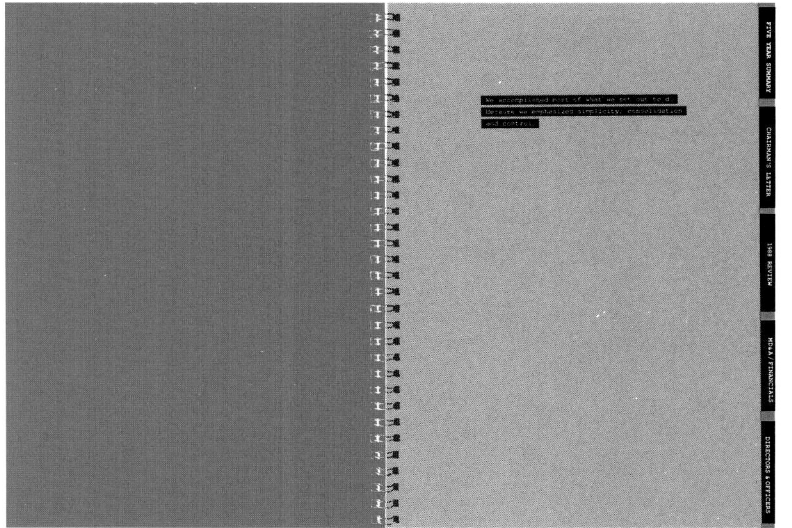

FIVE YEAR SUMMARY

Year ended December 31, (dollars in thousands except per share data)	1988	1987	1986	1985	1984
Income statement data					
Net premiums written	$103,809	$100,841	$ 67,490	$ 27,890	$ 18,320
Earned premiums	$ 98,491	$ 97,936	$ 55,656	$ 25,783	$ 21,732
Net investment income	19,344	17,820	12,930	7,610	7,794
Realized investment gains	63	55	1,955	1,680	119
Service fees	2,380	5,377	3,795	1,773	2,065
Total revenues	$120,278	$121,188	$ 74,336	$ 36,846	$ 31,710
Net income (loss)	$ 13,743	$ 10,539	$ 5,855	$ 247	$ (8,495)
Per share	$1.61	$1.05	$.70	$.04	$(1.42)
Weighted average number of shares of common stock outstanding (in thousands)	8,560	10,042	8,396	6,475	5,992
Balance sheet data					
Total assets	$361,304	$334,488	$296,608	$172,546	$144,598
Reserve for losses and loss expenses incurred	169,785	123,148	99,144	63,669	49,772
Notes payable	7,000	7,000	-	2,500	2,500
Total stockholders' equity	134,535	139,709	139,007	52,198	26,951
Number of shares of common stock outstanding (in thousands)	7,675	9,039	10,016	6,221	3,701
Book value per share	$17.53	$15.46	$13.88	$8.39	$7.28
Certain GAAP financial ratios					
Combined ratio	105.2%	108.0%	119.5%	136.6%	179.4%
Net premiums written to surplus ratio	.77:1	.72:1	.49:1	.54:1	.68:1
Loss and loss expense reserve to surplus ratio	1.26:1	.88:1	.71:1	1.22:1	1.85:1

Dear Fellow Stockholder,

Trenwick Group Inc.'s financial performance continued to improve in 1988. Record earnings of $1.61 per share together with our stock repurchase program resulted in an increase in book value of $2.07 to $17.53 per share. In addition, we initiated a modest quarterly dividend and increased it by year end. Your Company's progress last year was the result of formulating a good plan in 1987 and sticking to it in 1988. We accomplished most of what we set out to do because we emphasized simplicity, consolidation and control.

Trenwick substantially completed the elimination of all operations and activities not centrally related to its sole business objective; becoming one of the handful of superior underwriting companies in the reinsurance business. We also streamlined the operating structure of our reinsurance business.

During the year we significantly reduced our operating expenses and improved our productivity. We met the challenge of maintaining morale while cutting staff. We eliminated redundant levels of supervision, insisting instead on higher levels of individual performance. Our staff benefited from a change that promoted both the

MANAGEMENT'S DISCUSSION AND ANALYSIS
OF FINANCIAL CONDITION
AND RESULTS OF OPERATIONS

Operations

Trenwick is primarily engaged in underwriting property and casualty reinsurance, produced by brokers, through its principal underwriting subsidiary, Trenwick America Reinsurance Corporation ("Trenwick America Re"). Trenwick America Re, a Connecticut domiciled reinsurance company, is licensed, authorized or approved to write reinsurance in 48 states and the District of Columbia and had statutory capital and surplus of approximately $109 million as of December 31, 1988.

In 1988, pursuant to Trenwick's plan to streamline operations and reduce costs, Trenwick America Re closed its New York facultative branch office and consolidated its facultative underwriting operations in Hartford, Connecticut. **During the year, Trenwick also completed the deactivation of all its operating subsidiaries other than Trenwick America Re and the relocation of its headquarters to Stamford, Connecticut.**

Effective September 30, 1987, Trenwick sold its Bermuda reinsurance company, Trenwick Reinsurance Company, Limited ("Trenwick Re") to Forum Reinsurance Company Limited ("Forum"). In consideration for the sale, Trenwick received a promissory note from Forum for approximately that company's book value. Trenwick Re's operations have been included in Trenwick's consolidated financial statements for the first nine months of 1987. Trenwick Re underwrote substantially all of Trenwick's reinsurance business prior to 1985. In January 1989, Trenwick completed a commutation of all of its historical reinsurance of Trenwick Re and received payment of the note from Forum. No material gain or loss was realized by Trenwick on these transactions, which have settled all obligations between Trenwick and Forum.

15

DIRECTORS & OFFICERS

TRENWICK GROUP INC.
CONSOLIDATED BALANCE SHEET

December 31,	1988	1987
(dollars in thousands)		
Assets		
Fixed maturity investments, at amortized cost (market value, $269,123 and $216,833)	$274,721	$219,476
Short-term investments, at cost which approximates market value	33,642	38,027
Total investments	**308,363**	**257,503**
Cash	216	826
Investment income receivable	6,787	5,100
Balances receivable from ceding reinsurers	6,388	9,520
Reinsurance recoverable on paid losses	2,543	2,040
Deferred policy acquisition costs	7,018	4,801
Deposits with reinsurers	2,251	6,249
Deferred income tax charges	7,490	4,071
Funds under management	11,290	31,081
Other assets	8,958	13,297
Total assets	**$361,304**	**$334,488**

24

December 31,	1988	1987
(dollars in thousands)		
Liabilities and stockholders' equity		
Liabilities		
Reserve for losses and loss expenses incurred	$169,785	$123,148
Unearned premiums	26,713	21,395
Reinsurance balances payable	3,914	1,902
Income taxes payable	-	8,061
Note payable	7,000	7,000
Policyholders' deposits	11,290	31,081
Other liabilities	8,067	2,192
Total liabilities	**226,769**	**194,779**
Stockholders' equity		
Preferred stock, $.10 par value, 1,000,000 shares authorized; none outstanding		
Common stock, $.10 par value, 15,000,000 shares authorized; 7,675,179 and 9,038,658 shares outstanding	768	904
Additional paid-in capital	110,215	127,545
Retained earnings	23,598	11,371
Notes receivable on stock purchases	(46)	(111)
Total stockholders' equity	**134,535**	**139,709**
Total liabilities and stockholders' equity	**$361,304**	**$334,488**

The accompanying notes are an integral part of these statements.

25

DIRECTORS & OFFICERS

Note 3
Investments

Fixed maturity investments as at December 31 comprise the following:

	1988		1987	
(dollars in thousands)	**Book Value**	**Market Value**	**Book Value**	**Market Value**
Tax exempt bonds	$166,448	$164,895	$104,421	$104,220
U.S. government securities	76,287	73,997	84,682	83,567
Other taxable bonds	31,986	30,231	30,373	29,046
Total fixed maturity investments	**$274,721**	**$269,123**	**$219,476**	**$216,833**

During the twelve months ended December 31, 1988 all investments were income producing.

The components of net investment income for the years ended December 31 were as follows:

(dollars in thousands)	1988	1987	1986
Fixed maturity investments			
Tax exempt bonds	$ 9,497	$ 4,926	$ 1,252
U.S. government securities	6,414	6,912	4,801
Other taxable bonds	2,385	4,290	4,202
Short-term investments	1,775	2,731	3,272
Equity in earnings of affiliate	-	-	97
Gross investment income	**20,071**	**18,859**	**13,624**
Less investment expenses	727	1,039	694
Net investment income	**$19,344**	**$17,820**	**$12,930**

Realized gains on sale of investments for the years ended December 31 were as follows:

(dollars in thousands)	1988	1987	1986
Fixed maturity investments	$63	$55	$1,921
Short-term investments	-	-	34
Realized investment gains	**$63**	**$55**	**$1,955**

For the years ended December 31, 1988, 1987 and 1986, changes in unrealized (losses) gains on fixed maturities were approximately $(2,955,000), $(7,187,000) and $2,749,000, respectively, which are not reflected in the

32

financial statements. Had the unrealized gains been realized, an income tax provision of approximately $934,000 would have been recorded for the year ended 1986 which would have resulted in net realized (losses) gains on fixed maturities of $(2,955,000), $(7,187,000) and $1,815,000, respectively, for the three years then ended.

Trenwick paid investment advisory fees of approximately $200,000 and $296,000 for the years ended December 31, 1987 and 1986, respectively, to Conning & Company, an affiliate of a director of Trenwick.

Note 4
Other Assets

Other assets comprise:

(dollars in thousands)	1988	1987
Investment in affiliate, at cost	$6,300	$ 6,300
Note receivable	-	3,800
Other receivables	374	1,438
Premises and equipment, net of accumulated depreciation and amortization of $1,183 and $654	1,402	1,275
Goodwill, net of accumulated amortization of $352 and $277	376	451
Prepaid expenses and deposits	506	33
Total	**$8,958**	**$13,297**

Through a private offering in August 1987, Trenwick purchased approximately 20% of the outstanding common stock of Investors Insurance Holding Corporation, a property and casualty insurer, for $6,300,000. This investment in affiliate is being accounted for at cost as Trenwick does not significantly influence the operating or financial decisions of Investors Insurance due to the large shareholding of another stockholder. Income from this investment will be recorded in the period dividends are declared.

Effective September 30, 1987, Trenwick sold its Bermuda reinsurance subsidiary for approximately that subsidiary's net book value. Accordingly, Trenwick recorded no gain or loss on disposition and has consolidated the operations of that subsidiary through the nine months then ended. In

33

DIRECTORS & OFFICERS

CLIENT:
TRENWICK GROUP INC.

DESIGN FIRM:
FRANK C LIONETTI DESIGN

ART DIRECTOR:
FRANK LIONETTI

DESIGNER:
MARISSA VON GRETENER

PHOTOGRAPHER:
FRANK WHITE PHOTOGRAPHY

PAPER SELECTION:
CHROMKOTE 2000, VINTAGE VELVET, POSEIDON

PAPER MANUFACTURER:
CHAMPION, POTLATCH, MOHAWK

PRINTER:
BEAUVAIS PRINTING

NUMBER OF PAGES:
48 PLUS COVER

SIZE:
8 5/9" x 11"

TYPE SELECTION:
BAUER BODONI, COURIER

JAMES BILLETT, JR., CHAIRMAN, PRESIDENT, CHIEF EXECUTIVE OFFICER, TRENWICK GROUP, INC., STAMFORD, CONNECTICUT

In the 1988 annual report we were reporting on the progress of the company. We intended this report for the stockholders and we wanted to present them with a simple message: The company is determined, it is stable, and it is no-nonsense. This is a working annual report, with the spiral binding for easy use, and I personally did all of the highlighting in yellow that was used as a part of the design. This annual report reflects the Trenwick style.

FRANK C. LIONETTI, FRANK C. LIONETTI DESIGN, INC., OLD GREENWICH, CONNECTICUT

The Trenwick Group had been diversifying over the years and many changes had occurred at the company, some due to the nature of the reinsurance business. The design concept for this annual report was to generate a report that looked in some way like the Trenwick offices. We decided to "underdesign," which is very difficult to do. The spiral-bound book even had blank, lined pages for notes. We did this on the company Macintosh, and we made constant refinements to give it an understated look. We ended up with a functional-looking annual report. In essence, the company loved the concept.

JAMES BILLETT, JR., CHAIRMAN, PRESIDENT, CHIEF EXECUTIVE OFFICER, TRENWICK GROUP INC., STAMFORD, CONNECTICUT

Im Geschäftsbericht für 1988 ging es um den Fortschritt unserer Firma. Er richtete sich an die Aktionäre, und wir wollten eine einfache Aussage machen: die Firma ist zielbewusst, stabil und seriös. Dieser Jahresbericht sollte funktionieren, die Spiralbindung erwies sich als praktisch, und ich selbst hatte mich um die optische Unterstreichung der wichtigsten Dinge gekümmert. Dieser Jahresbericht reflektiert den Stil von Trenwick.

FRANK C. LIONETTI, FRANK C. LIONETTI DESIGN INC., OLD GREENWICH, CONNECTICUT

Die Trenwick Gruppe hat im Laufe der Jahre diversifiziert, was viele Veränderungen mit sich brachte, von denen einige mit dem Rückversicherungsgeschäft zusammenhängen. Wir entschieden uns für eine sehr zurückhaltende Gestaltung. Der spiralgebundene Bericht hat sogar einige leere linierte Seiten für Notizen. Wir benutzten einen Macintosh-Computer und überarbeiteten die Ergebnisse immer wieder, um das gewünschte gestalterische «Understatement» und einen funktionell wirkenden Jahresbericht zu bekommen. Die Firma war von dem Konzept begeistert.

JAMES BILLETT, JR., CHAIRMAN, PRESIDENT, CHIEF EXECUTIVE OFFICER, TRENWICK GROUP INC., STAMFORD, CONNECTICUT

Dans notre rapport annuel pour 1988, nous avons fait état des progrès de notre société. Nous avons destiné ce rapport à nos actionnaires en leur délivrant un message très simple: l'entreprise est résolue d'aller de l'avant, elle est stable, et elle ne perd pas son temps. C'est un document de travail à reliure spirale, et j'ai personnellement veillé à la mise en vedette des éléments du design. Ce rapport annuel reflète fidèlement le style Trenwick.

FRANK C. LIONETTI, FRANK C. LIONETTI DESIGN INC., OLD GREENWICH, CONNECTICUT

Le Trenwick Group est engagé depuis des années dans un processus de diversification qui a impliqué de nombreux changements, certains dus à la nature même de la branche de la réassurance. Le concept retenu pour le design de ce rapport annuel tendait à faire de ce document un élément intégré dans le travail. Nous avons donc décidé d'en faire moins plutôt que trop. Nous l'avons réalisée sur notre Macintosh en l'affinant au fur et à mesure pour la rendre encore plus neutre au plan du design. Le résultat a été un rapport annuel à l'aspect fonctionnel. Pour l'essentiel, la société en a été enchanté.

F. van Lanschot Bankiers nv Annual Report 1988
Figures and numbers
An annual report revolves around numbers and amounts. Both are made up of figures. The theme for the illustrations in this report is the image of special significance as attributed to figures throughout all the cultures and centuries.
The numeric sequence of 1, 1, 2, 3, 5, 8 and so on – drawn up in the twelfth century by the Italian mathematician Leonardo Fibonacci – is based upon natural relationships and patterns. The illustrations in this report are meant as a link to this sequence. The A4 format of this annual report is also part of a series of standardised sizes based upon a harmonious numeric sequence.

Deputy General Managers (continued)

R.L. Meezen
J.P.A.M. van Roon
J. van der Schans
Mrs J.C. van Tol-van Streepen
A. Tonnaer
A.G.H. Veeke
R. Verdam
F.J. Versteijlen
L. Visser
E.J.M. Weyers
A.M.M. Willems

Key Figures
Amounts in thousands of guilders (consolidated figures)

	1988	1987	1986	1985	1984
Shareholders' funds	236,907	219,471	204,296	166,271	153,079
Group funds and subordinated loans	380,446	331,069	307,875	238,011	202,258
Negotiable paper and non-subordinated loans	1,629,586	1,415,043	1,323,790	1,126,417	995,225
Savings accounts, Deposits and Creditors (including banks)	4,624,402	4,241,635	4,218,493	4,238,852	4,088,220
Advances to or guaranteed by the Government	1,690,883	1,458,783	1,487,094	1,252,013	1,295,555
Bills of exchange, Advances against securities and Other advances	2,981,975	2,802,092	2,696,856	2,600,282	2,413,132
Total assets	6,685,086	6,210,359	6,228,019	5,943,631	5,474,342
Income	174,072	165,203	155,954	147,602	138,858
Expenditure	116,720	108,437	99,746	91,671	87,615
Gross profit	57,352	56,766	56,208	55,931	51,243
Transfer to the Provision for general risks	22,500	22,500	22,500	25,000	28,500
Net profit	27,301	24,280	24,092	22,138	18,244

7 Key Figures

Savings accounts recovered somewhat from the outflow in the previous financial year (up by 5.2%). Our range of savings products appears to be adequately matched to the demands of our customer base. Savings accounts at notice in particular went up. The 'Investors' deposit' and the 'Income deposit', introduced in 1987, – offering a comparatively high return – are also meeting an increasing demand. Total funds placed with the bank by its customers *(Savings accounts, Deposits* and *Creditors)* rose by 7.1% *(1987: 5.4%)*.

Negotiable paper and non-subordinated loans increased by 15.2%. The amount of savings and bank certificates issued by our bank stayed at virtually the same level as in the previous year. The growth in this balance sheet item was caused in part by another issue of an Australian dollar loan. This issue, with the accompanying currency and interest swap, contributed to a reduction in our funding costs.

Capital market

Securities and New Issue activities
Business on the Amsterdam Stock Exchange during the early months of 1988 was certainly dominated by the crash in October 1987. Private investors were initially cautious. Nevertheless, internationally there was an upward trend in prices. The monetary measures implemented to cushion the consequences of the sudden price falls on stock markets seemed to pay off. Good corporate results and the growing number of mergers also had a positive influence. From June onwards, when it became clear that the recovery in share prices was of a more lasting nature, non-professional investors began entering the market on a larger scale. The general price level on the Amsterdam Stock Exchange closed the year 37.6% higher than it was at the end of 1987.
Share turnover on the Official Market fell by almost 25% to some *f* 121 billion; bond trading, however, went up by 19%. Accordingly, trading as a whole did not differ appreciably from the volume achieved in 1987. Turnover on the Parallel Market was less rosy; not even the sharply lower level of 1987 could be matched.

The effects of the October 1987 crash were reflected above all in the number of introductions on the Amsterdam Stock Exchange. Disregarding investment funds and companies listed abroad, only four companies obtained a listing on the Amsterdam Stock Exchange during the year.
In terms of contract volume, turnover on the European Options Exchange fell by about 23% in 1988. Nevertheless, the number of outstanding options has constantly risen in recent years. No other conclusion can be drawn than that investors are making more use of options as a tool in their longer term investment strategy. Interest for index contracts and along with them futures on the same indexes – which are dealt in via the EOE subsidiary Amsterdam Financial Futures Market – similarly increased.

The developments outlined above naturally affected our securities business. The turnover in shares on behalf of customers remained below the 1987 level. Nevertheless, our position in the professional market was consolidated and the number of foreign customers increased. Our bond market operations grew and so did our involvement in new bond issues.
The range of option instruments for our portfolio management services to institutional investors was more widely used. This specialist service is thought of as worthwhile.

16 *Report of the Management Board*

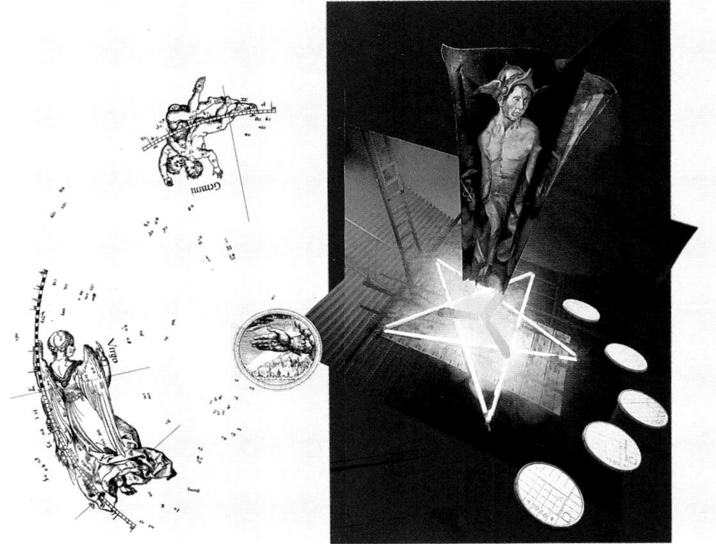

Profit and Loss Account

For 1988

In thousands of guilders	1988	*1987*
Other income and expense	12,404	*11,146*
Net profit of subsidiary companies	14,897	*13,134*
Net profit	**27,301**	***24,280***

Consolidated Balance Sheet as at 31 December 1988

After appropriation of profit

In thousands of guilders **Assets**	1988	*1987*
Cash and money at call	54,047	*68,130*
Treasury bills	–	*20,568*
Banks	566,277	*388,101*
Securities and syndicates	1,179,585	*1,309,787*
Advances against Treasury bills and/or securities	199,611	*254,606*
Bills of exchange	52,766	*36,038*
Advances to or guaranteed by the Government	1,690,883	*1,458,783*
Other advances	2,729,598	*2,511,448*
Investments in and advances to subsidiaries and affiliates	129,866	*81,752*
Premises and equipment	82,453	*81,146*
	6,685,086	***6,210,359***

In thousands of guilders **Liabilities**	1988	*1987*
Issued and fully paid up share capital	85,000	*85,000*
Reserves	151,907	*134,471*
Shareholders' funds	**236,907**	***219,471***
Outside shareholders' interests	7,921	*7,483*
Group funds	244,828	*226,954*
Subordinated loans	115,618	*104,105*
Total group funds and subordinated loans	**360,446**	***331,059***
Negotiable paper and non-subordinated loans	1,629,586	*1,415,043*
Savings accounts	1,055,659	*1,003,363*
Deposits	1,238,751	*1,115,741*
Creditors	1,435,606	*1,363,067*
Banks	894,386	*759,464*
Other funds taken up	70,652	*222,622*
	6,685,086	***6,210,359***
Contingent liabilities arising from guarantees issued	265,178	*251,118*
Contingent liabilities arising from irrevocable documentary credits	57,121	*46,267*

CLIENT:
F VAN LANSCHOT BANKIERS NV

DESIGN FIRM:
UNA

ART DIRECTOR:
HANS BOCKTING

DESIGNER:
HANS BOCKTING

PHOTOGRAPHER:
LEX VAN PIETERSON

WRITER:
F VAN LANSCHOT BANKIERS NV

PRODUCTION MANAGER:
UNA

TYPOGRAPHER:
HANS BOCKTING

PAPER MANUFACTURER:
CONDAT, FRANCE

PRINTER:
ROSBEEK BV, NUTH, THE NETHERLANDS

NUMBER OF PAGES:
60 PAGES

SIZE:
210 X 297 MM

A.W. JONKER, GENERAL MANAGER SECRETARY, F. VAN LANSCHOT BANKIERS, JN'S-HERTOGENBOSCH, THE NETHERLANDS

For F. van Lanschot Bankiers, the annual report is basically a presentation of yearly figures and a summary of the state of affairs for that year. The report also must represent, in a subtle way, the atmosphere and the character of the bank, which is a modern bank offering quality service to a select group of clients. This is a priority, and the annual report has to reflect this quality. For the 1988 annual report a theme suggested by UNA, the designers, was a treatment of the theme "Meaning of Figures." The reactions to the final annual report were positive. In fact, the financial press in this country commented that this annual report was "unique amongst annual bank reports in The Netherlands."

HANS BOCKTING, UNA, AMSTERDAM, THE NETHERLANDS

Since our client did not have a specific theme in mind, we suggested "figures" and we concentrated on the meanings and interpretations that the various cultures have attributed to numerals throughout the ages. We started with intense research on this theme and we discovered the relationship between various occult, mystical and religious patterns. We then combined photography with images from various sources. Through this, all sorts of intriguing connections became evident. Visualizing these was one of the most interesting and satisfying parts of the design process. This visual approach made a very complex concept accessible.

A.W. JONKER, GENERAL MANAGER SECRETARY, F. VAN LANSCHOT BANKIERS, JN'S-HERTOGENBOSCH, NIEDERLANDE

Für F. van Lanschot Bankiers ist der Jahresbericht vor allem eine Präsentation der Jahresergebnisse und eine Zusammenfassung der Geschäftslage. Der Bericht muss ausserdem unaufdringlich die Atmosphäre und die Art der Bank, einer modernen Bank, die einer distinguierten Gruppe von Kunden hervorragenden Service bietet, zum Ausdruck bringen. Das ist einer der wichtigsten Aspekte. UNA, die Design-Gruppe, schlug für den Bericht des Jahres 1988 «Die Bedeutung von Zahlen» als Thema vor. Die Reaktionen auf den fertigen Jahresbericht waren positiv. In der Finanzpresse war sogar zu lesen, dass dieser Bericht «unter den Jahresberichten von Banken in den Niederlanden einmalig» sei.

HANS BOCKTING, UNA, AMSTERDAM, NIEDERLANDE

Da unser Kunde an kein spezielles Thema dachte, schlugen wir «Zahlen» vor und konzentrierten uns auf deren Bedeutungen und Interpretationen in den verschiedenen Kulturen der Geschichte. Wir begannen mit intensiven Recherchen und entdeckten Verbindungen zwischen verschiedenen okkultischen, mystischen und religiösen Verhaltensmustern. Wir kombinieren Photos mit Bildern aus verschiedenen Quellen. Dadurch wurden alle möglichen Verbindungen deutlich, deren visuelle Umsetzung zum interessantesten Teil der Gestaltung gehörte. Die visuelle Interpretation machte das sehr komplexe Thema leicht zugänglich.

A.W. JONKER, GENERAL MANAGER SECRETARY, F. VAN LANSCHOT BANKIERS, JN'S-HERTOGENBOSCH, PAYS-BAS

Aux yeux de la Banque F. van Lanschot, le rapport annuel constitue en principe une présentation des résultats de l'exercice, ainsi qu'un résumé de la marche des affaires. Le rapport est également censé restituer de manière subtile l'atmosphère et les caractéristiques propres de cette banque moderne dont un groupe de clients haut de gamme s'attache les services de qualité. Le rapport se doit de refléter cette qualité. Le thème que nous a suggéré le groupe de design UNA pour 1988 tournait autour de la «signification des chiffres.» Les réactions ont été positives. En fait, la presse financière est allée jusqu'à dire que ce document est «unique parmi les rapports annuels bancaires publiés aux Pays-Bas.»

HANS BOCKTING, UNA, AMSTERDAM, LES PAYS-BAS

Notre client n'ayant pas déterminé de thème particulier, nous lui avons proposé celui des «chiffres» en nous concentrant sur la signification des nombres au cours des âges dans les différentes civilisations. Cela nous a coûté pas mal de recherches avec, à la clef, la révélation des associations numériques à teneur occulte, mystique et religieuse. Nous avons alors combiné des photos avec des images provenant de diverses sources. Il en est résulté d'intriguantes associations entre toutes sortes de nombres. Les visualiser a représenté l'aspect le plus intéressant du processus de design. Cette approche a clarifié un ensemble sémantique fort complexe.

WARNER COMMUNICATIONS, INC.

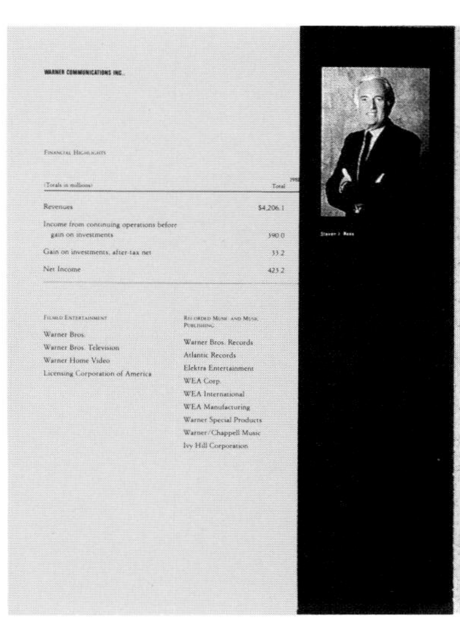

Eight years ago, we devoted several pages of WCI's annual report to technological advances that were revolutionizing home entertainment. At that time, cable television, videocassette players and car tape decks were about to give consumers unprecedented control over how they would be entertained.

That was 1980. Today, 1980 is ancient history. ▸

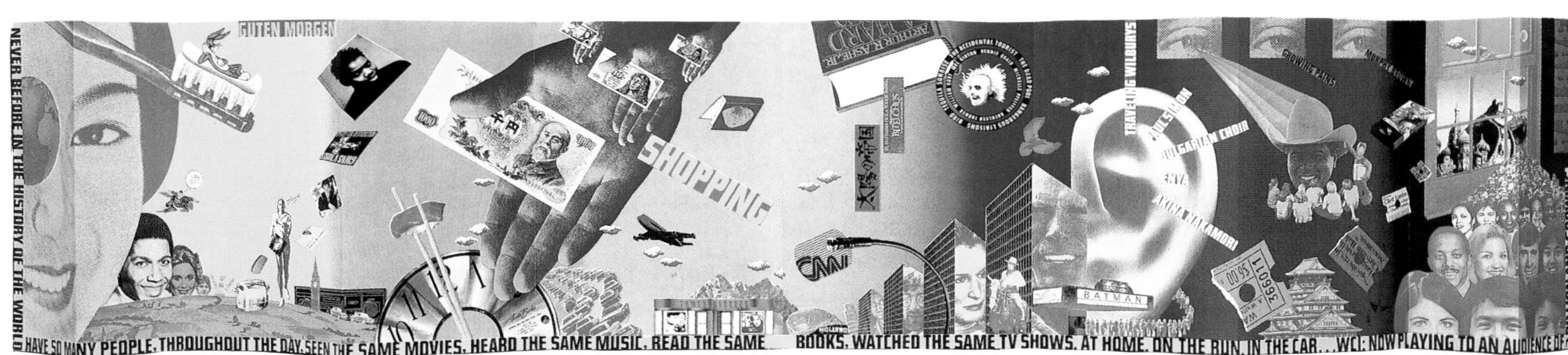

c. Atari

The assets, subject to certain liabilities, of the home computer and home video game businesses of Atari Holdings, Inc. were sold to Atari Corporation ("Atari") in 1984 in exchange for Atari securities. In November 1986, WCI received approximately $36 million in cash from the proceeds of an Atari public offering and 14,200,000 shares of Atari common stock in exchange for the Atari securities that were received in 1984. The cash WCI received in exchange for the original consideration was included in the 1986 after-tax gain on discontinued operations of $22.1 million, or $.16 per share.

WCI's common stock interest in Atari is accounted for by the cost method, is carried in the balance sheet at zero cost and, based on the market price of a share of Atari common stock, had a market value of approximately $80 million at December 31, 1988.

3. Investment in BHC

In January 1984, WCI acquired preferred stock convertible into 42.5% of the common stock of BHC, a subsidiary of Chris-Craft Industries, Inc. ("CCI"), in exchange for 15,200,000 shares of WCI Series B convertible preferred stock. As of December 31, 1988, wholly-and-partially-owned subsidiaries of BHC have purchased 8,542,200 shares of WCI common stock and 7,084,744 shares of WCI Series C convertible preferred stock. After giving effect to the shares of WCI common stock issued in the Lorimar acquisition on January 11, 1989, CCI had approximately 15.5% of the voting power of the outstanding voting securities of WCI and, if the Series B stock is converted into common stock, CCI would have 19.4% of such voting power.

Pursuant to the Shareholders Agreement among WCI, CCI and BHC, so long as their interests in BHC voting securities is 25% or more, CCI and WCI are not permitted, directly or indirectly, to own or operate any television or radio broadcasting station or related broadcast properties or any cellular mobile telephone service, except through BHC.

WCI does not include any income or loss recorded by BHC from its ownership of WCI securities when WCI records its equity in BHC's results. In the years ended December 31, 1988, 1987 and 1986, WCI's equity in BHC's results on an after-tax basis amounted to losses of $3.1 million, $1.6 million and $.3 million, respectively. BHC paid dividends to holders of its common and preferred stock in August 1987, of which WCI received $21.8 million.

The excess of WCI's investment over its equity in the underlying net assets of BHC is being amortized over forty years and amounted to $119.7 million (net of amortization of $16.6 million) at December 31, 1988.

4. Inventories

Inventories consist of:

December 31, (Millions)	1988 Current	1988 Noncurrent	1987 Current	1987 Noncurrent
Film productions for theatrical exhibition:				
Released, less amortization	$ 16.3	$ –	$ 17.1	$ –
Completed and not released	12.0	–	5.7	–
In process	–	151.1	–	149.7
Film rights for television exhibition, less amortization	331.8	138.4	299.4	138.5
Recorded music and music publishing	85.9	–	57.2	–
Publishing and related distribution	12.9	–	10.6	–
TOTAL	$458.9	$289.5	$390.0	$288.2

The total cost incurred in the production of theatrical and television films during 1988, 1987 and 1986 amounted to $706.4 million, $641.1 million and $621.5 million, respectively, and the total cost that was amortized amounted to $667.2 million, $583.3 million and $548.3 million, respectively. The unamortized cost of released theatrical and television films included in inventories at December 31, 1988 amounted to $430 million, more than 90% of which, based on management's estimate of film revenues yet to be earned, is expected to be amortized during the next three years.

5. Cash and marketable securities

Cash and marketable securities consist of:

December 31, (Millions)	1988	1987
Cash and cash equivalents	$144.3	$294.0
Marketable securities, at cost	84.3	147.7
TOTAL	$228.6	$441.7

Marketable securities include equity and debt securities having an aggregate market value of $85.4 million and $149.6 million at December 31, 1988 and 1987, respectively. Realized gains on marketable securities were not material.

6. Other assets

Other assets consist of:

December 31, (Millions)	1988	1987
OTHER CURRENT ASSETS		
Advance royalties and participations	$104.6	$ 71.1
Prepaid expenses	36.8	36.5
TOTAL	$141.4	$107.6
DEFERRED CHARGES AND OTHER ASSETS		
Music copyrights and cable franchise costs	$413.6	$317.9
Goodwill	187.6	125.1
Other assets	86.9	73.0
TOTAL	$688.1	$516.0

Accumulated amortization of intangible assets at December 31, 1988 and 1987 amounted to $130 million and $94.4 million, respectively.

7. Accounts payable and accrued expenses

Accounts payable and accrued expenses consist of:

December 31, (Millions)	1988	1987
ACCOUNTS PAYABLE AND ACCRUED EXPENSES		
Accounts payable	$ 252.7	$ 173.2
Participations and royalties	595.7	533.7
Accrued expenses	398.5	375.0
Contractual obligations	106.8	157.8
Accrued salaries and wages	114.4	100.8
Theatrical and television advances	20.4	38.0
TOTAL	$1,488.5	$1,378.5
ACCOUNTS PAYABLE DUE AFTER ONE YEAR		
Contractual obligations	$ 106.0	$ 180.9
Accrued expenses	177.7	165.6
Deferred income taxes	131.0	116.2
Participations and royalties	59.5	50.5
Other	78.9	30.8
TOTAL	$ 553.1	$ 544.0

Contractual obligations include current and noncurrent estimated liabilities of $47.7 million and $31.4 million, respectively, at December 31, 1988 and $81.8 million and $79.4 million, respectively, at December 31, 1987 in respect of various partnerships and license agreements ("film financing ventures") under which a portion of the funds used in producing and distributing certain motion pictures has been provided. The noncurrent amount at December 31, 1988 is estimated to be paid principally in years 1990 to 1993.

32

33

CLIENT:
WARNER COMMUNICATIONS INC.

DESIGN FIRM:
PENTAGRAM

PHOTOGRAPHER:
CAROL FRIEDMAN

ILLUSTRATOR:
GENE GREIF

WRITER:
JOHN BERENDT

PRINTER:
GEORGE RICE & SONS

JOAN NICOLAS, DIRECTOR OF INVESTOR RELATIONS, WARNER COMMUNICATIONS INC, NEW YORK, NEW YORK

For the Warner Communications Inc. 1988 annual report, the main theme was to show the global scope of our business. The message was that Warner creates and distributes entertainment products throughout the world. Visually, the report really captured this theme in an innovative way. The response was very positive to this annual report.

PETER HARRISON, PENTAGRAM DESIGN, NEW YORK, NEW YORK

For the Warner Communications Inc. 1988 annual report, we decided to make it entertaining. Based on the remarks of Steven Ross, the Chairman, we wanted to show the trends he said were beginning to emerge, namely the growth in the Pacific area, Europe and the United States. The company was positioned to take advantage of these trends. Also, there were staggering new gadgets that were bringing these things forward. So the idea we developed was to show all of this in a time line, showing one day in the life of a person in the world. We combined the copy as part of the illustration, creating a foldout with text on one side and the time line on the other.

JOAN NICHOLAS, DIRECTOR OF INVESTOR RELATIONS, WARNER COMMUNICATIONS INC. NEW YORK, NEW YORK

Der thematische Schwerpunkt des Jahresberichtes 1988 für Warner Communications lag beim globalen Umfang des Geschäftes: Warner produziert und vertreibt Produkte der Unterhaltungsindustrie in aller Welt. Dieses Thema wird im Jahresbericht auf ganz innovative Art visuell interpretiert. Die Reaktionen auf diesen Bericht waren sehr positiv.

PETER HARRISON, PENTAGRAM DESIGN, NEW YORK, NEW YORK

Den Jahresbericht 1988 für Warner Communications Inc. wollten wir vor allem unterhaltend machen. Ausgehend von den Angaben des Vorsitzenden Steven Ross, wollten wir die Trends aufzeigen, vor allem das Wachstum im pazifischen Raum, in Europa und den USA. Die Firma hatte neue Geräte auf den Markt gebracht, die diese positive Entwicklung unterstützten. Wir beschlossen, dies alles im Zeitablauf darzustellen, indem wir einen Tag im Leben einer Person zeigten. Wir machten den Text zum Bestandteil der Illustration: es handelt sich um einen Ausleger mit Text auf der einen Seite und der Zeitkurve auf der anderen.

JOAN NICHOLAS, DIRECOTR OF INVESTOR RELATIONS, WARNER COMMUNICATIONS INC. NEW YORK, NEW YORK

Pour le rapport annuel de Warner Communications Inc. 1988, le thème principal consistait à dévoiler l'envergure planétaire de nos opérations, à faire passer comme message le fait que Warner crée et distribue ses produits de spectacles à travers le monde entier. Au plan visuel, ce rapport a interprété ce thème de manière novatrice, d'où des réactions très positives.

PETER HARRISON, PENTAGRAM DESIGN, NEW YORK, NEW YORK

Pour le rapport annuel 1988 de Warner Communications Inc., nous avons décidé d'adopter un style distrayant. En nous basant sur les propos du P.-D.G. Steven Ross, nous avons voulu souligner la tendance à la croissance notée dans les pays du Pacifique, en Europe et aux Etas-Unis. Nous voulions également rendre compte de développements technologiques étonnants. D'où l'idée de montrer le tout à travers le portrait d'une journée dans la vie d'une personne. Nous avons agencé le texte de manière à en faire un élément de l'illustration sous forme d'un dépliant comportant le texte d'un côté, l'histoire chronologique de l'autre.

WCRS

UNION GIVES STRENGTH ▫ FOR THE WISE MAN LOOKS INTO SPACE AND HE KNOWS THERE IS NO LIMIT TO DIMENSIONS ▫

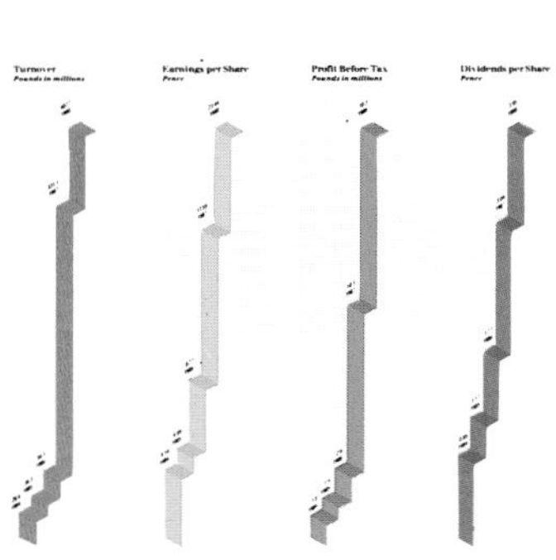

MAN IS SO MADE THAT WHEN ANYTHING FIRES HIS SOUL, IMPOSSIBILITIES VANISH ▫ YOU MIGHT AS WELL

CHAIRMAN'S STATEMENT

A LEAP YEAR FOR WCRS

This company has a culture where we drive ourselves forward less by giving ourselves pats on the back, and more by giving ourselves kicks up the backside. A fly on the wall at some of our management meetings might forget he was listening in on what is, arguably, one of the most successful companies founded in the last decade.

But once a year, at least, it is perhaps appropriate to put such useful self-criticisms aside and allow all our 3,500 people to take due credit for what we have achieved.

It is not just the remarkable profit increase (up 81%). Or the increase in earnings per share (up 33%). Or the growth in dividend (up 30%) to satisfy our demanding shareholders.

The figures fail to capture the spirit and vision of this "enterprise of entrepreneurs." It is this that is the ultimate asset that provides the intellectual capital for our business.

Peter Scott, our Chief Executive, reports elsewhere on the achievements of the year. I would like to give counterpoint to that by reminding you of the vision that will provide even more exciting years, and even more impressive results, in the future.

2

FALL ON YOUR FACE AS LEAN OVER TOO FAR BACKWARD ▫ IT IS A WRETCHED WASTE TO BE GRATIFIED WITH MEDIOCRITY

The vision is simple: to create a network of first generation companies with the energy, enthusiasm and insight to provide total communication solutions to the needs of world businessmen. This vision took several important steps forward in the year under review.

First, by the addition of the new entrepreneurs who chose to become part of our enterprise. In particular, the joining with Bélier and SGGMD from France brings a new dimension of first generation business and energy to the Group.

Second, the completing of the key parts of our multinational advertising network means that this entrepreneurial energy can be released onto the world's stage.

Already we work for 33 of the world's 100 largest advertisers. We will do even more work for these and for others, as we are the only network where every component in each country is a first generation advertising company. Perhaps in a decade or two we may worry that our vitality may be threatened by the management arthritis that currently affects our rivals. But today our suppleness is not stiffened by bureaucracy. We are a good 100 years younger than JWT and intend to stay that way.

There is a third part to our vision that is of growing importance. It builds upon the fact that we are an enterprise of entrepreneurs. But goes beyond the application of this just to advertising. For it recognises that the very concept of "advertising" is an unreal boundary in communication.

That to define our business in terms of advertising is to risk making the same mistake the railroads made in the 19th century when they failed to see they were actually in the transportation business. Which is why our vision extends so far into communication that today advertising represents scarcely more than 50% of this Group's business. It is because our business is young and alive that we are more able to sense the growing needs of our clients to develop rapidly into new areas.

So our major move into media buying reflected the wish to provide the leverage of scale in this area when in others we provide the

3

WHEN THE EXCELLENT LIES BEFORE US ▫ A MAN IN A BOW TIE IS TRUSTWORTHY, HONOURABLE AND CUTE ▫

leverage of creativity. Or why we have chosen to grow in international sponsorship to anticipate the new world of promotion where the old division between above and below the line becomes a meaningless blur.

Looking through this year's annual report, you will find that we have found new pearls to string on our necklace. Like Corporate Graphics (who have so skilfully designed this report) or Cohn & Wells whose Direct Marketing skills will be used to distribute it amongst the world's client prospects.

Which brings me to the final and perhaps most important part of this vision. All these remarkable entrepreneurs in this Group feed off each other. We challenge, we stimulate, we disagree, we agree, we compete, we respect and we create an environment where merely to manage effectively is inadequate. To leap beyond management to creation is our goal.

1987/88 was a year in which we were able to live up to our own unreasonable expectations of ourselves.

I can promise you we will be equally unreasonable in those expectations in the coming year which will complete this Group's first decade. I am confident it will not be our last.

Robin Wight
Chairman

ROBIN WIGHT: CHAIRMAN

4

OUR COMMON LUST FOR LIFE ▫ THERE IS NOTHING NEW UNDER THE SUN, BUT THERE ARE LOTS OF OLD THINGS WE DO

JERRY DELLA FEMINA

IF I'M GOING TO BE OWNED, I WANT TO BE A PRIZED POSSESSION.

I started my career breaking rules—in some circles I'm even known as a rebel. But the truth is, I'm a risk taker (in my mind a rebel looks backward and a risk taker looks forward) and that's what shows in our advertising. When we're really good as an agency is when we take risks and break the rules, when we're willing to try something different.

Whenever we've trusted our instincts we've created ads I've really loved... breakthrough advertising that really worked for our clients... ads that broke the rules.

Certainly you need marketing data. And, of course, you must know what the consumer thinks. But, armed with that information and a willingness to break rules, you can turn out advertising that both wins creative awards and sales awards.

For example, our ads for Blue Nun were funny and effective featuring spokespeople who admitted they knew nothing about wine. For Perry Ellis fragrance, we had a handsome confident-looking model who revealed he was as frightened and insecure as the rest of us. For LifeStyle condoms, we tackled AIDS as a problem when no one in the U.S. was willing to discuss it in advertising. And certainly our award-winning "Liar" ads for American Isuzu Motors break every rule of automobile advertising.

But the trick is not just in breaking the rules; it's in knowing when to break the rules and when to trust your instincts—whether it's writing an ad or selling an advertising agency.

When it became clear to me a number of years ago that I wanted to see something in the form of money after all these years in the business, I decided to take the plunge and try to be acquired. The acquisition process is a lot like dating; if you actively go out and look for someone no one wants you, but if you don't appear to be looking, then everyone wants you. We were lucky enough to have a number of people who were courting us.

I would have meetings with these people, and after the meetings they would make wonderful offers. But I never could figure out why I always came away feeling that I wasn't interested. After a while I began to question whether I was really interested in selling the agency. What I finally realised was that I was talking to people who were not like me. It's not that I'm a hot house flower that has to be in a perfect environment—but we weren't even on the same wavelength. I knew that any of these would be a partnership that could only be, at best, a marriage of convenience and I wasn't ready for that.

No one could ever understand that what I wanted was for the agency to continue to do the kind of work that we had been doing since the 70's—to continue as a good, strong creative agency. I wanted to be acquired, but I didn't want to lose the independence we had.

That showed me where my priorities were. It was clear that what I was really interested in was the agency. The financial part of it was secondary, important but secondary. So when we found out that WCRS had bought the Creamer agency and was interested in us, I was wary. We danced around each other for a while and then went to dinner at the Four Seasons one evening. We

5

Balance Sheets
at 30 April 1988

	Notes	Group 1988 £000	Group 1987 £000	Company 1988 £000	Company 1987 £000
Fixed Assets					
Tangible assets	13	16,303	10,131	326	3,341
Investments	14	6,713	733	97,133	56,455
		23,016	10,864	97,459	59,796
Current Assets					
Work in progress		154	799	–	–
Motor vehicle fleet		1,411	1,689	–	1,587
Debtors	15	65,406	52,005	16,069	11,875
Investments	16	767	8	625	–
Cash at bank and in hand		4,971	9,328	–	6,165
		72,709	63,829	16,694	19,627
Creditors					
Amounts falling due within one year	17	74,149	63,406	12,849	17,625
Net Current (Liabilities)/Assets		(1,440)	423	3,845	2,002
Total Assets Less Current Liabilities		21,576	11,287	101,304	61,798
Creditors					
Amounts falling due after more than one year	18	11,398	10,496	3,500	5,481
Provisions for Liabilities and Charges	19	442	710	737	340
Minority Interests		3,095	3	–	–
		6,641	78	97,067	55,977
Capital and Reserves					
Called-up share capital	20	4,359	3,518	4,359	3,518
Share premium account	21	579	1,405	579	1,405
Goodwill reserve	21	(11,386)	(10,808)	–	–
Merger reserve	21	–	–	86,762	47,184
Profit and loss account	21	13,089	5,963	5,367	3,870
		6,641	78	97,067	55,977

The Notes on pages 46 to 62 form part of these financial statements.

P J Scott, C R Stern
Directors

22 August 1988

44

Consolidated Statement of Source and Application of Funds
for the year ended 30 April 1988

	1988 £000	1988 £000	1987 £000	1987 £000
Source of Funds				
Profit on ordinary activities before taxation and extraordinary item		18,253		10,108
Extraordinary item		(283)		–
		17,970		10,108
Adjustments for items not involving the movement of funds				
Depreciation	2,549		1,458	
Profit on sale of fixed assets	(68)		(74)	
Profit retained in related companies	(1,125)		(218)	
Exchange translation adjustments	554		(64)	
		1,910		1,102
Total generated from operations		19,880		11,210
Funds from other sources				
Issue of Ordinary shares*	28,668		2,319	
Issue of Convertible Preference shares*	248		1,845	
Issue of loan stock*	1,526		–	
Sale of fixed assets	780		761	
Increase in long-term finance	–		10,317	
Investment by minority	8,000		–	
		39,222		15,242
		59,102		26,452
Application of Funds				
Additions to tangible fixed assets*	9,980		10,521	
Net movement in fixed asset investments*	9,929		461	
Goodwill on acquisition of subsidiaries*	31,550		10,808	
Decrease in long-term finance	624		–	
Taxation paid	4,137		5,997	
Dividends paid	2,372		1,005	
		58,592		28,792
		510		(2,340)
(Increase)/Decrease in Working Capital				
Motor vehicle fleet	278		(1,378)	
Work in progress*	645		(779)	
Debtors and prepayments*	(14,659)		(39,269)	
Investments	(759)		–	
Creditors and accruals*	6,580		50,526	
		(7,915)		9,100
(Decrease)/Increase in Bank and Cash Balances		(7,405)		6,760

**Summary of the effects of the acquisition of subsidiaries and deferred consideration payments during the year*

	£000		£000
Tangible fixed assets	964	Issue of Ordinary shares	81
Current assets	12,145	Issue of Convertible Preference shares	248
		Cash paid and issue of loan stock	31,679
	13,109		32,008
Creditors and provisions	(12,651)	Goodwill	(31,550)
	458		458

The Notes on pages 46 to 62 form part of these financial statements.

45

Client:
WCRS Group, plc

Design Firm:
Corporate Graphics

Art Director:
Bennett Robinson

Designers:
Bennett Robinson, Erika Siegel

Photographer:
Gordon Meyer

Illustrators:
Robert Risko,
Dian Friedman,
Seymour Chwast

Writer:
Rita Jacobs

Production Manager:
Francie Moseley

Typographer:
PDR

Paper Selection:
3 Crowns Grey

Paper Manufacturer:
LOE Gloss

Printer:
George Rice & Sons

Number of Pages:
66 plus cover

Bennett Robinson, Corporate Graphics, New York New York for the WCRS Group, PLC, London, England

The 1988 annual report for the WCRS Group was unusual for us because WCRS became our parent company, and we were in the role of being the client and the designers. As a worldwide advertising group, WCRS, of course, has risen in the firmament like a shooting star. We had an input meeting with top management. Usually, with clients, this could take all day. Our meeting took two minutes. The co-chairman had told us to do something "irreverent," so we decided to show dramatically that this was a young, vital firm abounding in energy. We used the photographer, Gordon Meyer, to capture this energy with the principals of the companies on both sides of the Atlantic.

Bennett Robinson, Corporate Graphics, New York, New York für die WCRS Group, PLC, London, England

Der Jahresbericht 1988 für die WCRS-Gruppe war für uns eine ungewöhnliche Aufgabe, weil WCRS zu unserer Muttergesellschaft geworden war. Dadurch waren wir gleichzeitig Auftraggeber und Designer. Als weltweite Werbegruppe war WCRS natürlich wie ein Meteor am Firmament erschienen. Ein Mitglied des Vorstandes beauftragte uns, etwas «Respektloses» zu machen, und wir beschlossen deshalb, ganz dramatisch darzustellen, dass es sich um eine junge, vitale, dynamische Firma handelt. Wir beauftragten den Photographen Gordon Meyer, dies in Aufnahmen der beiden Direktoren der Firmen auf beiden Seiten des Atlantiks einzufangen.

Bennett Robinson, Corporate Graphics, New York, New York, pour le WCRS Group, PLC, Londres, Grande-Bretagne

Le rapport annuel 1988 du WCRS Group a constitué une mission inhabituelle en ce sens que WCRS est devenu notre maison mère et que nous avons donc joué le double rôle de client et de designer. En tant que groupe publicitaire mondial, WCRS a connu une ascension phénoménale. Le co-président du groupe nous a chargé de réaliser quelque chose d'«irrévérencieux», ce qui nous a amenés à tenter une présentation dramatique de l'énergie qui abonde au sein de cette jeune entreprise pleine de vitalité. Nous avons eu recours au photographe Gordon Meyer pour capter cette énergie en images au contact des dirigeants du groupe des deux côtés de l'Atlantique.

ANNUAL REPORT PHOTOGRAPHY

PHOTOGRAPHIE FÜR JAHRESBERICHTE

PHOTOGRAPHIE DES RAPPORTS ANNUELS

87

ANNUAL REPORT PHOTOGRAPHY

PHOTOGRAPHIE FÜR JAHRESBERICHTE

PHOTOGRAPHIE DES RAPPORTS ANNUELS

87

PHOTOGRAPHER:
HENRY GILPIN

ART DIRECTOR:
DAVID BROOM

DESIGNER:
KIMIKO MURAKAMI CHAN

DESIGN FIRM:
BROOM & BROOM, INC.

CLIENT:
CALIFORNIA CASUALTY GROUP

◁ Photographer:
Scott Morgan

Art Director:
Jim Berté

Designer:
Jim Berté

Client:
Nichols Institute

Photographer:
Rodney Smith

Art Director:
Bennett Robinson

Designers:
Bennett Robinson, Erika Siegel

Design Firm:
Corporate Graphics

Client:
H.J. Heinz Company

ANNUAL REPORT PHOTOGRAPHY

PHOTOGRAPHIE FÜR JAHRESBERICHTE

PHOTOGRAPHIE DES RAPPORTS ANNUELS

88

PHOTOGRAPHER:
HANS NELEMAN

ART DIRECTOR:
WILIAM SIEGHART

DESIGNER:
WILLIAM SIEGHART

DESIGN FIRM:
FORWARD PUBLISHING

CLIENT:
DATA LOGIC

Photographer:
Scott Morgan

Art Director:
Robert Miles Runyan

Designer:
Michael Mescall

Design Firm:
*Robert Miles Runyan
& Associates*

Client:
Computer Science Corp.

PHOTOGRAPHER:
ARTHUR MEYERSON

ART DIRECTOR:
LOWELL WILLIAMS

DESIGNERS:
BILL CARSON, CINDY WHITE

DESIGN FIRM:
LOWELL WILLIAMS DESIGN

CLIENT:
PRIME CABLE

ANNUAL REPORT ILLUSTRATION

ILLUSTRATION FÜR JAHRESBERICHTE

ILLUSTRATION DES RAPPORTS ANNUELS

87

ILLUSTRATOR:
DAVID WILCOX

ART DIRECTORS:
ROGER COOK,
DON SHANOSKY

DESIGNERS:
ROGER COOK,
DON SHANOSKY,
ROBERT FRANKLE

DESIGN FIRM:
COOK & SHANOSKY ASSOCIATES, INC.

CLIENT:
THE SQUIBB CORPORATION

ILLUSTRATOR:
JOHN VAN HAMMERSVELD

ART DIRECTORS:
PETER HARRISON, HAROLD BURCH

DESIGNERS:
HAROLD BURCH,
PETER HARRISON

DESIGN FIRM:
PENTAGRAM

CLIENT:
WARNER COMMUNICATIONS, INC.

ANNUAL REPORT ILLUSTRATION

ILLUSTRATION FÜR JAHRESBERICHTE

ILLUSTRATION DES RAPPORTS ANNUELS

88

Illustrator:
David Wilcox

Art Director:
Bennett Robinson

Designers:
Kevin O'Neill,
Shelly Samuelson

Design Firm:
Corporate Graphics, Inc.

Client:
Charles Stark Draper Laboratory

▷ Illustrators:
Vincent Perez,
Tim Lewis,
Justin Carroll

Photographers:
Michele Clement (figures)
Terry Heffernan
Jeff Corwin

Art Director:
Kit Hinrichs

Designers:
Kit Hinrichs,
Karen Boone

Design Firm:
Pentagram

Client:
National Medical Enterprises

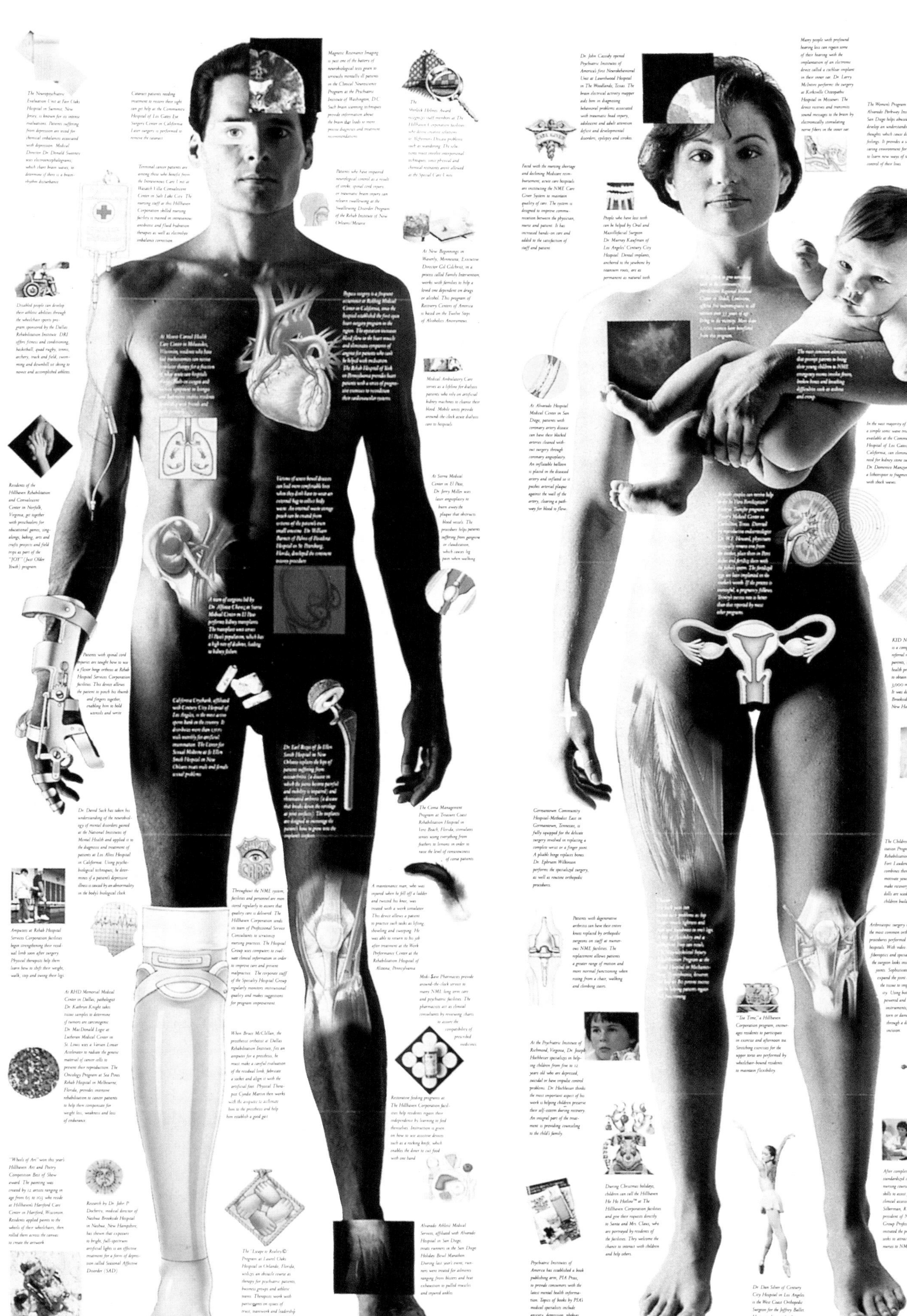

ILLUSTRATOR:
DOUG FRASER

ART DIRECTORS:
DOUGLAS JOSEPH,
RIK BESSER

DESIGNER:
DOUGLAS JOSEPH

DESIGN FIRM:
BESSER JOSEPH

CLIENT:
LINCOLN BANCORP

Illustrator:
Andrea Baruffi

Art Director:
Monica Little

Designer:
Paul Wharton

Design Firm:
Little & Company

Client:
United Healthcare Corp.

INDEX

VERZEICHNIS

INDEX

ART DIRECTOR INDEX

CLIENT INDEX

DESIGNER INDEX

PHOTOGRAPHER INDEX

ILLUSTRATOR INDEX

CALL FOR ENTRIES

FOR GRAPHIS' INTERNATIONAL YEARBOOKS

GRAPHIS DESIGN

ALL ENTRIES MUST ARRIVE ON OR BEFORE NOVEMBER 30

Advertising: Newspaper and magazine
Design: Promotion brochures, catalogs, invitations, record covers, announcements, logotypes and/or entire corporate image campaigns, calendars, books, book covers, packages (single or series, labels and/or complete packages)
Editorial Design: company magazines, newspapers, consumer magazines, house organs
Illustration: All categories may be black and white or color

GRAPHIS ANNUAL REPORTS

ALL ENTRIES MUST ARRIVE ON OR BEFORE JANUARY 31/APRIL 30

All material printed and published in connection with the annual report of a company or other organization.
Design, illustration, photography, typography, as well as the overall conception of the annual report are the criteria to be judged.
In order to do justice to this complex medium, we will present double-page spreads from the annual reports selected which are exemplary in their design and/or illustration.

GRAPHIS PHOTO

ALL ENTRIES MUST ARRIVE ON OR BEFORE JUNE 30

Advertising Photography: Advertisements, promotional brochures, catalogs, invitations, announcements, record covers, calendars.
Editorial Photography for press media – journalism and features – for books, corporate publications, etc. on the following subjects: fashion, cosmetics, architecture, arts, nature, science, technology, daily life, sports, current affairs, portraits, still life, etc.
Fine Art Photography: Personal studies
Unpublished Photography: Experimental and student work

GRAPHIS POSTER

ALL ENTRIES MUST ARRIVE ON OR BEFORE APRIL 30

Culture: Posters announcing exhibitions and events of all kind, film, theater, and ballet performances, concerts etc.
Advertising: Posters for fashion, cosmetics, foods, beverages, industrial goods; image and self-promotional campaigns of companies and individuals
Society: Posters which serve primarily a social and/or political purpose; from the field of education; for conferences and meetings; as well as for political and charitable appeals.

GENERAL RULES

THESE ARE APPLICABLE TO ALL BOOKS MENTIONED.

By submitting work to GRAPHIS, the sender expressly grants permission for his publication in any GRAPHIS book, as well as in any article in GRAPHIS magazine, or any advertising brochure, etc. whose purpose is specifically to promote the sales of these publications.

Eligibility: All work produced in the 12 month period previous to the submission deadlines, as well as rejected or unpublished work from this period, by professionals and students.

A confirmation of receipt will be sent to each entrant, and all entrants will be notified at a later date whether or not their work has been accepted for publication.
All the winning entries will be reproduced in a generous format and in four colors throughout.
By submitting work you qualify for a 25% discount on the purchase of the respective book.

What to send:
Please send the actual printed piece (unmounted but well protected). Do not send original art. For large, bulky or valuable pieces, please submit color photos or (duplicate) transparencies.
Please note that entries cannot be returned. Only in exceptional cases and by contacting us in advance will material be sent back.

Entry Fees:
For each single entry: North America: US$ 10.00 West Germany: DM 10,00 All other countries: SFr. 10.00
For each campaign entry of 3 or more pieces: North America: US$ 25.00 West Germany: DM 25,00 All other countries: SFr. 25.00
Please make checks payable to GRAPHIS PRESS CORP. Zurich, and include in parcel.
These fees do not apply to students, if copy of student identification is included.
(For entries from countries with exchange controls, please contact us.)

How and where to send:
Please tape (do not glue) the entry label provided (or photocopy) – with full information – on the back of each piece. Entries can be sent by airmail, air parcel post or surface mail. **Please do not send anything by air freight.** Declare "No Commercial Value" on packages, and label "Art for Contest". The number of transparencies and photos should be indicated on the parcel. (If sent by air courier, please mark "Documents, Commercial Value 00.00").

Thank you for your contribution. Please send all entries to the following address:

GRAPHIS PRESS CORP., DUFOURSTRASSE 107, CH-8008 ZURICH, SWITZERLAND

FÜR DIE GRAPHIS JAHRBÜCHER

GRAPHIS DESIGN

EINSENDESCHLUSS: 30. NOVEMBER

Werbung: In Zeitungen und Zeitschriften
Design: Werbeprospekte, Kataloge, Einladungen, Schallplattenhüllen, Anzeigen, Signete und/oder Imagekampagnen, Kalender, Bücher, Buchumschläge, Packungen (einzelne oder Serien, Etiketten und/oder vollständige Packungen)
Redaktionelles Design: Firmenpublikationen, Zeitungen, Zeitschriften, Jahresberichte
Illustration: Alle Kategorien, schwarzweiss oder farbig

GRAPHIS ANNUAL REPORTS

EINSENDESCHLUSS: 31. JANUAR/30. APRIL

Alle gedruckten und veröffentlichten Arbeiten, die im Zusammenhang mit dem Jahresbericht einer Firma oder Organisation stehen.
Design, Illustration, Photographie, Typographie und die Gesamtkonzeption eines Jahresberichtes sind die beurteilten Kriterien.
Um diesem komplexen Medium gerecht zu werden, werden aus den ausgewählten Jahresberichten verschiedene typische Doppelseiten gezeigt, die beispielhaft für die Gestaltung und/oder Illustration sind.

GRAPHIS PHOTO

EINSENDESCHLUSS: 30. JUNI

Werbephotographie: Anzeigen, Prospekte, Kataloge, Einladungen, Bekanntmachungen, Schallplattenhüllen, Kalender.
Redaktionelle Photographie für Presse (Reportagen und Artikel), Bücher, Firmenpublikationen usw. in den Bereichen Mode, Kosmetik, Architektur, Kunst, Natur, Wissenschaft und Technik, Alltag, Sport, Aktuelles, Porträts, Stilleben usw.
Künstlerische Photographie: Persönliche Studien
Unveröffentlichte Aufnahmen: Experimentelle Photographie und Arbeitenvon Studenten und Schülern.

GRAPHIS POSTER

EINSENDESCHLUSS: 30. APRIL

Kultur: Plakate für die Ankündigung von Ausstellungen und Veranstaltungen aller Art, Film-, Theater- und Ballettaufführungen, Musikveranstaltungen.
Werbung: Plakate für Mode, Kosmetik, Lebensmittel, Genussmittel, Industriegüter; Image- und Eigenwerbung von Firmen und Einzelpersonen
Gesellschaft: Plakate, die in erster Linie einem sozialen oder politischen Zweck dienen, auf dem Gebiet der Ausbildung und Erziehung oder für die Ankündigung von Konferenzen und Tagungen sowie für politische und soziale Appelle

TEILNAHMEBEDINGUNGEN

DIESE GELTEN FÜR ALLE AUFGEFÜHRTEN BÜCHER.

Durch Ihre Einsendung geben Sie GRAPHIS ausdrücklich die Erlaubnis zur Veröffentlichung der eingesandten Arbeiten sowohl im entsprechenden Jahrbuch als auch in der Zeitschrift GRAPHIS oder für die Wiedergabe im Zusammenhang mit Besprechungen und Werbematerial für die GRAPHIS-Publikationen.

In Frage kommen alle Arbeiten von Fachleuten und Studenten – auch nicht publizierte Arbeiten – welche in den zwölf Monaten vor Einsendeschluss entstanden sind.

Jeder Einsender erhält eine Empfangsbestätigung und wird über Erscheinen oder Nichterscheinen seiner Arbeiten zu einem späteren Zeitpunkt informiert.
Alle im Buch aufgenommenen Arbeiten werden vierfarbig, in grosszügigem Format reproduziert.
Durch Ihre Einsendung erhalten Sie 25% Rabatt auf das jeweilige Jahrbuch.

Was einsenden:
Bitte senden Sie uns das gedruckte Beispiel (unmontiert, aber gut geschützt). Senden Sie keine Originale. Bei unhandlichen, umfangreichen oder wertvollen Sendungen bitten wir um Farbphotos oder Duplikat-Dias.
Bitte beachten Sie, dass Einsendungen nicht zurückgeschickt werden können. Ausnahmen sind nur nach vorheriger Absprache mit GRAPHIS möglich.

Gebühren:
SFr. 10.00/DM 10,00 für einzelne Arbeiten
SFr. 25.00/DM 25,00 für Kampagnen oder Serien von mehr als drei Stück
Bitte senden Sie uns einen Scheck (SFr.-Schecks bitte auf eine Schweizer Bank ziehen) oder überweisen Sie den Betrag auf PC Zürich 80-23071-9 oder PSchK Frankfurt 3000 57-602.
Diese Gebühren gelten nicht für Studenten. Bitte schicken Sie uns eine Kopie des Studentenausweises.
(Für Einsendungen aus Ländern mit Devisenbeschränkungen bitten wir Sie, uns zu kontaktieren.)

Wie und wohin schicken:
Bitte befestigen Sie das vorgesehene Etikett (oder eine Kopie) – vollständig ausgefüllt – mit Klebstreifen (nicht mit Klebstoff) auf der Rückseite jeder Arbeit. Bitte per Luftpost oder auf normalem Postweg einsenden. **Keine Luftfrachtsendungen.** Deklarieren Sie «Ohne jeden Handelswert» und «Arbeitsproben für Wettbewerb». Die Anzahl der Dias und Photos sollte auf dem Paket angegeben werden. (Bei Air Courier Sendungen vermerken Sie «Dokumente, ohne jeden Handelswert»).

Herzlichen Dank für Ihre Mitarbeit. Bitte senden Sie Ihre Arbeiten an folgende Adresse:

GRAPHIS VERLAG AG, DUFOURSTRASSE 107, CH-8008 ZURICH, SCHWEIZ

POUR LES ANNUELS INTERNATIONAUX GRAPHIS

GRAPHIS DESIGN

DATE LIMITE D'ENVOI: 30 NOVEMBRE

Publicité: journaux et magazines
Design: brochures de promotion, catalogues, invitations, pochettes de disques, annonces, emblèmes, en-têtes, campagnes de prestige, calendriers, livres, jaquettes, emballages (spécimen ou série, étiquettes ou emballages complets)
Editorial Design: magazines de sociétés, journaux, revues, rapports annuels
Illustration: toutes catégories en noir et blanc ou en couleurs

GRAPHIS ANNUAL REPORTS

DATE LIMITE D'ENVOI: 31 JANVIER/30 AVRIL

Tous travaux imprimés et publiés en relation avec le rapport annuel d'une entreprise ou d'une organisation.
Les critères retenus pour l'appréciation sont le design, l'illustration, la photo, la typo et la conception d'ensemble des rapports annuels.
Afin de rendre justice à ce média complexe, nous présentons diverses doubles pages types des rapports annuels sélectionnés en veillant à ce qu'elles soient représentatives de la conception et/ou de l'illustration.

GRAPHIS PHOTO

DATE LIMITE D'ENVOI: 30 JUIN

Photographie publicitaire: annonces, brochures de promotion, catalogues, invitations, pochettes de disques, calendriers
Photographie rédactionnelle pour la presse (reportages et articles), livres, publications d'entreprises, etc. dans les domaines suivants: Mode, arts, architecture, nature, sciences et techniques, vie quotidienne, sports, l'actualité, portraits, nature morte, etc.
Photographie artistique: études personnelles
Photographie non publiée: travaux expérimentaux et projets d'étudiants

GRAPHIS POSTER

DATE LIMITE D'ENVOI: 30 AVRIL

Affiches culturelles: annonçant des expositions et manifestations de tout genre, des projections de films, des représentations de théâtre et de ballet, des concerts et festivals.
Affiches publicitaires: pour la mode, les cosmétiques, l'alimentation, les produits de consommation de luxe, les biens industriels; publicité institutionnelle et autopromotion d'entreprises.
Affiches sociales: essentiellement au service d'une cause sociale ou politique dans les domaines de l'éducation et de la formation, ainsi que pour l'annonce de conférences et réunions et pour les appels à caractère social et politique.

MODALITÉS D'ENVOI

VALABLES POUR TOUS LES LIVRES CITÉS.

Par votre envoi, vous donnez expressément à GRAPHIS l'autorisation de reproduire les travaux reçus aussi bien dans le livre en question que dans le magazine GRAPHIS ou dans tout imprimé relatif aux comptes rendus et au matériel publicitaire concernant les publications GRAPHIS.

Sont acceptés tous les travaux de professionnels et d'étudiants – même inédits – réalisés pendant les douze mois précédant le délai limite d'envoi.

Pour tout envoi de travaux, nous vous faisons parvenir un accusé de réception. Vous serez informé par la suite de la parution ou non-parution de vos travaux. Tous les travaux figurant dans l'ouvrage en question sont reproduits en quadrichromie dans un format généreux.
Votre envoi vous vaut une réduction de 25% sur l'annuel en question.

Que nous envoyer:
Veuillez nous envoyer un exemplaire imprimé (non monté, mais bien protégé). N'envoyez pas d'originaux. Pour les travaux de grand format, volumineux ou de valeur, veuillez nous envoyer des photos ou des diapositives (duplicata).
Veuillez noter que les travaux ne peuvent pas être retournés, sauf dans des cas exceptionnels et si vous nous en avisez à l'avance.

Droits d'admission:
SFr. 10.00 pour les envois concernant un seul travail
SFr. 25.00 pour chaque série de 3 travaux ou davantage
Veuillez joindre à votre envoi un chèque tiré sur une banque suisse ou en verser le montant au compte chèque postal Zürich 80-23071-9.
Les étudiants sont exemptés de cette taxe. Prière de joindre une photocopie de la carte d'étudiant.
(Si vous résidez dans un pays qui connaît le contrôle des changes, veuillez nous contacter préalablement.)

Comment et où envoyer:
Veuillez scotcher (ne pas coller) au dos de chaque spécimen les étiquettes ci-jointes (ou photocopies) – dûment remplies. Envoyez les travaux de préférence par avion, ou par voie de surface. **Ne nous envoyez rien en fret aérien.** Indiquez «Sans aucune valeur commerciale» et «Echantillons de spécimens pour concours». Le nombre de diapositives et de photos doit être indiqué sur le paquet. (Pour les envois par courrier, inscrire «Documents, sans aucune valeur commercial».)

Nous vous remercions chaleureusement de votre collaboration. Veuillez faire parvenir vos travaux à l'adresse suivante:

EDITIONS GRAPHIS SA, DUFOURSTRASSE 107, CH-8008 ZURICH, SUISSE